MW01617797

Sinews of Survival

Betty Kobayashi Issenman

Sinews of Survival

The Living Legacy of Inuit Clothing

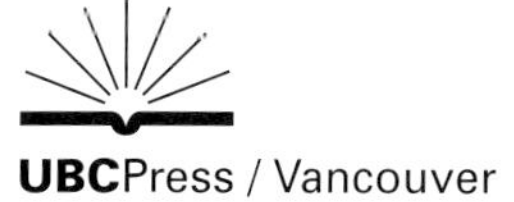

UBCPress / Vancouver

Published in association with
Études/Inuit/Studies

Printed in Canada on acid-free paper ∞

ISBN 0-7748-0596-X (HARDCOVER)
ISBN 0-7748-0599-4 (PAPERBACK)

Canadian Cataloguing in Publication Data

Issenman, Betty, 1921-
Sinews of survival

Includes bibliographical references and index.
ISBN 0-7748-0596-X(bound); ISBN 0-7748-0599-4 (pbk.)

1. Inuit – Costume. 2. Inuit – Material culture. I. Title.

GT1605.I88 1997 391'.0089'9712 C97-910494-7

UBC Press gratefully acknowledges the ongoing support to its publishing program from the Canada Council for the Arts, the British Columbia Arts Council, and the Department of Heritage of the Government of Canada.

Set in Figural and Meta
Printed and bound in Canada by Friesens
Copy-editors: Camilla Jenkins and Barbara Tessman
Proofreader: John Eerkes
Cartographer: Eric Leinberger
Inuktitut translation for maps: Avataq Cultural Institute
Indexer: Annette Lorek
Designer: George Vaitkunas

UBC Press
University of British Columbia
6344 Memorial Road
Vancouver, BC V6T 1Z2
(604) 822-5959
Fax: 1-800-668-0821
E-mail: orders@ubcpress.ubc.ca
http://www.ubcpress.ubc.ca

Illustraton on page vi Two men from Iglulik in caribou-skin clothing. They are photographed near Mittimatalik, NWT, to which they travelled overland in 1988.

This book has been published with the support of the following sponsors:

Avataq Cultural Institute
Department of Indian Affairs and Northern Development, Canada
Fur Council of Canada
Fur Institute of Canada
Hydro-Québec
Inco Limited
Jackman Foundation
Kativik School Board
Lytton Minerals Limited
Makivik Corporation
McLean Foundation
Nunavut Tunngavik Incorporated
Nunavut Wildlife Management Board
Placer Dome Canada Limited
Telesat Canada

For more infromation on the sponsors listed above see page 266.

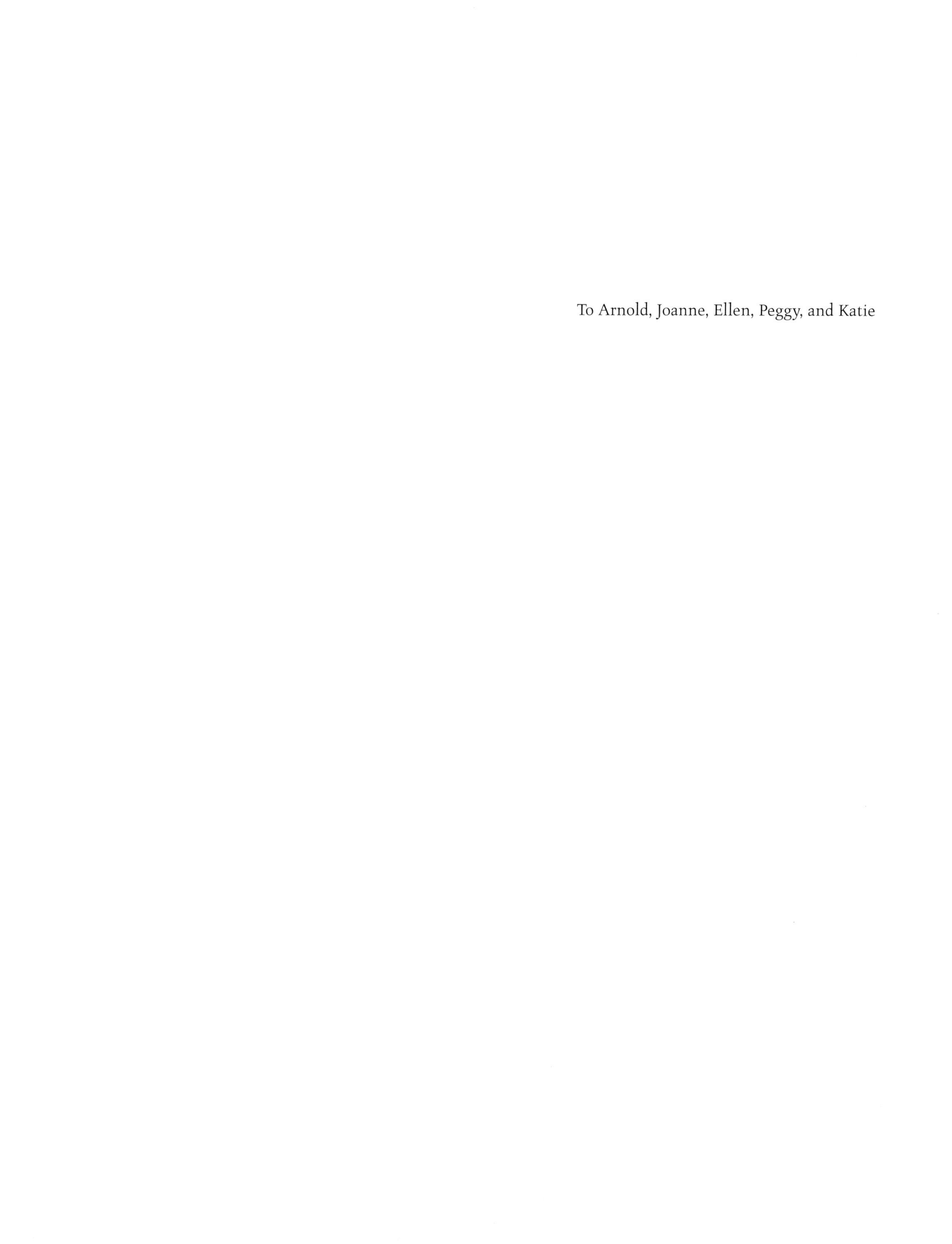

To Arnold, Joanne, Ellen, Peggy, and Katie

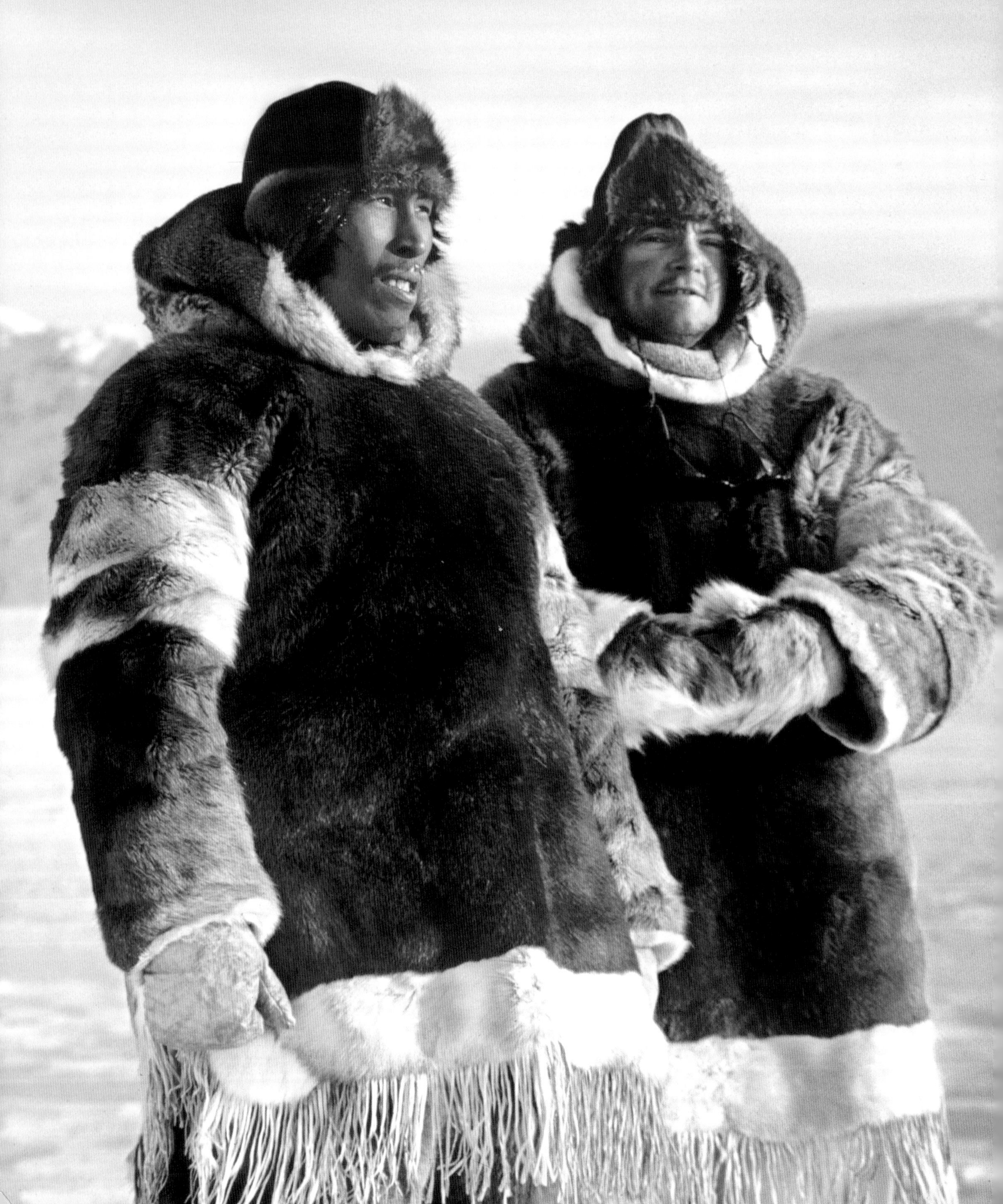

Contents

Maps and Figures

Maps

Figures

Preface

Sinew – *ivalu* – is the thread that Inuit use to sew their skin clothing, a key element in Arctic survival. The word evokes many images: of strands that reach into antiquity, out of which the Inuit culture evolved; of lines of communication across the northern lands; of strong, resilient fibres that hold families and communities together; of powerful bonds between humans, wildlife, and the land; of filaments transformed into symbols; and of links between the generations.

Studies about the Arctic have burgeoned worldwide in the last two decades, and Inuit clothing has received a share of this attention. Nonetheless, the apparel is little known to the vast majority of southerners.[1] This book seeks to overcome the deficiency by exploring Inuit skin clothing as protection, identity, and culture bearer, three roles that it has played from past eras until today. By studying this one aspect of Inuit society we discover a way to appreciate the culture as a whole.

As protection, the clothing is peerless. By meeting the challenge of one of the world's harshest climates it has enabled the Inuit and their forebears to survive for thousands of years. The sophisticated technology and skill used by both hunters and seamstresses to produce the garments have been passed from generation to generation and are a living legacy to our modern world.

Inuit costume also makes visible the clothing traditions of each country in which the people live and of the groups within each land. The diverse styles have permitted the Inuit to retain their identity, even though they are a tiny fraction of the world's population. Skin clothing acts as a carrier for an enduring, complex culture, based on a vast body of knowledge and an intimate mastery of every nuance of northern living. In other words, the garments embody spiritual, social, and artistic conventions, both prehistoric and historical.

The use of fur garments in the Arctic has declined, although fur and skin boots are still seen everywhere. Some people who choose a traditional lifestyle or who live in villages more affected by severe climates continue to dress in furs, often in combination with clothes made of woven materials. In winter hunters and trappers, both men and women, will carry a set of skin clothing with them on their expeditions. In summer, and all year round in parts of the North – such as Labrador and southern Alaska – where milder climates prevail, skin clothing for day-to-day purposes has not been worn for many years. But in some hamlets and towns fur clothing production has begun to flourish, partly because of renewed pride in the culture and a desire to preserve the heritage.

Yet the principles of clothing construction common to all Inuit continue, whether fur, wool, or vegetable or synthetic fibres are being used. Since contact with non-Inuit started in the thirteenth century (McGhee 1992, 16), the Inuit have taken from other societies materials and often items of clothing viable for their way of life, while retaining their own basic precepts of clothing production. They choose under what conditions they use dress of non-Inuit origin.

I spoke with many Inuit women, who generously shared their knowledge and their insights. I learned that in some communities several aspects of clothing manufacture and history are in danger of being lost; skin garment production has diminished in the face of many influences in today's Arctic, and the elders who are the guardians of the heritage are dying, often without having passed their wisdom to the young. Younger women sometimes told me that they did not possess a knowledge of the time-tested lore, a situation that encouraged me to think that documentation on skin clothing would be of interest to Inuit as well as to non-Inuit. I learned as well that there has been a revival of instruction in methods of Arctic survival for the rising generation, including how to harvest and process skins to transform them into clothing.

This work draws together in one place information scattered in reports, articles, journals, and books written over the centuries in several countries, including Inuit writings. I have drawn on this corpus of literature mainly through the Centre for Northern Studies and Research, the McLennan Library, and the Lawrence Lande Collection, all at McGill University, Montréal. I also consulted libraries at the following institutions: the Arctic Institute of North America, Calgary; the Avataq Cultural Institute, Lachine and Inukjuaq; the Bibliothèque Nationale du Québec, Montréal; the Boreal Institute for Northern Studies at the University of Alberta, Edmonton (now the Canadian Circumpolar Institute); the Hochelaga Institute, Montréal; Indian and Northern Affairs Canada, Ottawa; Kativik School Board, Montréal; the McCord Museum of Canadian History, Montréal; and the University of Calgary.

The earliest collection of data that lists and compares cultural elements in Inuit, Chukchi, and Koryak societies is found in Birket-Smith's tables (1929, Part 2, 234-94).[2] Of all the bibliographies on the Arctic developed more recently, the ASTIS [Arctic Science and Technology Information System] *Bibliography,* published by the Arctic Institute of North America, Calgary, proved most useful.[3]

I examined many collections of Inuit clothing and tools in museums and other institutions.[4] My most important study took place at the McCord Museum of Canadian History, where I was able to make a detailed examination of their invaluable collection of Inuit clothing and tools. Research also took me to the following institutions: the American Museum of Natural History, New York; the Arctic Institute of North America, Calgary; the Bata Shoe Museum, Toronto; the Eskimo Museum, Churchill; Glenbow Museum, Calgary; the Manitoba Museum of Man and Nature, Winnipeg; the Ministère des Affaires culturelles, Québec; the Musée de la civilisation, Québec; the Musée des Soeurs Grises, Montréal; the Museon Museum, The Hague; the Museum of Mankind, British Museum, London; the Peabody Museum of Salem, Massachusetts; the Provincial Museum of Alberta, Edmonton; Rijksmuseum voor Volkenkunde, Leiden; the Royal British Columbia Museum, Victoria; the Royal Museum of Scotland, Edinburgh; the Royal Ontario Museum, Toronto; the Scott Polar Research Institute, Cambridge, England; Université Laval, Ste-Foy; and the Winnipeg Art Gallery.

Many institutions sent me lists of their holdings of Inuit clothing. Among them are: Art Galleries and Museums, City of Dundee; Bristol Museums and Art Gallery, England; the Canadian Ethnology Service of the Canadian Museum of Civilization, Hull; Dartmouth College, Hanover; Hancock Museum of the University, Newcastle-upon-Tyne; the Hokkaido Museum of Northern Peoples, Abashiri City; the Logan Museum of Anthropology, Beloit, Wisconsin; Maidstone Museum and Art

Gallery, England; Manchester Museum, University of Manchester; the Mathers Museum, Indiana University, Bloomington; the Milwaukee Public Museum, Wisconsin; the Museum of Anthropology, University of Michigan, Ann Arbor; the National Museum of Ethnology, Osaka; the Peabody Museum of Natural History, Yale University, New Haven; the Perth Museum and Art Gallery, Scotland; the Provincial Museum of Alberta, Edmonton; the Royal Ontario Museum, Toronto; the San Diego Museum of Man; the Ulster Museum, Belfast; and the University Museum, University of Pennsylvania, Philadelphia. I also used the studies of Arctic ethnological museum collections found in Bockstoce (1977), Taylor (1974a), and VanStone (1984, 1985a, 1985b, 1989, 1994), and in many exhibition catalogues.

The rich, extensive photographic collections about the Arctic yielded many images to illustrate the text. Photographic archives examined were those of the Avataq Cultural Institute;[5] *The Beaver*, Winnipeg; the British Museum; the Canadian Museum of Civilization; Hudson's Bay House, Winnipeg; the Institute of Alaska Native Arts, Fairbanks; the Inuit Cultural Institute, Arviat, NWT; the McCord Museum of Canadian History; the Manitoba Museum of Man and Nature; the Manitoba Provincial Archives, Winnipeg; Ministère des Affaires culturelles, Québec; the Museum of Mankind, Ethnology branch of the British Museum; the National Archives of Canada; the Notman Photo-graphic Archives, McCord Museum; the Oakes-Riewe Photography Collection, Arviat and Winnipeg; the Old Dartmouth Historical Society Whaling Museum, New Bedford; Yolande Perrault, Montréal; Bernard Saladin d'Anglure, Québec; and the Winnipeg Art Gallery. The General Synod Archives, Anglican Church of Canada, sent me photocopies of their index of Inuit photographs. The Photographic Archives of *Them Days Magazine*, Happy Valley, Labrador, and Mystic Seaport Museum, Connecticut, sent photocopies of relevant images.

Some material in this book first appeared in *Études/Inuit/Studies*, the McCord Museum of Canadian History catalogue for the exhibition *Ivalu: Traditions du vêtement inuit/ Traditions of Inuit Clothing*, and *Threads* magazine. The text mainly discusses clothing from Arctic Canada. Earlier drafts contained sections on the dress of Siberian Yupiit, Alaskan Inupiat and Yupiit, and Kalaallit, but I realized that each country's costume deserved at least one book to deal adequately with the rich material available. I have retained the many references to and images from the non-Canadian circumpolar countries to enable the reader to savour something of their cultures and to understand differences and commonalities. I have chosen not to pursue the subject of Aleut dress. This vast area has been and is being dealt with by Alaskan and Russian scholars, both Native and non-Native.

For the place names throughout the text, I have used the Inuktitut words as designated by the Inuit. The glossary of place names at the end of the book provides further information.

Just as I have been helped by the wisdom of the Inuit and by colleagues from north and south, I hope this work will provide a record and a stepping stone for future studies by Inuit and non-Inuit. When we look at Inuit clothing – prehistoric, historical, modern – which illuminates the human condition, we can celebrate the achievements of the Inuit peoples, who created the garments and tools of survival with devotion and eloquence.

Acknowledgments

This work originated, although I was unaware of it at the time, on the shores of Kinngait Fiord, near Pangniqtuuq, Baffin Island. There, in the summer of 1978, we came upon elegantly dressed Inuit women, wearing shimmering white *amautiit,* babies on their backs. Although I had studied costumes of the world, the clothing of the Inuit was never mentioned either in traditional courses in the South or in the accompanying literature. I soon realized that its existence was unknown to most dwellers of non-Arctic lands.

Over the many years of my research I encountered a generosity of spirit among the Inuit and Arctic scholars. Their openheartedness can hardly be repaid by a mention of their names. Throughout the book, credits have been given in captions and text. These individuals and institutions, and the great numbers of people from North and South who shared their insights and showed me their archives and collections, have my deep appreciation.

At the outset I wish to recognize the invaluable contributions to world civilization made by the peoples of the Arctic who created the clothing and tools of their ancient culture. Among the Northerners who helped me understand the clothing and its place in the circumpolar countries are Tatyana Achirgina from Anadyr, Chukotka; Steve and Anaoyok Alookee of Taloyoak; Helen Siwooko Carius of Anchorage; Martha Greig, from Ottawa; Leah d'Argencourt Idlout of Mittimatalik; Mark Kalluak, from Arviat; Rhoda Karetak, from Kangiqliniq; Lucy Kayuliq of Salluit; Lucy Meeko, of Kuujjuaraapik; Jeela Alikatuktuk Moss-Davies, past president of Pauktuutit, the Inuit Women's Organization; Sarah Naluktuq, from Inukjuaq; Ellen Maarit Nakhalajarvi of Oulu, Finland; Annie Napayok, from Arviat; Anne Nuorgam of Oulu, Finland; Tommy Owlijoot, from Arviat; Sala Padlayat, Caroline Palliser, Nellie Palliser, and Siasi Irqumia Smiler, all of Kativik School Board, Montréal; Charlotte St. John, from Arviat; Michael Shouldice, also from Arviat; and Sally Qimmiu'naaq Webster of Qamanittuaq and Ottawa.

I have identified the persons shown in photographs wherever possible. Sometimes my extensive inquiries failed to bring results, and for this I am sorry. I gain comfort from the fact that efforts by governmental and Inuit organizations to obtain names for anonymous Inuit are having some success.

The staff and volunteers of the McCord Museum of Canadian History contributed in many ways to the evolution of the project. My thanks go to Jacqueline Beaudoin-Ross, the late Margaret Carroll, Conrad Graham, Moira McCaffrey, John McElhone, Pamela Miller, Catherine Rankin, and Stanley Triggs and his staff at the Notman Photographic Archives.

Many persons connected with other museums and institutions shared their research, helped immeasurably with information, books, references, archives, and images, and showed me their collections. My gratitude is extended to: Dixie Alexander, Institute of Alaska Native Arts; Claus Andreason, Greenland National Museum; Ian Badgley, Avataq Cultural Institute;

Sonja Bata, Bata Shoe Museum; Serge Bedekian, Fédération des Coopératives du Nouveau Québec; John Bennett, *Inuktitut Magazine*; Peter Bettenhausen, Museon Museum; Joanne Brandford, Ithaca; Lorraine Brandson, Eskimo Museum; Cunera Buijs, Rijksmuseum voor Volkenkunde; Jean Flanagan Carlo, Institute of Alaska Native Arts; Liza Churchill, Glenbow Museum; Richard Conn, Denver Art Museum; Sylvie Côté-Chew, Avataq Cultural Institute; Philip Cronenwett, Dartmouth College; Bernadette Driscoll, Winnipeg Art Gallery; Rose Dufour, Université Laval; William Fitzhugh, Smithsonian Institution; Mabel Generous, Institute of Alaska Native Arts; the late Robert Gessain, Musée de l'Homme; Keld Hansen, Greenland National Museum; Elmer Harp Jr., Dartmouth College; Ada-Rachel Hopkins, Bata Shoe Museum; Heinz Israel, Staatliches Museum für Völkenkunde; Mina Jacobs, Anchorage Museum of History and Art; Veronica Johnston, Leeds City Museum; Aune Kamarainen, Helsinki; Jonathan King, Museum of Mankind of the British Museum; Nobuhiro Kishigami, Hokkaido University; Rosemarie Kuptana, Inuit Tapirisat of Canada; Kenneth Lister, Royal Ontario Museum; Stephen Loring, Smithsonian Institution; Karen McCullough, Arctic Institute of North America; Judy McGrath, Pakenham, Ontario; Charles Martijn, Ministère des Affaires culturelles, Québec; Marthe Marleau, National Archives of Canada; the late Winifred Petchey Marsh, Newmarket; Gerda Møller and Poul Mørk, National Museum of Denmark; Murielle Nagy, Inuvialuit Social Development Program, Yukon North Slope; Jill Oakes, University of Manitoba; Jarich Oosten, University of Leiden; Leif Pareli, Norsk-Folkemuseum, Oslo; Yolande Perrault, Montréal; Katherine Pettipas, Manitoba Museum of Man and Nature; Rick Riewe, University of Winnipeg; Susan Rowley, Scott Polar Research Institute; Bernard Saladin d'Anglure, Université Laval; Doris Saunders, *Them Days Magazine;* Peter Schledermann, Arctic Institute of North America; Barbara Schweger and Douglas Stenton, Canadian Circumpolar Institute; Ailsa Shimotakahara, Montréal; Ulli Steltzer, Vancouver; Henry Stewart, Tokyo; Callum Thomson, Newfoundland Museum; Beth Turcy, State University of New York, Binghamton; James W. VanStone, Field Museum of Natural History; Gillian Vogelsang-Eastwood, Stichting Textile Research Centre; the late Frère Jacques Volant, Eskimo Museum; Malcolm Wake, Royal Canadian Mounted Police Museum; Virginia Watt, Canadian Guild of Crafts Quebec; and Darlene Wight, Winnipeg Art Gallery.

The following staff members were particularly helpful: Dorothy K. Burnham, Judy Hall, Odette Leroux, Robert McGhee, Robert Pammett, and J. Garth Taylor, all of the Canadian Museum of Civilization; Charles Arnold, Pat Freeman, John Hannigan, Tessa Macintosh, Toni Riley, Tina Sangris, and Walter Slipchenko of the Government of the Northwest Territories; Margaret English, Jeanne L'Espérance, Helga Goetz, Maria Muehlen, and Marie Routledge of Indian and Northern Affairs Canada; Marie-Paule Robitaille and Céline Saucier of the Musée de la civilisation. Parks Canada supplied much information on textiles used in the Arctic.

Many years ago Lydia Black of the University of Alaska at Fairbanks encouraged me to investigate the work of Russian scholars. Their contributions to the literature have profoundly influenced my perceptions. I am most fortunate to have corresponded and spoken with ethnologists from Moscow and St. Petersburg who also gave me books and images. They are Valentina Gorbatcheva of the State Museum of Ethnography of the Peoples of the Russian Federation, St. Petersburg; the late Ilja S. Gurvich, Valery Tishkov, and Mariya Yakovlevna Zhornitskaya of the Institute of Ethnography, Moscow; and A.P. Sudakov of the publishing house Proveshcheniye, Moscow.

Some literature on northern themes is available only in the Inuit, Russian, or Scandinavian languages. A number of people cheerfully rendered translations. The most extensive work was performed by the eminent, modest Louis-Jacques Dorais. My appreciation goes to him and to Olga Boutenko, the Consulate General of Sweden, Mary Craig and the staff at the Fédération des Coopératives du Nouveau Québec, the late Nina Farmer, Shoko Ochiai Galand, Marina Goussalova, Mark Kalluak, Inge Nielsen, Astrid Shoenauer, John Hannigan and Walter Slipchenko and staff at Circumpolar Affairs, Indian and Northern Affairs Canada.

I thank the many institutions and individuals who granted me permission to quote from their works. Among them are the Avataq Cultural Institute, Asen Balikci, Canadian Arctic Producers, Canadian Museum of Civilization, Canadian Stage and Arts Publications, the Fédération des Coopératives du Nouveau-Québec, Anne Fienup-Riordan, Indian and Northern Affairs Canada, *Inuktitut Magazine,* Robin McGrath, Caroline Palliser, the San Francisco Craft and Folk Art Museum, Ulli Steltzer, and James VanStone.

Several colleagues read early drafts of this work, in whole or in part. Their trenchant suggestions assisted me to correct, refine, and redirect parts of the content. My thanks go to John Bennett, the late Alan Cooke, Mark Kalluak, Robert McGhee, Judy McGrath, Tommy Owlijoot, and J. Garth Taylor. I am particularly indebted to Lydia Black for her reading of the manuscript during a demanding year for her, and who used her outstanding erudition along with a ruthless pencil to enable me to proceed to the final draft. The anonymous readers to whom UBC Press sent my manuscript made most constructive suggestions, for which I thank them. Of course, all errors and omissions are my responsibility.

In the early stages of the project, Margaret Issenman, graphic designer, devoted a great amount of time and energy making suggestions about the images and design. I am most grateful to her for her generosity and for her enthusiastic fellowship.

The financial assistance of the Canada Council is gratefully acknowledged.

I am beholden to the late Jack Cram, Jan Echenberg, Lorraine Fairley, Maynard Gertler, Harry Gulkin, Alan Herscovici, John McGrath, and Ruth Rohrlick for their most helpful advice and assistance. Many thanks to Christine Dolezsar, Carie Lerette, and Betty Maggiorino for their clerical assistance in typing earlier drafts. Jennifer Tung gave valuable time to make sure that the manuscript was properly copied.

I deeply appreciate the sponsorship and collaboration of François Thérien and Louis-Jacques Dorais, editors of *Études/Inuit/Studies.* The staff of UBC Press, in particular editors Jean Wilson, Camilla Jenkins, and Barbara Tessman have made our association a very happy one. We are all indebted to Rebecca Yates, project coordinator and fundraising consultant, who worked cheerfully and tenaciously to bring our mission to a successful conclusion.

My three daughters, who would not countenance any suggestion from me that, in a mood of despair and self-pity, I abandon my work, have my profound affection. I dedicate this volume to them and to Arnold Issenman, who was the first to read the text. He has given continuous loving encouragement, criticism, and suggestions. His strength and devoted support made it possible to complete this work.

Map 1.1 Inuit groups and their territories

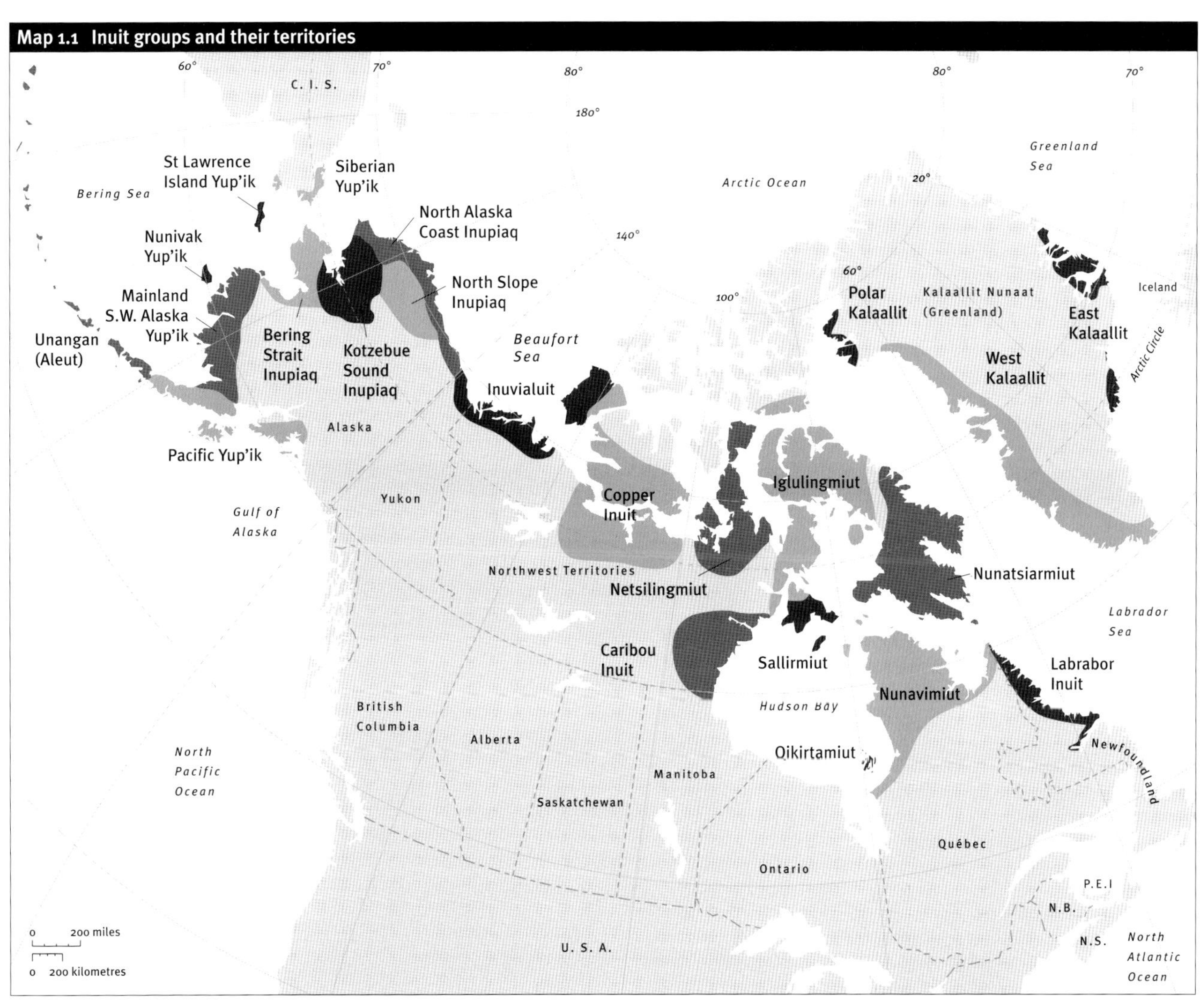

Map 1.2 Yup'ik, Inupiat, and Unangan (Aleut) communities

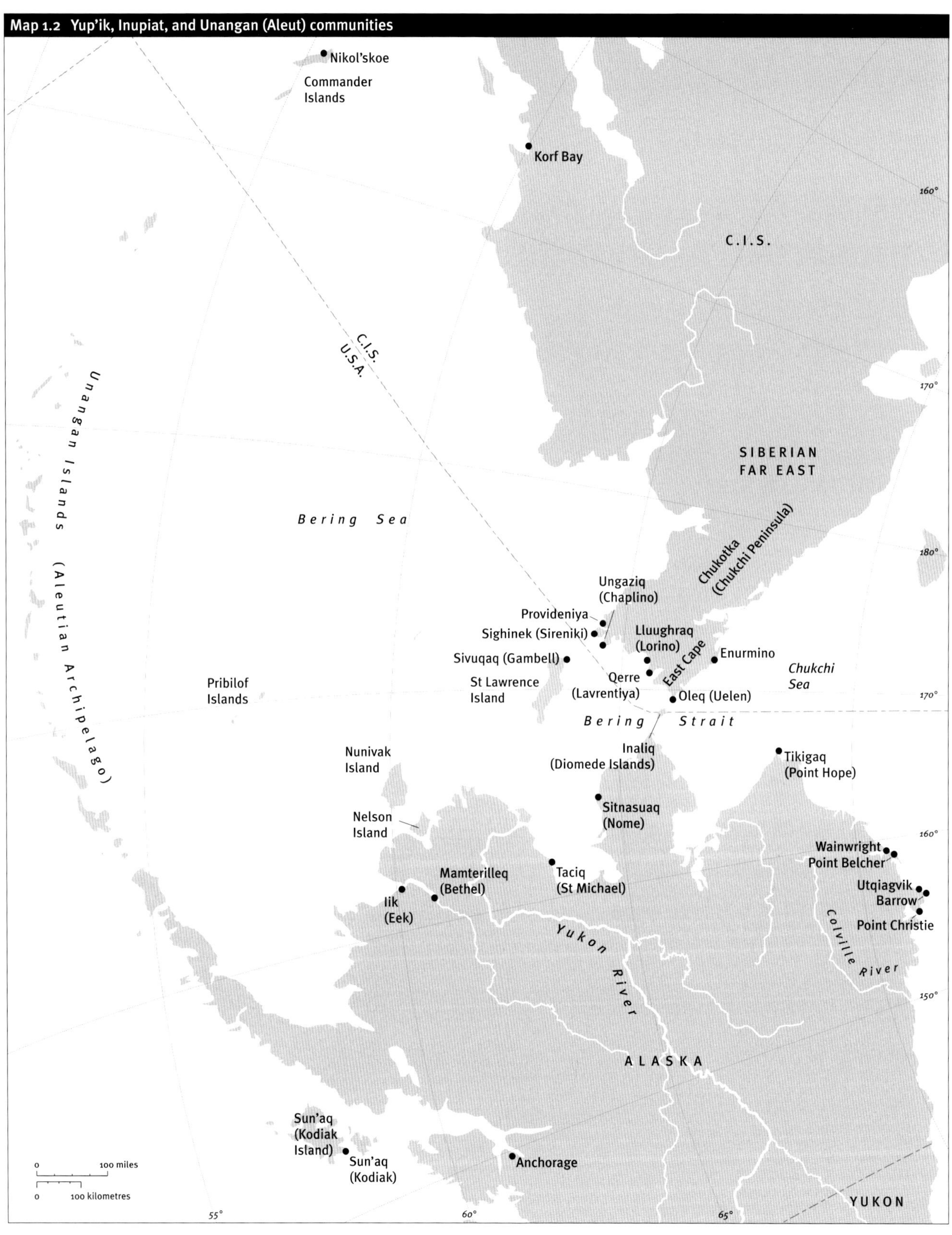

Map 1.3 Inuit communities in Canada and Kalaallit Nunaat

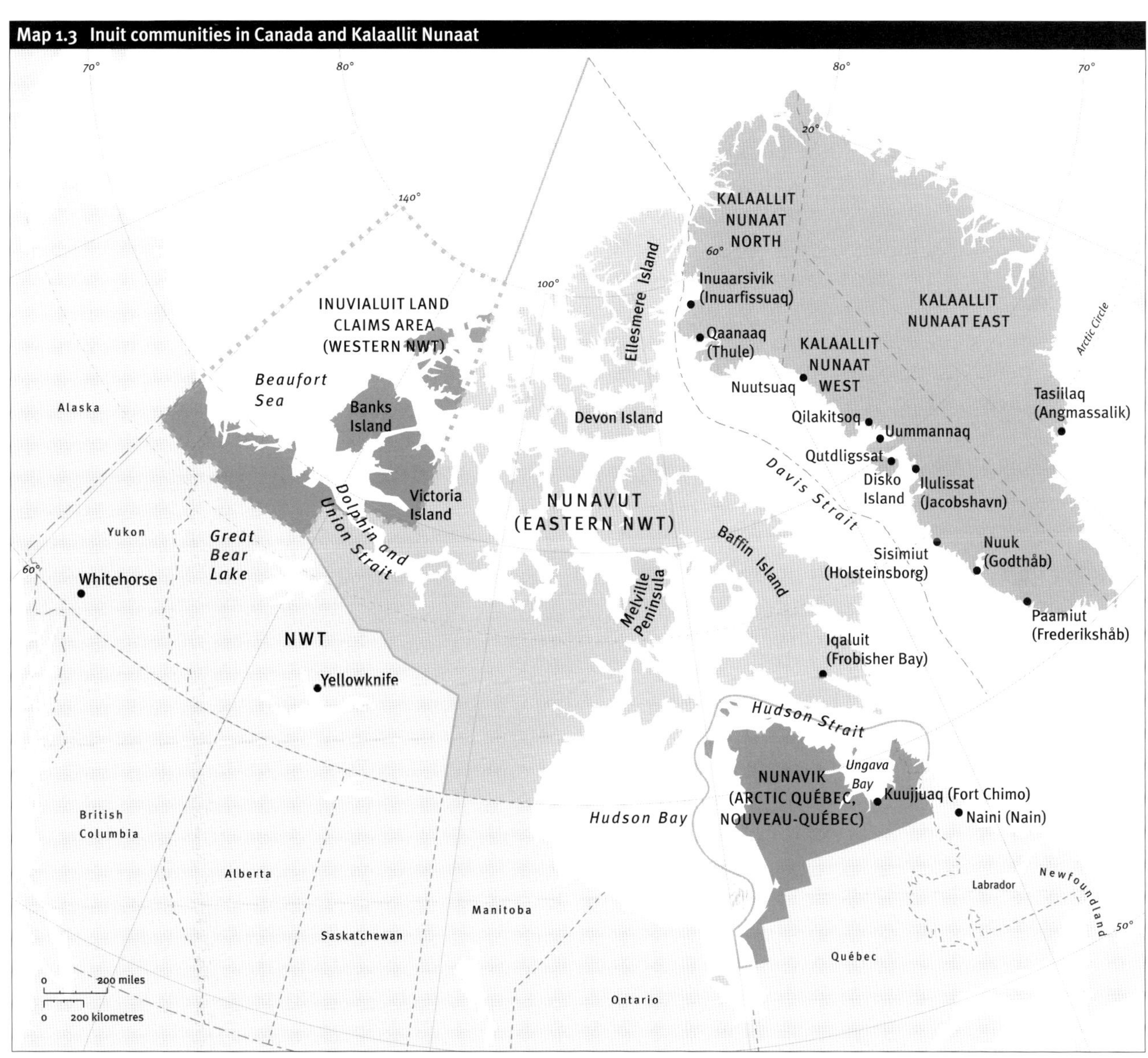

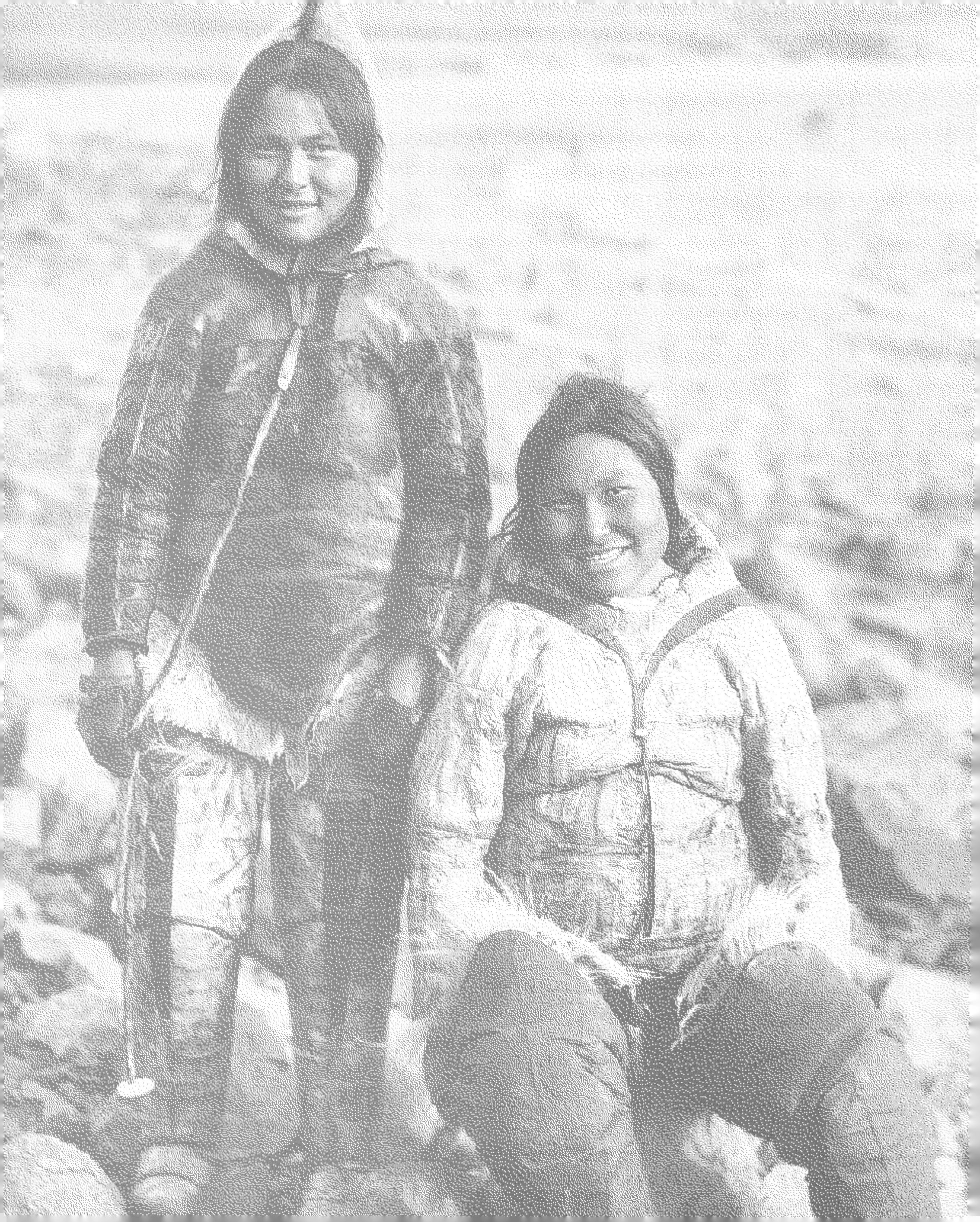

Our ancestors survived on the land and the sea, depending only on animals. It was not always easy for them, but they survived through many dangerous journeys and bitterly cold winters. They not only survived for themselves, they also survived for the future.

Mike Angutituak of Kangiqliniq[1]

When I was a child, we had clothes made from caribou and would wear store-bought clothes only in the spring and summer. When I was an adult and wore store-bought clothes in the wintertime, I would be very cold. [Sometimes] caribou were not readily available ... Our men ... had to go hunting far away just to get clothing to wear ... Our children had diapers from caribou and our blankets were made from caribou, and just from the heat of the seal oil lamp we were warm enough at night in the igloo.

Martha Angugatiaq Ungalaaq of Iglulik[2]

CHAPTER 1

THE INUIT: TIME AND SPACE

SKIN CLOTHING was one of the factors that ensured Inuit survival in the Arctic over thousands of years. Because of its functional excellence and often magical enchantment, the clothing constitutes a distinguished legacy from the Inuit to the human family.

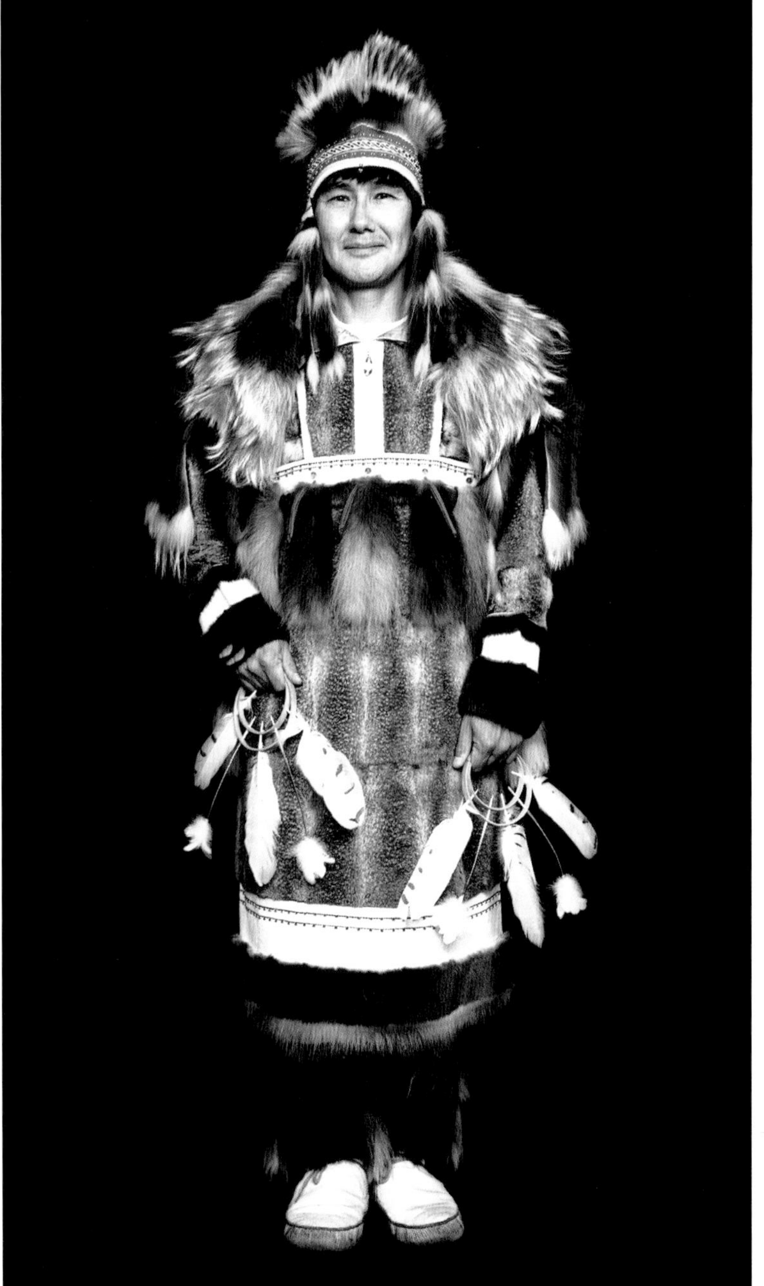

INUIT LANDS, LANGUAGES, AND POPULATION

The Inuit live in four circumpolar lands – Chukotka in northeastern Siberia, Alaska, Canada, and Kalaallit Nunaat – that straddle the Arctic Circle and stretch halfway around the globe. The area is mainly above the tree line, and in some parts of it one of the world's harshest climates prevails.

The word 'Eskimo,' by which the Inuit used to be designated, appears to have its origins in the language of the Montagnais Indians, with the meaning 'snowshoe-netter.' For some – who believed erroneously that it was derived either from an Algonquian word meaning 'eaters of raw flesh,' or from a French word for 'excommunicated' – the term was pejorative (Damas 1984a, 5-7). That judgment caused the Canadian government and some other institutions to use the word 'Inuit' instead by the late 1970s.

The people who were called 'Eskimo' now prefer to use whichever word means 'people' in their own language: Yuit or Yup'ik in the coastal areas of Chukotka in the Confederation of Independent States (CIS), on Sivuqaq, and in central and southwestern Alaska; Inupiat[3] in northern Alaska; Inuit in the Canadian Arctic; and Kalaallit in Kalaallit Nunaat. In order to present a

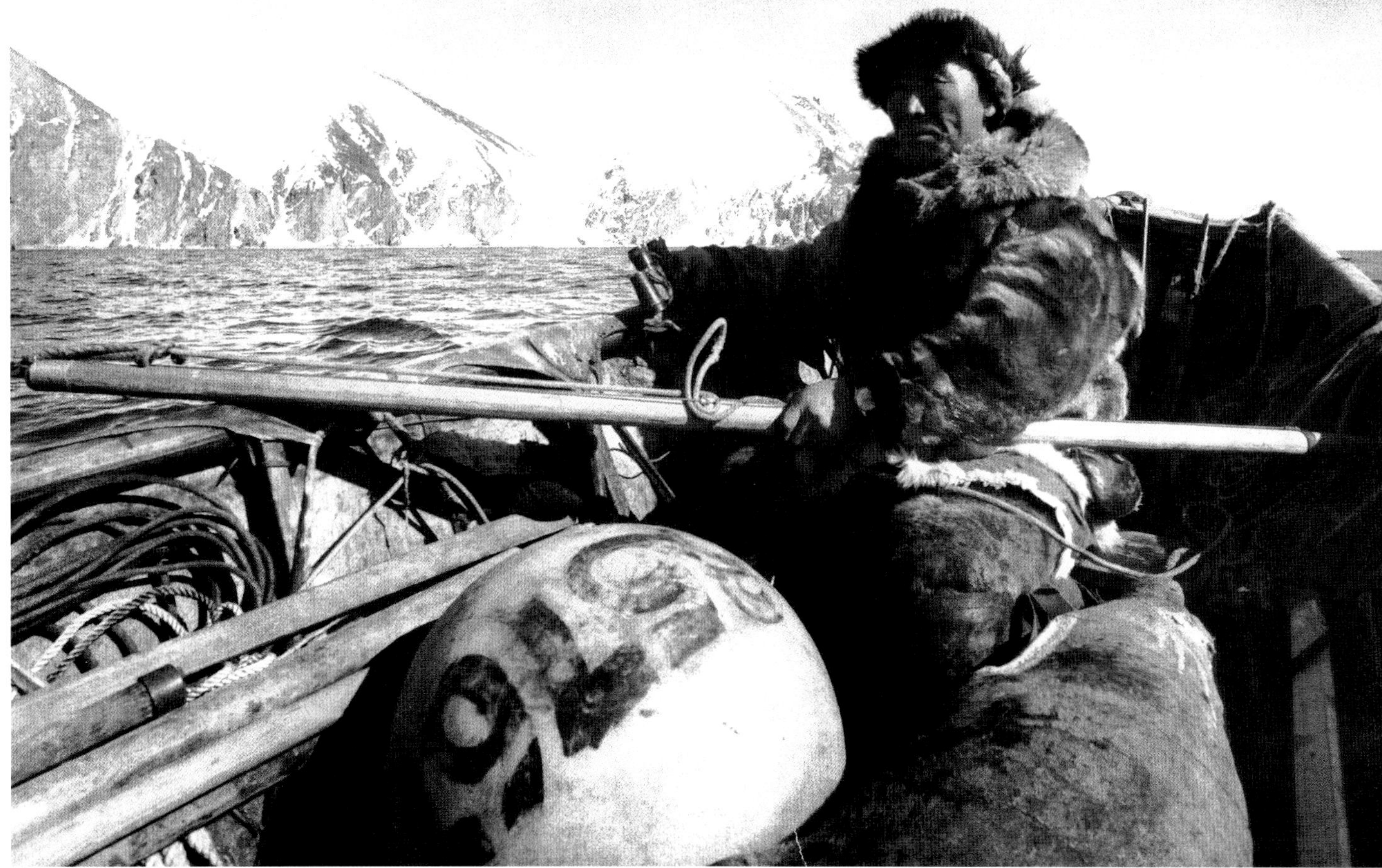

Above A Bering Sea Siberian Yup'ik hunter wears a reindeer-skin parka and trousers and a separate fur cap.

Opposite Chuna McIntyre, a Yup'ik artist and choreographer of Eek, Kuskokwim Bay, Bering Sea, Alaska, 1996, wears his traditional men's parka, called a *Kay'urrutalek* — 'One with arm bands.' The parka is composed of Arctic squirrel, river mink, land otter, Arctic wolf, wolverine, seal, and caribou skins. The decoration includes birds' feet and ochre, a red earth paint. McIntyre says, 'This parka reflects my family lineage. Our late Grandmother, Augilnguq, determined the designs, according to our family position and traditional history.'

unified nomenclature, the 1977 Inuit Circumpolar Conference in Barrow, Alaska, deemed that all present-day people formerly described as Eskimos should be called Inuit.[4] Some people in Alaska who refer to themselves as Yup'ik or Inupiat find the word 'Inuit' problematical and continue to use 'Eskimo' in common parlance (Fienup-Riordan 1990, 5; Jolles 1994, 108).

When social scientists and some Inuit use the word 'Eskimo,' they refer not only to all the present-day people who speak the languages of one of the Eskaleut subfamilies but also to ancient peoples whose remains indicate that they were ancestral to or bearers of the Eskimo tradition. When these scholars use the word 'Inuit,' on the other hand, they allude both to the present occupants of the area from the coasts of Chukotka to Kalaallit Nunaat and to their immediate forebears, who descended from the Thule culture peoples. The world Inuit population, defined most broadly, divides approximately as follows: Siberia, 1,600; Alaska, 50,600 (including 10,300 in urban areas); Canada, 32,400; Kalaallit Nunaat, 51,650 (Alaska Native Language Center 1995).[5]

The language of the more than 136,000 Inuit in the four circumpolar countries has two branches: Yup'ik and Inuit-Inupiaq. Yup'ik, which consists of five languages, is spoken on the coasts of Chukotka in Siberia and in southern Alaska. Inuit-Inupiaq, consisting of several dialects, is spoken in northern Alaska and across Arctic Canada to Kalaallit Nunaat (Woodbury 1984, 49, 56).

In June 1986, Thomas Suluk, a Canadian Inuk and a member of parliament, and Georges Erasmus, former national chief of the Assembly of First Nations, Canada, had a meeting with some Siberian Yupiit.[6] In an emotional statement to the press, Suluk said, 'We managed to have a bit of broken conversation in which some words were

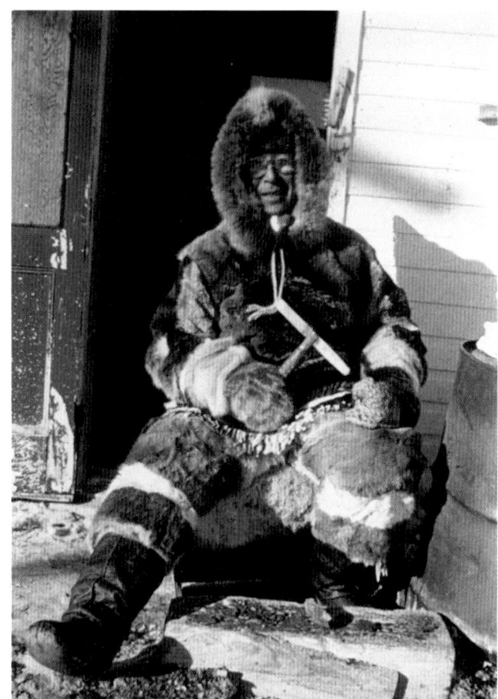

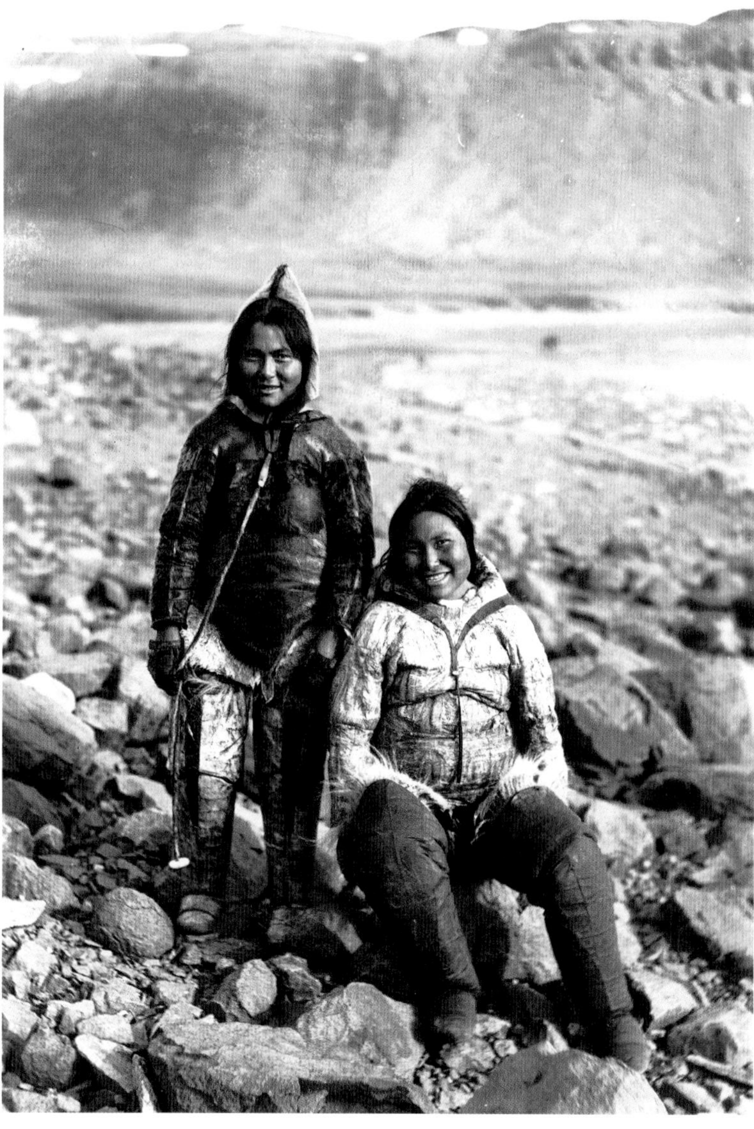

Above Simeonie Aqpik, an artist from Kimmiruk, NWT, 1988, wears caribou parka and trousers, sealskin mitts, and waterproof boots of dehaired sealskin.

Below Two young Inuhuit women from North Kalaallit Nunaat in 1909. Standing is Arnaruniak, seated is Inalliak. Both wear anoraks with small tips at the front and hip-high boots trimmed with bear fur. Arnaruniak wears a separate hood. Inalliak's anorak is made of birdskin.

similar ... The simple fact that we could understand some ... words represented for me a great occasion' (Martin 1986).

ORIGINS

Palaeo-Eskimos crossed from Asia to Alaska, although we do not know if they came 10,000 years ago via the Bering land bridge or about 5,000 years ago by boats or on the ice (McGhee 1987, Plate 11). From archeological sites we know that prehistoric Arctic peoples went on long journeys along well-established routes to trade obsidian, copper, silica, amber, and meteoritic iron, some as early as 1200 BC in the Coppermine River area (Wright and Carlson 1987, Plate 14).

PREHISTORY OF THE CANADIAN INUIT

The prehistory of Canadian Inuit is customarily divided into three periods: Independence I of the High Arctic (ca. 2000-1600 BC) and Pre-Dorset culture (ca. 2000-500 BC); Dorset culture (ca. 500 BC-AD 1500); and Thule culture (ca. AD 1000-1600).[7] The Historic Era is frequently dated from the seventeenth century to the mid-twentieth. Contemporary Era usually refers to the years from the 1950s to the present.

Pre-Dorset migrants from Siberia occupied the eastern shores of the Bering Strait, from where they spread rapidly along the Arctic coasts from Alaska to Kalaallit Nunaat. Some anthropologists propose, however, that the Pre-Dorset culture in the eastern Arctic has a separate origin and history from that of the western Arctic Palaeo-Eskimo culture. They postulate an east-west spread of another Pre-Dorset tradition that manifested itself in Arctic Canada and Greenland (Stewart 1989). The Dorset culture developed from the Pre-Dorset some time between 1000 BC and 500 BC and peaked about AD 1000.

The Dorset culture was later gradually overwhelmed by the Thule culture people, who moved rapidly from northern Alaska across Canada to Kalaallit Nunaat in the eleventh and twelfth centuries and south to northern Labrador as late as the fifteenth and sixteenth centuries. There is evidence of widespread trade among Thule peoples. The iron, both meteoritic and European smelted, found in some of their sites probably came from Kalaallit Nunaat. We also know that soapstone articles were transported from the central Canadian Arctic to the east, and then some time after AD 1200 traded westward to the northern Alaska coast. Iron found at western Arctic archaeological sites such as Memorana, on the west coast of Victoria Island, NWT, may have come from Siberia by way of Alaska (McGhee 1984, 369-76).

The Inuit, in retelling their history, refer to people whom they call Tuniit, who are believed to be Dorset and Thule culture bearers (Innuksuk and Cowan 1975, 15, 17):

There were two kinds of Tuniit: those who lived in more recent times, and those who lived even before them ... There used to be a camp [of Tuniit] called Sannirut near Pond Inlet. The Inuit took their land and the Tuniit had to leave ... They

were like the Inuit, except stronger and bigger, and the Inuit could understand their language.
Kuppuq of Ikpiarjuk

Today, you can see their tent rings all over and sometimes you find the little soapstone pots and qulliit *[lamps] that they carried inside their long coats. We used to be told that their best hunters were very scarred because the men did their cooking under their long coats when they were out seal hunting, and those that caught the most seals were cooking all the time.*
Atoat of Ikpiarjuk

The bearers of the Thule culture are believed to be the immediate forebears of present-day Inuit. The culture was remarkably uniform across northern North America and Kalaallit Nunaat. Arctic climates began to cool in the northern hemispheres after about AD 1200, however, culminating in the Little Ice Age between approximately 1650 and 1850, and the Thule culture suffered with the change. The populations of most sea animals, especially some species of whales and seals, decreased or even disappeared – the ringed seal, which can live under the sea ice, is an exception – and took with them a way of life.

The transition from the Thule to the Inuit culture brought with it a collapse of the cultural homogeneity exhibited by Thule remains. The Inuit gave up whale hunting as a main occupation and became fishers, and hunters of caribou, seals, and walrus. Each place developed its own way of life in response to local conditions of climate and resources (McGhee 1978, 103-7). The differences along the continuum of Inuit distribution were not significant in degree but were sufficient to distinguish, by dialect or by style of clothing, the origin and group membership of a person.

INUIT GROUPS IN CANADA

There are today nine major Inuit groups in Canada, each associated with a locality and each of which has its own historical development. A tenth group, the Sallirmiut, who inhabited Southampton Island, NWT, was swept by an epidemic in 1902 in which almost everyone perished. Within the present groups are several subgroups, defined by the Inuit according to where they live. The ten groups, more or less from west to east, are the Inuvialuit, Copper Inuit, Netsilingmiut, Iglulingmiut, Sallirmiut, Caribou Inuit, Nunatsiarmiut (Baffinland Inuit), Nunavimiut (Québec Inuit), Qikirtamiut (from Sanikiluaq), and Labrador Inuit.

The Inuit population of Canada, a total of 32,400, is distributed as follows: Northwest Territories, 20,800; Nunavik, 8,100; Newfoundland, 1,900; and the remaining 1,600 scattered through other provinces (Alaska Native Language Center 1995; Canada 1991, 90). Legislation to create Nunavut – meaning 'our land' – as a territorial government has been introduced in the Canadian parliament. Native peoples' land claims have changed borders, and with them population estimates. As of 1991, the Inuit population of Nunavut was estimated at 17,500. The Inuit population of the

Inuvialuit Land Claims area, a territory separate from and west of Nunavut, numbers 2,500 (Dickerson and McCullough 1993, 2).

ARCHAEOLOGICAL EVIDENCE OF CLOTHING

Many tools for clothing manufacture have been found at the archaeological sites, making the production of tailored fur clothing a probability even though direct evidence is not available. While we have no positive proof of trade in furs – their impermanence leads to loss of the evidence – we can postulate from the historical record and present-day research that furs and skins have been part of inter-Native exchanges for thousands of years.

Finds of clothing or its fragments from bygone ages in the Arctic are rare.[8] We do not know what the most ancient ancestors of the Inuit wore, but on the basis of figurines, tools, cut and sewn skins, Inuit narrative, and images rendered by Europeans, we are able to theorize that their clothing, particularly that of the Thule culture bearers, was similar to the apparel of later periods.

Figurines

The oldest evidence suggesting the development of clothing suitable for the Arctic comes from the CIS, but its relationship to later pre-Inuit cultures is, at best, indirect. Russian scholars believe that in the Upper Palaeolithic Age, 30,000 to 40,000 years ago, hunter and gatherer societies had to create tailored fur clothing to be able to hunt in winter (Okladnikov 1964, 14; 1970, 24). Some postulate that with population growth, food in traditional areas became insufficient, and the nomads began to move farther north. Although the new areas were rich in game – fox, reindeer, and arctic grouse – the very cold climate necessitated some adaptation. They learned to produce fire, possibly using the bow-drill, and began to prepare skins, to sew fur clothing, and to build warm dwellings.

Palaeolithic sites at Buret' and Mal'ta, CIS, dated 23,000 to 24,000 years ago have yielded important archaeological data (Michael 1984, 39; Okladnikov 1941). Among the finds at Buret' is a statuette interpreted as a woman dressed in a tailored skin garment.[9] Four clothed figurines discovered at Mal'ta are considered to exhibit fur clothing, girdles, shoulder belts, back pouches, and headdresses (Abramova 1967, 67, 89).

The Dorset era has produced many statuettes, a number of them with representations of clothing.[10] A distinguishing feature of the clothing of some of these figurines is a high, upright collar on a hoodless parka. This style is found on figurines excavated from sites in Kalaallit Nunaat, Labrador, Nunavik, and the eastern part of the Northwest Territories.[11]

Some Dorset carvings can be interpreted as human figures dressed in long apparel with a pointed hood, although the matter is not without controversy. One such sculpture has been described as having 'the shape of a Late Dorset triangular point hafted onto an incomplete arrow shaft or harpoon head ... [or] as a caribou hoof ...

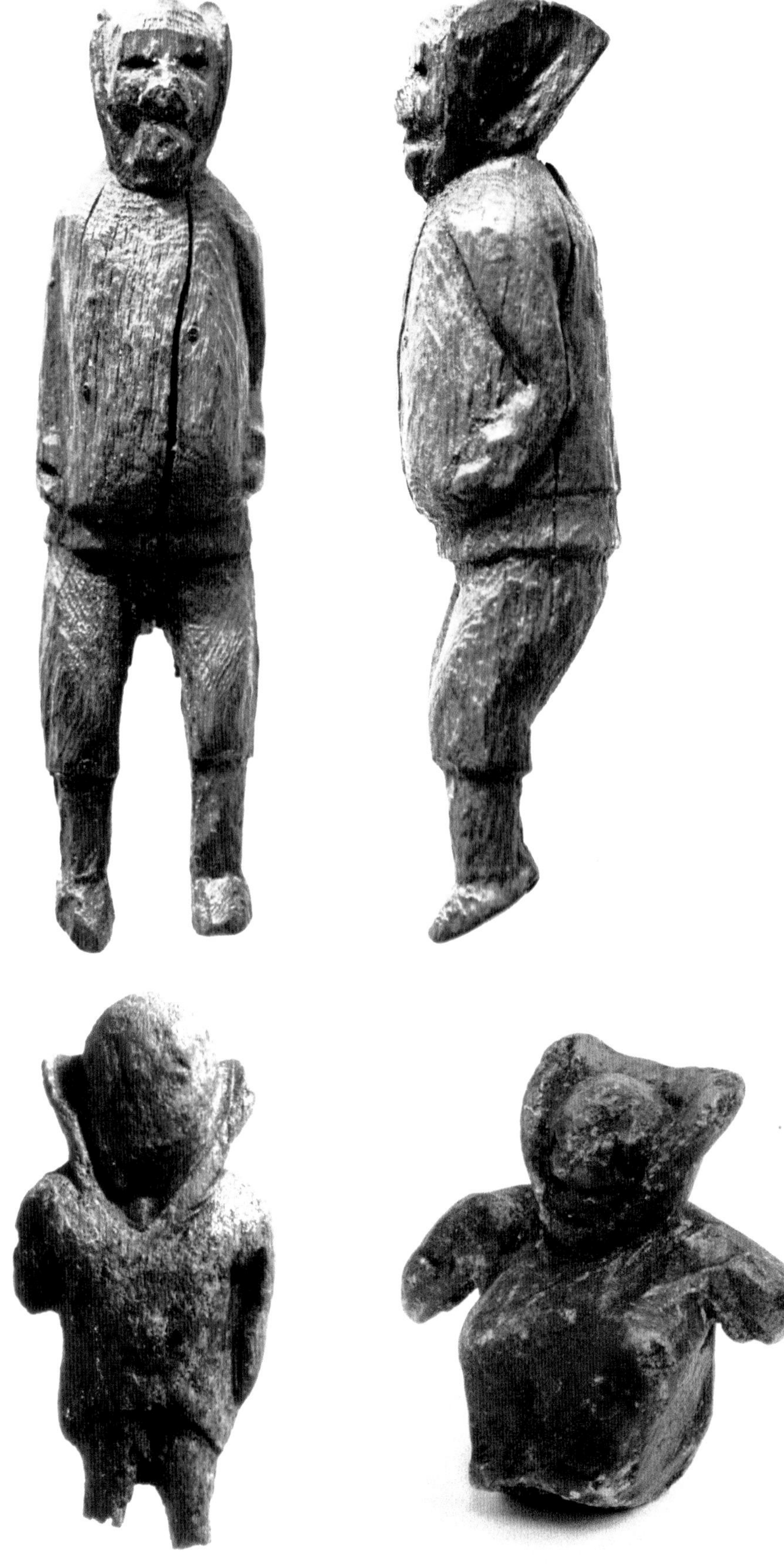

Above Wooden figurine, 7.8 cm, probably Late Dorset, AD 500-1000. Collected at Porden Point, Devon Island, NWT, by Robert McGhee in 1975. The carving depicts 'a person dressed in kamiks, trousers to just below the knees, double parka with the inner reaching to the hips, the outer to the waist, and a V-shaped collar (looking from above) extending to the top of the head' (McGhee, written communication 1982).

Below left Antler figurine, 2.9 cm, Dorset, AD 500-1500. Found at the Tuvaaluk Site, Diana Island. The even bottom edge of the parka suggests that the figure is male.

Below right Soapstone figurine, 3 cm, Late Dorset, AD 1350-1500. Found on Shuldham Island, Labrador, by William Fitzhugh in 1978.

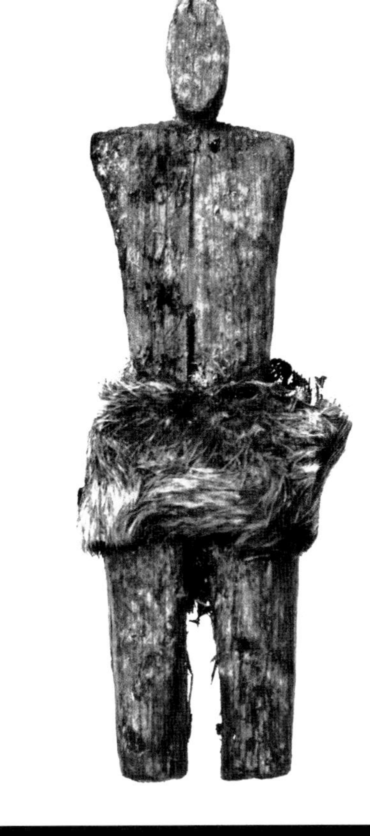

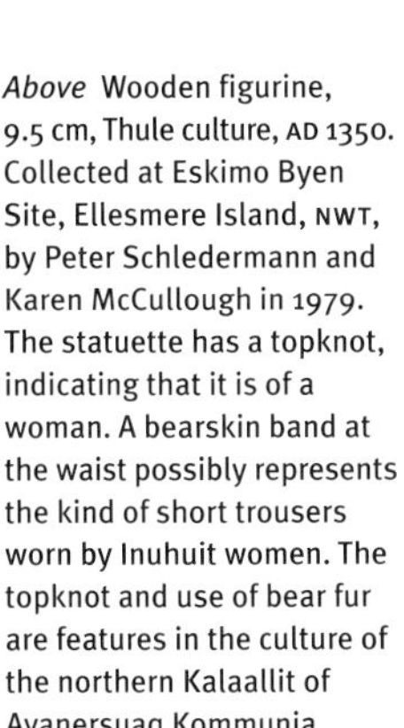

Above Wooden figurine, 9.5 cm, Thule culture, AD 1350. Collected at Eskimo Byen Site, Ellesmere Island, NWT, by Peter Schledermann and Karen McCullough in 1979. The statuette has a topknot, indicating that it is of a woman. A bearskin band at the waist possibly represents the kind of short trousers worn by Inuhuit women. The topknot and use of bear fur are features in the culture of the northern Kalaallit of Avanersuaq Kommunia.

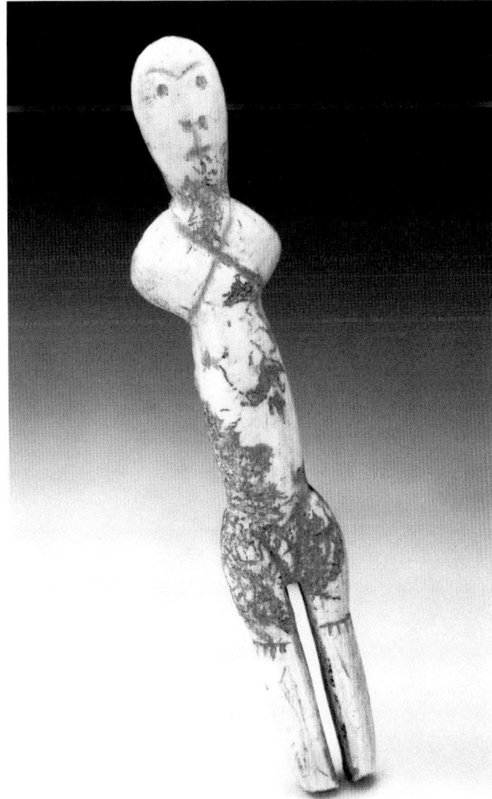

Below Ivory figurine, 8.5 cm, Thule culture, AD 1000-1600. Collected at the Bay of God's Mercy, Southampton Island, NWT. Incised on the statuette are straps that cross the chest, possibly to represent the cord of the amaut. The outline of the pelvis and navel are visible. Markings at the top of the high boots suggest a fur border. The facial markings seen on this figurine are unusual for a Thule culture statuette.

[or] as a swimming seal' (Thomson 1985, 47). Statuettes associated with the Thule culture are usually faceless and have knobs to represent arms (Sproull 1977, 23-8, passim).

Clothing Tools: Microblades, Uluit, Needles, and Needlecases

Incontrovertible evidence of clothing manufacture by prehistoric Arctic peoples from 2000 BC to the Thule and post-Thule eras comes to us in archaeological finds of tools such as *uluit* (referred to in the singular as *ulu,* meaning woman's knife), scrapers, needles, needlecases, thimbles, and thimble holders.[12] It is sometimes possible to ascertain the era from which such artifacts originate by the site of discovery, carbon dating, thermoluminescence testing, and by their shape, materials, and the methods by which they were produced. Since some archaeological material was gathered in the early days without corroborating evidence, however, researchers cannot always be certain about placing an artifact within a specific era.

The masterpieces of the Independence I and Pre-Dorset people are their precise, miniature, jewel-like, chipped stone tools (McGhee 1978, 37-43, 123-5). Their microblades, skin scrapers, bone awls, and ivory needles and needlecases suggest that they made tailored skin clothing. Tools that could scrape and sever skins were made from quartz or chert. Microblades, struck from a specialized core of chert, were parallel-sided flakes with very sharp edges. Tiny spalls or splinters, removed from a tool called a burin, formed blades with chisel-like cutting edges. Such blades in themselves probably served as cutting or carving tools, or could be placed on the side or end of a scraper. The Independence I culture of Kalaallit Nunaat (2050-1700 BC) gives evidence of skin dressing and clothing production: 'Hides were worked with large triangular convex end scrapers often having strongly flared ears or spurs. Tailored clothing was sewed with thin round-eyed needles made from goose or small mammal limb bones with the aid of bone bodkins. Needles were stored in tubular bone cases' (Fitzhugh 1984, 529).

Excavations from 1961 to 1963 on Baffin Island of artifact complexes from the earliest Pre-Dorset to the Dorset era (carbon-dated sites ranged from 2500 BC to AD 480) suggest that the Dorset culture developed directly out of the Pre-Dorset. This evolution indicates an efficient technological equilibrium over a continuum of 3,000 years – a unique event in North American material history. Pre-Dorset stone tools became increasingly miniaturized in, for example, the southern Baffin region: 'The implication is that hand motions in tool fabrication and use were highly skilled, highly controlled in terms of pressure and placement of the tool, and that most of the effective action came from strong finger motions rather than those of wrist and arm. Under such conditions ... [an] Eskimo woman [had] no difficulty sewing stitches less than one half millimetre apart' (Maxwell 1973, 301-2).

Dorset finds, which include uluit, scrapers, microblades, needles, and needlecases, attest to skin preparation and clothing manufacture. Miniature blades struck from a core of chert, for example, were discovered on Ellesmere Island in 1977-9. Dated between 2500 BC and AD 1000 and measuring 2.5 to 7.5 centimetres in length, these jewel-like blades were inset or lashed into handles of bone or ivory, and used for scraping and cutting skins.

The crescent-shaped knife known as the ulu, sometimes called the semi-lunar knife, is found in many eras and in many parts of the world (Boas [1927] 1955; McGrath 1992; Mason 1891; Porsild 1915). In Inuit societies it is used to skin and cut up seals, to process and cut hides, and to prepare food. The Kachemak III culture bearers of the Pacific Eskimo region, Alaska, for example, whose tradition spanned the first millennium to about AD 1000 and thus occurred within the Canadian Dorset era, produced stone uluit of the semi-lunar form (Clark 1984, 139-41).

At least three forms for the handle of the ulu appear in assemblages of clothing tools from the Thule culture bearers: the handle and blade in one piece; the wide handle, which has a socket into which the blade is secured; and the handle with a stem, or tang, at the end of which the blade is fastened. The last of these is probably the prototype for the T-shaped or tanged handle of historical and contemporary uluit (Mathiassen 1927, Part 2, 73). The last two forms of the ulu have continued to be used in the Historic and Contemporary eras, the one-piece grip being associated more particularly with tools in Siberia, Alaska, and the Inuvialuit Land Claims area. A Thule culture ulu found near Mittimatalik has a whalebone handle with a slate blade fastened to it by

Above Stone tools, Pre-Dorset, ca. 2000-1600 BC. Found at Port Refuge, Devon Island, NWT. Clockwise from left are one sidescraper (2.6 cm), two endscrapers, three burin spalls, and three microblade fragments.

Below Tools, Dorset, ca. 500 BC-AD 1500. From various Arctic sites. Left to right are two microblade fragments, two ivory needles, an endscraper, and a comb (6.3 cm).

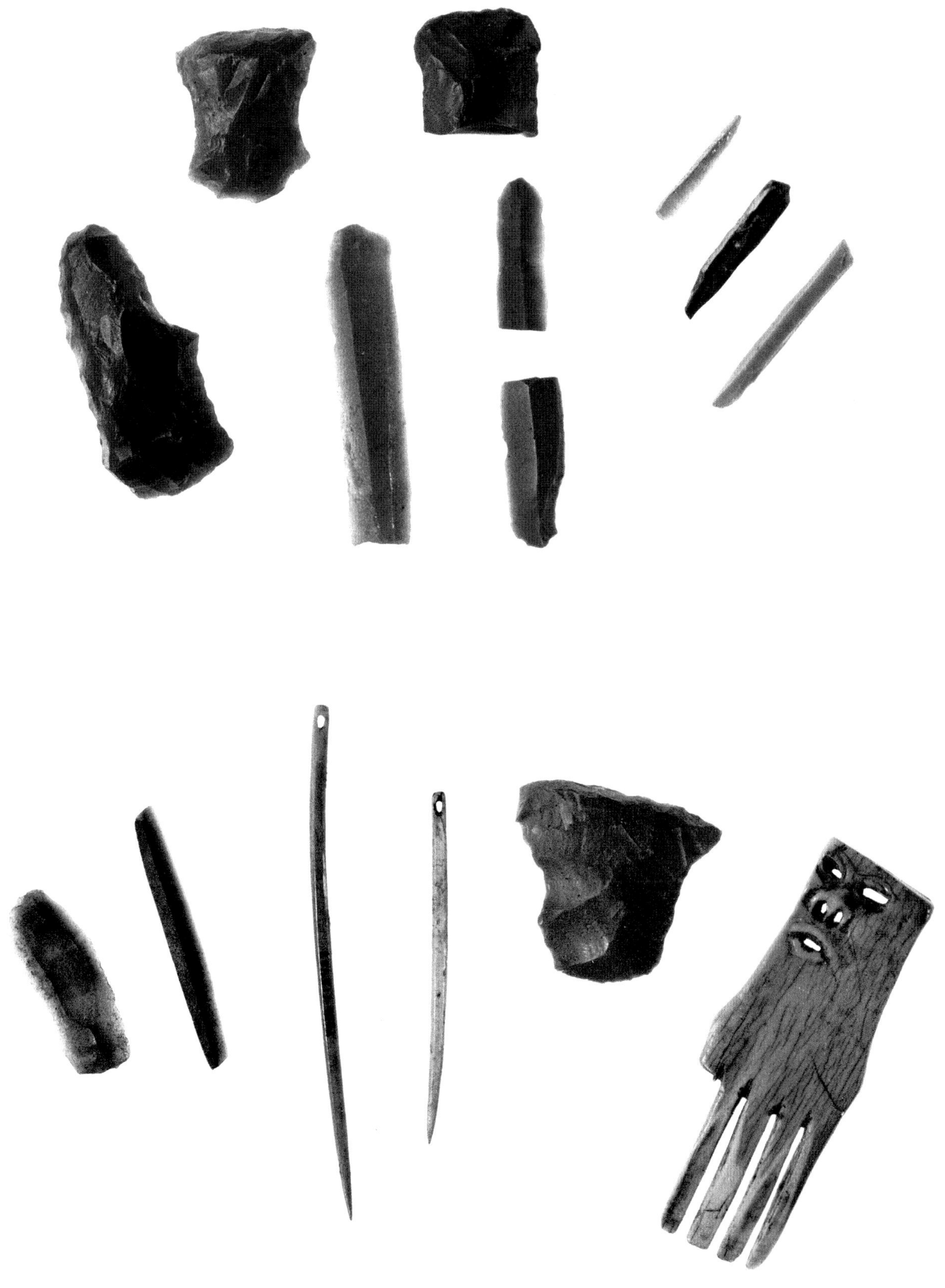

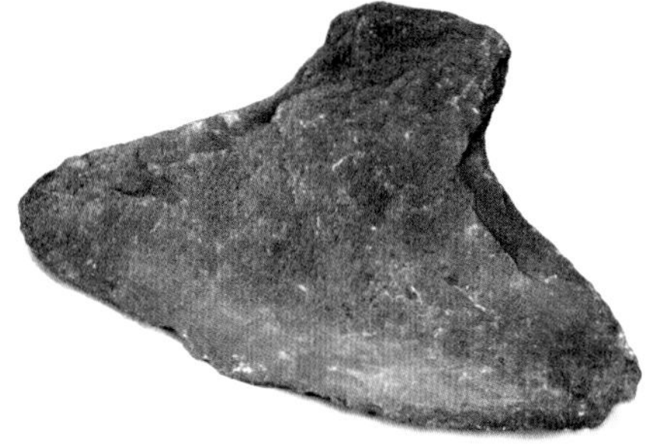

Slate ulu, 13 cm, Thule or immediate post-Thule culture. Collected by C.E. Wilcox on the north side of Strathcona Sound, NWT, in 1925-6. Tang and blade are in one piece.

baleen, a testament to the whale-hunting economy of the Thule culture bearers (Mathiassen 1927, Part 1, 173).

Generally, Pre-Dorset needles have oval cross-sections and round eyes that appear to be drilled with a rotary motion from either side. Needles found at Dorset sites, however, are distinguished by a cross-section that is variously quadrangular, lenticular, rhomboid, or lozenge shaped. The eyes are elongated and are made by gouging from either side of the needle until the indentations meet to make a hole (McGhee, personal communication 1985). For about 200 years during the Early Dorset era, according to a proposal by Jorgen Meldgaard, the double-pointed needle was the only type used in Arctic Canada and Kalaallit Nunaat. Between about AD 500 and AD 600 the needle gradually reverted to some of the features found in Pre-Dorset needles: the eye at the distal end, the point at the proximal end, and with a rounder eye and cross-section than the Dorset form (Meldgaard, personal communication 1983).[13] Thule needles and needlecases differ from their counterparts in previous eras. For the most part they have a rounder cross-section and rounder eyes than Dorset era needles.

As with uluit, needlecases are found dating from prehistoric to historical times and in many countries. Inuit women and their ancestors stored their fragile needles in cases made of bone or ivory, which were either tubular or carved with various forms. 'Winged' needlecases made their appearance in the Thule era. They disappeared from use except for the Sallirmiut of Southampton

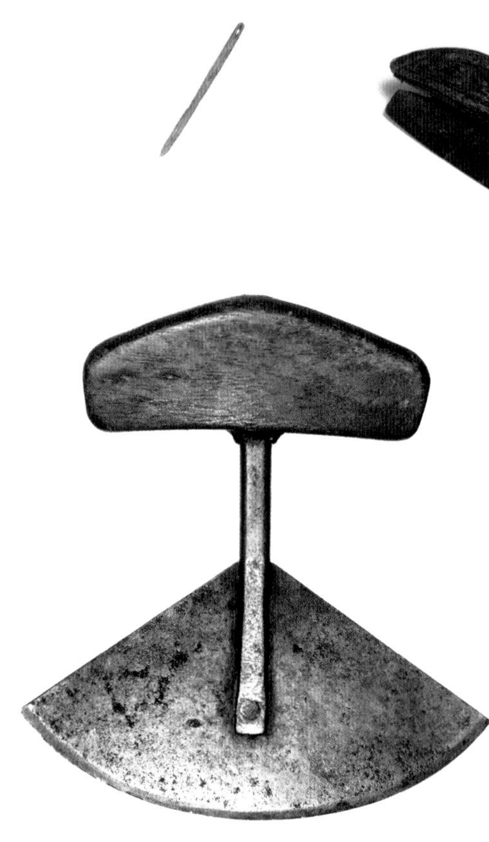

Above (Clockwise from top left) Wooden and stone ulu, 13.5 cm, Thule culture, AD 1000-1600. Collected in the Central Arctic by J.J. O'Neill. Whale bone ulu handle, 10.5 cm, Thule culture, AD 1000-1600. Collected in the Canadian Arctic by the Arctic Institute of North America, Calgary. Fossilized ivory and stone ulu, 8.2 cm, Punuk, Old Bering Sea culture, AD 600-1200. Collected in Alaska by Claudia Ferguson. Bone needle, 5.5 cm, Middle to Late Dorset culture, AD 1-1000. Found on Diana Island, NWT. Some of the earliest uluit have a wide grip with a socket or groove into which the blade is driven, glued, or sometimes held with lashing.

Left Wooden and steel ulu, 10.5 cm, Historic Era, Iglulingmiut, 1958. Collected at Naujaat, NWT.

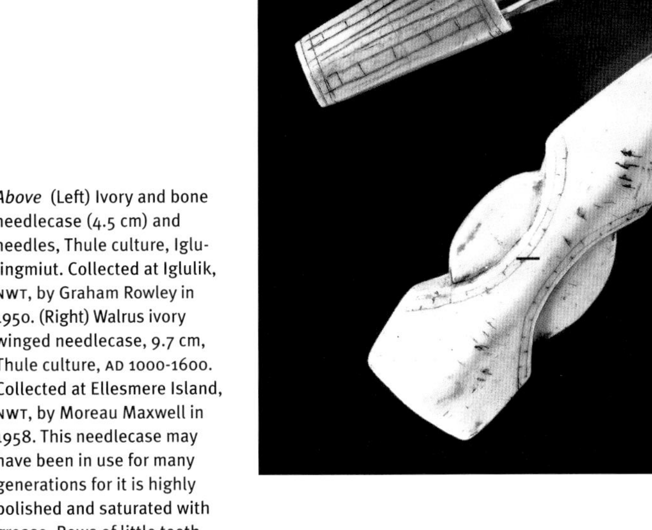

Above (Left) Ivory and bone needlecase (4.5 cm) and needles, Thule culture, Iglulingmiut. Collected at Iglulik, NWT, by Graham Rowley in 1950. (Right) Walrus ivory winged needlecase, 9.7 cm, Thule culture, AD 1000-1600. Collected at Ellesmere Island, NWT, by Moreau Maxwell in 1958. This needlecase may have been in use for many generations for it is highly polished and saturated with grease. Rows of little teeth marks suggest its secondary use as a baby pacifier (Maxwell 1960, 62).

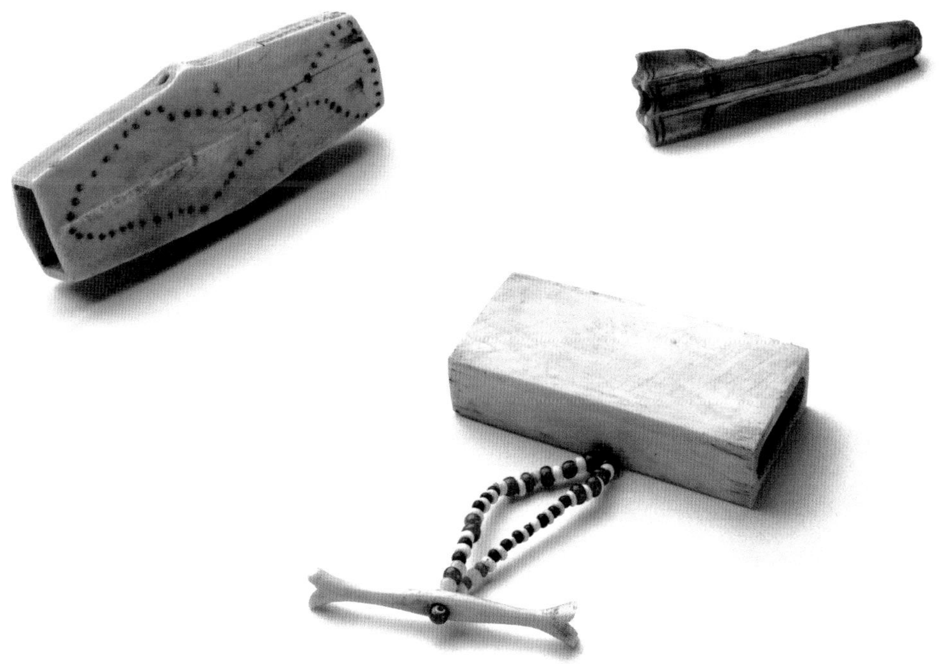

Below (Clockwise from top left) Ivory needlecase, 7.2 cm, Nunavimiut, mid-nineteenth century. Collected from the east coast of Hudson Bay, Nunavik, by Dr. W.B. Malloch. The hollow centre was packed with dried moss into which needles were inserted for safekeeping. Ivory needlecase, 6 cm, early nineteenth century, Inupiat (north Alaska). Collected by Claudia Ferguson. The flukes at one end and the small nobs toward the centre evoke the tail and flippers of a whale. Ivory and bead needlecase with thimble holder, 5.5 cm, Nunavimiut, late nineteenth century. Collected from the east coast of Hudson Bay, Nunavik.

Opposite above Parka made from sea mammal intestines and fur, sewn with sinew complete sleeve 35 cm, Thule culture, AD 1200. Collected on Skraeling Island, NWT, by Peter Schledermann and Karen McCullough, 1978. The pattern of this gutskin (waterproof coat) is similar to those of the Historic and Contemporary eras. The strips of gut in this parka are vertically aligned. Fur surrounds the face opening. The hood back is gathered and is anchored to the main part by root-like extensions.

Opposite below Caribou-skin hood, sewn with sinew, 33 cm, Thule culture. Caribou-skin and sealskin boot, sewn with sinew, 31.5 cm, Thule culture. Caribou-skin and sealskin child's mitten, sewn with sinew, 15.8 cm, Thule culture. All collected at Devon Island, NWT by Robert Park in 1985. The hood, made from numerous pieces of caribou skin, fur to the inside, is designed to be worn close to the head. A skin thong acts as a drawstring at the face opening. The boot leg consists of seven vertical panels of caribou skin, fur to the outside. The sole appears to be made of dehaired seal skin; the toe is fully gathered, the heel only slightly. The mitten, of caribou skin with fur to the inside, is made up of the three-piece pattern used by contemporary Inuit. The traditional fourth piece trims the wrist with seal fur. The back of the hand piece comes over the hand edge.

Island and the Inuhuit, or Polar Inuit, of Kalaallit Nunaat, who used them into the twentieth century. The 'wings' are side-protrusions of several shapes.[14] Some scholars propose that the wings are vestiges of human arms or represent the tail of the bowhead whale. This would reflect Alaskan heritage, as needlecases in that part of the Arctic were often carved in the shape of a human figure or a whale.

Historic Era Inuit used similar needlecases of hollowed bone or ivory in different designs inherited from their Thule culture forebears: cylindrical or straight-sided, both of which sometimes widened or bulged slightly at the centre-sides of the longitude. Others were carved in the shape of animals or sea creatures. Attachments sometimes included a marrow spatula, which could be used either to scoop marrow out of bones or to put pleated creases in the soles of boots, an open-ended thimble, and a thimble holder to prevent loss of thimbles. The needles were kept safe in moss or in a narrow hide strip that the seamstress or hunter pulled in or out of the case.

Prehistoric Clothing

Archaeological sites throughout the Arctic have yielded several finds of frozen skin and clothing fragments and of whole pieces. While investigations place the majority of these artifacts in the Thule era or slightly later, some cut and sewn skins from Dorset times have been discovered. The patterns, seams, and stitches of clothing from past eras show an unmistakable connection to those of the Historic Era.

High Arctic, Canada

The era to which boot fragments from Igloo Point, Ellesmere Island, belong is problematic. From the fragility of the skins they could conceivably be ascribed to the Dorset culture, but that is unlikely (Robert Pammett, personal communication 1993-4). Nonetheless, a sealskin boot fragment from the Nanook archaeological site in the Kimmiruk area, Baffin Island, is dated 200 BC. Its components are identical to those of modern boots: bearded sealskin sole, harp seal instep, and ringed seal upper, sewn with sinew (Maxwell 1984, 366).

Parts of a sealskin boot attributed to the Thule culture was found in the frozen earth at the bottom of a house ruin near Mittimatalik, NWT. Its pattern is similar to that of boots from the Historic and Contemporary eras. The upper, made of one piece, has one longitudinal seam sewn with sinew. It is topped by a skin casing to hold a plaited sinew cord.[15] The sole is made of bearded seal skin. The women of Mittimatalik to whom the archaeologist showed the fragments said that the large coarse stitches led them to believe that the sewing was accomplished with a bone needle (Mathiassen 1927, Part 1, 183).

Excavations at Ellesmere Island produced clothing from the Thule culture bearers, ca. AD 1200, all sewn with sinew. A waterproof coat made of sea mammal intestines shows much in common with Inuit gutskins of the twentieth century. Although it was badly chewed by animals, a good part is intact (Peter Schledermann, personal communication 1990).[16] The design of the coat and of

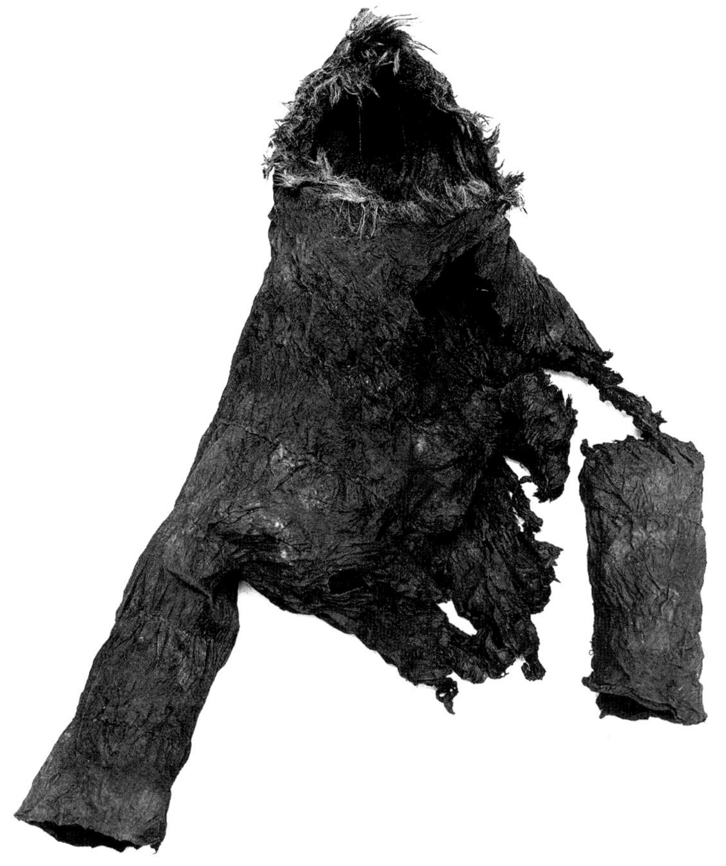

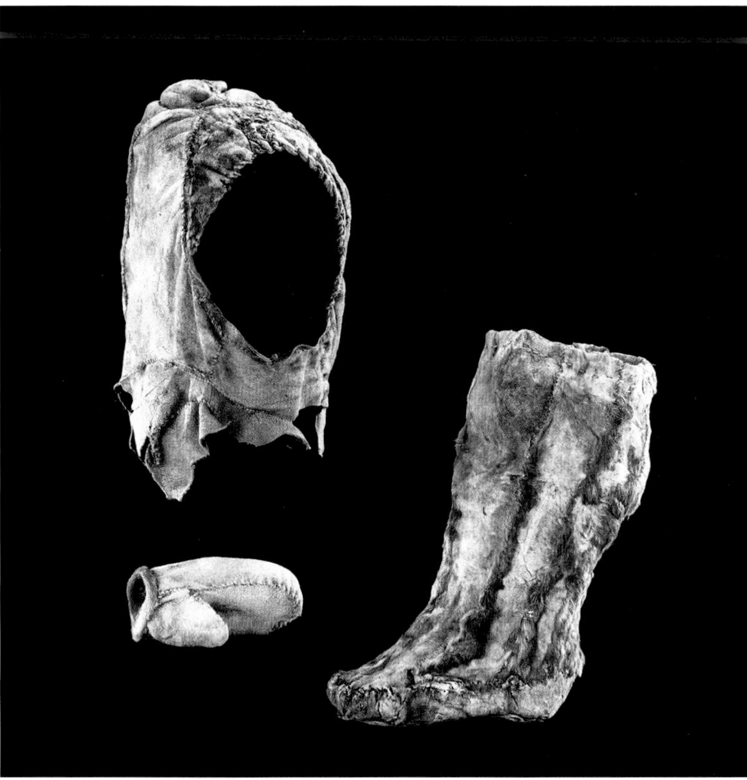

sealskin boots found in the same area suggests a link to the Inuhuit who used to live on Ellesmere Island and continue to live in Avanersuaq Kommunia – 'the place farthest north' – in northern Kalaallit Nunaat. At Smith Sound, only forty-eight kilometres of water separates Canada and Kalaallit Nunaat.

Explorations in 1985 on Devon Island, NWT, brought to light several pieces of clothing from a Thule era site, including a hood from a parka, a woman's boot, and a child's mitten. Restorative measures have revealed more fully the stitches and patterns, which in general correspond to seams and forms used today (Segal and Newton 1990).[17]

Qilakitsoq, Kalaallit Nunaat

In 1972 two Kalaallit hunters came upon eight bodies, of six women and two children, preserved by natural mummification in a dry, cold rock cavity at Qilakitsoq, western Kalaallit Nunaat. Their discovery ranks as one of the most valuable revelations about ancient Inuit and their clothing.[18] Carbon dating of the graves and artifacts points to approximately AD 1475. After completion of the research in Denmark, the artifacts discovered at Qilakitsoq were returned to Kalaallit Nunaat, where they are now in the care of the Greenland National Museum at Nuuk.

An analysis of the skin clothing found on and with the bodies at the Qilakitsoq site revealed that the 500-year-old seal skins were treated in the same way as are modern Kalaallit skins: scraped, washed, stretched, and dried. Published accounts indicate that

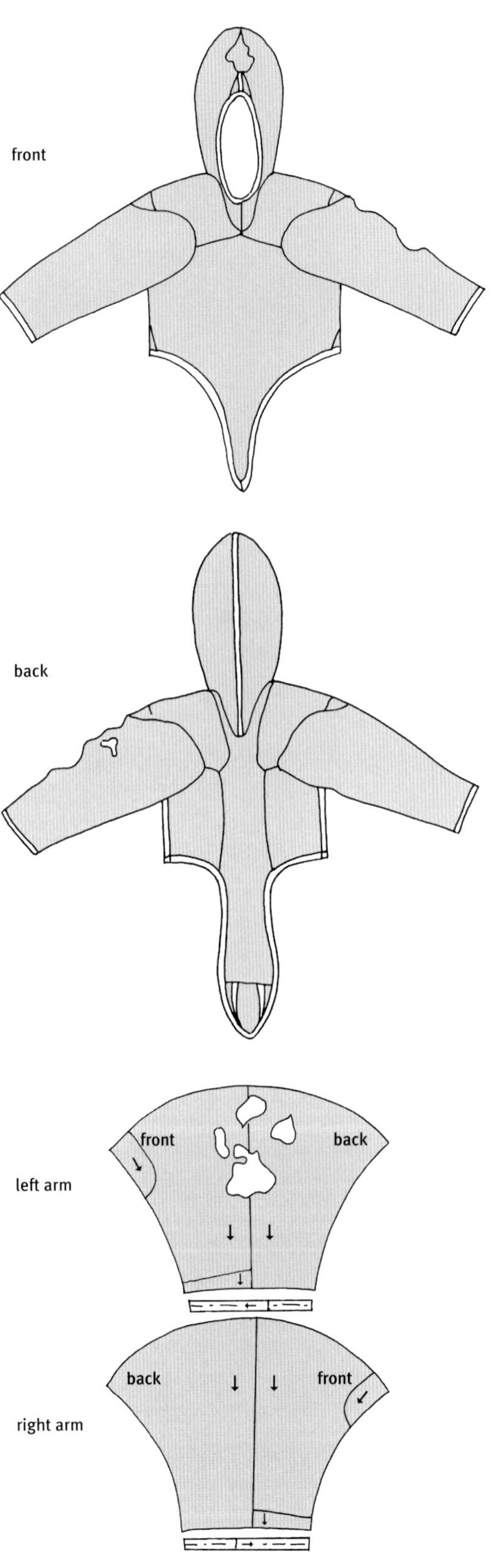

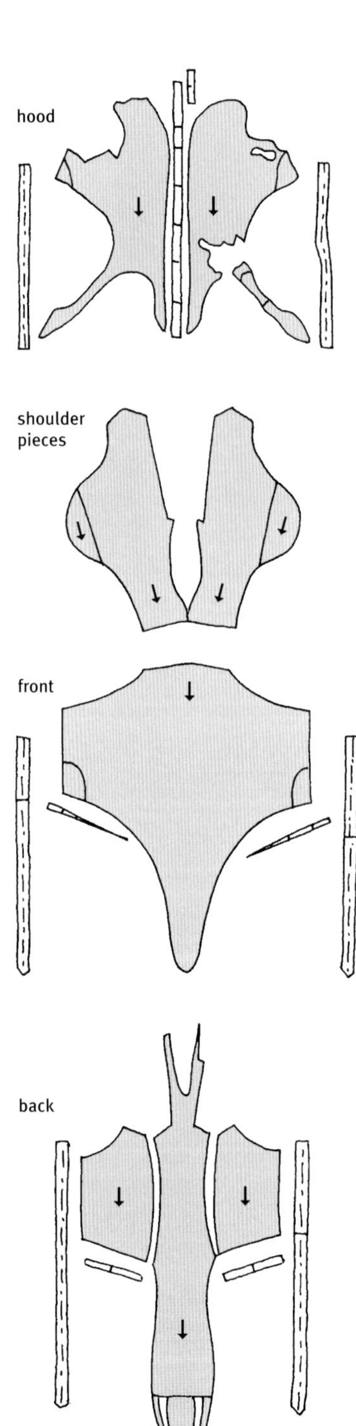

Figure 1.1
Pattern drawing of woman's jacket, Kalaallit. Arrows indicate fur flow. *Based on drawings from Greenland National Museum, Nuuk.*

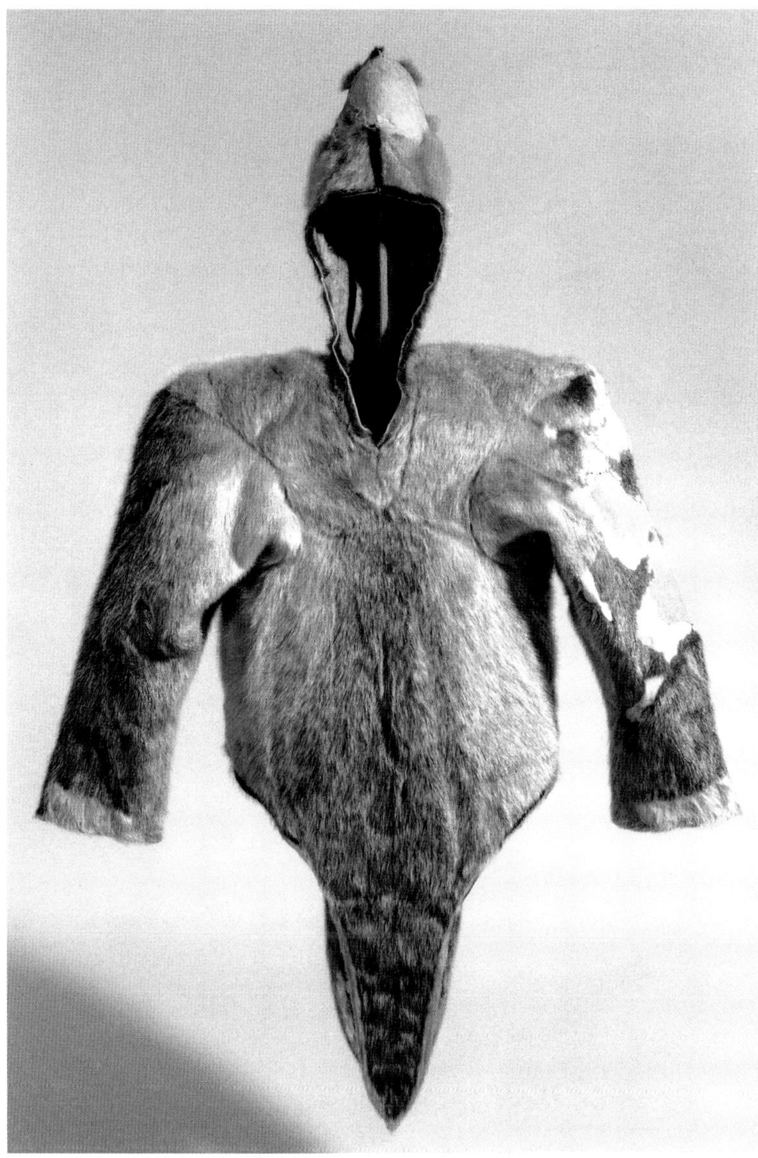

Left and below Woman's sealskin jacket, sewn with sinew, back about 130 cm, Kalaallit, ca. AD 1475. Found at Qilakitsoq, West Kalaallit Nunaat, by Hans and Jokum Grønvold, 1972. The jacket manifests features found in historic Kalaallit clothing and in other parts of the Arctic: a high, shallow hood anchored back and front into the main body by projections; a long, ovulate back tail; loose, seamless shoulders with dropped sleeve; and the use of dark and light skins, which may symbolize the seal. (See figure 1.1 for pattern.)

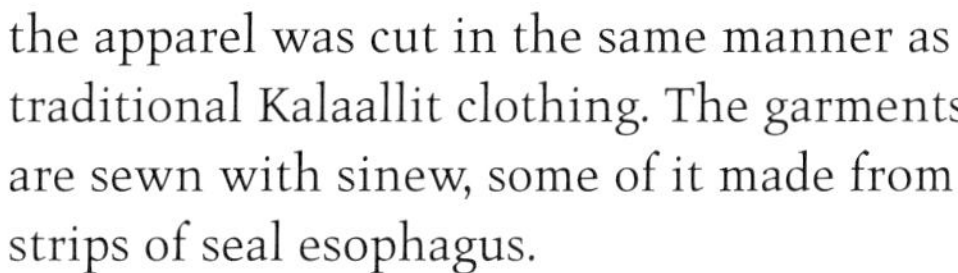

the apparel was cut in the same manner as traditional Kalaallit clothing. The garments are sewn with sinew, some of it made from strips of seal esophagus.

The skins of two seal species, the ringed *(Phoca hispida)* and the harp *(Phoca groenlandica)*, make up the outer apparel. The inner layer is made of bird skins, feathers facing inward. The boots are made with dehaired seal skin, the stockings of seal or caribou fur. Drawstrings for the boots are made of braided sinew. Small articles inferred to possess protective powers were found on the bodies or among the clothes.

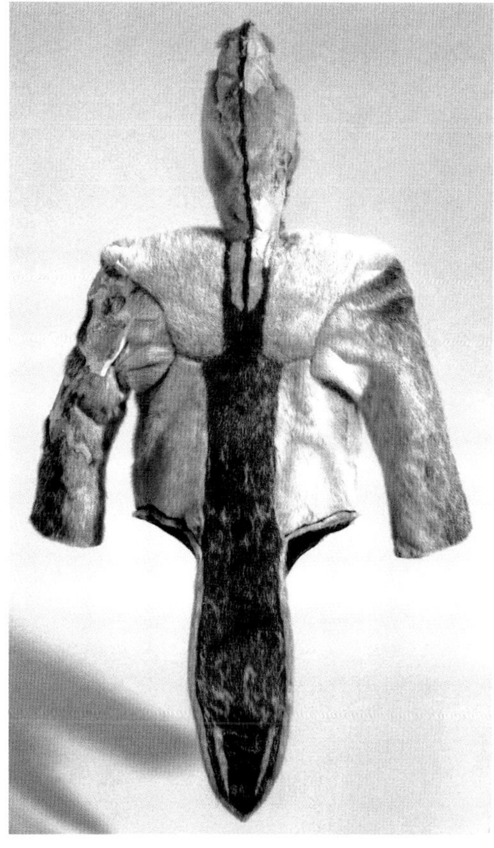

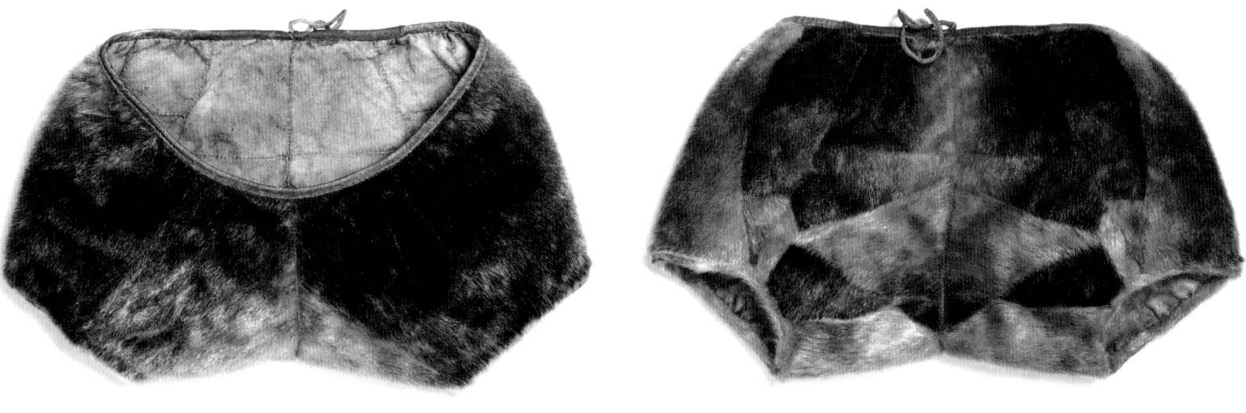

Figure 1.2
Pattern drawing of woman's housepants, Kalaallit. Arrows indicate fur flow. *Based on drawings from Greenland National Museum, Nuuk.*

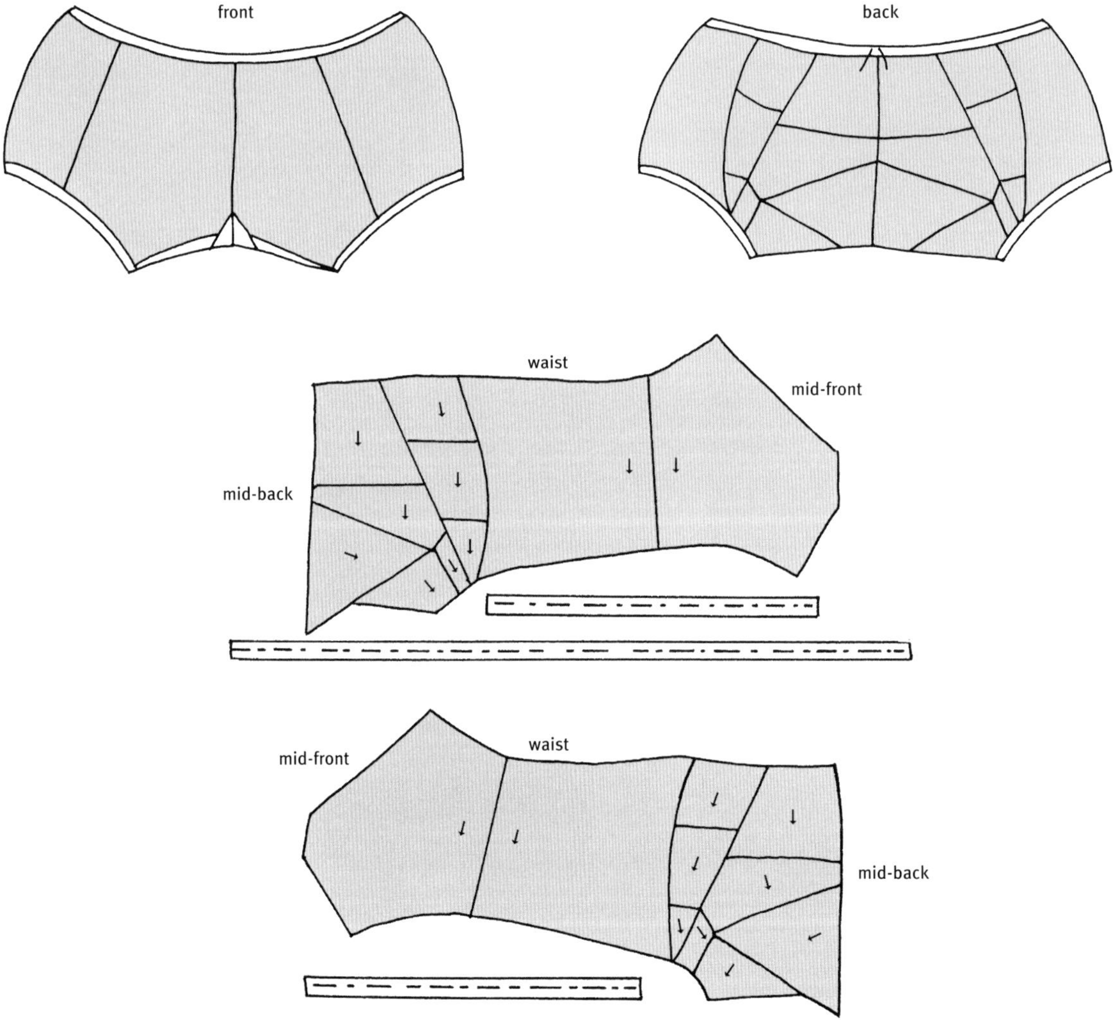

front

back

waist

mid-front

mid-back

waist

mid-front

mid-back

Opposite above Woman's sealskin housepants, sewn with sinew, back seam 28.5 cm, Kalaallit, ca. AD 1475. Found at Qilakitsoq, West Kalaallit Nunaat, by Hans and Jokum Grønvold in 1972. The short trousers are fashioned out of two symmetrical halves of eleven pieces each, joined by a centre seam. (See figure 1.2 for pattern.)

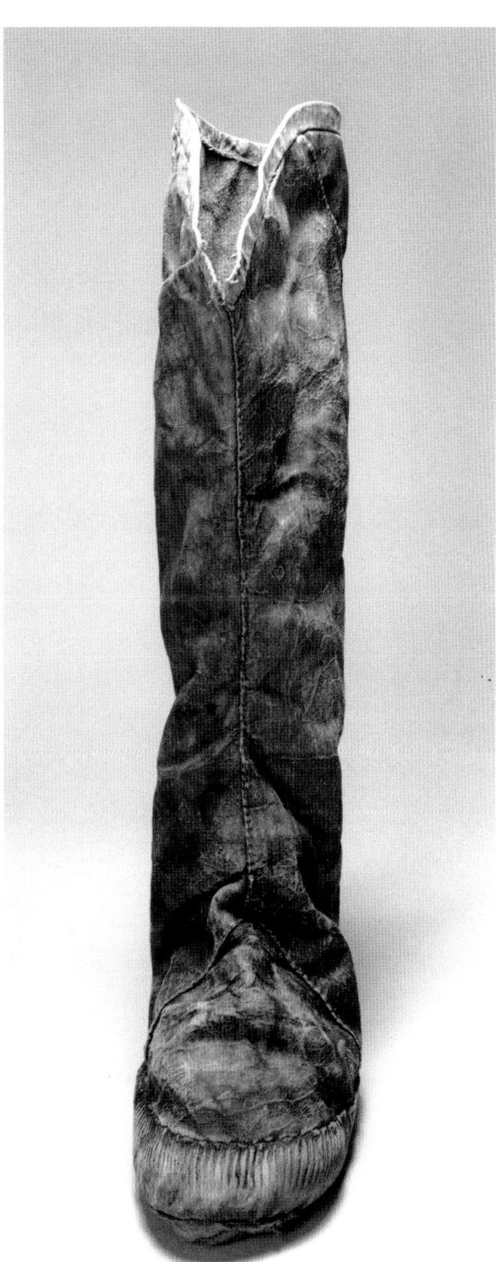

Right Woman's waterproof boot of dehaired seal skin and grass insulation, sewn with sinew, 41 cm, Kalaallit, ca. AD 1475. Found at Qilakitsoq by Hans and Jokum Grønvold in 1972. The leg has one seam running centre front and dividing at the instep to run to each side. The turned-up sole has fine pleats front and back, with a loop on each side for an ankle thong. A layer of grass for insulation was found inside the foot.

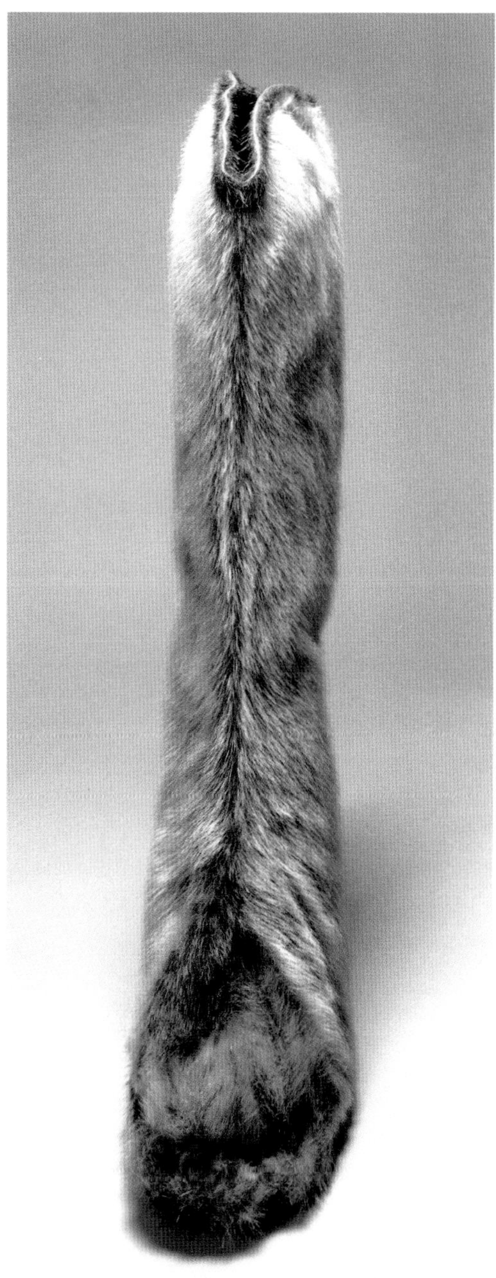

Far right Woman's sealskin stocking with grass insulation, sewn with sinew, 43 cm, Kalaallit, ca. AD 1475. Found at Qilakitsoq, West Kalaallit Nunaat, by Hans and Jokum Grønvold in 1972. Stockings were usually worn with the fur to the inside. This one is shown inside out to reveal the seal fur and the pattern. The hair on the leg points down, while the sole hair points forward.

Utqiagvik, Alaska

Excavations from 1981 to 1983 at Utqiagvik, Alaska, brought to light what may be the earliest examples of Kakligmiut clothing.[19] Kakligmiut territory consisted of a small section of the North Alaska coastal plain from Point Belcher to Point Christie, and extended approximately fifty kilometres inland. Carbon dating of bones placed a house ruin and its contents at approximately AD 1510. The clothing, as with the thousands of artifacts recovered, is considered to be different from the earlier Birnirk and Thule periods but from people ancestral to the Inupiat (Dekin 1984, 149). A ceramic shard examined by thermoluminescence tests was dated roughly AD 1530. The bone analysis date was later considered possibly suspect due to the chance of contamination by 'old' carbon. The estimated date is now given conservatively as AD 1500-1826, although scientists look forward to future refinement of the chronology (Hall and Fullerton 1990, 3:270-1).

The excavations were conducted by the North Slope Borough, Barrow, Alaska, with the cooperation of the whole community. The archaeology department of the State University of New York at Binghamton helped to set up and supervise the team for the Utqiagvik Archaeology Project. After study, all the excavated materials were restored to the community and the human remains given a proper burial.

At the Utqiagvik archaeological site, it appears that a house was destroyed nearly 400 years ago by overriding sea ice. In the house ruins the excavating teams, which included Inupiaq elders, discovered two well-preserved bodies and three skeletons, all female. The human remains were unclothed but covered with clothing and skin bedding robes, leading to the conjecture that the catastrophe occurred during sleeping hours.

The clothing and clothing-related tools found at the site are linked to the traditional Kakligmiut clothing complex known historically. Forty-eight complete or nearly complete garments were recovered. Thus the collection is the earliest and largest of any Kakligmiut archaeological clothing acquisitions. Its importance is further enhanced by the fact that it is made up of working dress and clothing in different stages of use, all sewn with sinew.

The findings reveal a high correlation between the costume found at the archaeological site and traditional Kakligmiut clothing known historically, and show that Kakligmuit clothing appears to have remained unchanged from about AD 1500 to about AD 1850. Furthermore, these archaeological discoveries contradict proposals of the ethnohistorians who assumed that Kakligmiut clothing underwent radical changes after AD 1850 due to western influence. The style changes occurred some time before western contact and came to northern Alaska partly through the inter-Native trade network. The traditional patterns of the clothing remained the same. It appears that after non-Native contact, customarily placed at 1826, the clothing did not change greatly. Rather, non-Inupiaq materials were gradually and selectively used.

Woman's caribou-skin outer coat, sewn with sinew, about 111 cm (without hood), Kakligmiut, ca. AD 1530. Found at the Utqiagvik Archaeological Site, Utqiagvik, Alaska, 1981. Part of the parka's back hood and body is missing. The hood, made of light-coloured fawn skin, is anchored to the main body by 'roots' or tusk-like extensions. The flaps are closer in appearance to those of Canadian amautiit than to later Alaskan clothing. The sleeves have the distinctive underarm gusset associated with North Alaskan and Inuvialuit clothing collected in the late nineteenth and twentieth centuries. (See figure 1.3 for pattern.)

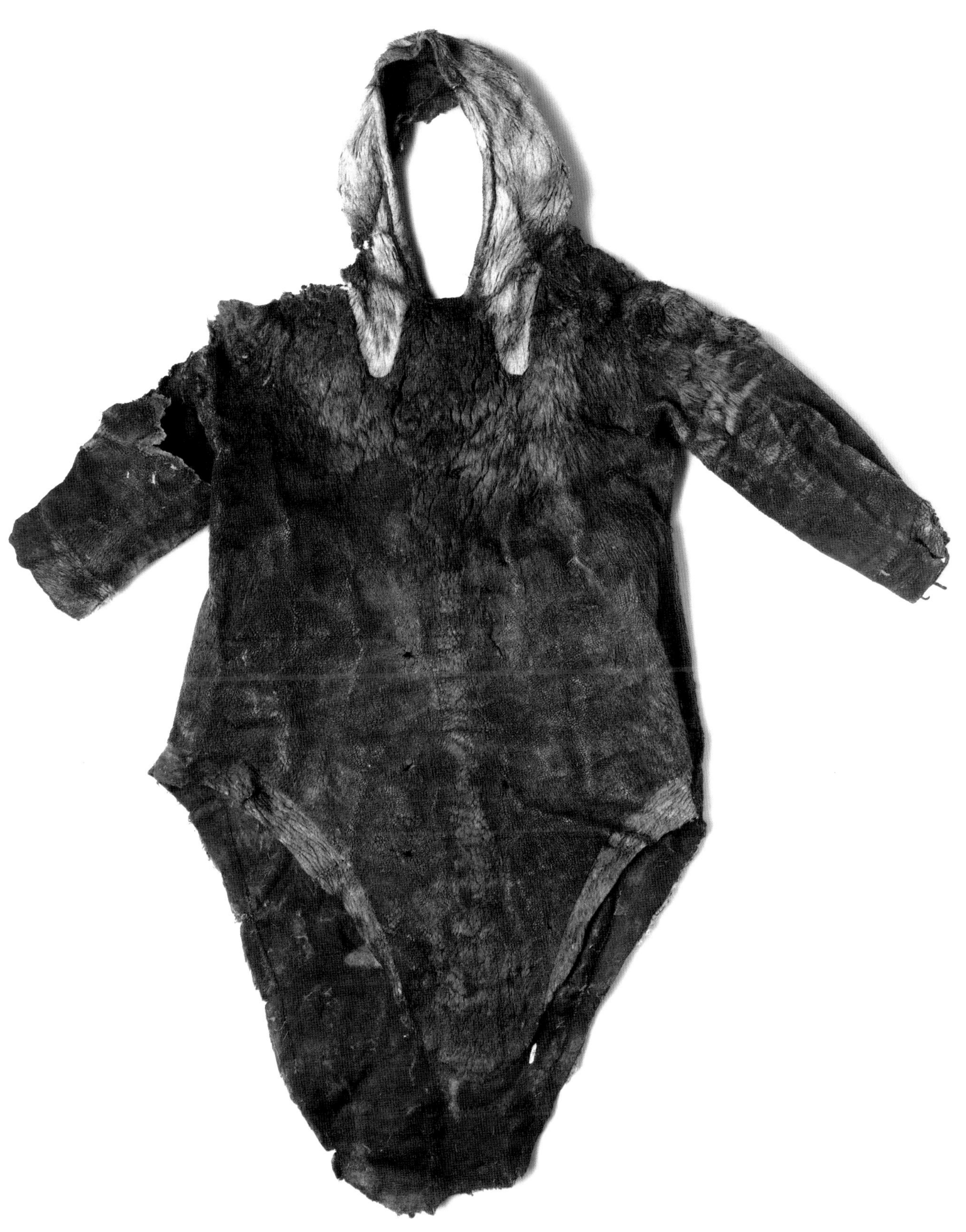

Figure 1.3
Pattern drawing of woman's outer coat, Utqiagvik Archaeology Project BAR2-44-55710, Kakligmiut. *Based on a drawing by Beth L. Turcy.*

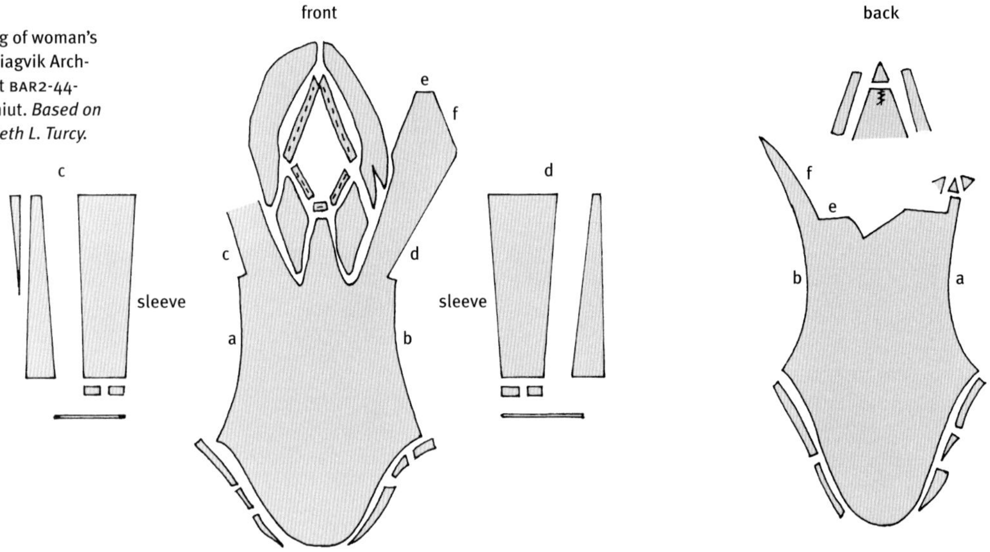

Figure 1.4
Pattern drawing of man's outer coat, North Alaska Inupiaq. *Based on a drawing from Murdoch (1892, 117).*

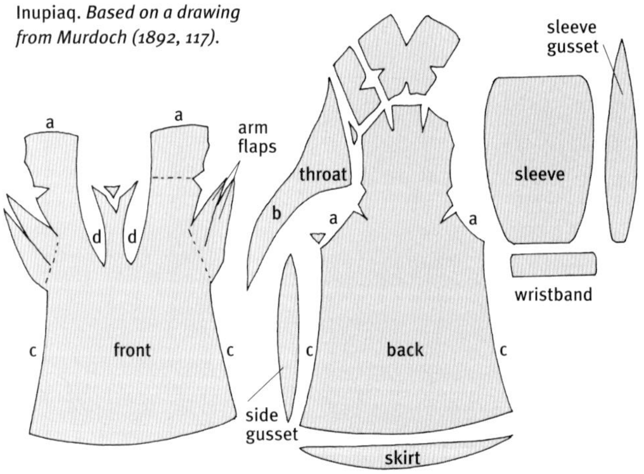

Figure 1.5
Pattern drawing of child's outer combination pants, Utqiagvik Archaeology Project BAR2-44-54150, Kakligmiut. *Based on a drawing by Beth L. Turcy.*

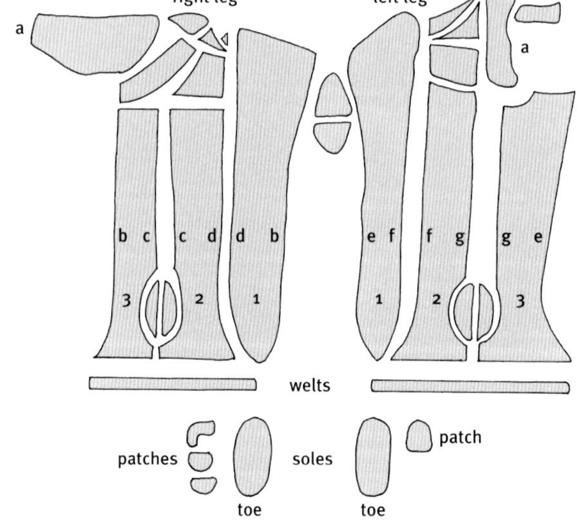

Figure 1.6
Pattern drawing of boot, Utqiagvik Archaeology Project BAR2-44-54739. The pattern consists of two pieces: the upper and the sole. A median seam runs down mid-centre front of the leg, and crosses diagonally to the outer edge of the boot to meet the edge of the sole — a pattern found in Kalaallit Nunaat. *Based on a drawing by Beth L. Turcy.*

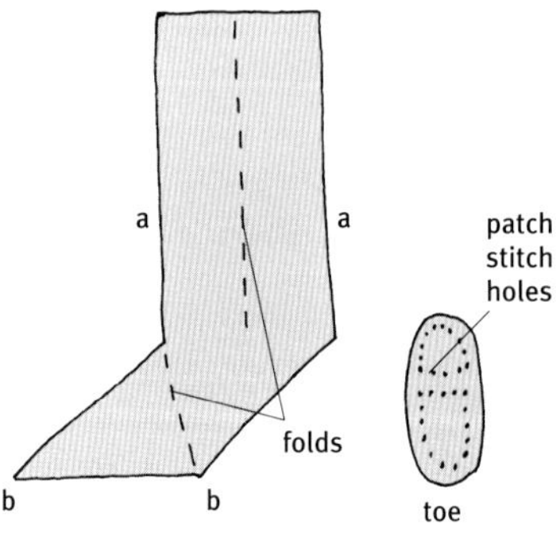

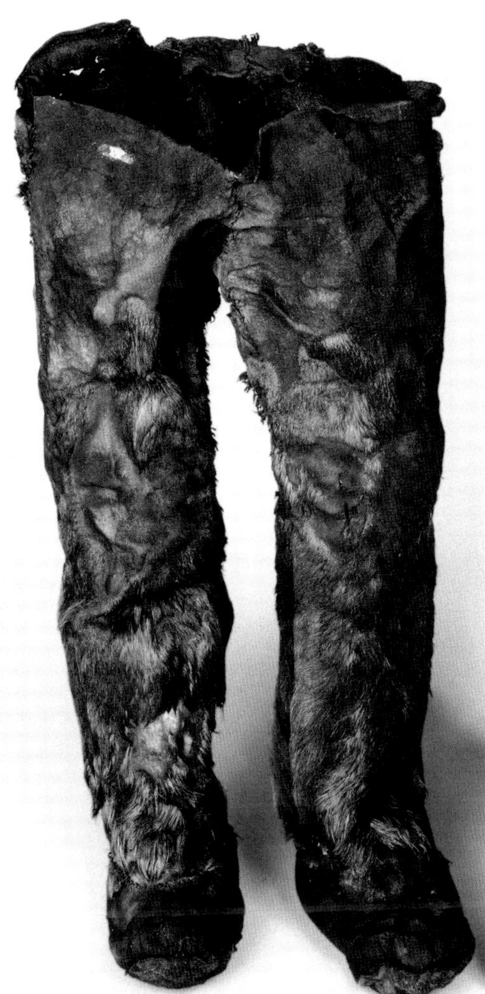

Above Caribou-skin and dehaired sealskin child's trousers with feet, sewn with sinew, 62 cm, Kakligmiut, ca. AD 1530. Found at the Utqiagvik Archaeological Site, Utqiagvik, Alaska in 1981. Overcast and waterproof stitches of sinew were found in the footwear seams. Historic and modern Inuit boots use the same skins, seams, and stitches. (See figure 1.5 for pattern.)

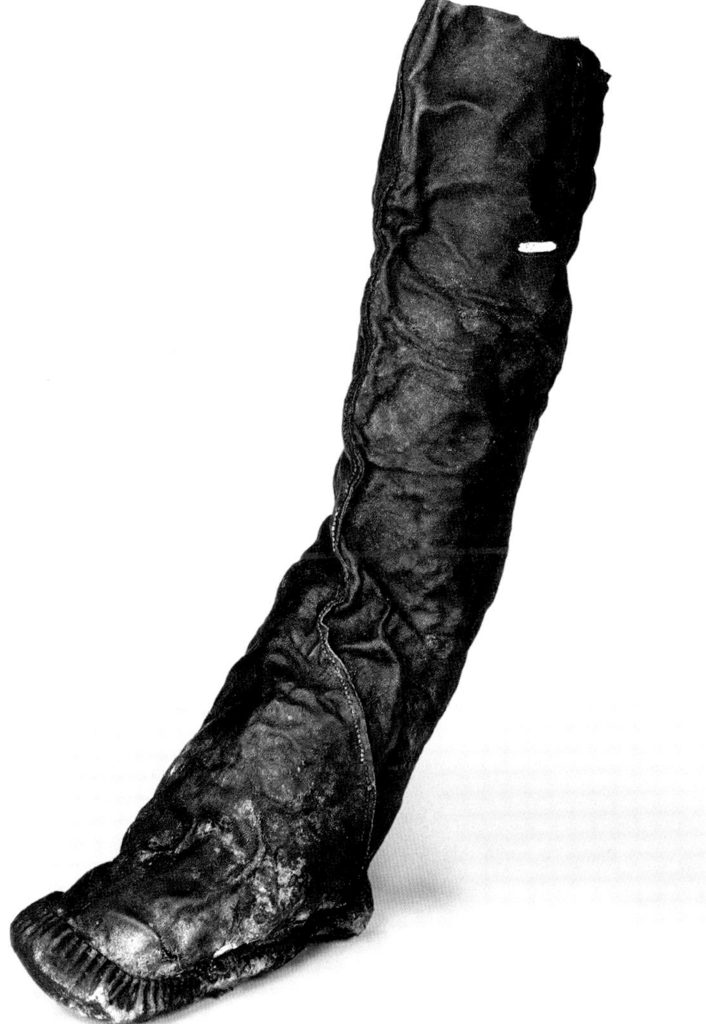

Right Dehaired sealskin and baleen waterproof boot, sewn with sinew, 51 cm, Kakligmiut, ca. AD 1530. Found at the Utqiagvik Archaeological Site, Utqiagvik, Alaska in 1981. The waterproof boot has a bearded sealskin sole that is crimped at toe and heel. Two loops are cut into each side of the sole to hold an ankle-thong (missing). Insulation of shredded baleen found inside the foot of the boot reflects the whale-hunting economy of the Kakligmiut. (See figure 1.6 for pattern.)

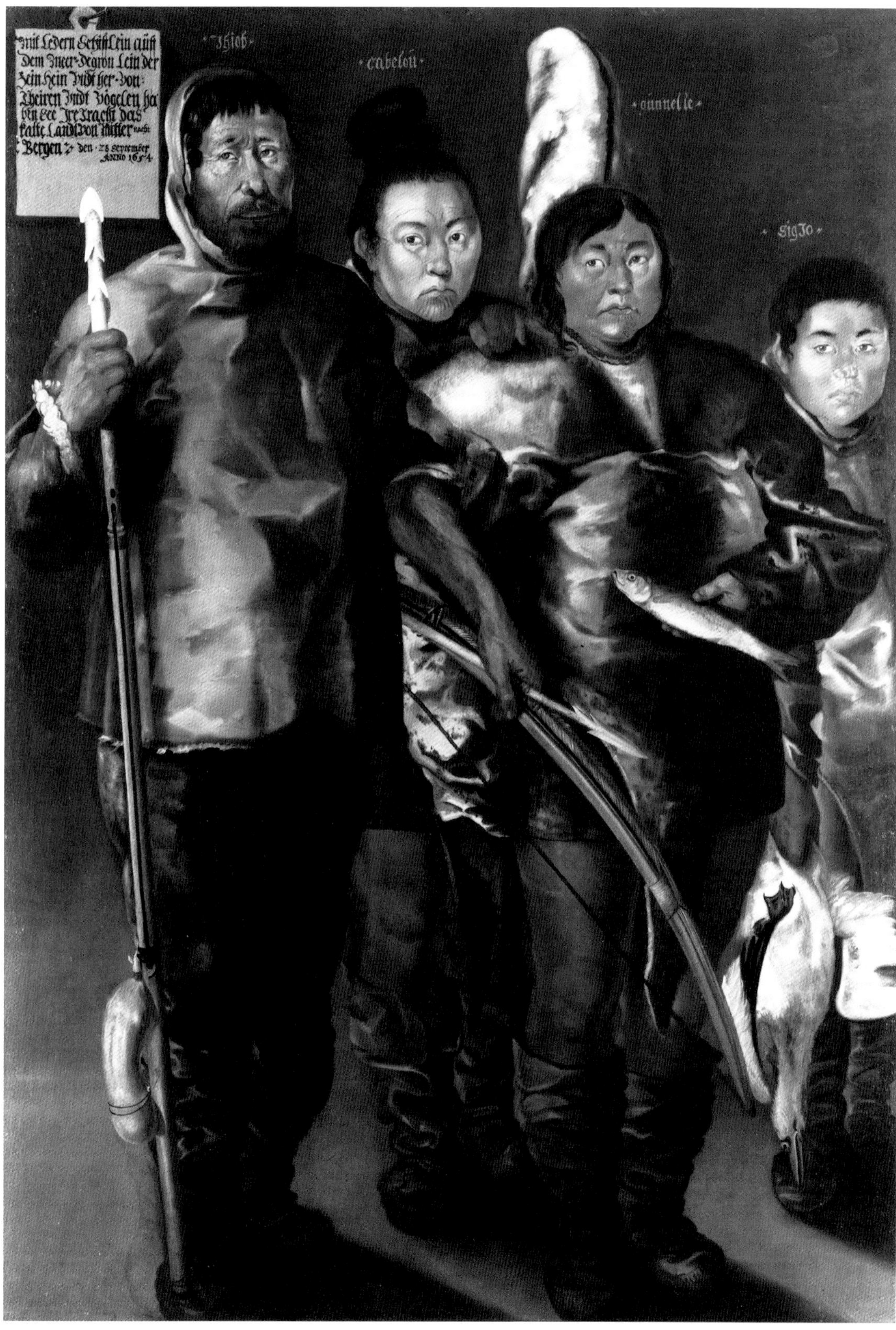
Bergen den 28 september ANNO 1654
Ihiob
cabelou
sigjo

Four Greenlanders kidnapped in 1654. Painting by Salomon von Hauen, Bergen, 1654, oil on canvas, h. 168 cm.

In the selection, the Kakligmiut demonstrated that they knew the superiority of their clothing and rejected most aspects of outsiders' dress because it was not suited to their purposes (Trucy 1986, 220, 221).

A SEVENTEENTH-CENTURY IMAGE

A seventeenth-century European painting rendered in 1654 is the oldest known of Kalaallit people. The clothing appears to have many of the same features as that of the Qilakitsoq mummies of the fifteenth century. The painting shows four Inuit who were abducted, in a most tragic event, from Nuuk Fiord area by Dutch-born David Dannell, the captain of a Danish trade ship (*Études/Inuit/Studies* 6 [1982]; Kaalund 1984, 135; National Museum of Denmark, written communication). The prisoners' portrait was commissioned at Bergen, where the ship stopped on the way to Copenhagen. The man, Ihob or Juppaa, died after they again set sail. His daughter Kabelau, the woman, Kunilik or Gunneling, and the thirteen-year-old girl Sigoko all died later in Copenhagen.

The clothing worn by the Kalaallit in the seventeenth century has much in common with the apparel found with the eight bodies at Qilakitsoq in the fifteenth century. Juppaa's jacket is hooded and edged with fur. It has roomy, dropped shoulders. His dehaired sealskin boots appear to be made in the traditional manner known today, with soles that come up the sides of the foot and are crimped at toe and heel.

Kunilik is shown wearing a closed jacket with a very high hood. The hood has a stripe that runs up the mid-front to the peak and continues down the back of the hood. (A view of the back can be seen in Bencard [1989].) The seams attaching the shoulder piece to the main body of the coat are lowered to the chest, away from areas of stress. A V-shaped root is found below the chin to anchor the hood and give width across the chest.[20] The jacket's front has a long, narrow extension with an arrow-like tip that reaches the knees. The trousers are short, leaving a space between them and the boots, which come only to the knee. The same placement of light and dark skins seems to appear in the clothing in the painting and in that of the Qilakitsoq mummies.[21]

There is ample evidence that the ancestors of the Inuit fashioned skin clothing that helped them survive in their Arctic lands under daunting conditions. In their migrations they brought with them a sophisticated technology and artistry, a formidable lore that they passed to future generations.

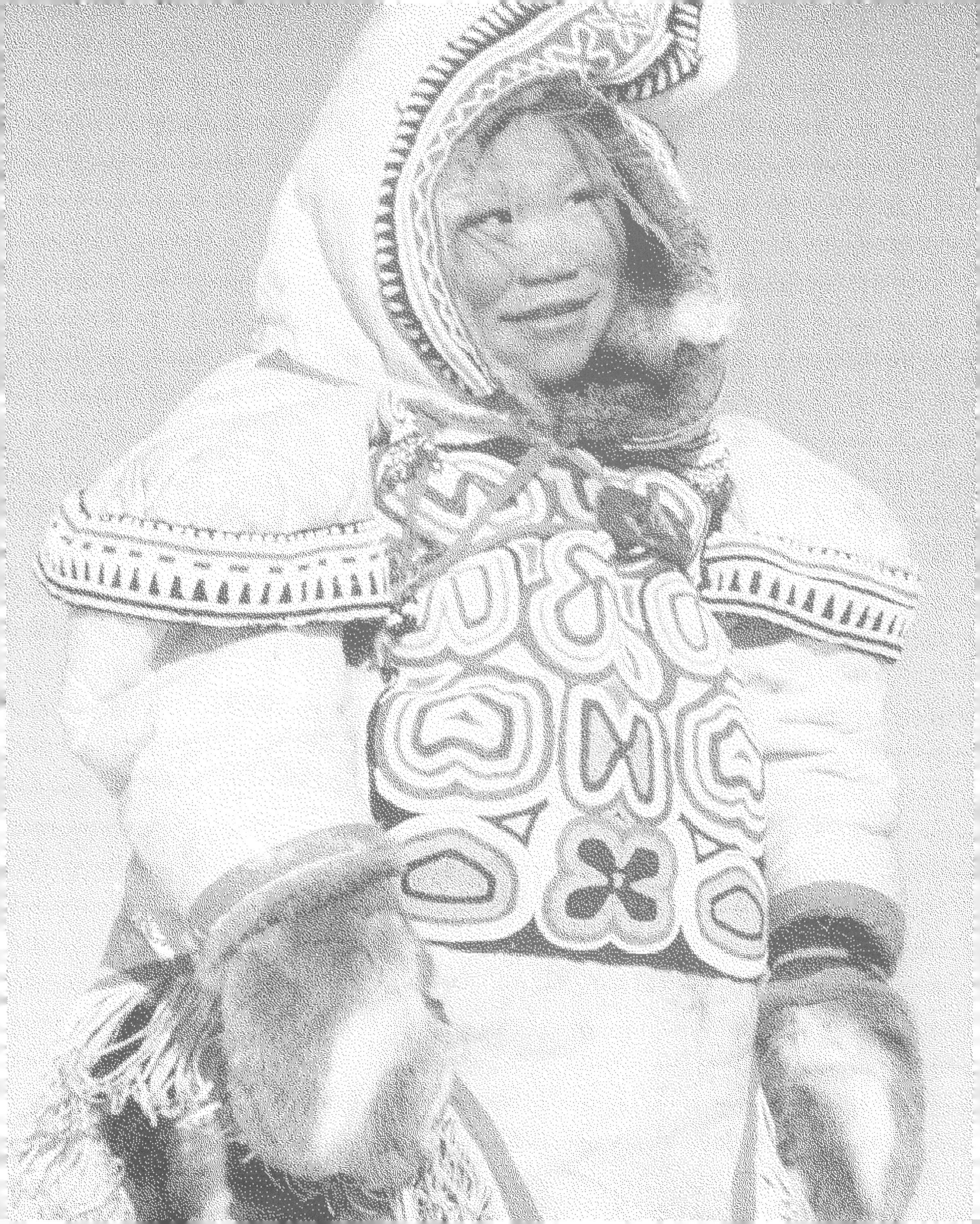

Glorious it is to see
The caribou flocking down from the forests
And beginning
Their wandering to the north.
Timidly they watch
For the pitfalls of man.
Glorious it is to see
The great herds from the forests
Spreading out over plains of white.
Glorious to see.
Yayai – ya – yiya.

Glorious it is
To see the great musk oxen
Gathering in herds.
The little dogs they watch for
When they gather in herds.
Glorious to see.
Yai – ya – yiya.

Glorious it is
To see long-haired winter caribou
Returning to the forests.
Fearfully they watch
For the little people,
While the herd follows the ebb-mark of the sea
With a storm of clattering hooves.
Glorious it is
When wandering time is come.
Yayai – ya – yiya.

Netsit of Umingmaktuuq[1]

Chapter 2

From Earth, Sea, and Sky

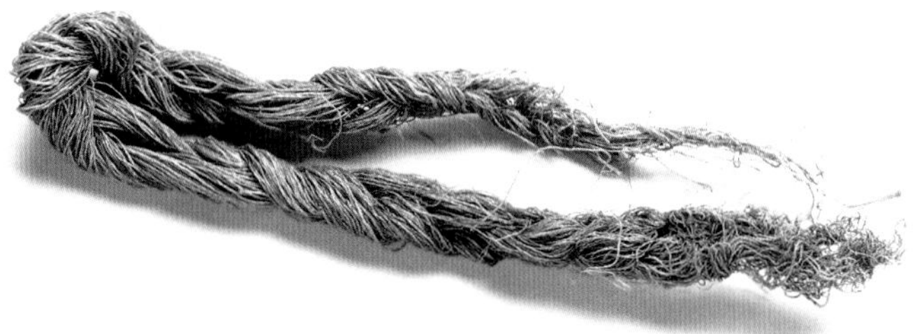

Above Sinew (ivalu), Inupiat, early twentieth century. Collected at Barrow, Alaska, by John A. Grose. Sinew is made from the fibrous tendons found along the spinal column and back legs of the caribou. It can also be made, for example, from the esophagus of seal or waterfowl, intestines and rectal canal of sea mammals and bear, and even the covering of a whale's tongue.

Opposite Man's parka (90 cm), trousers (40 cm), mitts (20 cm), and boots (40 cm), made from caribou, polar bear, seal, and fox skins, sewn with sinew, Inuhuit, ca. 1945. Collected at Qaanaaq, Kalaallit Nunaat North. The hair growth on caribou is twice as dense as on seal skin.

Except for the Yupiit of Alaska, the Inuit employ caribou and seal skins in the main for their clothing. They also use, depending on season and locality, hides of wolverine, wolf, musk-ox, bear, fox, ground squirrel, marmot, and dog. The Yupiit use the skins of smaller animals for the most part. In the past, the feathered skins of birds became coats and trousers and are still used today to insulate apparel and for other special purposes. Intestines and other membranes, tendons, bones, tusks, antlers, teeth, feathers, claws, and beaks are all used for clothing and its decoration. In former times, the Inuit dug up mammoth bones and tusks and turned them into men's and women's tools, ornaments, and amulets.[2] When living in the traditional way, the Inuit use almost every part of the animal or bird.

FROM THE EARTH

Caribou

Tuktu, the caribou *(Rangifer tarandus),* represented by several subspecies, is found in Europe, Kalaallit Nunaat, North America, and Siberia. In Europe and Siberia herders refer to both wild and domesticated subspecies as reindeer. Caribou and reindeer are one genus of the deer family *(Cervidae)* (Graves 1985; Stenton 1991b; Whitehead 1972).

The subspecies differ somewhat in coloration, which satisfies social and aesthetic demands in clothing manufacture. Peary caribou in Canada's High Arctic, for example, are almost all white. Coloration of herds located farther south in the Canadian Arctic changes seasonally with the moult, from black to deep brown in the spring and early summer to cream, grizzled, or grey for the winter pelage. In general, the neck fur and long ventral mane on the throat are cream coloured, while the belly, flank, and ventral tail surfaces are white, as are the markings on the rump and the leg just above the hoof. Both sexes bear antlers, although those of the male are larger. Antlers are bone, and when growing are covered by a vascular skin popularly called velvet. They are shed annually and rapidly replaced.

The caribou's coat has two kinds of hair: long, coarse guard hairs cover short dense hairs that are fine and soft. Each guard hair has a mesh-like core that surrounds dead air spaces. The trapped air supplies excellent thermal insulation. At the base of the guard hairs, where they emerge from the skin, the short hairs intertwine to form a layer that cold and moisture cannot penetrate. Heat is captured in and among the hairs when a person wears caribou skin next to the body since the pockets of dead air warm up from body heat. Although the fur appears bulky, much of its volume is made up of trapped air. The hide of caribou and reindeer is thinner, and thus lighter in weight and more supple, than that of other members of the deer family. The hide has a relatively low oil content and thus sheds with dampness (McElhone 1984a, 6-7).

The caribou supplies more than hide and fur. Dorsal tendons found along the spine and back legs produce *ivalu,* the sinew used for thread and cordage. Antler velvet was once used by men to tie back their hair. Antler, hard yet resilient and relatively easy

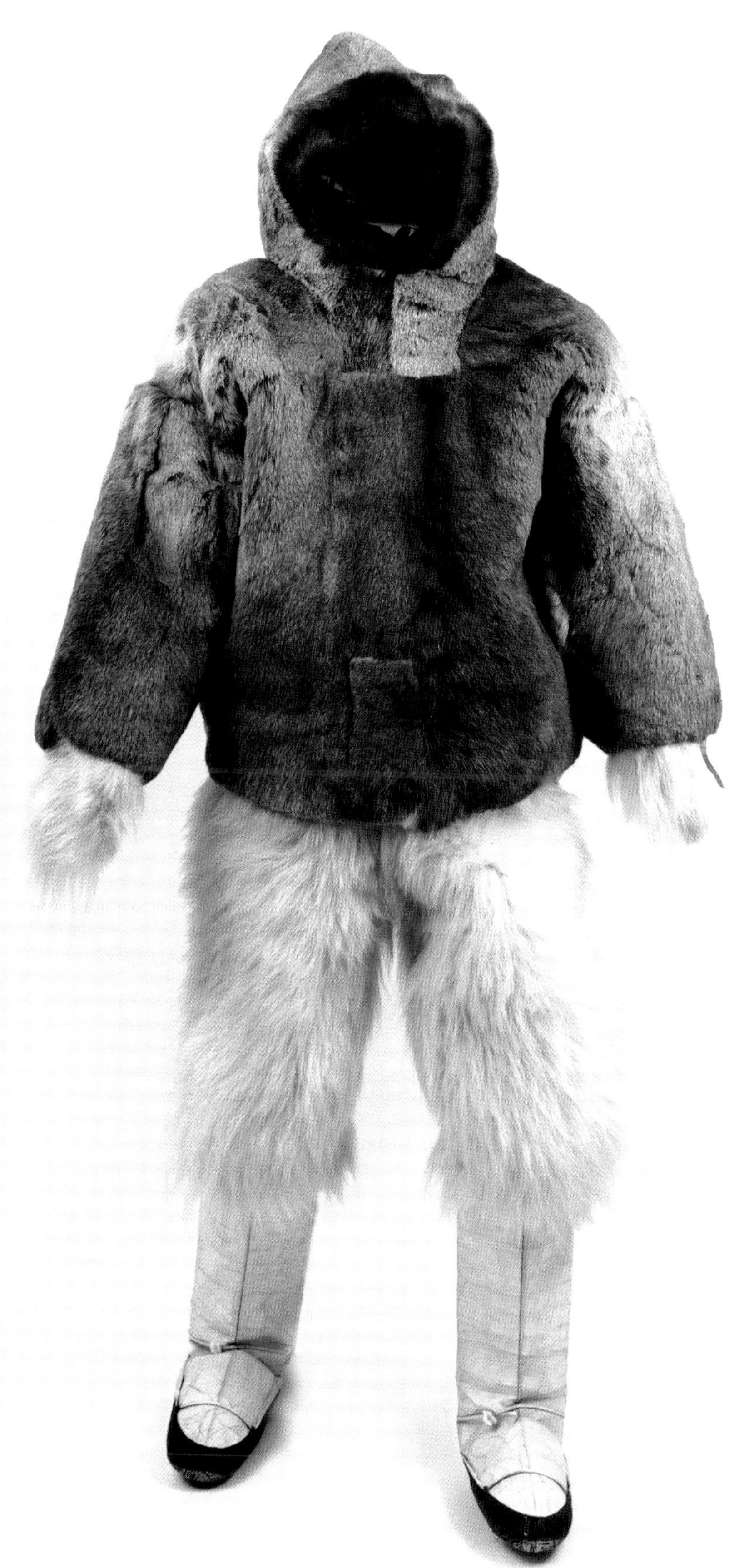

to work, provided tools (Hahn 1977, 343-4; Forsyth 1985, 12-15). Drilled, bent, or pierced, antler became a part of composite tools (Balikci 1970, 15). Bones had many uses. The sharpened femur of the caribou's hind leg became a *sakuuti,* a skin scraper. Bone, with marrow removed, then weathered and polished, became a needlecase. Incisor teeth and bones were carved into pendants.

Other Arctic Fauna

Nanuq, the polar bear *(Ursus maritimus),* is found all over the circumpolar areas (Durner and Amstrup 1995; Graves 1983). Its skin has an outer coat of guard hairs, underneath which is mixed a dense mass of shorter hairs. The central core of the guard hair shaft, full of membranes, traps air that acts as insulation. Polar bear skin has another quite remarkable feature. It functions as 'a natural collector that converts part of the solar-radiation spectrum into heat with an efficiency exceeding 95 percent' (Mirsky 1988, 26). The core of each guard hair traps ultraviolet light and conducts the radiation to the black surface of the skin, where it is absorbed, supplementing the heat generated from inside the body of the bear.

Because of its long guard hairs, *qavvik,* wolverine, is favoured for ruffs, as are *amaruq,* wolf, and *qimmiq,* dog. The husky's winter coat has long, thick guard hairs that cover a mat of short, wool-like fur. Dog skin does not shed when wet and is not easily damaged by moisture and subsequent drying.

The peoples of northeastern Siberia, particularly the Evenk and Even, utilized dog fur for decorative borders. The Itel'men preferred

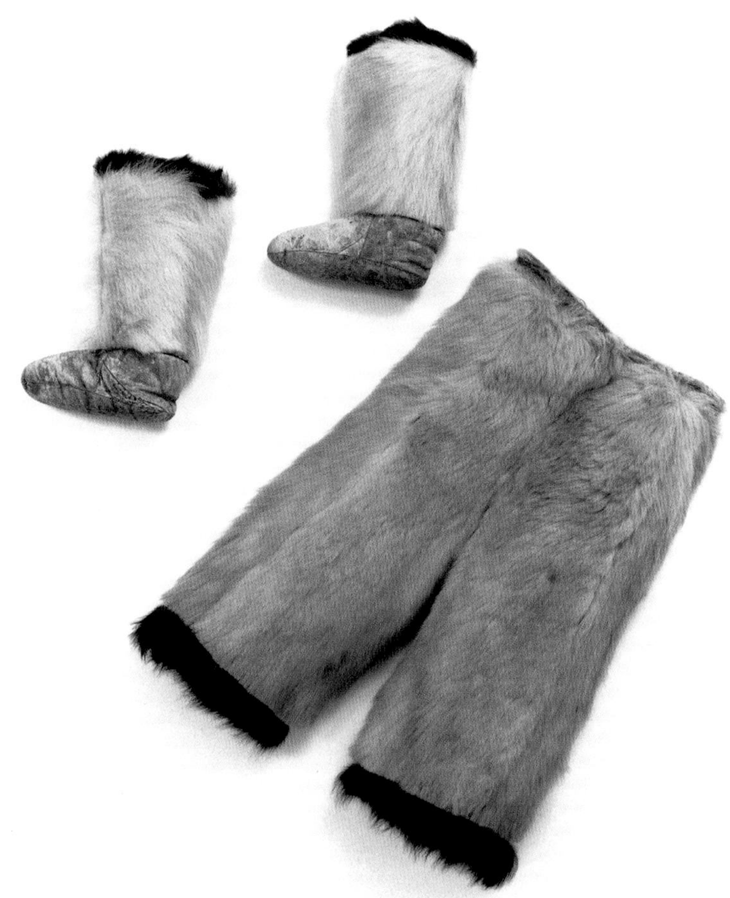

dog skin to caribou, which becomes a matted tangle and loses much hair when exposed to moisture. Dog fur makes a warm covering and will last four years when worn daily, in contrast to the caribou's one-year duration (Hatt 1969, 11).

Inuit elders, discussing clothing at a conference, agreed about the efficiency of fur (Nungak 1983, 126, 116, 132):

The best garments that were ever worn were made of caribou hides.
Isa Qupirqualuk of Purvirnituq

The best and the warmest fur that could be used around the parka is dog skin.
Paulusie Aupaluk of Akulivik

I've never worn polar bear skin or eaten walrus or whale. I have worn all other skins. Dog fur is very good as mittens and boots.
Isa Kasudluak of Inujjuaq

The skin of *tiriqaniaq,* Arctic fox *(Alopex lagopus),* has various uses. It can be made into a ruff for 'warm-weather' parkas and makes a fine hunting cap. Kalaallit women wore coats and trousers of fox skin, as we know from suits from AD 1460 to the 1960s (Holtved 1967, 49-50, 52-3; Kaalund 1984, 32, 133). The coat required at least ten skins (National Museum of Denmark 1955, 50). As Daisy Watt of Kuujjuaq points out, 'Fox belly fur can be placed inside duffle socks to keep feet warm. Women should also have fox fur under their breasts to keep warm while breast-feeding in the cold' (Nungak 1983, 128).

The long hair of *umingmak,* musk-ox, was useful on caps to keep off mosquitoes. Because of the density and length of the hair, it also made excellent bedding. Now, musk-ox hair is sometimes used for muffs. Today musk-ox down, said to be more valuable than cashmere, is used for knitting and is sold commercially.

In some areas of Alaska the skins of small animals such as marmot *(Marmota caligata)* and the arctic ground squirrel *(Spermophilus parryii)* are used to make upper garments and decoration. Small animals, more numerous and readily available than caribou, have soft, glossy fur. Thus the skins are both easier to obtain and to process.

Trousers (89 cm) and boots (42 cm) made from polar bear, wolverine, and seal skins, sewn with sinew, Nunavimiut, ca. 1911-13. Collected possibly at Kuujjuaq or Kangiqsuk, Nunavik, by Robert Flaherty. Polar bear fur, though bulky, is extremely warm, is water resistant, and does not shed with dampness.

FROM THE SEA

Seal

Of the four main kinds of seals available in the Arctic, *nattiq,* the ringed seal *(Phoca hispida),* and *ugjuk,* the bearded seal

Noah Pewogatok of Iglulik, NWT, 1986, scrapes bearded sealskin to make his lines. Since it is summer, he wears a lightweight parka with sealskin trousers and boots.

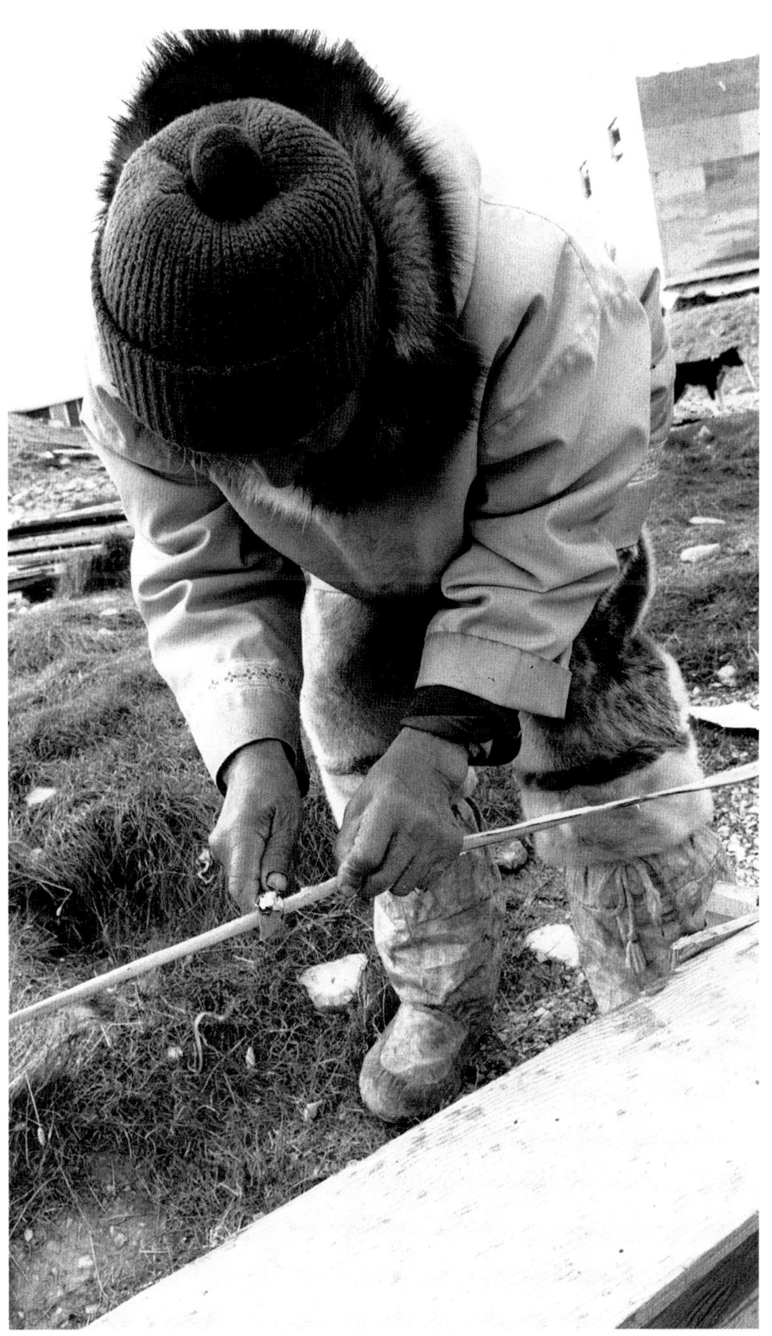

(Erignathus barbatus), are the most available and useful, being found on the coasts of the Arctic Ocean and the adjoining seas. The ringed seal has a population estimated at close to 5,000,000 and is the most abundant sea mammal in the Canadian Arctic (Forsyth 1985, 109). The harbour seal *(Phoca vitulina)* is not as prolific but has a wide distribution, from the Arctic coasts to as far south as Baja California, Mexico. The Siberian Yupiit use the skin of this seal, called 'nerpa' in Russian and sometimes referred to as the sea-calf or spotted seal. The Kalaallit consider the skin of the harbour seal to be the finest for trousers, often given by a hunter to his betrothed (de Neergaard 1987, 82).

Qairulik, the harp seal *(Phoca groenlandica)*, is found in the northeastern Arctic on the edges of the ice pack in northern Hudson Bay, Baffin Island, Kalaallit Nunaat, Nunavik, and down the Labrador coast to south of Newfoundland. Clothing has reportedly been made of skins of harp seal, but documentation about the extent of its use is scant.

A Canadian government team tried to study seals from the air by using infrared photography, which detects body heat. The seals thwarted their endeavours and remained undetected since their natural insulation prevents almost all loss of heat (Mirsky 1988, 26). The protective qualities of ringed-seal clothing are excellent. Sealskin parkas and trousers were traditionally worn in spring and summer by many Inuit groups, for seal skin weighs less than caribou skin. It is full of oil and therefore water repellent, and it does not shed when damp. Its porosity, which allows body humidity to escape, makes it an ideal substance for boots and for clothing worn at the ice edge and seashore, in the kayak or boat, and at lakes and rivers. Ringed-seal boots are used winter and summer. The seal intestines, like those of many sea mammals, were used – and in some places still are – to make waterproof garments to wear over the basic outfit.

The hide of the bearded seal is extremely tough and thick. The skin from the back gives soles for boots used in winter and summer, as well as for laces, belts, thongs, and lashings. The intestines are used for the manufacture of gutskin coats. Many women consider that the esophagus of bearded seal makes the softest, thinnest hide. In the past it was used to make sewing bags (Wilder 1976, 17).

Other Creatures of the Water

Qilalugaq, the beluga or white whale *(Delphinapterus leucas),* can furnish sinew. The skin has limited use in clothing manufacture. In some parts of the Arctic, for example in Sanikiluaq and among the Inuvialuit of the Mackenzie Delta area, the skin was used for boot soles. On the west coast of Hudson Bay, however, whale skin is considered unsuitable for soles (Mark Kalluak, personal communication 1985).

Sinew from *tuugaalik,* the narwhal *(Monodon monoceros),* is preferred by some seamstresses because of its length and strength. The narwhal also supplies ivory from its long, spirally twisted horn – actually the canine tooth in the male. *Aiviq,* the walrus *(Odobenus rosmarus),* provides ivory for sewing tools, toggles, and ornaments. Its intestines are still sought occasionally by Yup'ik seamstresses for making waterproof parkas. In Alaska, in the past, both fresh- and saltwater fish supplied material for boots, mitts, and waterproof parkas and bags, but documentation about Canadian use of fish skin is scant.[3]

FROM THE SKY

Birdskin clothing has been produced by all Inuit groups. Some elders claim that bird skins are warmer than the skins of caribou. In Canada the skins of *mitiq,* the eider duck *(Somateria mollissima),* were employed mainly by Inuit in Sanikiluaq and by the Nunavimiut of the hamlets on the east coast of Hudson Bay and the coast of Ungava Bay. Bird skins furnished coats and trousers with feathers either to the inside or outside. 'Duck skins ... were placed inside boots for insulation. They were very warm. Bird skins were used as all kinds of garments, even as parkas,' attests Allie Patsauq of Inukjuaq (Nungak 1983, 112). The skin, bones, and feet of other birds – auk and auklet, cormorant, guillemot, ptarmigan, loon, puffin, swan, and goose – were used for clothing, tools, containers, amulets, and decoration. In the 1980s and 1990s, communities in Nunavik and Sanikiluaq produced birdskin clothing as part of the movement to preserve this tradition.

The down of eider ducks provides a light, resilient, warm material. The down feathers are concealed in many birds, such as gulls and ducks, forming a thick undercover close to the skin under the long feathers.

Above Distinguished artist Davidialuk Alasuaq Amittu, 1910-76, of Purvirnituq, Nunavik, 1971, is wearing an eider duck coat made by Miaji Qassik and Maina Imirqutailaq. The winter parka is trimmed with dog and seal fur. He also wears gauntlet-type ringed-seal mitts, trousers, and waterproof boots.

Below Loonskin shoes sewn with sinew, 30 cm, Iglulingmiut, mid-twentieth century. Collected by Jacques-Marie Volant, o.m.i., Iglulik, NWT. Duckskin moccasins were very warm and were often worn by seal hunters on the outside of their boots (Mina Napartuk of Kuujjuaraapik, Nunavik, in Nungak 1983, 110).

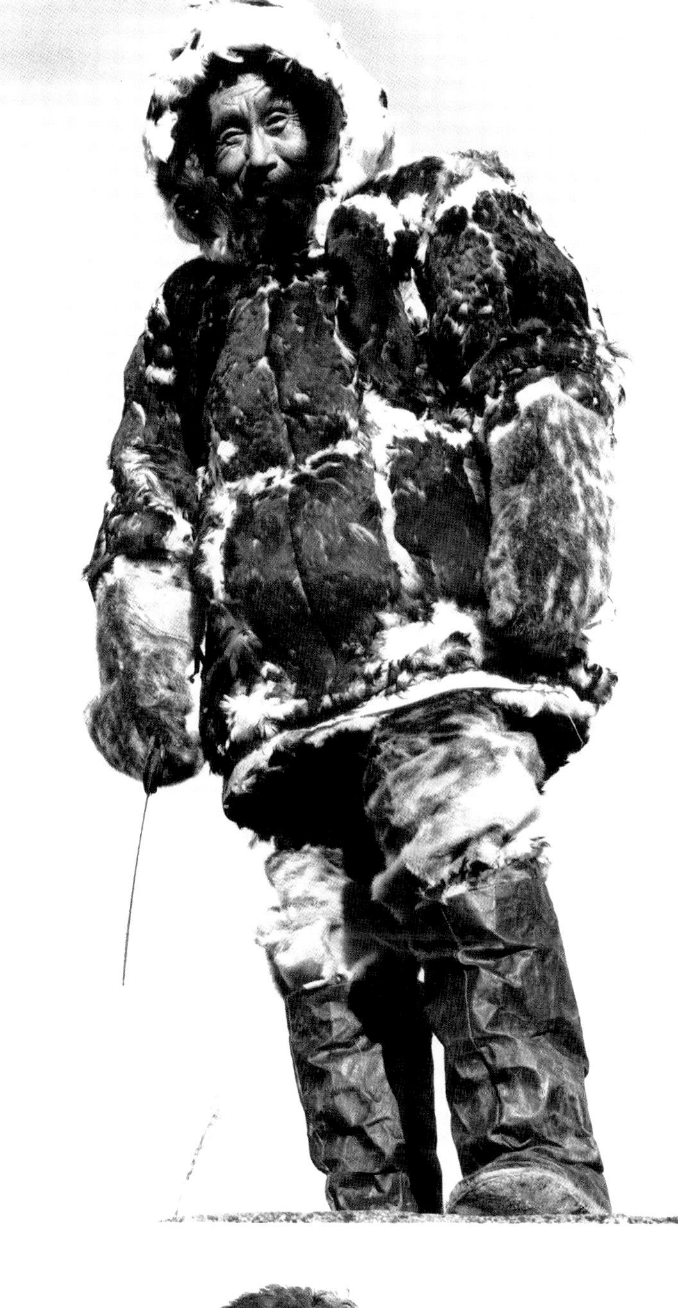

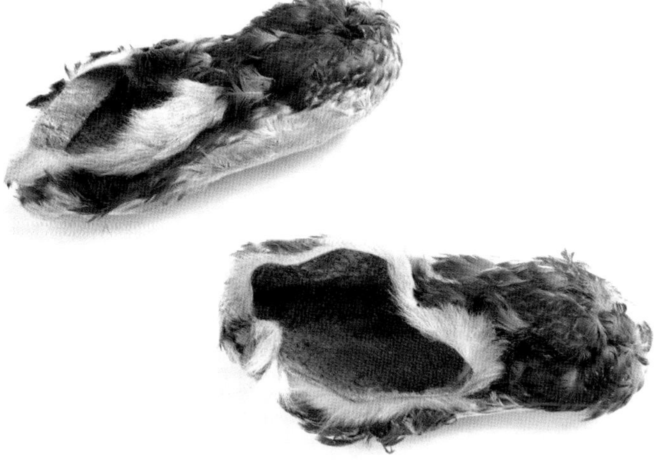

The barbs of down are long, loose, and fluffy, giving warmth without weight.

The female plucks the down from her breast and puts it in the nest to form a blanket for her eggs. Once the chicks have left the nest, the down can be collected. Down collecting is the least costly type of resource use, without any loss to the duck population.[4]

PRINCIPLES OF CLOTHING CONSTRUCTION AND FUNCTIONALITY

No matter where the Inuit live – Siberia, Alaska, Canada, Kalaallit Nunaat – their clothing is fashioned according to common principles. The apparel conserves heat, eliminates humidity, controls temperature, prevents ingress of water and wind, and has durability, all characteristics that meet the rigours of Arctic environments.[5]

Insulation and Heat Conservation

The insulative properties of caribou fur and the design of the clothing make it possible to live comfortably in deepest winter, when the sun is barely visible for months and temperatures below -40°C are common for weeks at a time. The Inuit are equally at ease in parts of the Arctic with milder climates and in spring and summer, when they wear one layer of fur clothing or fabric clothing sometimes combined with furs. The furs they do wear are often lighter weight, such as those of seal, summer-gathered caribou, ground squirrel, and marmot.

Used in the cold, dry months of winter, autumn-harvested caribou skins insulate the body superbly.[6] The skin is dense partly because it has no sweat glands.[7] In winter two layers of clothing are worn: the inner layer with fur next to the body, the outer layer with fur to the exterior. The design of the garments uses the principle of warm air capture. The model provides loose attire that contains the body-heated rising air like a bell, with few openings to allow heat escape. It has no front opening, is hooded with a snug neckline, and is secured at the face. Ruffs at face, wrist, and edges of coat and trousers further enclose the warm air. Fringes of inner and outer layers interlock, adding more insurance against heat loss (Jeela Alikatuktuk Moss-Davies, personal communication 1985). The back, longer than the front, tucks under the wearer when he or she is seated, to prevent blowing snow and wind from getting access and to stop the snow under the seat from melting.

If the wearer becomes too warm, the hood is thrown back. Looseness in the fit of coat and trousers over the hips and at the waist permits cold air entry from the bottom to replace the warm air that escapes through the slackened neck and hood, warming the face as it leaves. When a hunter stands still, however, he or she sometimes wears a *tapsiq*, belt, around the waist to keep out the wind. Skin belts are made in the same way as the cord around the *amaut* that supports the child, and as lines for harpoons, dog harnesses, and lashings.[8]

Humidity and Temperature Control

As important as coping with heat loss is contending with build-up of humidity inside the clothing, a factor in body temperature control (McElhone 1984, 7; Riewe 1975; Stefansson 1958).[9] The solution to this problem marks an important distinction between Inuit and Euro-American clothing.

The body constantly emits an invisible water vapour called transpiration, which becomes visible at low temperatures. Pull a hand out of a mitt at -50°C and steam rises from the palm and the finger tips. When the body is at work or overheated by too many clothes, the sweat glands produce a liquid called perspiration. At a certain point depending on the temperature both inside and outside the clothing, the moisture condenses and becomes hoarfrost. This 'dew point' can be located on the outside of the outer garment or between the layers of clothing where the cold from the outside meets the warm vapours from the inside. The fur, made of a keratinous substance, does not absorb moisture, and the hoarfrost, or ice crystals, are easily beaten off.

The ruff around the hood is also an instrument of temperature and humidity control. In cold temperatures the breath forms frost and ice on the face and headgear. The Inuit know that soft furs of even length such as fox and hare turn into solid ice when covered with vapour. The best ruff is made from wolverine fur, taken as a strip from across the animal's shoulders. The hair is long and uneven. When breath strikes this hair, it forms hoarfrost that is easily shaken free by brushing once or twice with the hand every ten or fifteen minutes. Moreover, the hair reduces the effect of the wind by creating eddies that reduce wind velocity. Thus a warm micro-environment is maintained between the face and the hood (Riewe 1975, 29). Wolf and dog fur have the same effect.

In very cold weather children wear a *manuilitaq*, a small piece of caribou or other fur, in the hood opening to catch the rime from the breath. The skin is taken out and dried when the child comes in from the cold.

By any and all means the extremities must be kept warm and dry. Layers of fur and skin are worn on the feet, but the Inuit insert additional padding inside the stockings, most often grass gathered in the summer. 'Dried grass was worn not because there was nothing else to wear,' remarks Lydia Tukai of Inukjuaq, 'but because it made good insulation against the cold ... I even wore guillemot skin boots inside my outer boots' (Nungak 1983, 112). Grass or other materials such as caribou hair or bird feathers continue to be used to absorb the humidity from the feet. It is taken out to dry when work is over.

The drawstring at the boot top keeps out snow or water. It can also be loosened or tightened for temperature control. If the feet become too hot, the warm air can rise up through the trousers and coat and escape via the neck.

The hands are carefully protected by mitts with fur to the inside or outside, according to need. 'When we make fur for a parka, we leave off the stomach of a fox. Hunters should take along the stomach fur when they go out. Thumbs easily get cold when riding a Ski-doo. When a piece of fur is placed inside mittens, it will keep fingers warm,' says Daisy Watt of Kuujjuaq (Nungak 1983, 128).

Should body humidity build up in woolen clothing, the wool becomes wetter and wetter and loses its insulative quality. The moisture eventually freezes in Arctic climates, and the apparel becomes a suit of ice. The absorption of humidity by wool and other non-keratinous materials adds immeasurably to the weight of clothing or sleeping bags. Moisture-laden materials require great quantities of heat to dry. When some explorers experienced the Arctic winter, they donned more and more layers of woolens because they did not understand the necessity to get rid of humidity on the inside of their garb. They became colder as the cloth absorbed the moisture from the body. When their clothing froze and there was no way to dry it out, it sometimes became their shroud.

Inuit skin clothing shields the body against water as well as wind. Seams are sewn with firm, small stitches of sinew. In particular, some footwear and mitts are sewn with a waterproof stitch called *ilujjiniq* that seals the foot seams (Hadlereena et al. 1986; Issenman 1990, 60-1; Oakes 1987b; Oakes and Riewe 1995; Pharand 1974, Plate 10).[10]

In case of an accidental fall through the ice the Inuit know what to do:

Men sometimes fall into water so we usually pack extra clothes for them when they go hunting. What you have to do when you get wet is wring your duffle socks well and pour the water out of your boots. You turn your socks inside

out, wring them, stamp on them and slap them with a stick repeatedly. Then you allow them to freeze, while keeping your feet covered. You have to do it fast so that you don't get too cold. Once the socks are frozen you remove the ice by slapping your socks against something hard. They'll become dry if you do that.
Akinisie Novalinga of Purvirnituq[11]

Form Fulfils Function

An intricate construction process is involved in making skin clothing, which appears in different styles across cultures. The cut and tailoring of Inuit costume create garments that are loose yet fitted when necessary and that admirably meet the requirements of hunter and mother.[12] Hood construction, with its close fit and drawstring, ensures clear peripheral vision. Capacious shoulders allow the wearer to carry out complex tasks. Looseness allows air to circulate between the body and the clothing. The garments flap when the hunter works or runs so that the interchange between the inside and outside air keeps the body cool and dry.

Looseness at the base of the man's parka is achieved by flaring, by inserting gores, and by making slits. The placement and stylistic treatment of the slit can sometimes help determine the origin of a garment.[13] These openings at the base also help to reduce the time necessary to pull on clothing, a feature essential to hunters, who must act speedily once game is sighted.

The number of main parts of the pattern is kept to a minimum, resulting in few major seams. Thus heat loss and the chance of splits are reduced. Most parkas have no back neck seam; the back of the hood and body are one. A dart lets the seamstress decrease the size of any part for better fit.

Durability

The traditional style of life demands a set of new clothes for each of the two seasons, since furs usually last a year when worn daily. A rich man, a successful hunter, can have two or more sets of clothing for himself and his family, and he must also provide for the less fortunate in the community. Old clothing, at least in the old days, was not simply discarded but was used for work clothes, bedding, or to provide material for repair of other garments. Last year's inner layer could be worn as next year's summer outfit. Old boot leggings were made into socks. Old bedding provided material for trim and repairs.

The seamstress understands the qualities of the skin from the different parts of the animal and cuts the clothing appropriately for longer endurance (Conn 1955, 1974; Saladin d'Anglure, Mautaritnaaq, and Mark 1979).[14] The head and neck skin, which is tough and curved, often forms the back of the hood. The elastic part of a caribou's skin near the shoulder is used over the human shoulder. The curved rump skin becomes the seat of the trousers. The durable forehead or leg skin, the hind legs being larger and more hardy, is made into boots and mitts. The upper part of the leg, which has longer hair, supplies the back of the mitten, and the lower part gives shorter, tougher hair for the palm. The forehead hair can be transformed into

Amauti made from caribou, seal, and dog skins, and beads, sewn with sinew, 192 cm, Nunavimiut. Artisans: Surra Baron, Surra Annanack, and Claire Etook of Kangiqsualujjuaq, Nunavik; beadwork by Ayanaylitok of Salluit, Nunavik, ca. 1979. Complex tailoring methods are evident in this piece of clothing. The hood and baby-pouch are formed by joining opposing-curved seams and by inserting wedges of various sizes. A long edge, curved or straight, is gathered to a shorter edge to furnish a voluminous shoulder, to make the pouch, or to give ease at the neck or sleeve. (See p. 157 for front view.)

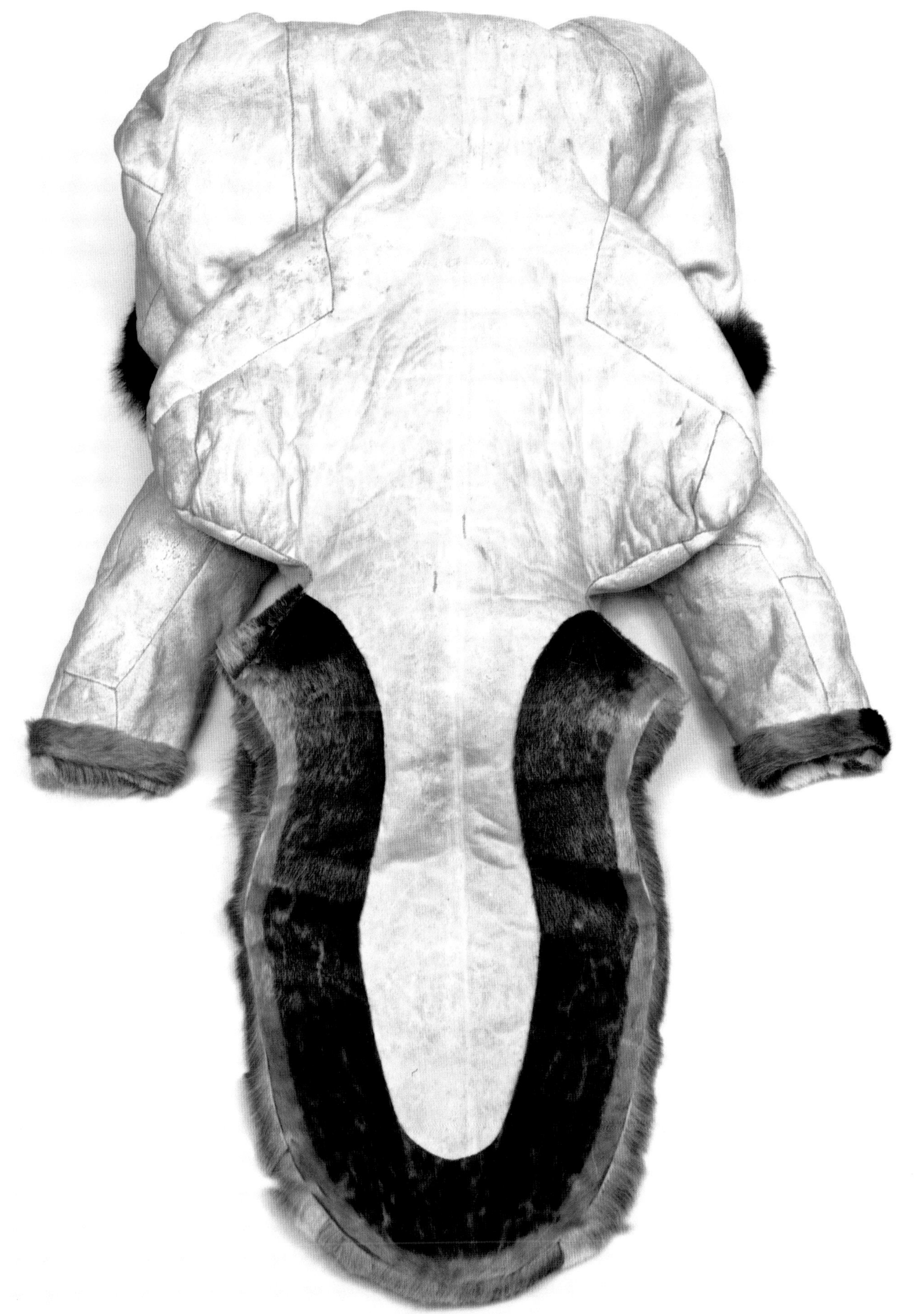

excellent winter boot soles and patches. Long-lasting bear or bearded seal skin is used for boot soles or for repairs.

The placement of major seams in areas of less stress ensures long life to the outfit. The conventional European armhole is not used, for the Inuit pattern attaches the sleeve to a dropped shoulder that may come to the mid-upper arm. A piece of the sleeve in some coats runs up the underarm into the main body, doing away with a seam at a place of tension. Shoulder seams are lowered off the shoulder. In earlier times, this seam occasionally was eliminated by using one skin for front and back.[15] Side seams of coats and trousers are made off centre.

Maintenance

Skin clothing requires great skill to maintain. It must be kept cold and dry to inhibit the bacterial action that causes decay and to keep it from becoming brittle or losing hair. Grease or blood from game impairs insulation quality and appearance and must be removed as quickly as possible by rubbing the stains with snow and then beating them out. Excessive perspiration or a fall through the ice can cause damage, but this can be averted by slow drying.

The *tiluqtut,* or snow beater, and drying rack are two important implements to rid clothing of humidity. The snow beater is made of bone, ivory, or wood, the last of these often obtained from a shipwreck or driftwood. Before stepping into the home, Inuit beat the snow and frost from the outside of their clothes. If the inside of the clothing is very damp it is left outdoors to freeze, and then beaten. One form of drying rack was made of antler or, as it is today, of wood since both materials can be bent. Sinew or thong, criss-crossed over the frame, form a net to hold damp clothing and boots so that they can dry slowly away from the heat source.

Before use the next day all outfits are checked for needed repairs. If left unattended, damage can cause a critical situation for the hunter. While the hunter is away from camp, and if his wife has not accompanied him, he brings needle and sinew in his tool kit to repair splits and tears. It is crucial that boots be attended to the moment they are taken off. Holes and seams are carefully repaired. If the sole is thin or worn through, a piece of bearded seal skin is applied on the outside. To keep boots soft, which is important for durability as well as for comfort and warmth, they are rubbed over a boot softener or chewed.

The comparatively low weight of skin clothing, while not a 'principle of construction,' is an important quality. Hunters in search of game for weeks at a time, or families undertaking a long journey overland, must carry only essentials. A person dressed in a traditional caribou winter outfit carries about four kilograms in skins, which is about one-half the weight of southern-style clothing used in similar circumstances. In addition, the furs are full of air so that in case of an accidental fall into the water they become a buoyant life preserver.

Rubber or leather footwear is no match for the light-weight, energy-conserving sealskin boots that are worn all over the

Arctic. Inuit footgear, consisting of a pair of seal fur slippers, caribou stockings, and sealskin boots, altogether weigh about one kilogram, whereas a pair of winter boots with a felt lining, nylon upper, and rubber or synthetic complete foot, also worn by Inuit, weigh over two kilograms. To this weight must be added thick socks.

FROM HEAD TO TOE

Differences in sex, age, local origin, marital status, and role are reflected in clothing. Occasionally garments indicate the identity of the maker. A man's traditional double-layered winter outfit usually consists of nine articles of caribou-skin clothes, of seven named categories: a *qulittuq* (a closed, hooded parka with fur to the outside); an *atigi* (the same with fur to the inside); two pairs of *qarliik* (trousers); *pualuuk* (mitts); two pairs of *mirquliik* (stockings); a pair of *kamiik* (boots); and sometimes a pair of *tuktuqutik* (overshoes). The *amauti,* the married woman's upper garment, is similarly layered, and she wears one pair of trousers. The single woman's coat is sometimes called an *atigi.*[16]

The vocabulary relating to clothing is extensive. The use here of one term for each garment does not reflect the local dialects, the diversity, and the richness of the words in the Inuit languages descriptive of clothing. A few examples will indicate some of the complexities: '*Akuitoq:* man's parka with a slit down the front, worn traditionally in the *Keewatin* and Baffin Island areas'; '*Atigainaq:* teenage girl's parka from the *Keewatin* region'; '*Hurohirkhiut:* boy's parka with slit down the front'; '*Qolitsaq:* man's parka from Baffin Island' (Strickler and Alookee 1988, 175).

Although I use the word amauti generically for the woman's upper garment, it actually refers only to the parka with an *amaut,* a baby pouch.[17] At least a score of words describe *amautiit* that come from different localities, tell the age of the wearer, and have distinctive styles. Pharand (1974) discusses many clothing lexemes, of which only a few examples are: *aanngaarnisaq,* a coat from Iglulik, NWT, for carrying babies; *amaugaarjuk,* a coat with a narrow flat baby pouch, worn by elder women in Iglulik who are past child-bearing age and sometimes by unmarried girls; *angijurtaujaq,* an amauti from Mittimatalik with tapered hood, bulging sleeves, and no flaps; *akuarjuk,* the same, with long rounded flaps back and front; *nirukkaujaq,* an amauti from Sagliq with a wide, round, pleated hood, straight sleeves, and a baby pouch shaped for the infant to sit comfortably without the legs folded underneath; and *minguttinnaartuq,* a coat worn by young girls from Iglulik and Naujaat, distinguished from the atigainaq by the square shape of the flap at the back and by the absence of a fringe along the edge of this flap, which may be folded up (pp. 36-8).

The Qulittuq and Atigi

Both layers of the man's parka have a similar pattern. They are hooded with no front opening. Two flaps, a front and a longer back one, grace both inner and outer parka in most places in Canada. The flaps are now cut with an even edge, usually with a shallow curve. The back of the hunter's parka is longer than the front, sometimes only by five centimetres but usually by more. It forms a pad to insulate the wearer from the snow and prevents the wind from entering while he sits for long hours beside a fishing hole or gets caught in an unexpected storm. Capacious shoulders allow the arms to be drawn inside for warmth and provide ample room for the wide, forceful movements needed in the hunt.

Ruffs or facings keep out the cold and add comfort. The old-time parka had no pockets, and little articles were carried in a small bag around the neck or over one shoulder. The back of the parka sometimes had an *amakatservik,* a toggle sewn to the upper mid-back on which the hunter suspended his *amagattark,* a pouch for his smaller hunting tools.

The Amauti

The amauti, the woman's upper garment, is distinguished from the man's parka by the amaut – a part of the amauti at the top back, below the hood – where a child spends the first two to three years.[18] When the hood, which is usually voluminous, is pulled over the head, it can be folded to the windward side so that the woman's head is protected by three thicknesses of material. If the weather is cold and blustery, the hood is held in place by a strap which goes through a loop near the top, and tucks into the mother's waist.

In most Inuit groups in Canada, the front of the amauti has a *kiniq,* a flap or apron, which can reach to below the knees and then curve up over the hips into the back. Both the kiniq and the *akuq,* the tail or back flap, are short or long, wide or narrow, according to locality. Another style of amauti, the angijurtaujaq, has an even edge but still dips at the back. Ruff, fringes, and facings perform the same functions as in male clothing.

The amaut is an expansion or pouch that is an integral part of the amauti – there is no material between the mother and the child. Traditionally the infant nestles against the mother's bare back. A *qaksungauti,* a girdle of hide or braid, goes on the outside around the mother's waist and under the amaut to help support the child inside, while the roominess of the pouch allows the child movement and a certain independence of existence. A toggle at centre front and sometimes at the armpits holds the belt and distributes the weight of the growing child. A tapered waist contributes to warmth and security for the baby inside the amaut. If the baby becomes too hot, the hood can be opened or the baby can be brought outside for a little while to cool off.

The intimate contact with her child makes the mother aware of the baby's physiological and psychological needs (Driscoll 1980, 79). The ample shoulders allow her to bring her arms inside the amauti to move the baby from back to front for breast feeding, or she can turn the whole garment around so that the child sits in the amaut facing her. She can judge from the involuntary movements of the child when he or

Man's caribou-skin costume sewn with sinew, Netsilingmiut. The costume is made up of an outer parka (106 cm), stockings (70 cm), and shoes with hair inward (24 cm), collected by the Fifth Thule Expedition, 1921-4, led by Knud Rasmussen at Utkuhigjalingmiut, Back River, NWT. The gloves (25 cm) and skin belt with sixty-two small bones (105 cm) were collected by the Gjoa Expedition, 1903-6, led by Roald Amundsen in King William's Land. The man's parka has slits at the hip or the front so that it is comfortable to sit in and can easily be pulled over the head.

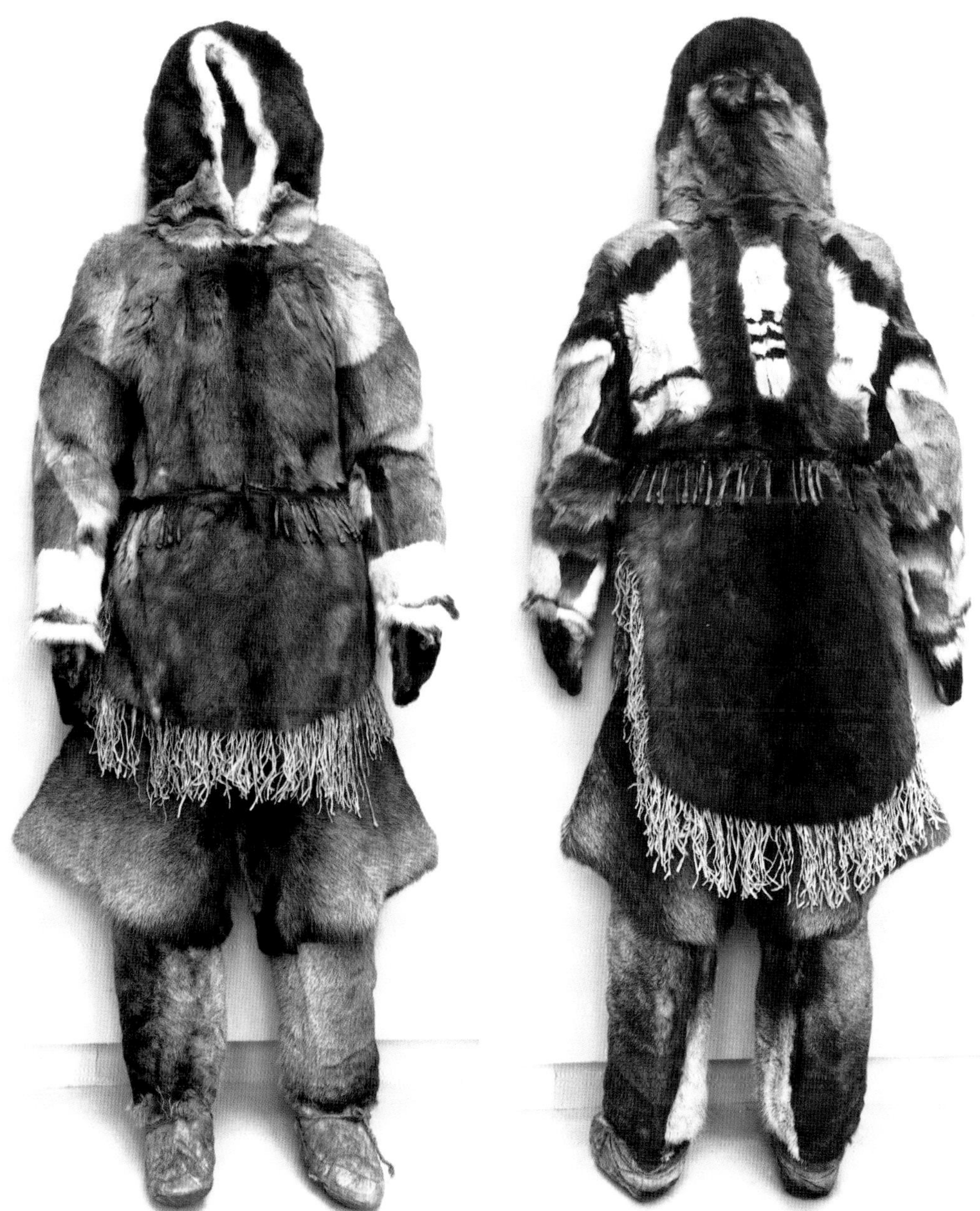

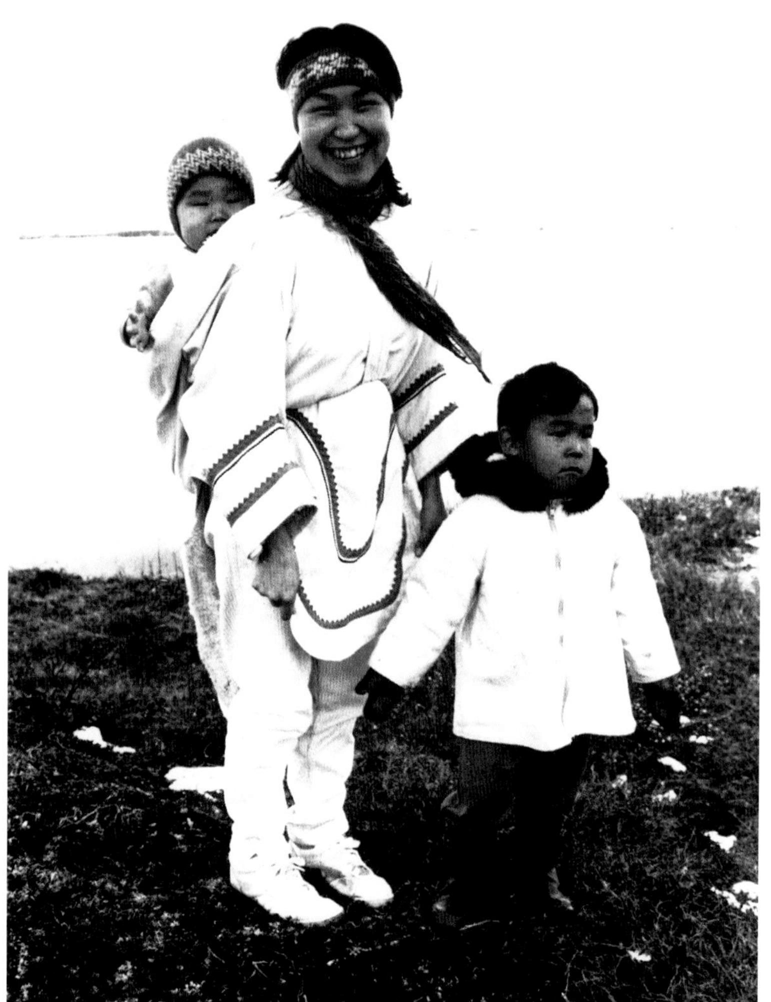

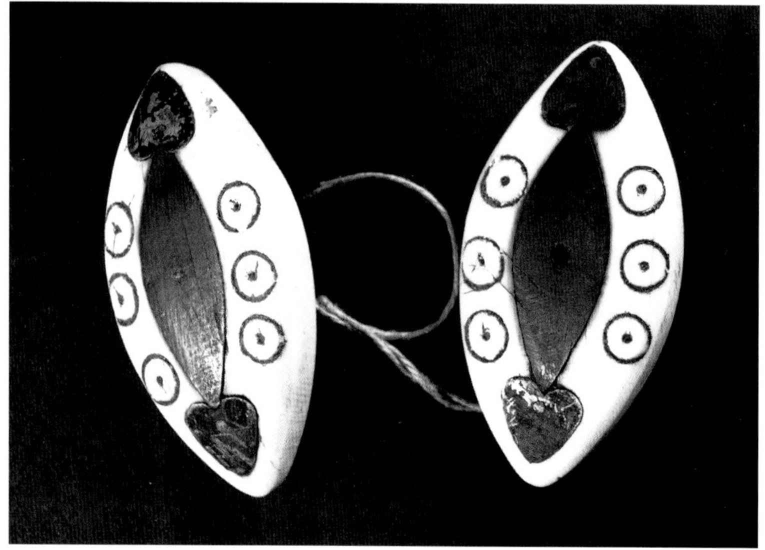

she needs to eliminate, for which the mother places the child in front of her, protected by the apron and not exposed to the cold. Prior to the advent of disposable diapers, *maniq* (moss) was used to line the garment to absorb urine or feces in the case of accidental discharge inside the amaut.[19] A piece of caribou fur also served as a diaper (Aliyak 1991, 44).

Desiccated wood helped the infant have a comfortable stay in the amaut before the appearance of commercial powders. In the parts of the Arctic where wood was available, mothers would gather it when it was at the point of becoming powdery. They dried and hammered it and used it to dust the baby. If wood was not available, wood-soot was flaked into powder, but, understandably, it was not preferred (Freeman 1978, 61).

Qarliik

Qarliik, trousers, are worn by men and women. Men wear two layers in the winter; women wear one since they do not usually go on long hunting forays in deepest cold. Trousers are waist high and hang loosely on the hips, held up by a drawstring that comes through a casing to tie at the back. They have ruffs, fringes, or facings made of fur, which come down over the boots and stockings and trap the warm air as it rises from the boots. The seat can obtain its shape by using the rump skin of the caribou or by piecing with several gores. The shape of the leg can vary. If caribou is in short supply, or if seal or bear skin is used, the leg is shaped more or less like a cylinder. A more comfortable style uses a bell-bottom cut, which

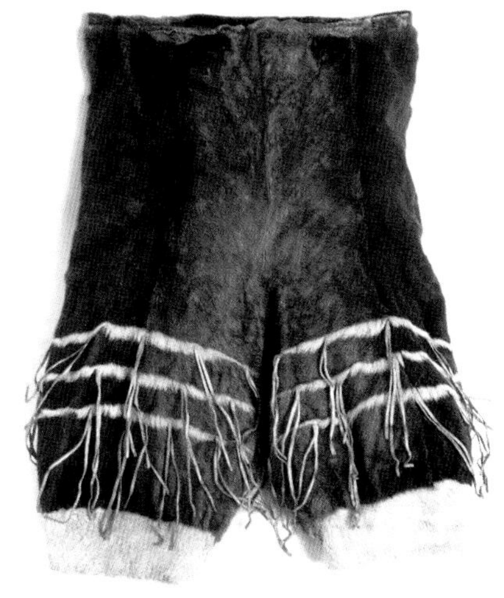

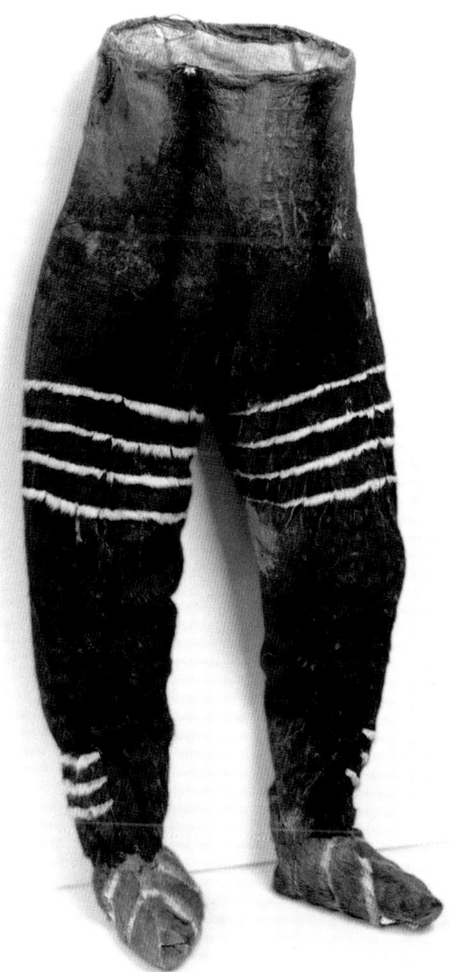

Opposite above Lillian Shamee and her two sons, at Arviat, NWT, in 1988. The shape of the amaut, which varies by locality, determines the position of the child's legs. Inside the amaut, an infant may draw the legs up or sit with them crossed. Older children can dangle their legs or wrap them around their mother's waist.

Opposite below Ivory ornamented toggles with inlay, 7.5 cm, Caribou Inuit, early twentieth century. Collected by E.W.Hawkes at Igluligaarjuk, NWT, 1914. The amauti belt passes through an opening at the back of the toggles to hold the belt at the neck and armpits.

Above Caribou-skin trousers, sewn with sinew, 84 cm, Copper Inuit, early twentieth century. Where the leg-piece attaches to the upper part of the trousers, the seamstress inserts decorative strips of contrasting-coloured fur, and sometimes fringes or dangles made of dehaired hide. The inserts strengthen the seams and add to the visual enjoyment. The white fur bands (pukiq) reflect the white markings on the animal's legs.

Below Trousers with feet, made from caribou skin, cord, 130 cm, Copper Inuit, early twentieth century. A rare example of *atartaq*. The white fur insertions at thigh, ankle, and foot echo the markings of the caribou.

allows the air to circulate when the wearer is running and can be wrapped around the leg when he or she is sitting (Manning and Manning 1944, 165). If trousers are worn with fur to the inside, caribou calf is the most comfortable material. If the wiry fur of adult polar bear is used, men wear a G-string made of Arctic fox fur to prevent chafing.

Formerly, if their boots were hip high, women wore trousers shorter than men's (Birket-Smith 1945, 152-7). Among the Copper Inuit, in the old days, men and women sometimes wore a one-piece combination of legging and boot. In Nunavik women's caribou-skin trousers could extend to the armpits. When caught in the cold away from home they pulled the pants over the shoulders and used them as a sleeping bag (Myers 1980, 141).

Hoods and Hats

Hats separate from the parka are worn by Siberian Yupiit and some Kalaallit. In Canada, many Inuit wear a cap under the hood. On social occasions, such as dances, a hat may be worn with the hood thrown back. In the mosquito season, when the weather is too warm to use a hood, the cap is draped with a scarf that covers the neck and as much of the face as possible. In the old days, the styles were of the hood or bonnet type and a kind of round cap called a calotte by non-Inuit.

Pualuuk

In winter men can wear two sets of caribou pualuuk, mitts, but usually one layer is considered adequate and less clumsy. Caribou

Below Boy's hood of blanket cloth, caribou skin, beads, Caribou Inuit (?), early twentieth century. Collected by Superintendent John Douglas Moodie at Kuugjuaq, Manitoba or Katiktalik, NWT in 1903-5.

Right Cap, double-layered, with wolverine fur outside and reindeer fur inside, 42 cm, Siberian Yup'ik, late nineteenth or early twentieth century.

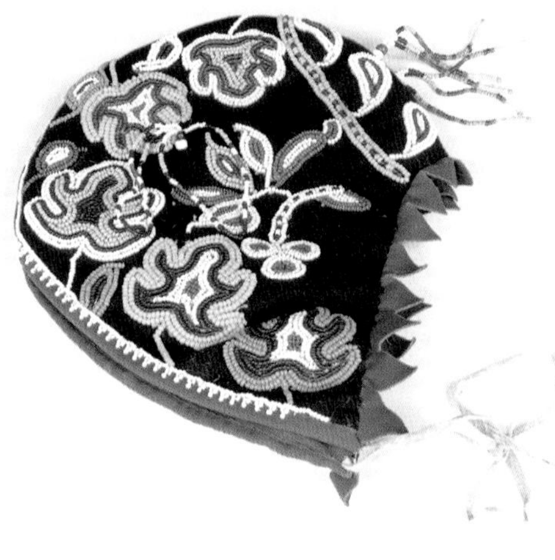

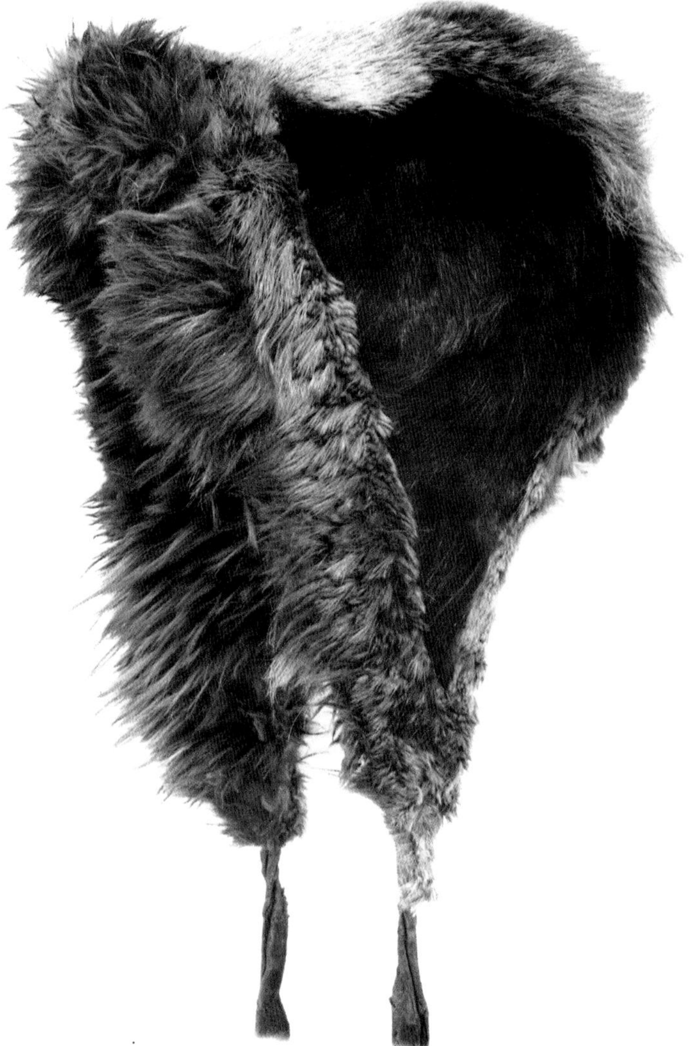

Figure 2.1
Hood patterns, Northeast Siberian Yup'ik. The bonnet pattern is found from Siberia to Canada, and possibly Kalaallit Nunaat. The Chukchi, Yup'ik, and Inuit made hoods with fur inside or out, or both. *Based on a drawing by T.B. Mitlyanskaya.*

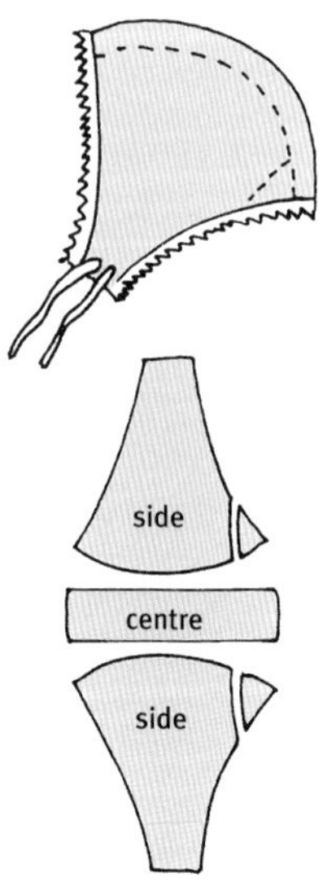

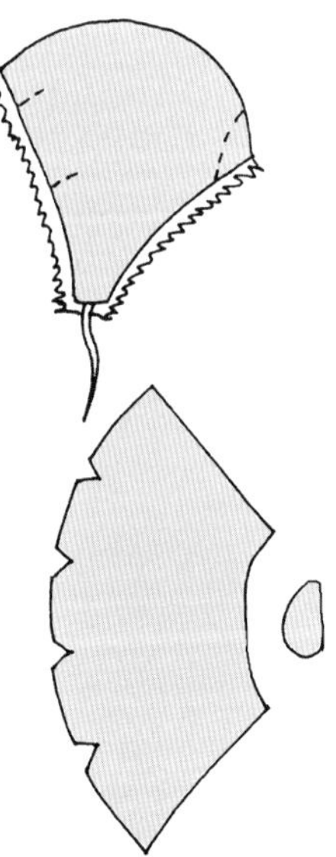

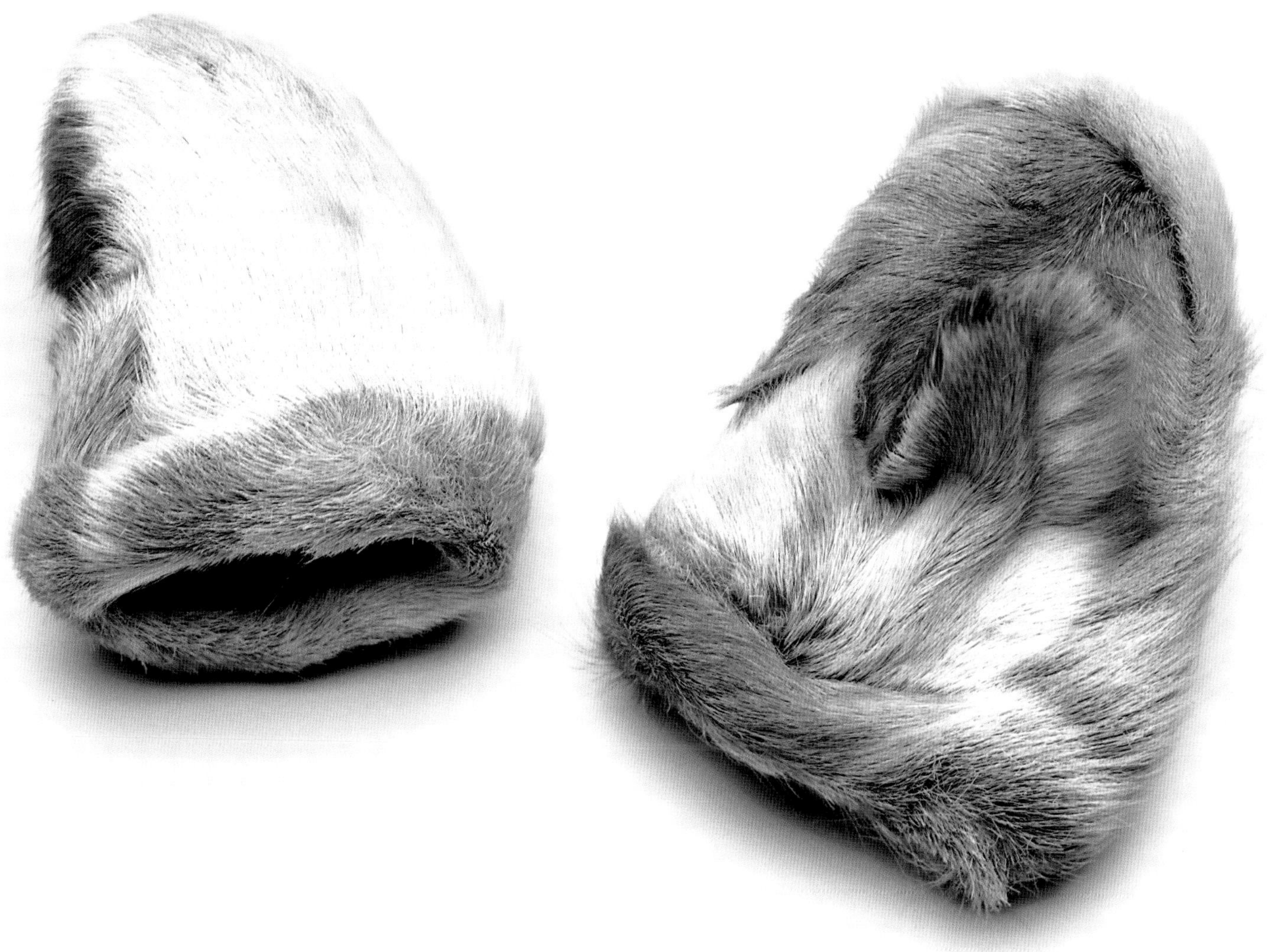

Caribou-skin mitts, sewn with sinew, 21 cm, Caribou Inuit, early twentieth century. Collected at Igluligaarjuk, NWT. These mitts are made of heavy caribou fur for winter wear.

leg skin is preferred for winter mitts since it is hard wearing and its short hair prevents moisture build-up. For tasks in warm weather and wet conditions, sealskin mitts are worn. Bear skin was favoured when icing sled runners in springtime because the hair does not shed with dampness. Palms made of depilated seal skin or with the fur flow running from the top toward the wrist improve the grip on, for example, harpoons, rifles, and dog traces.

A three-piece pattern for mitts is found all over the Arctic, usually with a fourth piece to make a strip at the wrist, although in Labrador and Siberia one- and two-piece patterns are known (Hawkes 1916, 48). The wrist of the mitt cuff is short, since the parka sleeve covers the mitt. The thumb is short and apposed, parallel to the palm of the hand. One half of the thumb is cut intact with the upper palm piece. The other half of the thumb is continuous with the lower palm, so that the root of the thumb, where the greatest movement and stress occurs, is seamless. The back of the mitt comes over the edge of the hand to the front and joins the palm in gathers that shape the mitt to the hand. Women's mitts were sometimes made of hare or fox skin with sealskin palms (Turner [1894] 1979, 54). An 'idiot' string, sometimes a harness, made of *singait* (braided sinew) or of thong can be attached to mitts and worn over the shoulders – not so idiotic when to lose a mitt can threaten life.

Footwear

The foot and leg coverings of the Inuit, more than other any item of their clothing, demonstrate their superb technology, complete comprehension of the animals used, and sensitive responses to their environment (Hadlereena et al. 1984; Hatt 1916, [1914] 1969; Jenness 1946; Oakes 1987; Oakes and Riewe 1995; Pharand 1974).[20] The footgear meets the challenges of weather, season, terrain, and function with maximum efficiency, comfort, and durability. Severe winter conditions or treacherous spring ice make their exacting demands on the Inuit seamstress. Boots must comply with terrain, whether gravel or rock, open sea or floe ice, wet or dry snow. Footwear must suit the occasion: the inland animal hunt, the wait by the seal hole, around camp or home, or the dance and special celebrations. Boots and stockings in many combinations have to guarantee warm, dry feet and legs.

Traditionally in the cold, dry winter months a person could don as many as five layers of footwear. He or she first pulled on *alirsiik,* caribou stockings with fur to the inside. Next could come *ilupirquk,* short socks of light-weight caribou skin or seal with fur to the outside. Then came *pinirait,* the second pair of stockings, fur to the outside.

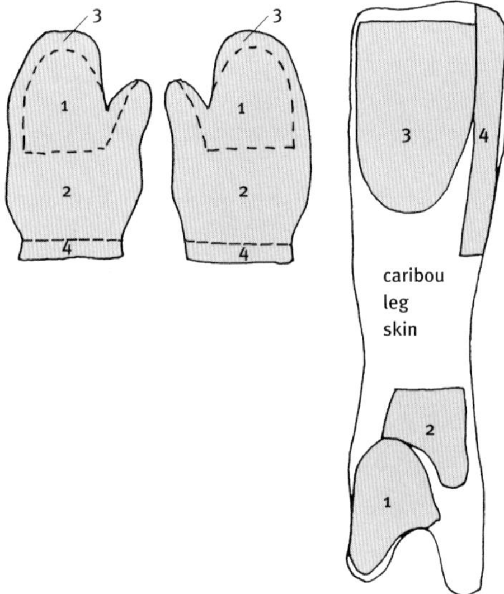

Figure 2.2
Pattern for mitts and layout on caribou leg skin, Nunavimiut. The fur on the legs of caribou, a browsing animal, becomes tough and wiry, making leg skin ideal for clothing such as mitts. The fur flow of the palm's upper part is down, while the flow of the palm's lower part with the thumb is up. This feature provides the hunter with a good grip on his or her equipment. *Based on a drawing by Tuumasikadlak.*

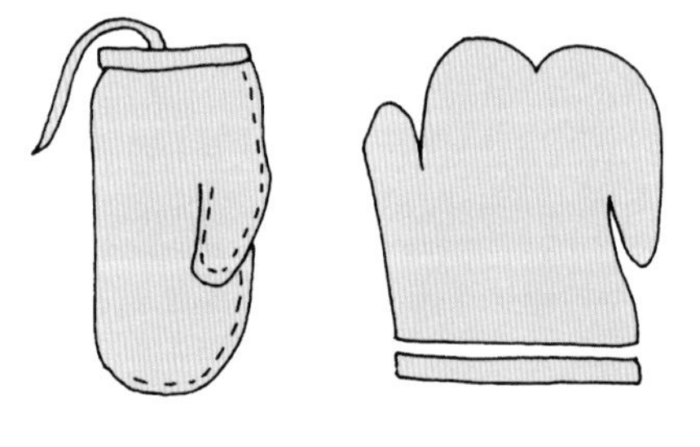

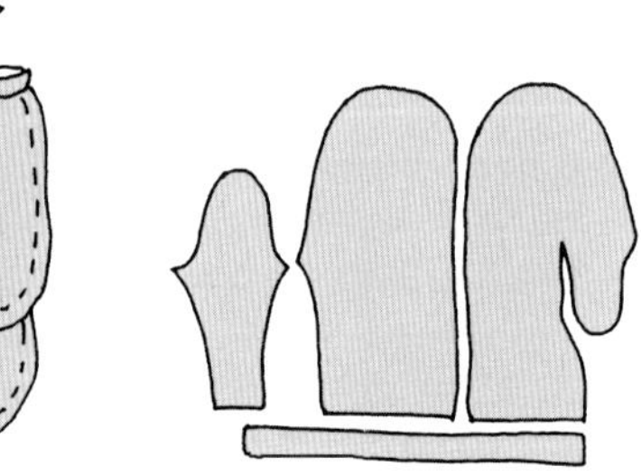

Figure 2.3
Two mitt patterns, Chukotka Yup'ik: a one-piece pattern and a three-piece pattern. Both patterns have a band at the wrist, which has a horizontal flow. *Based on a drawing by T.B. Mitlyanskaya.*

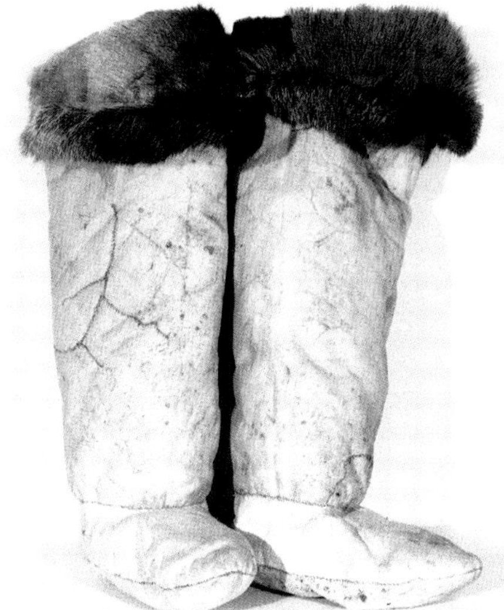

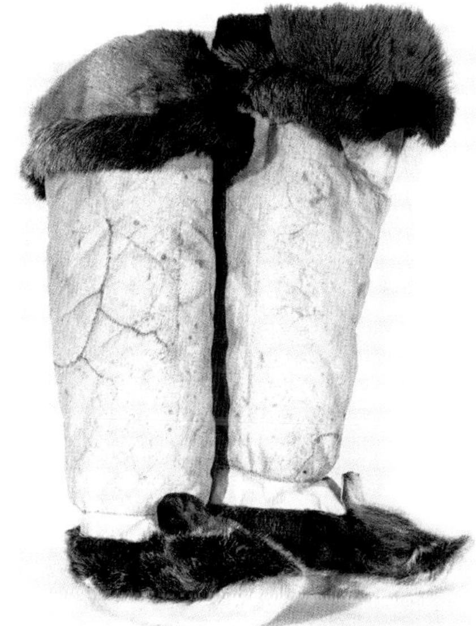

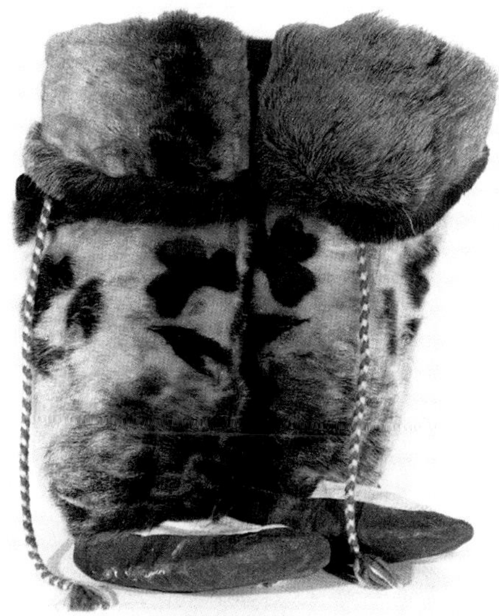

Winter footwear, Iglulingmiut.

Above Stockings, caribou skin, fur to inside (tops folded over), 61 cm.

Centre Slippers, seal skin, fur to outside, 26 cm, worn over stockings.

Below Boots, seal skin, cotton casing, wool drawstring, fur to outside, dehaired foot, 45 cm.

Artisan: Hanna Alooloo of Ikpiarjuk, NWT, 1987.

The boots cover the stockings and slippers. The boot has a ringed seal upper, fur to the outside, with one seam up the centre back. The foot of dehaired seal skin has an instep made of white, soft, freeze-dried seal skin and a sole of bearded seal. The foot is waterproof and has the distinctive sole that comes up the sides of the foot.

Over the stockings the hunter put on his boots, with fur outside. A *tuqtuqutiq*, an ankle boot, could be pulled over the kamiik. This last kind of boot provides excellent insulation. Made of heavy caribou skin, the fur is turned to the inside and an extra sole of sheared caribou fur is added to the outside.

The Copper Inuit covered their boots with shoes made of depilated seal skin. In these shoes, the sole was brought up over the sides of the foot and toes and formed to the foot by a series of exceedingly fine slits made by the removal of extremely narrow triangular slivers. The slits were joined to a V-shaped narrow tongue that ran down the middle of the instep. The heel was similarly slitted and strengthened by rows of fine stitches of sinew knotted at both ends.

In addition to caribou and seal skin, sheep skin is sometimes used. 'Sheepskin boots were called *kamipak*, but now they're called *marnguaq*. When I was young I didn't want to wear a caribou hide parka or sheepskin boots. I realized I needed to wear them when someone explained that I would be having duties which had to be done in the cold,' comments Sammy Nasak of Kangirsuk (Nungak 1983, 124).

Winter boots of caribou or seal can have a depilated sealskin foot with a furred upper. With the spring melt, *ipirautiik*, waterproof boots, replace the furry boots. These boots are made of dehaired, sometimes shaved, seal skin and are sewn with a waterproof stitch. For boots to be worn on ice or hard-packed snow, narrow strips of dehaired seal skin are sewn to the sole in puckers to form cleats or 'creepers.'

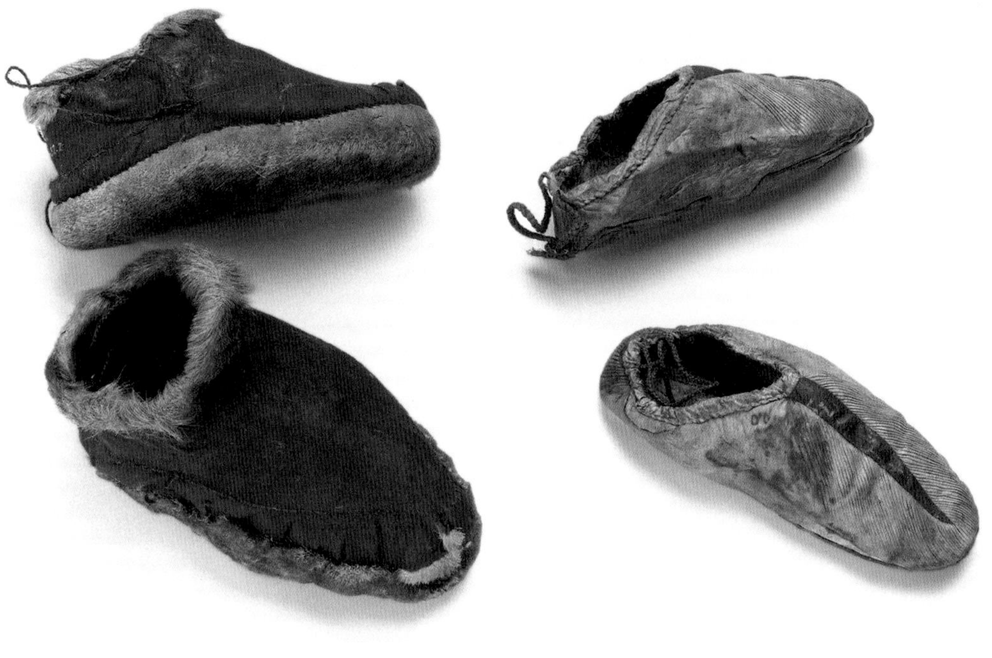

Above Caribou-skin ankle boots sewn with sinew (left), 27.5 cm, Caribou Inuit, Igluligaarjuk, NWT, early twentieth century. Sealskin shoes sewn with sinew (right), 24 cm, 25 cm, Copper Inuit, early twentieth century. The late Guy Mary-Rousselière notes that the boots 'may have come from Qamanittuaq, NWT, where an inland Caribou Inuit group live who have no bear or seal. They are made up of scraps of fur possibly indicating a time of scarcity and starvation' (personal communication 1985).

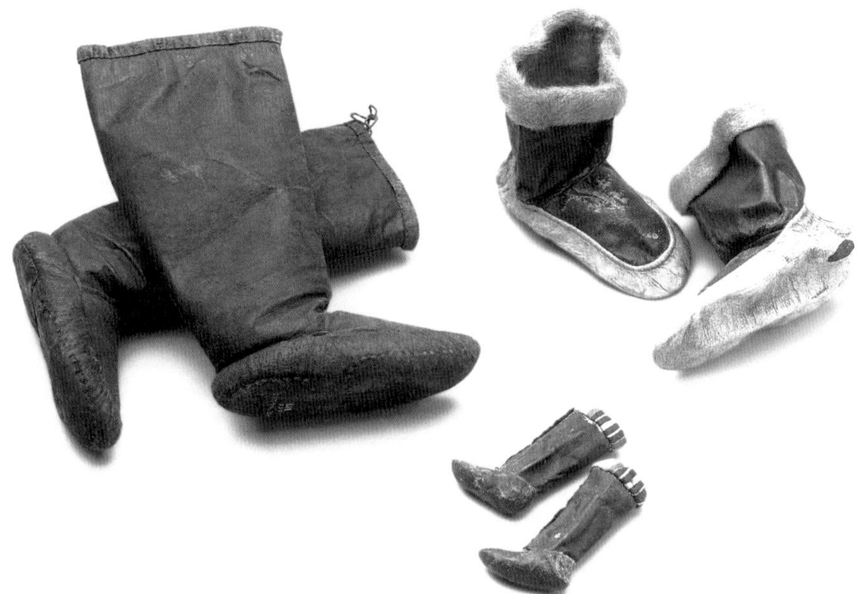

Below Waterproof boots. Sealskin and sinew boots sewn with sinew (left), 42 cm, Iglulingmiut, Naujaat, NWT, early twentieth century; sealskin boots sewn with sinew (right), 22 cm, Nunavimiut or Labrador Inuit, mid-twentieth century; sealskin and cotton infant's boots sewn with sinew (bottom), 15 cm, Nunavimiut, Ungava District, Nunavik, ca. 1860.

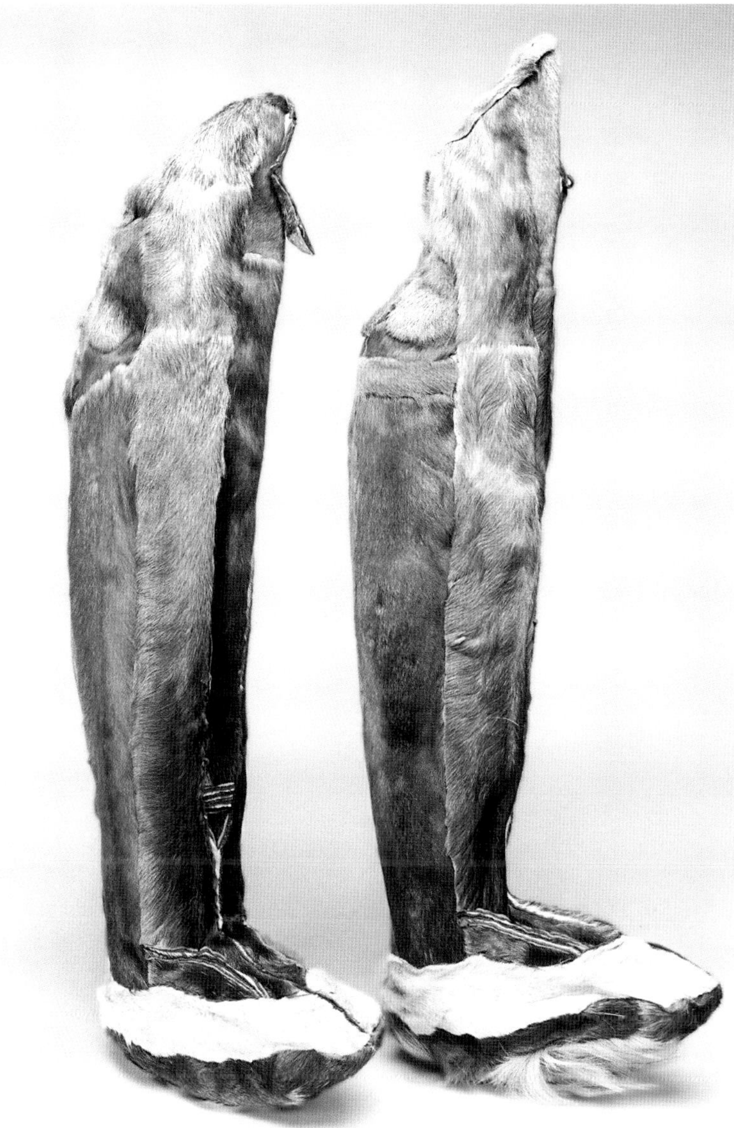

Women's boots, made of caribou skin, polar bear skin, stroud, sewn with sinew, 75 cm, Copper Inuit or Inuvialuit, ca. 1930. Collected by Percy Noad at Qurluqtuuq or Paulatuuq, NWT. In times past, boots were sometimes cut high and rose to a point with a thong that was tucked into the trouser waist by a caribou ear or toggle. The fur of the bearskin sole in these boots points forward to catch in the snow to give the wearer a sure footing.

Figure 2.4
Boot patterns, Nunavimiut. While the footwear is loose, it narrows at the ankle to hold the upper to the leg. A drawstring at the boot top can be loosened to allow heat and humidity to escape, or tightened to keep out wind and snow. *Based on a drawing by Tuumasikadlak.*

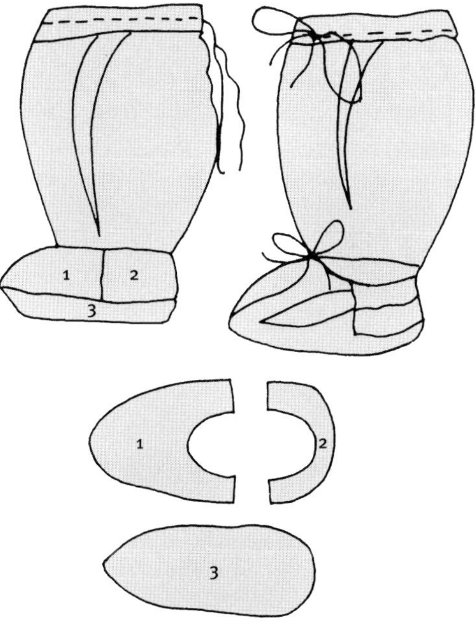

Inuit women's footwear was very distinctive. The early explorers of Canada were greatly enchanted by the women's hip-high, wide boots and stockings. No longer made, they are described in early writings and represented in images and in museum collections. Another kind of footgear for women had *quajjuk,* closed side pouches used to store small items for sewing or diaper material, for example.

A basic distinction exists between Inuit and Amerindian footgear. The soles of the Inuit boot cover the bottom and sides of the foot without seams or cuts. They are shaped to the contours of the foot at toe and heel by fine pleats and gathers and bend up to cover the edge of the foot. Indian groups such as the Apache, Navajo, and Pueblo peoples all made similar footwear. The soles of these boots do come up slightly at the sides but never more than about one centimetre, and they are never as deeply pleated as Inuit boot soles (Richard Conn, written communication 1989). Siberian Yup'ik and Alaskan Yup'ik and Inupiaq boot soles are particularly thick, sometimes reaching a depth of five centimetres.

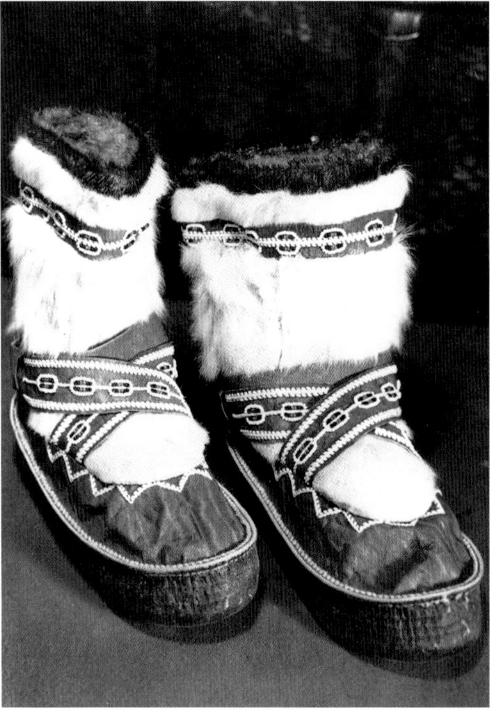

Above Man's boots, Siberian Yup'ik. Artisan: Mme. Kameya of Qerre (Lavrentiya), Chukotka, CIS, 1982. These boots, as well as several in the Forshtein Collection at the Museum of Peter the Great, St. Petersburg, demonstrate the deep edge of Northeastern Siberian boots. A similar pattern is found in Alaska, from where it moved in the early 1900s to the Copper Inuit areas (Hall, Oakes, and Webster 1994, 112).

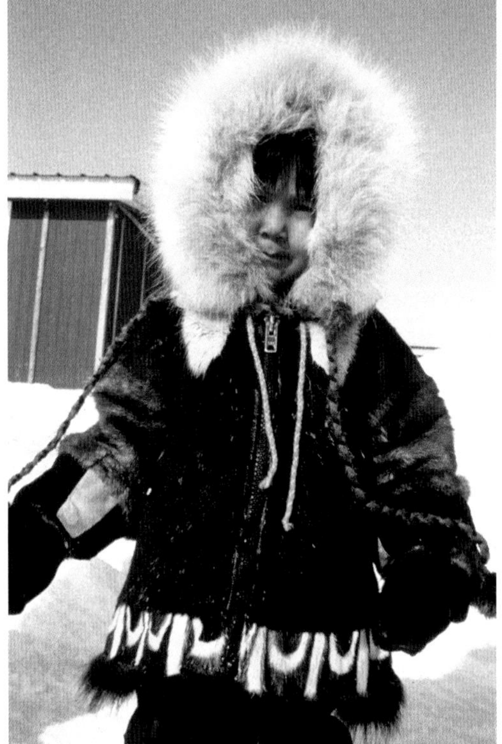

Below Sandra Hummiktuq of Uqsuqtuuq, NWT, 1992, wears a fur parka with a zipper. The wool drawstring keeps her hood close to her face on blustery days. Her mitts are secured by a braided wool cord that goes over her shoulders.

Opposite Caribou-skin infant's trousers sewn with sinew (24 cm), bonnet (19 cm), and parka (30 cm), Iglulingmiut, 1971. Artisan: Panikpakutsuk of Iglulik, NWT. The Yup'ik of Nunivak Island, Alaska, found a solution to keeping both mother and child comfortable while the youngster was still in need of a diaper. They made waterproof pants from the lining of a seal's stomach, which was strong and pliable. Moss inside the pants acted as a disposable diaper (VanStone 1989, 38).

Children's Clothing

Traditionally, in the case of an infant's premature birth, the mother and her helpers placed the baby in a seal bladder or a bird-skin pouch. The pouch would be hung over an oil lamp with a low flame. At least one premature baby was kept safe in the grandmother's sleeve (John Bennett, written communication 1992). The full-term infant's first few days might be spent naked in the mother's amaut or in a sack of caribou skin (Hawkes 1916; Mathiassen 1928; Pharand 1974; Saladin d'Anglure, Mautaritnaaq, and Mark 1979).[21] The first clothing, never made before the child's birth, could be of *illauq,* caribou foetal skin or skin of newborn calf that had died at birth. If the newborn child was clothed in a gown of bird skin, the bird was chosen according to the month of the child's birth: waterfowl in summer, ptarmigan in winter.

As the infant grew, the next set of clothes was made of other soft materials: a jacket of caribou fawn or fox skin; a hood from the skin of a hare's head; small boots of hare or fawn. After two or three years in the amaut, the young run-about acquired an *atajuq,* a hooded combination suit of caribou skin tied up the front, often with mittens, sometimes

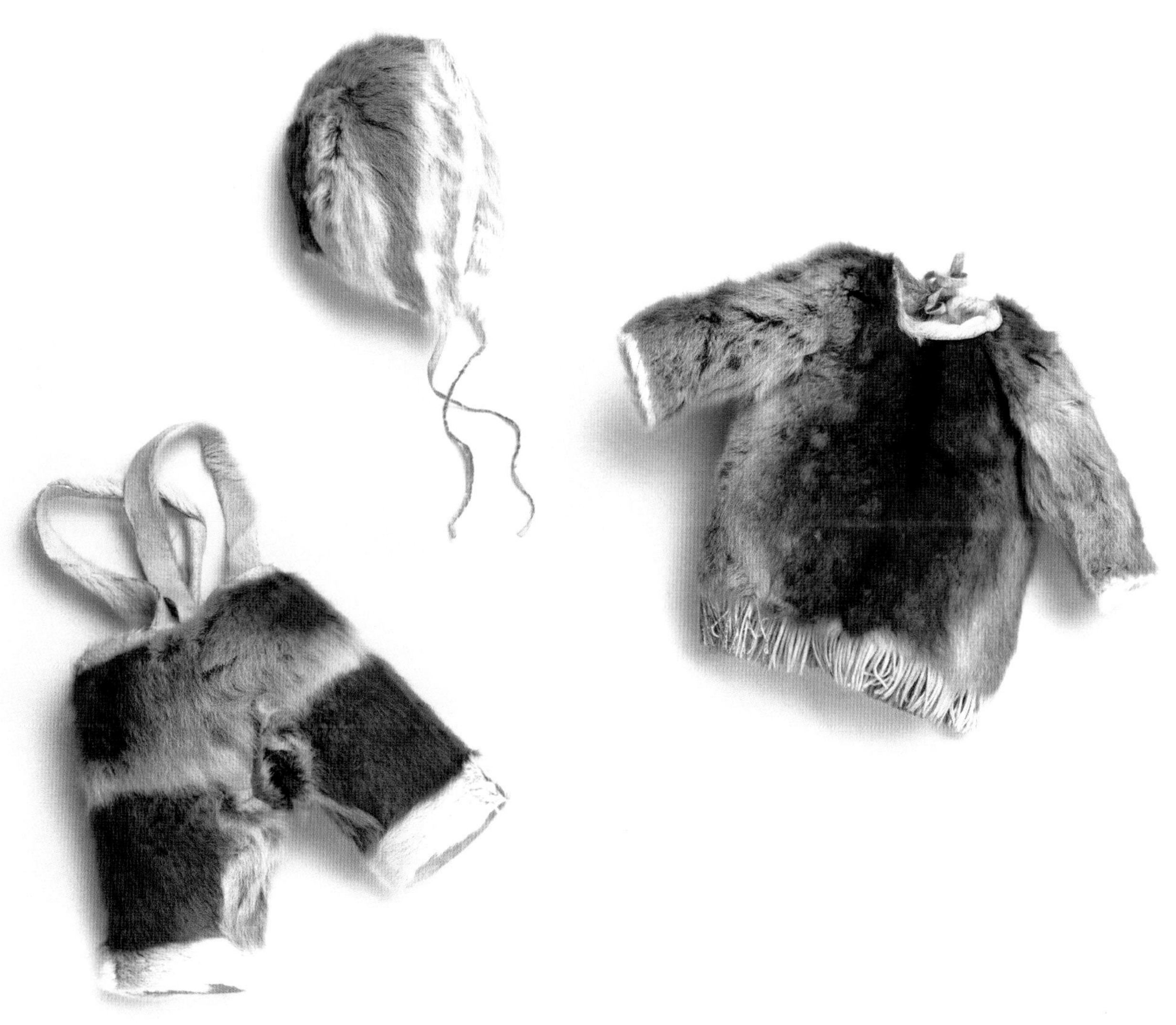

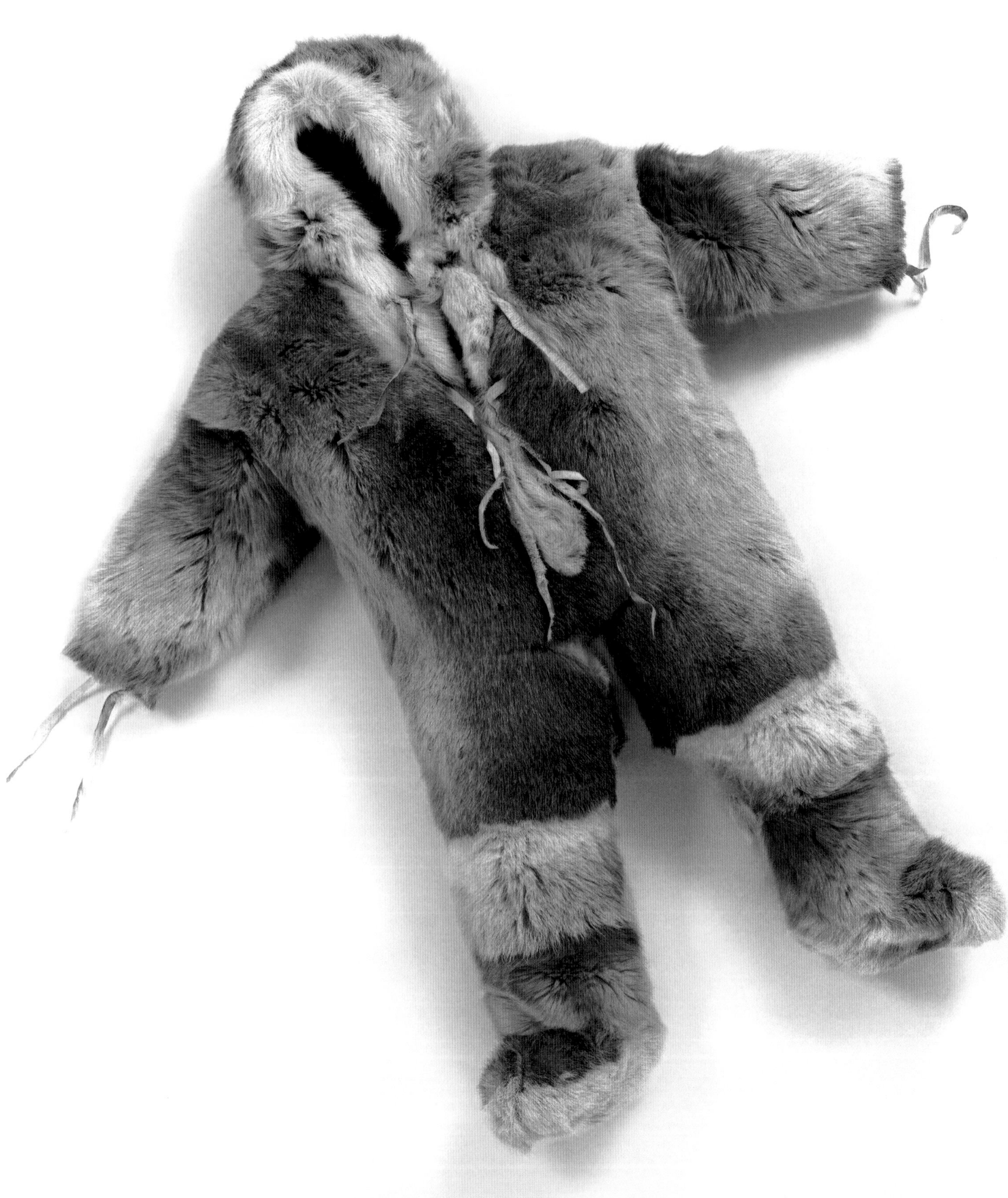

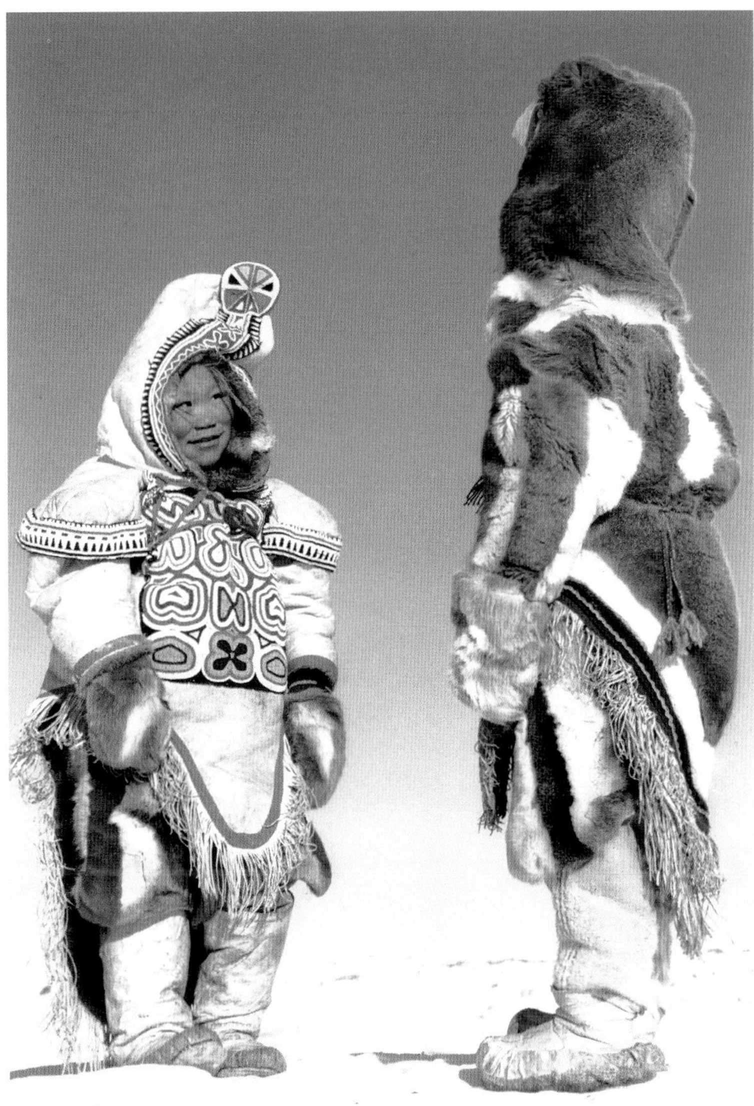

Opposite Caribou-skin child's suit sewn with sinew, 112 cm, Iglulingmiut, Iglulik, NWT, 1971. An opening at the back of the child's combination suit from about mid-hip to crotch allows for elimination. The aperture is made so that when the child squats, it opens; when the child stands, the overlapping edges fall back in place.

Above Two Caribou Inuit girls, Padlei, NWT, 1950. A small girl's parka either has no amaut or a very small one, and usually has short flaps in the back and front.

thumbless, and with feet attached. The older child wore separate parka and trousers fashioned like an adult's outfit. Today an Inuit mother or grandmother will make a fur suit or beaded *atigi* for their youngster. A good many children wear fabric clothing, sometimes augmented with a fur lining and ruff, or they dress in southern-style clothes with fur trim and down or synthetic insulation (Hall, Oakes, and Webster 1994, 105-22).

PERHAPS THE BEST ILLUSTRATION of the efficiency of Inuit garments is given in a story told by Vilhjalmur Stefansson (Stefansson 1958, 41). An elderly woman in northern Alaska went to gather driftwood about half a mile from home. She wore one layer of clothes, with fur to the inside – a 'warm' weather outfit. A gale descended and, feeling with her feet in the blinding whiteout, she found a small hillock. She took off her mittens to sit on so as not to melt the snow, pulled her arms inside the amauti, and with her back to the wind, settled herself leaning slightly forward with elbows on her knees so as not to topple over when she fell asleep. The storm lasted until late afternoon the next day, at which point she made her way home. No one thought much about her experience, except that some argued that she should have gone to the trouble of building a shelter such as a small *iglu*.

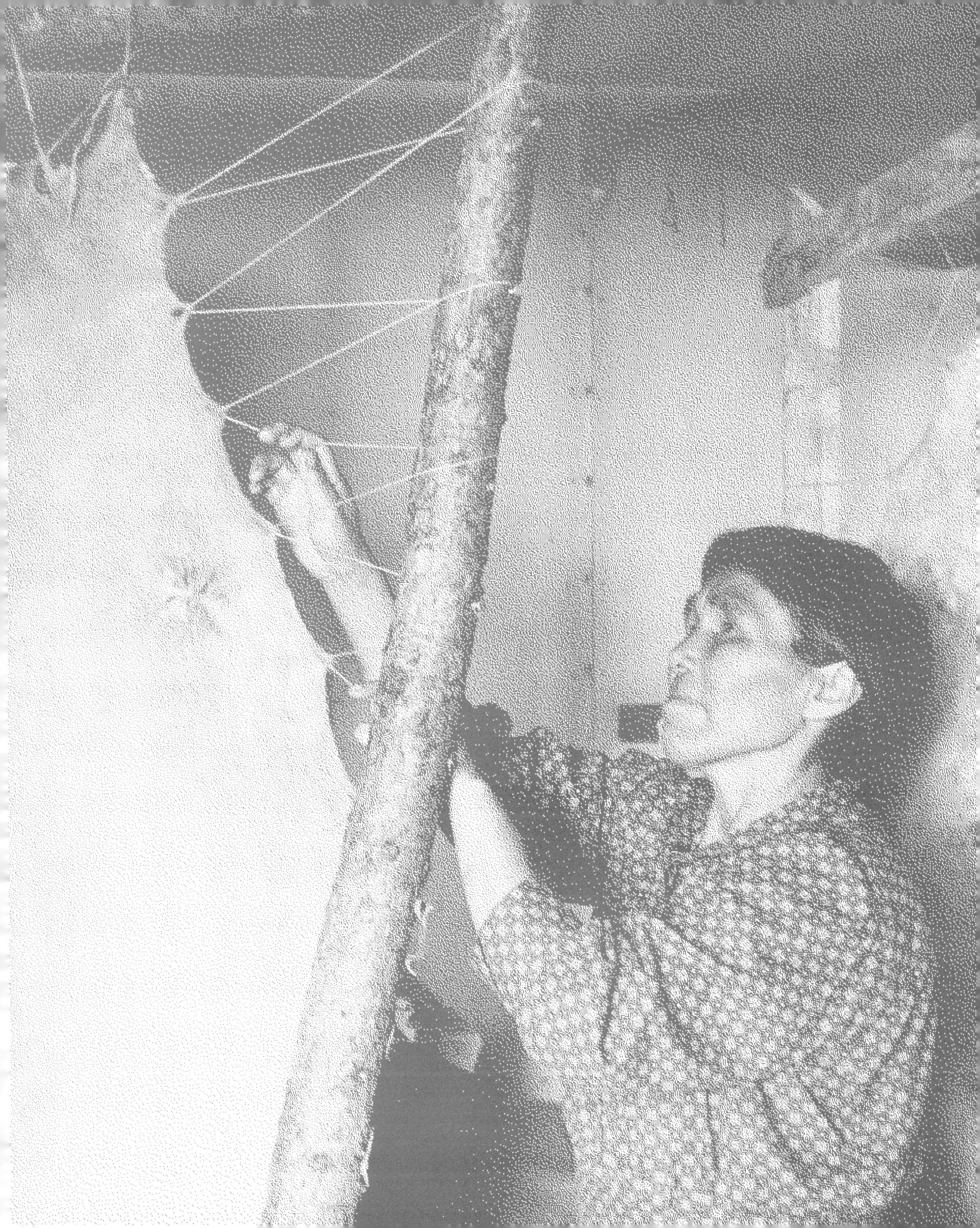

When a woman has her first child, her mother and her grandmother help her make her amautik ... That's how knowledge came through the generations.

Elisapee Kiliutak of Kangirsuk[1]

By the age of twelve, the girl's training began in earnest. She was now being taught how to make clothing and her mind was developing and she was becoming more considerate ... Her mother ... pushed her to learn about braiding, sewing clothes, scraping skins, cooking, tending the lamp, caring for clothing and many other things, such as the proper way to dry them.

Martha Angugatiaq Ungalaaq of Iglulik[2]

Chapter 3

Tools and Techniques

To clothe a family in the traditional manner required a complete knowledge of the animal cycles and the processing of skins. Man the hunter, woman the seamstress, grandparents, and children joined together in a year-round effort to produce the clothing. Subsistence activities centred on obtaining food and skins and governed the yearly economic cycle. The time for the main caribou hunt was usually from August to October. From December to May, seals and other sea mammals were hunted. The land-sea dichotomy reflected the seasons of the hunt and the time of light and dark.

The sewing season for winter clothes made of caribou skin was in October and November, after the hunt. Communities were anxious to complete the sewing before the light diminished and to ensure new clothing for the winter festivals. Just as important, in some communities, contact with caribou skins had to be completed before the start of sealing in order to comply with restrictions against mixing land and sea products.

Families would gather after the hunt for about four weeks of sewing. It was also a time to renew kinship bonds and friendships (Damas 1984b, 400). After the caribou-skin sewing was completed, the families would move in December from their inland site to sealing encampments near the sea and the floe edge. Large aggregations of families ensured that the maximum number of seal breathing holes could be watched and that other forms of marine animal hunting could be conducted.

TOOL MAKING

'My father made my tools. He could make ulus out of bone. I use the ulu for sealskin scraping, for cutting meat, cutting out the caribou parka, cutting out the sealskins to make kamiks, and to take the fat from musk ox and polar bear. If I did not have an ulu, I would not make anything,' said Martha Kiguktak of Ausuittuq (Steltzer 1985, 29). Men make the tools and the tools to make the tools.[3] They can fashion their own implements for hunting and fishing and skin-dressing and sewing tools for their wives and girlfriends. The care taken to make these implements and their ornamentation bespeak a pride and delight in the task.

In addition to the organic materials such as antler, ivory, horn, and wood out of which Inuit fashioned tools, inorganic components played an important part in tool making (McElhone 1984b, 3-5). Meteoric iron finds – there is a large deposit near Naujaat – supplied metal for blades. The iron was worked cold by hammering and filing. Ground copper was collected at various sites in the Arctic (Franklin et al. 1981). The copper, too, was cold-hammered, then folded, annealed, and filed. Metals were combined with organic materials to make composite tools. Once explorers, traders, and whalers came to the Arctic, the Inuit obtained heavy sheet tin and iron from 'refuse piles of some of the English ships of the Franklin Search Expedition' (Stefansson 1914, 98). They also collected brass from ships' fittings or from telescopes and steel saws from trade.

Wooden and steel ulu, 17 cm, Caribou Inuit, ca. mid-twentieth century. Bought in Arviat, NWT, 1986. Steel needle, 8.1 cm, ca. mid-nineteenth century, United Kingdom, manufacturer A. Shrimpton. The ulu is made from the blade and handle of a saw. The three-sided glover's needle (this one is size no. 12) is used in both the North and South for various kinds of sewing.

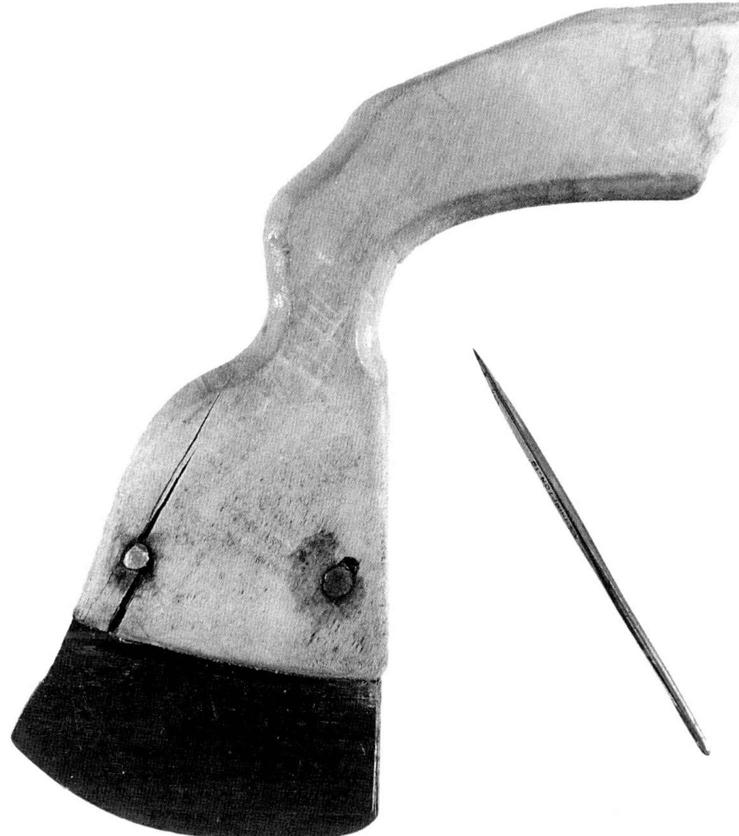

The Inuit hunter and seamstress still use traditional tools. As in the past, blades are frequently made from saw blades, obtainable at the local cooperative. One large saw blade can be cut up to make three to five uluit of different sizes (Condon 1985, 157).

CLOTHING IMPLEMENTS

Uluit

The ulu, sometimes called the semi-lunar knife, symbolizes the Inuit woman and her work. Every girl is given her own ulu, to be used by her alone (Freeman 1978, 47). In traditional life when she married she took her ulu and lamp to her husband's tent. When she died her ulu or its model accompanied her to her place of burial. The woman uses her uluit for flensing (skinning) and butchering a seal, slicing food, preparing and cutting skins and sinew, chopping moss, reeds, and tobacco, and cutting food. A large ulu can be used to butcher a seal or to scrape skins. The point of a small ulu can be used as an awl to make loops for boot thongs or for lacing a skin to a drying rack (Leah Idlout, personal communication 1984).

The ulu is made up of a handle and blade, both transverse.[4] The handle can consist of one to three pieces. The one-piece grip is simplest, where the blade is set directly into the handle, a form still used in the western Arctic. These handles are more or less cylindrical, but early ones were sometimes quite deep, with an opening to accommodate the fingers. A two-piece handle has a stem, called a tang, between the

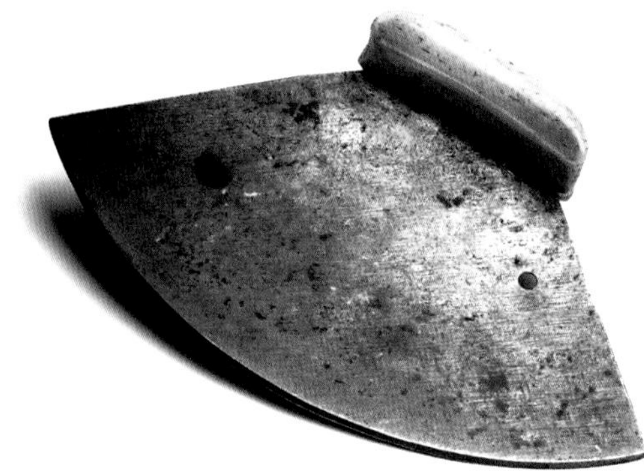

Left Ivory and steel ulu, 20.3 cm, Inuvialuit, late nineteenth century. Collected at Qikiqtaruk by Forbes D. Sutherland. The steel blade is cut from a saw and set directly into the ivory handle.

Below left Ulu of ivory, steel, brass, and baleen (?) inlay, 8.5 cm, Inupiaq or Yup'ik, early twentieth century. The two-piece handle of this ulu is composed of an ivory grip and a brass tang that is fastened by a rivet to the steel blade.

Below right Antler and steel ulu, 6.4 cm, Nunatsiarmiut or Nunavimiut, ca. late nineteenth century. The steel tang of this ulu is made of two pieces and set into the antler handle at the distal end. It is secured to the blade by an iron rivet. Very small uluit such as this one were used for fine work in hard-to-get-at corners or were given to a child.

grip and the blade. The three-piece has an intermediate part between tang and blade. The ulu's cutting edge is often characterized as crescent shaped or semi-lunar, but some Inuit groups, such as the Copper Inuit and those farther west, had blades that were fairly flat in the middle and curved only slightly at the ends. The blade can be shallow to deep and of different widths. The top edge has many shapes: right-angled, triangular, horizontal, or concave. When I asked Rhoda Karetak, an elder and renowned seamstress from Kangiqliniq, if she could tell from the shape of an ulu where it was from, she quickly drew a schema to indicate essential differences.

Each component of the ulu has changed over the centuries. The present-day shape brings together a number of factors for maximum efficiency (Porsild 1915, 106). The length of the handle approximates the width of the hand and provides a secure grip even if the handle is slippery from grease and blood. The length of the blade cutting edge is longer than the handle. When the blade is fixed to the handle by a single stem, the pliability of the wrist is fully used, and the blade's manoeuvrability inside the animal is assured. In some procedures and depending on the individual, the tang of the ulu comes between the second and fourth digit and the middle finger gives the required amount of pressure on the tang, which must therefore be neither too long nor too short. The tang allows a space between the handle and cutting edge and protects the fingers of both hands, since the left hand of the right-handed person holds

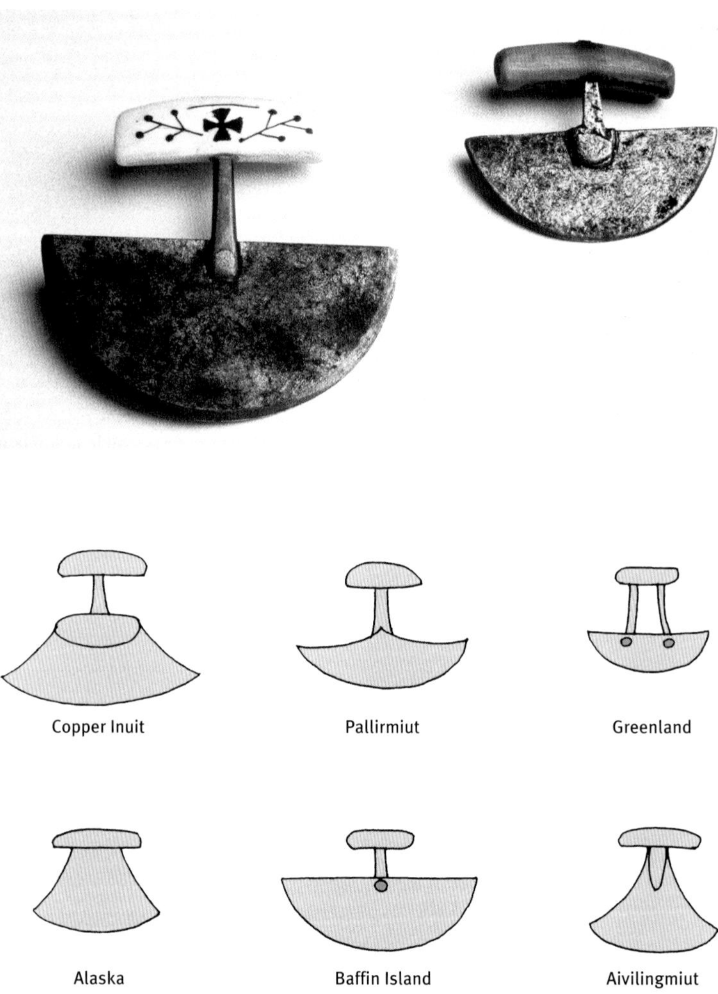

Figure 3.1
Ulu styles. Their shape tells where they come from. *Based on a drawing by Mrs. Rhoda Karetak, Arviat, NWT.*

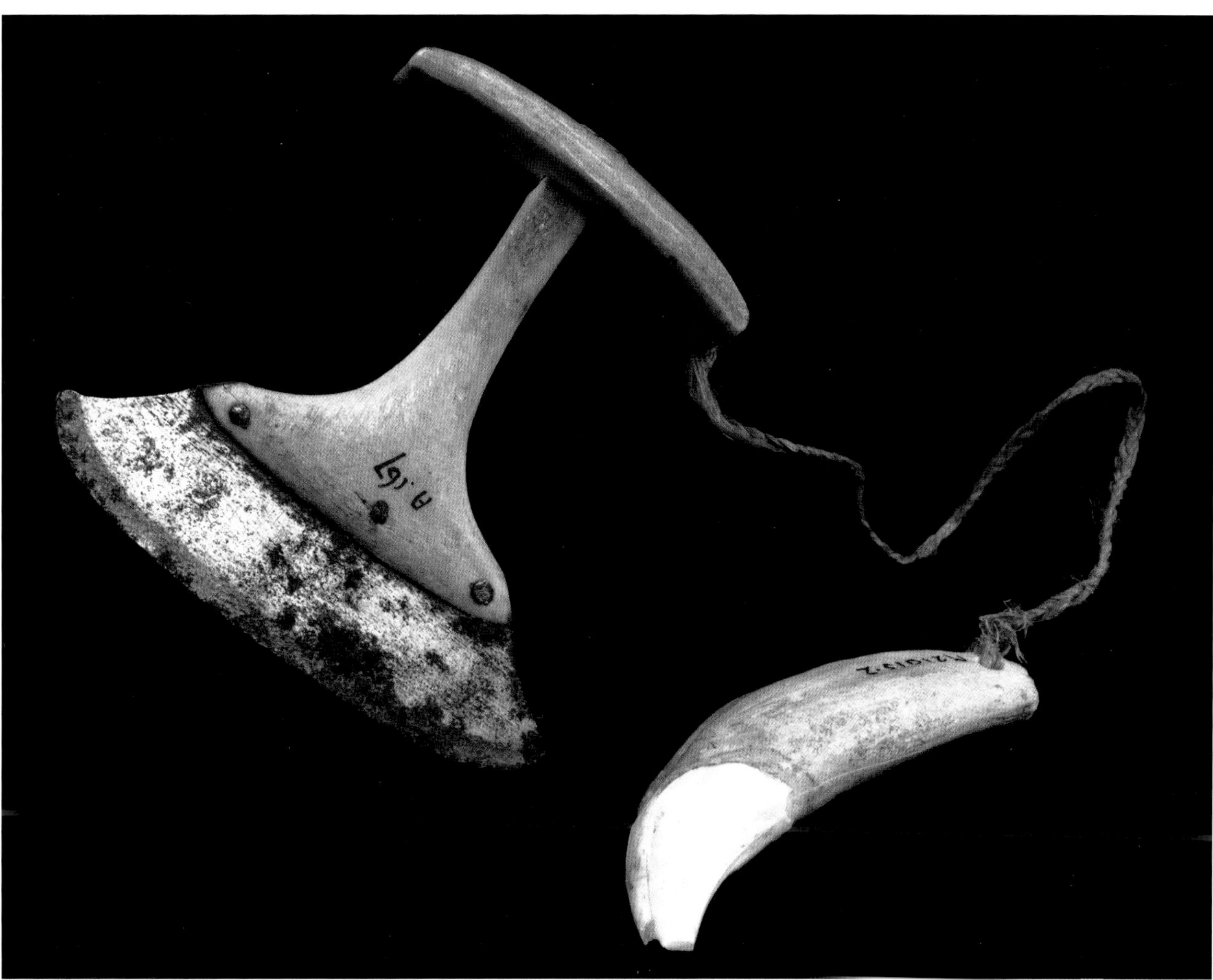

Ulu and blade sharpener of antler, metal, bear canine, and sinew, 8.5 cm, Copper Inuit, early twentieth century. Collected by the Arctic Institute of North America. The whetstone could be made of any close-grained stone. Molars of musk-ox or bear also served well, or a stick of copper mortised into bone or antler. By the early twentieth century, a fragment of a file or a rifle firing-pin were in common use (Jenness 1946, 83).

the skin or other object. The tang should be as thin as possible where it joins the blade so that there is no obstruction in cutting or scraping. The deep blade with adequate space between upper and lower edges protects the fingers and lasts longer since it wears away with use.

Men's and women's knives often had sharpeners attached to them by sinew: 'Some uluit are sharpened on one side of the cutting edge, some on both. An ulu honed on one side can be better controlled and is used for scraping. Such an ulu will not cut into the skin during the scraping and cleaning procedures. One sharpened on both sides can be razor-like and is best used to shave hair from or sever skins' (Jeela Alikatuktuk Moss-Davies, personal communication 1985).[5] It is possible that edge sharpening is not solely related to the function of the ulu. The Pallirmiut sharpened their blades on both sides, while the Aivilingmiut only on one side (Rhoda Karetak, personal communication, 1986). The man's knife, which he used to skin and butcher animals among many other tasks, had a lanceolate blade sharpened on both edges, although some Inuit groups, such as the Inuvialuit, sharpened knives only on one side (Stefansson 1914, 99). A short loop of seal skin was often added to the side of the handle so that the knife could be hung on the button of the coat or attached to a toggle on a bow case.

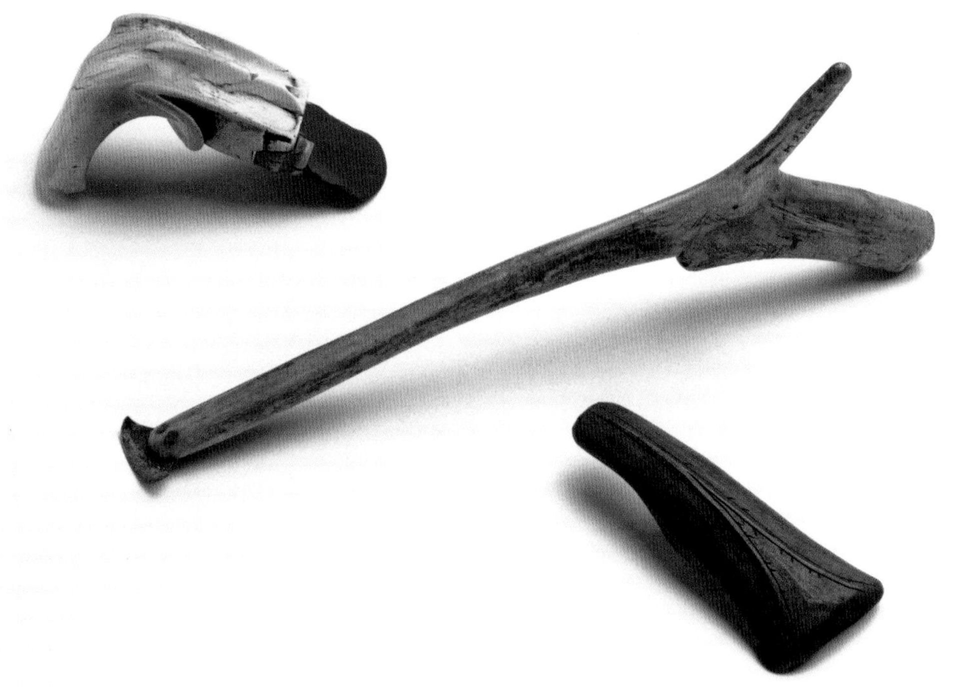

Ivory, slate, and iron skin scraper (top), 12.8 cm, Inuvialuit, late nineteenth century. Collected at Qikiqtaruk, Yukon, by Forbes D. Sutherland. Such scrapers were carved to fit the user's hand. Two indentations on top of the handle accepted the first two fingers. Grooves on the sides securely held the thumb and the third and fourth fingers around the scraper handle. The handle, whether of ivory or wood, was highly polished to make for comfort and a pleasing appearance. Antler, copper, and steel skin stretcher, softener (centre), 29 cm, Copper Inuit, early twentieth century. The Copper Inuit mounted a small curved-edged copper blade on a long handle made of antler for stretching and softening. Bone skin scraper (bottom), 11 cm, Inupiat, north Alaskan coast, late nineteenth century. Scrapers were made of stone, bone, antler, ivory, wood, or metal. Some scrapers had an even or only slightly curved edge.

Other Skin-Processing Tools

Scrapers, stretchers, and softeners have been used through the millennia to carry through the many steps needed to produce soft, long-lasting skins. These tools were used by Arctic peoples in conjunction with the ulu into the twentieth century, before being largely replaced by the ulu now used for most procedures. The forms of the instruments vary from era to era and from place to place, but their function and product are the same.

A blunt, scoop-shaped implement made from the shoulder blade of a caribou (or later of metal) removed flesh, fat, and oils from skins. A scraper made from bone or metal could stretch or soften skins. A sharper edge either dehaired the skin or removed a layer of it, according to the intended use of the finished product.

Skin-Processing Boards

Many kinds of flat surfaces, such as stone, whale bone, or wood, were used for the stages of skin preparation (Birket-Smith 1929, Part 1, 250; Boas [1888] 1964, 109; Myers 1980, 112; Pharand 1974, 21). In the past, when a woman had to carry her tools on frequent moves, the cutting and trimming board was only fifteen centimetres long and so fitted in the sewing pouch. A seamstress used to process skins sitting on her heels in front of the surface of stone or bone. Today she often uses a raised wooden board that slopes away from the body.

Needles and Awls

Arctic seamstresses eagerly adopted steel needles made available to them through trade and abandoned their fragile bone ones. To conserve the easily broken bone needles a seamstress employed an awl to start the hole for the stitch. An awl also made the large holes required in the seal skin that was to go on the drying frame or on skins for kayak covers.

Jenness reported that when he visited the Arctic in 1913-18, the Copper Inuit seemed to have no recollection of bone sewing

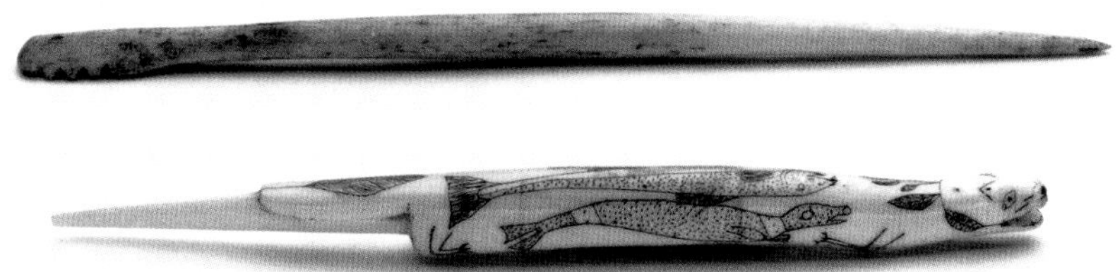

Bone awl (top), 14 cm, Copper Inuit, early twentieth century. Collected at Dolphin and Union Strait or Coronation Gulf, NWT, by J.J. O'Neill in 1914-16. Bone awl (bottom), 11.6 cm, Yup'ik, Southwest Alaska, early twentieth century. Awls were made of any strong material: the bones of seal, caribou, or bear, or the tusks of narwhal or walrus. If an awl was not handy, a pointed tool such as an arrowhead, a splinter of bone, or the corner of an ulu was used. The upper part of the awl was often decorated.

needles, and only remembered needles made from their native copper or iron ore (1946, 92). The copper needles, which were nearly square in cross-section, were disappearing from use due to the availability, through trade, of steel needles. Iron needles, hammered out in much the same way as the copper ones, were, at that time, still in common use. Today in the North, in addition to the round steel needle preferred for boot making, a three-sided metal needle – called a glover's needle – is in use. The edges make it easier to penetrate thick hides.

Needlecases

To store and protect her precious needles, the Inuit woman kept them in a container carved out of ivory or made from a hollowed bone. The needlecase, used from prehistoric time to the first part of the twentieth century, had two basic forms: a cylindrical and a rectangular. The shape, decoration, and tactile and visual qualities of needlecases attest to the skill and devotion of the men who carved them. The designs, usually incised with an engraving knife, reflect motifs used in the past from all over the Arctic.

The cylindrical needlecase had a wide distribution, from the Saami (the ancient and modern name for the peoples called Laplanders) across Siberia, and in Eurasia, North America, and Kalaallit Nunaat.[6] The most common type of needle storage using the tubular model was by means of a seal- or caribou-skin strap that passed through the length of the tube. The needles were stuck into the piece of hide, and the seamstress pulled it out of the tube to insert or withdraw her needles and in to prevent breakage or loss. The hide strip usually had a button or several attachments at both ends to pull it out or in, and to prevent it from coming out of the case. The simplest case came from the wing bone of a bird, sometimes the thigh bone of a swan. Such a small container was often carried by the hunter in his tool kit so that he could repair his boots or other clothing. Rectangular cases have been found along the west and east coasts of Hudson Bay, on Southampton Island, on Baffin Island, and in Labrador. The interior was hollow, and filled with moss. Sometimes a wooden or ivory stopper closed the case.

The Caribou Inuit, with the exception of one subgroup called the Qairnirmiut, appear not to have the needlecase in their material culture. Caribou Inuit women in Arviat, who belonged to the Pallirmiut subgroup, told me in 1986 that they had not heard of their people using needlecases. Instead, Caribou Inuit and some Nunavimiut kept their needles in tiny bags of caribou or seal skin, filled with moss and suspended from the neck.

Thimbles and Thimble Holders

The thimble is worn on the index finger and is used to push the needle from underneath the skin toward the user. It used to be made of a semi-circular piece of dehaired seal skin with a loop to encircle the digit. Another form was a cap of dehaired skin, preferably from the bearded seal or walrus, which covered the end of the finger. An open-ended kind of thimble was made of the small, circular toe bone of the caribou, of ivory, or of musk-ox horn (Mitchell and Van de Velde 1981). Metal thimbles with and without closed tips were greatly in demand from traders. Users first took the tip off metal thimbles themselves to make them open ended, but eventually this modification was done by traders themselves (Lydia T. Black, written communication 1990). If not available by trade, the European-style thimble became a model for ivory, horn, or bone ones.

A seamstress kept her open-ended thimbles safe by slipping them over a guard or holder attached to the needlecase or work bag. The simplest holder was made from a bird's leg bone. A common form was shaped like a bird with wings outstretched. A hole at the centre held a sinew or thong that attached the guard to the needlecase. Another kind of thimble guard is referred to by anthropologists as anchor shaped.[7] The centre or sides of such thimble holders feature posts or flukes over which open-ended thimbles were slipped and held secure. These guards were made of a single piece of ivory – an ingenious piece of carving.

One ethnologist has traced the distribution of the anchor-shaped holder (Birket-Smith 1929, Part 2, 282). He encountered it among the North Kalaallit and among the Iglulingmiut at Mittimatalik. Among the Copper Inuit this type of holder was used in the Thule period only (McGhee 1972, 104).

Another kind of holder, conventionally described as hook shaped, is found in Alaska and Kalaallit Nunaat, although the word 'hook' gives a poor idea of the style and execution of some of these holders. It is possible that Alaskan hook-shaped thimble holders had a double or triple function; they could function as belt hooks or fasten the entire needlecase to a woman's inner belt (Turcy 1986, 94-6).

Boot-sole Creasers

The boot-sole creaser, carved out of bone or ivory or fashioned from metal, was a slim, flat, blunt-edged instrument to pleat and smooth the gathers at the toe and heel of the sole when it was sewed to the boot upper. It was found only in certain areas, such as Kalaallit Nunaat, Labrador, Qurluqtuuq, and Alaska. The seamstress in other areas used her thumb to pleat the sole. Copper Inuit would often use the thumbnail, and gave it 'the magnificent name, *kamitik-sharарluk,* "my shoe-making tool"' (Jenness 1946, 95).

Marrow Extractors

Women possessed special instruments to extract marrow. Marrow of caribou bones was a dietary prize, and a man would please his wife or girlfriend by bringing her a gift of many marrow bones. The extractor was a narrow, spatulate instrument less sturdy than the creaser, sometimes found attached to the needlecase. It seems to be absent in many cultures of the eastern Arctic, with the exception of Kalaallit Nunaat. Among the Netsiliingmiut the extractors were widened at the top, flattened oval in cross-section, and had a suspension hole at the butt end (Taylor 1974a, 155).

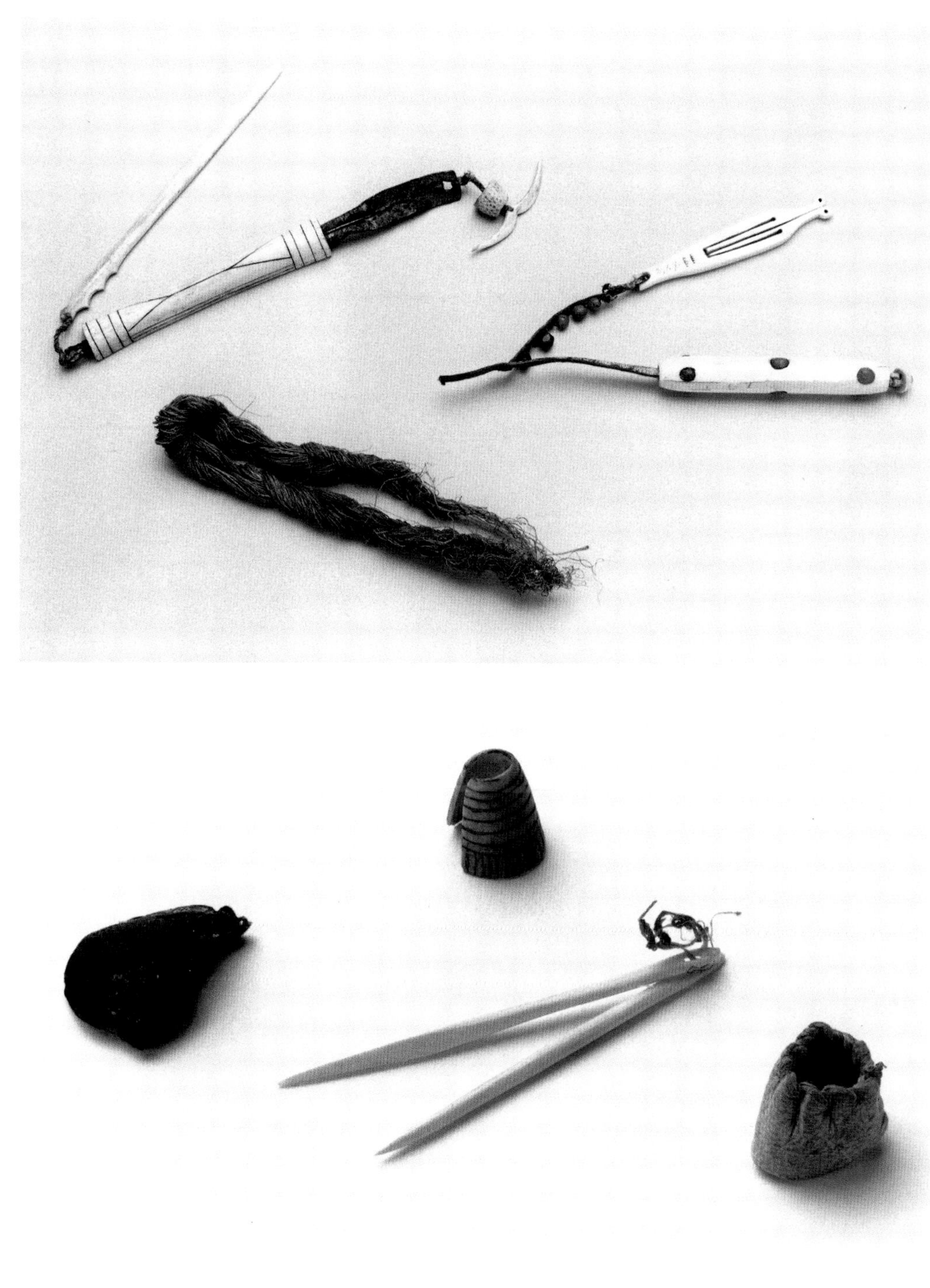

Above (Clockwise from top) Bone, caribou-skin, sinew, metal needlecase with marrow spatula, thimble, thimble holder, and needle, 13 cm, Copper Inuit, early twentieth century. Collected by J.J. O'Neill at Dolphin and Union Strait or Coronation Gulf, NWT. The marrow spatula could also function as a boot-creaser. The thimble is open-ended, the thimble holder is wing-shaped, and the needle held on a strap inside the case is four-sided. Ivory, hide, bead needlecase and thimble guard, 12.2 cm, Inuvialuit, mid-nineteenth century. Collected at Anderson River, NWT, by Roderick R. MacFarlane. Sinew, Inupiat, twentieth century. Collected at Barrow, Alaska, by John A. Grose. Sinew is loosely braided to keep it in order in the sewing bag.

Below Bone thimble (top), 2 cm, Copper Inuit, early twentieth century. Collected at Dolphin and Union Strait or Coronation Gulf, NWT, by J.J. O'Neill. Sealskin thimbles (left and right), 1.6 cm, 2.2 cm, Caribou Inuit, Igluligaarjuk, NWT, late nineteenth century. The Qairnirmiut, a branch of the Caribou Inuit, had a caribou-skin thimble for use when they were in the interior, and one of bearded sealskin when they were at the coast. Among some groups, this practice was in keeping with the custom that products of sea and land should not be mixed. Ivory needles, 7 cm, 7.5 cm, Nunavimiut, ca. 1900. Collected in the Ungava Peninsula, Nunavik, by Hugh Peck.

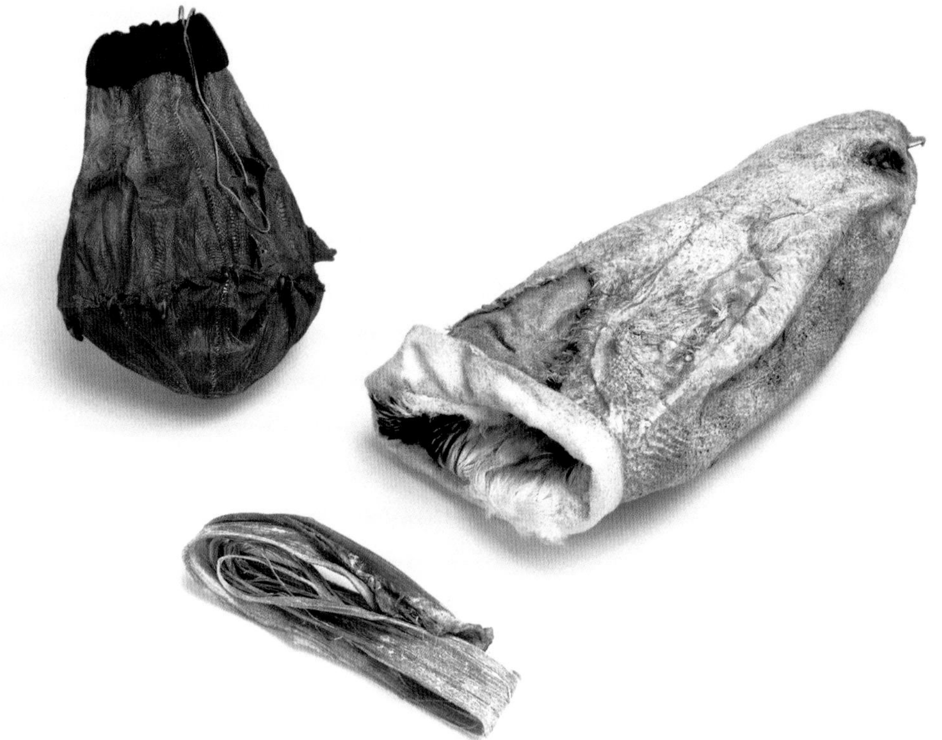

Sewing bag (left) of loons' feet, seal, cotton, sewn with sinew, 22.5 cm, Nunavimiut, Ungava Peninsula, Nunavik, late nineteenth century. The amount of work and the intricate sewing needed to form pouches of the skin of birds' feet make these bags rare objects. Sewing bag and tendon (right and bottom), loonskin, cotton, sewn with sinew, 42 cm, 73 cm, Nunavimiut, ca. 1979. Fish and bird skins are removed whole, and the fin or wing holes closed with stitches of sinew or thread. The feathers are turned to the inside or outside according to the wishes of the maker.

Some extractors had notches carved in the handle or were incised with motifs similar to or the same as those on needlecases. The significance of the number of notches and variation of their placement on these and other tools has not, to my knowledge, been studied.

Scissors

After contact with Europeans, the Inuit made scissors carved out of bone or antler. The cutting edges were sometimes made from thin strips of tin or sheet iron fastened to bone blades with copper rivets. Scissors are now used to cut fabric and small pieces of skin for trim or fringe and to clip fur to a desired length or depth for trim. They are not used to cut skins, since they would cut the fur at the skin's edges. The uneven lengths of fur would make every seam visible with a ragged appearance, whereas the seamstress chooses which seams to make invisible and which to emphasize by other means.

Containers

A woman's sewing bag or pouch held not only her tools but also sinew and tendon, patches of skin for repairs, and sometimes a comb, charms, and beads. A man's sewing items – a needle and needlecase, patches, and sinew – would be carried in his tool kit. When the Inuit were a nomadic people the pouch had to be accessible on the trail so that clothing and especially boots could be kept in good condition. The sewing pouch was made out of skins of fish, seal, caribou, or waterfowl such as loon and eider duck. Containers were also made from the skins of the split feet of swan or goose, or the flipper of the bearded seal. In some places women kept, and still keep, their sewing equipment in grass or wood baskets. In Canada, grasses are available in Labrador and around the shores of Hudson Bay and Ungava Bay.

Large bags, some one metre long, were used to store and transport clothing. Made of the skin of caribou or seal, the bag would be fitted with a carrying thong of hide or plaited sinew. In summer these sacks would be placed on high rocks so that animals such as dogs or foxes could not eat them. In winter they went into the cupboard-hole inside the iglu or in the outside storage place attached to the iglu.

CLOTHING PRODUCTION

Qalli Keatainak of Kangiqsujuaq sheds some light on the skill required for clothing production: 'When I was a child, all the clothing I wore was made of skins ... I was just beginning to sew clothing. I once started to cut patterns to make a pair of trimmed pants out of a caribou hide blanket. I was having so much trouble, I cried. I tried to learn the skills of my mother to make everything' (Nungak 1983, 121-2). Although the main processes for clothing production are based on precepts held in common all over the Arctic, schedules and procedures vary. Therefore only a general outline can be given for these extremely complex systems. Their exposition here has necessarily been simplified and steps omitted, most of which are described in great detail in the literature.[8]

Harvesting of Skins

Caribou

As Jeela Alikatuktuk Moss-Davies (personal communication 1984) remarks, 'The skins of caribou gathered in early September are preferred for clothing used in not too cold weather. The caribou fur obtained in late fall gets thick and makes good mid-winter clothes for hunters.' There are significant variations in hair length, density, colour, and skin thickness of caribou pelage, according to the animal's age, sex, health, size, diet, migratory routes, and the climate endured.[9] The fine, silky skin of the fetus or of the newborn calf taken in early spring at the calving grounds is used for infants' clothing. This skin is thin and soft, although not durable. For a few weeks in the summer the hair of the calf is short and glossy. Along the spine it becomes almost black, while on the belly very white. Some groups, such as the Copper Inuit, prefer this skin because of its fine, lustrous texture and because it is also suitable for special items of wear and for decorative purposes. Nuligak (1971, 120) tells of a June hunting trip in the Mackenzie Delta during which he and his four companions shot five caribou, including a calf whose fur was smooth and shiny. The men decided to hold a race for the prized calf skin. Nuligak won and was able to keep the skin for himself. The skins of adult caribou in spring and early summer are not suitable for clothing because botfly larvae have left perforations (Kelsall 1968, 269-74). The main hunt for caribou takes place in late summer and in the autumn when the animal still has fur that adheres to its skin and does not shed as much as winter fur. By this time the holes left by the botfly larvae have healed and the hair becomes long and thick, making it suitable for winter dress.

The sex of the caribou also has a bearing on the quality of the pelage and how it is used. The female experiences the summer

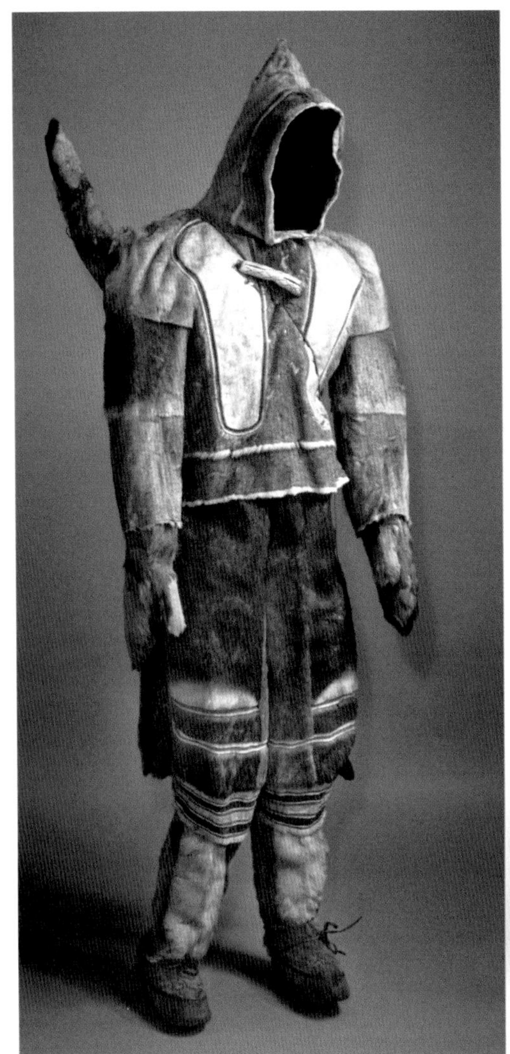

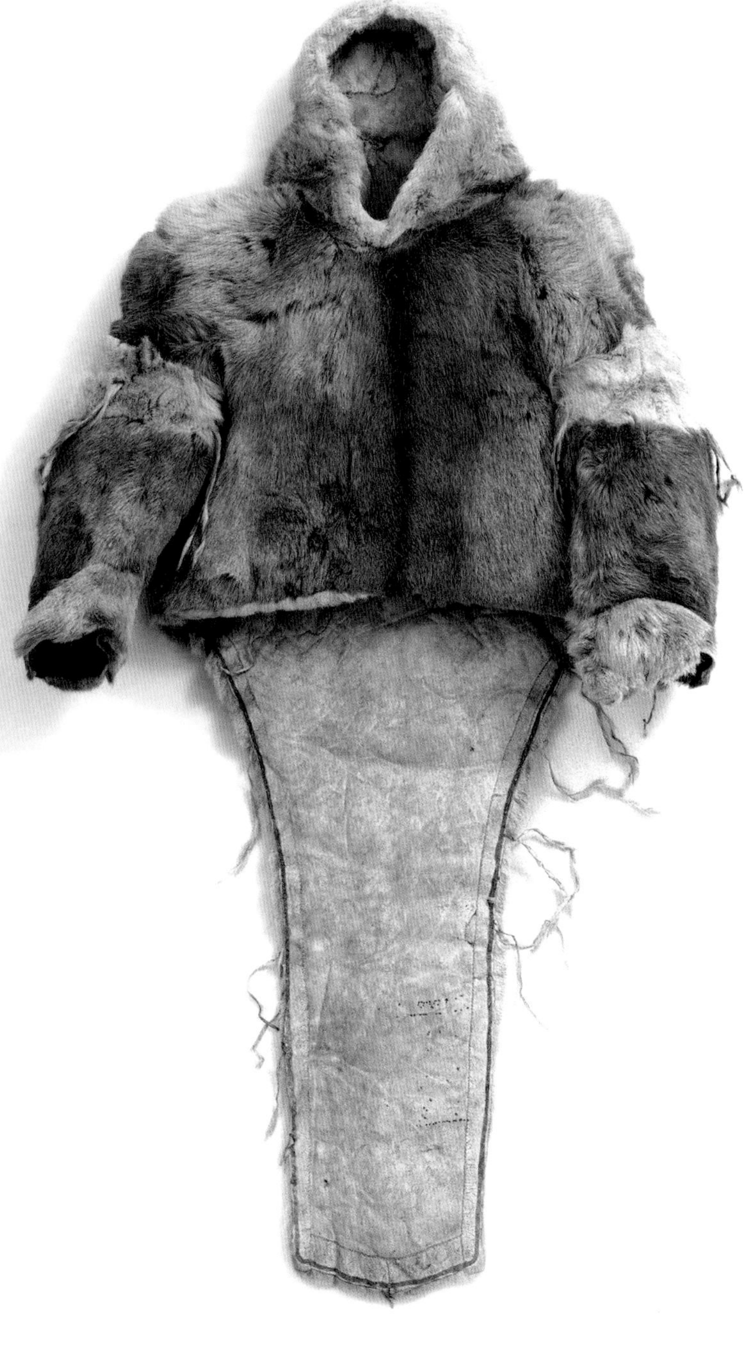

Opposite left Parka, 154 cm, trousers, 84 cm, mitts, boots, tool kit, snow goggles, of caribou skin, bone, sewn with sinew, Copper Inuit, 1850s. The costume, made of the fine, dark summer-gathered skins of caribou, was collected during one of the searches for Franklin.

Opposite right Man's caribou-skin parka, sewn with sinew, 152 cm, Copper Inuit, early twentieth century. Winter clothing, such as this parka, was made from the thick fur of caribou hunted in the autumn. Later, closer to winter, the caribou pelage becomes extremely heavy. The hair is brittle, sheds easily, and is suitable only for bedding and tents.

moult later than the male. The coat is lighter weight and tends to be kept for women's and children's clothing, while the male's is used for men's apparel (Vézinet 1980, 51). Stocking boots for a woman, for example, are made from the skin of a female caribou.[10]

The hunter removes the skin from the caribou by slitting the underbody from the tail to the throat, around the cheeks, eyes, and horns, and from the hock of each leg up to the belly incision. He then carefully separates the skin from the body in one piece, and lays it fur side down on the ground. If the horns are still in velvet, the hunter does not cut at the root of the horns, but pulls the skin over the horns so that the velvet remains on the head skin. An experienced hunter takes about one hour to skin and cut up an adult caribou. Blood stains are removed by rubbing the skin in snow. If the caribou has been taken in the water, the moisture is removed from the skin by blotting it in hard snow. A squeezing knife further presses as much water as possible out of the fur. These procedures lighten the load and shorten the drying time.

Before the Contemporary era most Inuit dressed in skins all year, and many caribou skins were needed to clothe an average family of five. The hunter had to take at least thirty caribou each year to meet minimum requirements (Vézinet 1980, 52).[11] Mitts and the many kinds of boots needed a minimum of the leg skins of fifteen caribou, without accounting for spares. These figures did not include the caribou that must be procured to provide bedding, tents, and food for the family and their dogs. More skins were required for extras, for clothing for festivities, or to help out the less fortunate ones in the community. Groups such as the Nunamiut of Nunavik's interior wore caribou clothing all year round and therefore needed an estimated fifty to sixty skins, including two and a half skins per person for bedding.[12]

Seal

Ringed seal are hunted for most of the year. After sewing caribou skins in late autumn and early winter, the Inuit move to the coastal areas to hunt seals at breathing holes in the new ice, at the floe edge, or in open water. The winter hunt at breathing holes requires a large number of hunters and their dogs: 'This aggregation [is] needed because of certain biogeographic characteristics of the seal. This air-breathing mammal keeps open any number of breathing holes through the thick ice and may use any one of them. Thus the larger the number of hunters attending each particular breathing hole in a restricted area, the better the chances for a speedy catch' (Balikci 1984, 418).

Sometimes a hunter waits all night for a seal to resurface to breathe. This method requires the finest insulation against the cold, especially on and under the feet. Lone hunters also stalk seals sunning themselves on the spring ice, by crawling slowly while imitating the seals' sounds and movements, aided by various implements and using fur accessories to slide more easily or wearing a white parka that acts as camouflage as well.

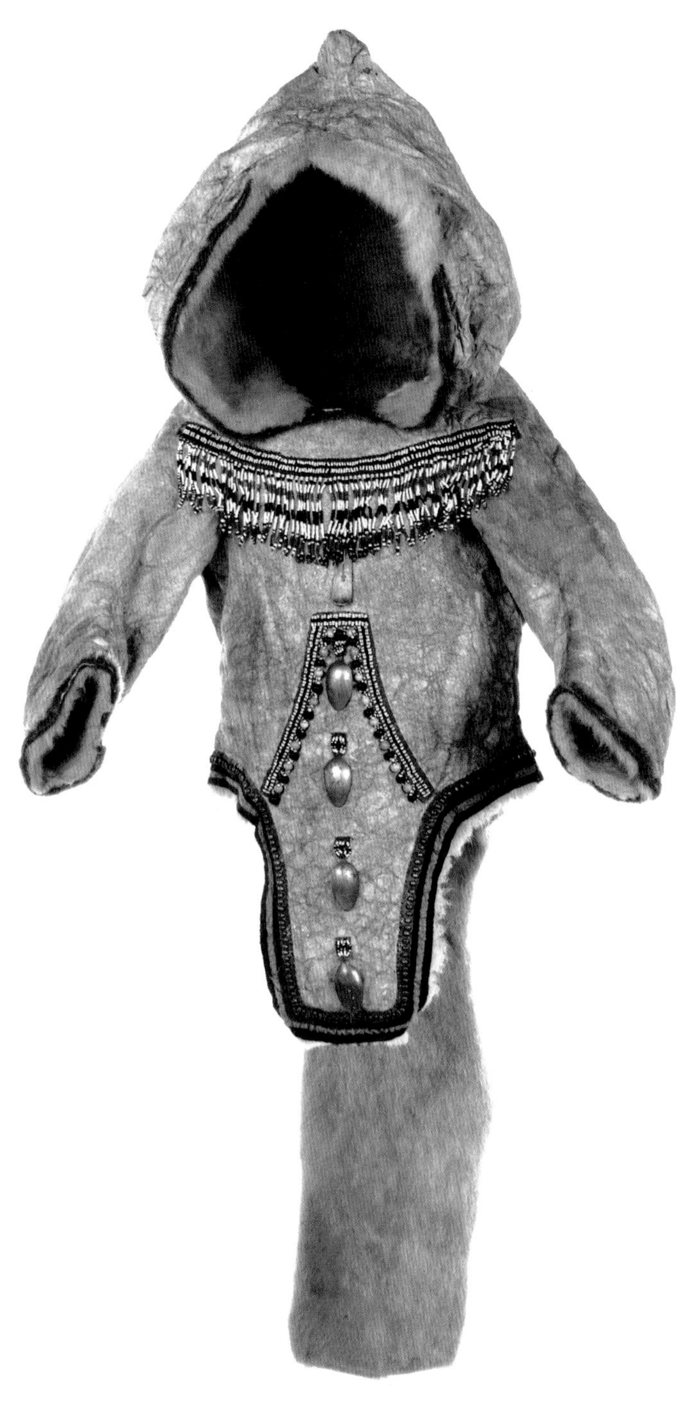

In Iglulik men skin and cut up the seal, although in other communities women perform this task. To skin the seal a cut is made along the mid-belly from chin to anus. Under the skin lies a thick layer of blubber, which in winter accounts for 40 per cent of the ringed seal's body weight. The man's knife or the woman's ulu separates the skin with the blubber from the flesh,[13] or alternatively leaves the blubber on the body, removing only the skin. Once the skin is removed, the body is cut up for food: 'The skins of young seals three to four months old, gathered from June to August, don't shed as much as those of old seals. They are easier to work to soften them. They are of a better quality too. Older seals have scars from a sea pest that penetrates the skin and makes a hole' (Jeela Alikatuktuk Moss-Davies, personal communication 1985).

Birthing of the ringed seal takes place in a cave under the ice, where the pups remain about two and a half months. The skins of the pups make fine stockings and inner slippers, especially for children, but are too fragile for boots. Ringed seals three to six months old have thick, soft, bushy, silver-tipped hair. The skins of these seals are used for garments on which the fur faces inward. Seals one year and older have strong skins: the fur becomes stiffer, silvery on the belly, and brown to black on the back, showing irregular whitish rings with a dark centre. The fur of young and adult seals is made into apparel with the fur facing outward, and into the uppers of boots.

The bearded seal is hunted for food and for its extremely thick and tough skin. The

Opposite Widow's amauti, of seal, beads, spoons, coins, lead, brass, and braid, sewn with sinew, 156 cm, Nunatsiarmiut, late nineteenth century. Collected on Baffin Island, NWT, by William Wakeham in 1897. The amauti is made of the skin of young ringed seal, fur to the inside. The type of beadwork fringe that decorates the chest from shoulder to shoulder is seen on amautiit in Baffinland and Nunavik (See page 148 for back view.)

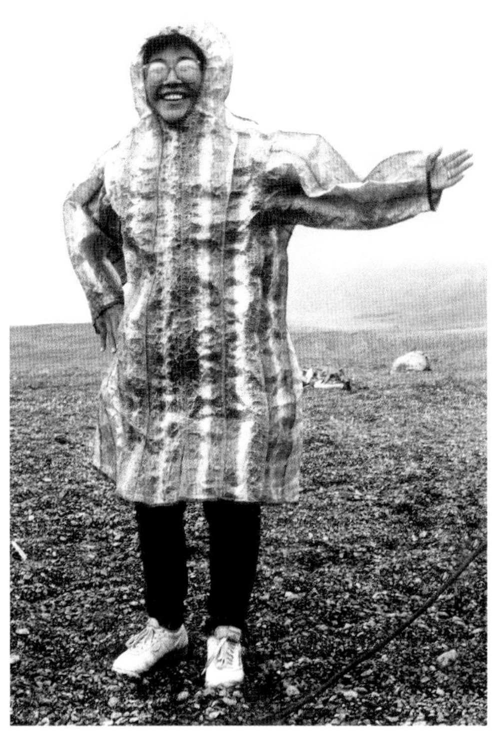

Right Rosemarie Kuptana wears a waterproof jacket of whale intestine made by Siberian Yup'ik, Sighinek, Chukotka, CIS, 1988. A freeze-dry method of treating intestine, called winter or cold tanning, produces an opaque, satiny, white quality. East Kalaallit also knew how to freeze-dry intestines to make them opaque. Today a few Yup'ik elders make and wear gut coats, but it appears that such coats are no longer made in Canada or Kalaallit Nunaat.

skin of the back is ideal for making boot soles. Bearded seal skin is also used to make laces, thongs, belts, harpoon lines, dog traces, and sled lashings.

Because it has been many years since whole families wore sealskin garments for part of the year, accurate figures about the total numbers of seal skins needed to clothe a family of five are not available. It is known that a hunter needed eight skins for his spring and summer parka and trousers. A family of five required the skins of six adult seals for warm-weather waterproof boots and mitts, which allowed for one extra pair each (Pharand 1974, 19).

Sea Mammal Intestines

'I know about the intestine strips to keep water off while riding a *qajaq* [kayak]. I remember my grandfather Naujaapik's *akuilitaq*.[14] I used to sit in front of him in his *qajaq*. My grandmother used to prepare a bearded seal rectal canal which she used as thread to sew *akuilitaq* with,' said Annie Aupaluk of Akulivik (Nungak 1983, 120). A hooded pullover parka made of sea mammal intestines was worn by men and women over their other clothes for protection against sea-spray or sleet, and for ceremonial purposes.[15] The gutskin parka formed part of the Inuit clothing complex in the four countries of the circumpolar Arctic and is still made on occasion in Siberia and Alaska.

On Sun'aq, Alaska, kamleikas came from the esophagus and intestines of whales, seals, sea lions, and bears. The tongue and liver membranes of the whale were also used. The skin of one whale's tongue produced eight kamleikas, but it was heavy and tore easily. Whale gut dyed black and trimmed with red was used by whalers on Sun'aq (Lydia Black, personal communication 1990). For Canadian groups from the Mackenzie Delta to the west coast of Hudson Bay, its recorded existence is rare.[16]

The material is resilient and tough, as we know from the way it functions inside the body with constant contraction and expansion under pressure. The orientation of the gut in the finished piece of clothing corresponded to the function *in vivo:* the exterior surface was used for the outside of the waterproof parka; the adjacent or inner surface went to the inside. Inside the animal body, the lumen or cavity of the intestine transports salt, water, and dissolved nutrients across the gut wall. This transport is primarily unidirectional, from the lumen side to the gut exterior (John McElhone, personal communication 1984). When the animal is living, capillaries pierce the gut wall but with death they close, making the intestine waterproof and resistant to decay (Morrison 1986, 17). Thus gutskin clothing allows humidity to escape from the inside and is waterproof from the outside.

The small intestine of a bearded seal can measure some twenty-two metres and of a walrus forty and a half metres. The width of sea mammal intestine, once split, varies according to the animal and its size, between seven and a half centimetres and fifteen centimetres. The upper section of a bearded seal intestine is sufficient to make one gutskin parka.

Polar Bear

The Polar Inuhuit of Kalaallit Nunaat use polar bear for clothing, especially for trousers, but examples of bearskin clothing are rare in Canada, partly because of the abundance of caribou and seal and partly because polar bear fur is bulky and wiry. In winter the polar bear's new coat is white, turning in spring and summer to a golden yellow. The various Arctic communities hunt the bear most often from winter to spring (Manning and Manning 1944, 159). The number of hunters needed to hunt one bear means that the pelt has to be shared among many, and often each hunter can obtain only a pair of mittens from the skin. One skin can provide three pairs of trousers. The Inuhuit hunter measures his length from knee to hip bone and a piece of skin is cut accordingly. If more than three hunters are present, a piece of skin to make half a pair for each man will be proposed but the fourth and subsequent hunters usually do not lower themselves to accept, and generously tell the men ahead of them to take enough for a whole set. The first man to reach the bear claims the 'mane,' the long hair on the back of the front legs, which is greatly treasured to trim women's boots (Freuchen and Salomonsen 1958, 396). Young bear is preferred, since the skin of older bear is stiff and uncomfortable.

Birds

From prehistoric times to the Historic era, Inuit in several parts of the Arctic relied on bird skins for their clothing. Today, birds are hunted mainly for food, and birdskin outfits are rarely made. However, when skins are 1equired,the harvesting methods are much the same as in earlier years.

For birdskin clothing, the Inuit have always preferred the skins of diving birds – eider duck, murre, cormorant, loon – since they are tougher than the skins of non-diving fowl. Traditionally, the Inuit hunted birds using a bow and a blunt-tipped arrow, a bolas, a net, a snare made of sinew or baleen, and a spear thrown from a board (Boas [1888] 1964, 103-5). Today, except for the bow and arrow, such weapons are still employed. The rifle is also used, but is not favoured because of the noisy disruption to the bird colonies (the Inuit protect the habitat and nests) and because the shots penetrate the skins. Eider duck can easily be captured when in the moult, for they rest flightless on the ground. However, wildlife management programs of organizations such as Makivik Corporation and the Canadian Wildlife Service control bird

Above A Yup'ik woman processes intestines at Sivuqaq, Alaska. Nunavimiut preferred the intestines of animals killed in October, when they had less fat and required less work to clean. Gutskin is exceedingly light: a parka weighs 170 to 200 grams. A gutskin coat can also act as a float in the water.

Below Amauti of eider-duck skin (male), skins of seal and dog, sewn with sinew, 84 cm, Nunavimiut, Sanikiluaq, NWT, 1972. Artisans: Maina Imiqqutailaq and Miaji Qassik.

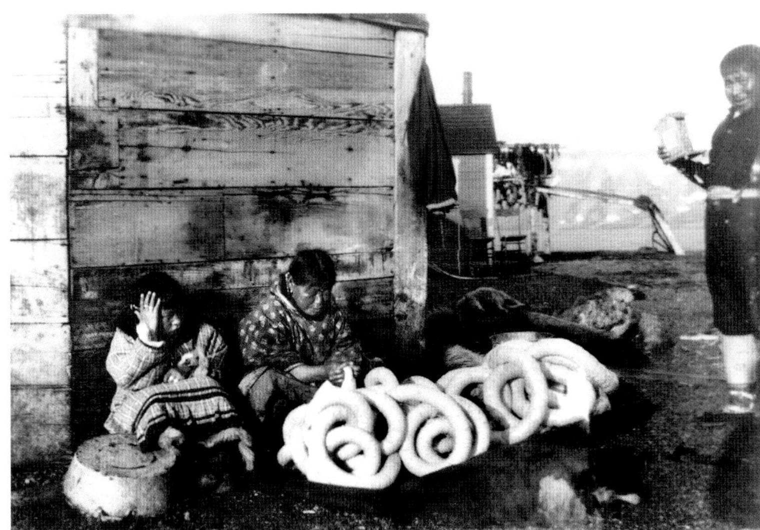

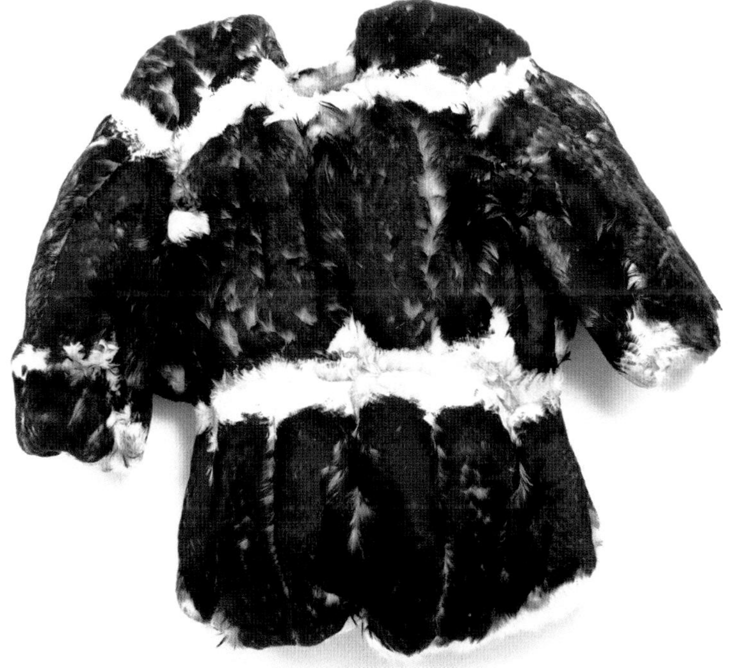

harvesting. Bird hunters are taught not to hunt in the spring, when the flocks are composed almost entirely of breeding pairs. The loss of breeding wildfowl can result in serious depopulation.

Skins of waterfowl come in many hues. The eider has five to eight centimetres of thick, downy plumage, the male being snowy white above and velvety black below, the female a rich brown with bars and blackish mottling that gives protective coloration. Female eider skins are more supple and lightweight than drake skins. The number of skins required varies with the size of the species and the kind of clothing sewn. A man's parka needs twenty to twenty-five skins; a woman's eider-duck amauti requires at least twenty-nine skins. Sometimes the long outer feathers are plucked, leaving skins with only the soft down remaining (Rosing 1986, 57; Pharand 1971b).

An inner parka found on one of the Qilakitsoq mummies is composed of the skins of five kinds of waterfowl. Skins with short, dense plumage are used at spots where warmth is most important, and more open-feathered skins are placed by the wrist and neck openings to let heat out (Moller 1989, 32).

Skin Preparation

In a 1987 interview for the Inuit History Project of Avataq Cultural Institute, Lucy Meeko of Kuujjuaraapik described skin preparation: 'There was a skin used by women to cut their patterns on and it was called *asimauttaq*. There is a board which is used to scrape sealskins on and it's called *sakivivvik.* A sharp utensil used by women to scrape fat off sealskins is called *sakuuguik* ... We used to sharpen ulus either with a knife or another ulu, today we use a sharpening flint.'

Before skins can be made into clothing they must be treated to become workable, soft, and long lasting. Untreated or incompletely processed skins will stiffen, rot, or split with use. Different stages of skin preparation involve treatment of the hair and of the various layers of skin: the epidermis, dermis or corium, and the subcutaneous tissue. Intensive 'elbow grease' is needed to scrape, rub, wring, stamp, and chew the skin to render it ready for clothing production. The order of procedures differs with each type of skin and the end use – whether for winter or summer wear, wet or dry conditions, workaday or festive garb. For the five-member family, when each member needed two sets of furs, the task of skin preparation needed some 300 hours of arduous work performed within a limited number of days (Pharand 1974, 10).

Caribou Skin

'I've dried caribou hides ... A hide that is going to dry on the ground had to be smoothly placed ... When it had become wet [from the rain], it needed frequent kneading, and scraping it again was the only way to make it soft. After scraping, it was then ready to cut into patterns,' explains Siasi Annanack of Kangiqsualujjuaq (Nungak 1983, 118). Caribou skins, once harvested, are set to dry as soon as possible. The leg skins can be left on or cut off to dry separately. The skins are spread, preferably outside, raised from the ground to allow air circulation (Nungak 1983, 118):

When caribou hides are brought we inspect them while they're damp ... Once they were dry, they were softened by using them as blankets. You had to be careful not to place them where it was too warm. The part of the skin that hair is stuck on is called sirliq [fascia or grain side]. When it was dry, it was scraped with a sharp scraper so that it was soft enough to be somewhat elastic ... It had to be kneaded and then with a sharp scraper it was scraped until it was nice and smooth.
Sarah Baron of Kangiqsualujjuaq

The lengthy process of scraping, wetting, and rescraping is repeated until the skins meet the desired quality. The women, sometimes aided by the men, first employ a blunt-edged scraper to remove the meat and fat particles on the connective tissues of the fascia (inner side), and start the skin on the way to pliability. Thus the skin does not shrink, crack, or stiffen. This very hard work may take three hours, and women who are over five months pregnant are exempted.[17] Once the tissues are removed, the skin is moistened, left for a day or so, scraped in the length and breadth, gently stretched, then rescraped with a sharp scraper or ulu.

'After the skin has been softened in this way, the woman then scrapes it again in all directions with a sharpened scraper *(sakuuti)*. This removes a thin layer of skin giving the surface a soft, fine texture. It is now ready for sewing' (Pharand 1974, 8). Sometimes the skin is depilated to make

Above **Leah Okatsiak of Arviat, NWT, 1993, scrapes a caribou skin with her ulu, demonstrating the hand and ulu position.**

Below **Leah Okatsiak chews a piece of caribou skin to complete the softening process.**

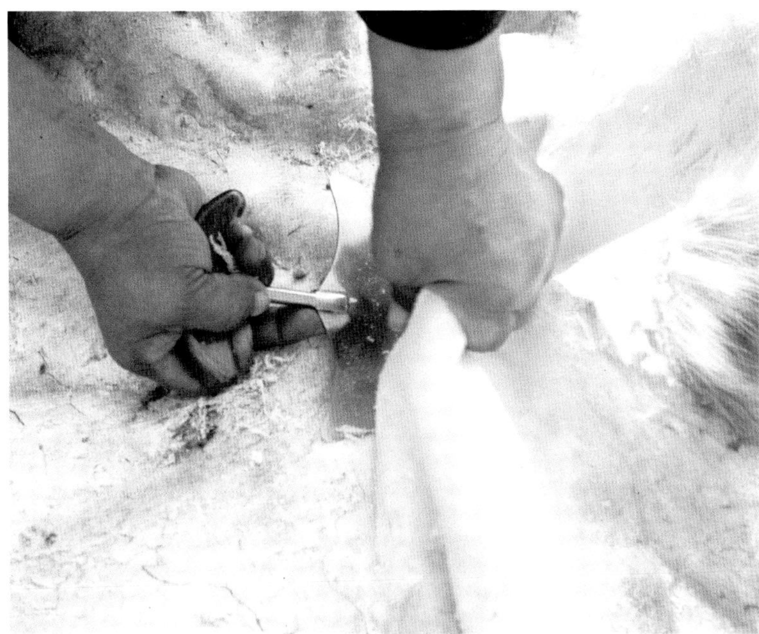

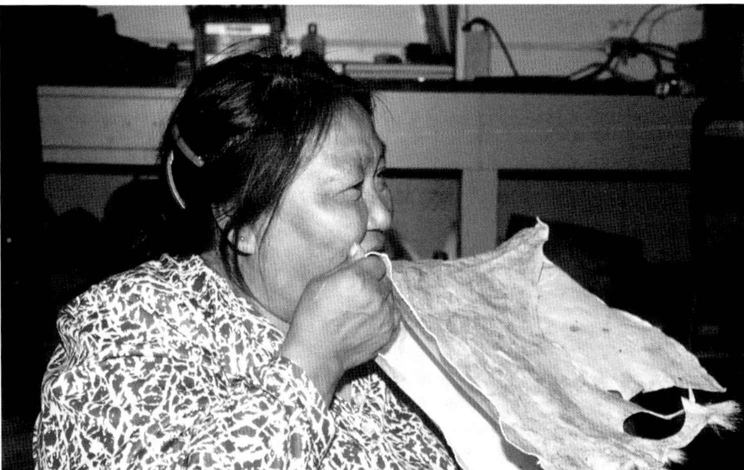

fringes or thongs. A rotting process, initiated by leaving the skin damp, dissolves the organic material between the epidermis and dermis. The timing has to be just right so as not to damage the corium, and then the hair is easily scraped or plucked off. The many steps involved in preparing caribou skins can take ten hours per hide. Nothing is left to chance in order to have soft, pliable, warm, and long-lasting skins.

If the leg skins have been put aside until ready for processing – skins are always stored in a cool place – they will be stiff and dry.[18] They are sprinkled with water, chewed, or kneaded vigorously, and scraped in the breadth with a blunt scraper. More than fifty hours of the seamstress's time is spent on preparing caribou leg skins to clothe feet and hands (Pharand 1974, 12).

The very fine fetal skin gathered in June and used for infants' clothes can also be put aside until ready for sewing. The seamstress will knead it so that it becomes soft and workable. One skin will clothe an infant, and the preparation takes about one hour.

The skins for the clothing of whaling crews in some parts of Alaska were not scraped or softened (Turcy 1986, 80-1). The subcutaneous tissues and fat were left on the hides to make them more waterproof. After the whaling season, the apparel was scraped clean, and then made pliable.

Seal Skin

Ungalaaq (1985, 8, 9) and Innuksuk and Cowan (1976, 89) contain testimony about the length of time it takes to treat seal skins and the complexity of the process:

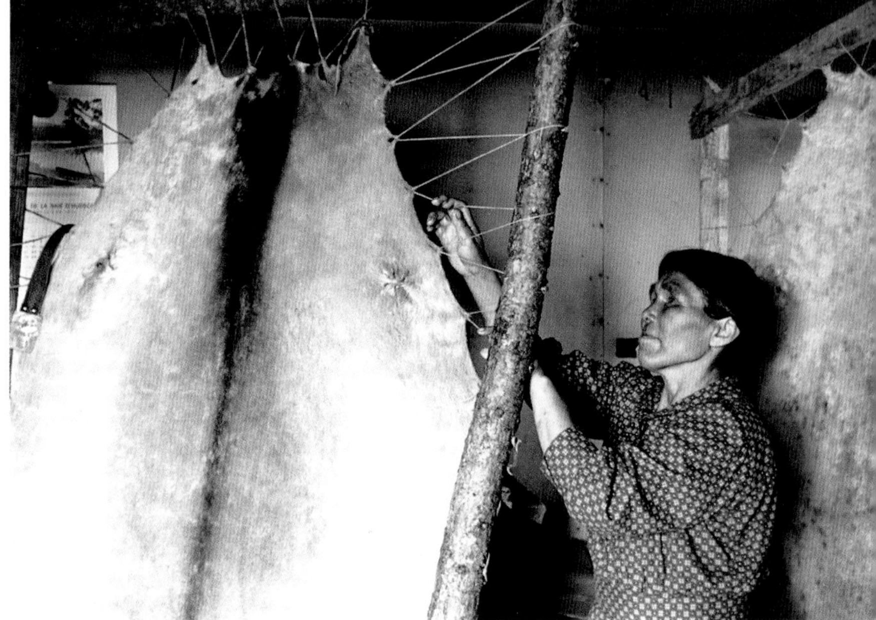

Young sealskins used to be cleaned, having every trace of grease removed. As soon as the membrane was removed, it was rinsed and then, after the water had dripped from the fur, it was dragged back and forth across some gravel or a smooth bed of rock ... Even at those times when they didn't have soap, they'd remove the grease very well. In the wintertime when sealskins were worked on, grease would be removed by rubbing the skin in the snow and beating it.
Martha Ungalaaq of Iglulik

I did nothing for four months ... except scrape sealskins. I scraped three hundred skins during all that time ... I was ill from scraping sealskins.
Oorebecca Issuqanqituq of Ikpiarjuk

Seal skin is treated in a similar manner to caribou, but the steps occur in a different order. Dead seals must not be left exposed to the sun even for half an hour prior to being skinned, for the hair will loosen and the skin burn. The skin must be washed in fresh water as soon as possible to clean away blood, salt, and fat to prevent the fur from yellowing. Once it is washed the skin sometimes is spread fur side down on a board that slopes away from the worker's body. The woman, or occasionally the man, scrapes away the fat and blubber, washes and rescrapes the skin, and then places it in an airy place to dry – over a line, on a frame, or staked to the ground. To string a skin to a frame or peg it to the ground appears to be a simple operation but is actually a complex piece of engineering whereby different amounts of tension, regulated by the length of the strings or by the

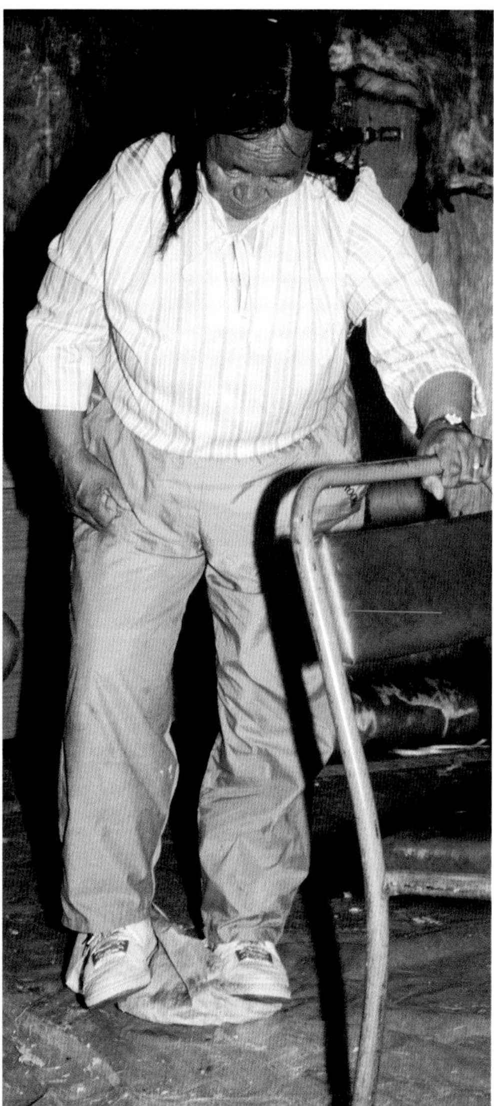

Above Jeannie Snowball (b. 1906) of Kuujjuaq, Nunavik, 1964, has attached seal hides to frames for drying. Depending on the season, drying can take anywhere from half an hour to a week. Testing for tension and dryness is carried out frequently. Mrs. Snowball is the renowned artisan, inventor of Ookpik, the snowy owl. The skins in this picture went toward the manufacture of Ookpiks, the little creature that became known internationally as a symbol of the Arctic.

Below Elizabeth Nibgoarsi of Arviat, NWT, 1993, stamps on a seal skin formed into a ball to soften it.

pegs, produce an evenly dried skin that has preserved its elasticity without distortions.

After drying, a skin must undergo further softening by folding it with the fur inside and chewing along the fold, stamping on it with the feet, and crumpling it until it has lost its stiffness. (If the stamping is done in a group everyone joins in with great merriment and song.) The skin begins to look whitish and is ready to be scraped again with a blunt scraper to stretch it gently. After that, it is ready to be cut. Seepola Nowdluk of Iqaluit explains the chewing process: 'The leg pieces have to be chewed to soften the skin. Chewing is an important part of kamik-making. As much as two days may be needed to chew all the pieces before they are sewn together. Without chewing, the skin would not be flexible enough to wear, and a sewing needle would not be able to penetrate' (Hadlereena, Hadlari, and Jensen 1986, 60).

If the hair is to be removed for waterproof footwear and mitts, the skin is plunged briefly into boiling water and the hair scraped away.[19] Another way to dehair skin is to fold it, hair to the inside, and place it in the sun for two weeks until decomposition sets in (Alariaq 1975, 1):

After the skin has been removed from the meat, slice off the blubber. Scrape on the skin (with a board under the skin). Then dip it in hot water, but do not let it stand long [so] as not to scald it. In doing that the fur is loosened and comes off when scraped again. Slice off the thin layer beneath the blubber that's on the skin with an ulu ... After it's dry, soften it by folding and stepping on it and when it becomes soft enough for chewing to soften. Do that and get it soft enough to cut. Then stretch it well with a tasiuktirut (that's an implement used for stretching the skin evenly).
Elizabeth Alariaq of Iglulik

A third method to produce waterproof uppers for sealskin boots is to shave the hair very carefully with a razor-sharp ulu, leaving the epidermis intact. After a day of drying, the skin turns black. When removed from the drying frame it is scraped, stretched, and softened.

A similar procedure produced 'waterskin,' which was used to make a waterproof combination suit found in North Alaska, Labrador, and Kalaallit Nunaat.[20] Waterskin is dehaired seal skin with the epidermis retained to prevent moisture penetration. This kind of skin preparation results in the dark colour seen in waterproof boots. The waterskin was sometimes impregnated with oil to improve its function.

The soft, paper-white, non-waterproof dehaired seal skin, *nalluaq,* used for the instep and decoration on boots and for trim on amautiit, is made by a freeze-drying method (Alariaq 1975, 2):

Scrape off the oily parts, soak it in hot water, slice off the thin layer on the skin and make holes along the edge. Cut out from the upper flipper out to the edge sideways from the flipper. Let out to dry on the ground with sticks passed through the holes where it will freeze. Put snow on top of the skin then scrape it off. When it's frozen take it off [the sticks].
Elizabeth Alariaq of Iglulik

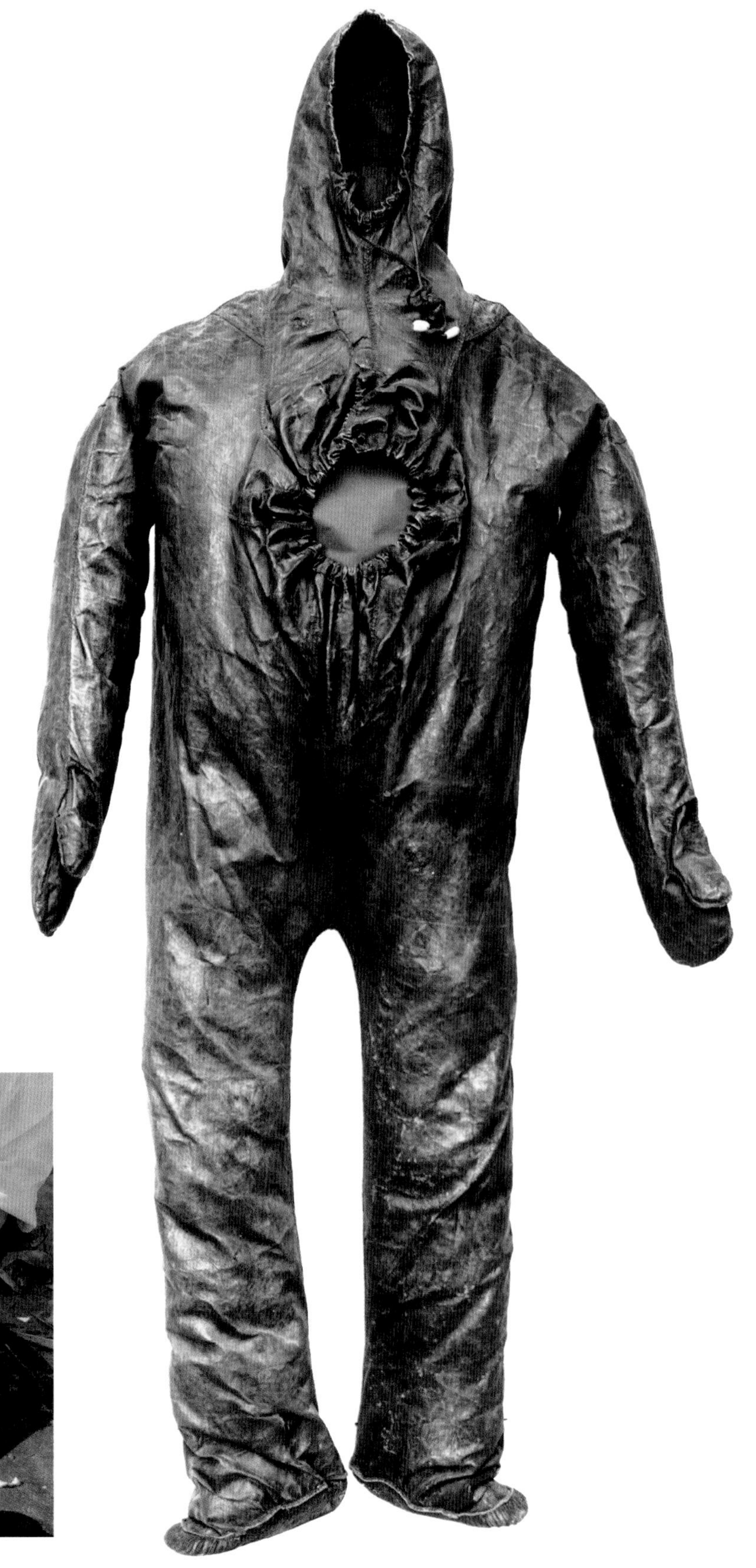

Right Sealskin, ivory, combination suit, 155 cm, sewn with sinew, West Kalaallit, early nineteenth century. Collected at Paamiut by J.P. Engholm. The 'waterskin' was a one-piece garment that combined hooded jacket, trousers, boots, and mitts. The Inupiaq suit from North Alaska had a face aperture wide enough for entry. The Kalaallit model had a round opening in the chest that allowed the wearer to ease himself inside, after which it was tightly closed by a drawstring. The suit could function as a life-preserver in case of an accident in the water.

Below Elizabeth Nibgoarsi shaves hair from the skin of ringed seal to make waterproof boots, 1993.

Man's sealskin boots, sewn with sinew, 52.5 cm, Kalaallit, ca. 1903. Cold tanning of seal skin results in a white, soft hide used for the instep and upper of some boots, and for decoration.

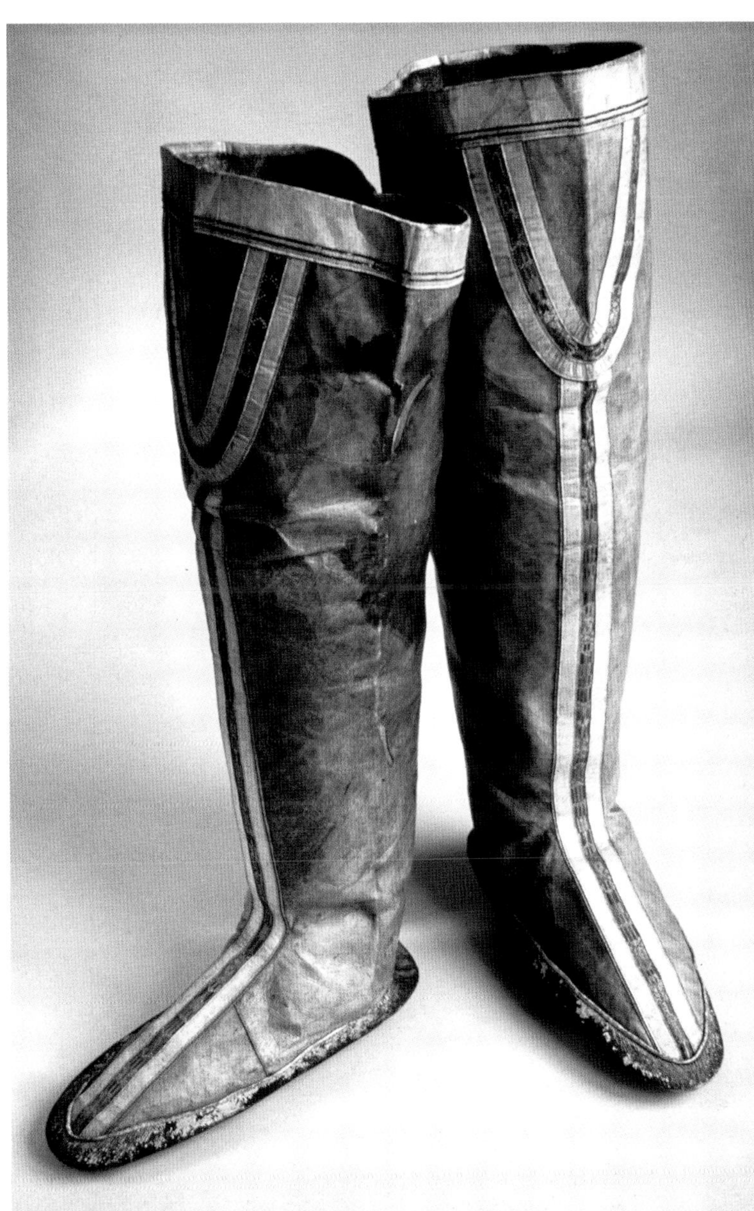

Nalluaq is hung outdoors to bleach in the sun and blowing snow. It must be kept frozen, and after complete drying it is ready to be cut to make boots or other items.

The skin of bearded seal, used mainly for soles, is treated as is ringed seal – cleaned, defatted, dried, scraped, and shaved. Since the skin is thick, drying takes a week. Once it is perfectly dry, the woman cuts out two large oval-shaped pieces approximately the same size as the soles she wishes to make. She then begins to chew and bite the two pieces of skin and bend them back and forth in all directions.

Many Inuit women still prefer to chew skins. Saliva has emulsifiers that facilitate the mixture of fat from the sea mammal skin with the water in the mouth. This emulsion can more easily penetrate the skin than water or fat alone, and deposits fat from the fascia into the dermis, thus softening the skin as it is chewed (John McElhone, written communication 1984). The process of chewing skins can wear down and blacken some women's teeth, as seen in old photographs. Discoloration of the teeth is caused by sand, often of quartz, picked up by the bearded seal in its interior and exterior as it browses on the sea floor for food using its flippers and thick, stiff whiskers to dig through mud and silt (Alan Cooke, written communication 1984).

Sea Mammal Intestines

Susie Kauki of Kangirsuk, Nunavik, discusses the traditional use of seal intestines: 'This *apuilitaq* (a strip of seal intestine) was a part of menswear ... Bearded seal intestine

Gutskin jacket of sea mammal intestines, hide, fur; thread; wool (?), sewn with sinew, 112 cm, Inupiat, early twentieth century. Collected at Cape Prince of Wales, Alaska, by R.G. Oliver in 1919. After processing, the upper gut of sea mammals becomes translucent. The lower intestine, the colon, becomes puckered and opaque when dry and is considered by some to be inferior (Wilder 1976, 16).

was scraped on the exterior and interior first. I soaked this one in semi-fermented oil. Once it was completed, the edges were trimmed with a strip of old waterproof hairless black sealskin boots. Its use became a thing of the past along with the *qajak*' (Nungak 1983, 120). Rita Pitka Blumenstein of Tununak, Alaska, conjures a picture of the much larger whale intestines: 'Imagine the intestine of a big mammal like the beluga! ... It's not transparent; it's white like cloth. They use it mostly for trimming like the tops of mukluks. They also use it for fringes, which symbolize the future generations' (Hickman 1987, 27).

Sea mammal intestines and other membranes such as those coating esophagus, rectal canal, or whale tongue skin undergo complex processing, including several washings, peeling inside and out, and scraping with a blunt scraper (Hickman 1987; Wilder 1976). More washing and rinsing take place until the water is clear. Then, with intestines, one end is tied, the tube inflated, the other end tied, and the sausage-like coils hung to dry. When completely dry, after about two days, the intestines are split longitudinally and rolled into tight bundles until they are used to produce a waterproof parka or other items, such as sinew. The material relaxes if dipped in water (Turner [1894] 1979, 58).

A freeze-drying method called winter or cold tanning gave an opaque satiny white quality to the intestines. The Siberian Yupiit of Sivuqaq preferred coats to be made of winter tanned gut because to them it was more aesthetic (Hickman 1987, 8). East Kalaallit also knew how to freeze intestines to make them opaque (Holm 1888, 61). The split, processed intestines must be well oiled and rolled up to prevent loss of pliability.

Gutskin is exceedingly light – a coat can weigh twenty-one to twenty-four grams. It was also used to make bags or windowpanes. When it was time to move on, the gutskin windowpane was easily rolled up, to be used in the next iglu. Inhabitants of the Colville River Delta area obtained windows made of bearded seal or walrus intestines by trading with Barrow Inupiat (Stefansson 1914, 85).

Polar Bear Skin

The fat is scraped off a polar bear skin with an ulu, but if much grease remains the skin must be washed before drying. To dry the skin, thongs are threaded through its edges to hold it to a frame where the air can circulate. Once the skin is dried it is cut out before being worked, for ease in handling. It is softened by wringing, squeezing, and chewing. The skin is then moistened with water on the flesh side, folded over with flesh sides together, and rolled up and tied for a day or two. Before it is again dry it is rescraped. The softest and whitest skins are obtained by freeze-drying, the skins preferably being left out all winter. Young bear is preferred, since the skin of older animals is stiff and uncomfortable.

Bird Skin

'Young loons when they are long and skinny make a good fit for slippers. When the skin is still wet, you pull out the long feathers. Then what is left are the short

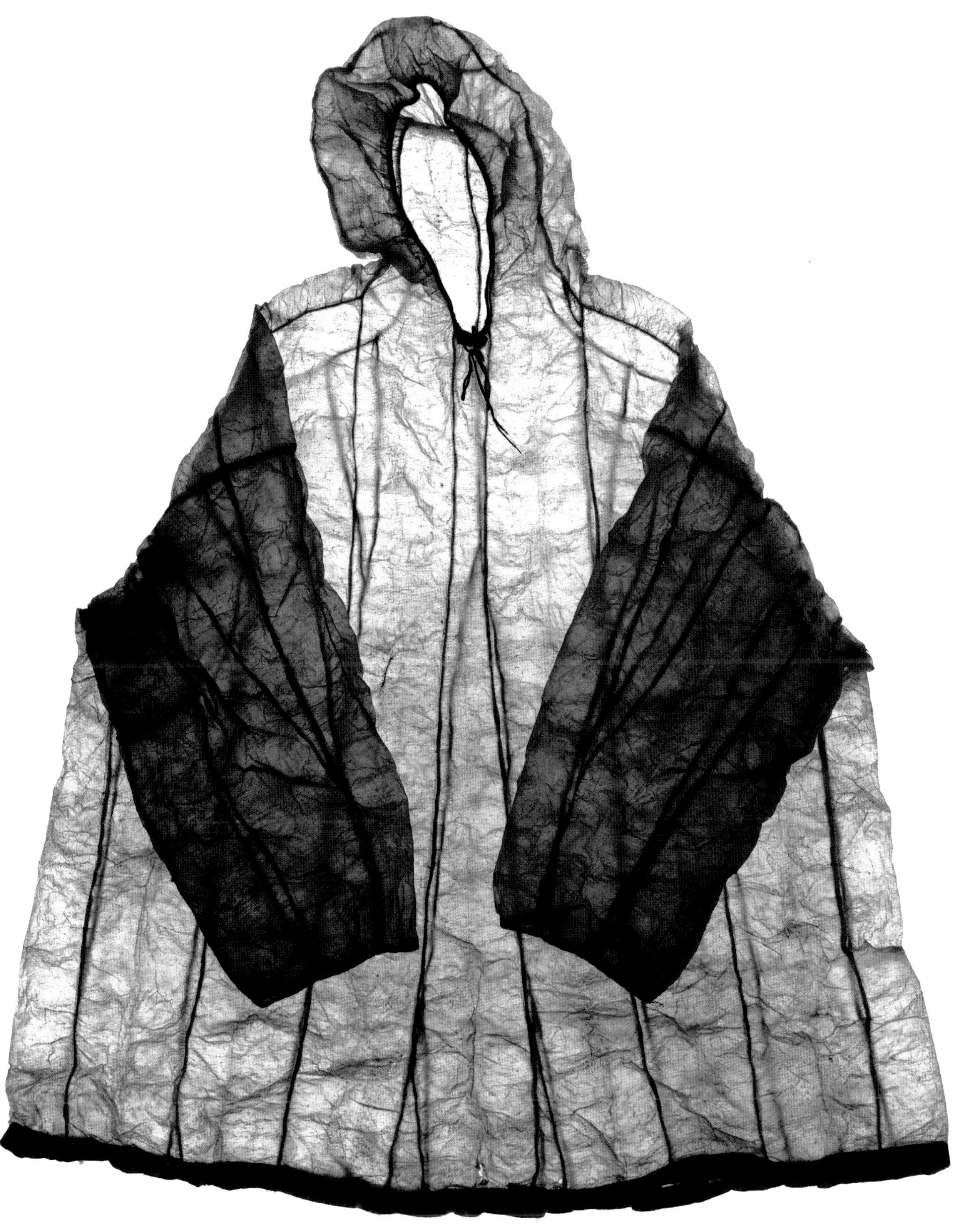

soft feathers and down' (Rhoda Karetak, personal communication 1986). Birdskin preparation follows in general the methods used for animals.[21] Women take charge of the procedures for skin removal and dressing. After scraping and drying, the skin becomes somewhat stiff. A method called 'gumming,' consisting of many small bites but not chewing, removes the fat, resulting in a soft skin. More fat removal takes place before the skin undergoes a cold tanning or freeze-drying process, during which it becomes creamy white. Then it is subjected to more drying and softening.

Ivalu

Lucy Meeko of Kuujjuaraapik discussed the use of sinew in her interview for the Inuit History Project of the Avataq Cultural Institute: 'Fibrous nerves were prepared to be used for thread ... A single tail of a seal contained enough fibrous nerves to be braided into a long line of thread. The best kind of thread that could be found were the fibrous nerves of a bearded seal ... They [the strands] looked so pretty if a black thread was braided along with them.'

Inuit thread comes from sinew that is made from animal tendons and from membranes of sea mammals and waterfowl. In the caribou, a bundle of dorsal tendons, *uliut,* lies immediately under the skin on either side of the vertebrae and attached to the tenderloins. Tendons are also found along the muscles of the back legs, but they are coarser than the dorsal ones and are used as lashings and lines in hunting and fishing gear. Fifteen dorsal bundles are needed for caribou clothing for a five-member family. The rest of the bundles acquired are used to sew sealskin clothing, tents, bedding, and kayaks.

In some places, sinew from the back of the narwhal *(Monodon monoceros)* or beluga whale *(Delphinapterus leucas)* is preferred. Narwhal sinews are about one metre long. Whale sinew is stronger than that of caribou but harder to split into fine strands (Brower 1899, 597; Jenness 1946, 86-7; Pharand 1974, 15; Wilder 1976, 18-19).

When caribou tenderloins are brought back to camp, the seamstress carefully separates the tendon bundles with her ulu. They resemble wide ribbons. She scrapes the tendons clean of flesh and fat, washes them, and sets them out to dry for a day. They are then put in her sewing bag or in a bag in the refrigerator, for they must be kept cool and not dry out completely. From the ribbon-like tendons come the strands of sinew. Caribou sinew can be split into four even finer filaments, called fibrons (Ailsa Shimotakahara, personal communication 1980). During sewing the fibres of the bundle are separated as required using the teeth or a thumbnail. Sometimes the seamstress separates the strands ahead of time and makes up braided bunches two and a half centimetres thick so that she can keep them untangled and proceed more quickly.

The separated fibres are sometimes run through the teeth and tested with the tongue to find weak or broken parts.[22] The sinew can be greased, twisted, or rolled on the cheek or thigh to make it even and smooth. Learning to twist sinew is difficult,

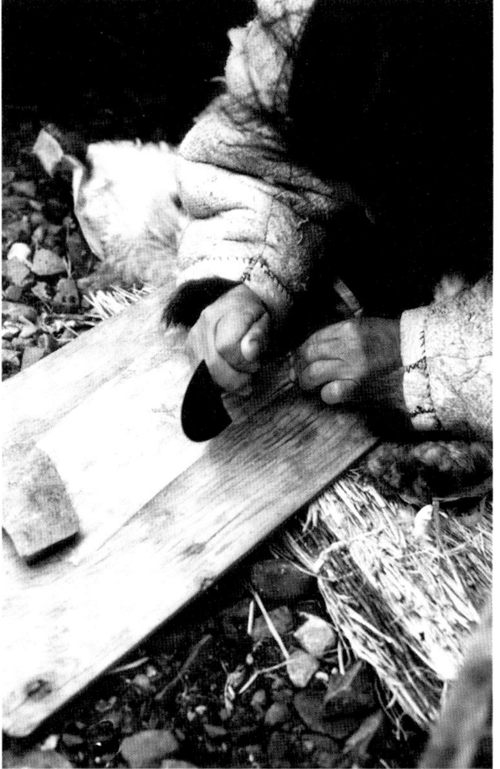

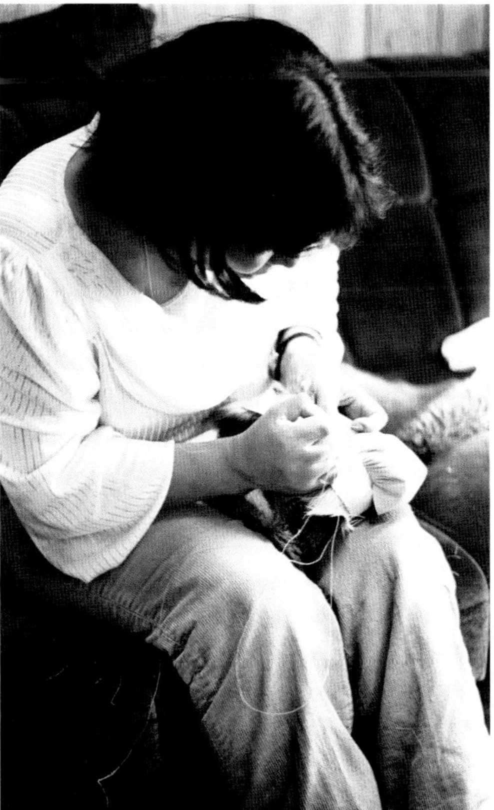

Above Maina Iqaluk of Purvirnituq, Nunavik, 1971, has prepared the membrane of waterfowl esophagus and cuts it with her ulu in thin strips to use as thread. She wears a birdskin amauti, feathers to the inside, and ringed sealskin trousers. Mrs. Iquluk is seated on a mat of grasses, and uses a cutting board.

Below In preparation for an exhibition at the Museum of Mankind, British Museum, 1986, Leonnie Qrunnut of Iglulik, NWT, sews part of a costume with sinew.

but once the skill is acquired it goes smoothly. It means getting the feel of the sinew, its thickness and size of twist. Inuit women twist sinew almost as southerners knit or crochet (Wilder 1976, 19).[23] The sinew has a grain, and the seamstress knows that snags form if it is drawn through the skins against the grain. The 'front' end is moistened with the mouth and tapered to go through the fine eye of the needle. The 'back' end is knotted when sewing, or traditionally, spliced to attach the old to the new.

Three-ply braided sinew, singait, makes fishing lines and drawstrings for boots. Four-ply cords are used for ice-hole fishing and for the stretching cords on drums. Harpoon lines have from four to eight strands braided together.

Although more and more women today use synthetic fibre, there is no completely suitable substitute for sinew. Linen, cotton, or synthetic thread can cut skins, as can dental floss. Being of even thickness, these threads cannot be tapered to fill the fine hole of the needle. The Inuit needle makes a smaller hole than the diameter of the sinew, so that the sinew completely fills the hole. Its superlative characteristic is that when damp, it swells and thus improves the waterproof quality of the seams.

MEASURING, MARKING, CUTTING, AND SEWING

Caribou skins are ready for sewing about a week after the last caribou has been brought in. In a good season, there are enough skins to choose from for the various needs of the

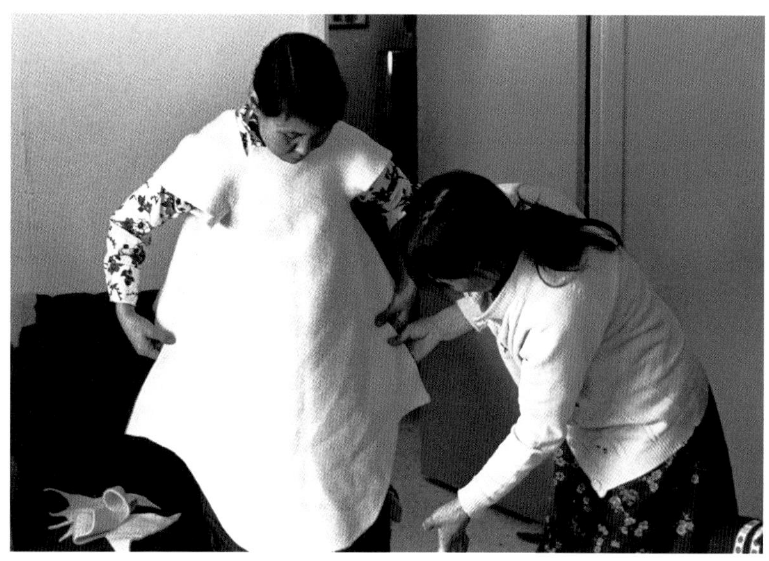

family. Sealskin clothing production takes place in the spring, usually toward the end of April when the sun is no longer low. Birdskin clothing manufacture begins after the fall harvest of waterfowl in September.

Measuring

Traditionally the Inuit seamstress does not use a standardized pattern to make an outline on the skin. Each piece of clothing is made to fit one particular individual, and an old garment can serve as a model for a new one. The oldest method of developing a pattern, still used, is by measuring with hand and eye. The apparently quick and simple hand and eye measurement is deceptive. An extremely complex system of pattern development that takes many years to master is at work. The procedures necessary to develop each part of each piece of each pattern differ from group to group and among individuals. The seamstress looks carefully at the prospective wearer, up and down, front and back. Then she measures with her hand. The most noticeable hand measurement is the hand spread between the tip of the thumb and of the middle finger but there are many other spans, and for smaller items such as boots some measurements are made using the space between, for instance, the finger or thumb joints (Oakes 1988; 1991, 118-21).[24]

Some seamstresses use a strip of skin, a length of knotted sinew, or a piece of string and put it against the wearer and then on the fur to be cut. Some now make their own paper or cardboard patterns after using the hand and eye method. The paper patterns

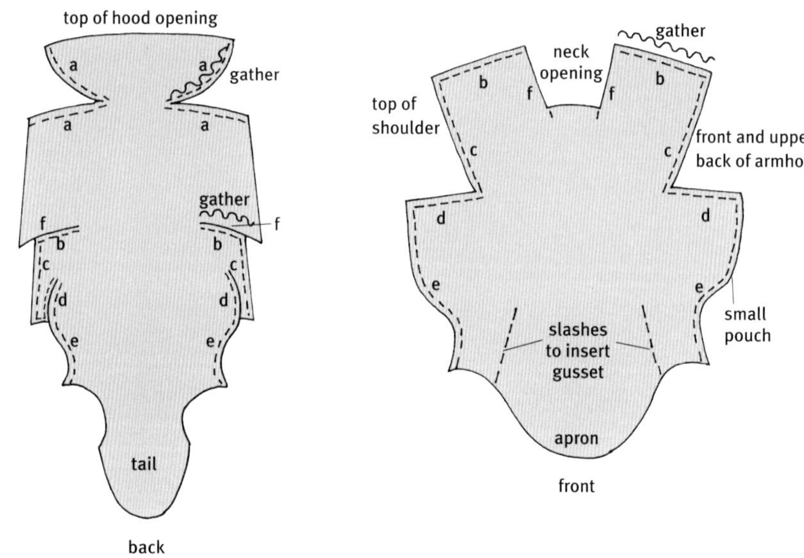

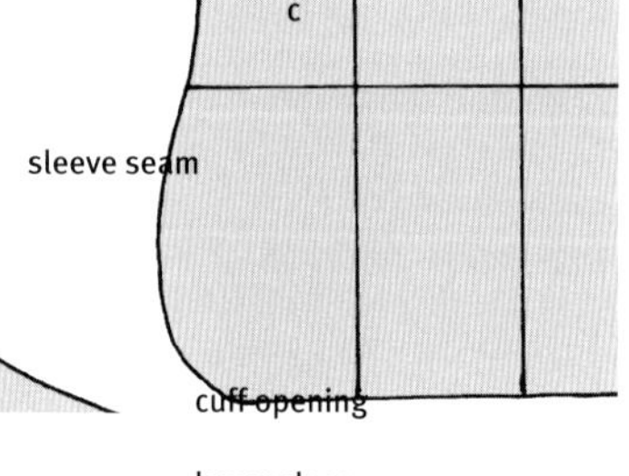

Figure 3.2
Pattern for a girl's amauti designed by Lucy Meeko of Kuujjuaraapik, Nunavik, in 1988. The style is that of the Nunavimiut. It has a large, wide hood, rounded side bulges for the amaut, a long back flap, and a shorter flap at the front shaped like an inverted bell. *Based on a drawing by Donna Kern.*

Elisapee Kiliutak of Kangiqsuk, Nunavik, 1979, fits an amauti for a friend. She cuts one half of the garment and then uses the cut part, folded over, to make the other side. All leftover skin is saved for piecing, inserts, trim, and repairs.

help in the instruction of young people, particularly since daughters now seldom learn sewing skills in very early childhood.

Lucy Meeko, an elder from Kuujjuaraapik, when demonstrating skin sewing, decided to make a small girl's amauti out of caribou skins provided.[25] She first marked and cut a pattern freehand out of brown paper folded down the middle. As she went along she adjusted the proportions and curves according to her inner vision. The evolution of this configuration can only be described as a dynamic gestalt.

Marking

The skins are first marked down the middle by biting or pinching. In the old days the outline of the garment could be made by an edged ivory tool and today sometimes with a ballpoint pen. The clothing is symmetrical, and corresponding parts match just as on the animal. The middle of the skin on the animal is the middle of the front or back of the garment.

Before the seamstress cuts the pattern pieces from the skin, she knows which way the fur must flow for each part. Usually in the finished garment the flow goes from top to bottom.[26] An exception is sometimes made in the front of the inner amauti, which has the fur to the inside. The fur flow goes from bottom to top so that the garment does not ride up from the weight of the child. At the same time, the flow inside the amaut, the baby pouch, must be down, so that the fur will not irritate the child. The strip of fur or hide that constitutes the fringe, ruff, or inner band attached to the edges of hood, sleeve, trouser leg, or garment body has a horizontal fur flow. This band prevents the skins from curling, gives warmth and strength, and can be highly decorative. The band imparts strength not only because it adds another layer to the edge but also because skin is harder to tear against the grain than in the length.

The flow of feathers in birdskin clothing is in the main from top to bottom. Because the bird's densest feathers are at its neck and chest, however, and would cause discomfort from overheating if placed at the wearer's neck, the feathers of the skins at the top front of the parka or amauti flow up, so that the lower or leg end of the bird skin, which has looser, more open feather density, is at the wearer's face. The top of the hood is made up of female skins since they are more supple and lightweight than those of the male. The feather alignment of the middle skin at the hood top is from back to front, thus helping the hood adhere better to the head (Pharand 1971b).

When boots are made, the pattern pieces are indented or scratched into the prepared skin or outlined with a pen. In most Arctic communities the fur flow for men's boots runs vertically top to bottom while for women's boots the fur runs diagonally or horizontally. The uppers of men's sealskin boots ideally are cut so that the dark fur of the adult seal is at the back of the boot, and the silvery grey sides and belly fur go around the sides and centre front where the seam is made. Sometimes the whole boot is silver, and the seal's dark back is used for the decorative bands and inserts.

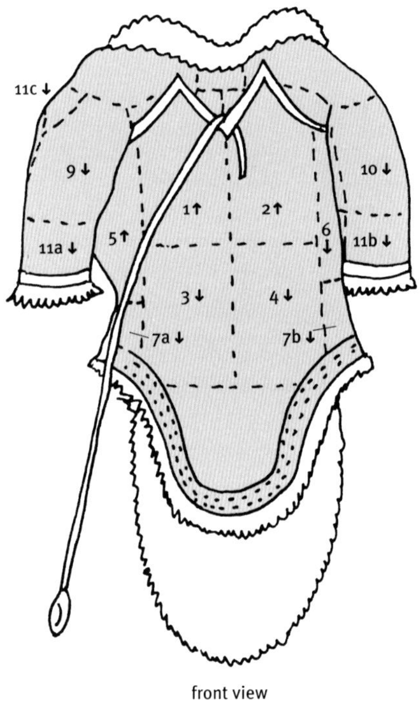

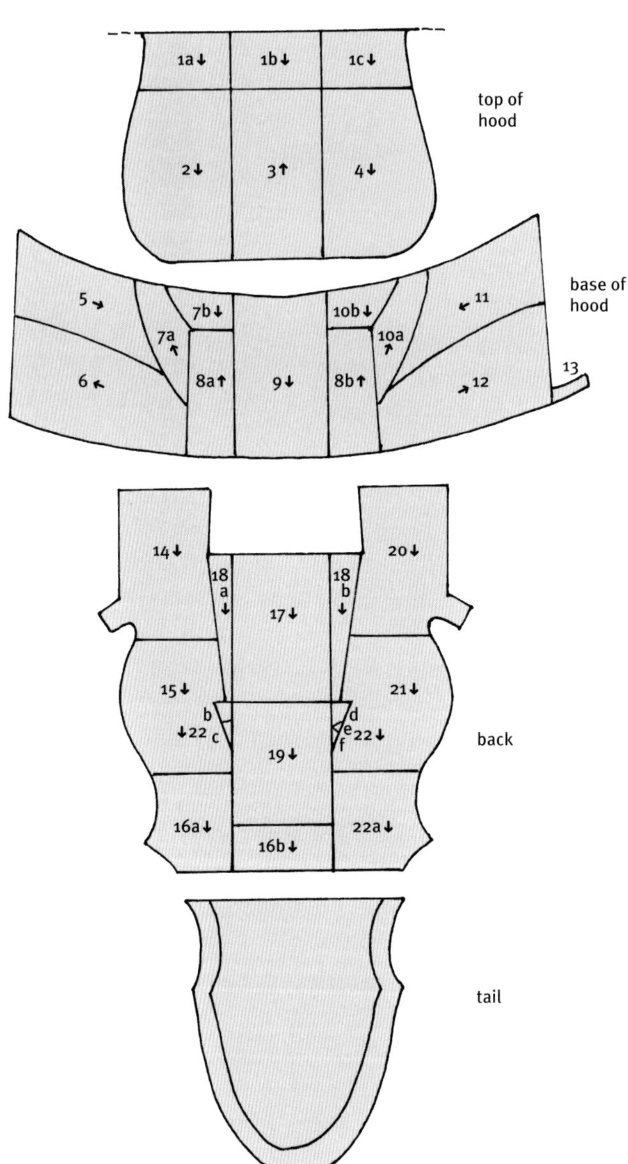

Figure 3.3
Pattern for inner amauti made by Maina Iqaluk and Caroline Kullualuk, Sanikiluaq, NWT, 1971, of skins of eider duck, seal, and dog, with metal and beads. Arrows indicate feather flow. *Based on a drawing by Sylvie Pharand.*

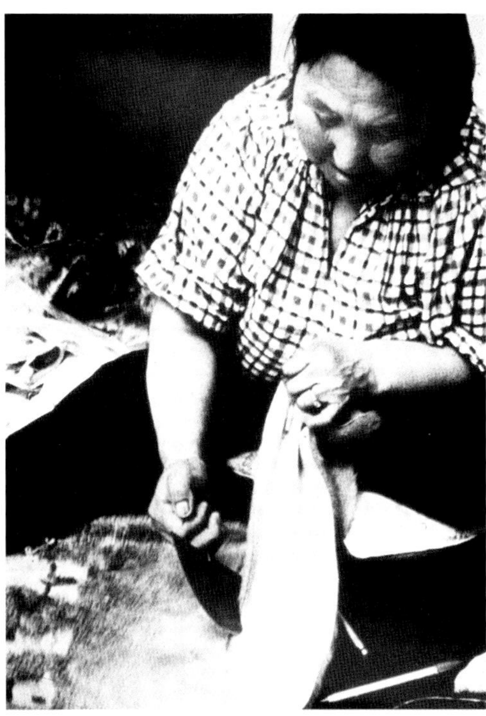

Maggie Alaku, Akulivik, Nunavik, 1978, cuts out a seal skin. While holding the skin for cutting, she is careful not to stretch it since an unevenness can develop, causing the costume to hang crookedly.

The boot sole is usually marked in six places (some communities favour four): at the beginning and end of the heel gathers and those of the toe, and at the mid-points of the length of the sole. During the marking and cutting, the pieces are chewed and otherwise softened and stretched with a blunt scraper to make them flexible. The edges of the soles are shaved to thin them so that they will be easier to gather and seam to the upper. The sewing commences from the inside of the boot. The steps described, all too briefly here, are not always taken in the same sequence in every community or by every seamstress.

Cutting

The seamstress continues to develop her pattern as she cuts the skin or fabric. Care must be taken not to skimp on the pieces, for if too small they have to be used for clothes for a smaller person. The seamstress must also ensure that 'The ulu ... [is] held straight up when cutting skins or the edges can't be sewn together properly' (Lucy Meeko, personal communication 1988). As well, 'There is a certain way to cut furs, for example the trim around an *amauti,* so it will lie flat but curve when required' (Jeela Alikatuktuk Moss-Davies, personal communication 1984).

The seamstress uses a razor-sharp ulu to cut skins. She sharpens it with a steel or another ulu very often during the cutting. If the skin is haired, she places the fur side down. She holds the ulu upright, starts the cut with the sharp point of the knife, and severs the skin smoothly in a motion away from herself. She holds the skin with one hand and lifts it enough to prevent the ulu from cutting off the hairs underneath. If the hair underneath is cut, the seams and stitches will be visible in the finished garment. Moreover, damaged hair prevents water and dirt from running off. As the pieces are cut, fittings take place to see what adjustments have to be made. The marking and cutting for one amauti may take one hour for an experienced woman.

Sewing

Four main stitches are employed when sewing skins: the overcast stitch, the tuck stitch, the running stitch, and the waterproof stitch. The most common is the overcast stitch, used on most garment seams. The fur sides are placed together, with edges even or slightly overlapping as in a felled seam. The stitches, which are very close, can neither be too tight, lest the skin tear, nor too loose, lest the seams work and split.[27] When seams are sewn with furred skins, the hair underneath must be spread and pushed to keep it from catching in the

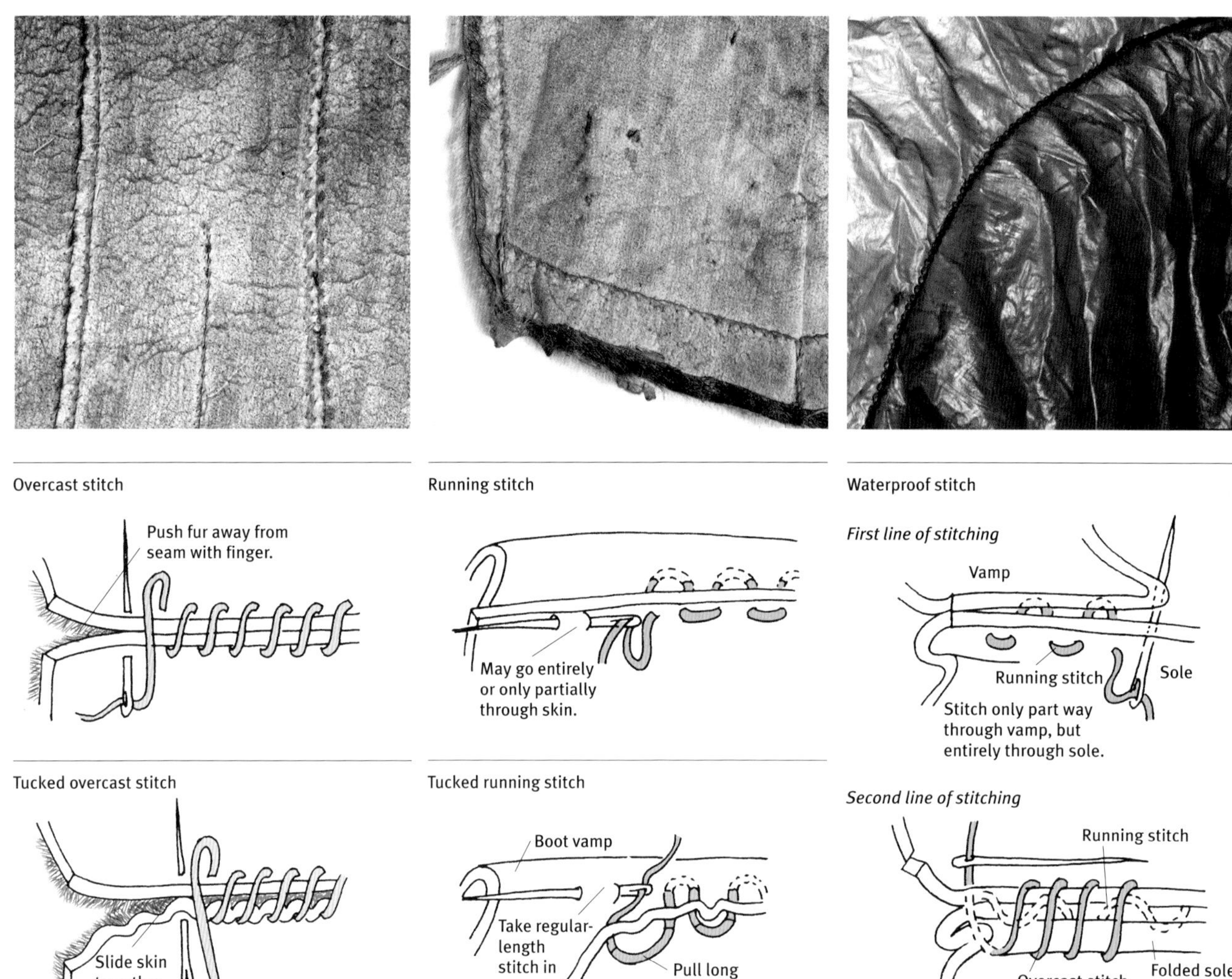

Figure 3.4
Illustration of five Inuit sewing stitches. *Based on a drawing by Donna Kern.*

seam and protruding on the flesh side. When a larger piece of skin must be joined to a smaller, such as for the amaut or at an elbow, a gathering or tuck stitch is employed. The running stitch is used to attach some facings, to insert coloured material between some seams, and to make rows of stiffening at the heels of boots. It sometimes passes between the skin layers and does not appear on both surfaces.

The stitch for which Inuit seamstresses are most famous is the waterproof stitch, of which there are several kinds. The most common, called ilujjiniq, is employed for seams of waterproof boots and sometimes for mitts (Pharand 1974, 15, Plate 10; Hadlereena et al. 1986; Manning and Manning 1944; Oakes 1987b; Oakes and Riewe 1995, 33). I would say this stitch is unequalled in the annals of needlework. Waterproof seams have two lines of stitching. In the first line, the needle goes part way through the first skin and entirely through the second. In the second line, the stitch goes right through the first skin and partly through the second. Some seamstresses, for the second pass, make the needle go only part way through both skins.

Opposite above Close-ups of Inuit overcast, running, and waterproof stitches.

Below Sealskin boot, sewn with sinew, Nunavimiut or Labrador Inuit, mid-twentieth century. Collected by Dr. Arthur Schwartz. The close-up of the boot toe shows the waterproof stitching. The seamstress gathers the toe and heel between her marked notches in fine crimps or pleats to form the sole, which comes up the sides of the foot. While in some parts of the Arctic, seamstresses use a boot creaser, others use their thumbs or other tool.

Thus the needle and sinew never penetrate both skins at the same hole. The sinew is threaded into a needle, the eye of which is filled by the sinew, thereby ensuring that the sinew packs the needle hole in the skin. The sinew swells with humidity, making the sealskin boot impervious to melting snow, ice, or water.

Another kind of waterproof stitch is often used for the gutskins made from the intestines of sea mammals. With the outer sides facing out and the inner sides together, the edges of the two skins are narrowly turned in. The needle and sinew go through the four layers using a running stitch. The stitches in these seams therefore do not penetrate the part of the garment exposed to moisture. This stitch can also couch decorative loops made of dark wolf-fish skin, grass, red-dyed or untanned seal skin, seals' bristles, the fine feathers of waterfowl, and more recently, thread.[28] These organic materials help increase the water-resistant qualities of the gutskins while having an ornamental function (Bockstoce 1977, 93; Hickman 1987, 8; Murdoch 1892, 122; Nelson 1983, 36-7; Wilder 1976, 95). The magnificent waterproof gutskins produced by Yup'ik and Unangan (Aleut) peoples combine technical prowess with an artistry evolved from an ancient heritage. The entire production of one sea mammal coat can take a month.

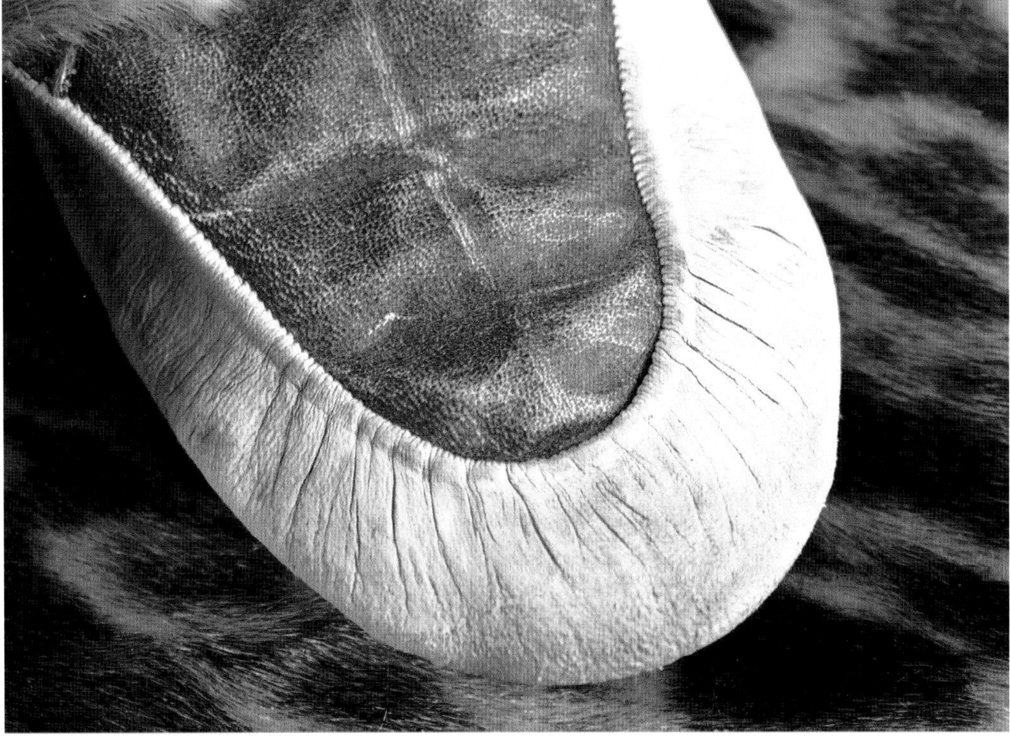

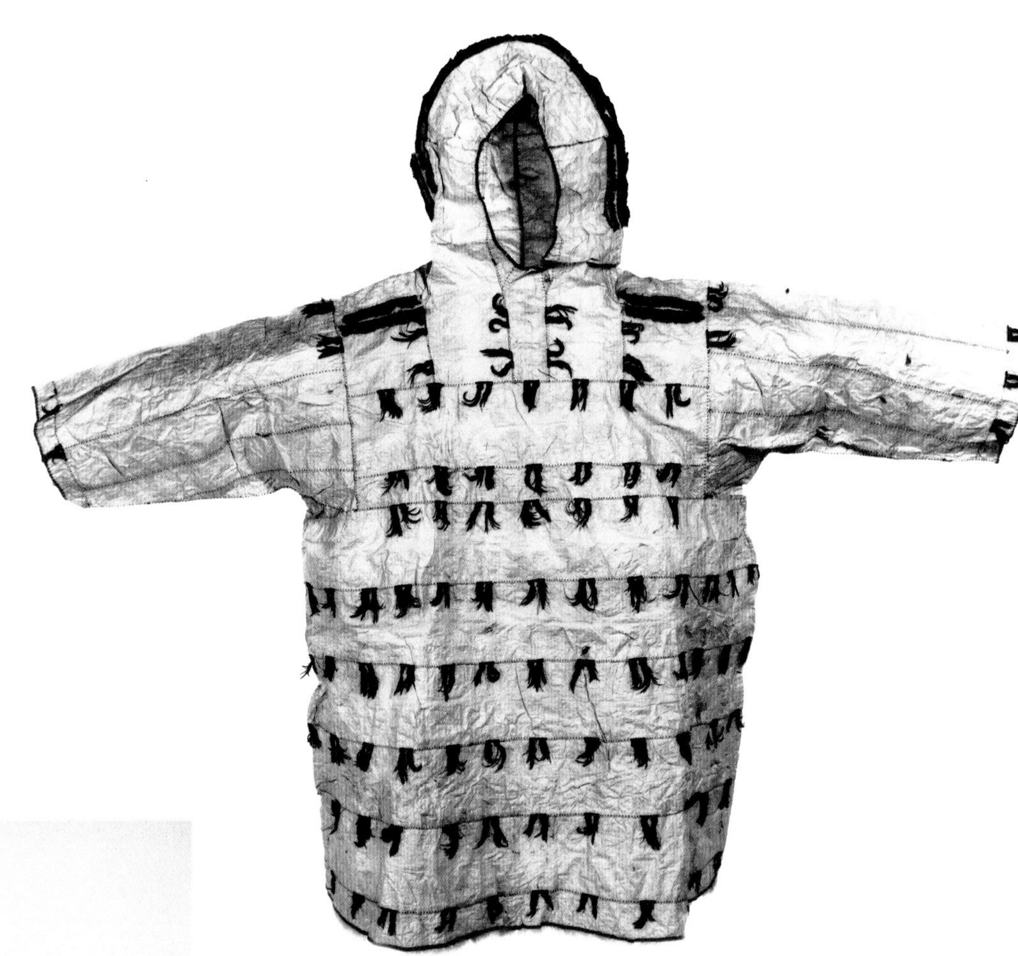

Right Gutskin, walrus intestine, auklet beaks and feathers, sewn with sinew, Yup'ik, twentieth century. Collected at Sivuqaq, Alaska, by Henry Collins in 1930. Sivuqaq gutskins are often decorated by spaced insertions of puffin beaks or of the bright orange-red horny sheath from the base of the mandible of the crested auklet, along with the dark brown or black curly feathers from the auklet's crests.

Below Lucy Meeko of Kuujjuaraapik, Nunavik, 1988, completes a girl's amauti made of caribou skin. Her sewing basket and ulu appear at lower left.

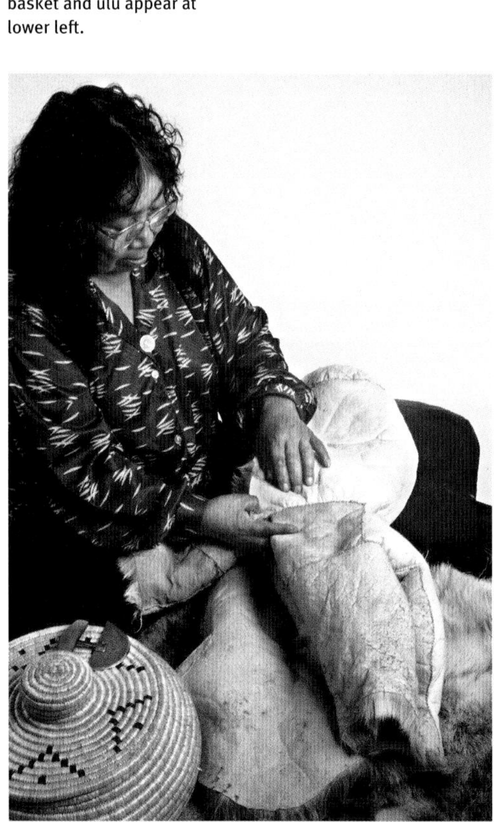

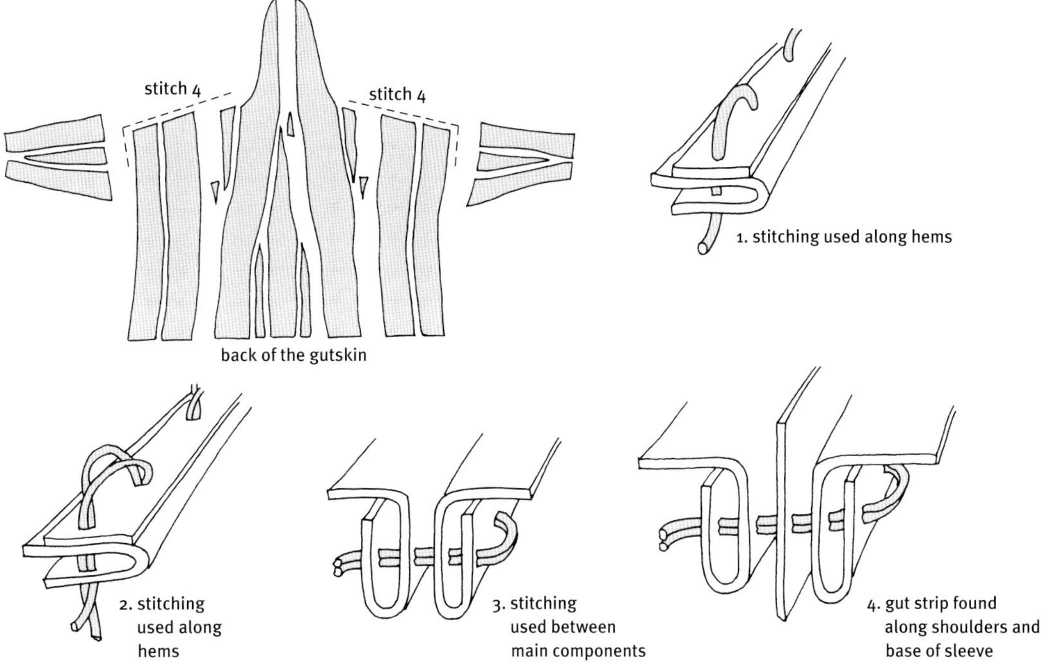

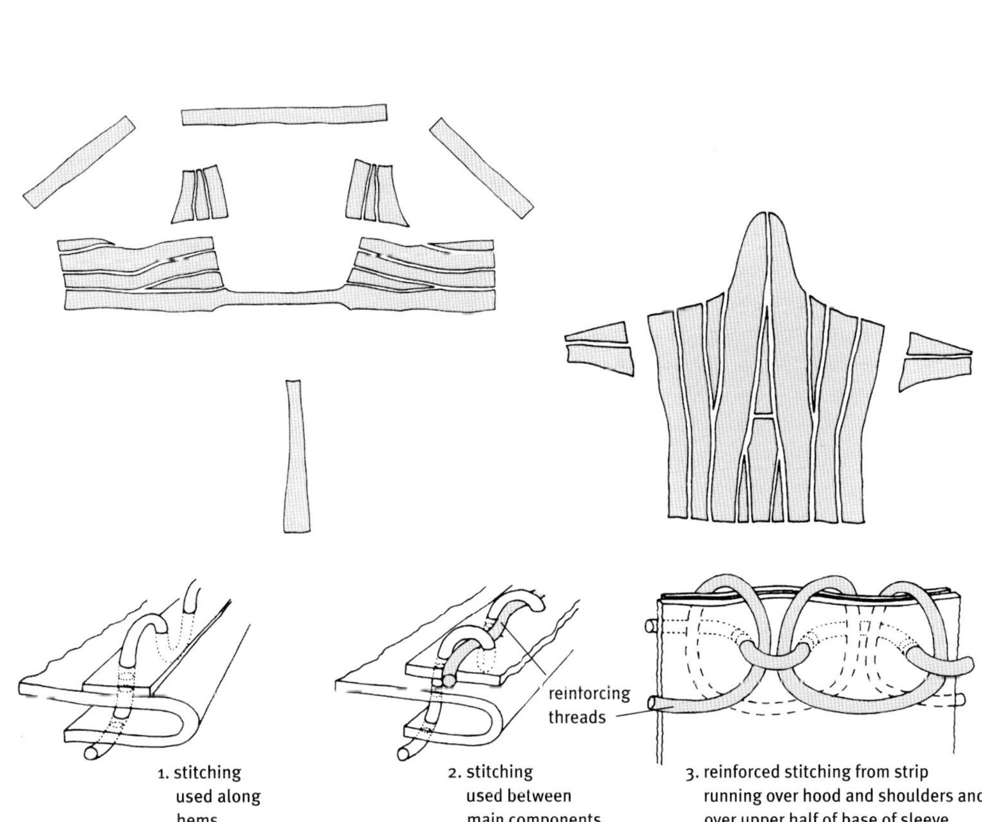

Figure 3.5
Illustration of pattern, seams, and stitches for two gutskins collected by Frederick Beechey at Kotzebue Sound, Alaska, between 1826 and 1827. The first, showing the back pattern and stitching, is 86 centimetres long. The second, showing front and back pattern and stitching, is 81 centimetres long. *Based on a drawing by John R. Bockstoce.*

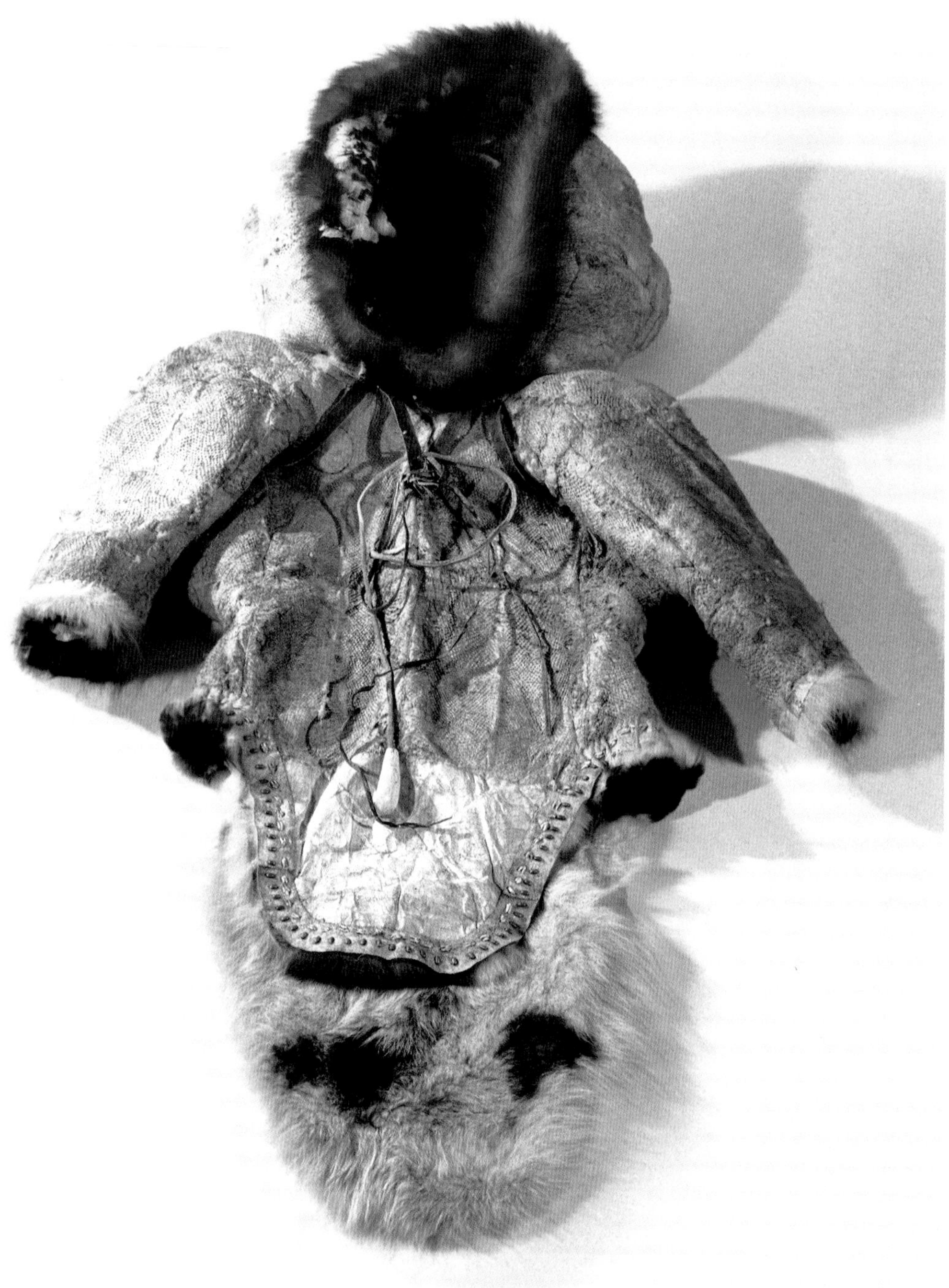

Front and back views of inner amauti, eider duck skins (four female, twenty-seven male), dog and seal skins, metal, beads, sewn with sinew, 122.5 cm, Nunavimiut, 1972. Artisans: Maina Iqaluk and Caroline Kullualuk of Sanikiluaq, NWT. (See figure 3.3 for pattern.)

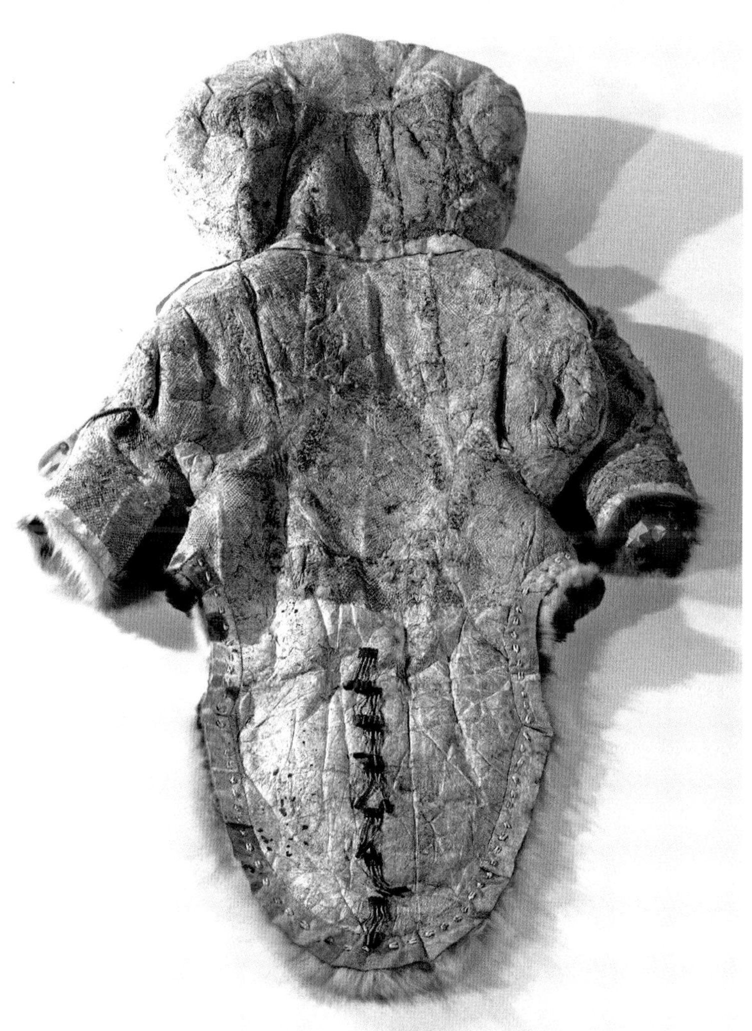

Minnie Aodla Freeman remembers when she was growing up in Sanikiluaq how much joy she experienced learning to sew. Her grandmother started her on boots she wished to make for her four-year-old brother. She recalls that it took her three days, whereas an experienced woman can make a pair of boots in one day (Freeman 1978, 91). Sewing an outer amauti of caribou skin can take fifteen hours, and a set of infant's clothes may take six hours. The intensive work of pattern development, cutting, and sewing caribou clothing for a five-member family can take at least 200 hours (Pharand 1974, 11). When we look at the multitude of elements that go into the production of one piece of clothing, we can understand why a woman is thirty-five before she can be considered an accomplished seamstress even though she begins to help with the skins and sewing as a child (Gubser 1965, 111).

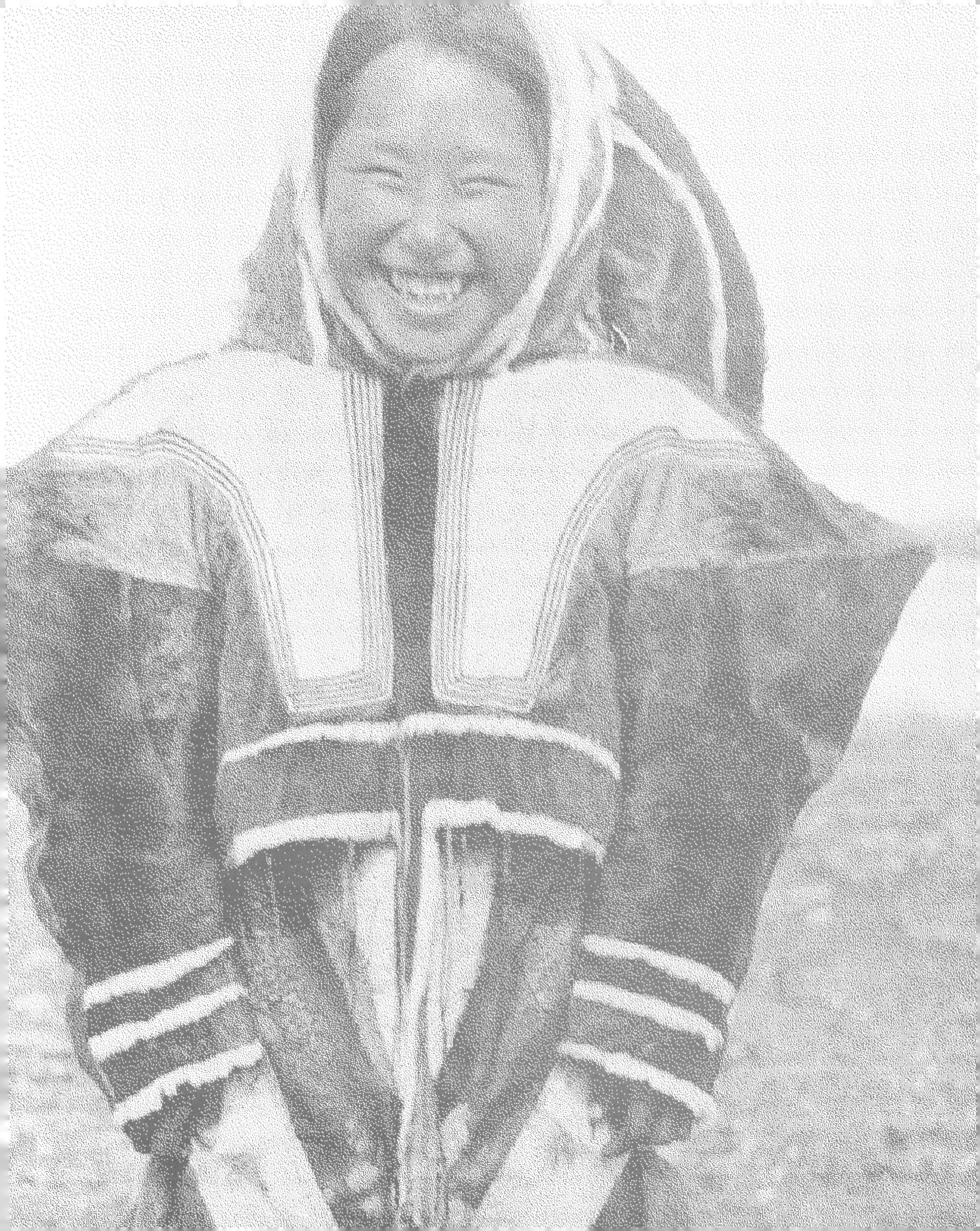

We know what kind of clothing should be worn to fight the cold.

Mina Napartuk of Kuujjuaraapik[1]

We still use the methods our ancestors used to make the clothing.

Akinisie Novalinga of Purvirnituq[2]

We are the people of the north and that will not change. So I can say that I am happy to see the children being taught in school more about the old ways, especially the language and sewing. I think as long as there are animals the girls should know how to look after the skins, to make clothes out of them because they will always be the best to wear in the winter time.

Evie Saviardjuk of Salluit[3]

Chapter 4

Inuit Style

Inuit clothing presents a great diversity of styles.[4] The attire tells the knowledgeable onlooker which country and which part of the country the person comes from, and in some instances the kin group, the person's sex, age, and often, for women, marital status. Important indicators on the parka are the hood or lack thereof, and hood shape; width and configuration of shoulders; presence of flaps front and back, and their shape; in women's clothing the size and shape of the amaut, the baby pouch; length and outline of the lower edge; and fringes, ruffs, and decorative inserts.

Several streams have influenced the characteristics of the garments. Motifs, designs, and styles from northeastern Siberia – the Chukchi, Koryak, Yup'ik – are found in some communities in Arctic North America. The Inuit's ancestors, particularly the most recent Thule, left their mark. The Inuit of the Historic era – a mobile population that always traded, worked, and socialized with neighbours and sometimes travelled to distant areas across the Arctic, often between continents – incorporated into their apparel whatever seemed useful or appealing. They took from Europeans, Russians, and non-Inuit North Americans what suited them, without compromising the basic efficiency and imagery of their attire.

CANADIAN INUIT AND THEIR CLOTHING

When describing the clothing of the ten Canadian Inuit groups, of necessity only general characteristics can be set forth. The many variations among the subgroups within each group defy the parameters of this book, and exceptions to general rules abound as the artisan produces clothing from materials available and out of her own creativity.

The Inuvialuit

Often referred to as the Mackenzie Delta Inuit, the Inuvialuit, as they now call themselves, inhabit the northwestern Arctic coast from Alaska to Avvaq.[5] Nineteenth-century records reveal that the indigenous population was divided among five subgroups, the largest of which was the Kittegaryumiut. Archaeological investigations in the territory of the Kittegaryumiut demonstrate that these ancestors of today's Inuvialiut maintained a uniform, rich, and distinctive culture from the fourteenth to the nineteenth centuries (McGhee 1974, 7-18, 93).

The forebears of the Inuvialuit shared their economy, their technology, and their culture with the North Alaskan Inupiat, with whom they mixed and traded from early times and who were part of the intercontinental trade network of the Bering Strait. The predecessors of today's Inuvialuit also crossed to Banks Island to trade with the Copper Inuit. As well, trading between North American Indians and Karngmalit, an Inuvialuit group centred in Paulatuuq, occurred before the advent of non-Inuit traders.[6] Goods found in the Mackenzie Delta area that could have come from inter-Native trade include metals, dentalium shells, and Russian trade beads.

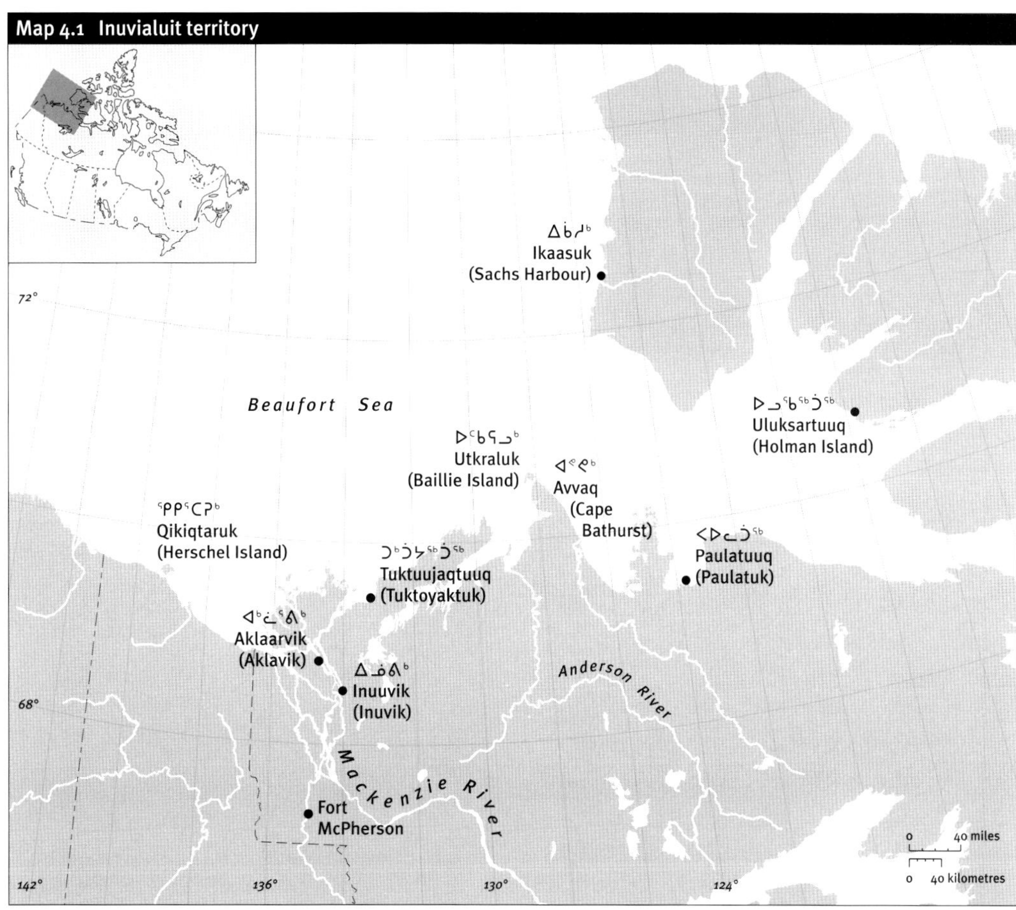

Map 4.1 Inuvialuit territory

Dentalium shells in particular were rare and highly prized, and were obtained by the Inuit only through trade. Some Californian Indian tribes used dentalium shells as a medium of exchange, but only those over 4.3 centimetres long.

Although the indigenous population of the Mackenzie Delta area numbered between an estimated 2,000 and 4,000 in the nineteenth century, a series of epidemics decimated the group. By 1910 only a few score survived, and they were deeply affected culturally and linguistically by the Alaskan Inupiat who had immigrated into the area during the boom times for whaling, 1889 to 1908, and with whom they intermarried (Smith 1984, 348). Baleen whales were hunted almost to extinctionby 1915, and the demand for baleen[7] and whale oil dropped when spring steel was invented and petroleum discovered, prompting some Inuvialuit to move to North Alaska in search of jobs other than those provided by whalers.

This loss of population was later offset by Inuvialuit who migrated from Utkraluk and Avaaq west to centres such as Tuktuujaqtuuq, some drawn by the establishment of a Hudson's Bay Company store in 1937. By 1995 the Inuvialuit population numbered about 2,400 people, some of whom gained employment in the exploration for oil and gas in the Beaufort Sea. Part of the community's renewable resources is a 13,000-head domestic reindeer herd, brought in by the Canadian government in 1929.[8] The herd's owners supply skins, harvested twice a year, to Inuit who cannot obtain the kind of skins they require for clothing.

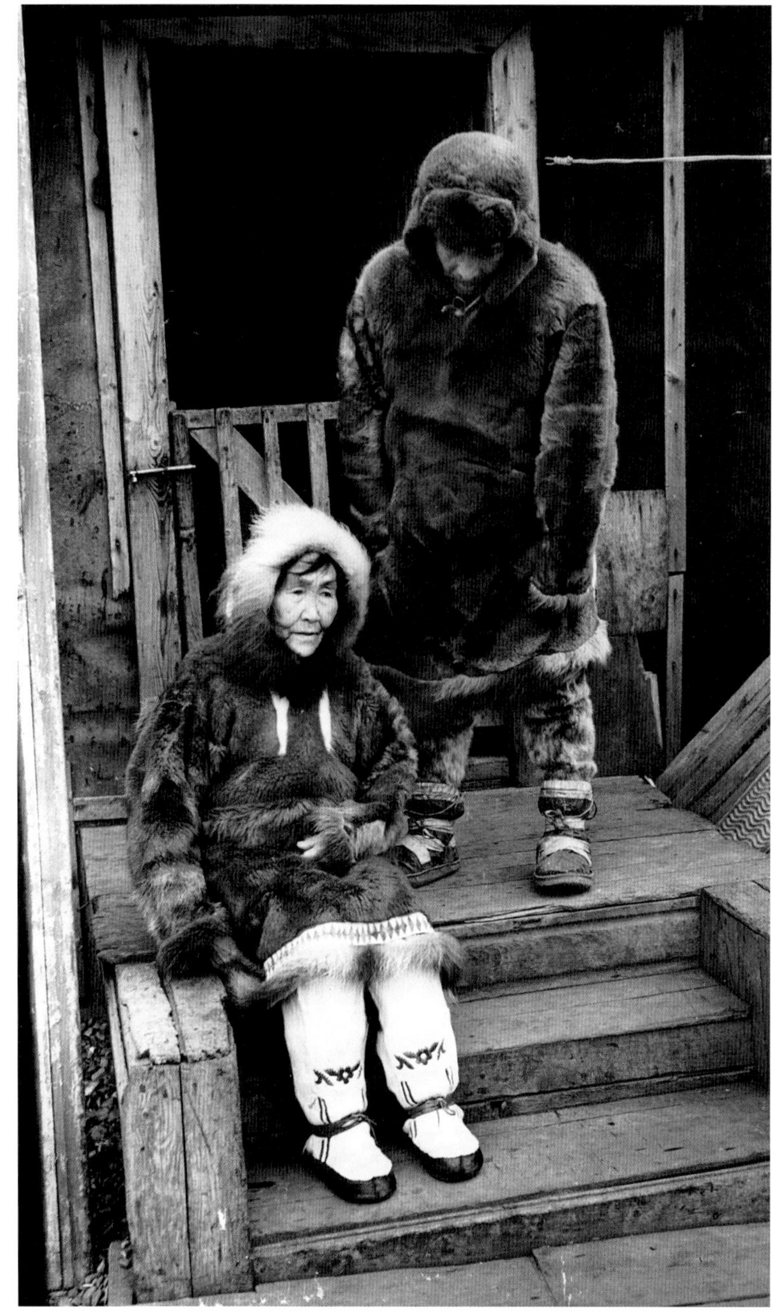

Clothing
In the early twentieth century some forms of Inuvialuit dress were more akin to the styles of Alaska and Siberia than they were to clothing found in the rest of Canada and Kalaallit Nunaat. Stefansson (1914, 139) reported that the Mackenzie area clothing styles had become so like Alaskan designs that only by detailed questions could he learn of any distinction.

Alaskan and Inuvialuit men's parkas were, and continue to be, substantially similar in style. The parka is a loose, flared pullover that reaches below the hip, with a round hood that comes forward from the face and is made of the animal's headskin. The lower edge is even and rounded.

The ruffs for hood, sleeve, and lower edges are made from the fur of long-haired animals such as wolverine and wolf. Some parkas have a modest hood ruff consisting of one or two fur layers. Another kind of ruff, known as a sunburst, has three layers sewn into a circle and then attached to the hood. The outer layer comes from the long hair of the wolf's back, the middle from the wolf's belly fur, and the section next to the face from wolverine or the dark fur of dogs.

It is not clear how long the trouser pattern persisted or when a change, if any, occurred. Trousers were knee-length and had a close-fitting cuff to which the pant leg was gathered.

When traders brought machine-woven textiles north, seamstresses sewed parka covers for their husbands. A strong twilled striped cotton called ticking was manufactured into a *silapaaq*, or snow shirt.[9] Worn

Opposite The Roshchenko family, who are Siberian Yup'ik living at Oleq, Chukotka, CIS, 1974. Inuvialuit attire continues to have much in common with Alaskan and Siberian Yup'ik clothing: use of caribou and reindeer skins and skins of smaller animals, long-haired ruffs, roots – described as 'walrus tusks' – into the chest, decorative fur mosaics at edges, and skin boots.

Right Man's parka of caribou skin, wolverine skin, blanket cloth, sewn with sinew, 108 cm, Inuvialuit, ca. 1900. Collected in the Mackenzie Delta area, NWT, by Forbes D. Sutherland in 1904. The front hood roots of this parka are made of the same deep brown fur as the trunk. Usually the roots are made of pukiq (white fur), but here contrast is achieved by the upward flow of the roots' fur. The band of fur mosaic that decorates the lower edge is made up of alternating light and dark geometric fur pieces sewn together by invisible stitches. The fur pieces are sheared to enhance texture and lustre.

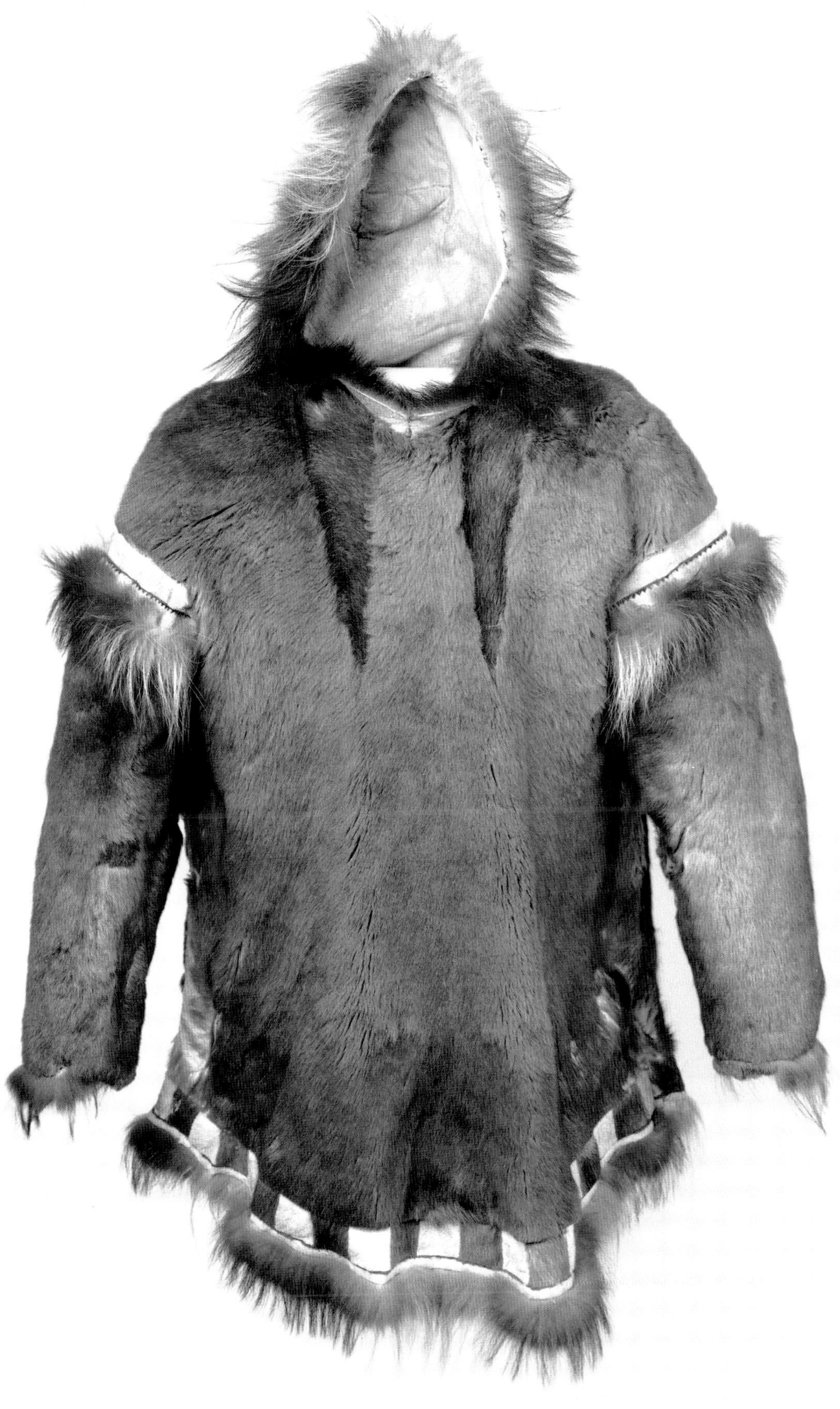

Caribou and stroud man's trousers, sewn with sinew, 69 cm, Inuvialuit, late nineteenth, ca. 1900. Collected in the Mackenzie Delta area, NWT, by J.L. Todd. Below the white fur cuffs are bands of sheared white caribou, between which are sewn red piping and saw-toothed stroud. In earlier times, the red in the decorative bands was achieved by inserting a row of tiny pieces of the red skin found above the eyes of the willow ptarmigan (Stefansson 1914, 140).

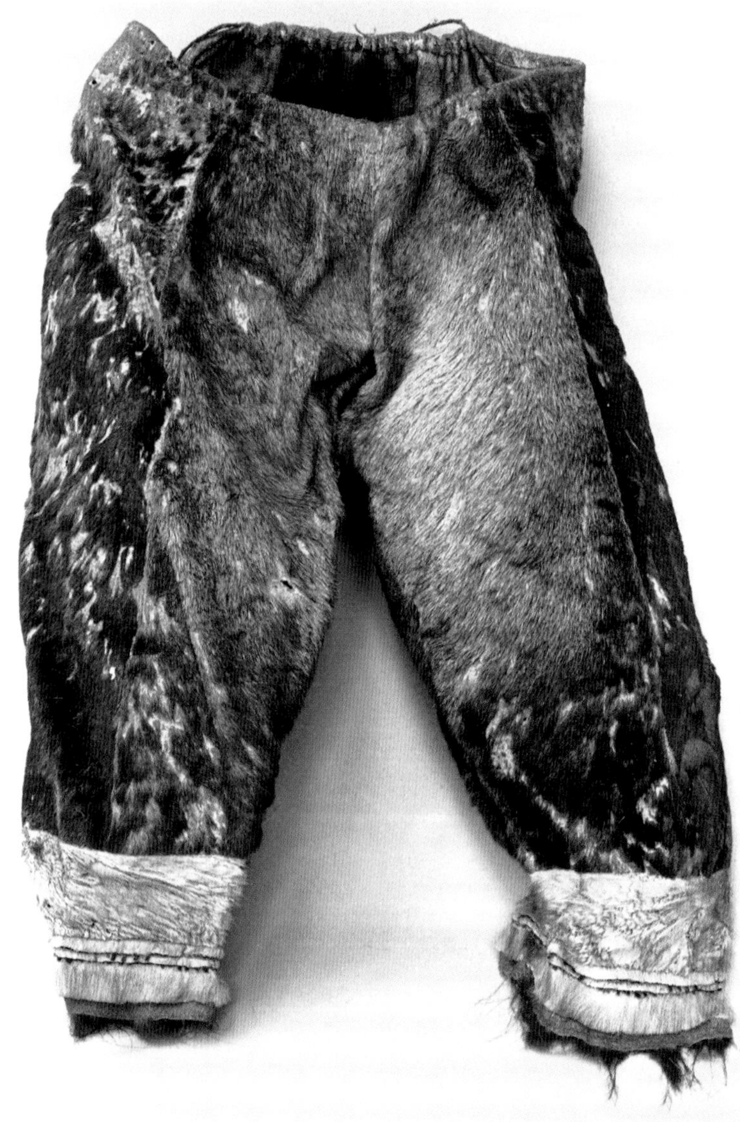

over the parka, the densely loomed fabric kept snow off the furs. The overall appearance of ticking is white, providing camouflage for the hunter.

Dance parkas had no hoods. Hats were worn for games, celebrations, and other social occasions. Gauntlet gloves and caps shaped like a pilot's helmet, called 'lindy' hats by the Inuvialuit, were inspired by aviator Charles Lindbergh, who made a solo airplane flight across the Atlantic in 1927.[10] Gloves worn on dress occasions were similar to Siberian and Alaskan gloves.

In former times the Inuvialuit sometimes used the skin of the beluga or bowhead whale for the soles of sealskin and caribou boots. Today the skin of bearded seal furnishes soles. Boots have drawstrings at the top and come to the knee.

The woman's parka style changed markedly among Alaskans and the Inuvialuit in both areas. The one known in the Mackenzie Delta area in the nineteenth and early twentieth centuries had a large hood and neckline, wide shoulders, narrowed waist, and long, broad flaps that rose in a gentle curve to the thigh. The large hood accommodated the woman's hair, which was sometimes piled in a coil on top of the head. The back of the amauti had a full cut over the back and neck rather than the pieced amaut known in other parts of Canada. Because of the fullness, a child could still be held against the mother's back, secured by the amauti cord.

Women's trousers were long and often striped, formed by sewing contrasting colours of furs together lengthwise, a style

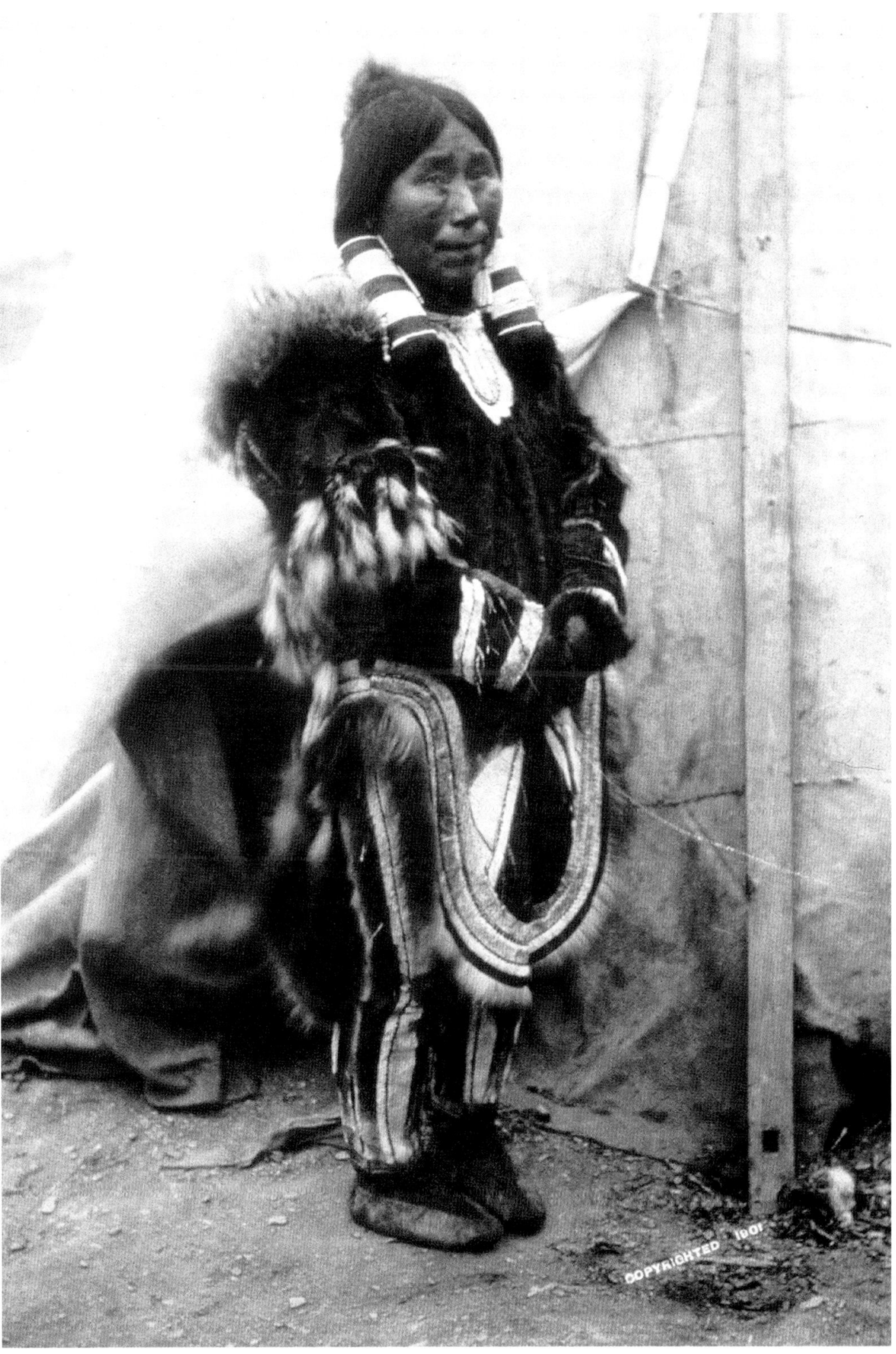

Inuvialuit woman in the area of the junction of the Peel and Mackenzie Rivers, NWT, ca. 1901. Typical of western Arctic costume of the time are the long, broad flaps back and front that are elaborately pieced, the long-haired ruff, the insert under the chin, the fur dangles at the seam where the sleeve joins the shoulder, and the bands that outline the garment. The trouser legs show decorative piecing. The woman has dressed her hair with hairsticks.

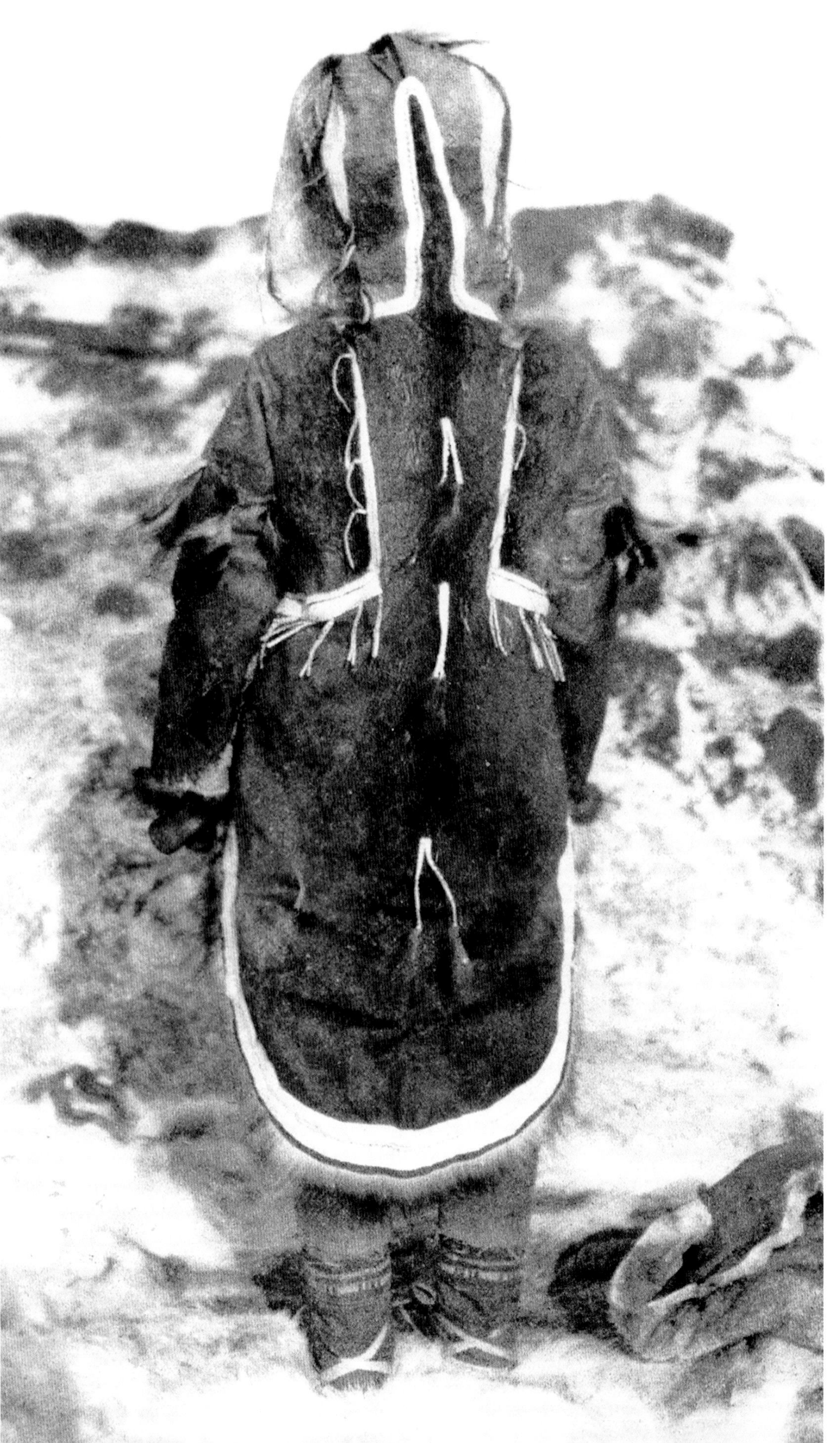

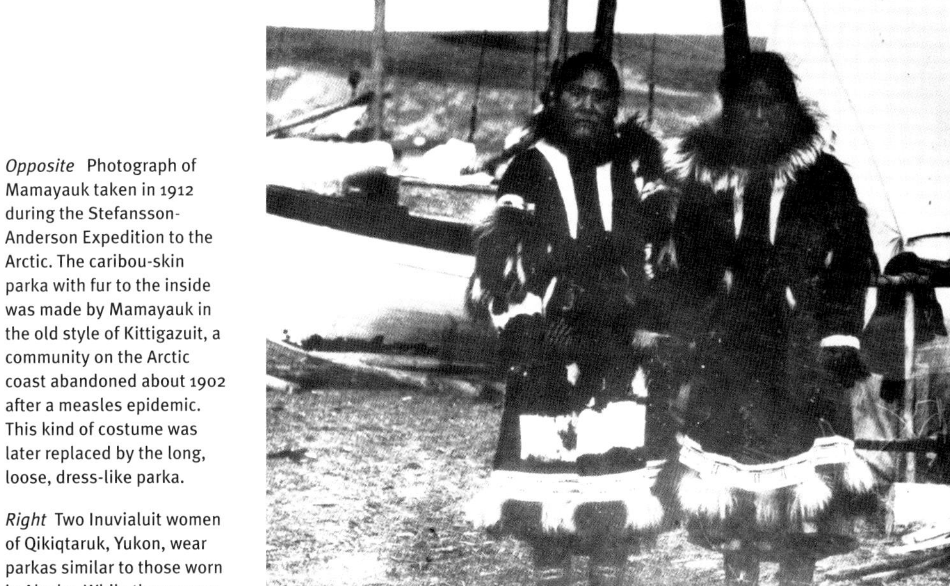

Opposite Photograph of Mamayauk taken in 1912 during the Stefansson-Anderson Expedition to the Arctic. The caribou-skin parka with fur to the inside was made by Mamayauk in the old style of Kittigazuit, a community on the Arctic coast abandoned about 1902 after a measles epidemic. This kind of costume was later replaced by the long, loose, dress-like parka.

Right Two Inuvialuit women of Qikiqtaruk, Yukon, wear parkas similar to those worn in Alaska. While the woman on the right wears a walrus (pointed root) pattern on her parka, the woman on the left wears a fish tail pattern (squared root ends) 'which, as Mrs. Persis Gruben of Tuktuujaqtuuq told me, is more like those of the Kittegaryumiut people in the Mackenzie Delta. The footwear of the woman on the right is akin to that made by Dene Indians. The woman on the left wears a parka made of reindeer skin which would have been available through trade ... at Herschel Island' (Murielle Nagy, written communication 1992).

known in Siberia. Women's hood ruffs were, and continue to be, like those of the men.

It is not yet clear when this style changed to the long, dress-like parka with the even edge that we know from at least the 1950s, and perhaps earlier. The Alaskan garment began about 1880 to lose the U-shaped flaps (Fitzhugh and Kaplan, 1982, 138). When some Alaskan families migrated eastward, their clothing became a model in parts of the western Canadian Arctic.

Inuvialuit clothing has several features that are not found in groups farther east in Canada. In the parka pattern, a gusset runs from the main part of the parka front into the sleeve at the underarm. This attribute does away with part of the armhole seam and gives width to the upper part of the sleeve. It secures the sleeve to the garment and adds strength, as do hood roots, to areas where movement places tension on the skins (see figure 1.4).

The roots descending from the hood into the chest of the parka help identify Inuvialuit clothing. This feature is now also found in Copper Inuit clothing, although it came to them via Alaska. Curiously, the parka depicted by John White in his image of a Nunatsiarmiut woman, 1567, displays these roots. Parkas of the Nunatsiarmiut known in later centuries do not have this design.

Another feature of Inuvialuit clothing, although not now exclusive to that group, is the trim used at the seam between the dropped shoulder and the sleeve, at the bottom edge of the coat and sleeve, and at the trouser cuff. The same layered strips of ornamentation are seen in Siberian Yup'ik and Alaskan clothing. The 'Delta trim' now found on cloth parkas all over North America derives from fur decoration found on the Inuvialuit parkas. The original Delta ornamentation used fur and hide and was later made up of small coloured pieces of

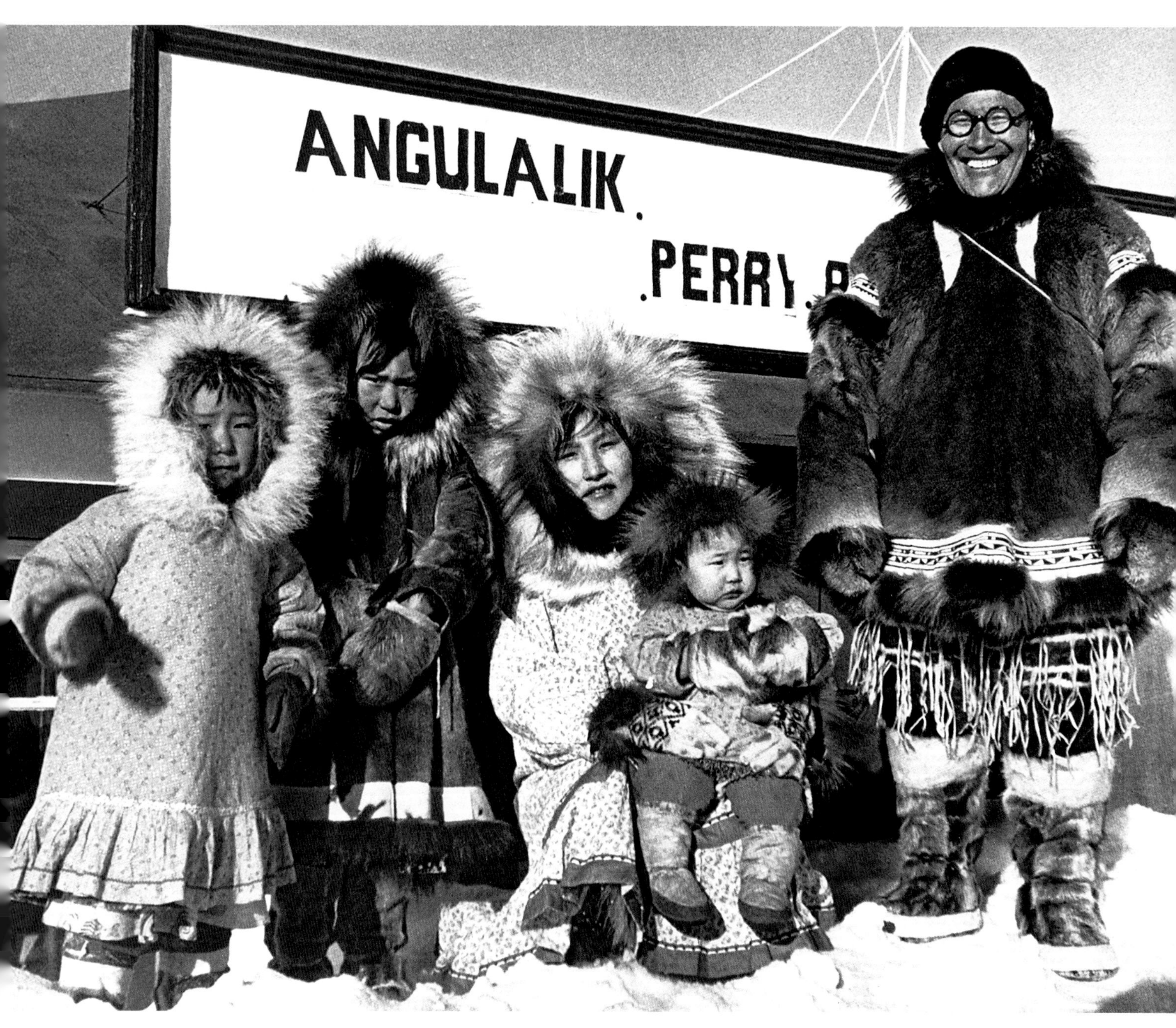
ANGULALIK.
.PERRY.

Opposite The Angulalik family in front of the Perry River trading post, NWT, 1950. From left to right: Mary, Margaret, Ekvana (Mabel), Lena, and Stephen Angulalik. Stephen Angulalik (1895?-1980), the operator of the trading post, wears caribou clothing made in the Inuvialuit style. His daughter Mary and wife Ekvana wear cloth Mother Hubbards over or lined with fur, while daughter Margaret wears a caribou-fur parka.

Right Man's coat of skins of reindeer and wolverine, wool yarn, sewn with sinew, 97.5 cm, Siberian Yup'ik, early twentieth century. Collected at East Cape, Chukotka, CIS, by G.B. Gordon in 1905.

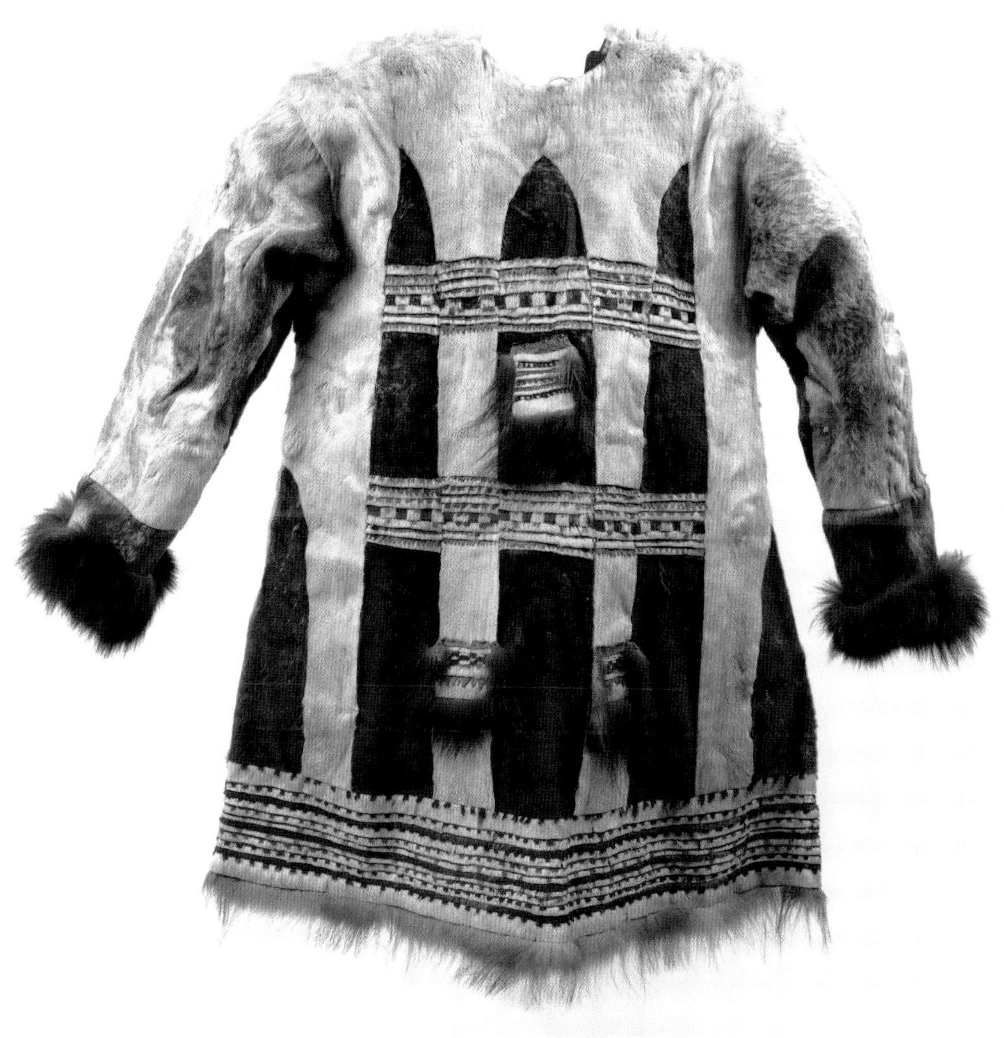

cotton bias tape, cut in half lengthwise to eliminate bulk, then cut in varying lengths to make the pattern.[11]

Inuvialuit fur decoration on the parka contributed to the development of the Mother Hubbard, the calico cover that has had over a century of evolution in the North.[12] It is possible that missionaries brought the Mother Hubbard to Alaska, from whence it came to the Mackenzie Delta area and points east. Many missionaries throughout the Arctic deemed that women should not show their trousers, and enjoined them not to remove their upper garments in the iglu and tent as was the custom. The Mother Hubbard began to be worn either under or over the amauti so that it concealed the trousers and fell below the edge of the furs to the boots or even lower. It often had a bottom flounce and ruffle at the shoulder decorated with Delta trim. By the late nineteenth century it was called the cloth parka. At that time more style-conscious women discarded the flounce as old fashioned. The popularity of the Mother Hubbard can be ascribed to several factors. The pattern is simple and enjoyable to produce, unlike the hours of work required to make fur garments. The material available from traders and whalers was exotic, and therefore appealing and valuable. The *kaliku,* as it was also called, proved a useful and easily washed cover over furs and could be worn by itself when women were performing hot, dirty work, such as flaying animals and dressing skins.

Waterproof parkas made of intestines of sea mammals were worn in the Mackenzie Delta area. Bertram Pokiak of

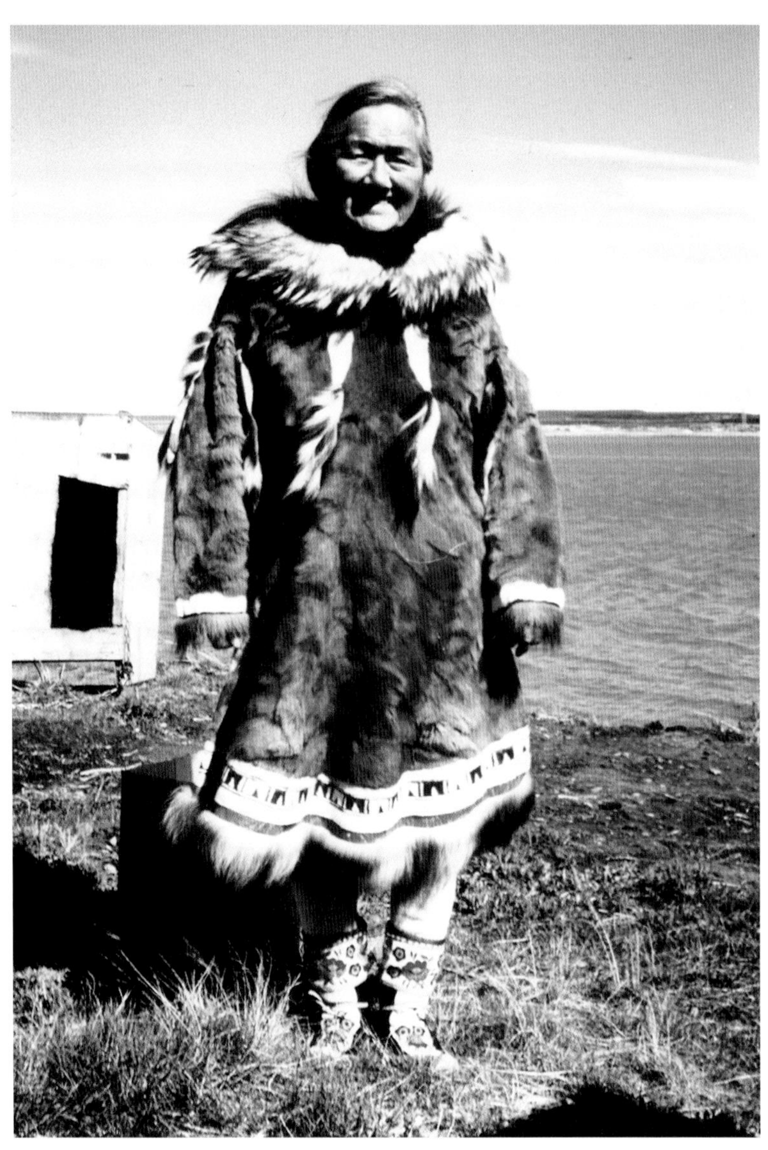

Mrs. Emma Gruben Fietchtinger of Tuktuujaqtuuq, NWT, 1991, wearing a parka she made herself.

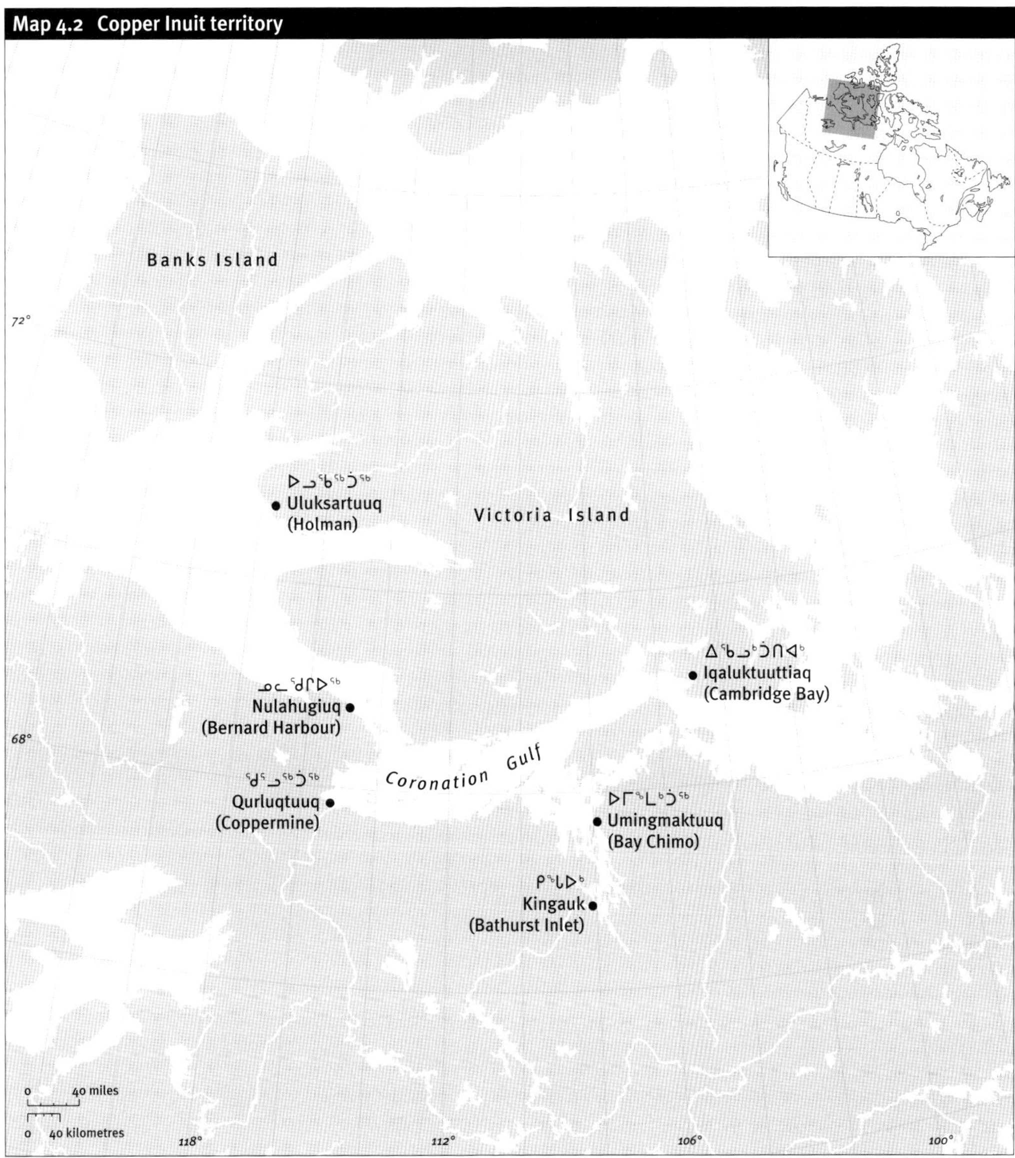

Tuktuujaqtuuq, writing in 1976 about the old days as related to him by his grandparents, mentions their use: 'Where driftwood was available, sod houses were made. The sides were covered with mud and more logs were piled on top of the mud. The roof was then covered with sod. Each house had one window and it was made with the intestines of whales or bearded seals. They also used these intestines to make parka covers to use as raincoats' (*Inuktitut* 1989, 70:37).

Fabric and synthetics have now largely replaced fur for both men's and women's clothing. With an increased concern to promote their cultural and artistic heritage, more women are making fur garments – for themselves and their friends, for special occasions, and for museums and other public displays.

The Copper Inuit

The territory of the Copper Inuit encompasses both sides of Coronation Gulf: north into Victoria Island and the south coast of Banks Island, and south to the heads of the rivers that lead into Qurluqtuuq and Umingmaktuuq. The 500 kilometres of coast west of their area was a poor hunting region and uninhabited, serving to isolate the Copper Inuit from the people and richer territories farther west. Nevertheless, the Copper Inuit groups who lived on or travelled to western Victoria Island and southeastern Banks Island met Inuvialuit from Avvaq who came to trade, and traditionally they traded with Caribou Inuit to the south (Csonka 1995).

Robert M'Clure's ship, *Investigator,* abandoned in 1853 on Banks Island, supplied wood, metal, and other European materials for many years. The nineteenth-century whalers of Alaska and Qikiqtaruk rarely penetrated as far east as Copper Inuit territories, so the Copper Inuit remained separated from non-Inuit influences longer than their compatriots to the west. It was in the first quarter of the twentieth century that trading ships from Alaska and Qikiqtaruk penetrated the area.[13]

Outsiders brought diseases to the Copper Inuit to which they had no resistance, among them influenza and typhoid. From 1929 to 1931 a tuberculosis epidemic caused the death of one in five persons in the Qurluqtuuq area. Diamond Jenness, who had been adopted as a son into an Inuit family, lost most members of the extended family.[14]

Today the Copper Inuit participate in the exploitation of oil, gas, and minerals in their area but still remain people of the tundra, where they hunt caribou, musk-oxen, fox, and bear, and of the sea, where they are experts at sealing.

Clothing

The Copper Inuit made their clothing of caribou skins except for a damp-weather coat and some boots manufactured from seal skin. The traditional patterns are no longer worn and were quite distinct from those of all other Inuit groups.[15]

The Copper Inuit preferred to use the dark, glossy, lightweight skins of caribou gathered in the summer for both inner and outer layers, and in winter wore over both an overcoat made of the heavy, creamy beige skins garnered in the autumn. Stormy weather demanded such a coat, since it came to the knee and sometimes below and was ideal for travelling. It overcame the disadvantages of the lighter weight clothing underneath. Another kind of outer coat made of seal skin and shorter than the travelling coat served for sealing in the spring and other tasks performed in wet conditions.

The parka was cut high and square across the waist, a feature that sometimes allowed cold to penetrate. It had a long, narrow, straight-sided tail, which descended at the back to below the knee, sometimes the ankle, and ended in a shallow V. Loops at the bottom edge allowed the tail to be folded to the waist at the inside by a toggle of wood or ivory when the day was warm or if the tail hampered work. The hood barely came forward of the cheek bones, fitted closely to the head, and was pointed. Instead of the long-haired ruff seen in the western Arctic, a band of white caribou fur, or sometimes several bands of alternating light and dark fur, graced the edge of the hood.

Man's caribou-skin parka and trousers, sewn with sinew, 154 cm, Copper Inuit, early twentieth century. Sometimes a finely fringed hide strip runs on the inside edge of the back waist and tail, or clusters of haired or dehaired caribou hide will dangle in groups of two, three, or four. Similar clusters fall from the shoulder seam. The leg is joined to the upper trouser by a band of dark fur, bordered top and bottom by a narrow strip of white fur from which hang clusters that form a fringe.

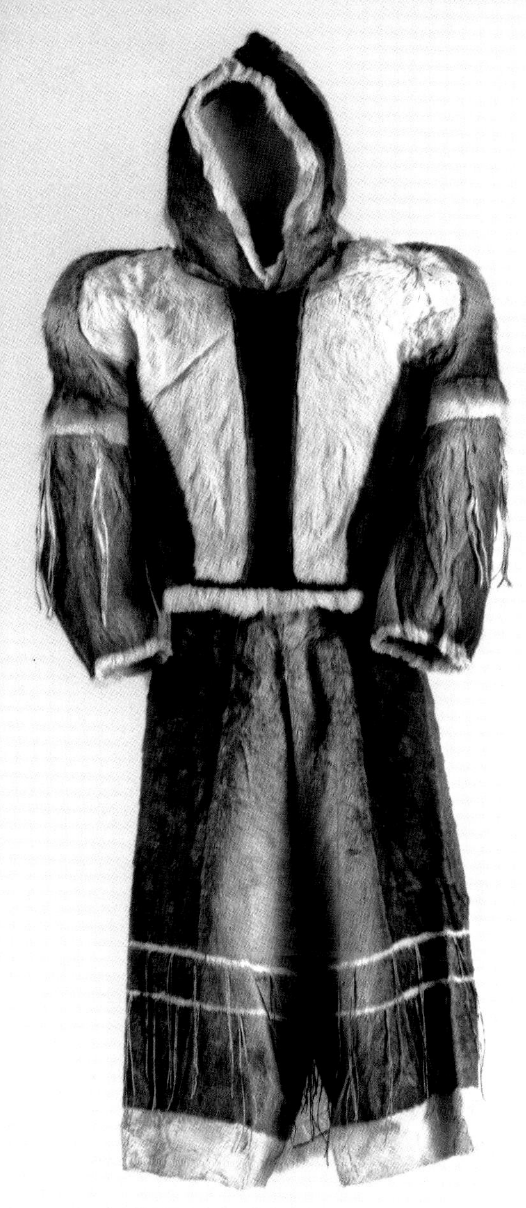

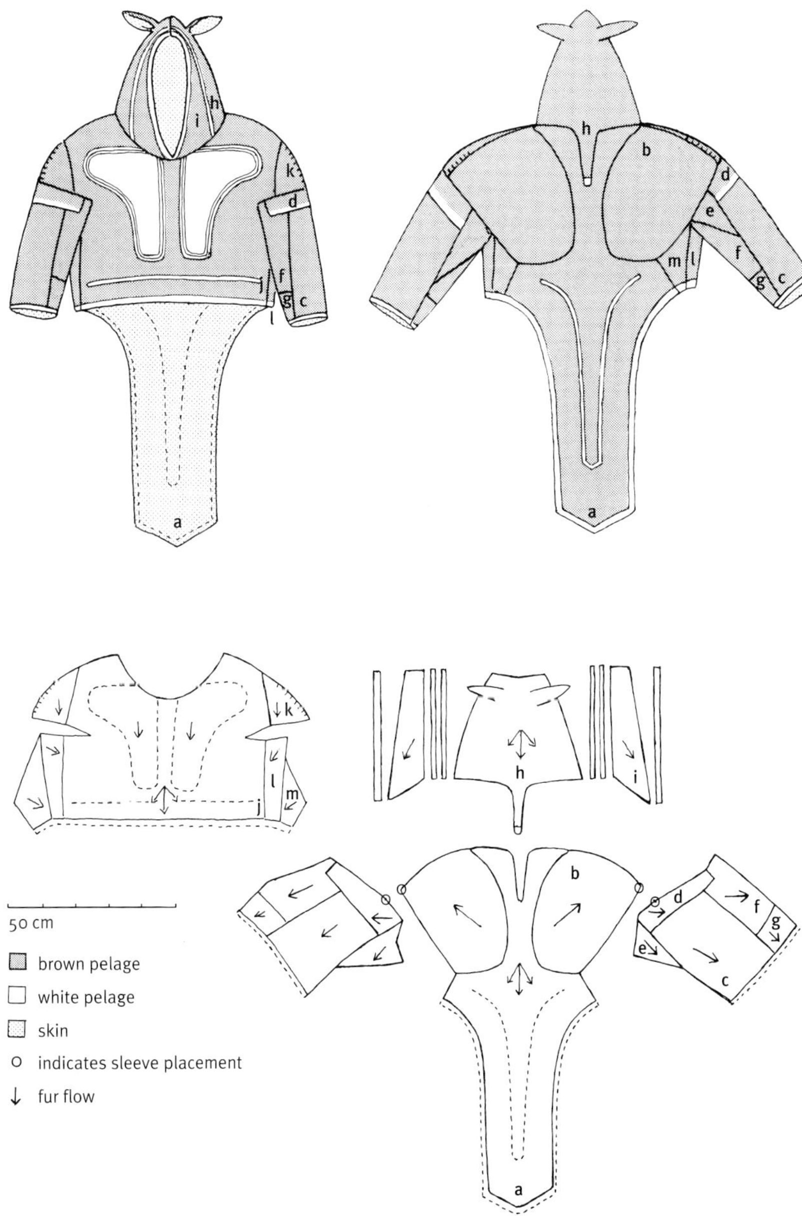

Figure 4.1
Pattern drawing of Copper Inuit man's outer parka. *Drawing by Dorothy K. Burnham.*

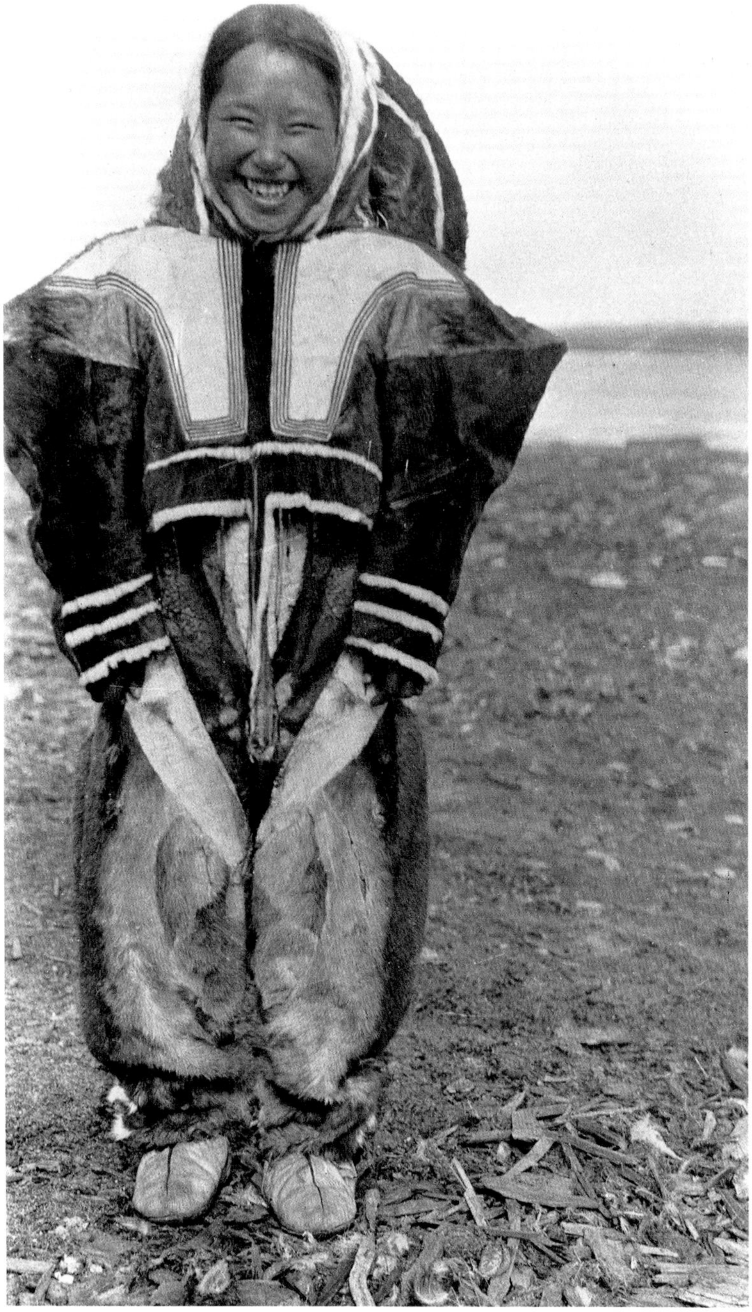

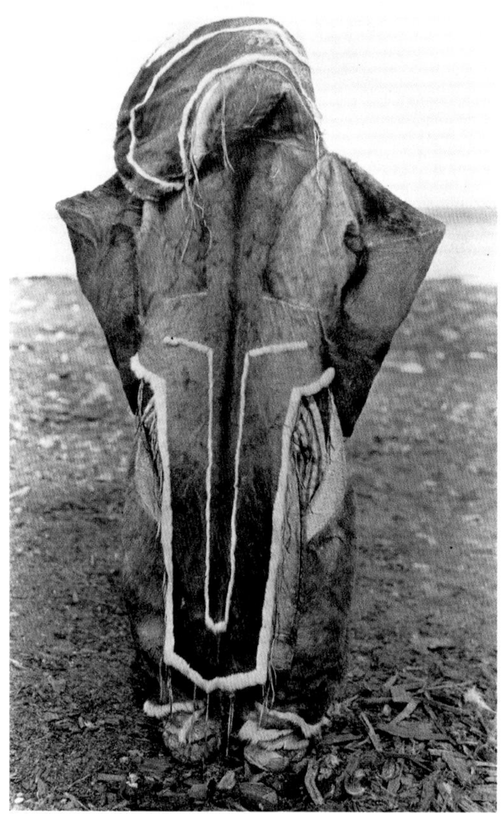

Jennie Kanaiyuk of Nulahugiuq, NWT, photographed here in 1916, was born in 1903 and died in 1931, a victim of tuberculosis. Her parents, Ikpukkuaq and Higilaq, adopted the anthropologist Diamond Jenness as their son, and Jennie acquired her English name through her relation to him. As his younger sister, Jennie made his fur clothes (Vanast 1991, 93). In this photograph she wears shoes over her boots. The inserts over the chest of Copper Inuit parkas were sometimes outlined in strips of red, black, and white bands, as in the amauti worn here.

Figure 4.2
Pattern drawing of Copper Inuit woman's outer parka. *Drawing by Dorothy K. Burnham.*

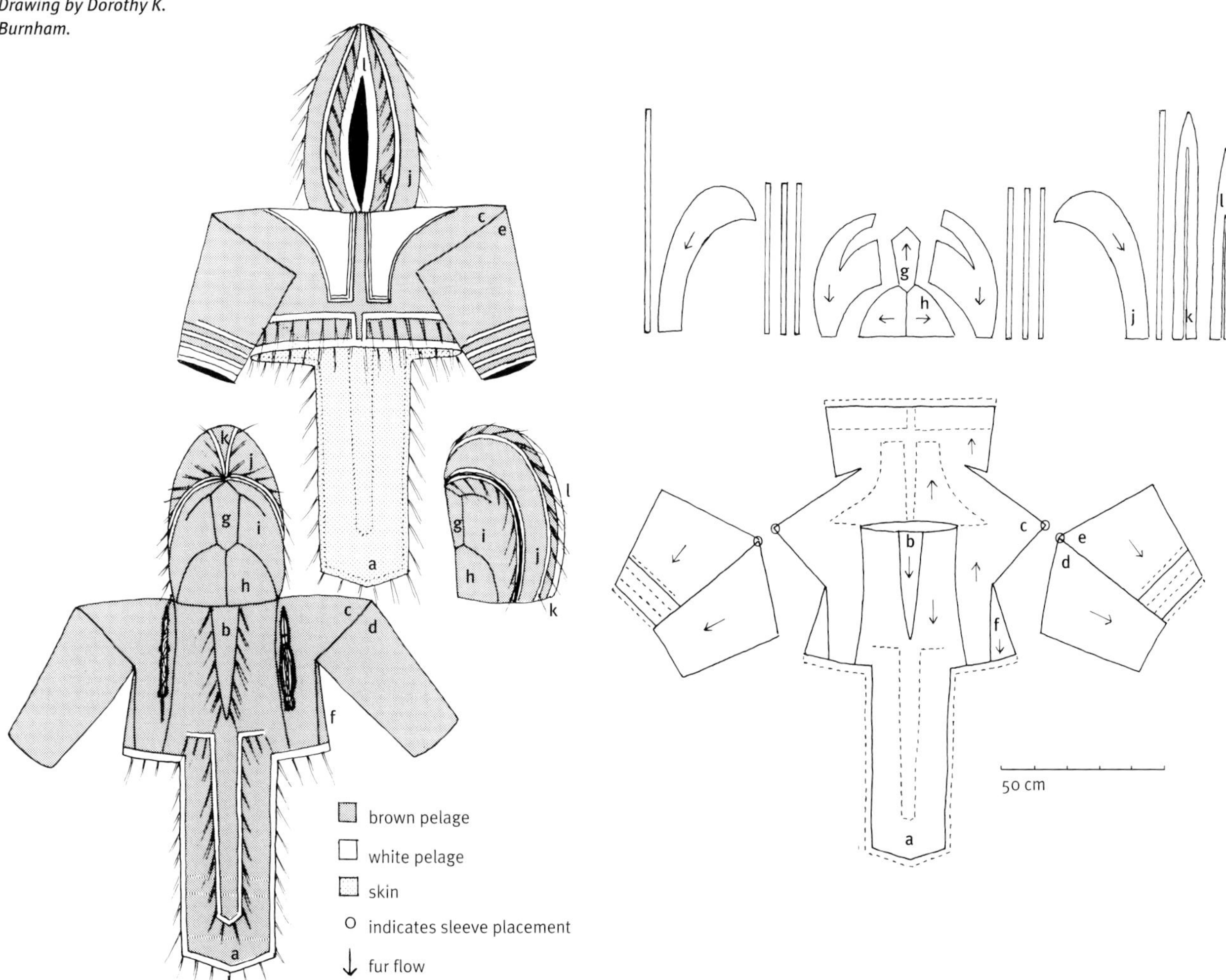

White fur inserts over the chest were, for men, broad and rounded at the shoulder and tapered toward the waist. Sometimes, possibly for workaday parkas, these inserts were close in shape to the narrow 'walrus tusk' hood roots. Some parkas, often those of children, had no chest decoration. The garment was outlined at hood, sleeve, waist, and tail with one or two bands of white fur. The seam joining shoulder and sleeve was inserted with one or two bands of white fur that circled the upper arm, strengthened the attachment of the sleeve to the body, and provided a fringe to which clusters of hide strips were often added.

The woman's amauti differed from the man's parka in some significant aspects. The hood was elongated with a small face opening. The hood back was made of concentric arcs, for shaping. To accommodate a baby, the back of the maturing girl's parka was expanded by inserting an oblong between the shoulders and widening the hood neck. When the woman married and bore children, pieces were added to the back pouch or amaut so that it was large enough to receive her offspring. The shoulder of the Copper Inuit amauti was extremely wide.

Caribou-skin boot, sewn with sinew (left), 52 cm, Copper Inuit, early twentieth century. Caribou-skin boot with lynx trim, sewn with sinew (right), 49 cm, Copper Inuit, early twentieth century. The outer stocking-boot of caribou reached to below the knee and was kept in place by a drawstring of braided sinew threaded through a top casing. Sometimes socks of caribou, duck, or loon were worn inside. Such boots served for travelling and were acceptable in the dance-house.

The sleeve joined the outside edge of the shoulder at approximately a ninety-degree angle, and the sleeve seam connected at an angle of about forty-five degrees. The sleeve had white fur bands at the forearms. The white chest inserts, for women, followed the sharp angles of the sleeve seams.

Men's trousers, worn in two layers in winter, had a high waist, especially important because of the short length of the parka front. Symmetrical pieces inserted at the seat and crotch, some of rump fur, provided fullness. Gores on either side of the leg produced a flared shape. The fur flow of the upper trousers went from top to bottom. The leg proper, joined at mid-thigh to the upper part, had a horizontal fur flow, a feature that reduced friction when the leg was in motion. The leg, which came over the boot top, was made in two styles. In one version, gores on either side of the leg produced a flared shape. This kind of leg could be joined to the upper trouser by a dark band of fur bordered top and bottom by a narrow strip of *pukiq*, white caribou fur, from which hide thongs dangle to form a fringe. The bottom edge of this style had a wide band of pukiq for strength, warmth, and decoration.

The second style was akin to the trousers of the Inuvialuit. At the lower edge of the leg, bands of dyed and natural-coloured skin formed a cuff that hugged the leg. A band of long-haired fur sewn to the cuff formed a fringe that met the boot top. A drawstring of singait went through a dehaired hide casing around the waist to emerge through two holes at the centre back. Copper Inuit men were known to have worn *atartaq*, a combination of trousers with stockings or boots.

Women, too, wore two pairs of trousers in winter, unlike the practice in other Inuit communities, where they wore only one pair. The trouser leg was shorter than that of the men, for the women wore high stockings and boots. The outer trousers of women were decorated, often with contrasting stripes down the outside of each leg and sometimes with a triangular insertion of white fur at mid-front waist, which formed a unified pattern with the inserts on the amauti and the high stockings. Women secured their stockings and boots with a loop and toggle at the top that tucked into the waistband of the trousers.

One kind of caribou boot for men worn with fur to the outside, called kamikpak, was decorated with vertical or horizontal alternating light and dark bands. These boots were worn with an overshoe (Asen Balikci, personal communication 1984).

Women's boots and stockings differed greatly from those of men. Made of caribou, except for the sealskin waterboot, they fitted foot and ankle as usual, then expanded like a funnel rising over the hip to the waist. The boots tapered to form a strap that tucked into the trouser belt. They were pieced at thigh and buttocks for fullness, and in the curved seams that joined these pieces the seamstress sometimes inserted the creamy fur from the animal's rump to form a decorative fringe. The foot was made of leg fur for strength and was sewn on separately at the ankle. Women, like men, wore shoes over their fur boots and stockings.

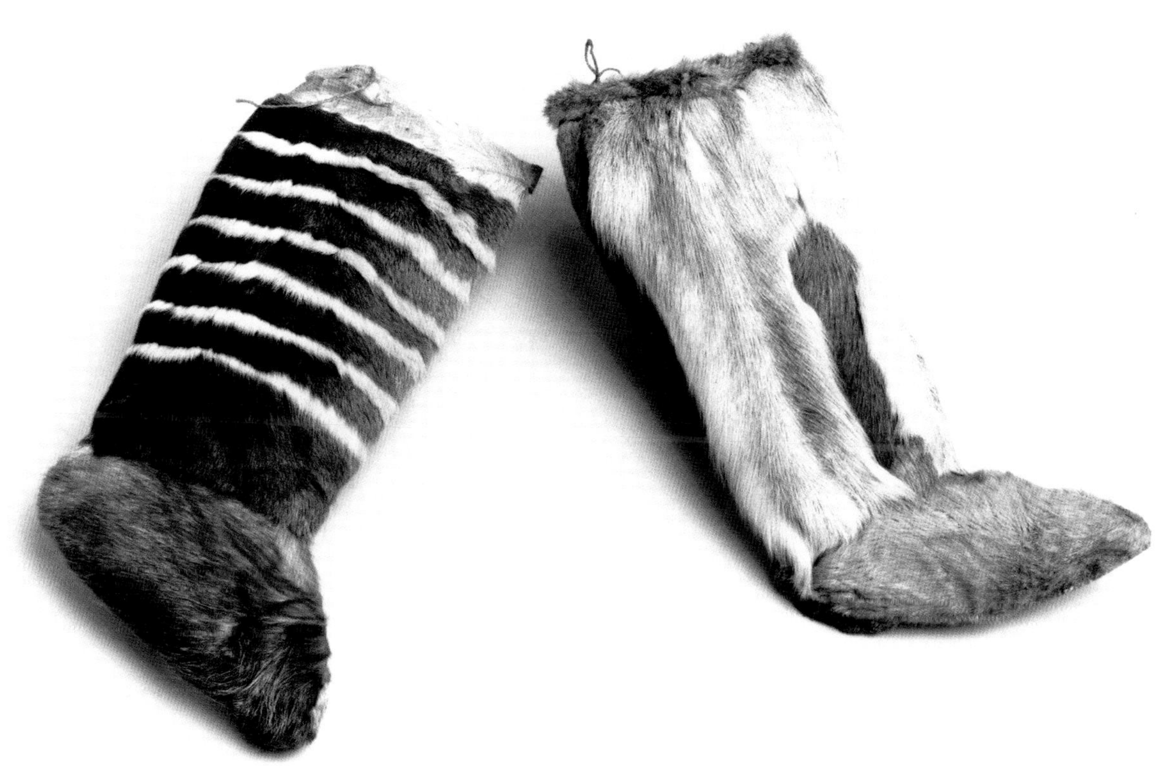

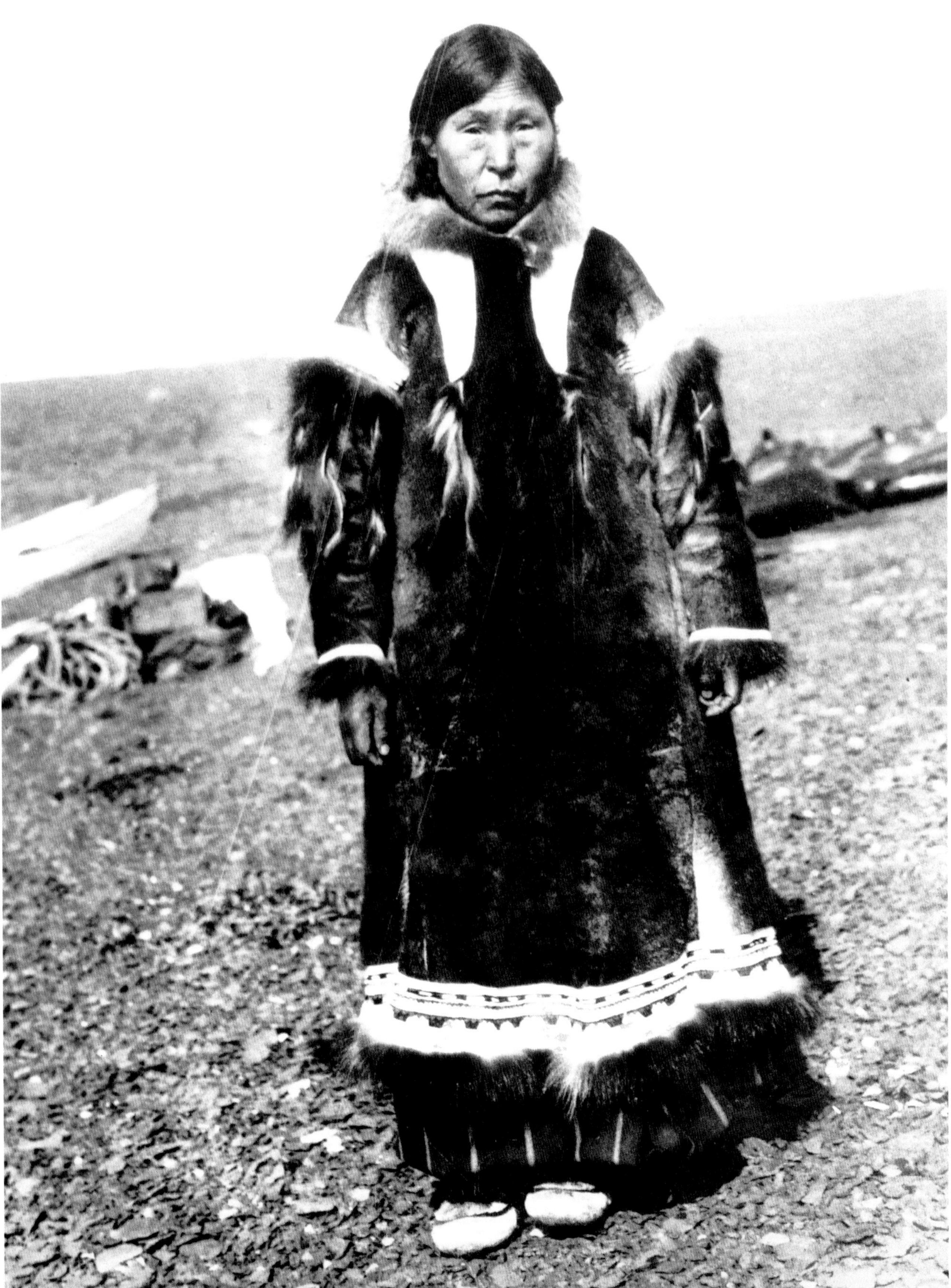

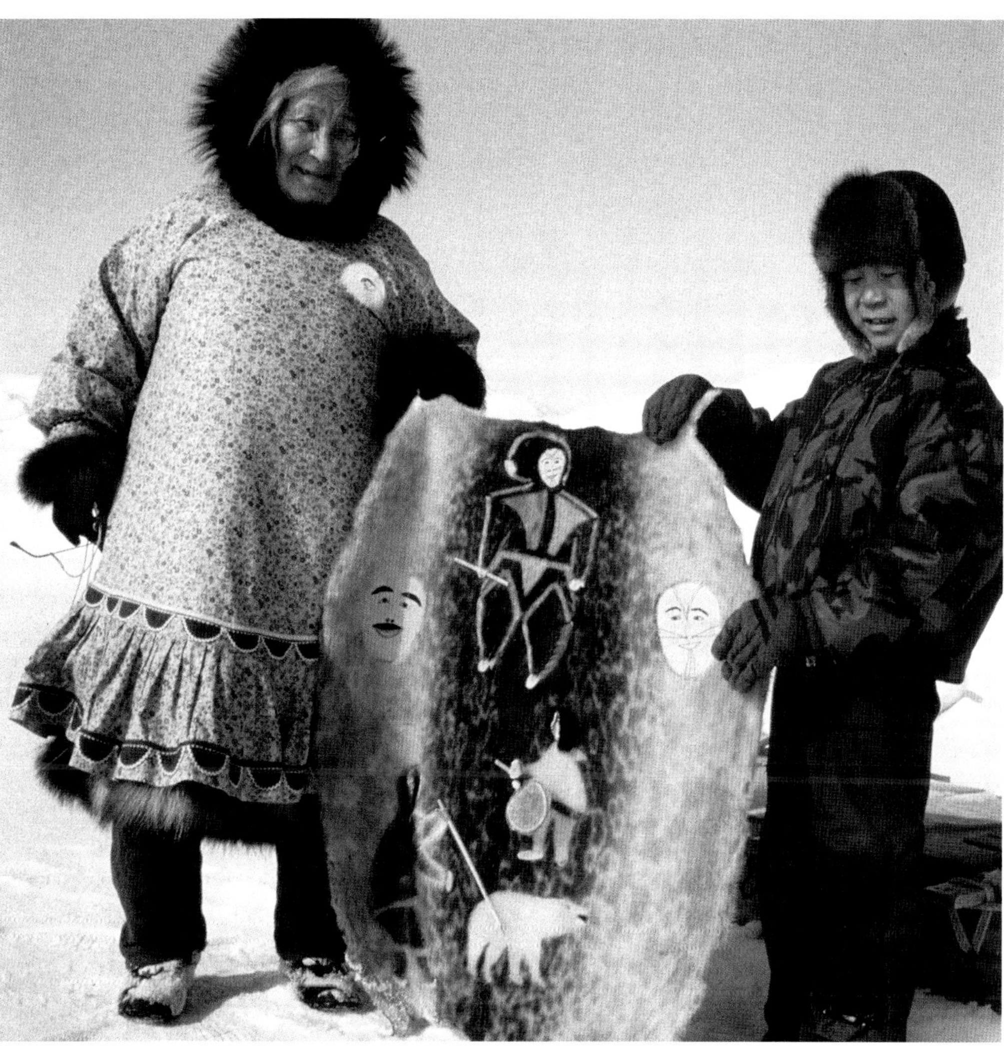

Opposite Mrs. Qimniq Klengenberg's North Alaskan parka contrasts sharply with the traditional Copper Inuit clothing she encountered when she first came to the Coronation Gulf area in 1916. She wears an ankle-length skirt under her parka. Photograph taken ca. 1924.

Right Nellie Hikok of Qurluqtuuq, NWT, 1992, and her grandson hold a sealskin wall hanging. Their clothing combines furs and fabric.

Style Changes

After the whaling industry collapsed in the early part of the twentieth century, Inupiat from Alaska and Inuvialuit from the Mackenzie Delta region migrated to the Coronation Gulf area. The influx resulted in marked changes in the clothing of the Copper Inuit.

An important influence was the family of a Danish born ship's pilot, Christian Jorgensen Klengenberg, and his Inupiaq wife Qimniq (Jones 1996). Qimniq came from Wainwright Inlet, Alaska (Jenness 1922, 241). The family migrated to the Coronation Gulf area in 1916, and their eldest daughter, Etna, taught Copper Inuit seamstresses how to cut and assemble the Mother Hubbard style, common in Alaska, out of fur and fabric (Oakes 1987a, 6-10). The style spread quickly throughout the area, and by at least the 1930s and 1940s was firmly established among the Copper Inuit. The fur parka made in the Mother Hubbard style is now called the *puuq* (Strickler and Alookee 1988, 38, 174-5). It goes below the knee, is roomy, and is cut in an A-line to flare at the bottom. The fabric puuq has a sunburst ruff of fur at the hood and is trimmed with fur at the wrist.

Map 4.3 Netsilingmiut territory

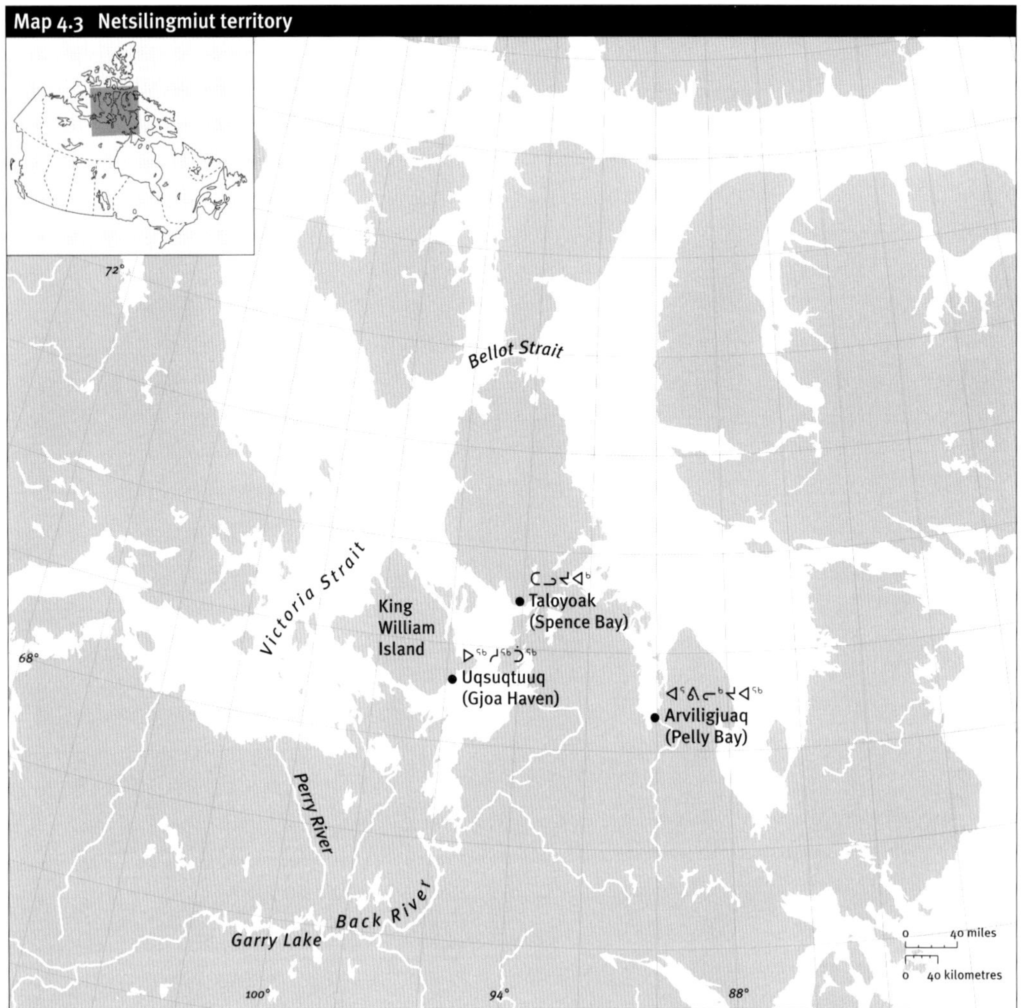

Opposite Ablooshirjuaq and his family lived in Arviligjuaq, NWT, an area in the eastern part of Netsilingmiut territories that abutted on Iglulingmiut lands. Photograph taken in 1926.

The Netsilingmiut

East from the Copper Inuit live the Netsilik Inuit, the People of the Ringed Seal, or Netsilingmiut.[16] Their vast territory of 23,000 square kilometres extends from Victoria Strait in the west to Arviligjuaq in the east, and from Bellot Strait in the north to Garry Lake deep in the western section of Keewatin. Their land is an Arctic desert, and in winter the long-lasting low temperatures cause the sea ice to freeze to a depth of over two metres. Seven small, highly mobile bands used to roam these immense territories, sometimes joining forces for hunting and fishing.[17]

Situated almost at the centre of the Canadian Arctic, the land of the Netsilingmiut is a crossroads of eastern and western cultural exchange among the Inuit (Judy McGrath, personal communication 1983). Studies of the many variations in fur clothing patterns suggest origins in these central areas, where the paths of distribution merge from and radiate out to east and west (Hatt [1914] 1969, 52).

The first non-Inuk of European origin to reach the Netsilingmiut areas was Captain John Ross, whose expedition arrived in the paddle steamer *Victory* in 1829. The Netsilingmiut helped the explorers – hunted with them, supplied food and skins, and taught them how to cross the land by dogsled. In the early twentieth century the Netsilik women sewed clothing for

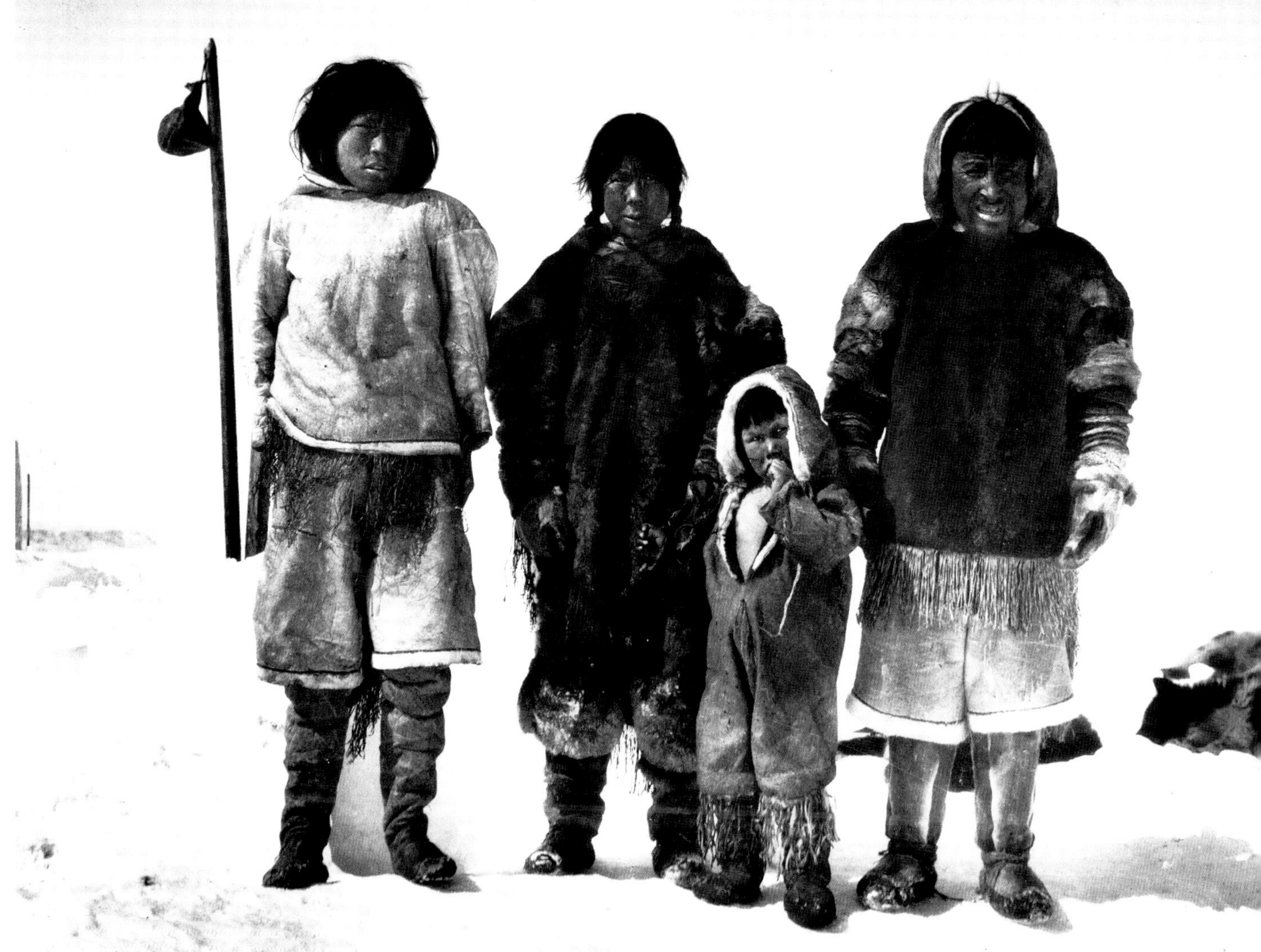

members of Amundsen's Gjoa expedition. Unfortunately, lack of comprehension of the subtleties of the clothing prompted the men to remove the fur trim, which caused the furs to curl at the edges (Amundsen 1908, 1:256). The abandoned ships supplied iron and wood for many years. These materials provided good tools, including sewing implements, and were useful for trade with Copper Inuit neighbours, from whom they obtained copper.

Clothing

In the clothing of the Netsilingmiut gathered in the early twentieth century, stylistic differences are apparent between those who lived in the western part of their territories, close to the Copper Inuit, and those who lived proximate to the Iglulingmiut to the east. In general, however, their caribou clothing is distinguished from that of the Copper Inuit in several ways. The man's parka has a front flap that comes to below the waist or lower. The back flap is long, coming to the knee or lower. Both flaps are broad and curved at the lower edge. The hood is rounded – indeed, some have no top seam – and the face opening is small and forward of the cheeks.

The woman's amauti has a long, broad, rounded back flap, and a front flap that narrows to a rounded V that reaches mid-hip. The woman's amauti hood is high and full. Gussets from the hood extend into the

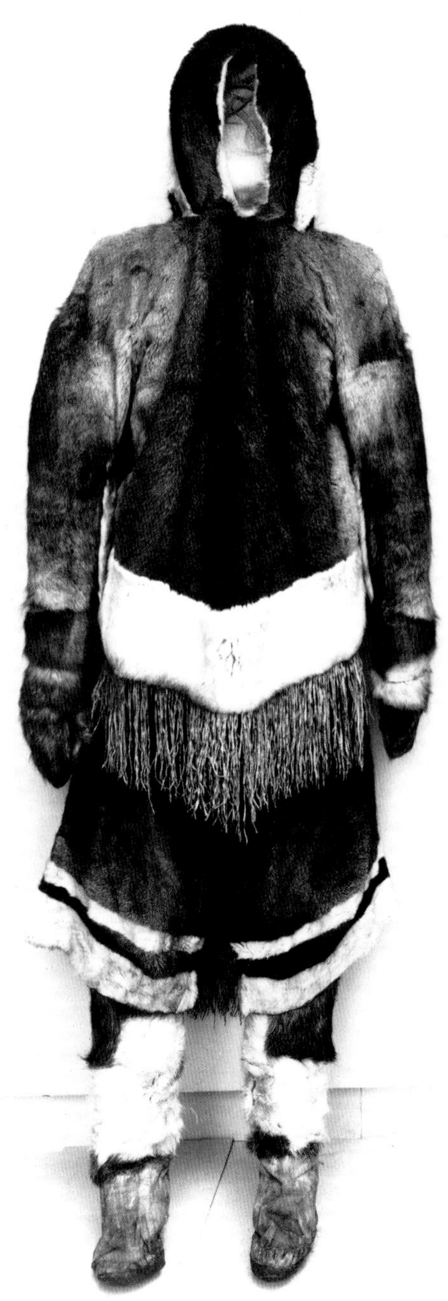

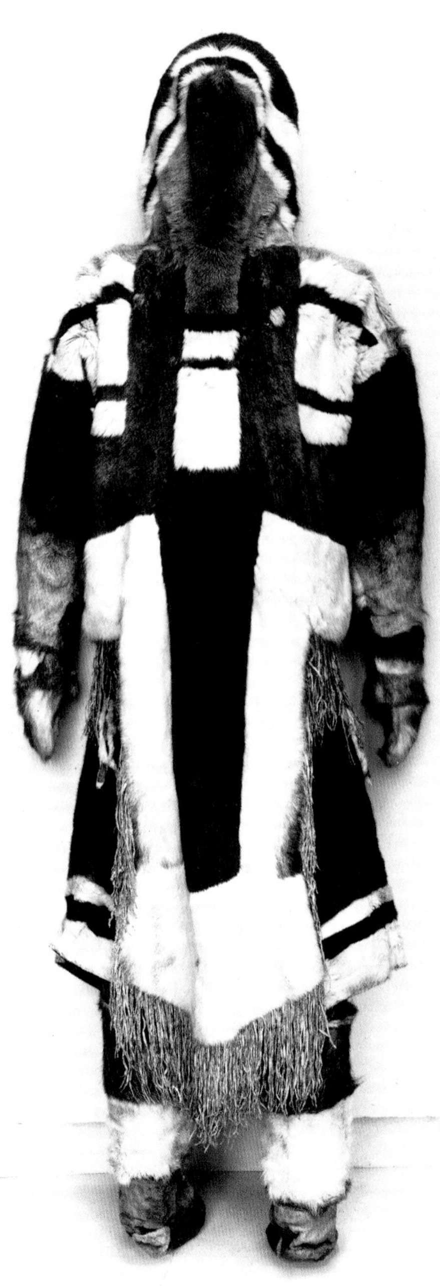

Below Caribou parka (132 cm), caribou trousers (82 cm), skin stockings, hair inward (44 cm), skin shoes, hair outward (23 cm), skin boots, leg with hair outward foot with hair inward (32 cm), Netsilingmiut (Utkuhigjalingmiut), Back River, NWT. Collected by the Fifth Thule Expedition to Canada and Alaska, 1921-4, led by Knud Rasmussen. Caribou mitts, 21 cm, Netsilingmiut (Qiqiqtarmiut of King William Island). Collected by Gotfred Hansen on Roald Amundsen's Gjoa Expedition 1903-6. This costume was collected from Netsilingmiut who lived close to Copper Inuit lands. It is assembled from different subgroups of the Netsilingmiut, using a man's parka and trousers and a woman's footwear.

Opposite Caribou amauti (168 cm), caribou trousers (80 cm), Netsilingmiut (Utkuhigjalingmiut), Back River, NWT; skin stockings (104 cm), skin boots (106 cm), Netsilingmiut (Qiqiqtarmiut), King William Island, NWT. Collected by the Fifth Thule Expedition to Canada and Alaska, 1921-4, led by Knud Rasmussen.

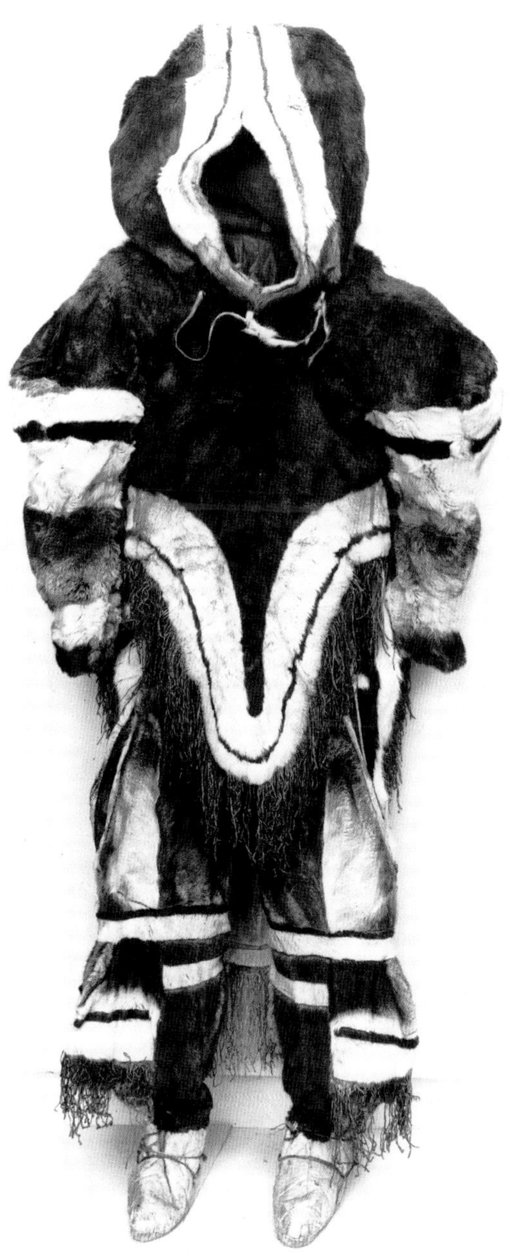

back to anchor the hood and form the baby pouch. The teenage girl's parka, since it has no amaut, is cut close to the body with a less capacious hood and shoulders. The back flap of the unmarried girl's parka is cut straight across at the lower edge (Judy McGrath, personal communication 1983).

The Netsilingmiut use the white fur of caribou extensively to strengthen and embellish their clothing. Broad bands interspaced with narrow dark ones grace the edges of flaps, sleeves, hoods, and trousers. Men's parkas are frequently decorated on the back with evenly spaced white squares across the shoulder blades, where amulets used to hang. A continuous dehaired caribou-skin fringe is placed around the lower edge of the parka, but in some cases the fringe consists of spaced clusters of hide strips.

The front of the man's sealskin parka is made of one skin, as is the back. It is cut evenly across the lower edges and is without flaps or side vents. Sealskin clothing was used in the kayak and in other damp conditions.

Men's trousers can be made of caribou or of seal. Women's trousers, like the parkas, are of caribou. Both men's and women's trousers are long, coming to below the knee to cover the boot top, and are flared. A one-piece set of waterproof trousers and boots made of waterskin – depilated seal skin – and sewn with the waterproof stitch was worn early in the century.

Men's and women's footgear is similar in the main to that of the Copper Inuit. Several caribou-fur boots from King William Island demonstrate an unusual pattern, however, in which the instep and sole are cut from a single piece of skin, thus eliminating a seam at the toe. The upper part of women's boots rose to the waist at the leg front and reached only to the knee at the back, unlike those of the Copper Inuit (Hatt [1914] 1969, 75, 130, Plate 14, Figures 2, 3). Waterproof sealskin boots continue to be used, as they are all over the Arctic. The seal fur is shaved from the pieces that make up the sole, instep, and leg, leaving the outer skin layer intact. The seams are sewn with waterproof stitches.

Because Taloyoak is a crossroads for Nunatsiarmiut, Caribou Inuit, Iglulingmiut, Copper Inuit, and Inuvialuit, many streams have influenced Netsilingmiut styles. Copper Inuit styles, which had absorbed patterns from Alaska and the Inuvialuit, inspired the Netsilingmiut use of a very full ruff and the Mother Hubbard style in fur and fabric. The straight lower edge for the amauti may have been inspired by styles from the Copper Inuit, although this kind of pattern was produced throughout the Arctic with contact. The back flap of some amautiit took on the appearance of those of the Nunatsiarmiut.

As in the past, men's parkas nowadays can be decorated on the back with evenly spaced white square inserts across the shoulder blades. Women's dressy caribou-fur Mother Hubbards can be decorated across the back with weasel tails. Some women's hoods have become voluminous and curve up to a peak at the back that ends in a small knob, reminiscent of the caribou's nose.

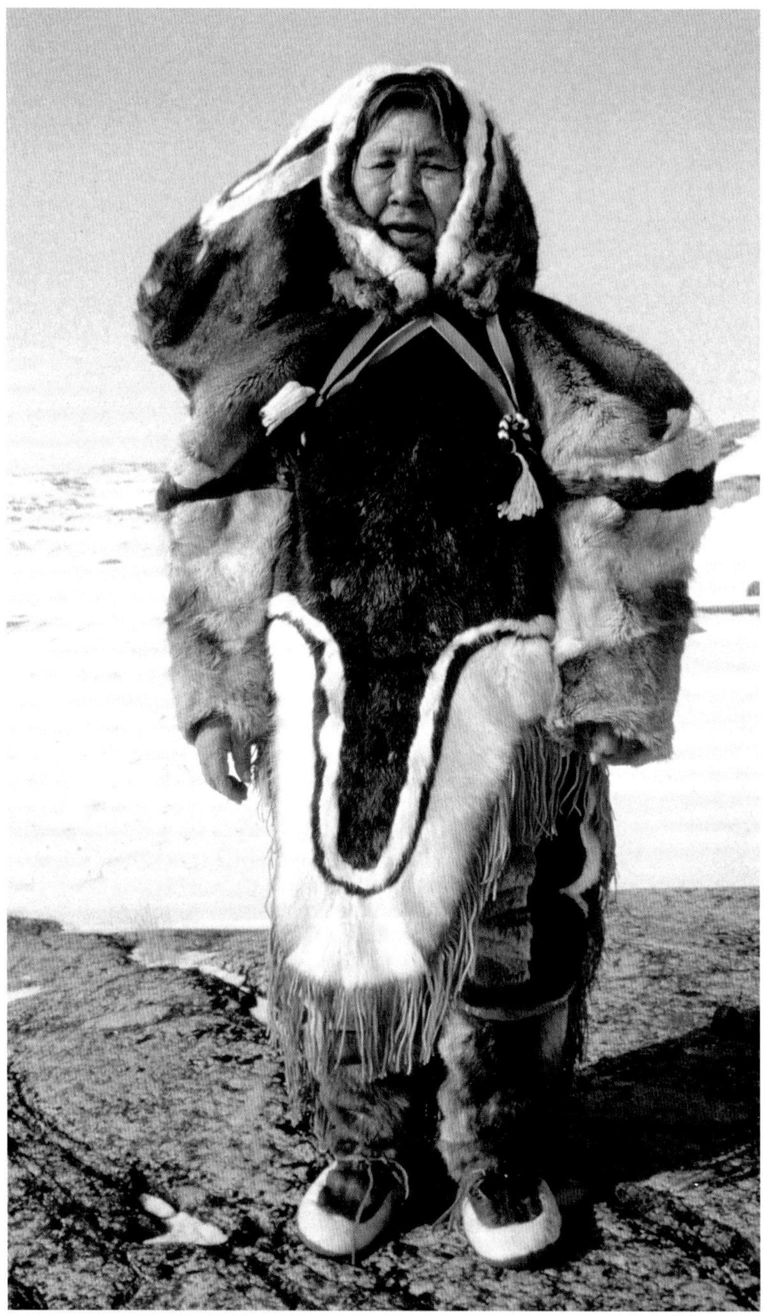

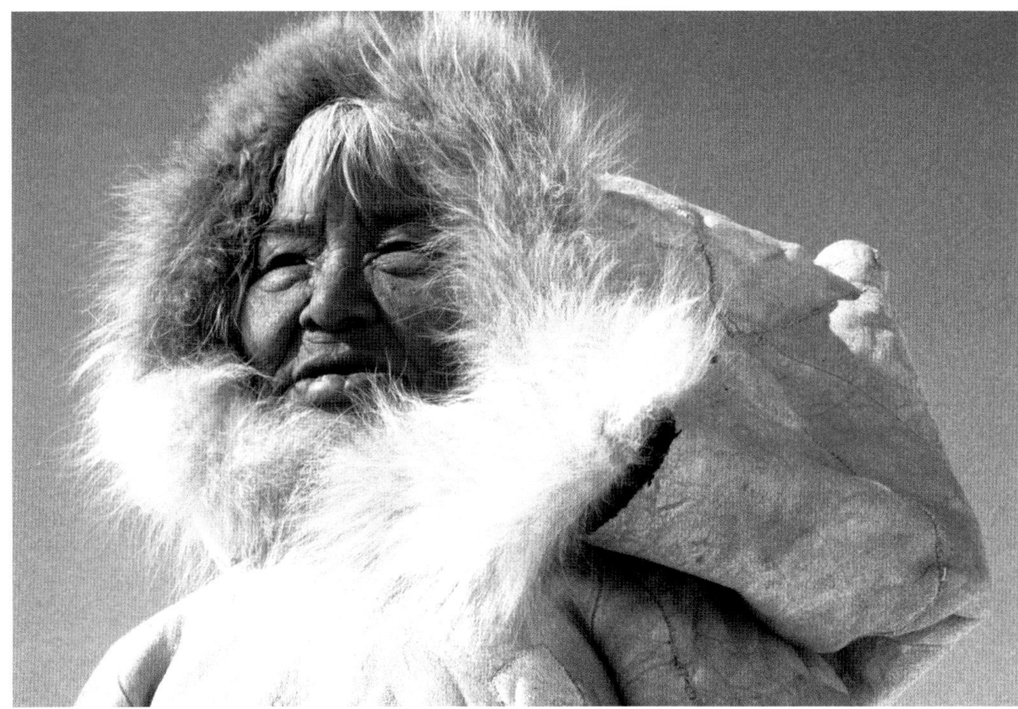

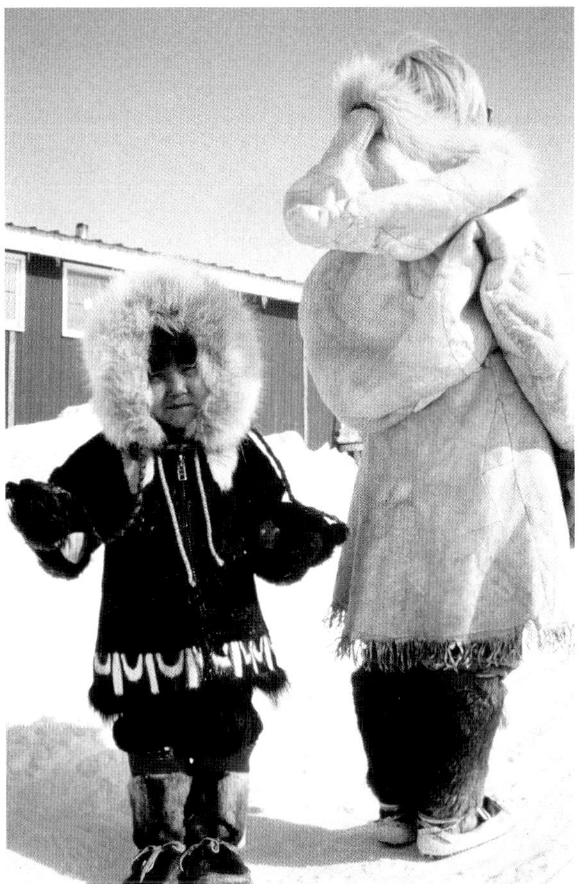

Opposite The caribou-skin amauti worn by Agnes Iqqugaqtuq of Arviligjuaq, NWT, 1992, displays the traditional toggles attached at the armpits that help counterbalance the weight of the child in the amaut.

Above The caribou skin amauti of Eva Teeltuq of Uqsuqtuuq, NWT, 1992, features the traditional deep hood and the more modern long-haired ruff.

Below Sandra Hummiktuq (left), 1992, wears a dress parka with a long-haired ruff, contrasting hood roots, and a fur mosaic at the base. A cord of braided wool is fastened to her mitts to prevent their loss. Eva Teeltuq (right) wears an even-edged caribou-skin amauti. Both are from Uqsuqtuuq, NWT.

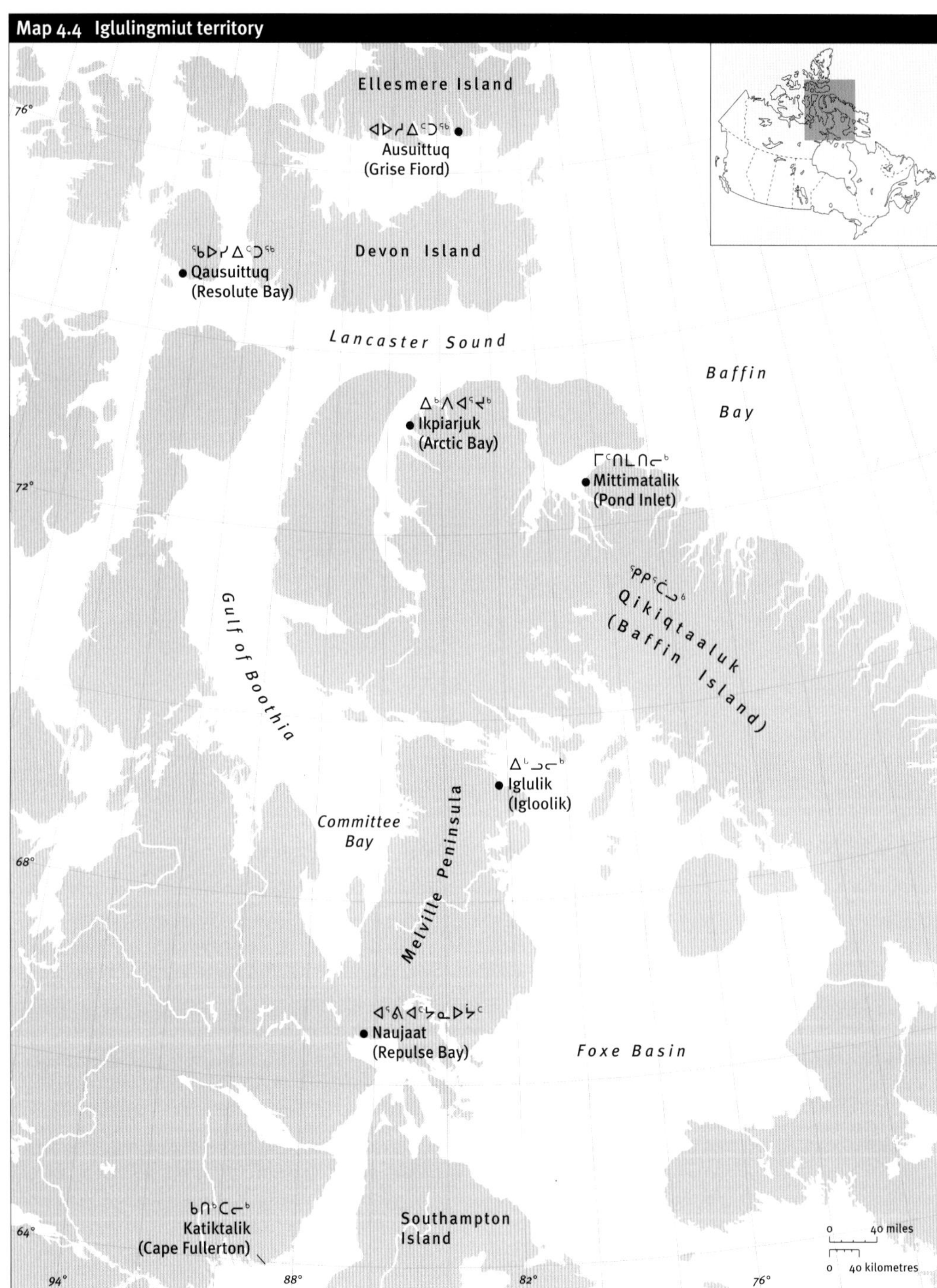

Map 4.4 Iglulingmiut territory

The Iglulingmiut

Although they take their name from the town of Iglulik, which is at the centre of their territory, the Iglulingmiut include numbers of subgroups that dwell in the vast areas of Devon Island and northwestern Baffin Island, south over the Melville Peninsula to Katiktalik at the northwestern reaches of Hudson Bay, and from Committee Bay in the west to Foxe Basin in the east.[18] North of Devon Island lies Ellesmere Island where, at Smith Sound, Canada is separated from Kalaallit Nunaat by only forty-eight kilometres of water.

These lands have provided rich archaeological data that have helped us trace human occupations that go back over the millennia. The area around Ikpiarjuk shows an occupancy by nomadic hunters from the west some 4,500 years ago. Pre-Dorset culture bearers came to Ausuittuq and the more northern parts of Ellesmere Island, and to the Iglulik area. Dorset and Thule sites and legends are known to present-day inhabitants. Elisapee Kanangnaq Ahlooloo of Kangiqlugaapik describes the area at the back of the house where she lived as a child (Innuksuk and Cowan 1976, 33):

Behind us were very old sod houses, built by our ancestors [known as Tuniit], where the women of our family used to go to look for artifacts. They found a lot of old things buried in the old campsites ... quliit *[lamps] and old soapstone pots, a sewn skin bag containing old robes ... and a pair of old boots ... Their needles were made from the leg bones of caribou ... Pieces of skin were used as thimbles.*

The Iglulingmiut territories are known for their riches of land and sea. Iglulik and the area of Naujaat is close to the largest walrus herd in the Arctic. Several kinds of seal are abundant, as are whale, polar bear, caribou, musk-oxen, and marine birds.

Clothing

Iglulingmiut clothing shows considerable variety in patterns and trim based on region, age, sex, and season.[19] Characteristic of outer caribou-skin attire for women and men is the use of contrasting white and dark fur on hood and sleeves as trim and on the back, where they may become a mosaic. Broad white bands border back and front flaps. There are continuous fringes of caribou-hide strips around the broad flaps.

The men wear different styles of parka: the back of one from Iglulik will be made of a single skin; another, typical of Naujaat, will have a black and white mosaic on the back. Adult men wear parkas with square front and back flaps coming to mid-hip. Some male adults and teenagers wear a different parka model. The front flap is cut high and rounded and the rear flap is elongated and square. There used to be a variety in the placement of the slits at the base of the coat: some mid-front, sides, or even three in the back. Now men's parkas have openings only at the sides. Some hoods of men's parkas have a single, oblong hood root at the back. The hood is pointed and fitted to the head.

Women's clothing, too, exhibits different styles according to the locality and the age of the wearer. The amauti of a mother from Iglulik has the characteristic wide shoulders, elongated hood, bulging sleeves, slightly tapered, long, rounded back flap, shorter tapering front flap, and expandable amaut. The amautiit of women from Mittimatalik have wide, pointed, tapered hoods, and some have long, rounded flaps, while others have even bases. The evenly based amauti, called an angijurtaujaq, represented a change from the traditional amauti pattern. It first appeared in whaling

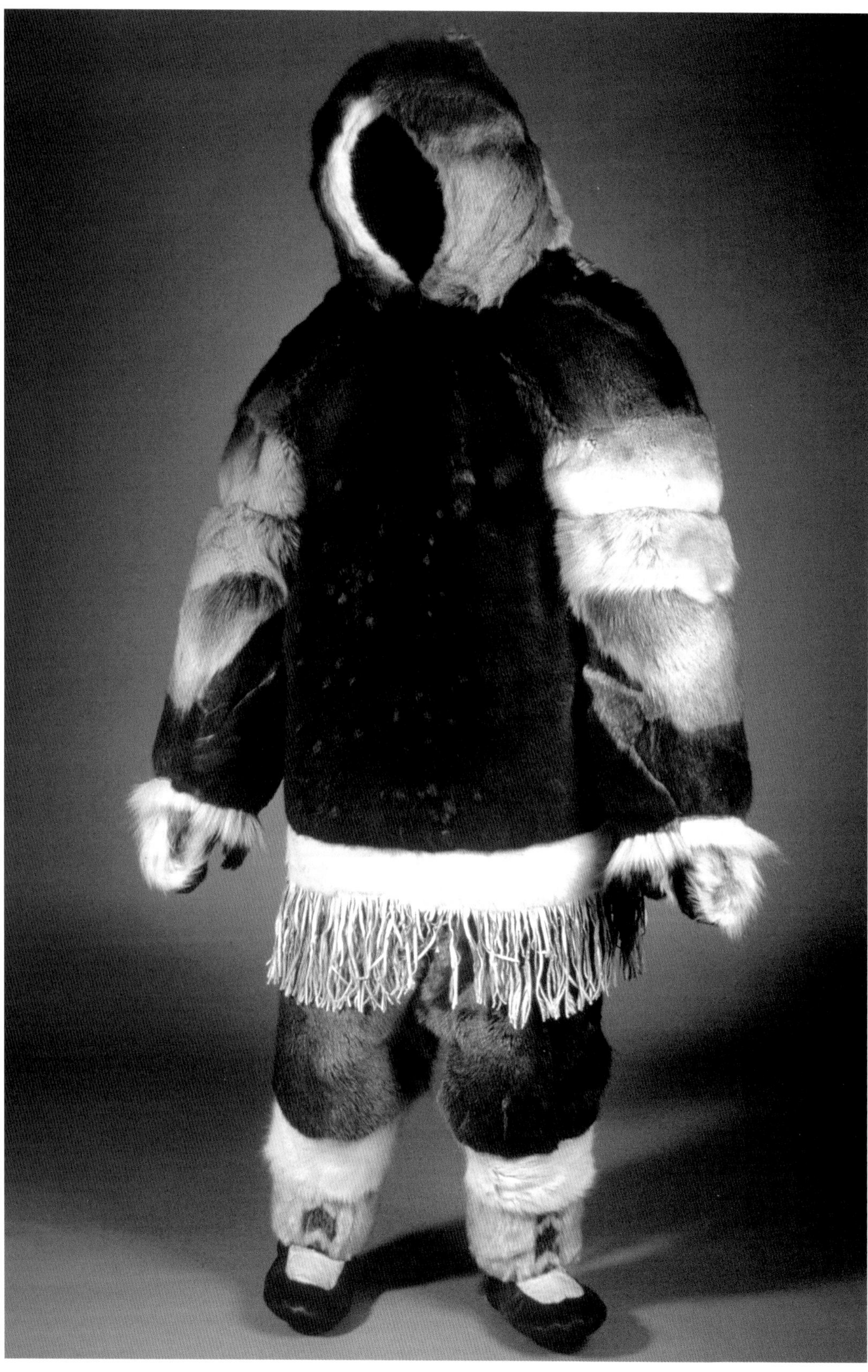

Opposite Man's caribou-skin parka, trousers, mitts, Iglulingmiut, 1986. Artisan: Leonnie Qrunnut of Iglulik, NWT. The costume was made for the exhibition 'Living Arctic' at the Museum of Mankind, British Museum. Man's caribou-skin and seal-skin boots, Iglulingmiut, 1986.

Right Caribou-skin and seal-skin amauti, trousers, mitts, boots, Iglulingmiut, 1986. Artisan: Sipora Piunngittuq Inuksuk of Iglulik, NWT.

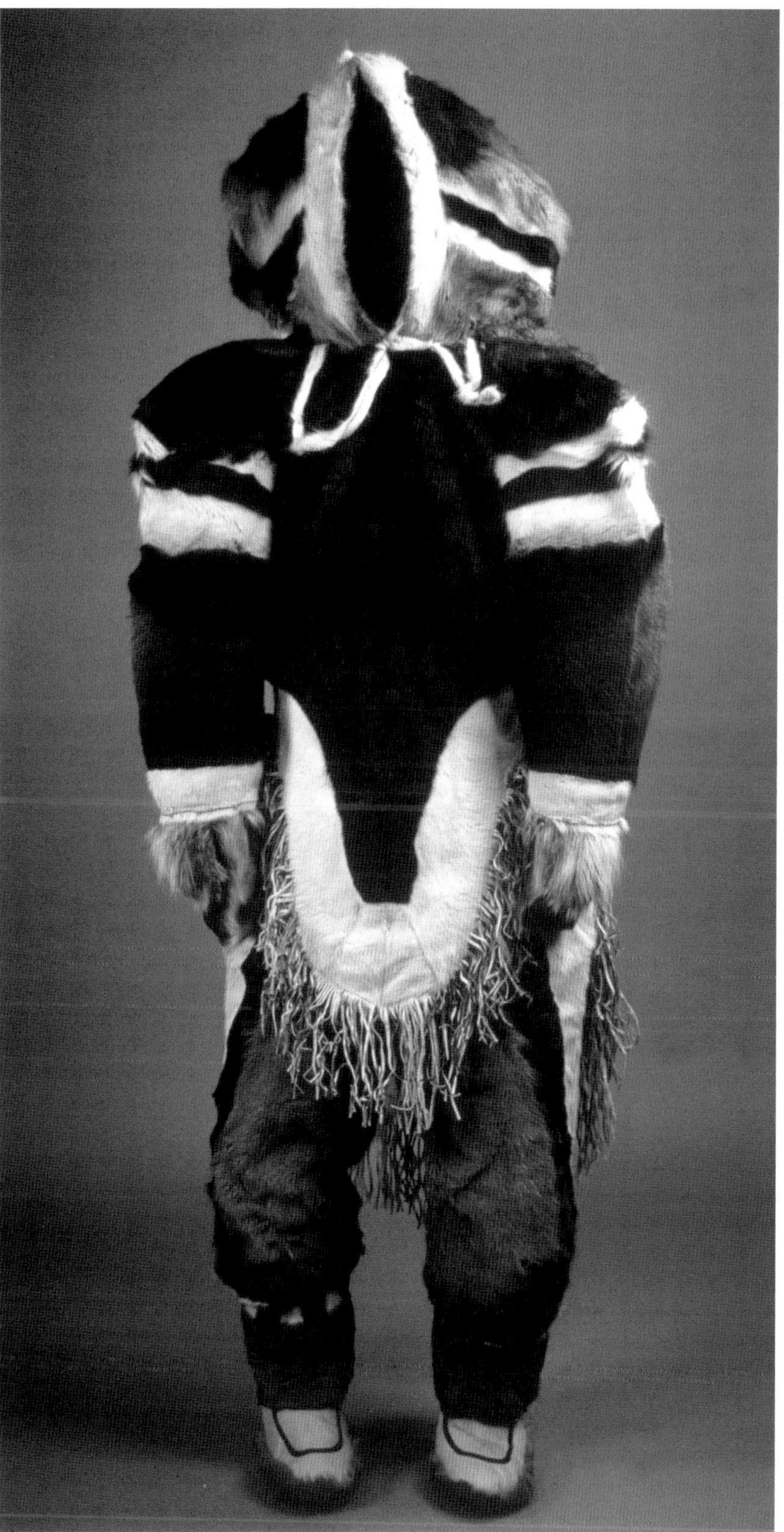

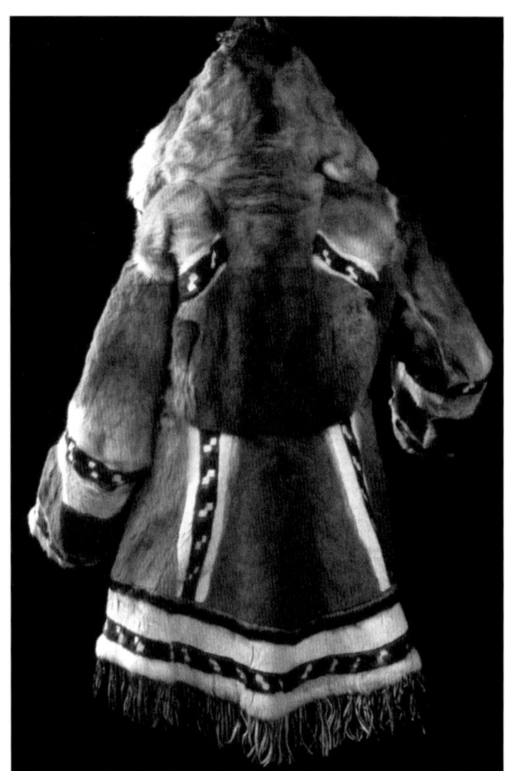

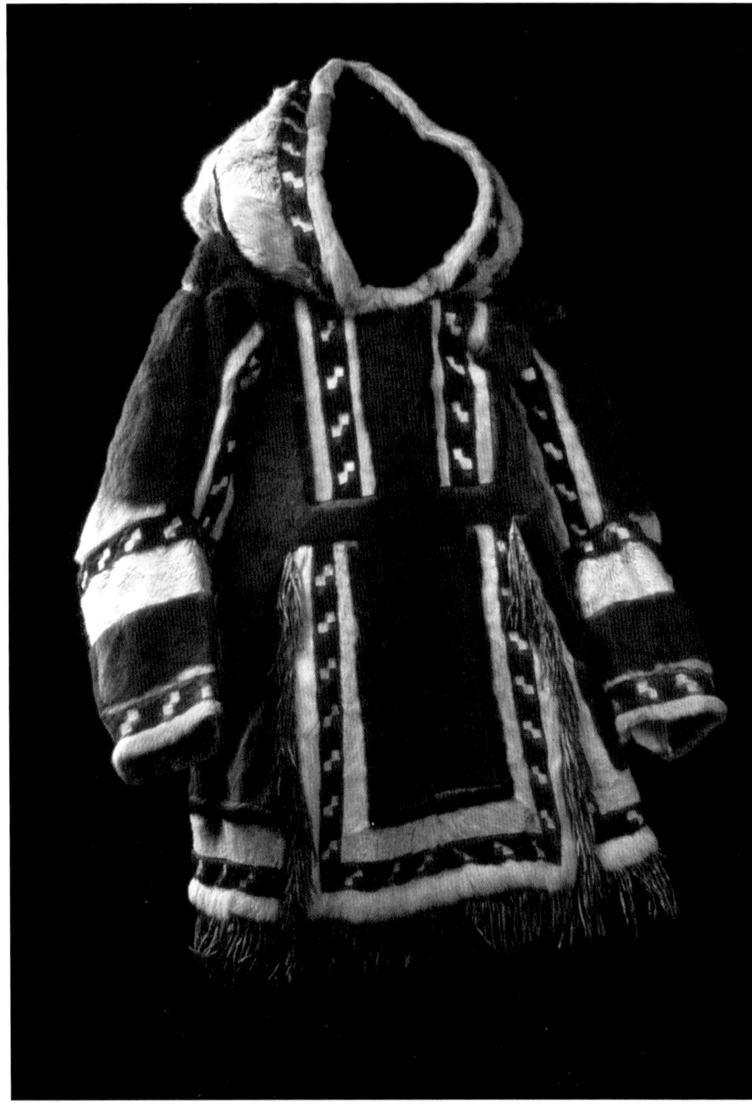

Left and above Caribou-skin amauti, sewn with sinew, 76 cm (excluding hood), Iglulingmiut, late 1920s. Collected probably at Mittimatalik, NWT, by Hugh Margetts. This coat is a fine example of a seamstress's artistry. The back of the softly peaked, ruffed hood has the animal's ears left at the top. The parka is decorated by a magnificent fur mosaic.

Opposite Three Inuit women from Ikpiarjuk wear amautiit, 1987. Two of the costumes are made of caribou fur, one of duffle.

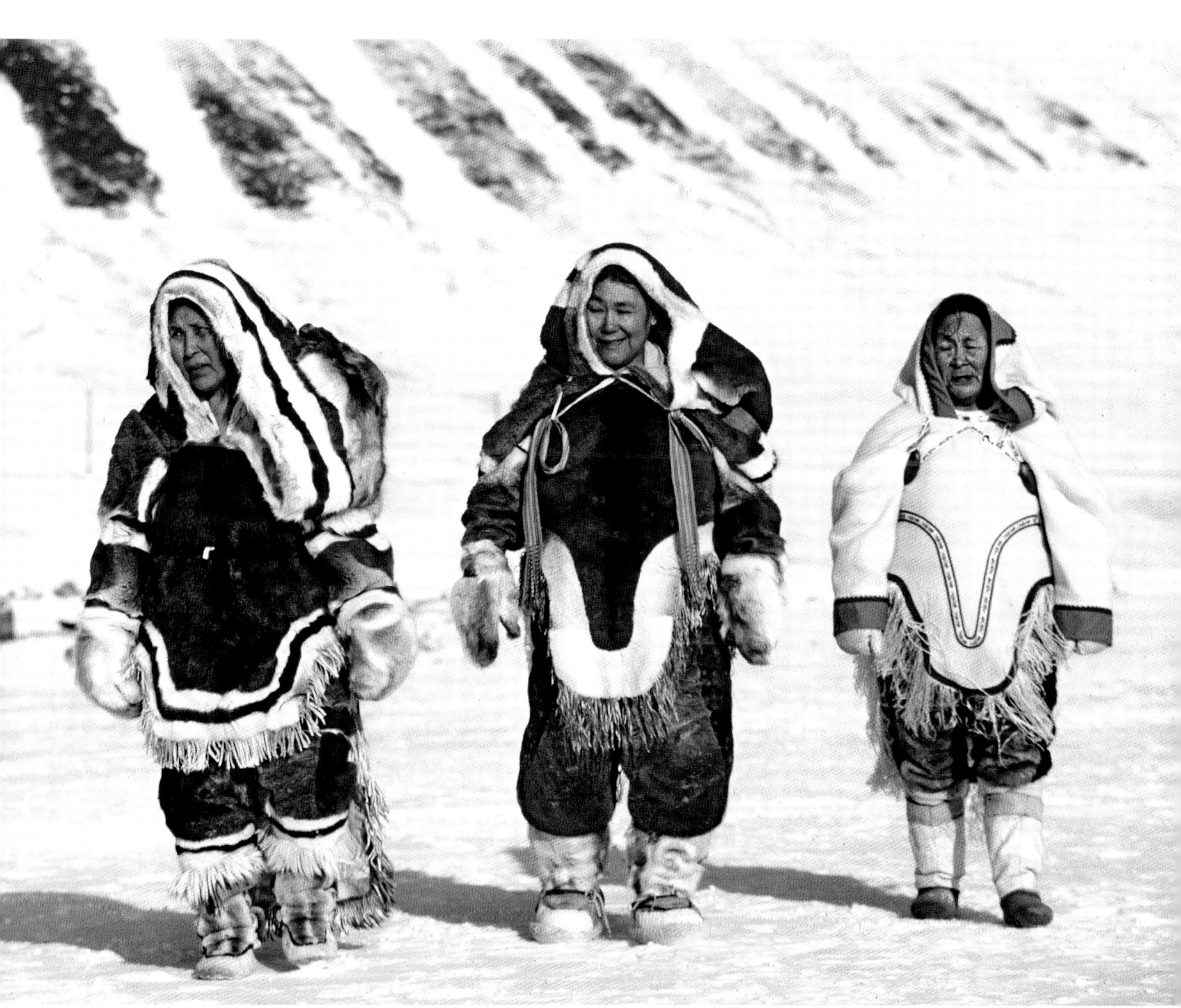

centres on Baffin Island in the late nineteenth century (Driscoll 1983, 147). The amautiit of the woman past child-bearing age and of the young unmarried girl usually have no back pouch and have all the characteristics of the adult female one, except they are less pronounced. The hood of young girls' parkas in most areas is small and round. The flaps are also small and often artfully decorated. The very small girl, like the boy, wears an atajuq, a one-piece suit of caribou in two layers with an opening in the seat.

Beadwork sometimes decorated the outside of men's and women's warm-weather caribou clothing, worn with the skin or smooth side on the outside. The woman's amauti was often elaborately ornamented, although some had only a simple edging on the sleeves and hood.

Men's and women's trousers are long and cut close to the leg. They do not exhibit the flared style of their neighbours.

Iglulingmiut women, in earlier days, wore an unusual boot with side pouches, although this style was not exclusive to them. The legging part of the outer boot was made of caribou skin and had fur to the outside, the boot part had fur to the inside, and the sole had fur to the outside. Between the knee and the ankle was a pouch or sack-shaped extension called a quajjuk, which extended out to the side. A warmer weather boot had fur to the inside, while the outside could be decorated. A woman would carry small articles in the quajjuk or pull her feet up into them to keep them warm while seated.

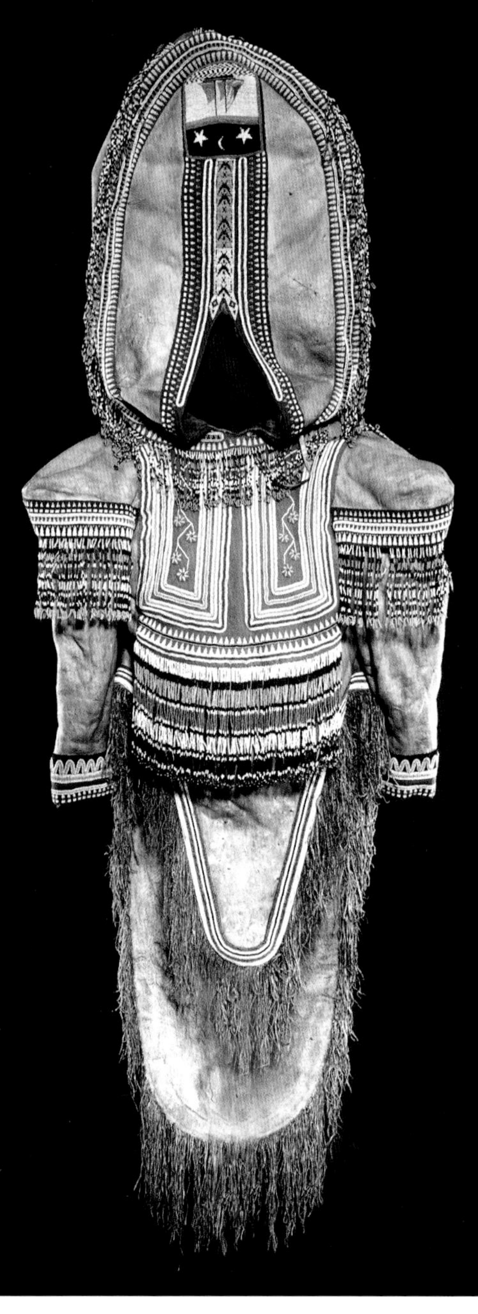

Amauti of caribou skin, beads, brass pellets, sewn with sinew, 188.5 cm, Iglulingmiut, ca. 1913. Collected at Naujaat, NWT, by Captain George Comer. The beadwork on inner amautiit outlines the face and hood, shoulders, flaps, and sleeve edge. Deep beaded fringes fall from around the hood, the shoulder bands, the chest panels, and the symbols on the back. For the history and analysis of the bead work of this amauti, see Driscoll 1984.

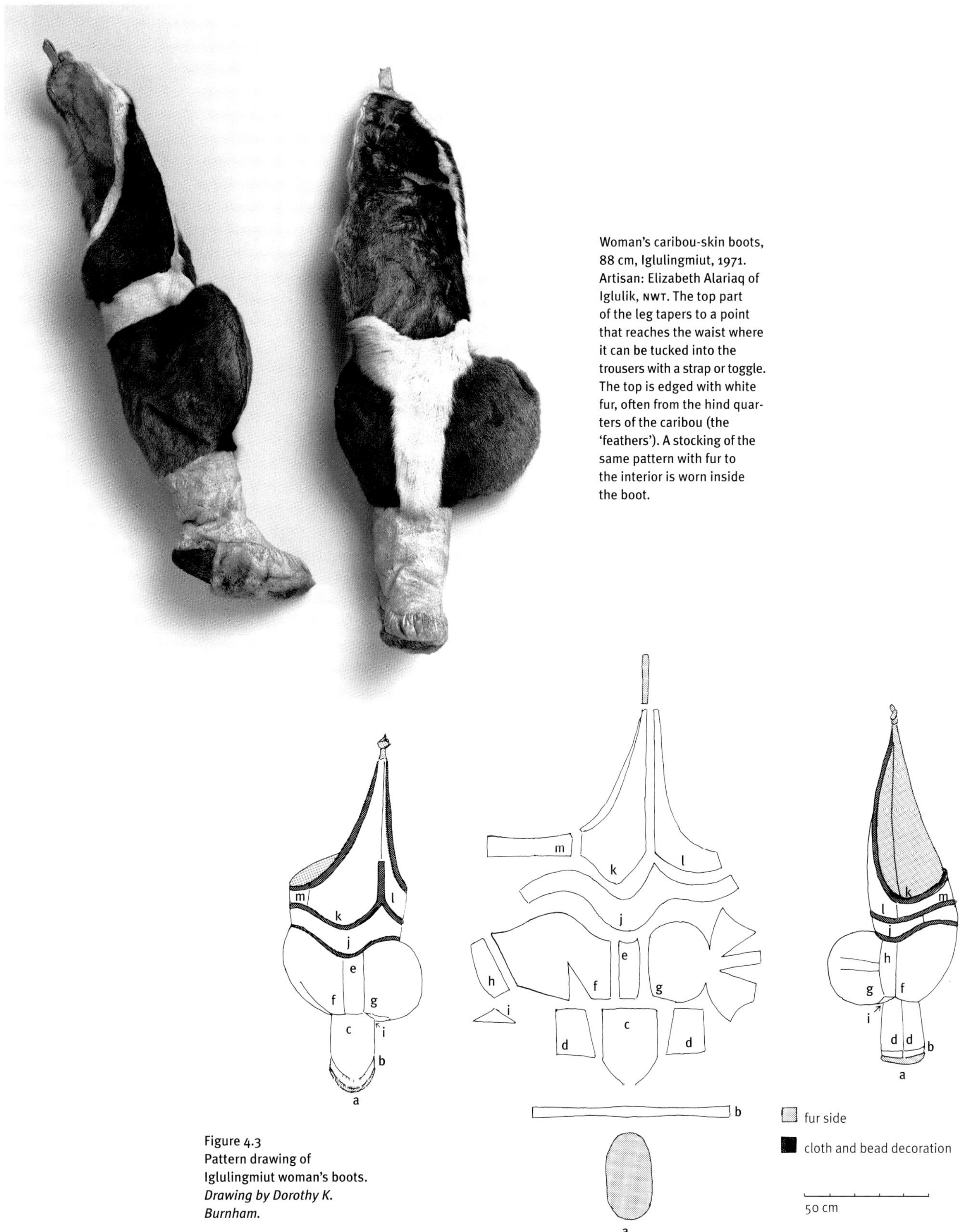

Woman's caribou-skin boots, 88 cm, Iglulingmiut, 1971. Artisan: Elizabeth Alariaq of Iglulik, NWT. The top part of the leg tapers to a point that reaches the waist where it can be tucked into the trousers with a strap or toggle. The top is edged with white fur, often from the hind quarters of the caribou (the 'feathers'). A stocking of the same pattern with fur to the interior is worn inside the boot.

Figure 4.3
Pattern drawing of Iglulingmiut woman's boots. *Drawing by Dorothy K. Burnham.*

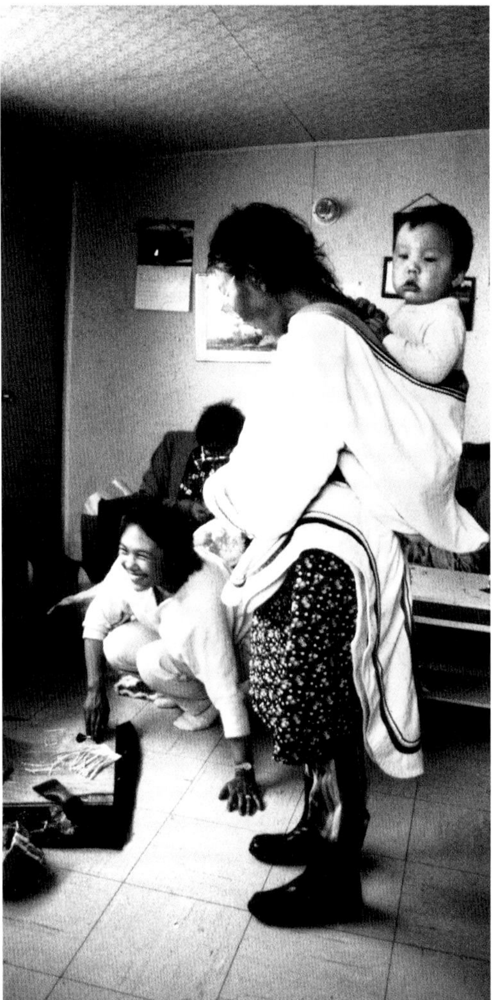

Left Rachel Kalliraq of Iglulik, NWT, 1986, with her grandson Shannon in her amaut, stands after making a skin fringe on her board.

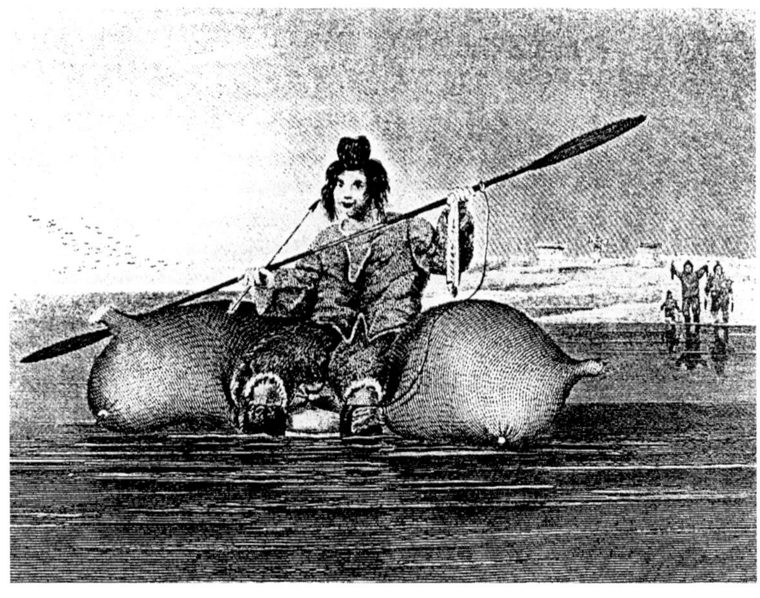

Below Engraving by Edward Finden of a drawing by G.F. Lyon (Lyon 1824, 54). In 1824 George Lyon, captain of HMS *Griper*, and his crew encountered Sallirmiut of Southampton Island. Neeakoodloo, who paddled out to the ship to greet them, wore a fur parka and trousers. The three inflated sealskins on which he sat were held together by sea mammal intestines, also inflated for buoyancy. Captain Lyon obtained from the Sallirmiut a very large sail made of gutskin strips. In return he gave them a knife.

Today, with more clothing made of natural and synthetic fibres, traditional styles exist alongside the modern, even-edged parkas. Many women sew amautiit that feature front and back flaps, decorated with braid and tape that replaces fur designs.

The Sallirmiut

Southampton Island and nearby Coats Island and Walrus Island were the home of the Sallirmiut, who no longer exist.[20] Their extinction, save for five individuals, came about possibly as a result of an undetermined disease brought by a crew member of the Scottish whaling ship *Active* in about 1902, when their number was estimated at fifty-eight (Mathiassen 1927, Part 1, 284). The last survivor died in 1948.

Several Inuit groups have sagas about the Tuniit, or Turnit, who inhabited the country before them. The legends say that the Tuniit lived in permanent winter houses and hunted whale and walrus. The men wore bearskin trousers and the women had long boots. Some Aivilingmiut, a branch of the Iglulingmiut, say that the Sallirmiut were the remaining Tuniit. The legends are substantiated by non-Inuit records noting that some artifacts used by the Sallirmiut are similar to those in assemblages from the Thule culture (Mathiassen 1927, Part 1, 285ff).

In 1955 and 1959, archaeologists examined the skeletons of forty-one males and fifty females recovered from Tunirmiut, one of the sites of the epidemic (Merbs 1983). The osteoarthritic patterning in the bones of the females correlates with activities in skin

Map 4.5 Sallirmiut territory

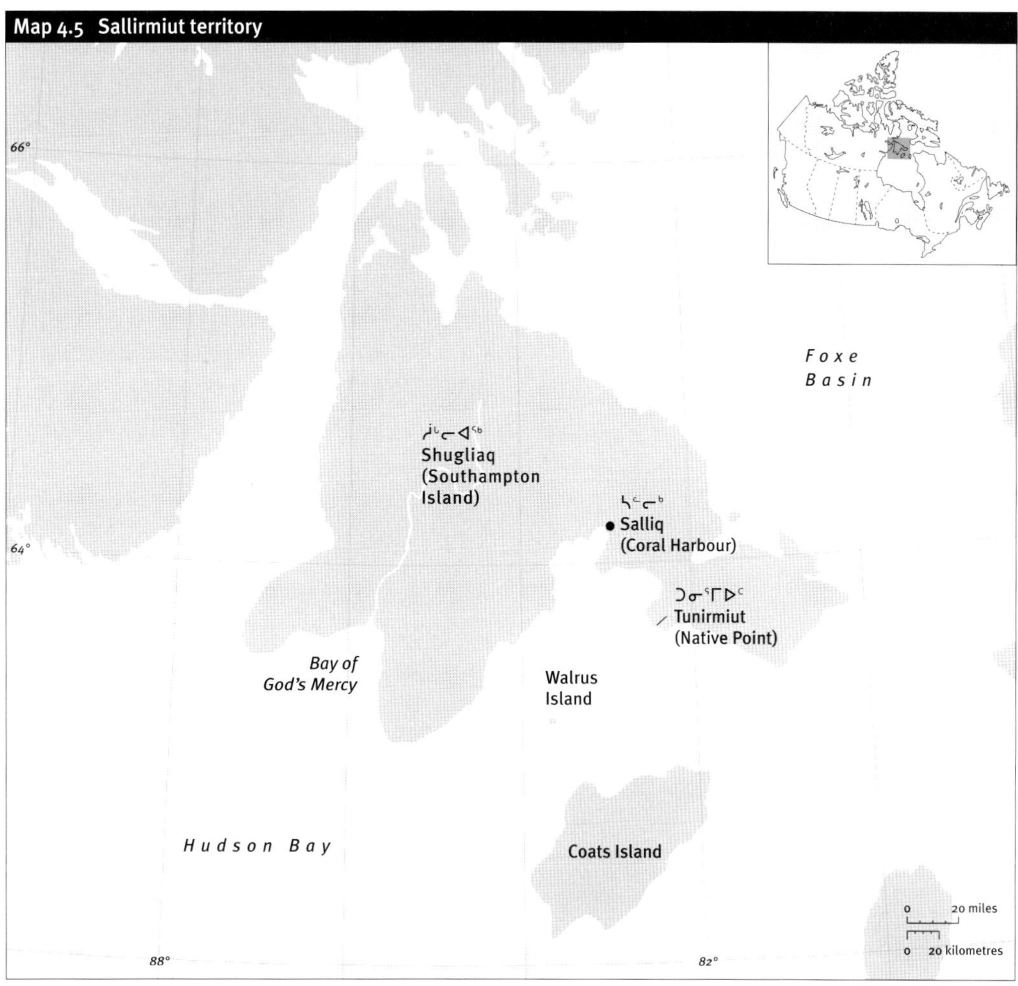

preparation and clothing production such as scraping, chewing, cutting, and sewing. There was evidence that women carried children or heavy loads on their back.

Captain George Lyon was the first non-Inuk seen by the Sallirmiut. In 1824, when his ship HMS *Griper* was off Salliq, a young male Sallirmiut, Neeakoodloo, came over the water to meet him. After some initial trepidation on the part of Neeakoodloo, the two exchanged goods, Lyon's beads being matched with dried salmon and a flint-tipped arrow from Neeakoodloo. The men at that time of year wore sealskin trousers and waterproof sealskin boots. They wore gloves of dovekie *(Plautus alle),* feathers to the inside. The women wore thigh wrappers and very high boots.

At the turn of the century Sallirmiut clothing showed features resembling those of the Inuhuit who live in Avanersuaq Kommunia in northern Kalaallit Nunaat. Therkel Mathiassen learned about the Sallirmiut by talking with the Inuit, in particular with the elder Saorre and with Angutimarik, an Aivilingmiut who lived in southwestern Southampton Island in 1902 and who lost children in the epidemic (Mathiassen 1927, Part 1, 272-4). He also studied photographs given to him by Captain John Murray, the owner of the whaling station at Cape Low.

The Sallirmiut man's outer parka of bear, caribou, or seal was cut straight at the bottom with no vents at the sides or back. The hood was small, shallow, and pointed.

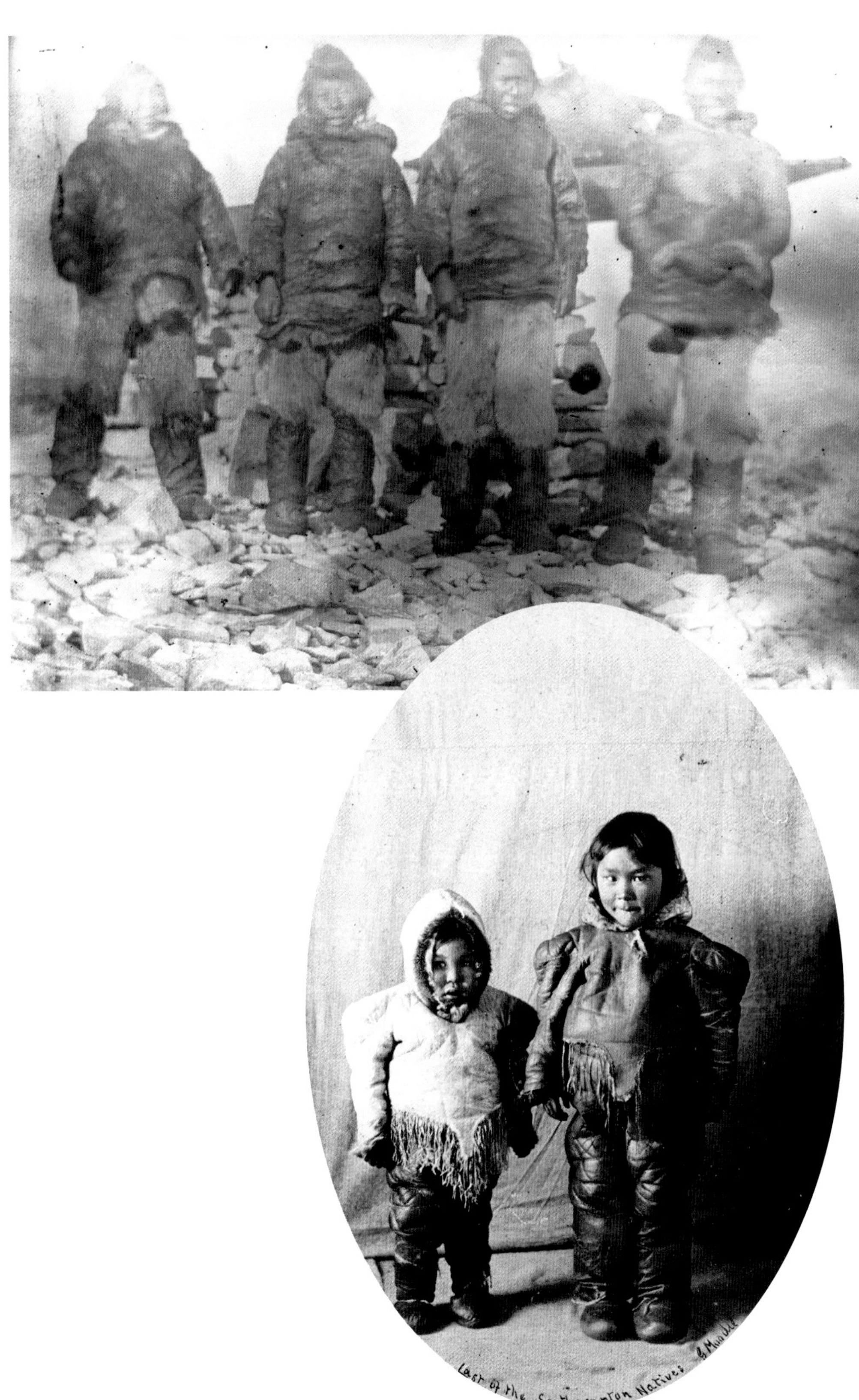

Above Four Inuit men, Southampton Island, NWT. The photograph was taken by Captain George Comer some time between 1897 and 1905. The print, taken from a glass-plate negative, is unclear, but it is possible to discern some details of the clothing, in particular what appear to be narrow-cut bearskin trousers that go below the knee to meet the boot. If the photograph was taken in the southern part of the island, the men would, in all probability, be Sallirmiut.

Below At least two children survived the epidemic of the winter of 1902-3 that claimed the group of fifty-eight Sallirmiut. The children were adopted by Aivilingmiut, a branch of the Iglulingmiut. When this photograph was taken, in 1908, they were probably with their adoptive family. They wear parkas and trousers with fur to the inside and waterproof boots. The clothing has some characteristics of the Aivilingmiut – the wide shoulders (these children must have been girls) and the fringe – but retains the front 'tip' that is common to Sallirmiut and Kalaallit, and also seen in clothing for Caribou Inuit children.

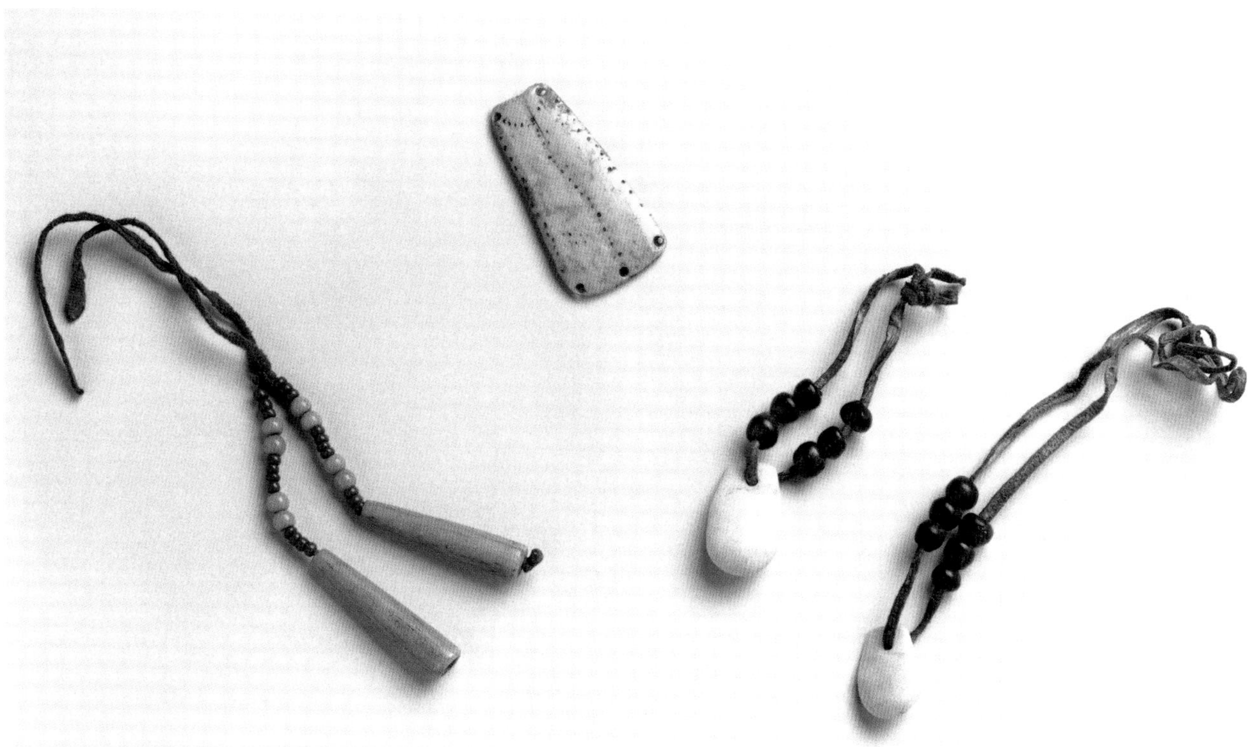

Hair ornament (top), 5.7 cm, Sallirmiut, late nineteenth, early twentieth century. Collected on Southampton Island, NWT, by John Kinnaird in 1925-6. The ethnographic records indicate that this kind of hair ornament was unique to the Sallirmiut. Carved conical or spherical pendants hung from holes at the base. The tablet is decorated with lines of dots, a form of ornamentation common in the Thule culture. Pendant / hair ornament (left) of bone, beads, and thong, 21 cm, Inuvialuit, late nineteenth century. Pendants / earrings (right), 16 cm, Inuvialuit, late nineteenth century.

The outer parka could have a seam at centre front, where the fur of the caribou underbelly formed a white stripe. The inner parka was made of caribou or young bear, fur toward the wearer's body. The clothing of the Sallirmiut did not have fringes on the lower edge of caribou-skin coats. Trousers were made of bear skin, hung on the hips and narrowed to below the knee. Winter boots had feet of seal skin and legs made of young bear with hair to the outside. Owing to gravelly terrain, a sandal of bearded seal skin was fastened to the sole. Stockings used inside the boot were constructed of skins of young seal, caribou, fox, or dog. The kayak parka of seal skin reached the hips, and along with this was worn a double pair of long mitts: the outer made of seal and the inner of seal or young bear with hair turned inward.

The woman's amauti, made of seal or caribou, had a short, narrow back flap about twenty centimetres long and ten centimetres wide and was cut almost straight across the front. The hood was short and wide. The trousers were quite short, although on journeys long bearskin trousers were worn. Women's boots, of dehaired seal skin, were very high and wide and stiffened with strips of baleen. They were fastened at the top into the trousers. Stockings of caribou or young seal lined the boots.

The child's one-piece suit was made of bear or seal skin, or more rarely of caribou or fox. The inner parka was often made of eider-duck skin worn with feathers next to the body. The neck was protected by a piece of bear skin.

The women of the Sallirmiut wore a unique pendant in their hair, coming to them from the Thule culture. Made of ivory, the thin plaque is less than six centimetres long. Two holes at the top corners held the sinew by which it was fastened to the head. Three holes at the base held small dangling spherical or conical carvings.

After the catastrophe of 1902, whalers brought Aivilingmiut to Southampton

Island from the mainland, although some were already established on the north part of the island. In 1924 the Hudson's Bay Company moved its post from Coats Island to Salliq, now the main centre, and brought Ugumiut from Baffin Island. As did the Sallirmiut, they and their descendants depend on the traditional maritime resources of the island – sea mammals, including beluga whale and walrus, and polar bear.

The Caribou Inuit

South of the Netsilingmiut and the Iglulingmiut live the Caribou Inuit, on land west of Hudson Bay.[21] Their territories extend from north of Igluligaarjuk south to the tree line, which at the coast reaches the Manitoba border, and from Hudson Bay on the east to Lake Ennadai and Dubawnt Lake and River on the west. The Caribou Inuit are made up of several independent groups: the Qairnirmiut, Dwellers of the Flat Land; the Hauniqtuurmiut, Dwellers Where Bones Abound; the Harvaqtuurmiut, People Where Rapids Abound; the Pallirmiut, People of the Willow, the largest group; and the Ahiarmiut, the Out-of-the-Way Dwellers. Each group has its own particularities in clothing, but some are so subtle that usually only seamstresses or members of the group can identify the differences.

Although the Qairnirmiut of Qamanittuaq are now the only inland Inuit community in the Northwest Territories, in former years the Caribou Inuit lived mainly in the interior, depending on caribou and musk-oxen and on lake and river fishing. They would come to settlements on the west coast of Hudson Bay in the warmer weather for brief periods either to trade, to work on whaling boats, or to hunt sea mammals.

Most groups lived close to the edge of survival. Even in the twentieth century some groups did not heat their snow houses with blubber lamps, which, among other aspects of comfort, made drying clothing easier. All groups suffered greatly if the caribou failed to arrive at the traditional hunting grounds. In the early 1950s when the migration pattern of the caribou changed, famine struck the Ahiarmiut, who lived near Lake Ennadai. There were some fourteen semi-nomadic families scattered over 130 square kilometres. They decided to walk out to the coast, a perilous journey of over 400 kilometres if measured as the raven flies. Some of the youngsters endured only because they were carried in their mothers' amauts (Belsey 1986; Elizabeth Karetak, personal communication 1986). In the late 1950s the Canadian government encouraged the Caribou Inuit to move to the coast and live in settlements, and these became permanent hamlets.

Clothing

The Caribou Inuit prefer the skins of caribou gathered in the summer when the pelage is light weight, strong, and warm. The very dark skins, which are gathered slightly earlier and are therefore thinner, less hard-wearing, and sleeker, are considered to be the most handsome.

The hood of the man's parka is pointed and can have a drawstring. When pulled

Map 4.6 Caribou Inuit territory

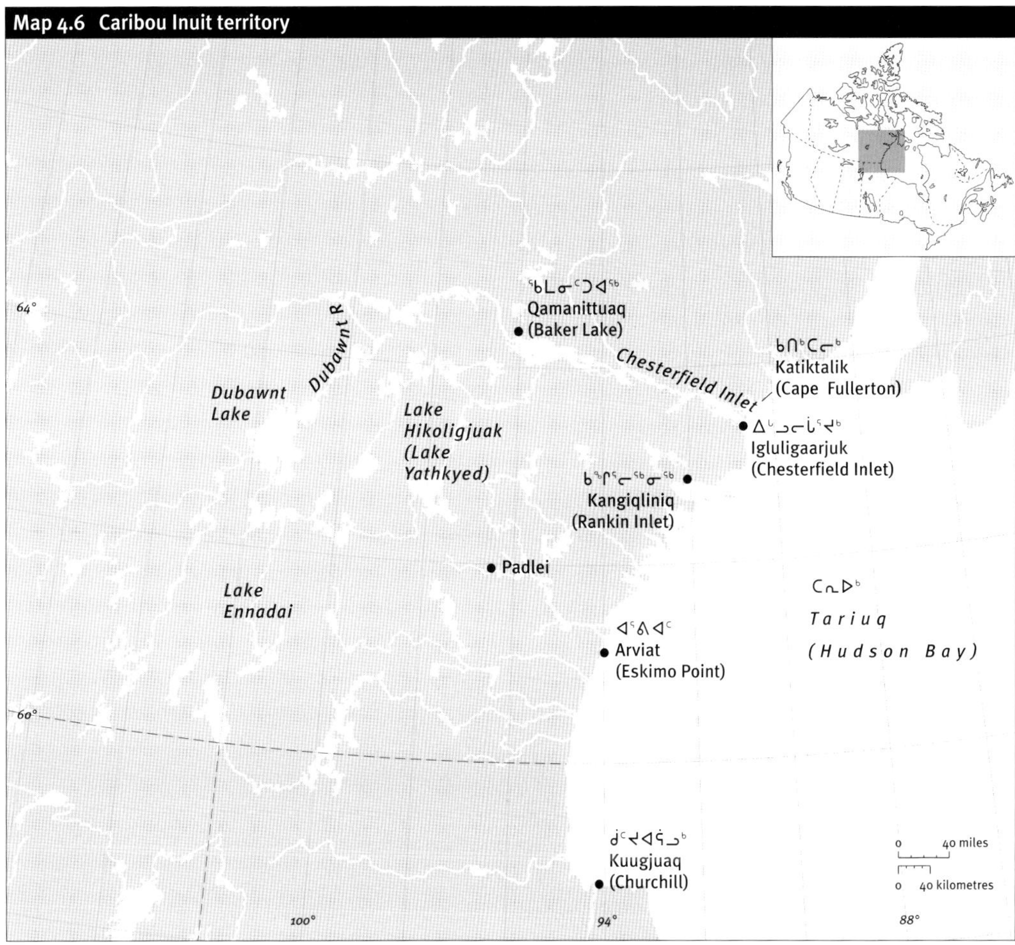

tight, this drawstring keeps the hood in place by looping the excess over a knob on the peak. In the past, though ornamentation of the man's inner parka could be very simple, beaded embroidery was often placed in the same positions as the fur mosaics and inserts on the outer coat. The parka worn by the Pallirmiut is slit up the sides, forming two broad U-shaped flaps front and back, the former reaching the thighs, the latter slightly longer. The Qairnirmiut parka sometimes has a shorter front flap and longer back flap. White fur bands decorate the hood, lower parts of the sleeve, and front and back flaps.

The woman's amauti has a very high hood that, when thrown back, can almost reach the hips. The hood of the outer coat is attached by wedge-shaped hood roots at the back. The shoulders are extremely broad and voluminous. The front flap of the Pallirmiut amauti comes to about the thigh and is narrowed and rounded – a tongue-like shape – whereas the back flap has a wide U shape, sometimes reaching the ankles. The amaut is carefully made with several sections: the side pieces are enlarged as the child grows. Pieces would be added during the year. Sometimes amautiit were worn for more than one season. The fur amauti can have elegant borders, chest panels, and mosaics made of white fur on the sides and back. Outer coats are fringed all around the flaps, and sometimes dangles of furred, white strips fall from the sleeves at the shoulder seam. The beadwork on inner amautiit outlines the hood and face, shoulders, flaps, and sleeve edge and replaces the

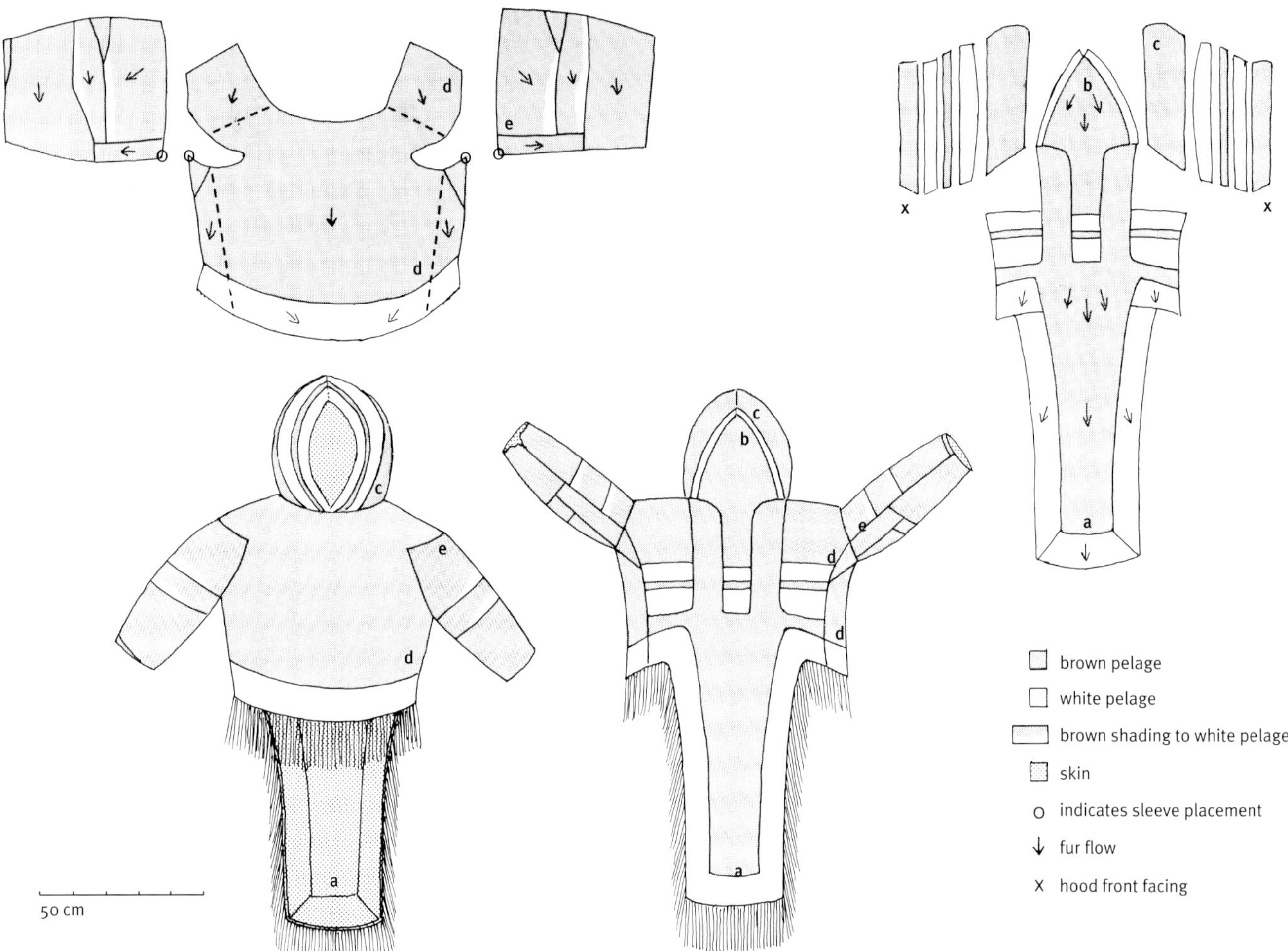

Figure 4.4
Pattern drawing of Caribou Inuit (Qairnirmiut) man's outer parka. ***Drawing by Dorothy K. Burnham.***

fur inserts that form the column up the centre front of the hood and over the chest.

Men's and women's trousers are made of caribou skin, the women wearing one layer, the men two for protection from the cold while hunting. The legs are loosely cut to allow unhampered movement as well as warmth when seated, as they can be wrapped around the thigh. The trousers have several gussets for fullness. Trousers are often well decorated with contrasting bands of dark and white fur at the lower leg and where the leg is sewn to the upper. The leg and inserts have a horizontal fur flow.

Today's footwear still resembles the traditional styles, especially when worn by the men and women who hunt and travel in the winter. Footwear is as follows from inside to out: a long pair of *alerti,* stockings with fur to the inside; some pinirait, the short socks mentioned earlier; kamikpak, the long boot with the fur to the outside; and tuktuqutik, the ankle boot with double sole (Rhoda Karetak, personal communication 1986). The mitts of the Caribou Inuit follow the same pattern found all over the Arctic.

The child once out of the amaut puts on the atajuq, the combination suit. A loose fur cap with a long, furry fringe to cover the neck can be worn in winter, and in summer a lighter cap or bonnet is worn. Under the chin is placed a small piece of long-haired caribou skin to catch the rime

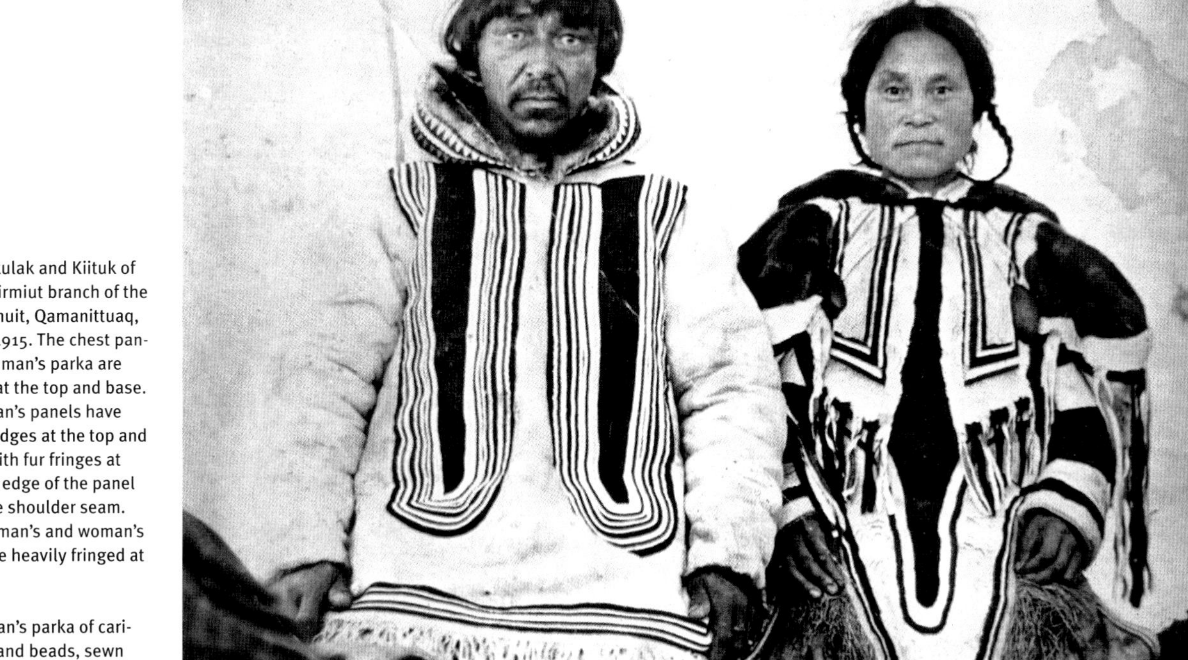

Above Akulak and Kiituk of the Qairnirmiut branch of the Caribou Inuit, Qamanittuaq, NWT, ca. 1915. The chest panels of the man's parka are rounded at the top and base. The woman's panels have straight edges at the top and bottom with fur fringes at the lower edge of the panel and at the shoulder seam. Both the man's and woman's parkas are heavily fringed at the base.

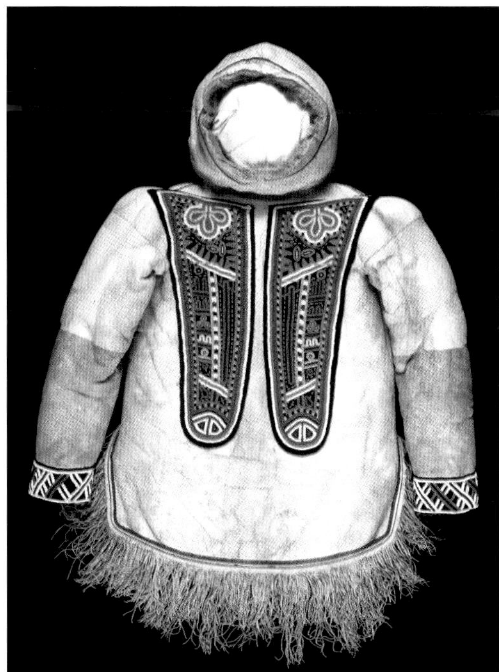

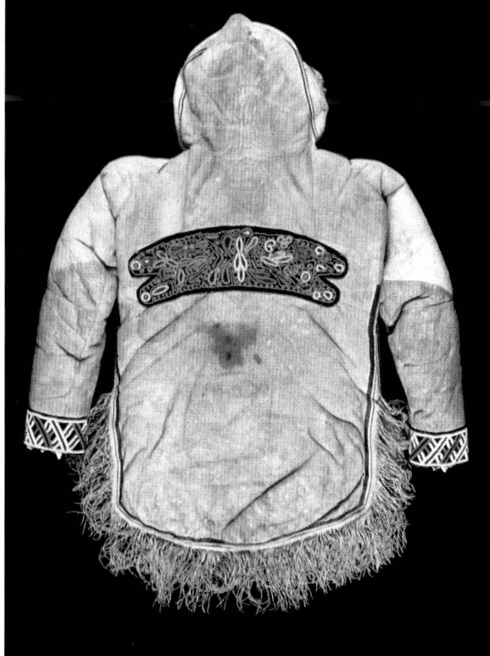

Below Man's parka of caribou skin and beads, sewn with sinew, Caribou Inuit (?), early twentieth century. Collected possibly at Kuugjuaq, Manitoba, or Katiktalik, NWT, by John Douglas Moodie, ca. 1903-5. The beaded back panel on men's inner parkas replaced the inserts of the outer fur on which amulets were placed.

Figure 4.5
Pattern drawing of Caribou Inuit (Qairnirmiut) woman's outer parka. *Drawing by Dorothy K. Burnham.*

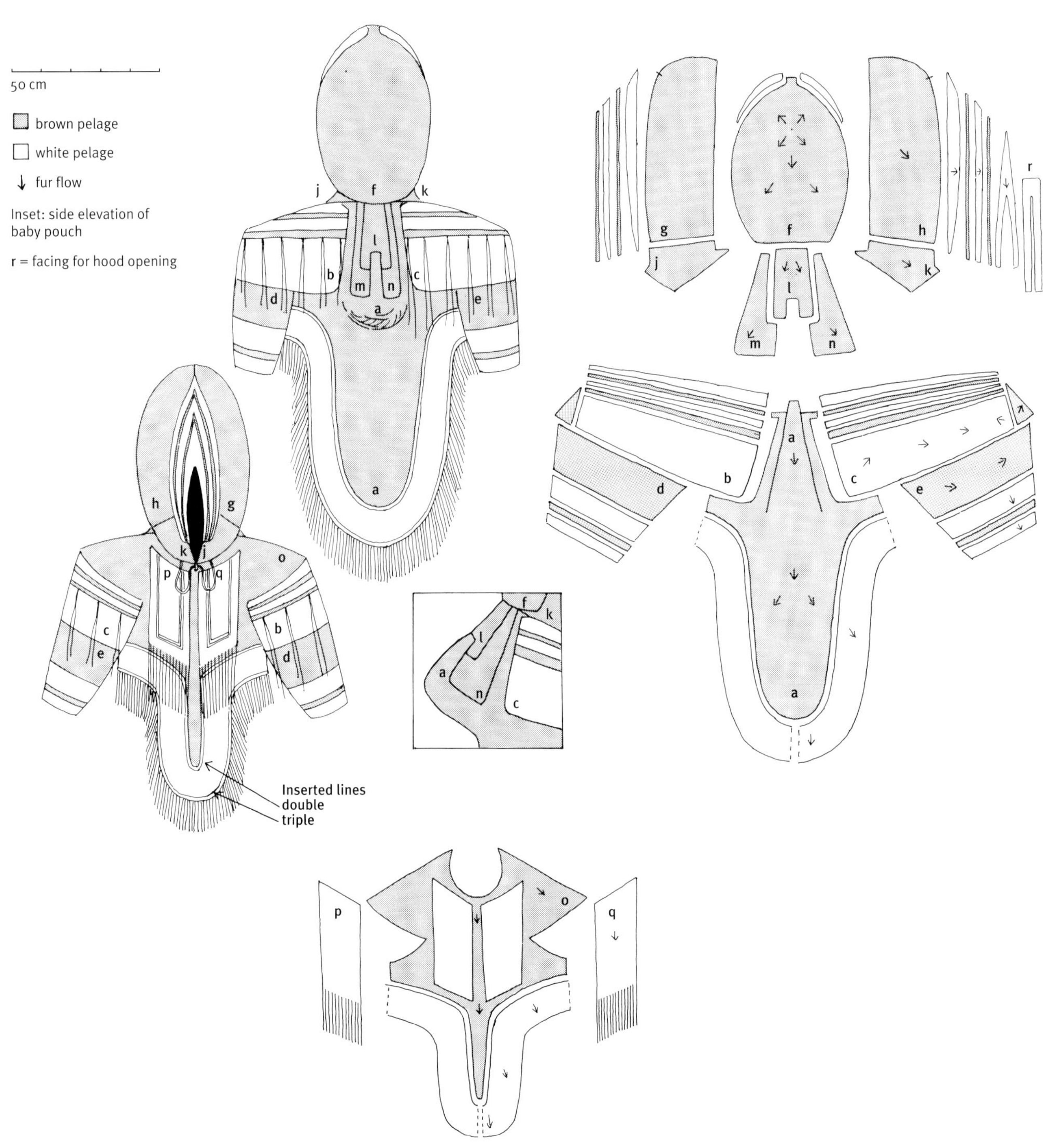

Below Jacob Ikinilik of Qamanittuaq, NWT, in 1987. M. Ikinilik, a Caribou Inuit hunter, wears a caribou-fur oufit, including long mitts.

Right Caribou-skin amauti, sewn with sinew, Caribou Inuit, late nineteenth century. Collected by D.T. Hanbury in 1899.

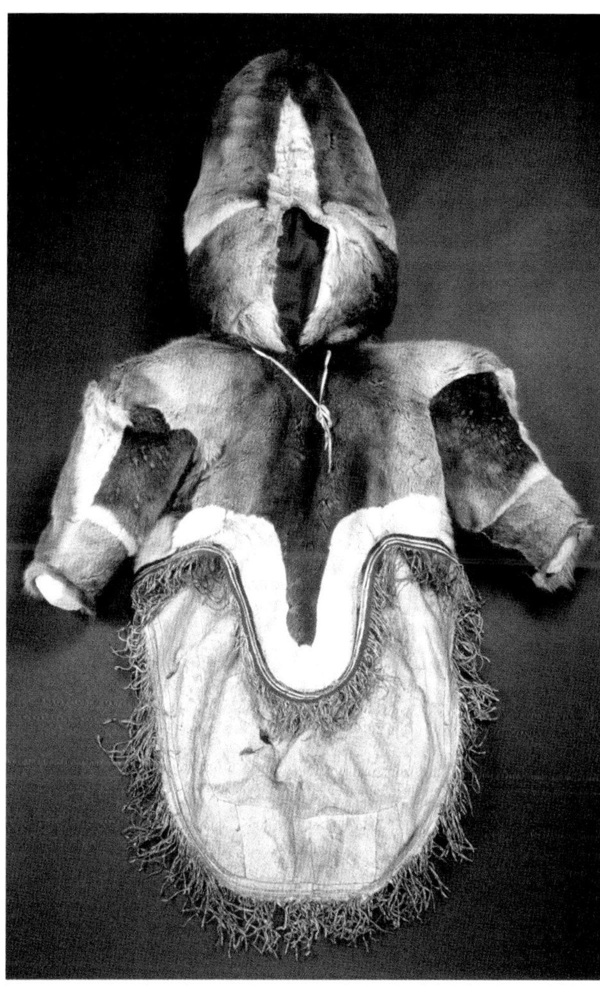

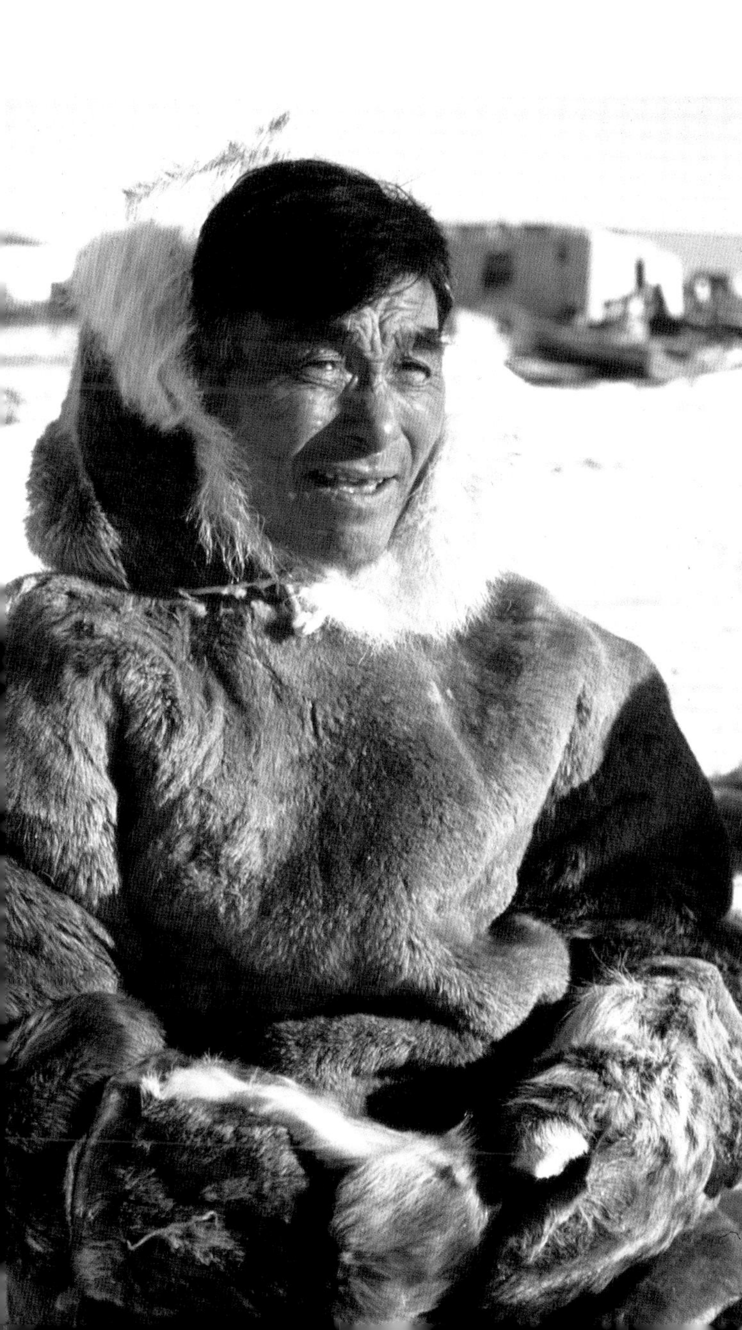

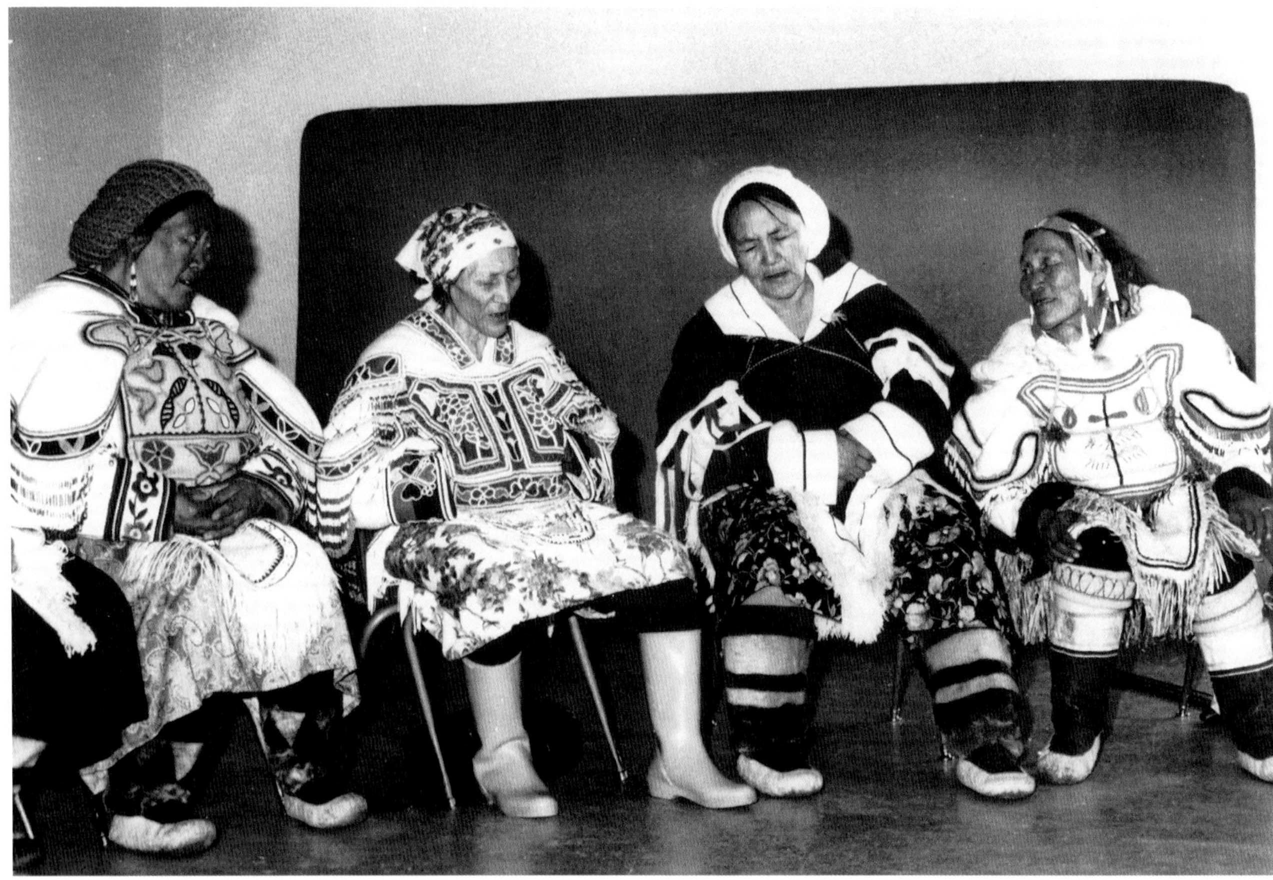

Singers at Arviat, NWT, in 1990. From left to right: Elizabeth Nibgoarsi, Helen Konek, Mary Anowtalik, and Annie Sewoee. The singers wear traditional fur and beaded amautiit. The beadwork can be removed in whole pieces since it is first sewn to duffle or hide and then affixed to the garment. It is passed on from generation to generation, and some beadwork has a long family and kin group history contained in it (Winifred P. Marsh, written communication 1983).

from breath vapours. Older children wear clothing modelled on those of adults but with abbreviated aspects.

Caribou Inuit clothing has evolved slowly and undramatically from the early part of the century to the present. The bottom edge of men's coats has lengthened, and the armholes continue to be roomy. Men no longer wear parkas with beaded decoration, but the back of fur parkas between the shoulder blades can have the traditional three squares of white inserts. Ruffs made from caribou fur surround the face on the outer parka. Women's skin parkas continue to be decorated with beadwork. Fabric amautiit follow traditional patterns.

The Nunatsiarmiut

The Nunatsiarmiut, the People of the Beautiful Land, occupy the southern two-thirds of Baffin Island, from north of Kangiqlugaapik to Hudson Strait.[22] While they do not differ sharply from the Iglulingmiut, who occupy the northwestern part of the island, in the matter of language the two groups consider themselves to be distinct from one another, a feeling substantiated in part by the difference in their clothing.

Thule culture bearers, who spread eastward from Alaska, occupied northern and southern sites on Baffin Island by about AD 1200. Three centuries went by before contact between Baffinland people and non-Inuit took place, when Sir Martin Frobisher arrived from Britain in 1576 in search of the northwest passage to India and China. Sir Martin was struck in the buttock by an iron-tipped arrow during a skirmish with local inhabitants. He captured one of the Inuit along with his kayak and took him to England, where Frobisher presented him at the court of Queen Elizabeth (Devine

Map 4.7 Nunatsiarmiut territory

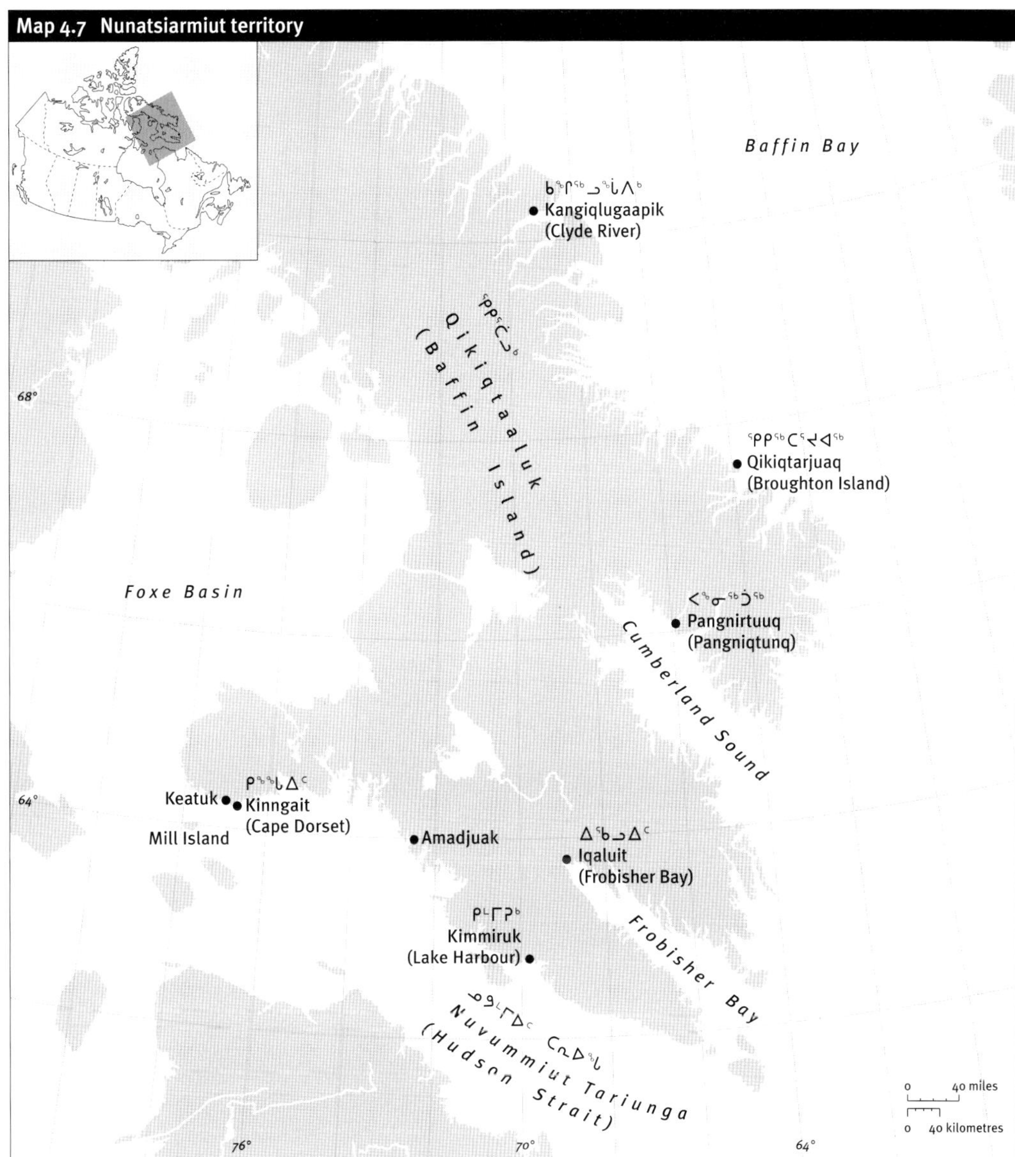

1982, 134). The following year Frobisher kidnapped a Baffinland man, woman, and child, all of whom, sorrowful to tell, died shortly after reaching England.

Clothing

Images of the Thule Eskimo descendants kidnapped and brought to England in 1576 and 1577 have been preserved in the water-colours of John White, who accompanied Frobisher to Baffin Island between 1576 and 1578.[23] While we cannot be certain that White's paintings are accurate in every detail, his fine attention to detail allows a view that written accounts do not. These pictorial records of sixteenth-century Baffinland dwellers are unique and invaluable, and possibly illustrate some aspects of the older Thule culture.

Frobisher's expedition arrived in the summer, when the Nunatsiarmiut were wearing light clothing made of seal skin. The man's parka in the images has a rounded hood with side pieces that extend into the front tongue or root below the chin. The shallow hood hugs the face and

Eskimo man (front), painting by John White, 1577, watercolour, 22.7 cm x 16.4 cm. Eskimo man (back) Sloan copy from John White, ink and watercolour, 33 cm x 21.8 cm. The parka front is hip length and has an even edge that curves to the back flap, which is long and tapered. The hood, both at the face and top seam, the neck opening and yoke, the wrists, and the lower edges are outlined with narrow light and dark bands. The boots appear to be waterproof, and have a drawstring that encircles the boot top just below the fur stockings.

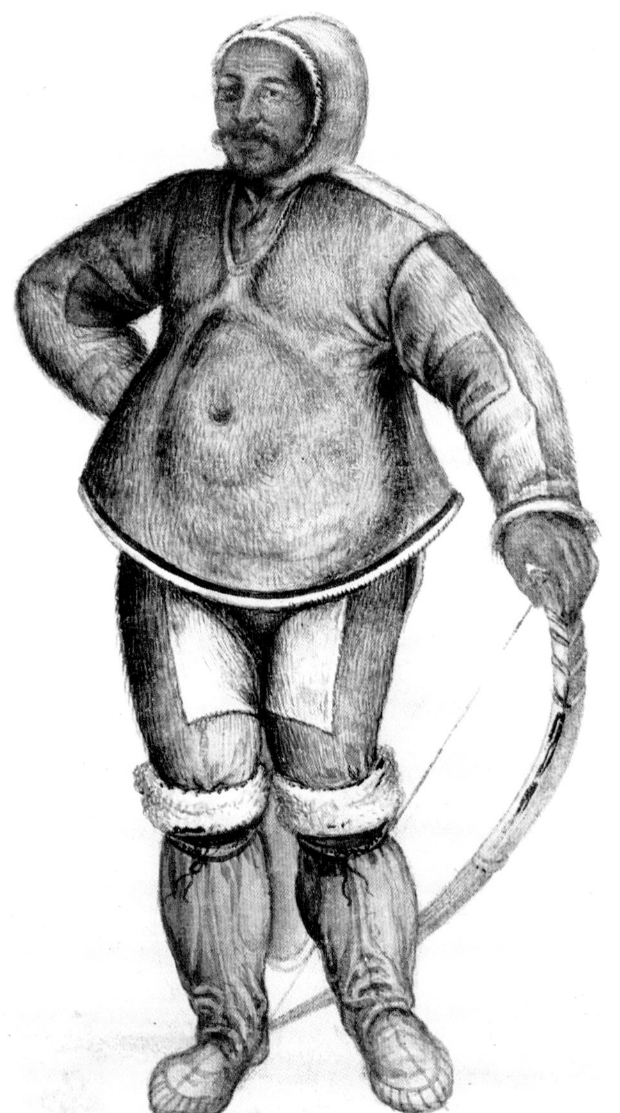

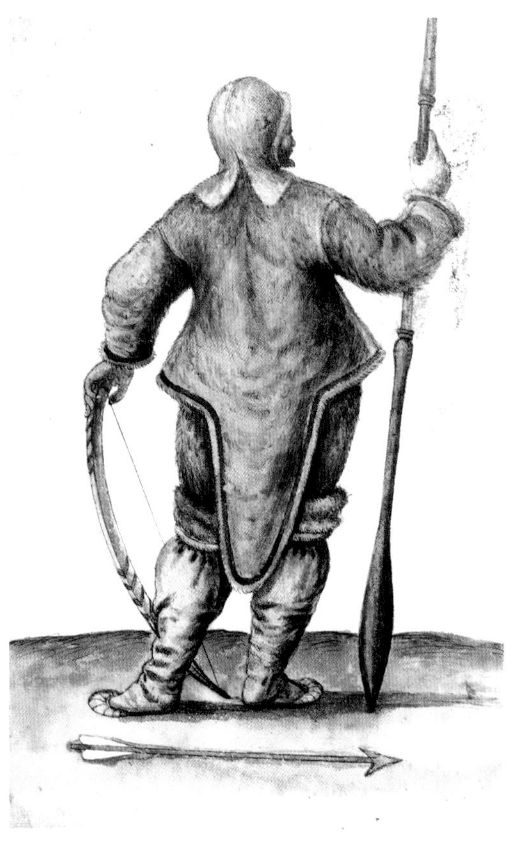

Eskimo woman and baby, painting by John White, 1577, watercolour, 22.2 cm x 16.6 cm. The amauti is decorated with light and dark bands around the hood, lower edge, and wrists, all with short fur ruffs.

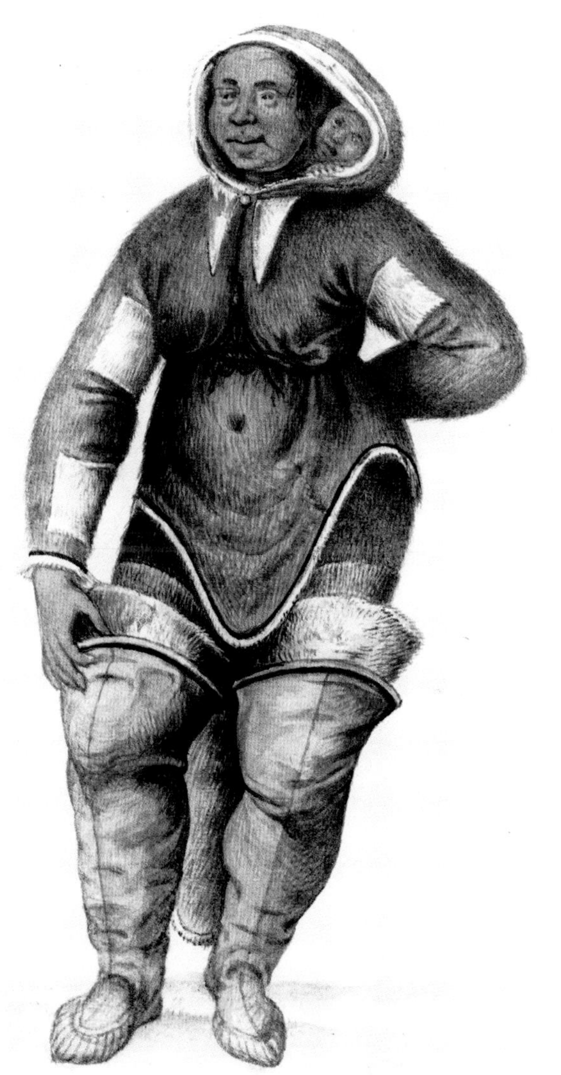

has a short-haired ruff. The parka's front edge comes to the hip and is even and rounded. Oblong insertions appear at the inner sleeve joint. The sealskin trousers tuck into the boots and are decorated with inserts of light-coloured fur on the inside of the thighs. The boots are dehaired, brown, and come to the knee.

The painting of the woman dressed in a sealskin amauti shows a child peeping out from the hood, which is wide and rounded. Two white, pointed hood roots, similar to Alaskan and Inuvialuit 'walrus tusks,' descend from the neck to the chest. At the chin is a toggle that helps fasten the belt of the amaut. The short front flap, shaped like an inverted bell, curves up over the top of the hip to the back, where the back flap extends almost to the ankle. The bottom edge of this flap appears narrowed and rounded. White oblong insertions appear on the upper and lower sleeve, proximal side. The trousers meet the footwear, but it is unclear if there is a thigh wrapper between the trouser leg and the stocking, which rises above the boot.[24] The dehaired sealskin boots and furred stockings are high, well above the knee, and widen at the top.

Two hundred years later White's observations were confirmed, with additional information that Inuit of the Savage Islands off the south coast of Baffin Island wore 'shifts of seals' bladders' (Ellis [1748] 1946, 31), a testimony to the use of gutskin parkas in the eastern Arctic. A pair of leggings collected in the Cumberland Sound area 350 years later could possibly have functioned as Thule culture 'draught excluders.'[25]

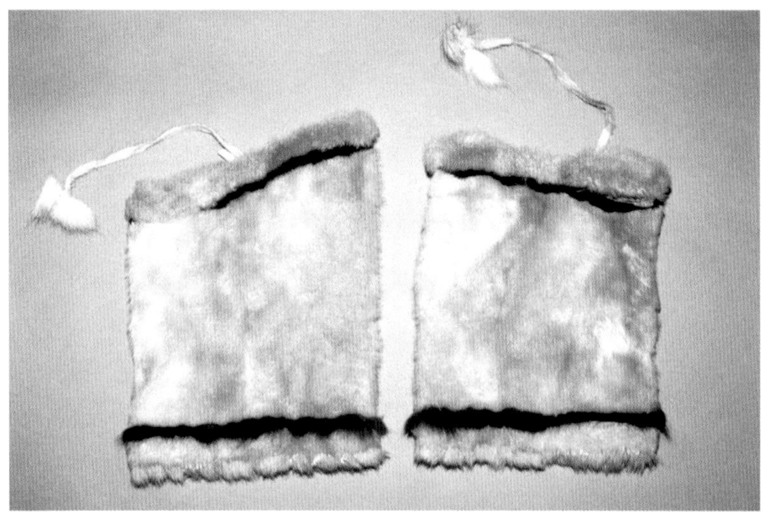

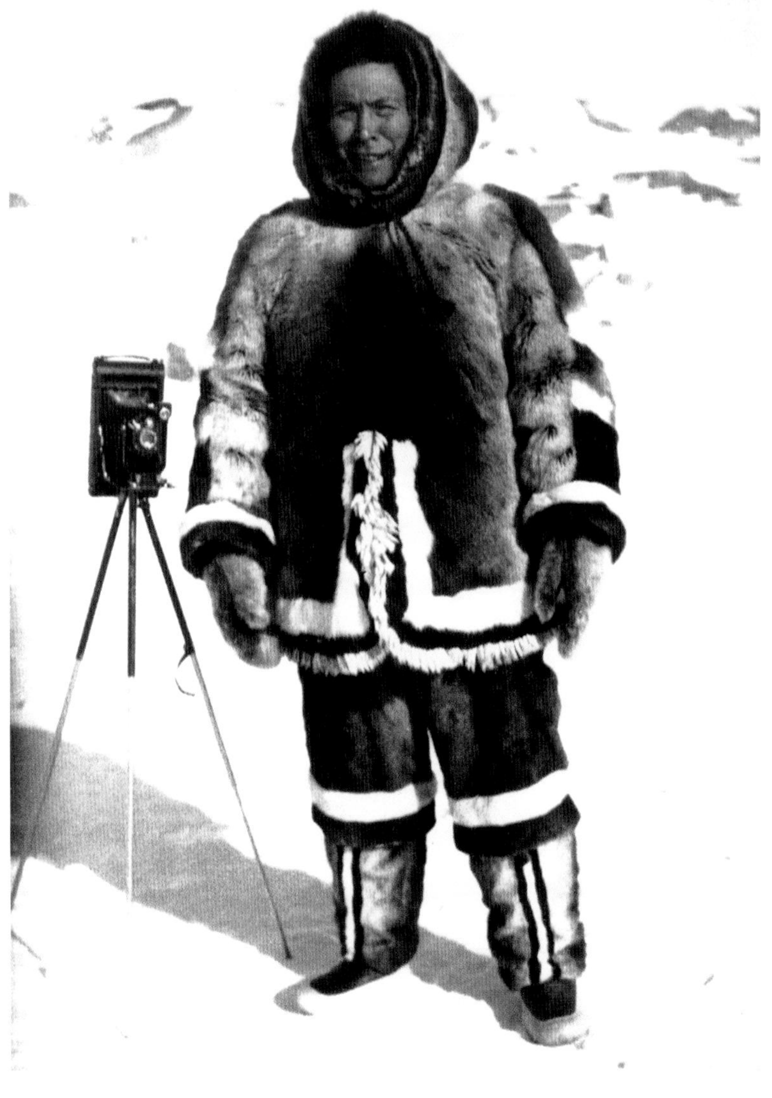

Women from Cumberland Sound wore short sealskin pants and thus would have needed protection between trouser base and boot top (Arnaujaq 1986, 11).

Toward the end of the nineteenth and in the twentieth century, the Nunatsiarmiut were wearing parkas with pointed hoods. The man's parka was thigh length, cut straight all round, and had a slit mid-front or at the sides. Retained from the past in sealskin clothing were oblong fur inserts of a contrasting colour at the upper sleeve and dark bands to outline garments and some seams.

The woman's amauti changed as well. The hood became pointed, wide, and roomy. At the back it was of one piece with the amaut, which was gathered at the base to form a spacious pouch.[26] The front flap became straight sided, came to the thigh, and was square at the base. The back flap reached the lower calf and had a squared bottom edge. As it came over the hips it narrowed slightly, curved out to a point part way down the length, then tapered with a slight curve to the base, the shape on each side something like a shallow keel, a design that persists to the present: 'The woman's amauti tail is square-cut in North Baffin – in Pangniqtuuq, Qikiqtarjuaq, Kangiqlugaapik, and Mittimatalik. The points in the sides of the tail help with folding it up which we do when the ice is slushy' (Jeela Alikatuktuk Moss-Davies, personal communication 1984, 1985). Women's clothing, like men's, was outlined with narrow bands of dark- and light-coloured fur.

Opposite above Woman's sealskin and cotton leggings, 37 cm, Nunatsiarmiut (Uqqurmiut), early twentieth century. Collected at Cumberland Sound, Baffin Island, NWT, by J. Dewey Soper 1924-5. These leggings are made with the soft fur of young seal and are lined with tan cotton. The longer peaked part of the legging comes at the centre front of the leg. The thong at the outer leg ends with a fur tuft, which would be tucked into the trouser waist.

Opposite below Peter Pitseolak (1902-73) of Kinngait, NWT, photographed by Aggeok, his wife, ca. 1946. His photographs and drawings constitute a visual history of south Baffin Island.

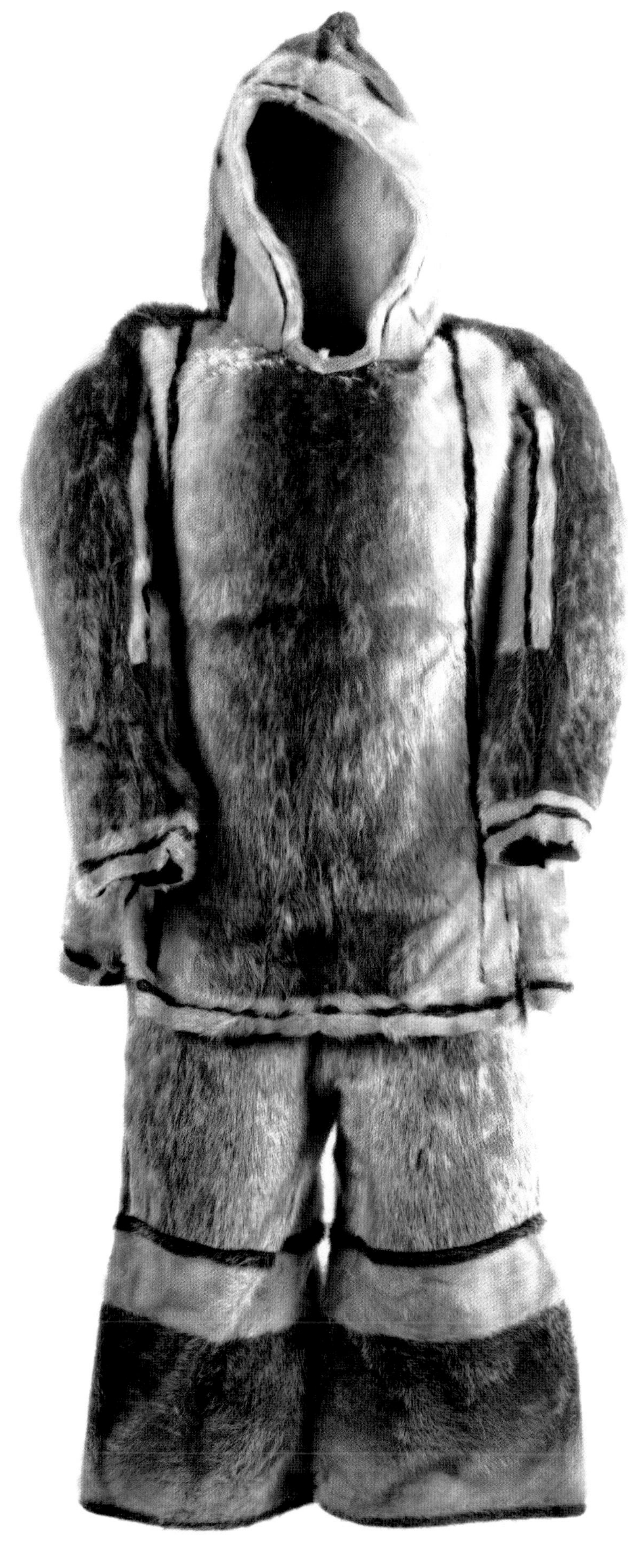

Right Man's parka (119 cm) and trousers (85 cm) of seal, canvas, and wood, sewn with sinew, Nunatsiarmiut or Nunavimiut, late nineteenth century. Collected at Cumberland Sound, NWT, or Hudson Strait coast, Nunavik, by William Wakeham in 1897. The dark bands that embellish the parka come from the deep brown fur of adult seal. Since it is very large, the outfit may have been made for a non-Inuk. In addition, there are some innovations, although this does not necessarily signify that the wearer was not Inuit. The parka has two welted pockets inserted into either side of the mid-front seams. The trousers have a three-button front fly closing as well as wooden buttons at the waist to hold braces. The buttons are of European manufacture (Jacqueline Beaudoin-Ross, personal communication 1985).

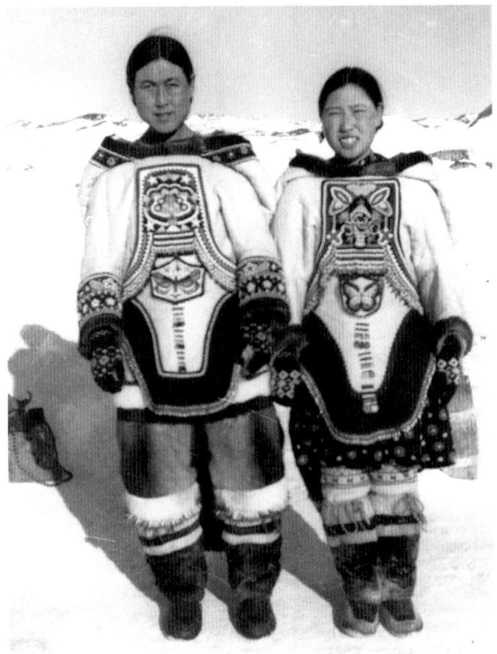

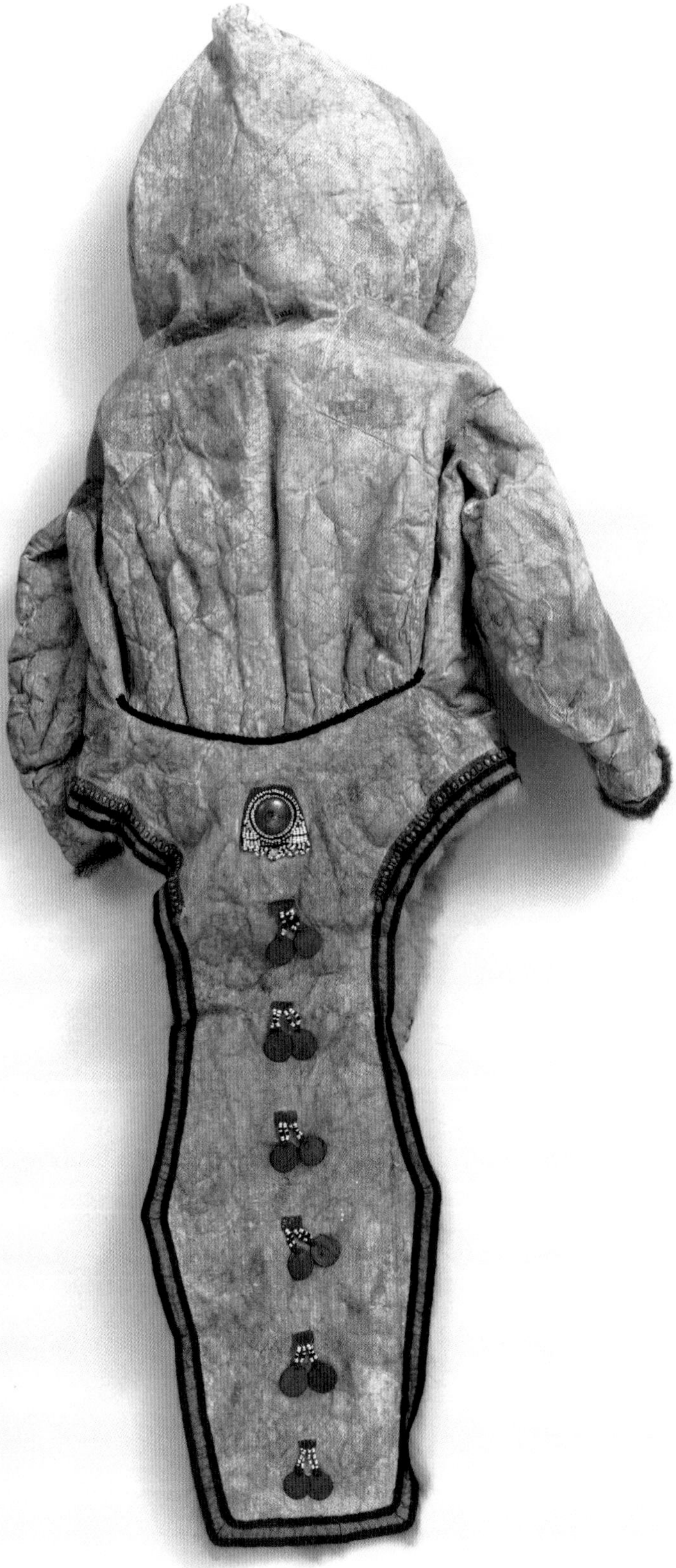

Some inner amautiit used to be decorated with beads, spoons, and pennies. The form of Baffinland beadwork was distinct from that found in the west. The top outline of the beadwork, as it rose toward the chest, more or less mirrored the outline of the front flap. By the 1970s, however, there was only one amauti in Kinngait trimmed with pennies: 'Eliya Panni carried her baby Anna in it and she says, "I was the only one in town who had one. Everyone knew when I was coming"' (Eber 1973, 37).

A child's sealskin parka from the late nineteenth century is an example of simplicity coupled with efficiency. The pointed hood is attached to the front by a narrow insert that dips under the chin. The back of the coat is of one piece with the hood. The

Opposite left Aggeok and Udluriak, Peter Pitseolak's wife and daughter, wear amautiik decorated with beadwork and pennies. Photographed by Peter Pitseolak near Kinngait, NWT, between 1942 and 1946.

Opposite right Back view of widow's amauti, of sealskin, beads, spoons, coins, lead, brass, sewn with sinew, 156 cm, Nunatsiarmiut, late nineteenth century. Collected on Baffin Island, NWT, by William Wakeham in 1897. (For front view, see page 72.)

Right Child's sealskin parka, sewn with sinew, 84 cm, Nunatsiarmiut, late nineteenth century. The dark skin of the seal's back is placed centre front and back and fades to the lighter belly skin at the sides. The hood's light coloured fur is placed near the face, the dark around the back.

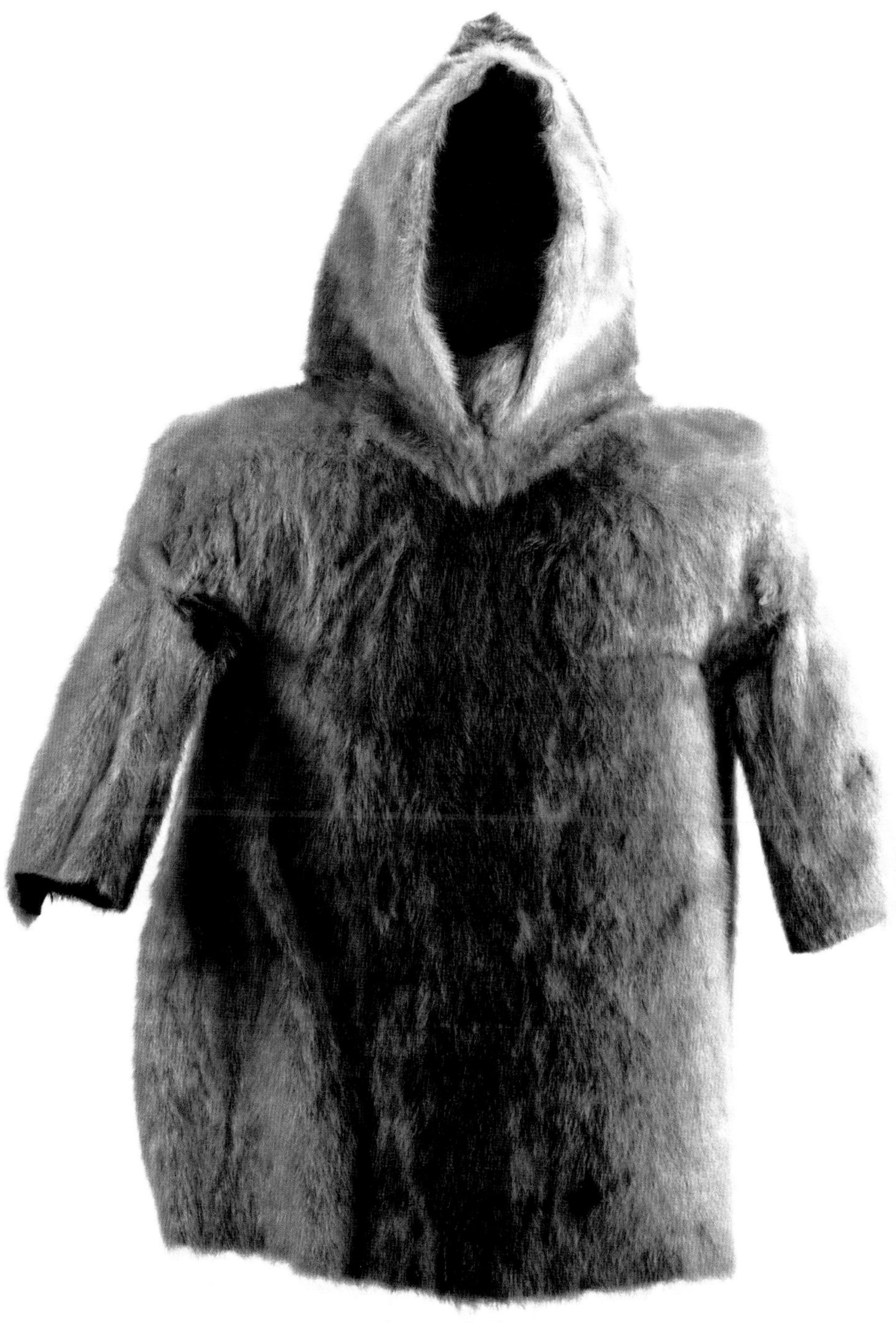

Below Hunters pull a seal from a breathing hole near Keatuk. Left to right: Kooyoo, Ashevak, Peter Pitseolak, Pingwartok. Photographed by Aggeok, developed by Peter Pitseolak in an iglu ca. 1944.

Opposite Inner and outer amauti of cotton, duffle, dogskin, tape, braid, and wool, 190 cm, Nunatsiarmiut, 1979. Artisans: Napachee and the Pangniqtuuq Sewing Co-operative. The inner amauti of duffle combined with the outer windproof shell of closely woven Grenfell cloth (polyester and cotton) provide superb protection for the wearer and child in the deep cold of south Baffinland.

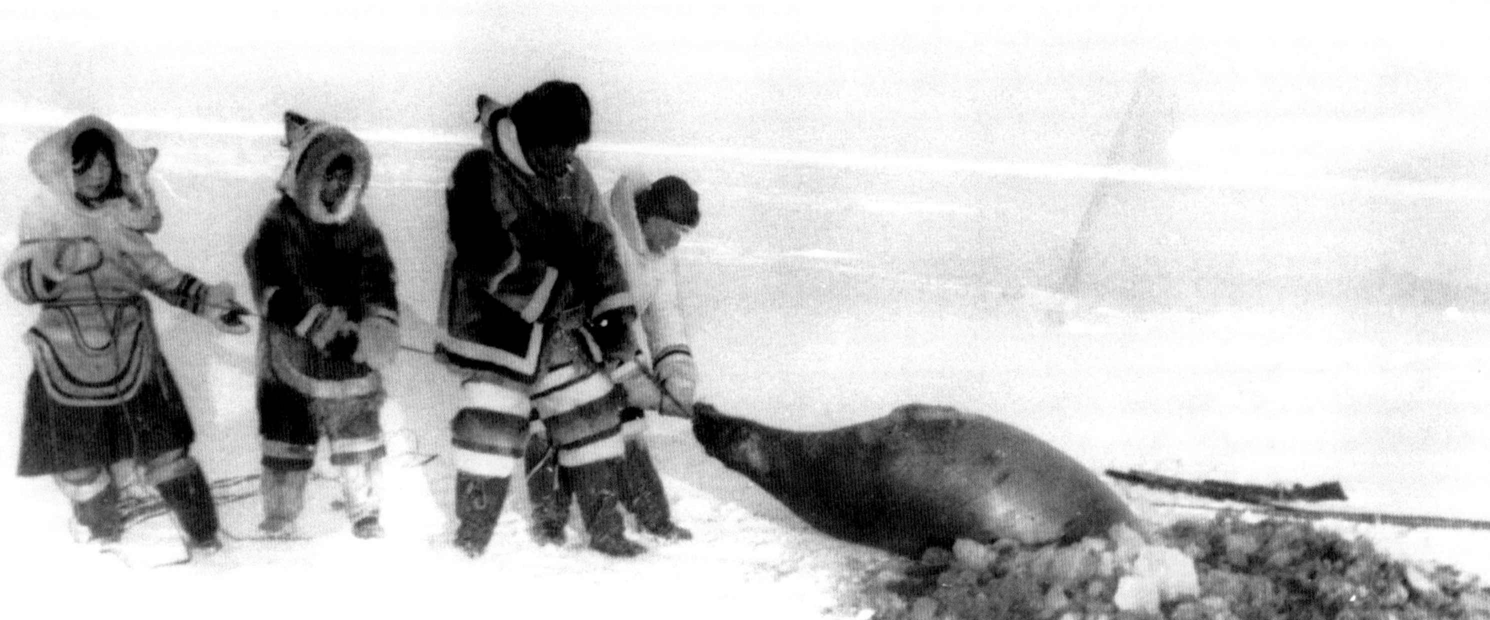

front, too, is made of one skin. The garment has a very small vent over the hip and flares where the front meets the back. Under the arm a triangular gusset is inset for ease.

The present-day style of the man's fabric parka from Baffinland takes its pattern from fur clothing. Called a *kukukpalik,* it is found all over the Arctic. Materials used side by side with furs are duffle, closely woven cotton, and synthetic blends.[27] The cloth parka is shorter than the one of caribou, comes over the hip, and has no slit in the side. The hood curves to a peak at the back and can be trimmed with wolf, dog, or wolverine if available. The even bottom edge and sleeves can have a fur trim, and braid or tape decoration. The cut of the fur or fabric amauti of the Nunatsiarmiut is preferred by many women in other localities because of its roomy comfort for mother and child. The hood is very deep and wide. The amaut has plenty of space for the child's feet and legs, for in addition to the large gathers at the base of the amaut small extensions are built in on either side of the base. The distinctive tail of the Nunatsiarmiut amauti has also been adopted in many parts of the Arctic.

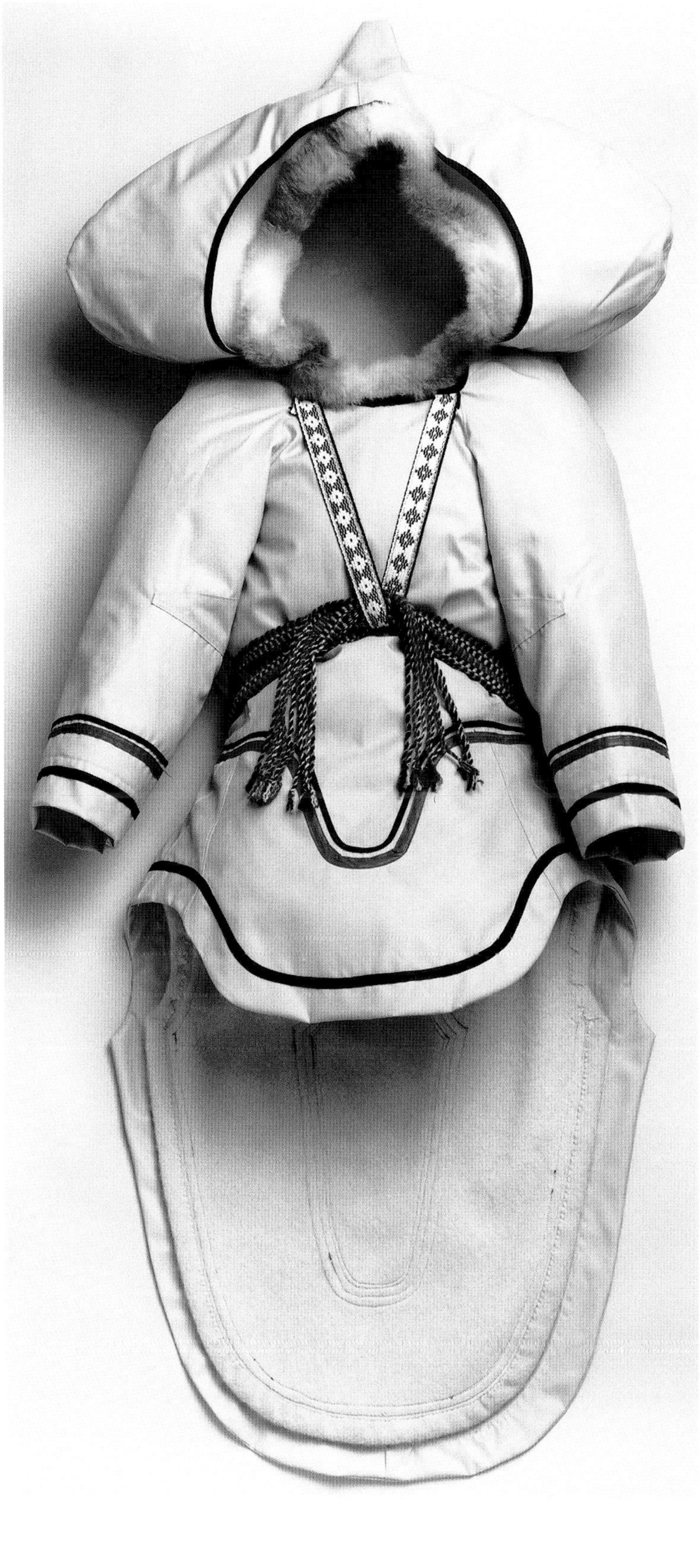

Below Mariano Aupalarjuk of Pangniqtuuq, NWT, 1992, who is playing a string game, is dressed in furs from the adult ringed seal.

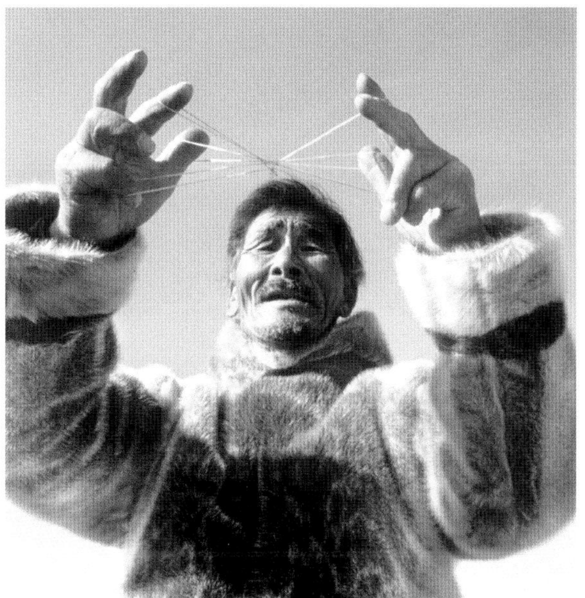

Map 4.8 Nunavimiut territory

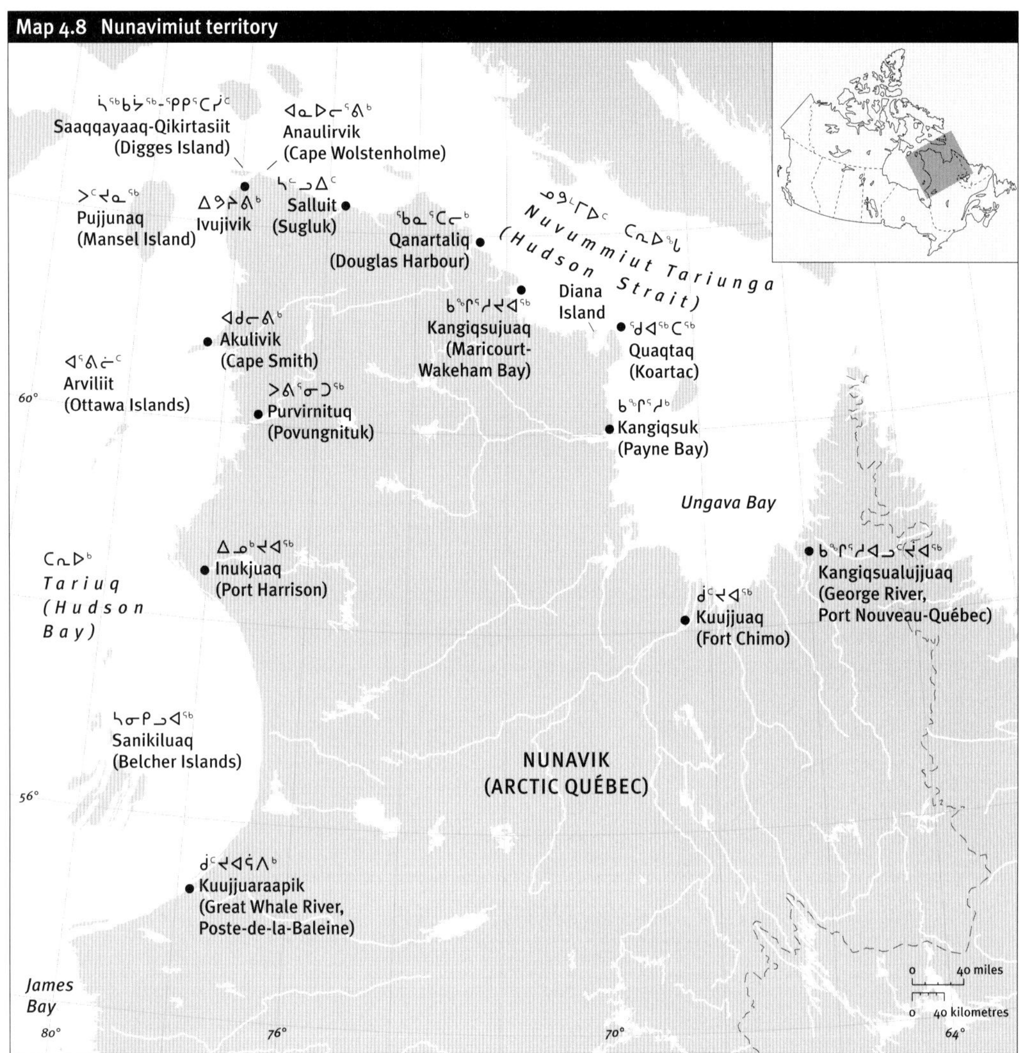

The Nunavimiut

The Inuit of Nunavik, or Arctic Québec, live north of the tree line in fourteen communities around the coast of Ungava Bay, the south coast of Hudson Strait, and the east coast of Hudson Bay. They call themselves the Nunavimiut.[28] There is evidence that in the past they were not all residents of the coastal areas who went to the interior only on occasional forays during the summer to hunt caribou. A hypothesis has been broached that Inuit called the Nunamiut – from the Inuit word *nuna,* meaning the interior lands – traditionally occupied the interior (Vézinet 1980, 9-11).

Clothing

There were distinctions in clothing among the Nunavik groups. The white edging of women's winter caribou parkas was narrow among the Tarramiut in the northwest areas of Québec and broad among the Inuit to the south. Thigh-length boots of dehaired seal skin were worn only on the east coast of Hudson Bay. On Mansel Island and Arviliit men's trousers and winter boots were made of polar bear skins, and occasionally children's and adolescents' parkas were made of fish skins (Saladin d'Anglure 1984, 482).

The first preserved image of the Nunavimiut was drawn in the eighteenth century. Unusual in men's clothing was a short,

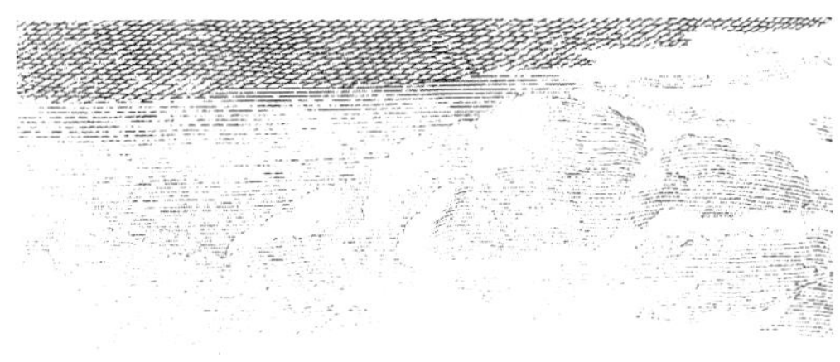

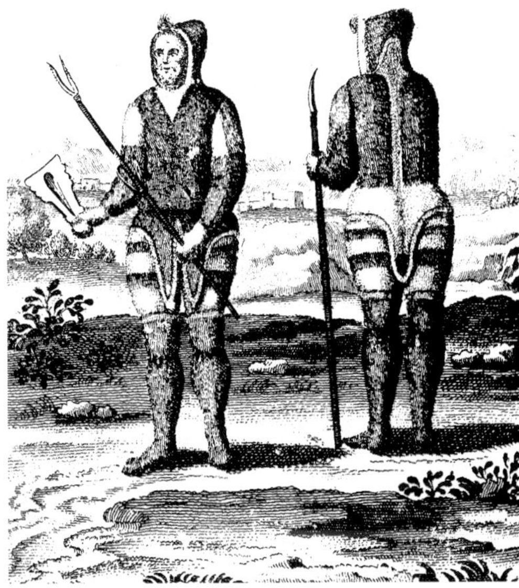

Above The first known depiction of Nunavimiut, early eighteenth century, at Anaulirvik, Nunavik, or Saaqqayaaq-Quikirtasiit, NWT, is a drawing of two men with hunting tools. Both the plant life and the construction in the background lend a European air. The clothing has features found in later images of male attire: a rounded hood, short-haired ruffs, hood root under the chin, inserts at the hood back and on the upper sleeve, a split at mid-front, and contrasting bands of fur at the edges.

Right 'Husband and Wife – Douglas Harbour – Man in Winter Dress (Oct. 28)' (William Wakeham 1898). The photograph may have been taken aboard SS *Diana* when Wakeham was on a tour of exploration for Marine and Fisheries Canada. The woman's amauti is decorated with strands of beads across the chest and with what appear to be lead drops around the edge of her flaps.

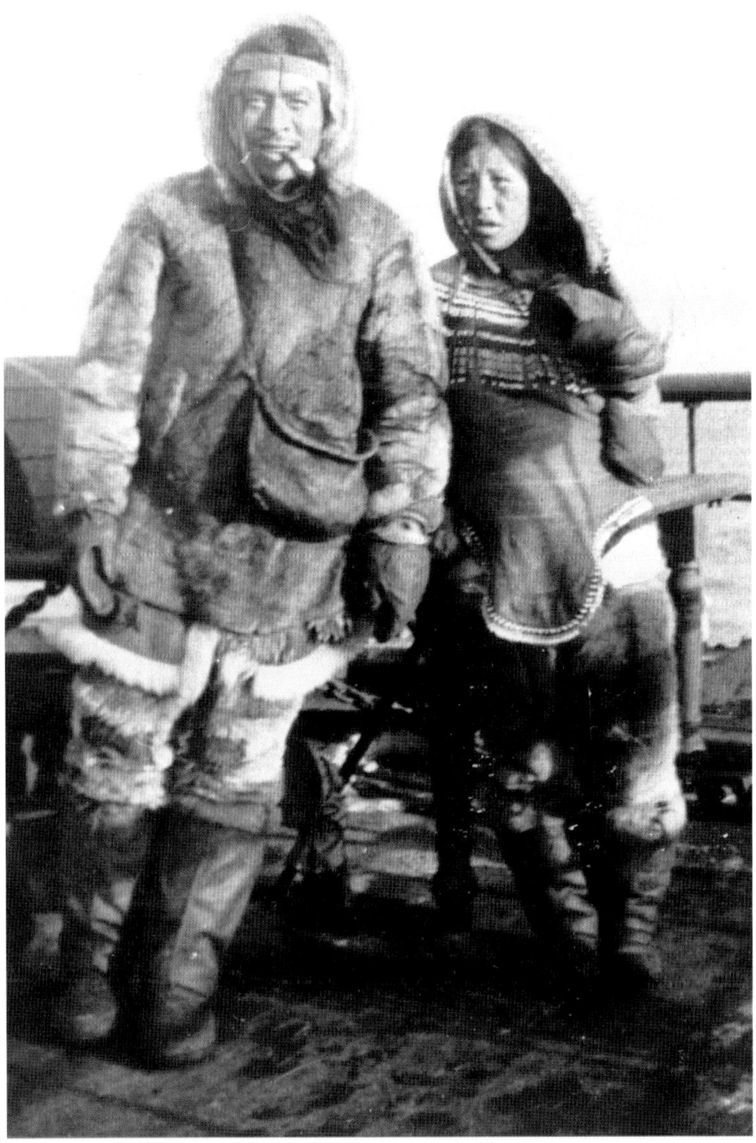

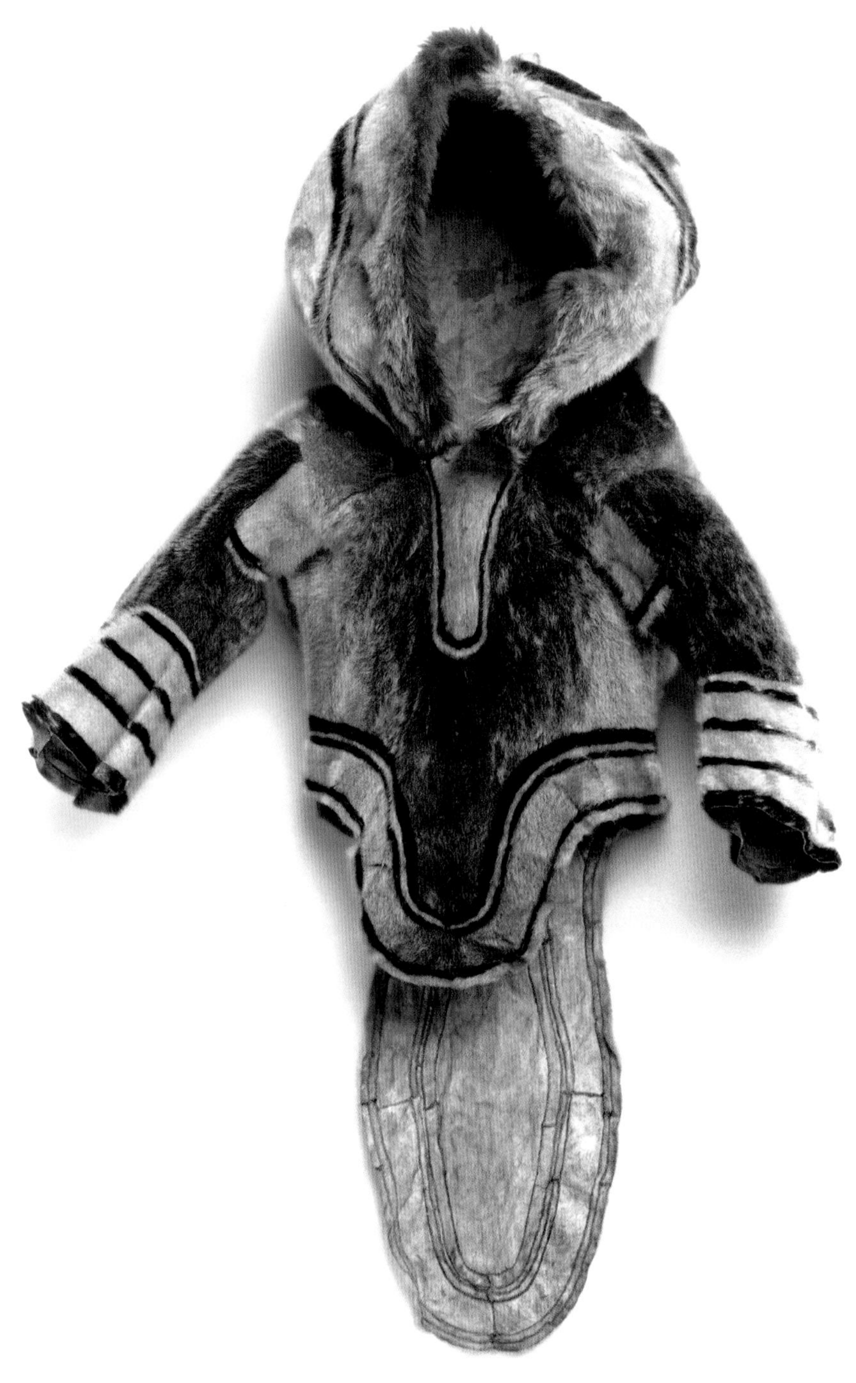

tapered flap at front and back of the parka, which curved up over the hip as do most Canadian women's amautiit. In the late nineteenth century Nunavimiut men's parkas still had the round hood cut close to the face, but they were even edged, came to the thigh, and were often split slightly up the mid-front. It is not known when the tail of the man's parka became reduced. The possibility has been proposed that shortening or eliminating the tail could have been an adjustment to the kayak (Hatt [1914] 1969, 37). In the kayak the Nunavimiut wore waterproof coats made of sea mammal intestines into the twentieth century.

An example of a Nunavimiut sealskin amauti from the late nineteenth century is identified as coming from Nunavik because of the shape of its tail, which is narrow, has a slight inward curve below the waist, and then curves out to end in a round base.[29] One of the North's most skilled seamstresses says that the old shape of the tail in Nunavik is said to be like the roof of a caribou's mouth (Rhoda Karetak, personal communication 1986). Another distinctive feature is the dark gusset inlaid on either side of the amaut at the top of the back flap, not seen elsewhere. The amaut is formed by cutting the top of the back very full. The base of the amaut is gathered and seamed to the top of the back flap to form the large pouch for the child.

A child's outfit from the early twentieth century made of young seal skin, fur to the exterior, shows the retention of the back tail, which lasted in men's clothing for some time. The dark outline on the inside of the back 'tip' is unusual.

Opposite Sealskin, dogskin amauti, sewn with sinew, 143 cm, Nunavimiut, late nineteenth century. Collected on the south shore of Hudson Strait (?) by William Wakeham in 1897. The amauti hood is deep and softly pointed with a ruff of dog fur. From its point a strip of dark adult seal goes along the top halfway to the front. Wide bands outlined with narrow dark and light strips decorate all the garment's edges. The inserts below the chin and upper arms are echoes from the first drawing of Nunavimiut in the eighteenth century.

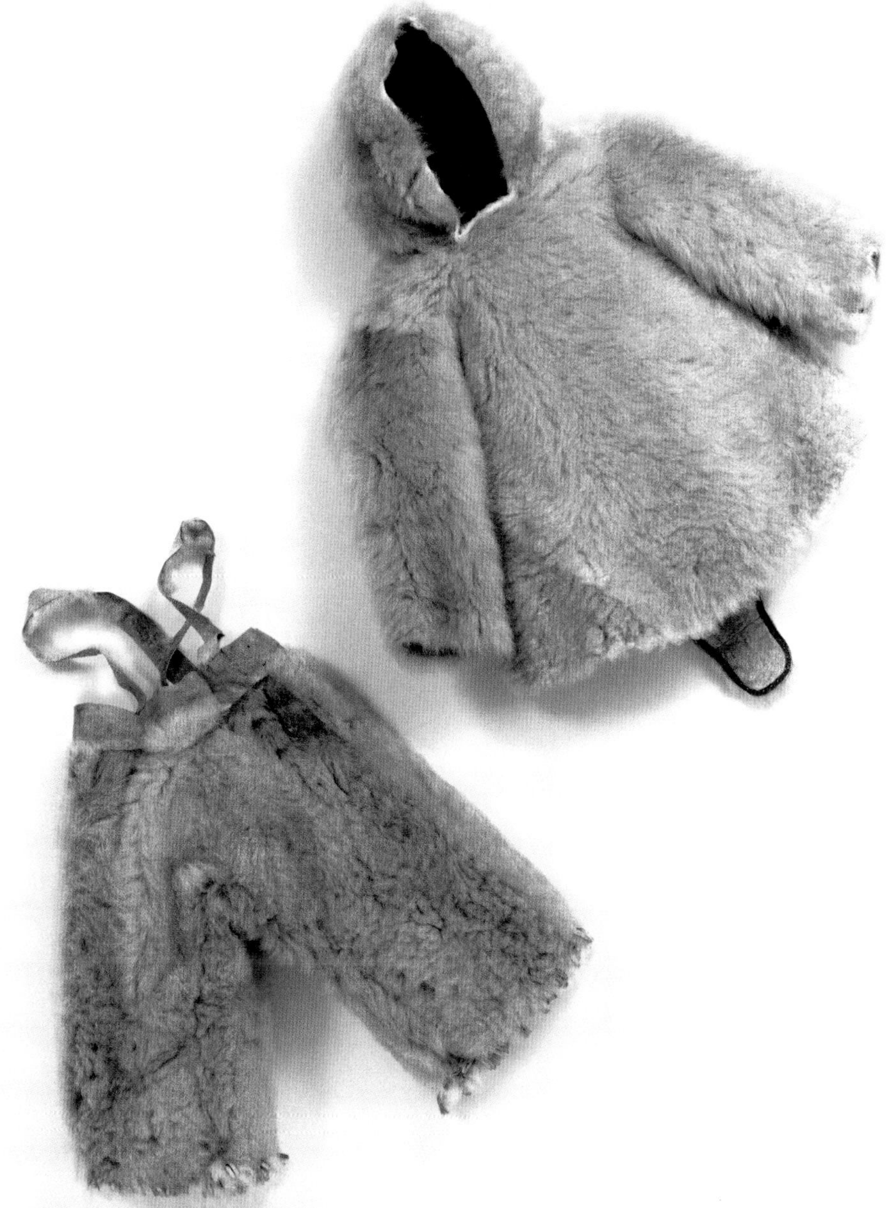

Right Child's seal coat (82 cm) and trousers (53 cm), Nunavimiut, early twentieth century. Collected possibly at Kuujjuaq or Kangiqsuk, Nunavik, by Robert Flaherty in 1911-13. The parka and trousers, of young seal, are simply made. The waistband of the trousers is of adult seal.

In the middle of the twentieth century, Nunavimiut clothing retained some aspects of the old and incorporated new elements. Still to be seen was the white root below the chin and contrasting inserts on the inner part of the sleeves. A continuous fringe graced the lower edges of garments. New by the 1950s were the broad flaps of the amauti with the 'keel' shape. Today's clothing brings in many pan-Arctic elements. The man's parka, whether of fur or fabric, continues to be hooded, closed, and loose and reaches the hip, where it flares. The hood of the woman's amauti is no longer pointed but round, wide, and deep. The shoulders and the amaut are voluminous. The front flap hangs below the knee and the back one reaches the ankle. Both are very broad and like the amaut reflect the style of the Nunatsiarmiut.

Sealskin boots, furred or depilated, continue to be made and worn alongside footgear of rubber or synthetic materials. As is true all over the Arctic, the Inuit know there is no substitute for their lightweight, breathable, warm skin boots.

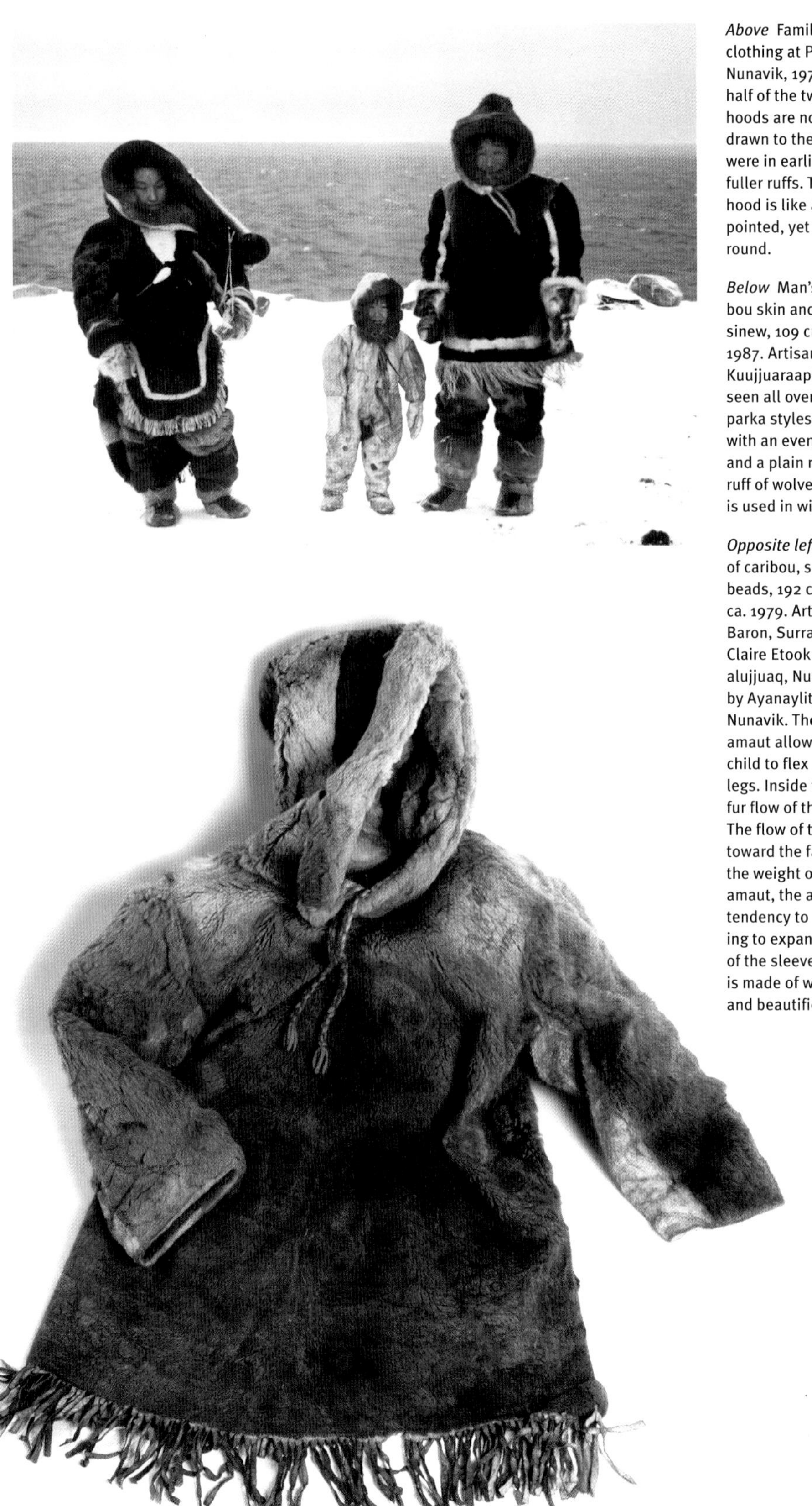

Above Family in caribou clothing at Purvirnituq, Nunavik, 1971. In the second half of the twentieth century hoods are not so closely drawn to the face as they were in earlier days and have fuller ruffs. The peak of the hood is like a knob: not pointed, yet not completely round.

Below Man's parka of caribou skin and wool, sewn with sinew, 109 cm, Nunavimiut, 1987. Artisan: Mary Cookie of Kuujjuaraapik, Nunavik. Now seen all over the Arctic are parka styles such as this one with an even bottom edge and a plain ruff. A long-haired ruff of wolverine, wolf, or dog is used in winter.

Opposite left Amauti of skins of caribou, seal, and dog, beads, 192 cm, Nunavimiut, ca. 1979. Artisans: Surra Baron, Surra Annanack, and Claire Etook of Kangiqsualujjuaq, Nunavik. Beadwork by Ayanaylitok of Salluit, Nunavik. The shape of the amaut allows the growing child to flex or extend the legs. Inside this amauti the fur flow of the back is down. The flow of the front is up toward the face so that, with the weight of the baby in the amaut, the amauti has less tendency to ride up. The piecing to expand the under part of the sleeve for enlargement is made of white caribou fur, and beautifies the inside. A wide ringed-seal band borders the front and back flaps. Sewn at one edge only with the outer edge free, the lustrous seal fur ripples as the wearer moves, catching the light and the breeze. (For a back view, see page 41).

Opposite right above Pattern illustration, sealskin appliqué on bleached caribou hide, 36.4 cm x 18.3 cm, Nunavimiut, probably from Inukjuaq or Purvirnituq, Nunavik, 1950, artist unknown. On the left side of the wall hanging, the artist has depicted a man's or boy's parka with pointed hood and even edge, trousers, and boots. The middle and right side show the pieces of the amauti with back flap to the ankle, and a pair of woman's boots.

Opposite right centre Woman's sealskin boots, sewn with sinew, 37 cm, Nunavimiut, 1981. Artisan: Mary Luuku of Ivujivik, Nunavik. The furred upper has the ancient tooth or triangle motif. The sole, depilated, is made of bearded seal. A drawstring goes through the top of the boot.

Opposite right below Nellie Amidlak with her son, one-year-old Kuuniluusi, in her amaut. She was one of the participants in the Traditional Skills Summer Camp Program near Inukjuaq, 1990. The program was organized by the Natturalik Youth Committee in cooperation with Avataq Cultural Institute, Makivik Corporation, and the Québec Ministère des Affaires culturelles.

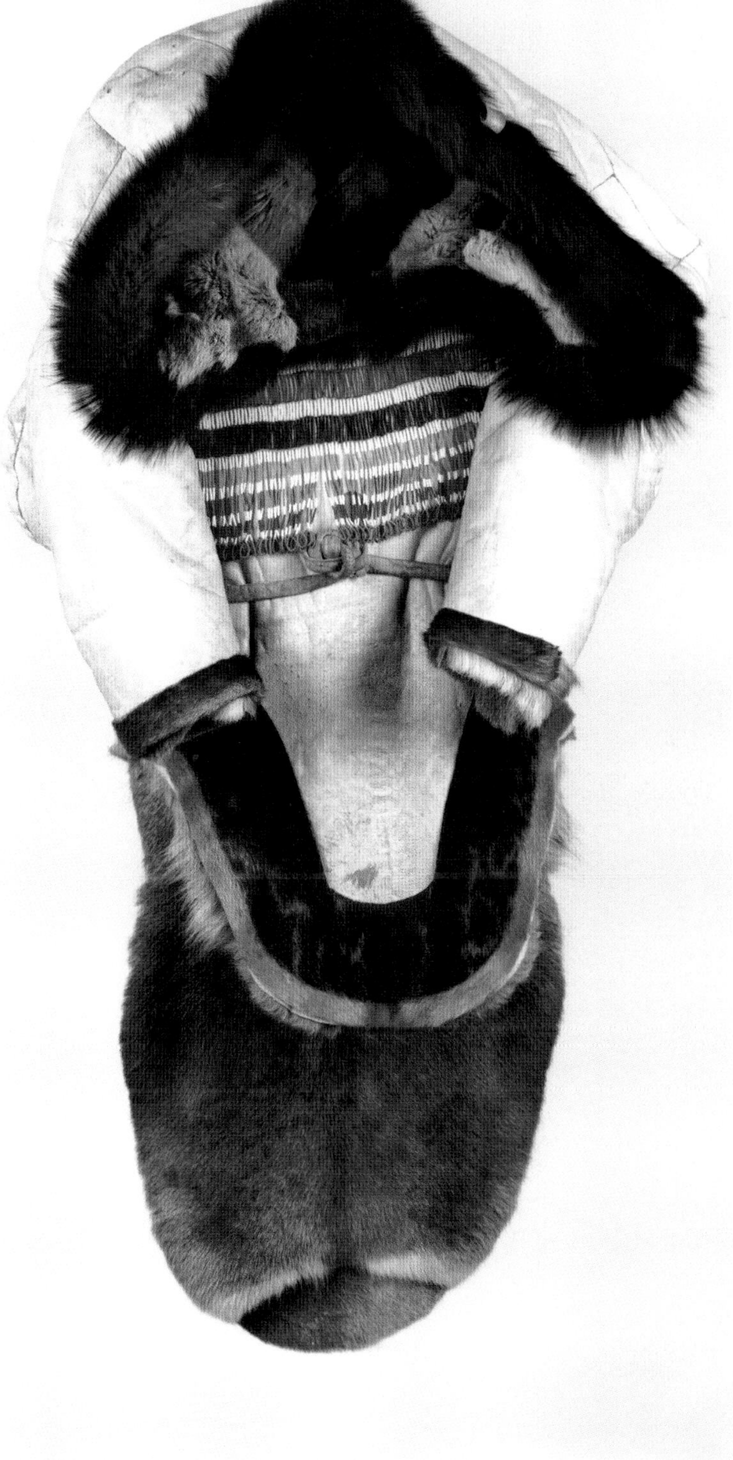

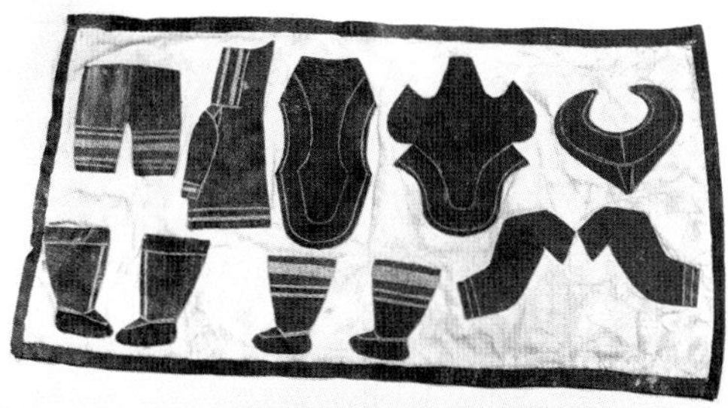

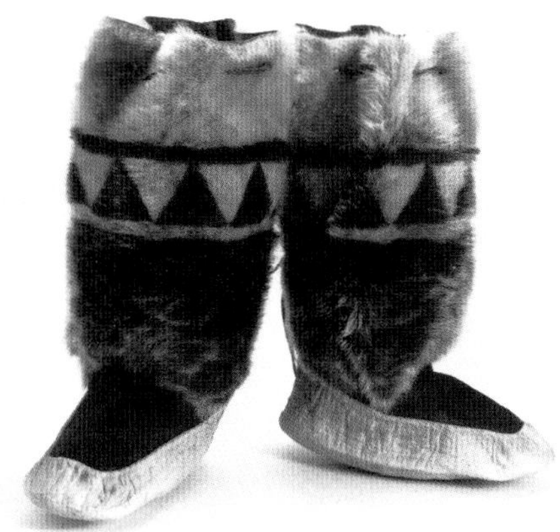

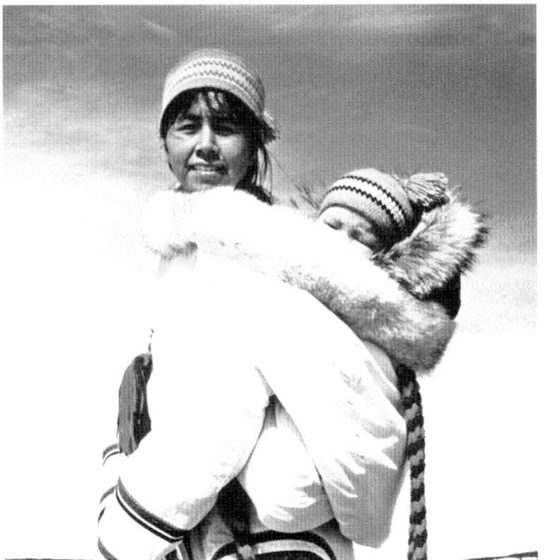

Map 4.9 Qikirtamiut territory

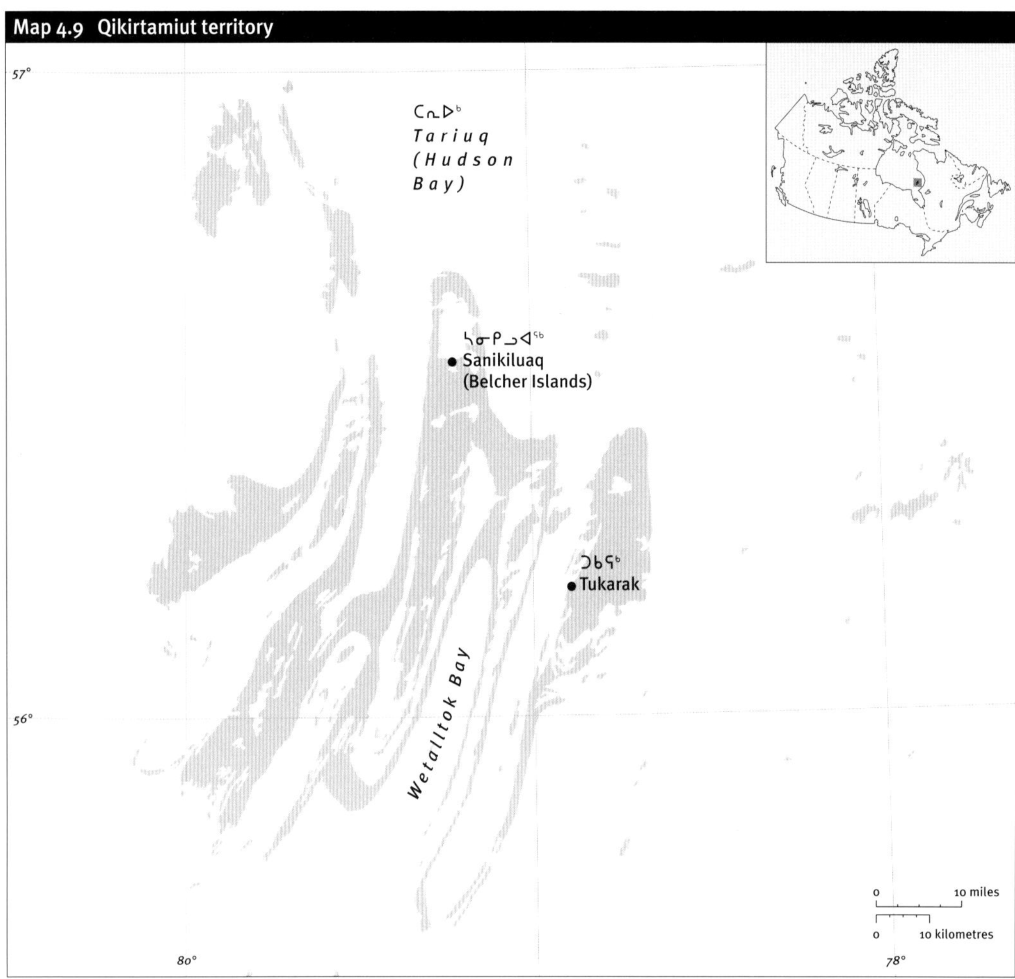

The Qikirtamiut of Sanikiluaq

Though Sanikiluaq as a political unit is today part of the Northwest Territories, the people share the culture of the Nunavimiut. They call themselves the Qikirtamiut, the People of the Islands.[30] The maze of islands, covering more than 8,000 square kilometres, was accurately described in a chart made in 1910 by Weetaltuk, the highly respected Inuk who was a Hudson's Bay Company pilot, boat builder, and artist.[31]

The Qikirtamiut were said to be little known by their kinspeople on the eastern shore of Hudson Bay. Nevertheless, they traded with Nunavimiut who travelled over the one hundred and thirty kilometres to the islands by sled once the ice had formed. This ice bridge lasted about six weeks. In 1840 some Inuit families from the Akulivik area and Sanikiluaq came to the Hudson's Bay Company trading post at Mailasikkut. They brought gifts of boots and sealskin lines for relatives and friends and items for trade including fox, wolverine, and caribou skins and parkas (Francis and Morantz 1983, 139).

Peter Kasudluak of Inukjuaq recalls his childhood when, after the family spent the summer hunting caribou in the interior, they would return in the fall to the coast. He says (Kasudluak 1995, 45):

On the trip back to the coast, we went to Kuujjuaraapik, passing through Sanikiluaq in order to trade caribou skins for qamutiks [sleds] with ivory runners from the Inuit who lived there.

They would also trade skins for Sanikiluaq dogs. Before accepting a dog, the men would test the dog by driving a sled with that dog pulling; that way, they would not trade too many skins for a poor dog.

Sanikiluaq is rich in sea mammals, polar bear, and waterfowl. Caribou used to be numerous on the archipelago, but some time in the late 1880s, after an extraordinary amount of snow, the weather turned mild and then just as abruptly turned cold. A thick coating of ice covered the land, preventing the caribou from grazing on their diet of lichens. They starved, victims of warm weather (Bruemmer 1971, 81).

Clothing

When the Qikirtamiut became bereft of caribou, they made their clothing from skins of marine birds and used skins of dog and seal for reinforcement and trim. *Mitigait,* eider-duck clothing, was worn double layered in winter. In summer the inner parka served, and when it depreciated it was turned inside out and became the outer garment worn over a new inner coat.

The pattern of the man's parka was loose to allow for air circulation and ease of movement. The skins formed a pattern according to density and colour of the feathers. They were first sewn together in horizontal bands, and then the tiers were matched to form hood, sleeves, and body.

The woman's amauti was also made up of tiers of bird skins that form the hood and front and back of the main body. The ruff of the capacious hood was often made of dog fur. The flaps were also sometimes made of dog skin. In the inner amauti pictured on page 160, the front apron comes to below the knee. The tail attaches to the main body at the hip and comes to the calf. Both flaps have a rounded base. The front apron border is ornamented with kidney-shaped lead drops. The back tail border is decorated with small .22-calibre cartridge shells. Down the middle of the tail run seven groups of pendants made up of beads and cartridge casings. The amaut belt on the outer amauti, held by the V-shaped strap over the chest, is fastened by a knot attached to a walrus ivory toggle. Ringed seal straps attached to the amauti perform several functions: to hold the amaut belt and go under the arms to distribute the weight of the child; to reinforce the back of the neck of the garment at the juncture of the hood and the amaut; to go under the amaut and around the waist to secure the child; and to hold the hood snug and to one side so that the wind cannot blow it off the head.

In winter women sometimes wore loose, hoodless birdskin parkas over hooded inner amautiit. The birdskin outer parka had feathers to the exterior, came to the hip, and was even edged. The neckline was wide for ease in pulling it over the spacious hood. An expansion over the back accommodated the amaut of the inner garment. Children wore birdskin outfits made of the very lightweight, supple skins of female waterfowl. Dog fur trimmed the hood, sleeves, and lower edges.

Boots were made with seal skin as in other parts of the Arctic. In former times

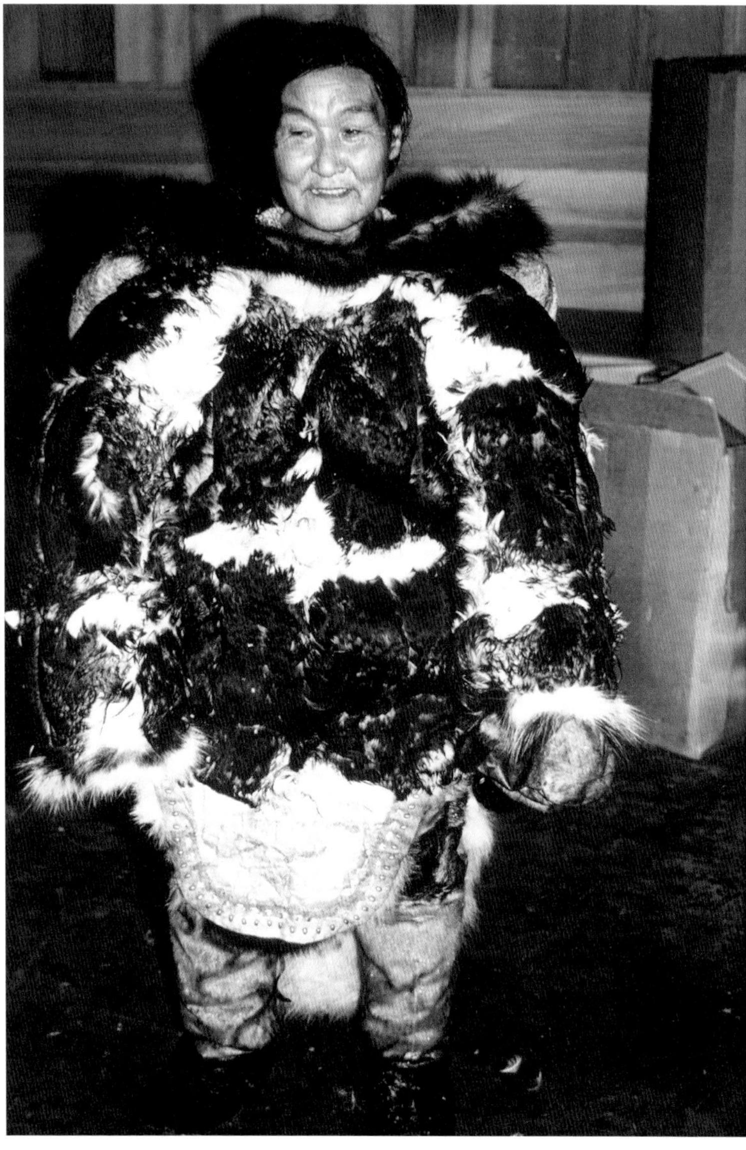

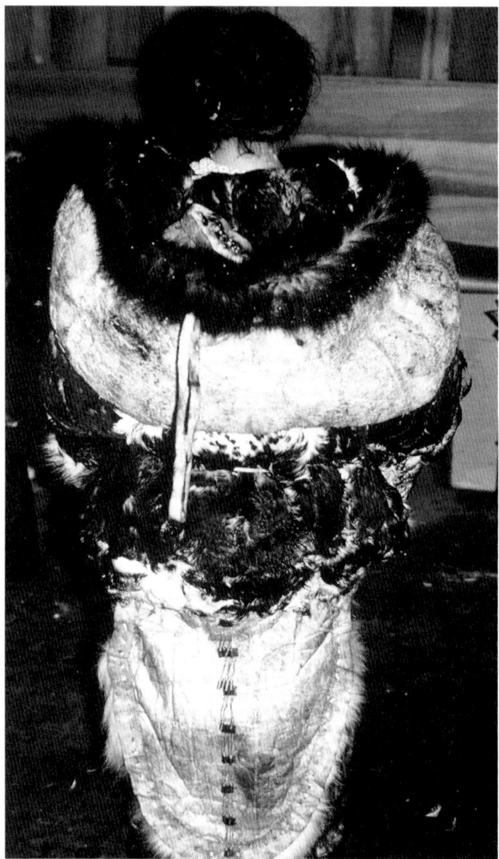

Opposite Maina Aquttuq Alasuaq of Purvirnituq, Nunavik, 1971, formerly of Sanikiluaq, wears inner and outer amautiik of eider duck skins, sewn with sinew, a winter outfit (inner amauti is seen on pages 94-5). The outer amauti (71.1 cm), feathers to the outside and hoodless, is composed of twenty-nine male eider-duck skins. Artisans: Maina Imirqutailaq and Miaji Qassik.

Right Davidialuk Alasuaq Amittu, Maina Aquttuq, and one of their children at Purvirnituq, Nunavik, in 1971. After graduating from the atajuq, the one-piece combination suit, the child wore a birdskin parka and trousers patterned like adult clothing. Children's clothing was made of female waterfowl (as seen here), which are softer and lighter, both in weight and colour, than the male.

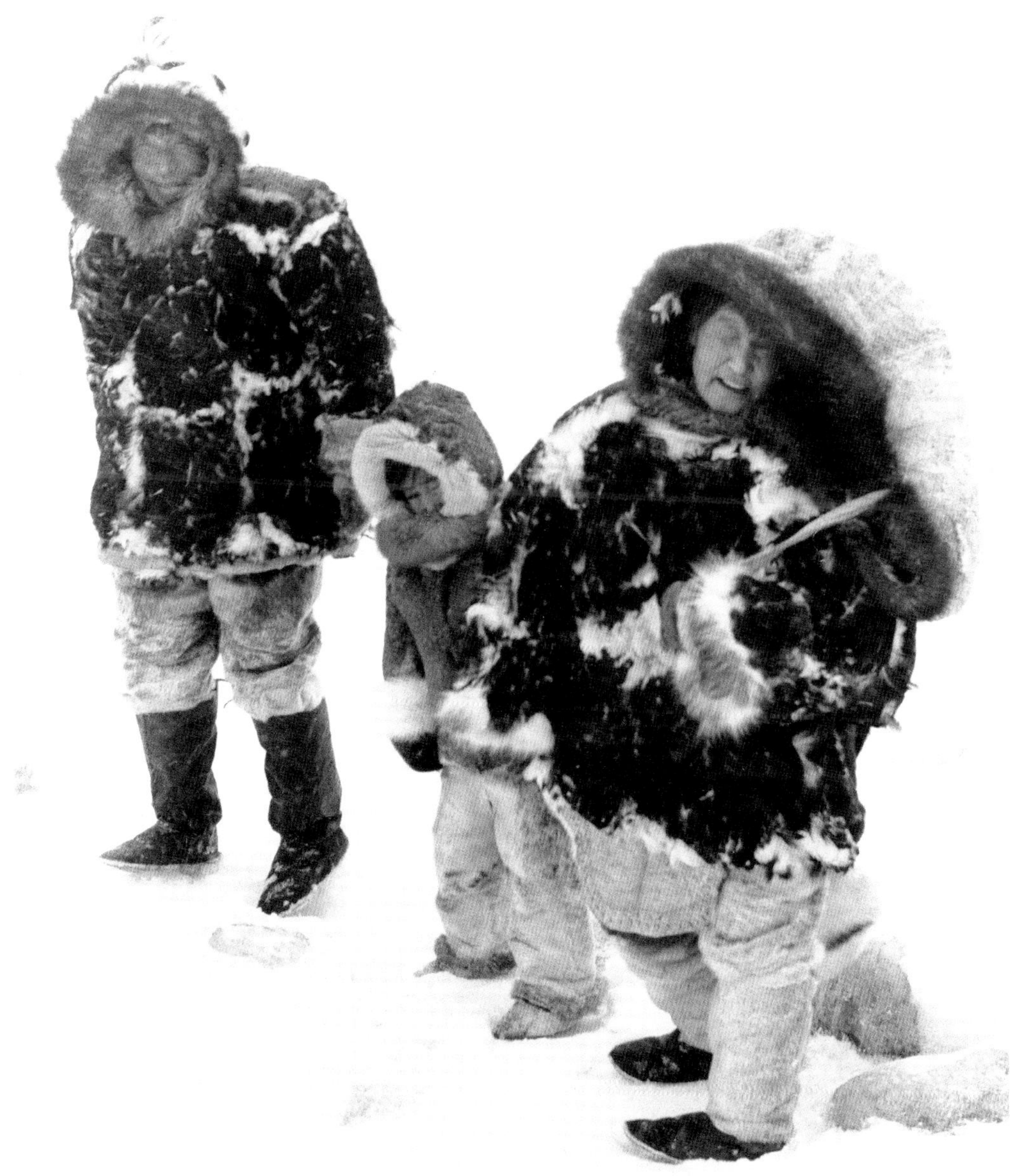

boot soles were made of whale skin. Fish skin, a strong substance, is still used for boots and bags (Edward Miller, Joanne Miller, personal communication 1991).

With the introduction of a reindeer herd several years ago, seamstresses began to use furred skins, although they still remember how to make parkas, trousers, and slippers of waterfowl. A renewed interest in making marine bird clothing has come about through projects sponsored by governments and cultural institutions and through the Qikirtamiut's wish to preserve their heritage (Douglas Nakashima, personal communication 1989).

The Labrador Inuit

The Labrador Inuit and their ancestors occupied much of the Newfoundland coast north of the Strait of Belle Isle, but now they live in coastal communities at and north of Hamilton Inlet.[32] The largest Inuit community is at Naini where Inuit constitute the majority of the population. The second largest group is at Vaali, and the remainder live mainly in Aqvituk, Maquuvik, Kikiaq, and Qipuqqaq. A number of settlements, no longer inhabited, were renamed by Moravian missionaries to bear names evocative of Biblical times: Ramah, Hebron, Zoar.[33]

In addition to visiting between the coastal communities, the Inuit who lived on the northern coasts of Labrador travelled to Nunavik to trade and for reasons of kinship. They also travelled inland seasonally to hunt the migratory caribou, the most important land animal. The Labrador Inuit have occupied more southerly regions than any other Canadian group, and possibly had contact with the maritime Archaic Indians and the Beothuk, but the evidence for any lasting influence is scant. Inuit of the Historic Era lived close to Algonquian groups and the Montagnais-Naskapi, but the effect on each other appears to have been negligible.

Clothing

Labrador Inuit used the skins of seal, caribou, polar bear, dog and, according to early eyewitnesses, eider duck for their clothing, although seal skins appear to have been more generally used due to a warmer and wetter climate than in other parts of the Arctic (Cartwright 1792, 144). The clothing exhibits similarities to that from Baffin Island, in particular from Exeter Sound and Cumberland Sound, and from Nunavik. Because of the 200-year association of Labrador Inuit with the Moravians and the long mixing with European settlers, however, Labrador Inuit are seen by the Inuit of the Northwest Territories and of Nunavik as being very different from them.

More frequently than among any other Arctic group, the Labrador Inuit were taken, forcibly or otherwise, to Europe and placed on exhibition. Some of these tragic events resulted in our early images of Labrador Inuit, with striking details of their clothing.[34] Handbills printed in closely similar versions in Augsburg, Nuremberg, and Stuttgart, Germany, in 1567 were the first depiction of Inuit by Europeans done from life. They advertised the exhibition of an Inuit woman and her child who were

First date refers to time of station establishment by missionaries of the Unitas Fratrum, commonly known as Moravians (J.G.Taylor 1984: 509, 511).

Map 4.10 Labrador Inuit territory

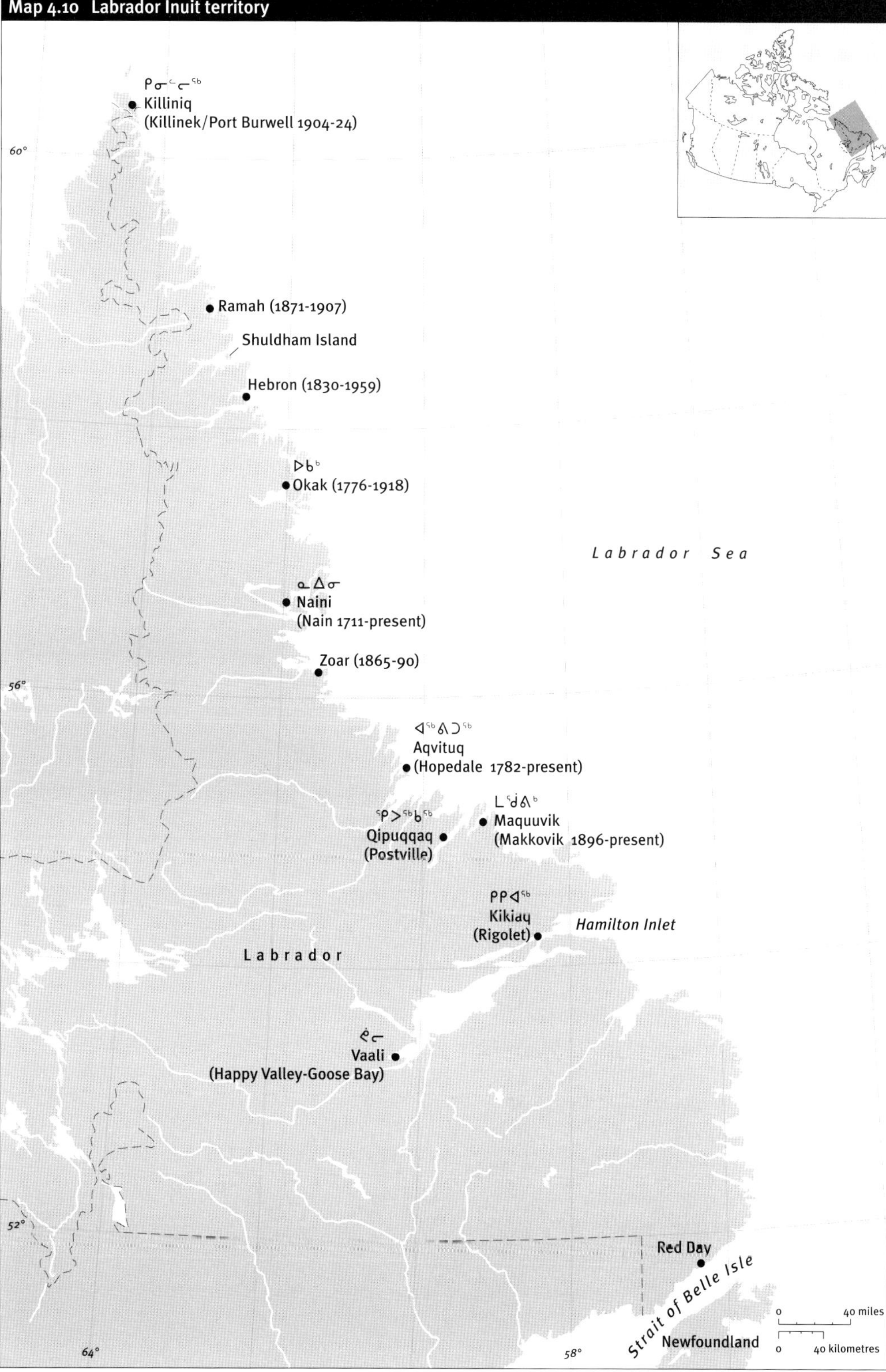

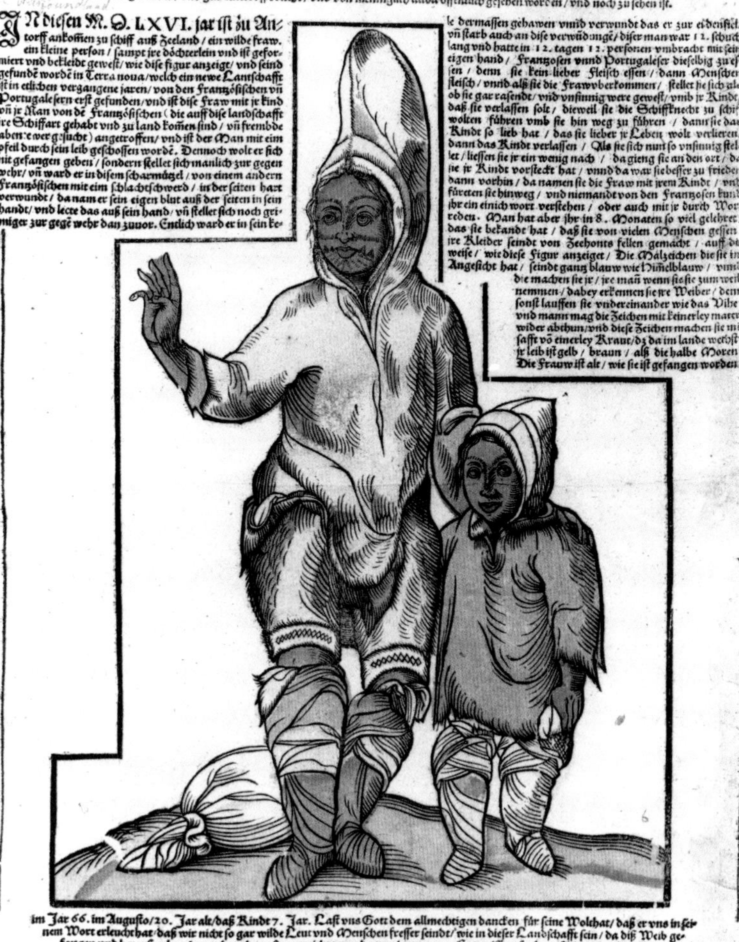

Warhafftige Contrafey einer wilden Frawen / mit jrem Töchterlein / gefunden in der Landschafft Noua terra genannt / vnd gen Antorff bracht / vnd von menniglich allda offentlich gesehen worden / vnd noch zu sehen ist.

IN disem M. D. LXVI. jar ist zu Antorff ankommen zu schiff auß Zeeland / ein wilde fraw. ein kleine person / sampt jre döchterlein vnd ist geformiert vnd bekleidt gewest / wie dise figur anzeigt / vnd seind gefundẽ wordẽ in Terra noua / welch ein newe Lantschafft ist in etlichen vergangene jaren / von den Frantzösischen vñ Portugalesern erst gefunden / vnd ist dise Fraw mit jr kind vñ jr Man von dẽ Frantzösischen (die auff dise landschafft jre Schiffart gehabt vnd zu land komen sind / vñ frembde abenteuer gesucht) angetroffen / vnd ist der Man mit eim pfeil durch sein leib geschossen wordẽ. Dennoch wolt er sich nit gefangen geben / sondern stellet sich manlich zur gegen wehr / vñ ward er in disem scharmützel / von einem andern Frantzösischen mit eim schlachtschwerd / in der seiten hart verwundt / da nam er sein eigen blut auß der seiten in sein handt / vnd leckte das auß sein hand / vñ stellet sich noch grimiger zur gegẽ wehr dan zuuor. Endlich ward er in sein kele dermassen gehawen vnnd verwundt das er zur erden fiel / vñ starb auch an dise verwũdungẽ / diser man war 12. schuch lang vnd hatte in 12. tagen 12. personen vmbracht mit sein eigen hand / Frantzosen vnnd Portugaleser dieselbig zu essen / denn sie kein lieber Fleisch essen / dann Menschen fleisch / vnnd als sie die Fraw vberkommen / stellet sie sich also ob sie gar rasendt / vnd vnsinnig were gewest / vmb jr Kindt / daß sie verlassen solt / dieweil sie die Schiffknecht zu schiff wolten führen vmb sie hin weg zu führen / dann sie das Kindt so lieb hat / das sie lieber jr Leben wolt verlieren / dann das Kindt verlassen / Als sie sich nun so vnsinnig stellet / liessen sie jr ein wenig nach / da gieng sie an den ort / da sie jr Kindt vorsteckt hat / vnnd da war sie besser zu frieden dann vorhin / da namen sie die Fraw mit jrem Kindt / vnd füreten sie hinweg / vnd niemandt von den Frantzosen kund jhr ein einich wort verstehen / oder auch mit jr durch Wort reden. Man hat aber jhr in 8. Monaten so viel gelehret / das sie bekandt hat / daß sie von vielen Menschen gessen / jre Kleider seindt von Zeehonts fellen gemacht / auff die weise / wie diese Figur anzeiget / Die Malzeichen die sie im Angesicht hat / seindt gantz blauw wie Himelblauw / vnnd die machen sie jr / jre mañ wenn sie sie zum weib nemmen / dabey erkennen sie jre Weiber / denn sonst lauffen sie vndereinander wie das Vihe / vnd mann mag die Zeichen mit keinerley materi wider abthun / vnd diese Zeichen machen sie mit safft võ einerley Kraut / dz da im lande wechst / jr leib ist gelb / braun / als die halbe Moren / Die Fraw ist alt / wie sie ist gefangen worden / im Jar 66. im Augusto / 20. Jar alt / daß Kindt 7. Jar. Last vns Gott dem allmechtigen dancken für seine Wolthat / daß er vns in seinem Wort erleucht hat / daß wir nicht so gar wilde Leut vnd Menschen fresser seindt / wie in dieser Landschafft sein / da diß Weib gefangen vnd herauß gebracht worden / denn sie gar nichts von dem rechten waren Gott wissen / sondern schier erger denn das Vihe leben / Gott wölle sie auch zu seinem erkentnis bekeren / Amen.

Getruckt zu Nürmberg / bey Hans Wolf Glaser.

Above Hans Wolf Glaser, handcoloured woodcut, Nuremberg, 1567. This handbill advertised the exhibition in Europe of an Inuit woman and her child. The dress depicted may be representative of the clothing of the Thule culture people, from whom the Labrador Inuit at that time were not too long removed.

Opposite Angelica Kauffmann, *Woman in Eskimo Clothing from Labrador* (ca. 1768-72), oil on canvas, 76.5 cm x 63.5 cm. The woman's amauti has a wide hood, which the artist depicts as draped about the face. The decorative bands and the wide, high boots are consistent with what is known of Labrador attire. The long, narrow back flap, seen in the almost ethereal figure in the background, is evocative of the shape of the tail of early Nunavimiut amautiit.

kidnapped from the Labrador coast by French sailors in 1566.[35] The clothing of the woman in the 1567 Augsburg handbill shows features in common with the garments of the Kalaallit kidnapped in 1654 from Nuuk Fiord. Notable characteristics are: the shape of the woman's hood, which is high, narrow, and rounded at the top with a dark stripe up the middle; the insert below the chin; the short trousers; and the knee-high boots.

The woman's very high hood and short trousers are not the kind of attire seen in paintings from the eighteenth century. Italian artist Angelica Kauffmann (1740-1807) resided in England from 1766 to 1781, and it is believed that her paintings *An Eskimo Man* and *An Eskimo Woman* depicted Inuit brought over from Labrador by Captain George Cartwright in 1772. Men's coats from the mid-eighteenth century to the twentieth have had a straight cut. Eyewitness accounts from the late seventeenth and early eighteenth centuries tell of men's coats with a tail on the back. It is therefore probable that the loss of the tail in some parts of the Arctic occurred in the early eighteenth century (Taylor 1978, 4).

A painting from the early nineteenth century entitled *A Moravian Missionary Conversing with the Eskimos at Nain, Labrador* includes male figures. All wear seal skins, consistent with the warm weather confirmed by the depiction of open water and a tent. The men wear parkas with pointed hoods and straight-cut, hip-length bottom edges. Their trousers appear to come to below the knee and are tucked into their boots. The woman's amauti has a pointed

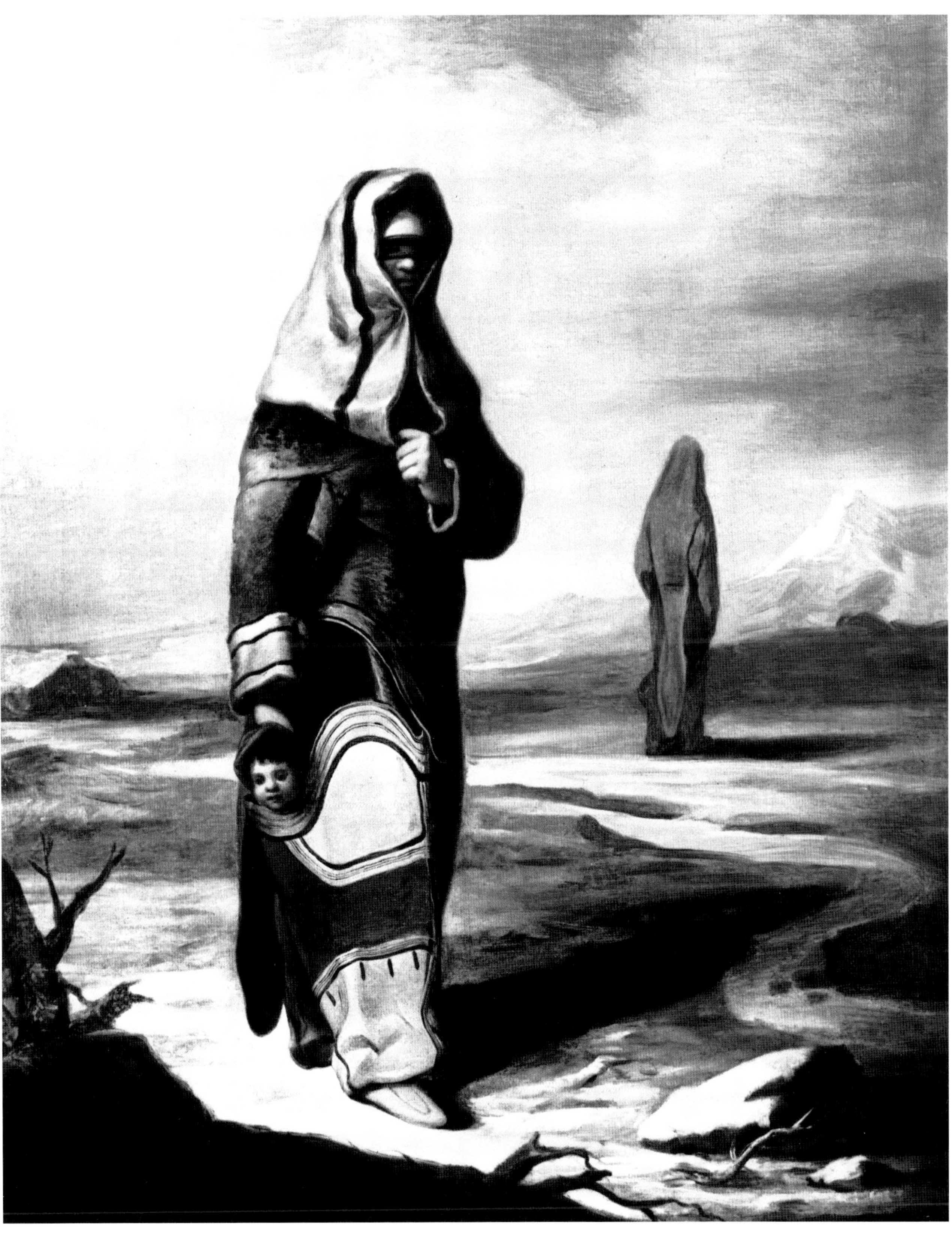

hood and shows ample evidence of beadwork, which is sewn at the edges of the front flap, rising from the edge of the flap toward the waist, and on the back flap. Her trousers, too, tuck into her boots, which appear to have a widened, decorative cuff.

Labrador Inuit continued to use seal- and caribou-skin clothing into the twentieth century. Sealskin parkas and trousers were ideal for seal hunting, for seal skin slips over the ice easily and makes the seal think that one of its kin is approaching. The man's parka, made of seal or caribou skin, was edged with dog or polar bear skin. The trousers were long and narrow. The man's caribou coat on the right-hand side of the photograph on page 168 has European adaptations: buttons at the waist for suspenders and a buttoned fly. The stockings, fur on the outside, have feet, fur to the inside. The woman's sealskin amauti has much in common with the earlier Labrador amauti pictured by Kauffmann and with that of the Nunavimiut of the late nineteenth century.

By the eighteenth century, however, European cloth and clothing had been introduced by missionaries, explorers, whalers, traders, and colonial administrators. Men began to wear duffle parkas or a cloth cover over furs or woolens. In northern Labrador and elsewhere in the Arctic this cotton cover is called a silapaaq: a light, hooded garment worn over a parka. The Labrador cover also goes by the name of cossack or dickie (for the Inuit word *atigi*), and is made of canvas.[36] With white overalls the outfit becomes a winter camouflage as well as good protection against the wind.[37]

Cloth amautiit gradually displaced skin garments. The Moravian Brethren initiated the use of a skirt or full-length dress under the amauti. A beaded or embroidered band was applied around the fur-ruffed hood of the cloth attire. Women wore lace caps for church activities. Before the widespread use of skirts and dresses, mole skin or dog skin trousers were sometimes worn by women instead of seal skin.[38] The mole skin was embroidered at the bottom edge. Some cloth amautiit retained the style of the skin garment: a pointed, wide, cape-like hood banded at the face with embroidery; a narrowed tail to the calf with soft curves; and narrow and wide bands that outlined the parka. Some women adopted a short, even-edged cloth parka much like the man's.

The clothing of Labrador Inuit whalers may be unique in Canada, for there are no records elsewhere in Canada that describe the garb worn by Inuit who waded into the water near the shore to cope with the whales brought in by the harpooners. It appears that a combination waterskin suit was worn for flensing whales (Taylor 1984, 515). The dead whale was towed to fairly shallow water near the settlement of the man who had lodged the first harpoon. The flensing was carried out in the water, and the suit insulated and kept the harpooners dry while they manoeuvred around the animal to cut it up. The pieces were carried to shore by kayak or towed by ropes and hooks. Other waterproof items were special mittens and chest-high wading pants that combined shoes and trousers. These pieces

A Moravian Missionary Conversing with the Eskimos at Nain, Labrador, 1807-ca. 1830. Painting by Mid.(?) Hall after Maria Spilsbury (1777-1820), watercolour on paper, 51.0 cm x 66.0 cm. The male parkas have no side-vents, a feature of Labrador clothing that contrasts with that of Baffin Island and other locales. The form of the beadwork on the woman's amauti appears to be similar to the design on a doll from near Kuujjuaq, Nunavik (Turner 1979, 95).

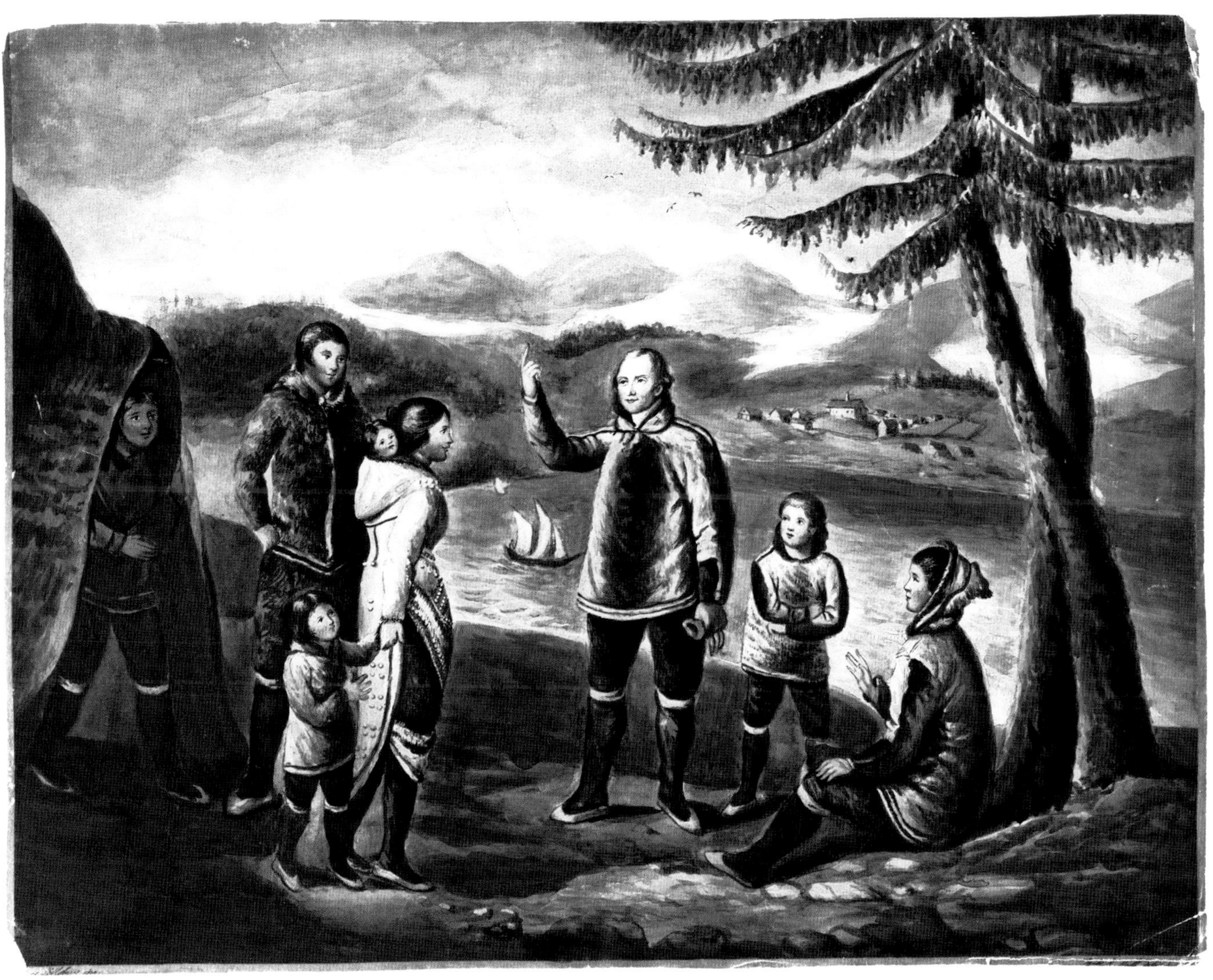

Woman's costume (left): sealskin amauti, sewn with sinew, 132 cm; sealskin outer trousers, sewn with sinew, 85 cm; inner trousers of caribou skin and sinew, cotton, 31 cm; sealskin boots, sewn with sinew, 85 cm; duffle stockings, 49 cm. Labrador Inuit, early twentieth century. Collected at Kiniliq, Labrador, before 1922 by H. Lindow. Man's costume (middle): sealskin and dogskin parka, sewn with sinew, 70 cm; sealskin and cotton trousers, sewn with sinew, 75 cm; boots of sealskin, cotton, and beads, 30 cm. Labrador Inuit, early twentieth century. This parka is made of harbour seal, the sleeves and hood edged with dogskin. Man's costume (right): parka of caribou skin and polar bear skin, sewn with sinew, 75 cm; trousers of caribou skin, cotton, buttons, sewn with sinew, 96 cm; caribou-skin stockings, sewn with sinew, 35 cm; caribou-skin shoes, sewn with sinew, 28 cm; sealskin outer gloves, sewn with sinew, 21 cm. Labrador Inuit, early twentieth century. Men's clothes collected at Hebron, Labrador, by H. Lindow before 1922.

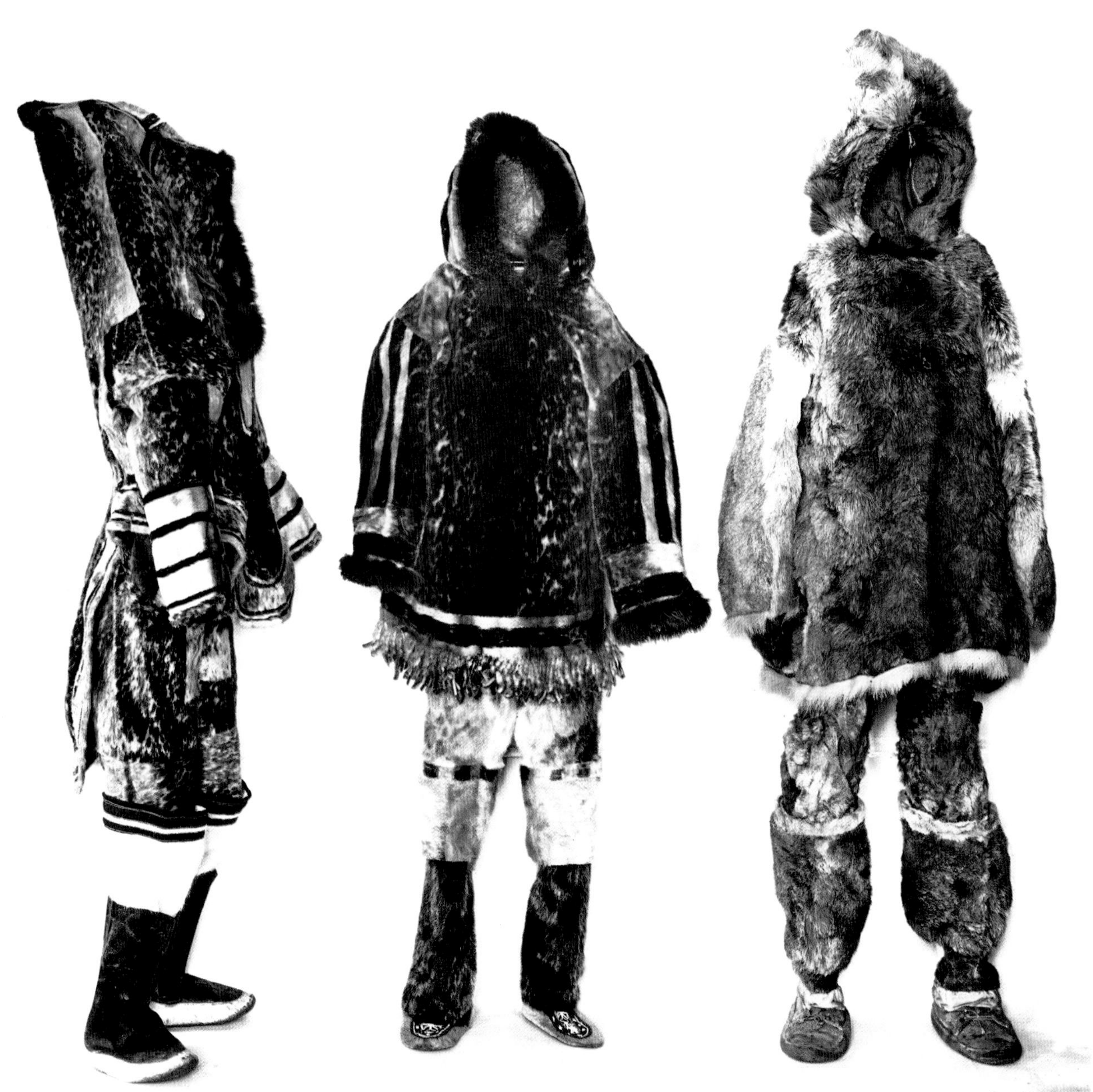

Above Three women, in dress suitable for church, wear lace caps and have long skirts or dresses under their amautiit, which are decorated with embroidered bands around the hood. Photograph taken ca. 1930, possibly on a festival day such as Christmas or Easter at the Moravian Church, Naini, Labrador.

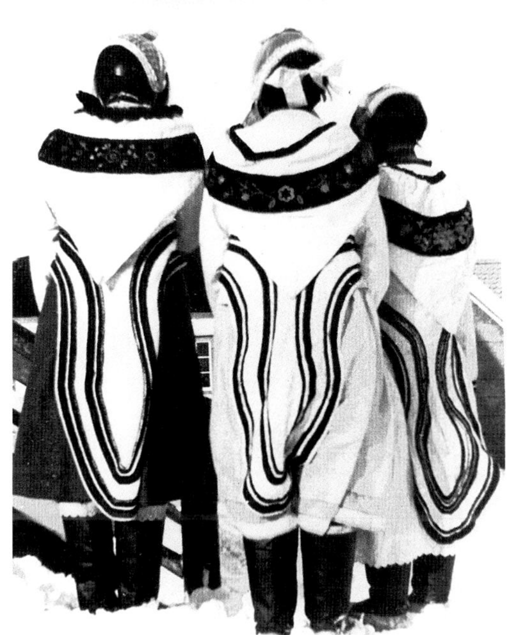

Below Group holding church confirmation certificates at Naini, Labrador, ca. 1930s. Front: Sam Brown. Back left to right: Ado Ikkiasiak, Dan Dan (Okak), unknown, Leah Dan, Mattius Igloliorte, Naeme Maggo. Men wear a hooded, fur-trimmed duffle parka or sometimes a cotton cover over fur. If sealing, the cotton garment was turned inside out to hide the braid trim.

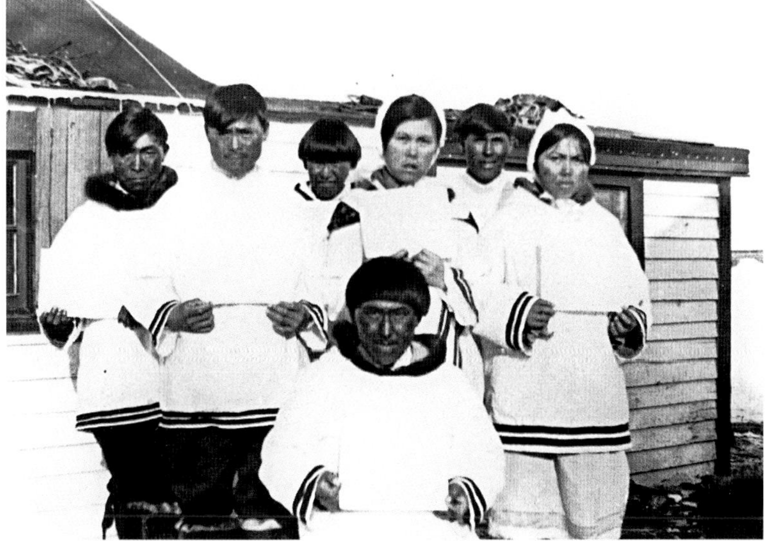

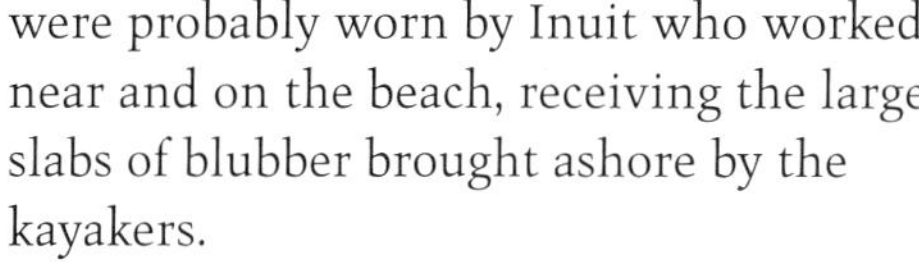

were probably worn by Inuit who worked near and on the beach, receiving the large slabs of blubber brought ashore by the kayakers.

Traditional fur clothing has gradually fallen into disuse over the past half-century, with the exception of sealskin boots, which continue to be worn by a few men and women. Women's boots are slightly wider at the top and have more ornamentation. Inside the boot a fur shoe can be worn; it is called a vamp if made of duffle. Some people still wear duffle parkas with cotton or synthetic covers. Women no longer wear the long-tailed amauti every day, although some have kept them from their youth and wear them on special occasions. Some adapt traditional patterns to make clothes to suit today's way of life.

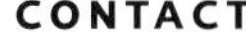

CONTACT

Within the Inuit Universe

Intercontinental Exchanges

Krupnik (1994, 13) describes an 'Inuit universe' that 'produced structures regulating trade and war, that built intertribal alliances and marriages ... [and] promoted the spread of languages.' Following centuries-old patterns the coastal Chukchi and Siberian Yupiit had direct contact with North American Inuit in the nineteenth century through working together on whaling vessels or via the trade networks.[39] American whalers who stopped for supplies at ports in Sivuqaq, the Diomede Islands, Point Hope, and Barrow signed on Chukchi and Inupiaq crew. Some made their headquarters at Qikiqtaruk, to which Inuvialuit moved in order to trade, to hunt marine animals, and to work as seamstresses. Coastal Alaskans traded artifacts with Sivuqaqiut and Siberians. These direct contacts influenced clothing patterns and motifs.

Women's work bags collected at Sitnasuaq and Cape Prince of Wales, both Inupiaq towns on the Bering Strait, may provide some information about nineteenth- and twentieth-century contacts between continents. The geometric patterns of alternating light and dark skin that decorate Inupiaq women's work bags also form motifs in the clothing of the Koryak, Chukchi, Yup'ik, and Inuit cultures: 'Native peoples from Alaskan settlements were attracted to Nome [Sitnasuaq] by opportunities to trade with gold miners and other visitors. Handicrafts from even more distant areas, including northeastern Siberia, reached Nome through native and non-native trading patterns and routes' (VanStone 1984, 451).

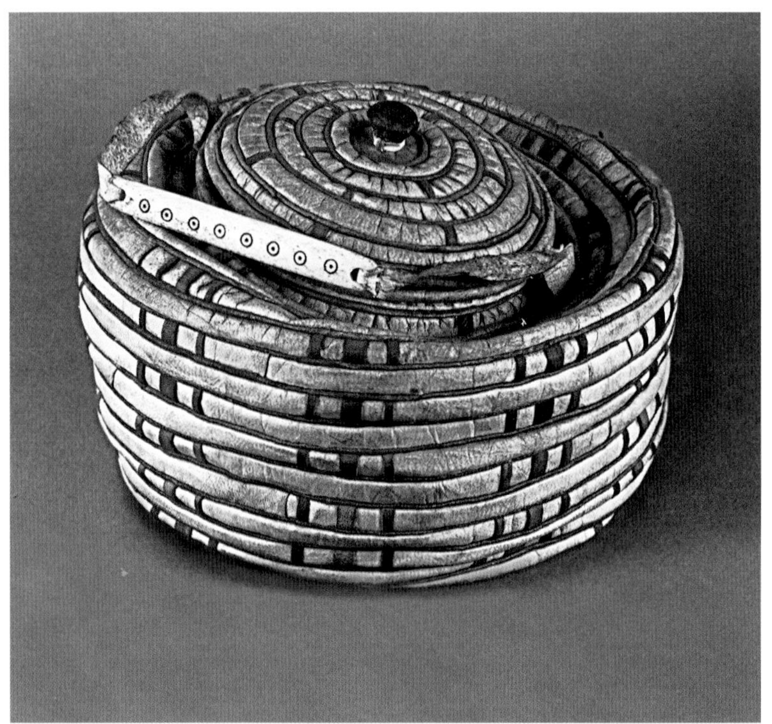

Sealskin and ivory work bag, 18 cm, Inupiat, early twentieth century. Sometimes called a sewing basket, the bag is made of narrow folded strips of dressed sealskin attached in coils. The bag has a lid and carrying strap with a decorated handle, circle and dot motif. Undressed sealskin blocks form the pattern. The welts between the strips are sewn by the same technique used in some Inuit boots.

Inland and Maritime Peoples

From Chukotka in Russia, across the North American Arctic to Kalaallit Nunaat, one of the most important trade patterns occurred between maritime and inland peoples. The necessity for each other's products set up reciprocal relationships. Maritime Inuit could supply sea mammal products such as seal skins, walrus ivory, and seal oil. The inland dwellers' harvest included caribou skins, antler, sinew, and products such as copper, soapstone, and meteoric iron. They did use caribou oil but preferred seal oil because of its superior qualities for heating, cooking, and medicine (Borré 1994).

Siberian Yupiit were and continue to be hunters of marine animals. These coastal peoples traded their products for reindeer skins from the Reindeer Chukchi, who were inland herders (Arutiunov 1988, 39, 40). Nunivak Islanders came to the mainland in summer to barter seal skins, blubber, and fox skins for tobacco. (Nunivak Island is about forty kilometres from the coast of Southwest Alaska.) In return, an *umiak* from the mainland would bring goods such as calico, ammunition, and needles to Nunivak (Lantis 1984, 210, 215).

In prehistoric and historical times, trade fairs drew thousands of Native peoples together at several important locations on the Alaska coast. These fairs were part of a Native trade network that stretched over 3,000 kilometres of the Arctic (Morrison 1992, 45, 46). Nigalik, the place where the Colville River flows into the Beaufort Sea, was the location of a well-known fair in northern Alaska (Hall 1984, 339). The mountain Eskimos would come to wait for the Utqiagvimiut, who lived in the territories near Barrow. At Nigalik inland dwellers would exchange their caribou skins and sinew for Utqiagvimiut seal oil, seal skins, and ivory. Clothing found at the Utqiagvik archaeological site has been dated, with reservations, ca. AD 1510. It was made of caribou with the exception of most of the footgear, which used seal, and one mitten made of polar bear hide (Turcy 1986, 265-319).

A pair of gauntlet gloves in the collection of the McCord Museum of Canadian History is similar in construction to gloves worn on dress occasions by Siberians and Alaskans. The pair comes from the Inuvialuit area of the Mackenzie Delta, and a route for them to reach Barrow has been postulated: the Malimiut of Norton Sound received gloves from Russia and took them to the Nunataagmiut of Kotzebue Sound, who in turn brought them to Barrow traders at the Colville River (Murdoch 1892, 125). From there the gloves could be carried east to the Inuvialuit of Canada's western Arctic.

Similar trade patterns between coastal and inland peoples are documented in the eastern Arctic. The coastal peoples of Nunavik conducted economic and matrimonial exchanges with peoples from the interior and from the islands in Hudson Bay (Saladin d'Anglure 1984, 479).[40] Inlanders needed ivory for weapons, tools, and utensils, and required bearded seal skins for boot soles, for which they exchanged their bales of caribou skins. Inuit from the islands were noted for their powerful dogs and walrus ivory. One islander offered his sled, shod in ivory, and its harness to an inlander in exchange for a bale of skins and a complete suit of caribou.

When Peter Kasudluak of Inukjuaq was a boy, his family, while hunting in the interior, lived with the Nunamiut. He comments on their clothing (Kasudluak 1995, 24):

The Nunamiut [inland people] had very beautiful clothing, well made and nicely decorated. Caribou fur is pretty if the fur is thin. I remember wearing that kind of skin. The women looked so pretty in their thin-furred caribou clothing. Their pants were decorated with white caribou chest skin. It took time to learn and much practice to make that beautiful clothing.

Encounters with the Saami

The Saami – indigenous peoples formerly called Laplanders by non-Saami – have had a special relationship to the Nunatsiarmiut, the Inuvialuit, and Alaskans (Beach 1994, 182). A few Saami reindeer herders and their families came to the eastern and western Arctic in the early part of the twentieth century. In 1921 they were brought to Baffin Island to teach Inuit the ways of raising domesticated caribou (Tuck 1954). The Hudson's Bay Company established reindeer herding at Amadjuaq on southern Baffin Island: 'The reindeer herd of six hundred and twenty animals had been brought across the Atlantic by the *Nascopie* ... four reindeer herders, their families, their dogs and their little sledges. After two years the project of reindeer herding was abandoned and the Laplanders returned to their own country' (Hinds 1984, 43). The Nunatsiarmiut referred to the Saami as 'the playing card people' because of their colourful coats and exotic hats and boots (Alan Cooke, personal communication 1986).

We have yet to discover what influence, if any, the Saami may have had on the clothing of Baffinland, Alaska, and the Inuvialuit areas where Saami herders brought Siberian reindeer from Alaska (Steltzer 1985, 75). The fur clothing of the Saami has several features in common with that of the Inuit.[41] The clothing is worn layered in winter. Preparation of sinew for sewing and skin-dressing methods resemble those of the Inuit (Jomppanen 1982, 98-105). Saami use stitches of sinew, many of which appear to be similar to those of the Inuit. From my observations, however, I would say that Inuit boot-sole construction and the waterproof seam and stitch are not used by the Saami for their boots. We do not yet know the details of boot construction of all groups across Siberia.[42] Was the Inuit boot, with its many refinements, a response to a maritime environment in which the hunt for sea mammals was highly developed, making waterproof boots and mitts an essential ingredient for survival? Do other maritime peoples have such waterproof footgear?

The Inuit and Amerindians

Some anthropologists have ascribed certain types of Inuit ornamentation to the influence of Amerindian tribes: plant-like motifs and single and double scrolls, some executed using beads. The scroll motif, found on Siberian and Indian artifacts (Ivanov 1963, 38-9, Speck 1914), is part of beadwork designs on Aivilingmiut and Pallirmiut clothing.[43] Where Indian and Inuit groups were in contact, they could have borrowed culture traits such as skin-dressing methods or beadwork from each other. However, beadwork was practised, for example, in the Hudson Bay area by the Inuit more than 100 years before the neighbouring Dene Chipewyans took up the art (Lorraine Brandson, Judy McGrath, written communication 1985). In general, Inuit designs and choice of colours are quite distinctive

Two Saami reindeer herders and a Canadian official who were part of a team to establish a herd of domesticated animals at Amadjuak, Baffin Island, NWT, 1921.

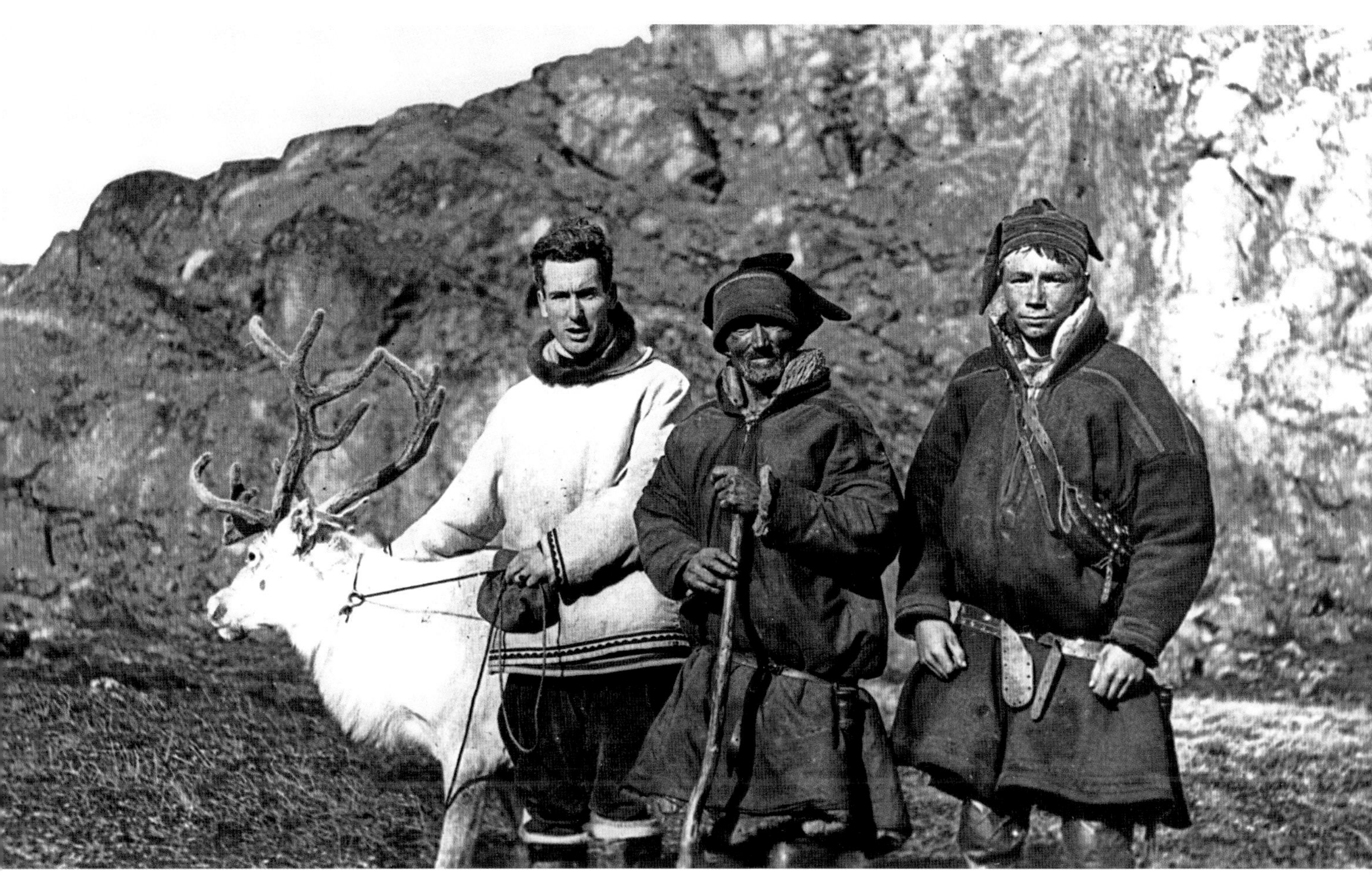

from those of Amerindians (Winifred P. Marsh, written communication 1983).

The answer to the origin of motifs held in common between Inuit and Amerindians may lie in Siberia.[44] The skins – or banners – spread over backrests used inside the tipis of the Plains Cree and Plains Ojibwa, for example, display several emblems seen in North American Inuit and northeastern Siberian artifacts (Brasser 1984, 56-63). Discs were sometimes sewn over or painted around the eyeholes of the buffalo hide. James Bay Cree used this ornamentation to indicate that the animal skin was considered to be alive and to impart speed and endurance to the hunter. Some banners have discs with a circle and dot motif; another has the splayed blades found in designs on Inuit artifacts.[45] Other emblems seen on banners and held in common among northern peoples are: tongue- or dome-shaped pieces, sometimes placed over the earholes in buffalo skins; the 'croix pattée,' a cross with splayed blades; and scrolls.

Contact with Outsiders

Contact between the Eastern Inuit and European cultures may have started with Eirik the Red in AD 980 (McGhee 1992). Eirik, outlawed from Iceland, explored the east coast of Kalaallit Nunaat and returned in AD 986 with twenty-five ships and 400 colonists. The last account of Norse colonies in Kalaallit Nunaat was dated AD 1410. Inuit arrived in Kalaallit Nunaat at least a century earlier (possibly before AD 1300), and co-existed with the Norse in the southwest for several generations.

About AD 1000, Eirik's son Leif voyaged to southern Baffinland or northern Labrador. The first mention of meeting Inuit was in AD 1266, when the Norse encountered traces of Inuit whom they called *skraelings*. At that time the Norse said that the Inuit had no iron and used stone knives and ivory weapons. The archaeological record shows, however, that in several Inuit villages in Arctic Canada, dating from the period before AD 1300, the Inuit had smelted iron, bronze, and copper. They traded walrus ivory, narwhal tusks, polar bear skins, and other furs, which the Norse exported to Europe.

Martin Frobisher's visits in 1576-8 were followed by a mass of hunters and explorers. By the year 1590 about 350 European ships were hunting seals between Baffin Island and Kalaallit Nunaat (Crowe 1974, 105). Over time, explorers came with hundreds of ships trying to find the Northwest Passage and searching for riches. These visitors, some of whom became settlers, introduced materials that became sought after by the Inuit. In 1717 the Hudson's Bay Company established a trading post at the mouth of the Churchill River, on the west coast of Hudson Bay, through the efforts of Captain James Knight. They also traded stores aboard ships that plied the northwest Hudson Bay coast. They would receive from the Inuit 'train,' or whale blubber, oil, baleen, and fox and caribou skins in exchange for knives, lances, fish spears, saws, beads, and needles. Missionaries, notably in Labrador, effected changes in styles for Inuit women, who were importuned to wear skirts and caps along with their traditional dress when going to church.

Stores expended between 1907 and 1909 from the American whaler *A.T. Gifford* included 1,017 yards of calico, 725 yards of drill cloth, 238 bunches of beads, 500 beading needles, 10,500 ordinary needles, 216 thimbles, one hand sewing machine, and 124 pairs of scissors (Ross 1975, 141). The Hudson's Bay and other companies, besides trading beads and articles for day-to-day use, brought in quantities of blanket cloth, or duffle. The Inuit made duffle into boot and mitt liners and used it as a substitute around camp for fur garments because of the relative ease with which it could be made into clothing.

EVOLUTION

Although outsiders brought new goods such as duffle and beads and one or two styles that were incorporated into Inuit dress, they brought about no lasting change to traditional principles of clothing construction across the Arctic; they only modified the outward appearance. The Inuit, knowing the superiority of their clothing to fulfil their requirements, conservatively selected from outsiders' cultures elements that suited their purposes.

Kakligmiut clothing styles, patterns, and materials from northern Alaska, for example, did not change from about 1500 to about 1850. A British naval expedition led by Captain F.W. Beechey was sent to northwestern Alaska in the summer of 1826 to await the arrival of the explorer John Franklin. Beechey anchored at Icy Cape and sent a long-boat or barge up the coast.

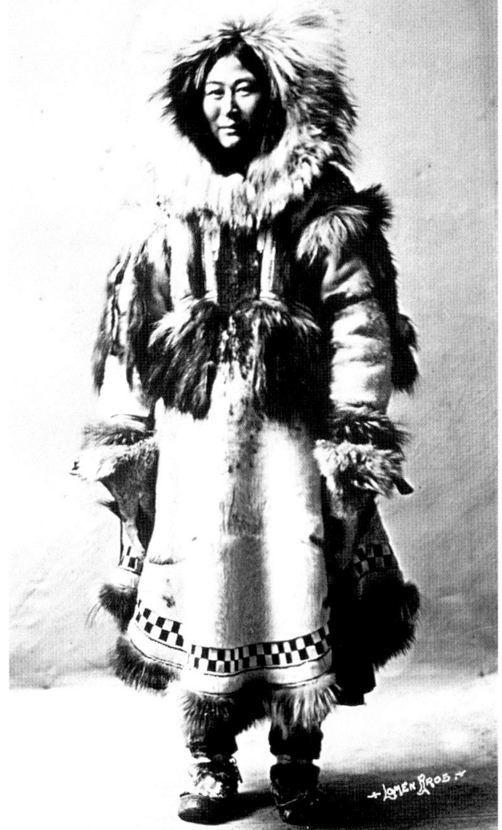

Nora, an Inupiaq girl, at Sitnasuaq, early twentieth century. Her parka appears to be made of domesticated reindeer.

By August it had reached Barrow, in the territory of the Kakligmiut. This is the first recorded contact that Kakligmiut had with Europeans. In 1848 the first American whaling vessel arrived. Direct contact with all these non-Inuit had little impact on the Inupiaq clothing complex (Turcy 1986, 220-2).

Similarly, the Norse presence and trade with Europeans had little effect on the clothing construction of the Kalaallit. Study of a Serermiut settlement near Ilulissat that existed from 1500 BC to AD 1850 has shown that the material culture, including clothing and related tools, did not change despite the presence of a Danish trading station. Later studies confirmed that the same clothing traditions continued into the twentieth century (Mobjerg and Caning 1986, 178, 184-6). The design of the sealskin clothing found at Qilakitsoq remained unchanged from the Thule to the Contemporary era. A small alteration occurred around 1909 when the coat developed a shorter tailpiece (Rosing 1986, 40), leading Canadian Inuit to call their kin in Kalaallitt Nunaat the Akukitormiut – the people of the small tailpieces.

The greatest influences on styles seem to have come from exchanges between Inuit groups and from migrant Inuit families who brought their own styles and methods into new groups.[46] Northeastern Siberian Yupiit worked on whaling ships and came in contact with Alaskan and Canadian Inuit. Inupiat from northern Alaska traded and attended gatherings with Yupiit from southern Alaska. Canadians learned and still learn from each other, assimilating elements that each group considers more efficient, artistic, or exotic than its own. One elder, Leah Arnaujaq of Igluligaarjuk, recalls that at the beginning of the century, when she was a young girl, a whaling ship approached the shore. She heard that they had picked up Inuit called Uqqurmiut – the name used by the people of Cumberland Sound, Baffin Island – as extra hands to help the crew: 'I boarded the ship and got a good chance to look at the people. I had never seen women wearing sealskin parkas and really short sealskin pants before, like those women did' (Arnaujaq 1986, 11). Mrs. Arnaujaq's experience of seeing a different style of clothing from her own still goes on today when Inuit from various parts of the world meet each other.

By the early twentieth century, Inuit men, when around camp in the summer, wore ready-made clothing obtained from the Hudson's Bay Company post. Women wore woolen shawls on short excursions or around camp. A shawl would be folded on the diagonal and placed over the shoulders of the traditional garment, sometimes substituting for the amaut to carry a child.

Crocheted woolen hats with tassels became the trademark of Nunavimiut men. This type of hat was worn under the hood, and it is possible to determine its origin from the geometric designs in the knit or crochet (Lucie Kayulik, personal communication 1986). Its use has spread to many parts of the Arctic. The hat's closely woven surface prevents wind penetration and allows the escape of humidity, and the double-layered base protects the ears. The tassel, worn at the front, acts to anchor the parka hood.

Inuit, in particular the elders, know some of the disadvantages in the use of woven or synthetic fabrics. On Qikiqtaruk the Inuvialuit considered 'white' men's clothing provisional at best. Their word for cloth pants was *kam'-mik-hluk,* which meant 'makeshift pants' (Stefansson 1909, 221). Introduced items of clothing were therefore adopted and modified. If a man wore a duffle parka or boots for hunting, he wore a cotton cover to prevent the snow from sticking. Absorption of humidity by woven or other non-native materials presents danger. 'Even if caribou garments get wet, you can allow the water to freeze and then slap it dry ... Moisture forms in a duffle parka if the outer shell is wind-resistant. The parka will get very cold when that happens,' notes Tumasi Kudluk of Kangiqsuk (Nungak 1983, 129).

Some non-traditional clothing has its disadvantages in extremely cold weather. A child carried in a duffle amauti can risk an upper respiratory infection if overheated, for wool absorbs body humidity and thus its insulative quality is reduced. If a parka or pair of trousers has a zipper with no lapover, cold air can enter. Metal and plastic zippers can break and snag. Metal freezes to the skin. Tight cuffs and waistbands prevent air circulation. Rubber and synthetic boots enclose body humidity. Synthetic materials and velcro closings are noisy, a handicap during the hunt.

Clothing filled with waterfowl down provides excellent insulation against the cold. Placed between layers of cloth, down effectively keeps the body warm, particularly if non-synthetic material is used on the inside and windproof material on the outside. This design, however, is less effective at regulating humidity. When the body becomes overheated through exertion, the down absorbs the body moisture.[47] If the wearer is out on the land for any length of time at low temperatures, the moisture freezes and the insulation is reduced, leaving the person at risk (Nungak 1983, 124, 127-8):

Garments made of duck down are very warm, but they should not be worn when hunting. When the garment gets wet, the down gets wet. The moisture will then touch the skin. When that happens it's unsafe when you're out in the cold. Many people have died of exposure, wearing duck down garments ... Duck down parkas are fine to wear in the community but shouldn't be worn while out of the community.
Mary Tukkiapik of Quaqtaq

Eider down garments are very good protection from wind if the shells are of the right material. Down garments made by non-Inuit are cold. I don't recommend them to be worn in extreme

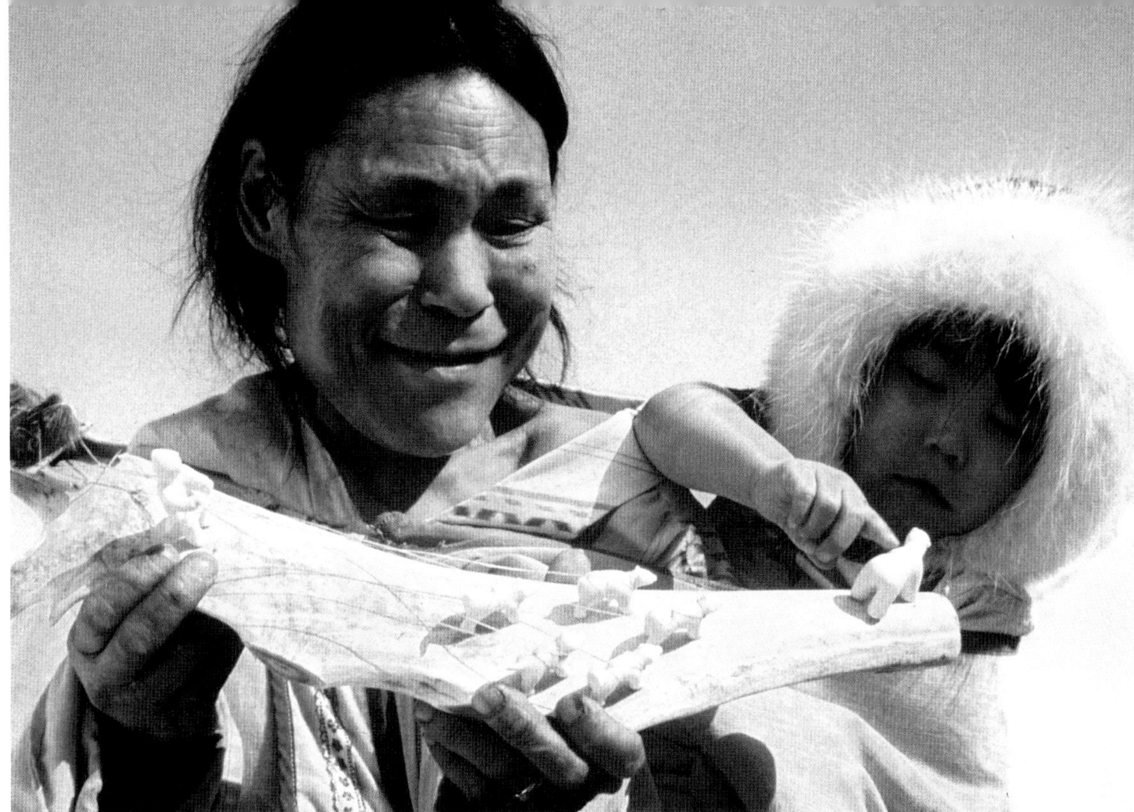

Emily Illnitok, an artist of Arviligjuaq, NWT, 1992, shows one of her carvings to her granddaughter who is safely ensconced in the amaut. Mrs. Illnitok wears a fabric amauti. The child's parka has a full fur ruff.

temperatures. Artificial down is used for fillings and the wind blows right through them.
Daisy Watt of Kuujjuaq

These disadvantages are overcome by choosing the time and place to use down-filled and skin clothing in combination with non-traditional gear. The clothing worn today is a blend of tradition and modernity.

The visitor to the Arctic is not likely to see fur clothing except in winter. Heated homes, offices, and schools require less insulated wear. Many outdoor jobs are dirty, and since the worker is often near a heat source, the use of furs is impractical. Clothing made of duffle, cotton, wool, and synthetic blends is easy to purchase and keep clean. Bought clothing conserves time and energy that would otherwise be needed to make skin garments and releases the person for cash-earning activities. Women who formerly worked full time to sew for and feed the family are now earning salaries in offices and schools, through science projects, or with film crews.

Traditional principles of form and function underlie the new attire made of woven vegetable, animal, and synthetic fibres that is often combined with furs. The garments are layered and loose. Parkas are hooded and ruffed. The amauti continues to be worn by mothers and daughters. Sealskin and caribou mitts and footwear are extensively worn. When out on the land for long periods in cold temperatures, the hunter takes along a set of furs to place over a fabric parka and padded ski pants. If the temperature is expected to go below −20°C, a sheepskin overshoe with fur on the inside and an extra sole with fur to the outside is pulled on. Festive times, such as drum dances, spring festivals, and Christmas celebrations, call for the donning of the most splendid furs.

Retention of fur clothing is not governed solely by its importance to physical survival and comfort, or because there is no adequate substitute. Despite varying norms about traditional clothing, the use of furs is a way to preserve ancient traditions and to identify with cultural values. It is a visual symbol of one's origin as a member of a dynamic and prestigious society whose roots extend into antiquity.

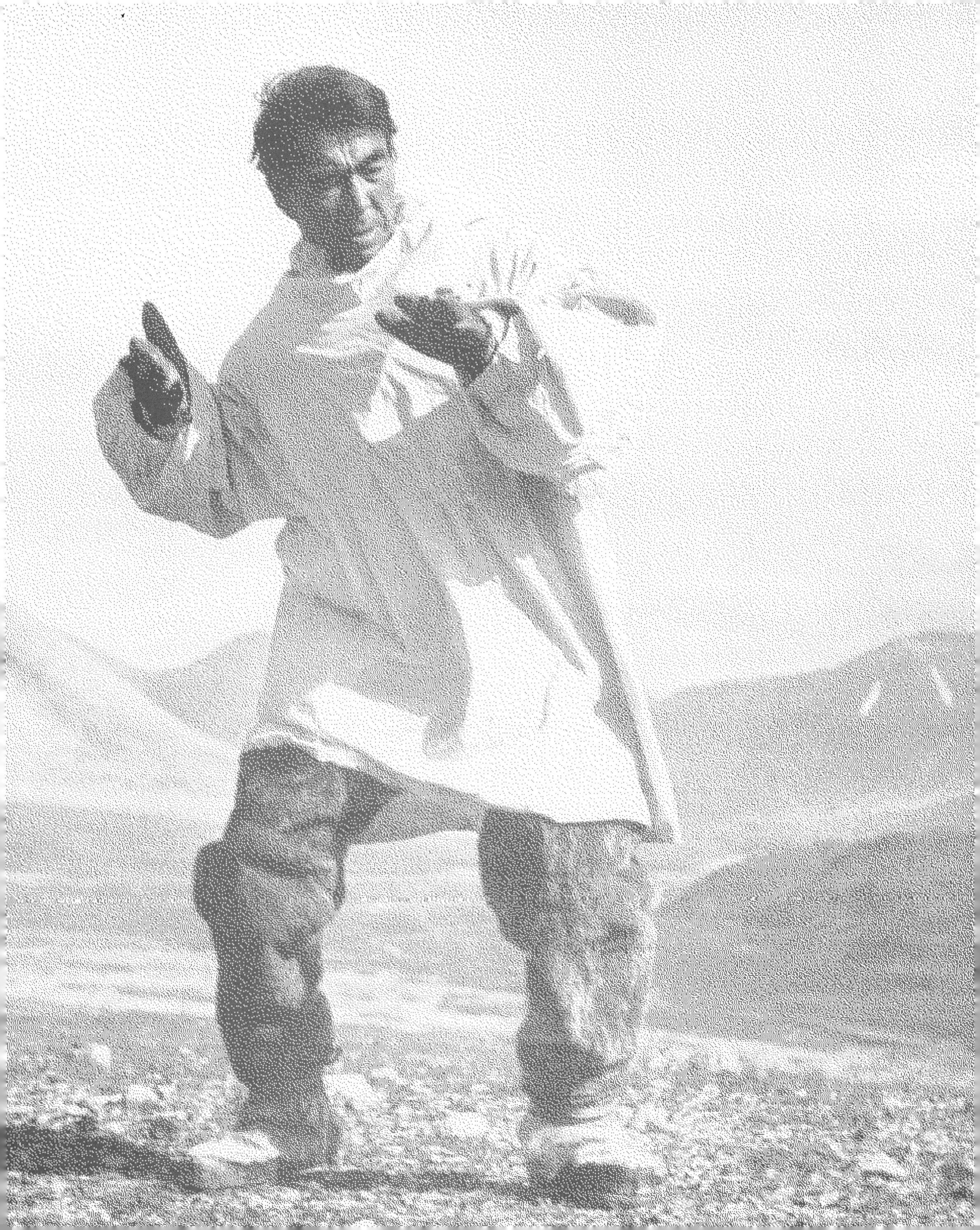

To be an Inuk woman a couple of decades ago wasn't complicated, for gender roles were clearly defined and religiously followed to survive up North.

You were a wife to your husband, a mother of your children, a housewife who cleans and cares for the animal skins and furs your husband brings back home from the hunt. You have dexterous skills which are essential for making clothes, for making transportation facilities and shelters, and you were trained at an early age.

I grew up when formal education had come up North, when our parents had no time to teach us traditional life-skills because we were at school all day.

We were told by our parents that the clothing they made reflects the life-force and would prevail over the environment and climate. Today, many influences that are foreign to us have invaded us. Our lives have gone from the nomadic age to technology in a few decades.

We were so caught up with our new life-style that we almost got engulfed by it all, though we realized in time that we almost allowed our culture and language to deteriorate before it was too late.

Kativik School Board I think played a part in helping to turn our history around by putting emphasis in Language and Culture programmes which they provide in the schools, where our culture teachers give courses from hunting skills to weather forecasting, from trapping to seamstress skills. We have pedagogical counsellors travelling to the communities to give help and support to our teachers.

We still sew our winter clothing and it's taught in our schools but skin and furs have been replaced by synthetic materials, eider down, and cowhide. But they are still much warmer than the store-bought ones.

A month ago I was very lucky to attend a National Inuit Women's Annual Conference, where it was like attending an Inuit national fashion show, for Inuit women from all over Canada wore their most stylish Inuit garments. I saw an Amautik which awed me greatly – I had seen photos of these meticulously decorated Amautiks, but I had never handled and tried one on, nor had I ever met the maker of such Amautiks.

The Amautik had the strangest effect on me: it was like finding a part of myself I never knew existed. It felt sacred, majestic. In it I saw a woman's patience, energy, ingenuity. I felt such pride, respect, and love and inspiration.

I had always been proud of being an Inuk and of my culture, but never felt all these emotions at once until I saw this Amautik. It was like history coming alive. And I daren't part with it.

Caroline Palliser of Inukjuaq[1]

Chapter 5

Spiritual, Artistic, and Social Traditions

THE COSMOLOGY of the Inuit has played an important part in the creation of their clothing. Their apparel, besides including indicators of role, gender, and age, contains references to spiritual beliefs, human-animal bonding and transformation, social and artistic traditions, and group identity.

SPIRITUAL BELIEFS

Cosmology

All the creatures that we have to kill and eat, all those that we have to strike down and destroy to make clothes for ourselves, have souls, like we have, souls that do not perish with the body, and which must therefore be propitiated lest they should revenge themselves on us for taking away their bodies.
Ivaluardjuk of Iglulik

In the Inuit world outlook, all living beings have a soul, and all things, even ideas, have a spirit.[2] Humans are integrated with and allied to all of nature. As long as humans show respect for animal life by observing certain customs, rituals, and rules, the animals will return again to be hunted anew. When a seal or a whale is caught, a solemn moment occurs when the hunter places fresh water made from melted snow in its mouth. The seal and whale are thirsty and come to land looking for a considerate hunter who will slake their thirst. This gesture of kindness to the soul of the animal will encourage its return.

In the past, upon killing a female animal, the hunter sometimes left a piece of caribou or seal skin to be used as a needlecase by the creature's soul. The dangerous and powerful polar bear, too, wanted gifts from humans. After being killed, the soul accompanied the skin into the dwelling for several days and was considered an honoured guest. Tools that the male or female bear desired were hung up with the skin. A female bear was especially eager to obtain uluit, skin scrapers, and needlecases. At the end of four or five days, the soul departed with the spirits of the tools and used them thereafter, having been propitiated and prevented from becoming an evil spirit. Today Inuit traditionally thank the animals who allow themselves to be caught. A hunter can kill as many animals as needed, but reckless destruction of herds can bring on retaliation in the form of famine. To show esteem, the hunter and his wife make certain that he wears clean and well-crafted clothing for the hunt.

In an important Inuit creation myth known across the Arctic, the most powerful spirit, the sea goddess Sedna, symbolizes the intimate liaison between humans and animals.[3] In some communities injunctions against certain sewing practices – whereby activities and products of land and sea were kept separate – arose from the prohibitions of Sedna. Sea animals had their origin in her fingers, and whenever her offspring were murdered she had to be placated. She disliked caribou, who were offensive to her, and humans were prohibited from bringing land animals into contact with her favourites, the sea mammals. Sewing seal skins had to take place in the spring and never along with the sewing of caribou

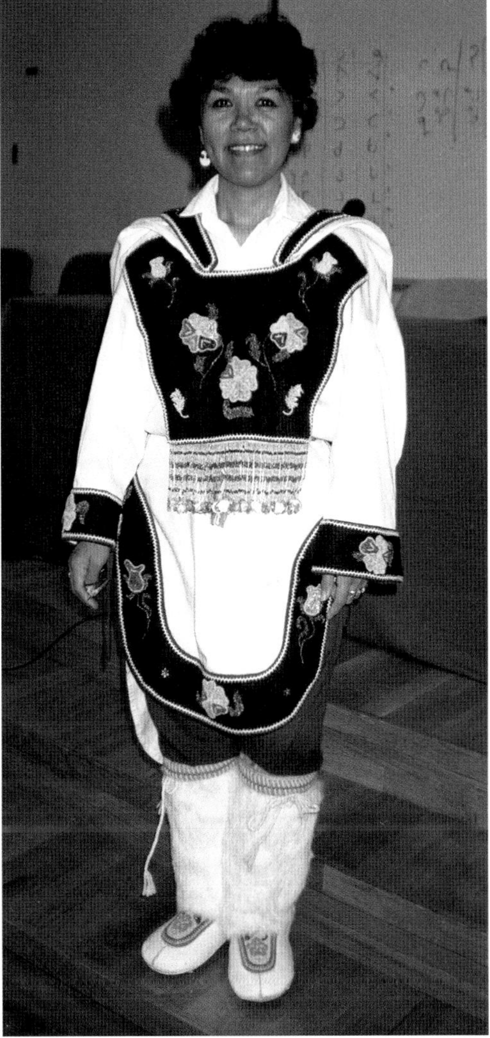

Caroline Palliser of Inukjuaq, Nunavik, is the former Coordinator of Language and Culture Programmes for Kativik School Board. She is seen at the First International Congress of Arctic Social Sciences, Université Laval, 1992, where she conducted the session on learning to speak Inuktitut. She wears an amauti she made herself.

clothing, lest the seals and their governor Sedna take offence. Caribou clothing had to be manufactured in the fall, before the hunt for seals and walrus.

Another version of the Sedna story reveals that when hunters fail to live in the right way, the sea goddess becomes depressed and refuses to comb her long hair. Sea creatures become entangled in her matted tresses and do not come to the surface where the Inuit can find them. A shaman can make a journey to the bottom of the sea to find out from Sedna what rule has been broken.

The Pallirmiut and other Caribou Inuit groups removed the fringe from their caribou clothing when they came to the coast of Hudson Bay for fear of flouting the sea goddess by reminding her of her fingers (Winifred P. Marsh, written communication 1983). The Labrador Inuit were forbidden to bring caribou sinews near a whale, or the weather would become so stormy that flensing could not take place. The Iglulingmiut smoked their tools and caribou-skin clothes over seaweed fires before they started their hunt for seals and whales. This procedure removed the odour of the land animals, and in return Sedna gave them a successful hunt. The absence of bone needles at some Dorset era summer occupation middens leads to the conclusion that similar sewing restrictions were observed by the ancestors of the Inuit.

Transformation

The seamstress combines superb technology with symbolic references to make visible the liaison between animals and humans. By donning fur and skin clothing, humans take on the form of animals and express their bond with the rest of the animal domain. They acquire the strength, knowledge, and powers of the animals' souls.

The way the dressed caribou skin is cut for human clothing helps to transform the person while giving the protection required. Once the white chest, belly, and rump skin is removed for symbolic references and decoration and the leg skins are cut off to make mitts and boots, the shape of the parka appears. The animals' ears and antler velvet are often left on the hood or back to maintain the resemblance to the animal and to transfer the qualities of the caribou to the human. The white chest fur of the caribou, *pukiq,* is used for inserts in the front of the coat. The contours of these inlays reflect the shape of the caribou's white dewlap. Placed over the breast of the human, they dramatize the chest of the caribou, under which beats its great heart. Pukiq bands outline the garment's back and front to manifest the human as animal. The rhythms achieved in the contours around the face, limbs, and corps, curving over hip and haunch and ending in graceful flaps, bring a vision of caribou moving in their great migrations.

Parka armbands made of light and dark stripes emphasize the difference between men's and women's roles. The bands on the man's upper arm signify his arm and shoulder muscles, so important in the hunt that is a joint venture between man and animal. Bands on the woman's lower arm indicate her use of the forearm for scraping skins and for fine sewing – her part in the transformation process. On trousers the caribou rump 'feathers,' the long white fur, signify the strength and flexibility of the muscles of human and animal. The markings on the caribou legs and feet, which give off thunder and lightning as the animal traverses the tundra, become part of footwear, assigning endurance and fleetness to the hunter.

Rosing (1986, 38-9, 45-8) proposes that the oblong insets decorating the arms and legs of clothing from Baffinland, Nunavik, Labrador, and Kalaallit Nunaat represent the animals' bones marked on the surface. (A remarkable example is the elaborate vertical band that graces the mid-front of

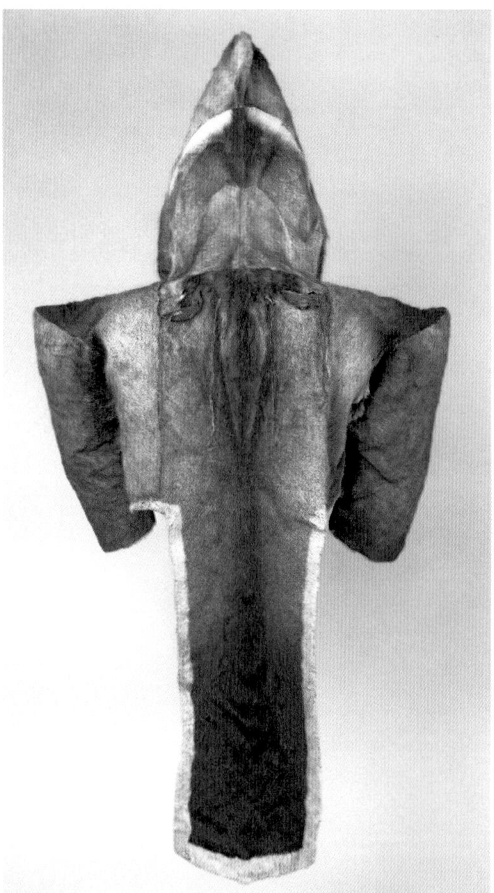

Above Girl's caribou-skin parka, sewn with sinew, 146 cm, Copper Inuit, early twentieth century. The hood, made from the animal's head skin, retains the shape of the head and nose. Between the caribou ears placed at the hood base dangle two tassels of dehaired strips.

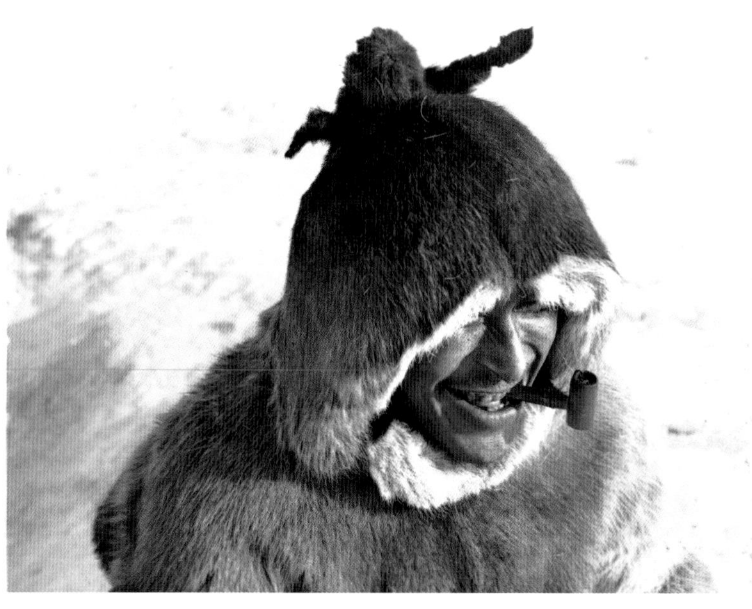

Below An Inuk of Naujaat, NWT, dressed in caribou, 1953. Antler velvet remains on the hood so that the wearer can appropriate the strength and majesty of the caribou.

Below Man's caribou-skin parka, sewn with sinew (154 cm), and trousers (84 cm), Copper Inuit, early twentieth century. Girls' parka (103 cm) and trousers (50 cm) of caribou skin, weasel skin, ptarmigan claws and head, sewn with sinew, Copper Inuit, early twentieth century. On the girl's parka, the third amulet is missing. The middle amulet consists of the head and claws of a ptarmigan wrapped in the skin of a caribou leg, to endow speed and endurance. The right-hand amulet, made of weasel, would give the girl's future sons strength and dexterity. Caribou ears placed below the amulets provided sharp hearing and therefore good hunting.

Right Woman's outer combinations of caribou skin (upper), dehaired sealskin (foot), sewn with sinew, Inupiat (Kakligmiut), ca. 1510. Collected at Utkiagvik, Alaska, by the Utqiagvik Archaeology Project team 1981-2. This pair of combination pants (boots and trousers in one) shows a representation of the caribou hock by piecing of light and dark furs.

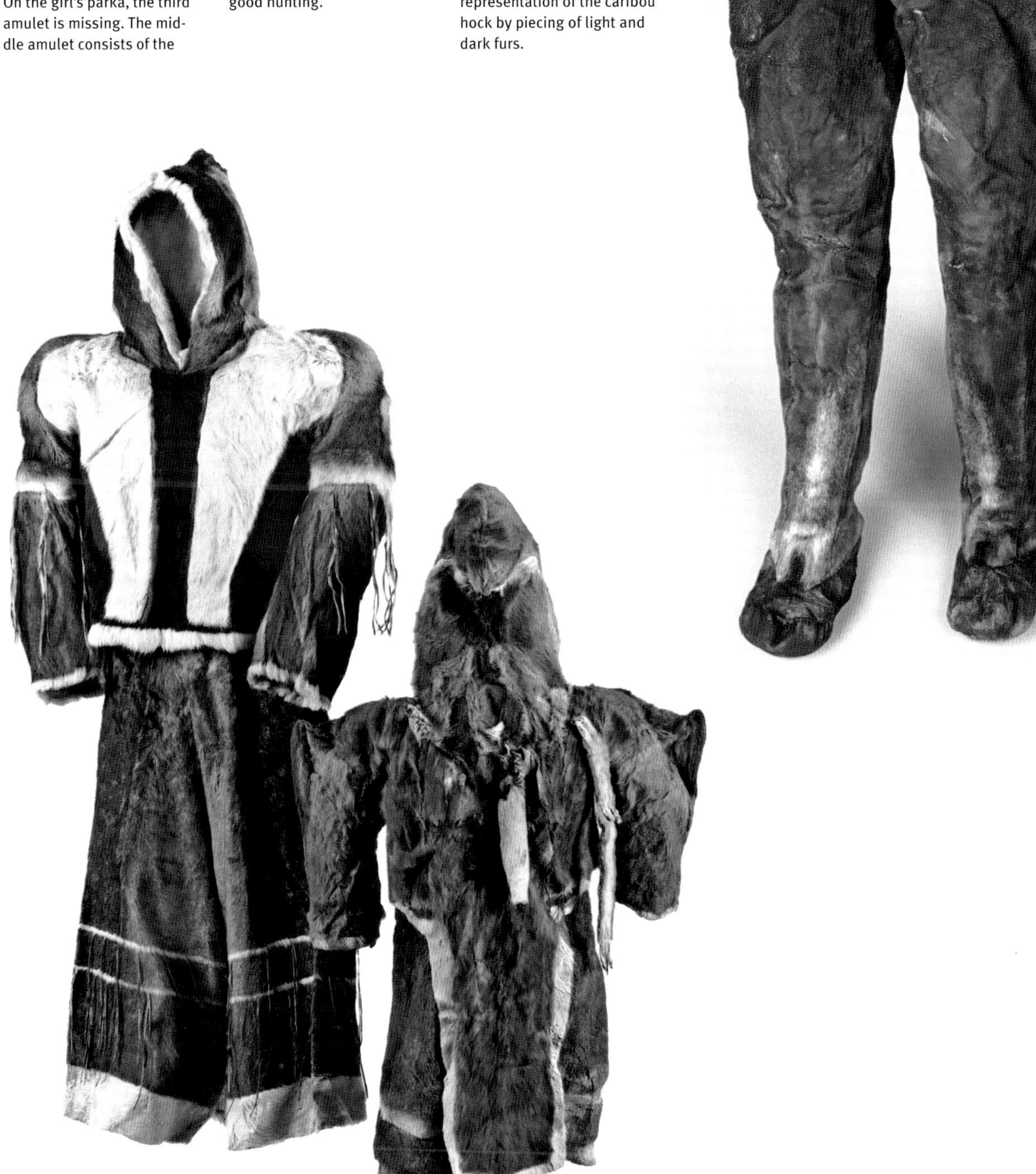

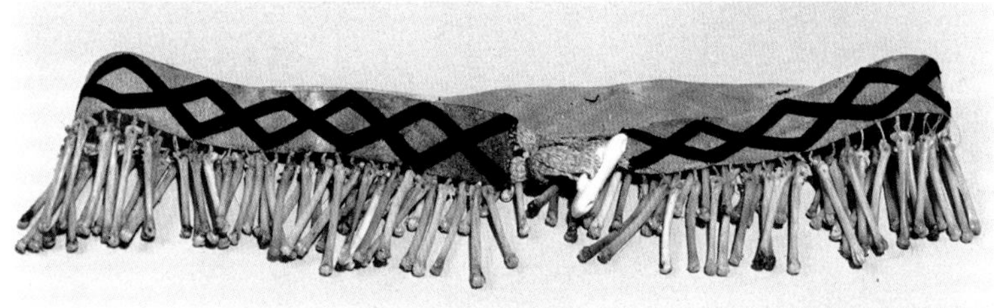

Above Shaman's belt of caribou skin, bone, cotton, ivory, stone, sinew, 92.5 cm. One hundred and six animal bones, each about five centimetres long, hang by sinew from this belt. The small metatarsal bones of fox or wolf ensured strong legs and speed.

Opposite Woman's parka of ground squirrel, wolverine, wolf, caribou, silk, cotton, sewn with sinew, 137 cm, Central Yup'ik, Alaska, ca. 1915. Collected at Taciq, Alaska, by Mrs. Oscar Priester. The skins of forty to sixty ground squirrels make up the coat. Fur from the top of the animals' heads forms the hood (Marcus Wiseman, personel communication 1985). Traditionally a pullover garment, the parka was split to make it easier to put on and take off, a design now used by some Inuit and non-Inuit.

trousers in Kalaallit Nunaat.) The narrow strip that distinguishes the hood centre symbolizes the animal's nose bridge. The sleeve stripes stand for its humerus or ulna, while those positioned at the edges of the costume's openings at the face, arms, and hips match the joints where the knife has cut the skin in order to roll it off the animal. The animal's soul is pleased that its coat changes the human into a member of the animal kingdom, a tribute that it rewards by returning to be hunted anew. The human, thus transformed, acquires the 'ability to move, warm and confident, through cold and storm' (Rosings 1986, 48).

Another symbol of bones on the surface of clothing is found in the chevron motif. The chevron, placed serially and running vertically on the back or front of garments, has been construed to signify the bones of humans and animals.[4]

Helping Spirits

While the human soul was considered to be powerful and the main source of all women's and men's strength, inevitably difficulties arose that could not be resolved by mortals alone. Each Inuk therefore had a helping spirit or 'familiar,' who aided the hunt and other ventures and protected the person from sickness and accidents.[5]

The familiar could be embodied in items worn on or in clothing, such as a carving, animal tooth, claw, or piece of skin, or an unusual *objet trouvé.* Amulets gained their efficacy from their resident spirit and they were exclusively for the use of the person who owned them. Some, made of animal parts and sewn to various places in the clothes, brought good hunting, the qualities needed to become a good hunter, and protection and power. Belts worn outside the coat carried amulets that invested the wearer with the qualities of the resident spirits.

Weasel skins, their representations, or other amulets hung across the back of the parka in series of three or five, gave the wearer speed and adroitness. Inuit mothers placed amulets on their children's clothing to ensure that a son would have success as a hunter or that a daughter would bear talented sons. The hunter who wore a pair of tiny boots on his back was assured that his own boots would last on a long trip, and tiny model boots are still made as gifts and souvenirs.

ARTISTIC TRADITIONS

There does not exist any word for 'art' in Inuktitut. A neologism for 'art' could be sanannguaniq, *'the fact of pretending to work.' A design on clothing is called* allaq *if its pattern is linear ... and* taaqsaq *(literally, 'blot' or 'stain') when the design has a rounder, fuller shape ... An artist or artisan would be a* sanannguati, *'one who habitually pretends to work.'*
Louis-Jacques Dorais, 1984

Decoration and Ornamentation

Clothing is ornamented by fur and skin inlay combinations of strips and bands, which form borders and inserts. Some bands and inlays are made up of geometrically shaped pieces of fur sewn together to form a mosaic. Beadwork on the outer, skin

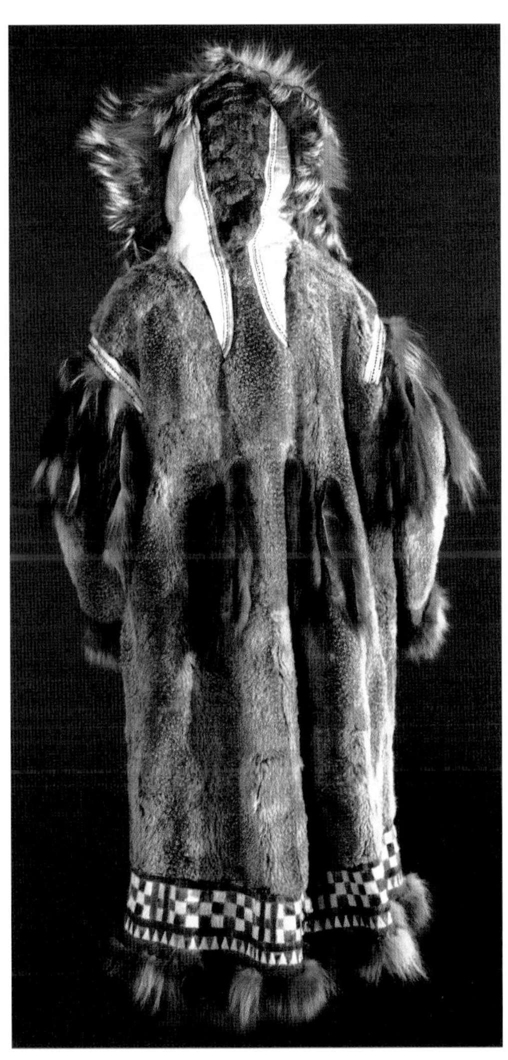

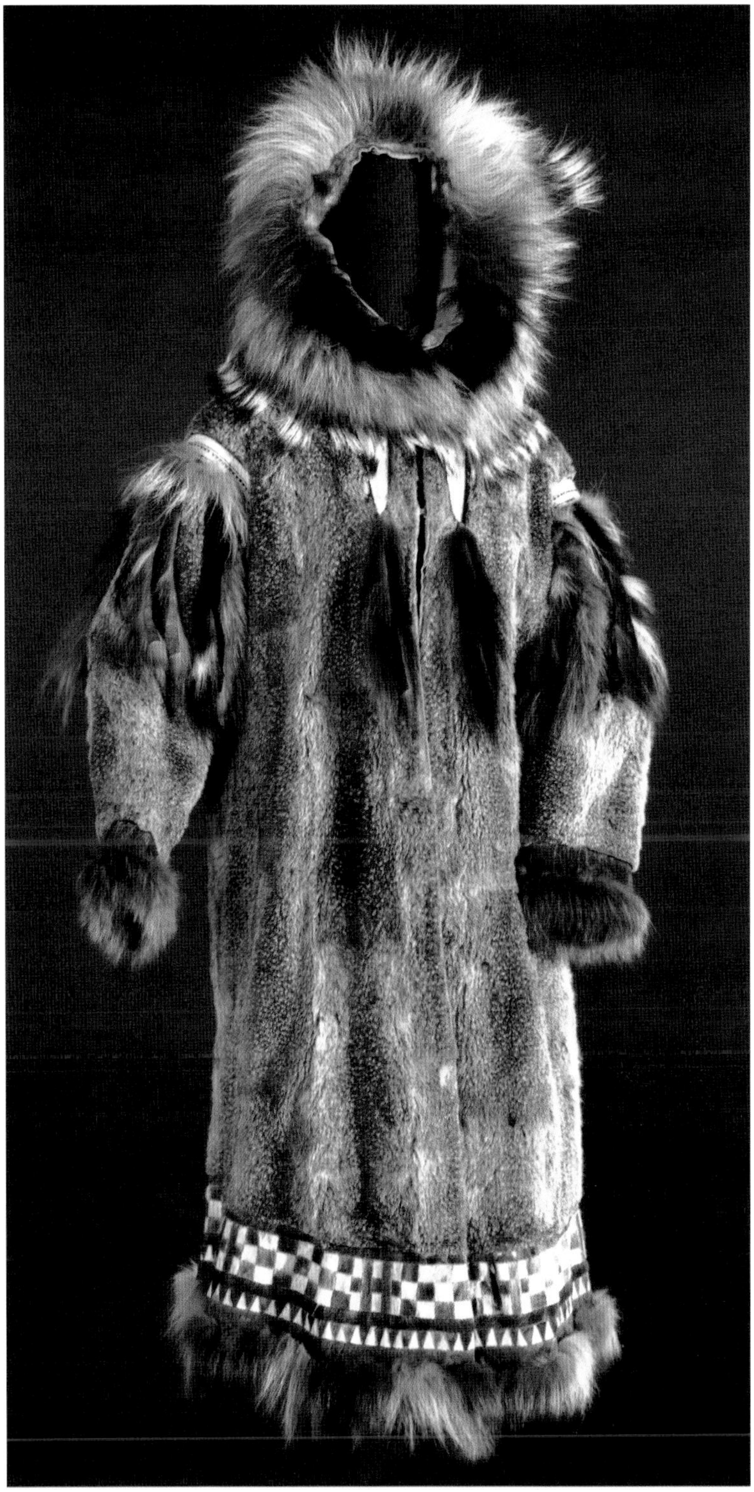

side of inner coats takes the place of the fur patterns of contrasting colours and of amulets, although fur borders are also applied to the skin side.

Borders and Inlays

The skills to prepare fur borders and inlays take many years to master. The different seasons and types of food intake bring many variations in fur colour and length. The animal's age and sex make for diversity of texture and strength. An accomplished seamstress gives lustre to the furs, achieves subtle colour combinations, matches light and dark furs attractively with invisible stitches, and shears the fur to varying depths. Some furs, when clipped, have an appearance like velvet. Matching or contrasting fur flow is important: 'Fur textures are exploited fully, in all possible combinations. There are many levels and types of pile, not just one shaggy fluff. The thick pile restricts folding and draping; thus light and shadow interest occur mainly through variations of texture introduced at seams and margins' (Brandford 1967, 87).

Borders, inlays, and other trim are formed in several ways: the apposition of horizontal strips with variations of clipped fur and shaved or dehaired skin; stroud and skin welts; wool and dyed skin tufts and tags; short- and long-haired fur fringes and dangles; and pieced light and dark furs. When textiles, braid, and tape became available in the Arctic, seamstresses used them to decorate skin, duffle, and cotton clothing.

The borders and inserts of Kalaallit skin clothing, formerly made of contrasting

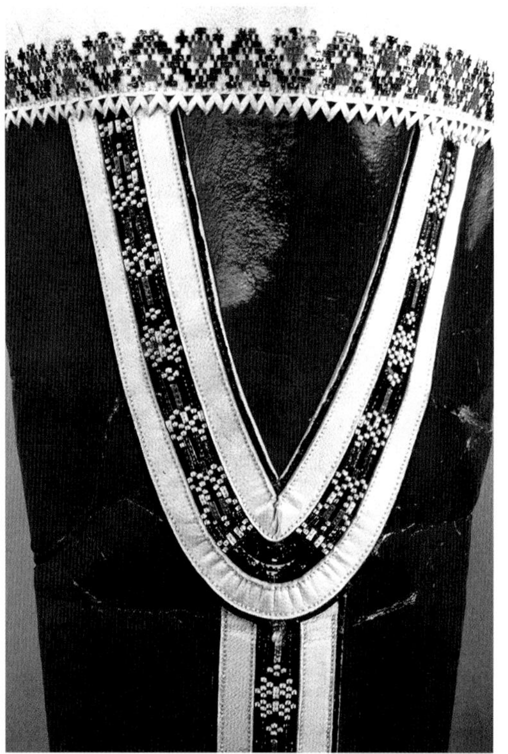

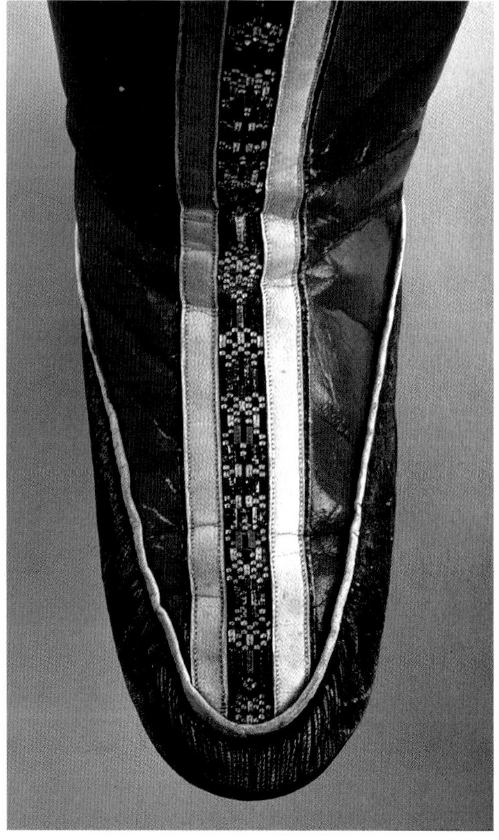

Woman's sealskin boot, sewn with sinew, 68 cm, West Kalaallit, 1955. Artisan: Laurie Jeremiassen of Qutdligssat, Disko Island, for her silver wedding anniversary. Collected by Sheila Romalis in 1982. Close-up views of 'skin embroidery' near boot top and on ankle and instep. The seamstress dyes cuttings of hide as she requires, then cuts out tiny pieces for 'embroidery.' The most popular colour, red, is obtained from brazilwood combined with alum.

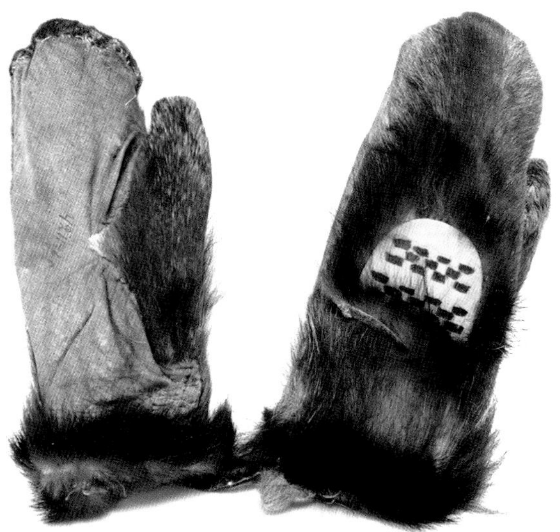

Caribou-skin mitts, sewn with sinew, 26 cm, Siberian Yup'ik, Chukotka, CIS, late nineteenth or early twentieth century. The back section of the mitts is double: the outer surface of caribou leg, the inner of fawn. The palm has fur to the inside. In the back, the seamstress has inserted a U-shaped piece of white hide through which are woven strips of dark skin that form a pattern of alternating rectangles, much like some of the designs in Delta trim in Canada.

colours of furs, are now made with narrow strips of dehaired and dyed skin.[6] This kind of decoration developed into *avittat,* skin embroidery. In the strict sense the method is not embroidery, since the patterns are not made by a continuous thread that passes through the skin to decorate the area. Actually the technique is an appliquéd skin mosaic so fine that it has been compared to, and sometimes mistaken for, the petit-point stitch.[7] Skin embroideries decorate Kalaallit boots and women's trousers.

With a small, sharp knife the Kalaallit seamstress cuts, freehand, fine strips of dyed skin, usually one millimetre wide. The pattern of the mosaic is made up of squares and rectangles one millimetre wide and three to five millimetres long. A stitch on each side of the square secures it; a rectangle requires more stitches between the secured ends. The patterns are handed down within the family, and can be traditional for a garment, for the age and sex of the wearer, or for a given locality. The variations of colours, shapes, and numbers and combinations of strips are infinite. Siberian Yup'ik women use a knife similar to the Kalaallit one for their skin decoration. It seems that this knife is not a part of women's tool assemblages in Canada.

A form of skin decoration held in common by some northern Siberians and Kalaallit is known as slit weaving and slit threading. In a band of fur or dehaired skin the seamstress makes a series of slits across the band that do not reach either edge. A contrasting colour of fur or hide is threaded through the openings and forms a series of squares or rectangles in many combinations.[8] The Kalaallit sometimes use this leather-threading technique, which gives an appearance akin to their skin embroidery and takes much less work. The technique is rare in Canada.[9]

Colours and Dyes

A variety of materials traditionally supplied colours for fur, skin, and fabric inserts.[10] The Copper Inuit and others obtained dyes from ores and outlined seams and inlays with dehaired caribou skin dyed red and black. The Kiluitturmiut, a branch of the Copper Inuit (*kiluittuq* means 'sewing-in-small-stitches'), inlaid red-dyed strips of skin between their fur mosaic patterns. They made the dye from soft pebbles, which they found on the beach and crushed and mixed with seal oil. Another dye, used by western Inuit, was ochre, a mineral of clay and hydrated ferric oxide. It produced pigmentation ranging from light yellow through red to brown. Alder bark was widely used by Arctic peoples such as the northeastern Siberians, Alaskans, and Kalaallit to obtain a red-brown colour. The Kalaallit also acquired red dye from washed-up spruce trees (Hatt 1969, 16). Lichen, moss, berries, and pond algae also supplied colours.

Dyed hair of animals and sea mammals was used as a decorative element, especially on the gutskins made by Asiatic Yupiit and other northeastern Siberians, Bering Sea Inupiat, and Unangan. Hair to be used for seam insertions and embroidery must have certain qualities, fulfilled best in the Arctic by the caribou. The hair 'must be long enough for easy handling; thick enough to be readily visible; white, or only very lightly pigmented, so as to accept dyes; and capable of being folded, flattened, or creased sufficiently to obscure the thread used for stitching' (Turner 1976, 16).

In addition to using dyed hide for seam inserts and outlines, Inuit artisans employed stroud and wool yarn. In past times the Qairnirmiut, a group of the Caribou Inuit, worked with the red web of guillemot *(Cepphus grille)* to obtain red motifs.

When colours other than those of the natural furs or skin are needed, red was the most widely used. 'For the ceremonial things, they'd have yarn tassels on the hood and shoulders. They would be red for suffering. Blood is for suffering,' asserts Rita Pitka Blumenstein of Nelson Island, Alaska (Hickman 1987, 23). Red ochre was sprinkled on graves, and grave articles had ochre paint on them. On the other hand, red was seen in clothing worn every day, at festivities, and by shamans, suggesting that its use had other meanings according to the occasion and the person's role.

Though aniline dyes were obtained from coal tar in 1856 and have been available for some time in the Arctic, Inuit women today sometimes soak dyes out of crêpe paper for their colours. Those who have learned to extract dyes from lichen and willow, moss, berries, sedge, and seaweed prefer them to commercial dyes for their brilliance and subtlety (McGrath 1977, 27).

Fringes, Pendants, Beads, and Beadwork

Fringes on caribou-skin clothing take several forms and enhance and enrich the garment. The simplest are made of furred or dehaired strips cut into a fringe and applied to the bottom edge or inserted into some seams of a parka or trousers by a running or overcast stitch. Most fringes run in a continuous line. Some fringes consist of spaced tassels that group two, three, or four narrow strips.

Sealskin clothing does not need skin fringes. It is worn in the warm weather, when there is less need to conserve heat by interlocking the fringes of double-layered furs to prevent wind entry.[11] Fringes are also traditionally prohibited near the sea, since they would remind the goddess Sedna of her lost fingers. Rita Pitka Blumenstein recalls the use of intestine of beluga to make fringes. When processed the gut looks like white cloth. In southwestern Alaska this kind of fringe symbolized the future generations (Hickman 1987, 27). Two groups whose clothing is fringeless are the Inuhuit of Kalaallit Nunaat and the now-vanished Sallirmiut of Southampton Island.

Bone and ivory pendants used to hang from the lower edges of sealskin parkas.[12] They helped finish the border as well as being ornamental and auditory, adding to the merriment at feasts and dances. They

Above Sealskin kamleika (gutskin), sewn with sinew, 119 cm, Siberian Yup'ik, Chukotka, CIS, late nineteenth or early twentieth century. A ritual gutskin with a vertical strip arrangement, the garment is trimmed at the edges and seams with dark red cloth and cinnamon-coloured ringed-seal skin. Dyed hair strips ornament the chest and simulate a belt at the waist, possibly a reference to that of the shaman.

Below Ivory pendants, 2.2 cm (left), Thule culture. Collected from various sites in the NWT, by the Archaeological Survey of Canada.

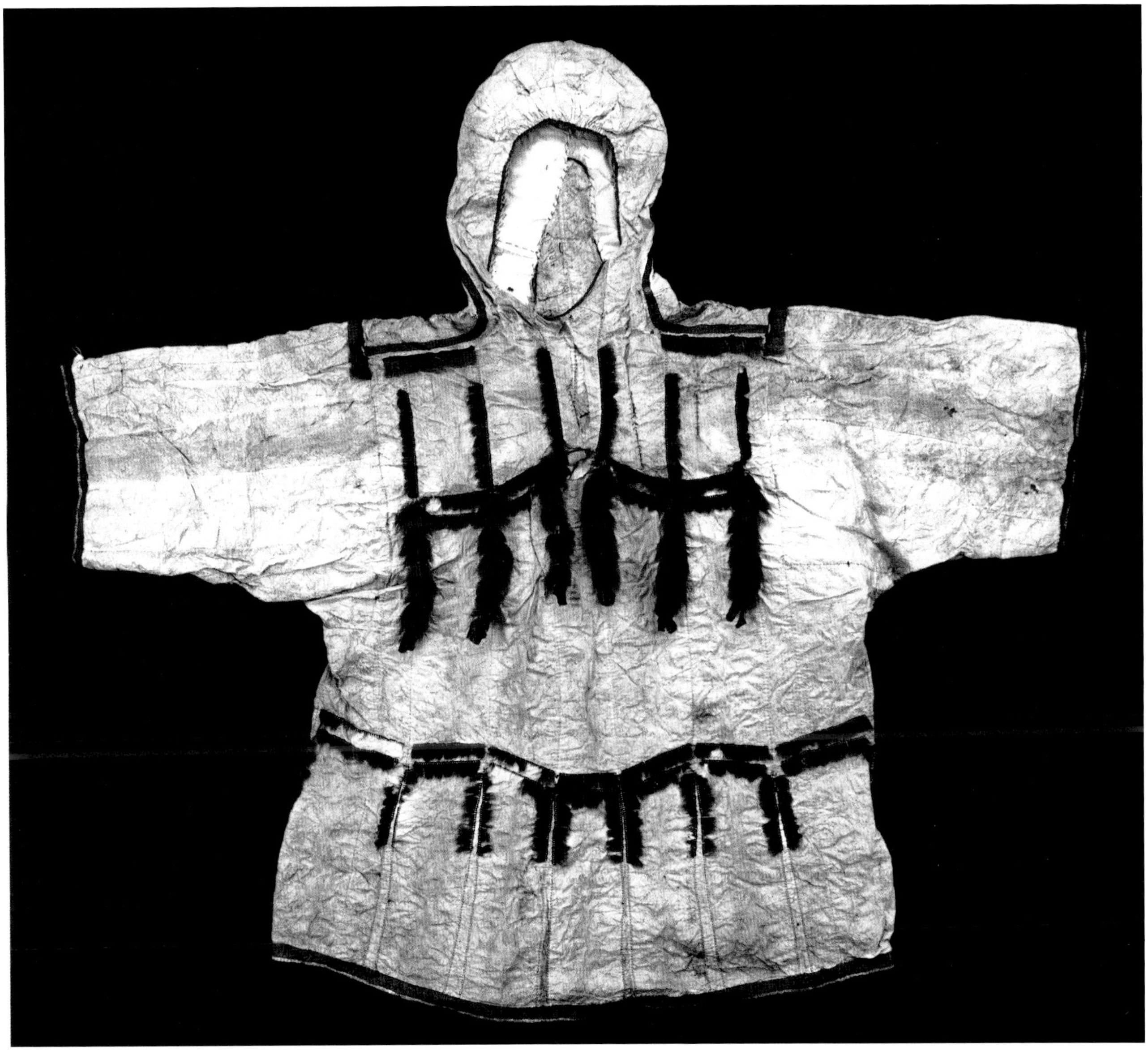

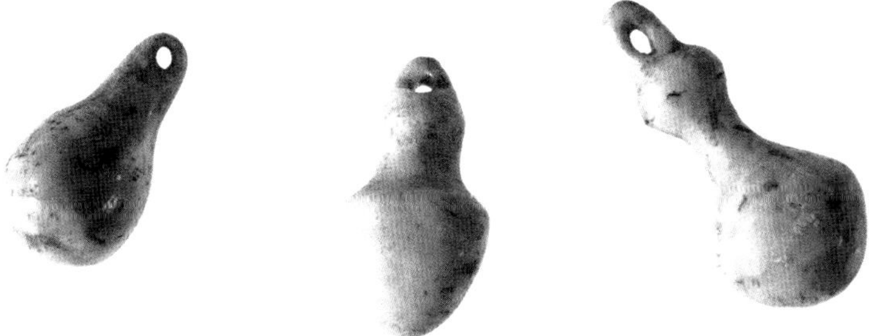

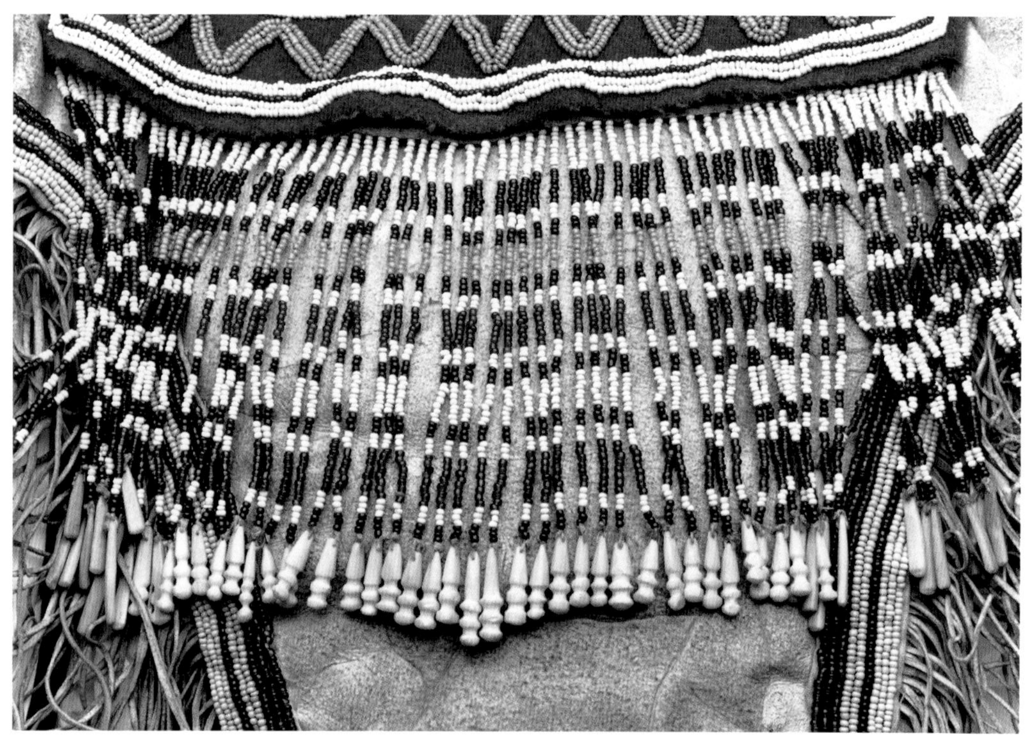

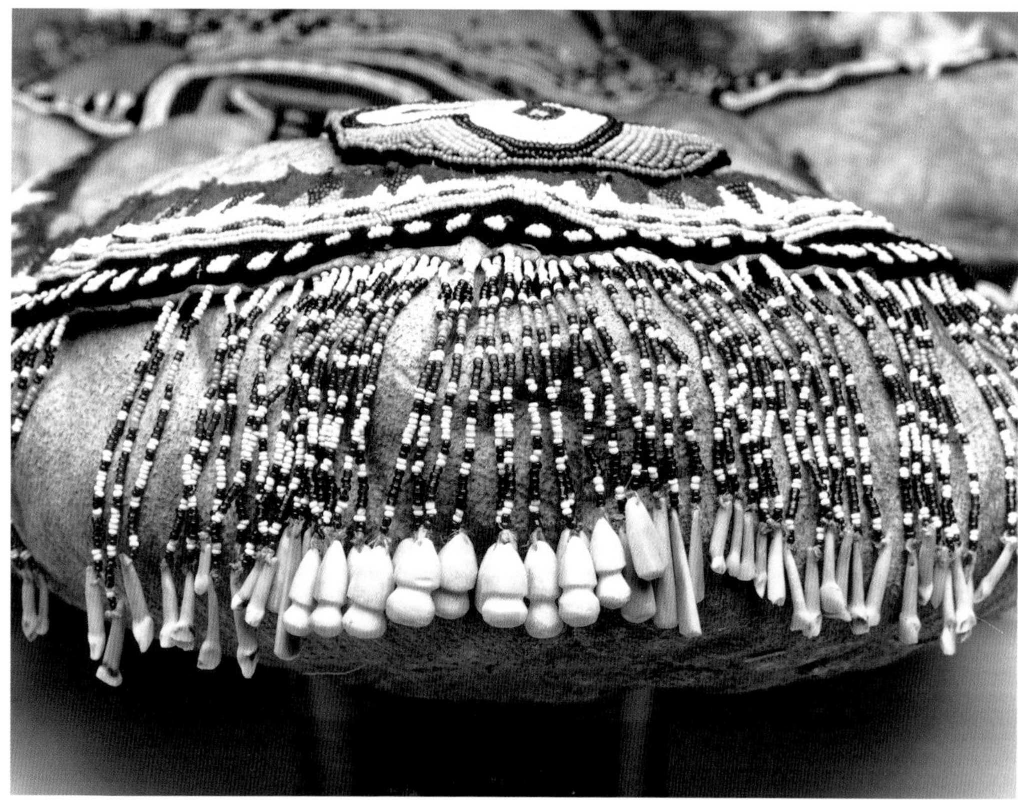

Amauti (detail) of caribou skin, beads, bone, blanket cloth, sewn with sinew, Iglulingmiut (Aivilingmiut), ca. 1930. For a full front view of the amauti, see page 193.

Above The detail from the front includes carved notched and flat bone pendants between 1.5 and 2.5 centimetres in length.

Below The detail at the top of the hood shows carved bone pendants (1.5 cm) and teeth (average 1.8 cm).

were also suspended from the ends of strings of beads. Some resembled pendants recovered from the Thule culture.

Pendants made of animal teeth, particularly the incisor teeth of caribou, were the most widely used. Teeth of caribou fawns are long and elegant, and are drilled at the root end for the suspension hole. Both men and women would drill hundreds for decorative purposes, such as dangling from the ends of beaded strings. The bow-drill lent itself to this task, women having smaller ones than men. 'Each woman made her own design ... In those days, if a woman had coins, she liked to decorate the back tail of her packing parka [amauti] with them. If there were no coins, her husband melted down a few of his lead bullets or some weights from the fishnet and shaped them into drops,' remarks Mosie Jayko of Kinngait (Strickler and Alookee 1988, 142).

With contact and trade, more materials became available for decoration: coins, pewter spoons, tin tags from plug tobacco, metal buttons, bullet casings, beads. To make the lead drops that the seamstress sewed to the amauti, her husband obtained spoons from the Hudson's Bay Company, melted them, and poured the fluid metal into a mould made of two slabs of soapstone to obtain the drops. After hardening they were pierced horizontally at the back so that the attaching sinew was invisible.

Some of the oldest pendants and beads known in the Arctic come from Kalaallit Nunaat. Dated 2000 to 1000 BC, some are carved of soapstone. More recent Kalaallit beads manufactured from materials at hand are made of animal bone, tooth, thoracic vertebrae of capelin, and cod otoliths.[13] Thule culture sites in Canada, ca. AD 1000, have yielded a few beads made of amber, stone, tooth, and ivory.

The use of beads applied to the skin side of furs, inset into tools, or in personal decoration became widespread in North America when quantities were brought from Russia and Europe by explorers and traders.[14] The rate of exchange, difficult now to determine, varied according to area, season, and who was involved in the negotiations. In the Norton Sound, Alaska, area two matching greenish-blue beads brought the non-Inuit trader three or four caribou skins (Jenkins 1972, 36-7). In other Alaskan coastal areas two beads were exchanged for three large bearded seal skins or a seal bladder full of whale oil. An impoverished Inuk who arrived at Barrow with one blue bead traded it for a sled and five dogs, ten slabs of baleen, five cross-fox skins, and one silver fox skin (Bockstoce 1977, 89).

The beads that arrived in Alaska and later in the Mackenzie Delta are called Russian or Siberian trade beads, but they were not made in Russia. Russians acquired the beads, which were manufactured in China or imported from Venice to Hong Kong by English trading companies (Dubin 1987, 274-5). Some beads came directly to North America from Venice through the Hudson's Bay Company posts.

The largest number of beads brought in by the HBC were seed-beads, sold in bunches of five or six strings each ten to fifteen centimetres long. At Fort McPherson, one beaver skin obtained one bunch of seed-beads (Orchard 1975, 101-2). The nineteenth-century seed-beads were larger than the ones traded in the twentieth century. The beads used in one Pallirmiut woman's amauti made in the 1940s were perhaps 100 years old, having been obtained in trade in the 1800s (Winifred P. Marsh, written communication 1983). A distinctive and much sought-after bead from Venice was called the Cornaline d'Aleppo. The Hudson's Bay Company distributed them all over North America so that they came to be known as 'Hudson's Bay beads' (Orchard 1975, 100). The Cornaline d'Aleppo was a tubular bead of opaque red glass wound over an opaque white or transparent green or yellow core. Because of its high price it was used sparingly, as found in the beadwork on a widow's amauti from Baffin Island.

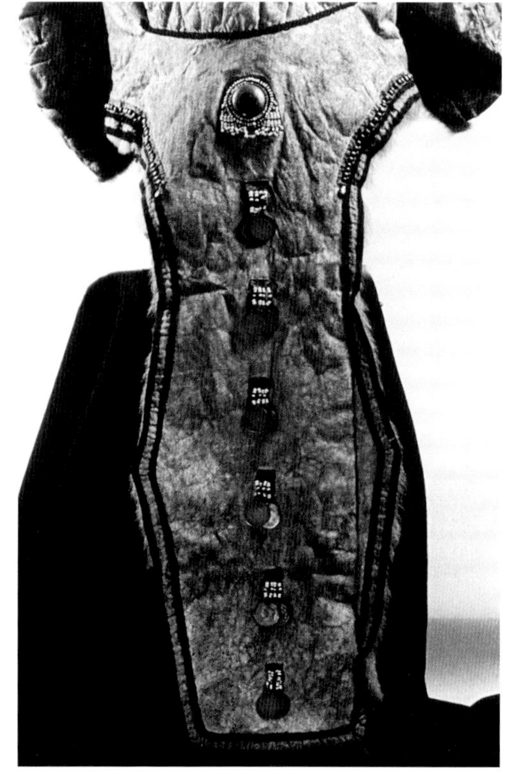

Widow's amauti (detail) of seal, beads, spoons, coins, lead, brass, and braid sinew, Nunatsiarmiut, late nineteenth century. Collected on Baffin Island, by William Wakeham in 1897. Oval-shaped lead drops are sewn to a sealskin strip applied to the borders of the front flap and top of the back flap. Surrounded with beadwork, a brass boss and six groups of two American one-cent pieces, dates 1848 to 1855, descend the amauti tail. The beadwork surrounding the boss (at the top of the tail) includes one rare bead called a Cornaline d'Aleppo. For a full view of the front, see page 72; for the back, see page 148.

Beadwork took much creative effort and time to accomplish: 'The beautiful geometric Padlimiut woman's attigi back and front was the work of a young woman who yearly picked her work to pieces in order to make a new outfit for herself and her husband' (Winifred P. Marsh, written communication 1983). In one style, the beads are first sewn to dehaired skin or to red or black stroud or other fabric that fits the area to be decorated (Strickler and Alookee 1988, 142). The beaded piece is then applied to the skin side of the garment. These panels and bands are removed and placed on new clothing once the original garment wears out, and are passed on from mother to daughter and to members of the extended family. For some time, beadwork has been applied only to women's clothing. Beaded panels form the central column that ascends the hood of the amauti; the cuff, coat, and hood borders; shoulder decorations; and chest ornamentation. The seamstress decides on the content of the decoration, drawing on group and family traditions, on personal experiences, and on her own imagination. Beadwork will often tell the maker or locality of origin. Caribou Inuit designs, for example, favour naturalistic, flowing, and rounded shapes, with lobes, scallops, and petals. Farther north among the Iglulingmiut are often found representational images.[15]

Young girl's amauti of caribou skin, beads, bone, and blanket cloth, sewn with sinew, 128 cm, Iglulingmiut (Aivilingmiut), ca. 1930. Collected north of Igluligaarjuk, NWT, by Clifford P. Wilson. The garment contains elements from both the Aivilingmiut and the Pallirmiut. The beadwork's motifs, lobes and rosettes, are reminiscent of those of the Pallirmiut. The flaps are like those of the Aivilingmiut – rounded and slightly tapered – in contrast to the more square-cut ones of the Pallirmiut. The amaut, which is too narrow and flat to accommodate a baby, was worn by Iglulingmiut women past the child-bearing age and, very occasionally, by unmarried girls. Consultants who suggested an Aivilingmiut provenance were Asen Balikci, Bernadette Driscoll, Rhoda Karetak, Judy McGrath, Winifred Marsh, and Annie Napayok.

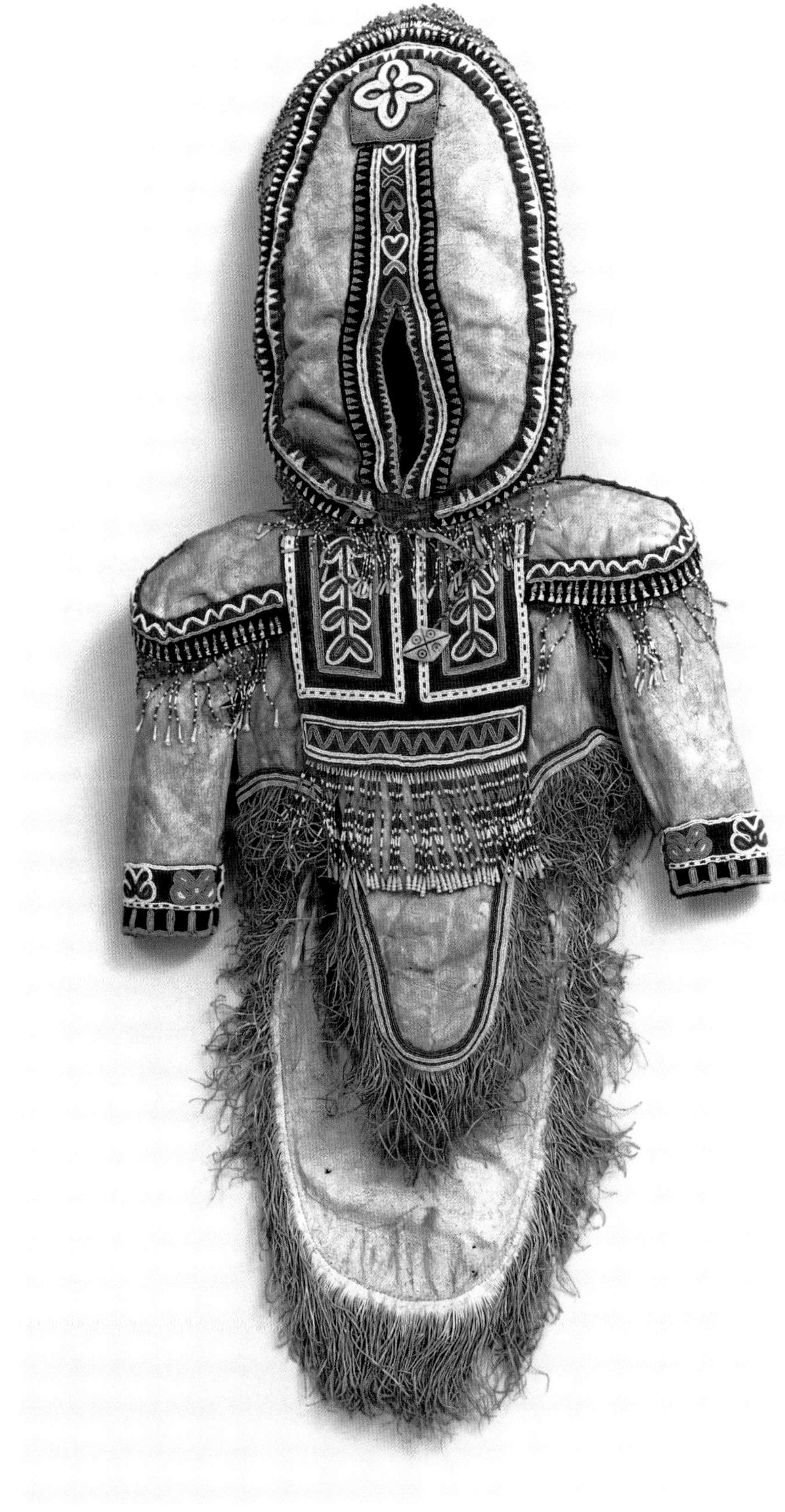

In Nunavik and Baffinland another style of beaded decoration exists alongside the beaded cloth appliqués. Strings of beads are attached across the chest of the amauti in alternating light and dark horizontal bands. Similar strings of beads fall from the lower edge of the chest panels and shoulder and hood bands of amautiit from the west coast of Hudson Bay. Tradition dictates that the beads are strung in a consistent repetition of juxtaposed light- and dark-coloured horizontal bands of certain widths. The same number and colours of beads on each string, traditionally made of sinew, produce the bands. The closely aligned sinews are anchored by a knot in a doubled strip of dehaired hide that is sewn either to the stroud or to the chest of the amauti. At the end of each string there can be a loop of beads, a caribou fawn's tooth, or a carved bone pendant. Beads were also set into tools, boxes, and jewellery and used for dolls' eyes.

Eastern and western Kalaallit obtained European glass beads in the 1600s and 1700s from Norse and later from Dutch whalers (Kaalund 1984, 123). They incorporated the beads into their clothing in borders, collars, and tassels. The national or festive dress of western Kalaallit Nunaat demonstrates the elaborate use of beads. The bead collar was small at the beginning of the twentieth century but has developed so that it often goes from over the shoulders almost to the waist. The patterns in the deep bead collar of the festive dress are geometric, or sometimes floral. The Kalaallit collar can weigh over a kilogram. Cape-like and with a net construction, it stretches open as needed to give width over the shoulders, adapting to the size of the wearer. The openings in the net are important to allow the spirits through to be in contact with the person (Sheila Romalis, personal communication 1982). American Indian groups have net-like beading weaves similar to the Kalaallit (Hansen 1979, 36-9; Orchard 1975, 139-48).

Motifs

The designs and motifs used on fur and skin clothing, and now on fabrics, have ancient roots that come from the ancestors of the Inuit.[16] Genetic, linguistic, and cultural complexes link the Inuit peoples of northeastern Asia, the North American Arctic, and Kalaallit Nunaat. The cultural connections among the northern parts of the continents stretch beyond the Yup'ik peoples who live on the Bering Sea to important northeastern districts of the CIS, notably to the Chukchi and the Koryak.

The ornamental designs used on artifacts of Eskimo-like peoples who existed around the beginning of the first millennium AD have been linked to a Palaeo-Eskimo tradition of arrow-like shapes, triangles, parallel and broken lines, and nucleated circles (Bronshtein 1986, 54). Double-headed artifacts have been discovered throughout the Arctic from the Thule era to the Historic era. The bicephalous formation persists in Arctic and Subarctic Siberia (Mundkur 1984, 451 and passim). The placement of a dot on the head gives the appearance of an animal, land or marine.

Studies of the design elements of Siberian peoples of later eras have demonstrated even

Opposite above Needlecase with thimble holder, ivory, thong, beads, and sinew, 12.2 cm, Inuvialuit, mid-nineteenth century. Collected in the Mackenzie River area, NWT, by Roderick R. MacFarlane. Blue 'Russian trade' beads decorate this tubular needlecase made of walrus tusk. The beads have been split along the threading hole and inlaid into the ivory. The anchor-type thimble holder is etched with lines that have five spurs each, a motif from the Thule culture, as is the double-headed formation at the top of the guard.

Opposite below Girl's festive costume, West Kalaallit, 1860. Collected by Gustav Holm. Anorak of skin covered with white cloth, decorated with ribbons of textile and skin, glass beads, 50 cm, Nuuk; sealskin trousers with skin embroidery, 22 cm, Sisimiut; skin boots with skin embroidery, 29 cm, Nuuk. Kalaallit women's anoraks in the 1800s show long loops of large beads that drop from around the hood opening, wrists, and lower edges. Beads became a part of the jewellery and of the hair-bands around women's topknots, the colour of which indicated their marital status.

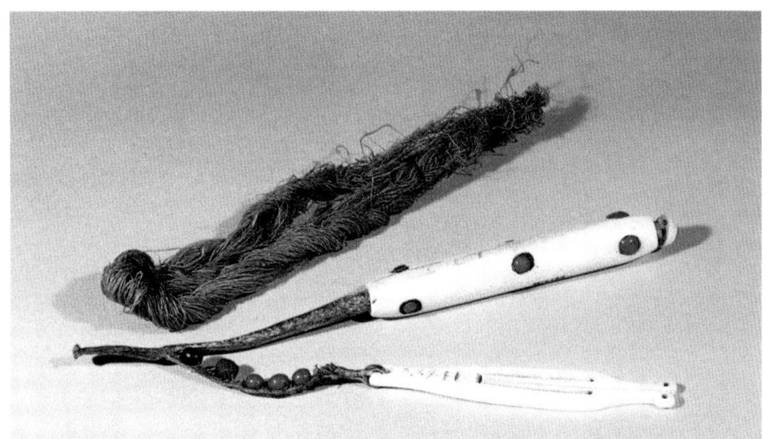

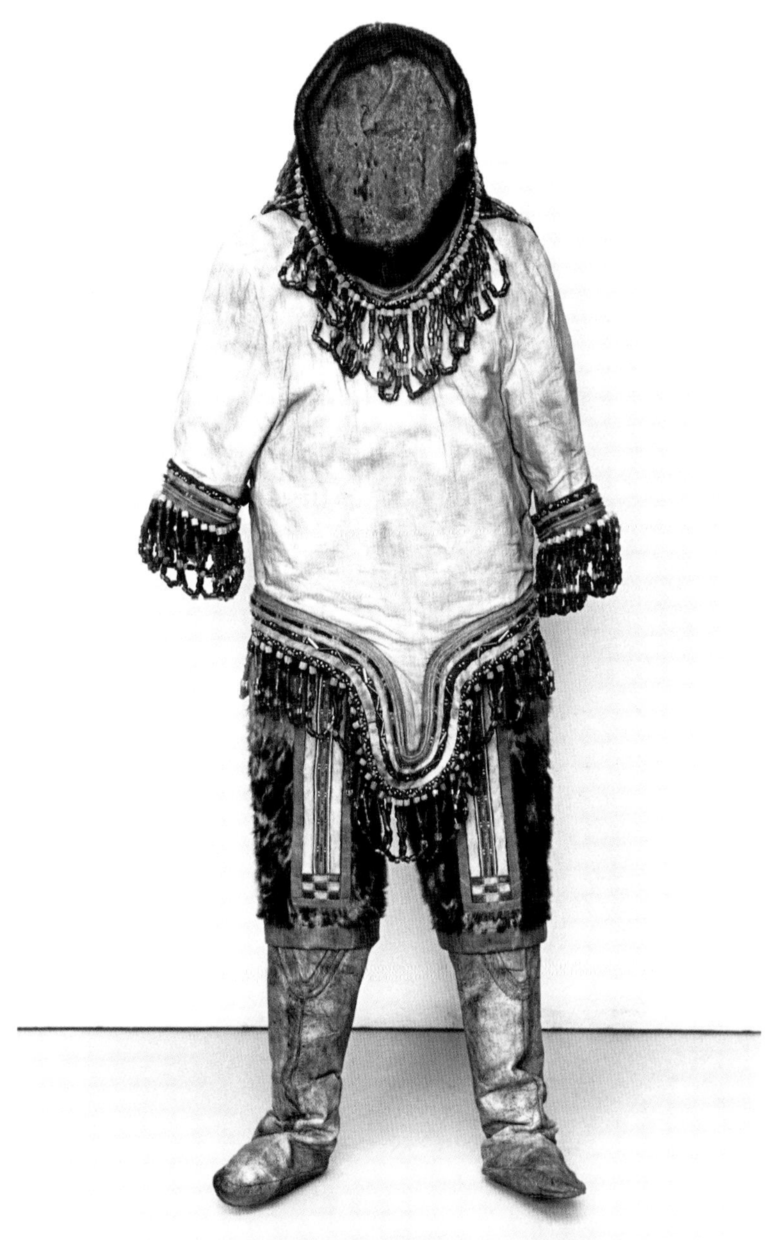

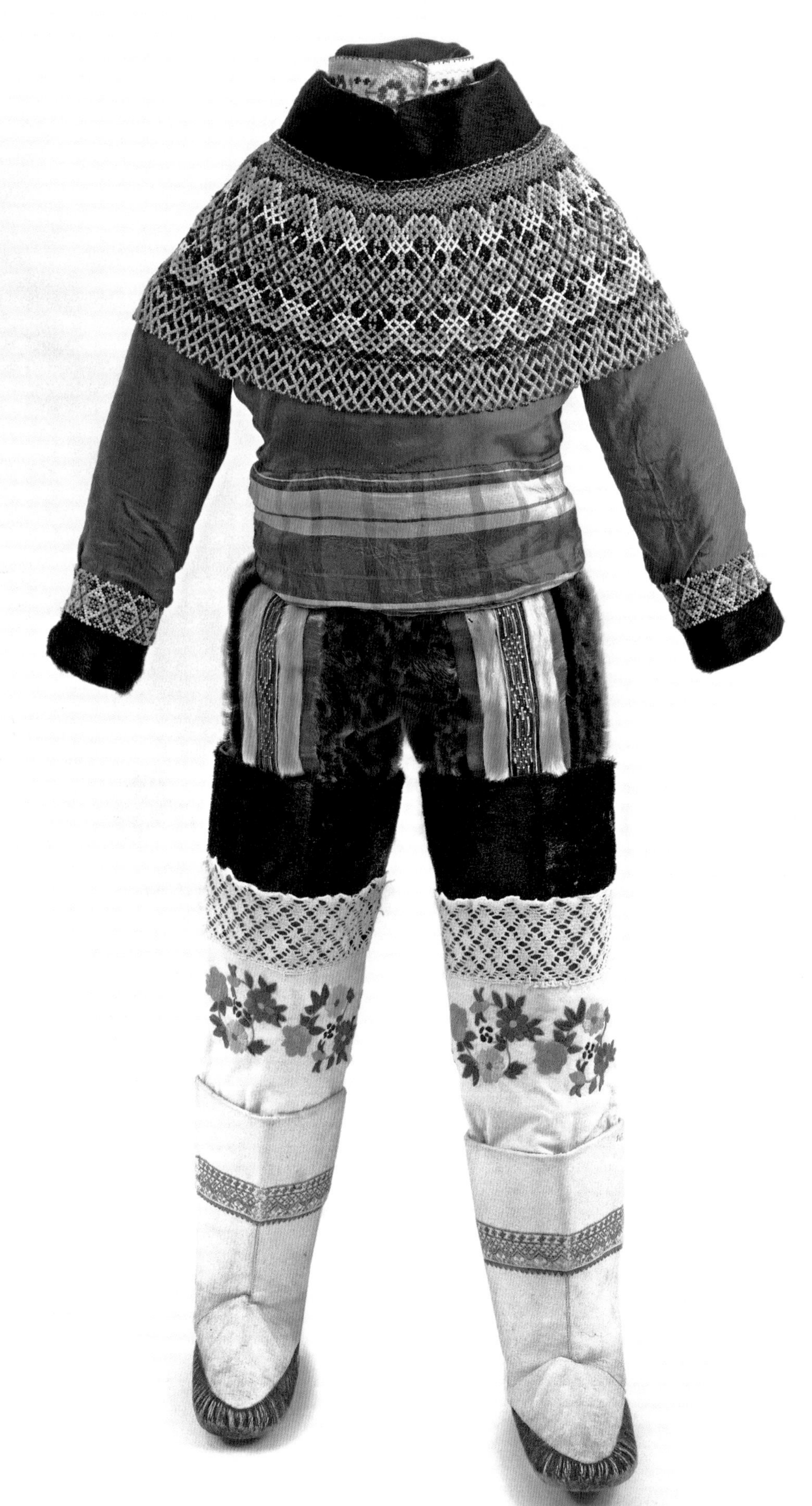

Opposite Girl's festive dress, West Kalaalit, ca. 1950. Anorak, 36 cm, and waist band are made of imported silk and decorated with a deep beaded collar and beaded cuff bands; the collar, cuffs, and stocking tops are of European black ox fur; the sealskin trousers, 17 cm, are decorated with traditional front strip of 'skin embroidery'; stocking with boots, 47 cm, are ornamented with lace and with silk and skin embroidery. Kalaallit national or festive dress is worn today by girls and women at Christmas and Easter, and for celebrations such as weddings and birthdays.

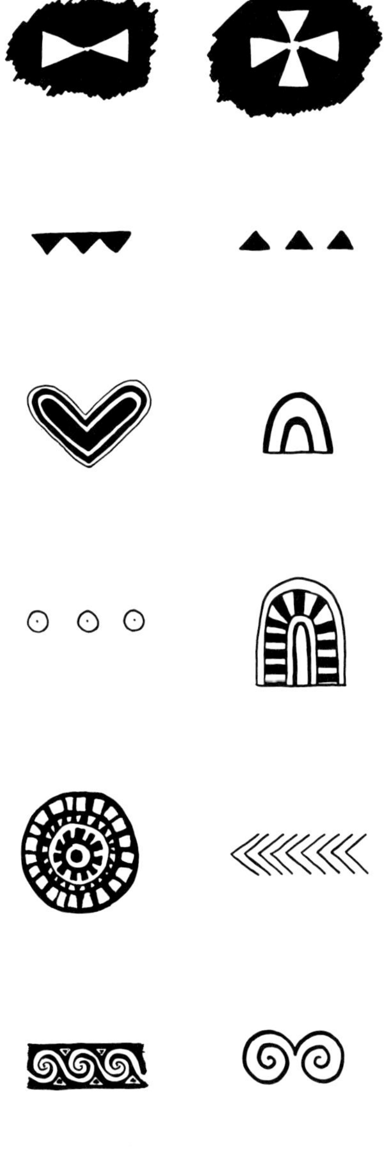

Figure 5.1
Design elements shared by Inuit and Northeast Siberians. *Drawing by Margaret Issenman.*

more shared motifs and techniques among Arctic peoples. Migrants to North America brought some of these cultural elements when they came to the North American Arctic. Cross-continental parallels in design components are a living testimony of peoples who passed on their traditions from parents to children over several millennia.

An important device, the nucleated circle, has been interpreted as a joint-mark, the joints of the human body being 'equivalent to the eyes as seats of the soul' (Schuster 1951, 19). Schuster proposed that the symbol became dissociated from its original function to develop into a decorative element. In the Central Yup'ik language, the circle with dot is designated *ellam iinga,* the eye of awareness: 'The circle and dot is a concrete metaphor for and means to achieve a dynamic movement between worlds, be it spiritual cycling, supernatural vision, or social transformation' (Fienup-Riordan 1987, 43-4). The nucleated circle is also found in Inuit clothing. The bone toggle of a belt of an Aivilingmiut amauti has the design in each quadrant of the rhombus. The Pallirmiut employed the device in their beaded side and back panels for parkas.

Engraving tools to make the circles are found in some circumpolar groups. The Chukchi, Koryak, and Yupiit use a two-pronged chisel with a wooden handle (Ivanov 1963, 172, Plate 102). One prong serves as a leg that revolves to form the circle, the other as a bit. The Netsilingmiut had an ornamentation drill called a *parparutariik.* This instrument had three points, each of a different length, so that circles could be

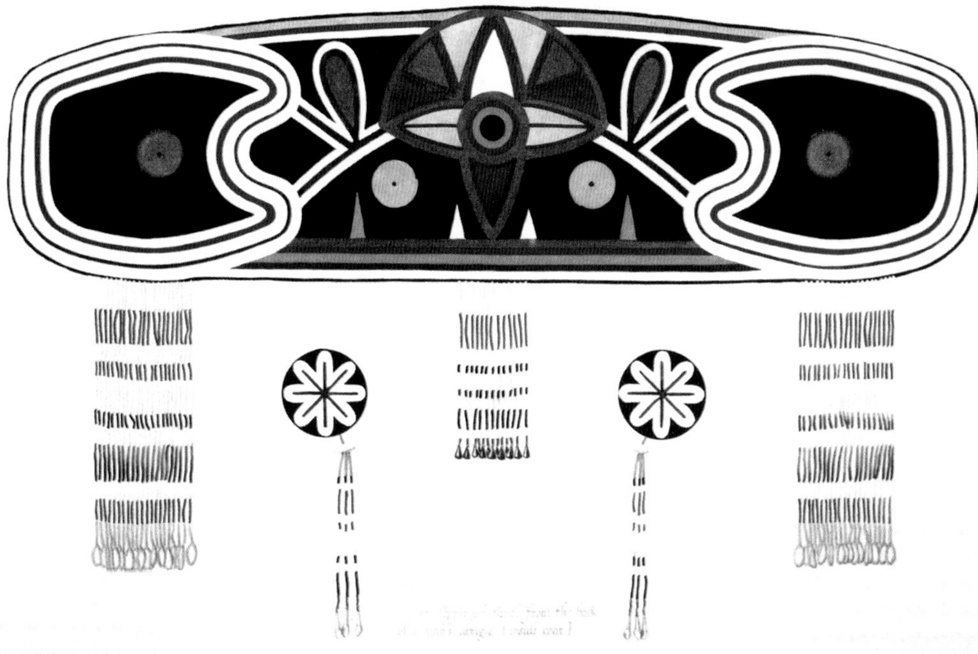

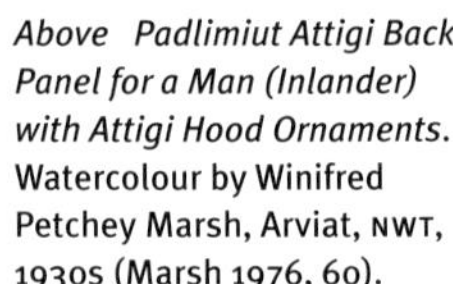

Above *Padlimiut Attigi Back Panel for a Man (Inlander) with Attigi Hood Ornaments.* Watercolour by Winifred Petchey Marsh, Arviat, NWT, 1930s (Marsh 1976, 60).

Below *Padlimiut Attigi Back Panels for Boys and Men.* Watercolour by Winifred Petchey Marsh, Arviat, NWT, 1930s. The artist comments that the symbols in the third panel, that of a boy, represent mosquitoes and the wearer's name (Marsh 1976, 61).

Opposite *Padlimiut Beadwork Borders for Hoods and Cuffs.* Watercolour by Winifred Petchey Marsh, Arviat, NWT, 1930s (Marsh 1976, 56).

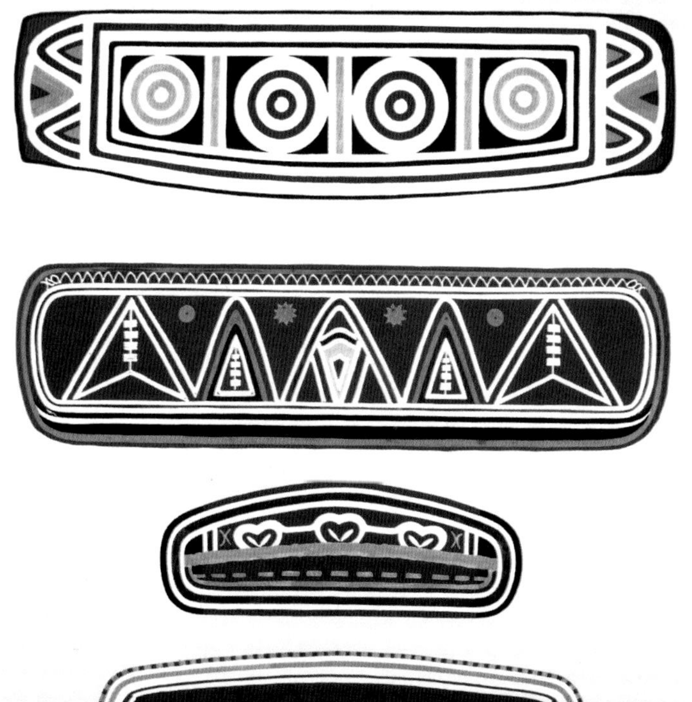

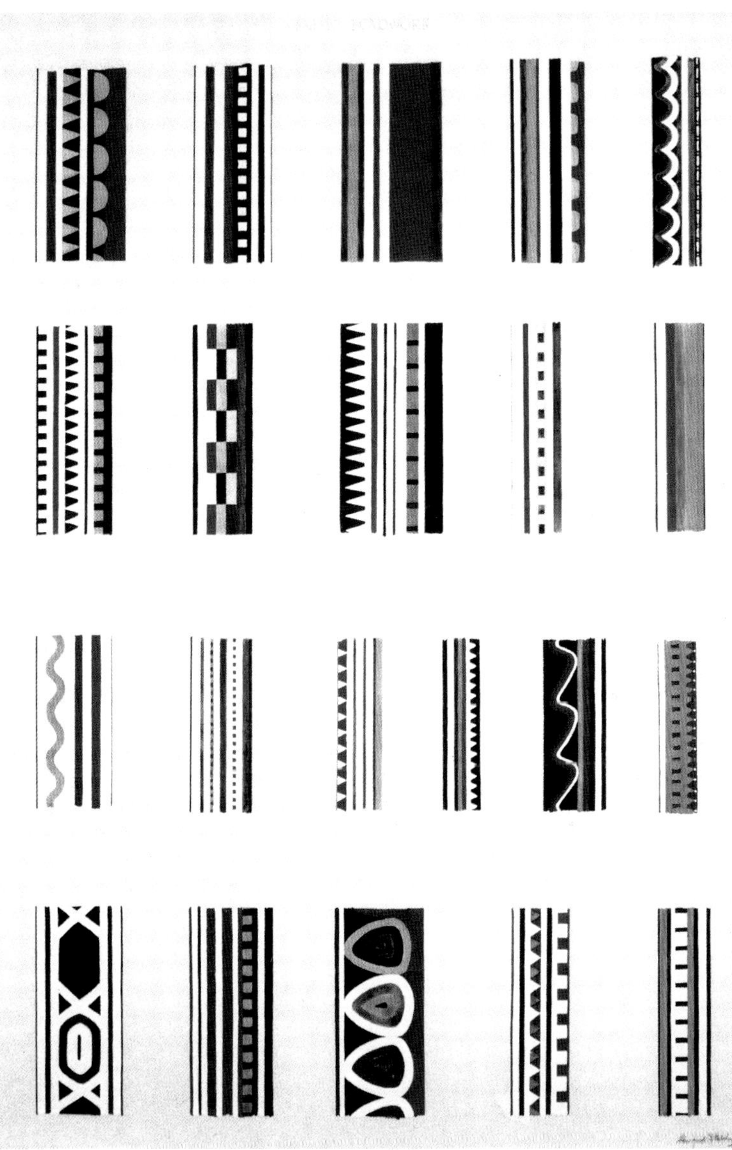

etched when the tool was revolved. Ornamentation of the type made by this implement was found on Eskimo combs, and also on the two toggles attached to the women's costume to hold the belt that secured the baby on the mother's back (Mitchell and Van de Velde 1981, tool kit no. 13).

The triangle or tooth motif and its variations are found on northern clothing in Siberia, North America, and Kalaallit Nunaat. It can become so narrow and elongated that it develops into a 'spur.' Thule culture carvers passed on the spurred or hatched line that appears in historical tools and clothing. Semi-circles, ovals, tear-drop, and tongue-like shapes are found on clothing across the Arctic. The Canadian Inuit are familiar with the latter shape because of the front and back flaps of their skin clothing, which are sometimes U shaped or can narrow to become a rounded or elongated V. The variety of possible designs is great. If two elongated 'tongues' are superimposed at right angles, for example, a heart shape, sometimes called a 'flanged heart,' results. Four tongues can make a cross-shaped rosette (Ivanov 1963, 255, Plate 149).

Inuit designs include plant-like motifs, scrolls, and what appear to be floral and foliate ornamentation.[17] Designs applied on some Siberian Yup'ik clothing are similar to the rounded, plant-like patterns formed in Paalirmiut beadwork. One form that has its origin in nature is the Paisley pine tree or cone shape.[18] The calicos traded to the North American first peoples very often carried the Paisley design, and the motif spread as well to Siberia.

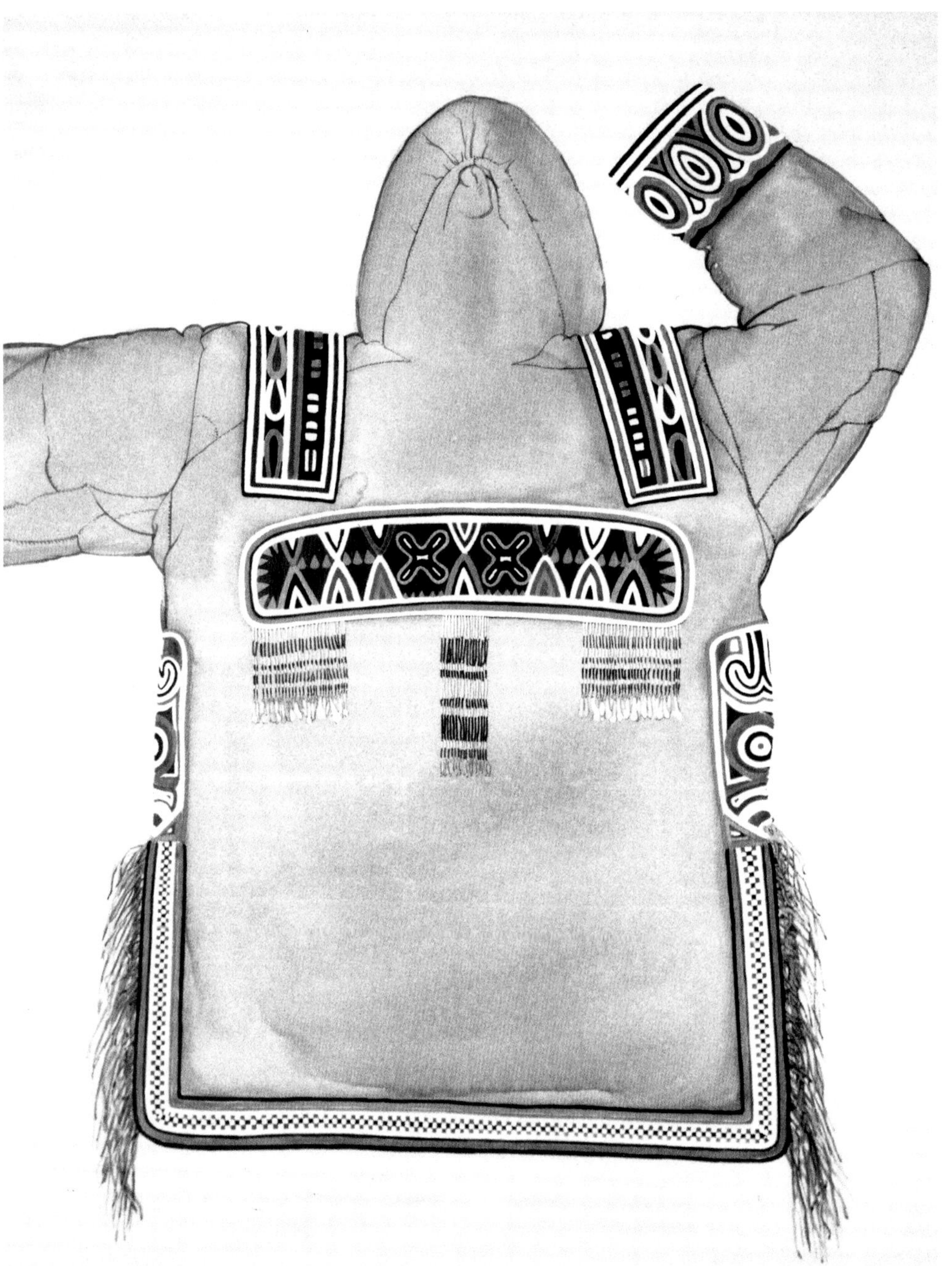

Left Padlimiut Man's Attigi or Inner Coat (Rear View). Watercolour by Winifred Petchey Marsh, Arviat, NWT, 1930s (March 1976, 55). The fringe on the lower edge is removed when at the coast to avoid offence to Sedna, the goddess of the sea. Three beaded decorations drop from the back panel, replacing the amulets that decorate outer garments.

Opposite Gloves of hide, cotton velvet, and braid, sewn with sinew, 30 cm, Inuvialuit, late nineteenth century. Collected in the Mackenzie Delta area by Forbes D. Sutherland. These gauntlet gloves, embroidered with trefoils, tendrils, and scrolls, are similar in construction to gloves worn on dress occasions by Alaskans and Siberians. The scroll, also called 'travelling wave' and spiral, is common among northerly groups in the CIS and occurs widely among all the peoples of the Lower Amur River, on the border between Russia and China (Ivanov 1963, 346-7, 387-91).

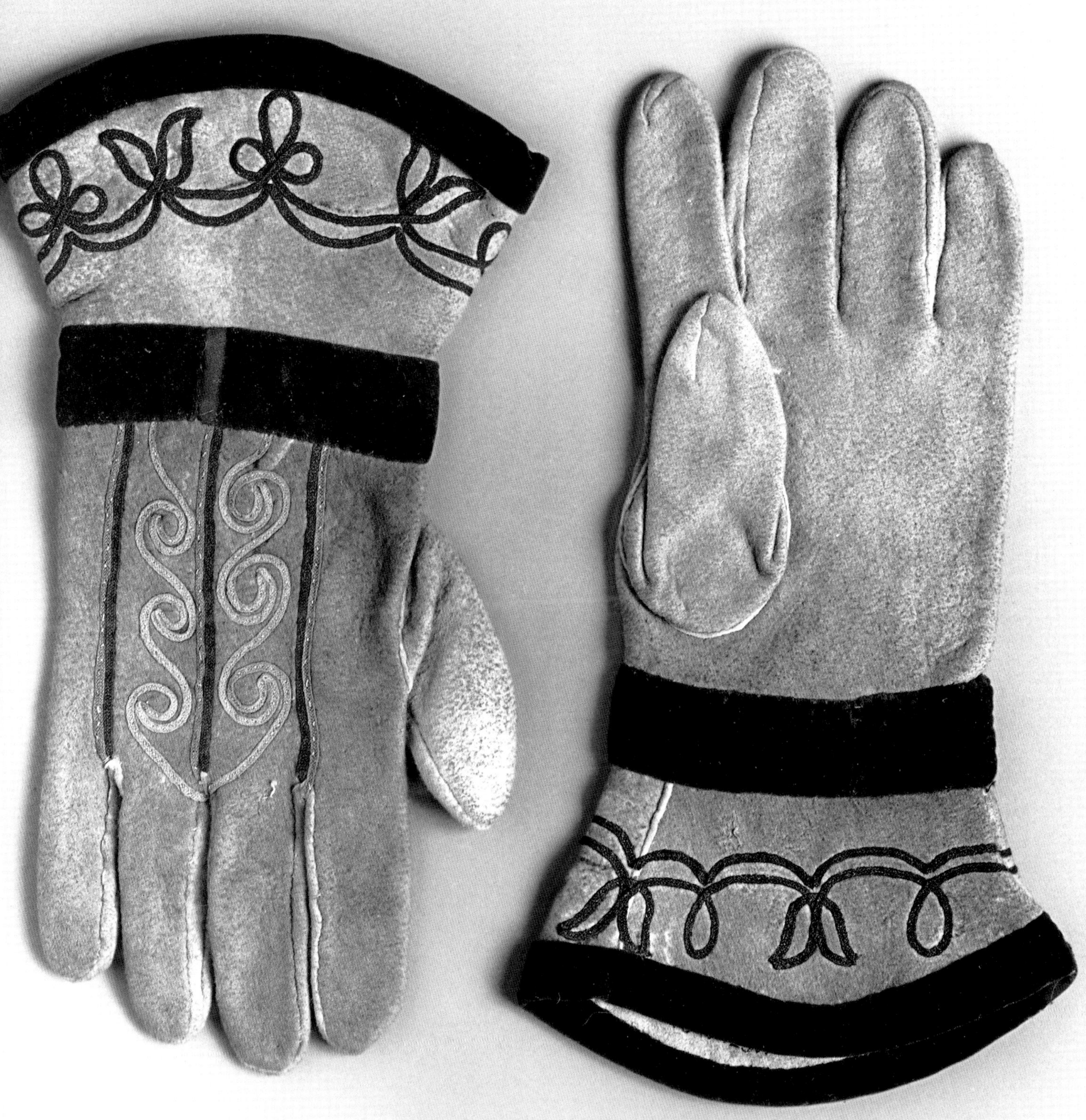

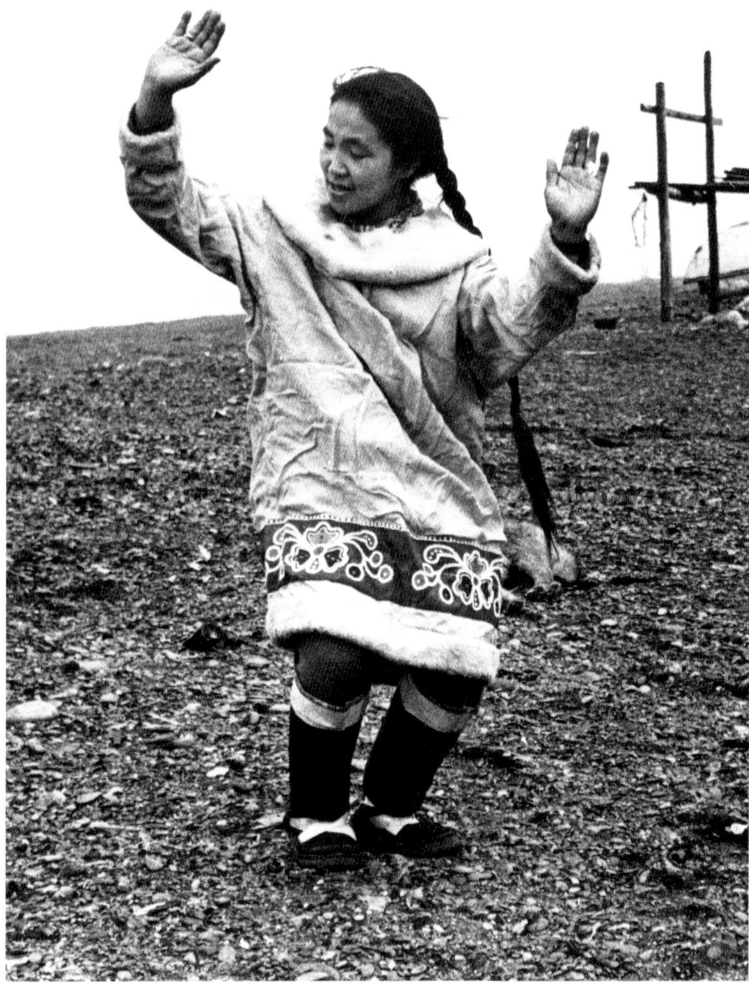

Left M. Ippi, a Siberian Yup'ik of Enurmino, Chukotka, 1974, dances wearing a fur parka and sealskin boots.

Below Doll of cotton, fur, skin, duffle, braid, and tape, 34 cm, Copper Inuit, ca. 1971. Artisan: Ida Uveluk Bolt of Qurluqtuuq, NWT. The Inuit described the Paisley design, seen here on the doll's costume, as 'a bunch of little stomachs.' The phrase translates as *aqiaruraq*, and has become the Inuit word for calico with a Paisley pattern (Strickler and Alookee 1988, 157, 175).

Opposite Kameya, a Siberian Yup'ik of Lluughraq, Chukotka, 1974, dancing. She wears traditional dress and sealskin boots as she sits on the shore reenacting the movements of whale hunters.

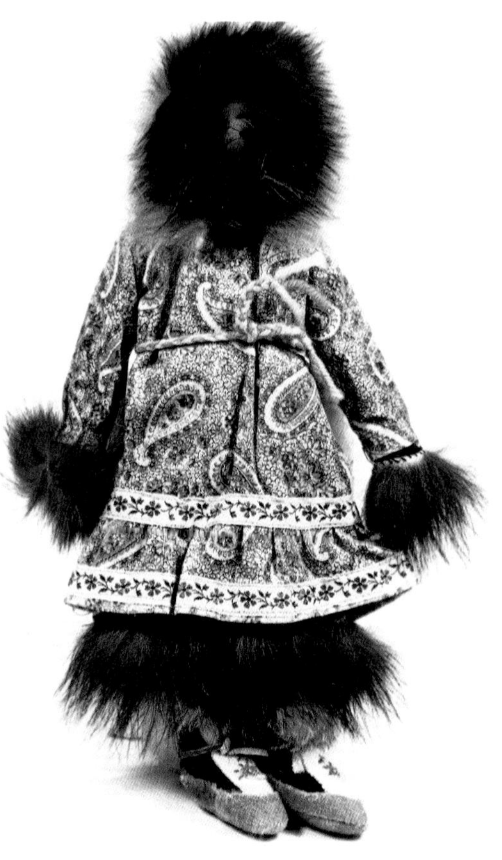

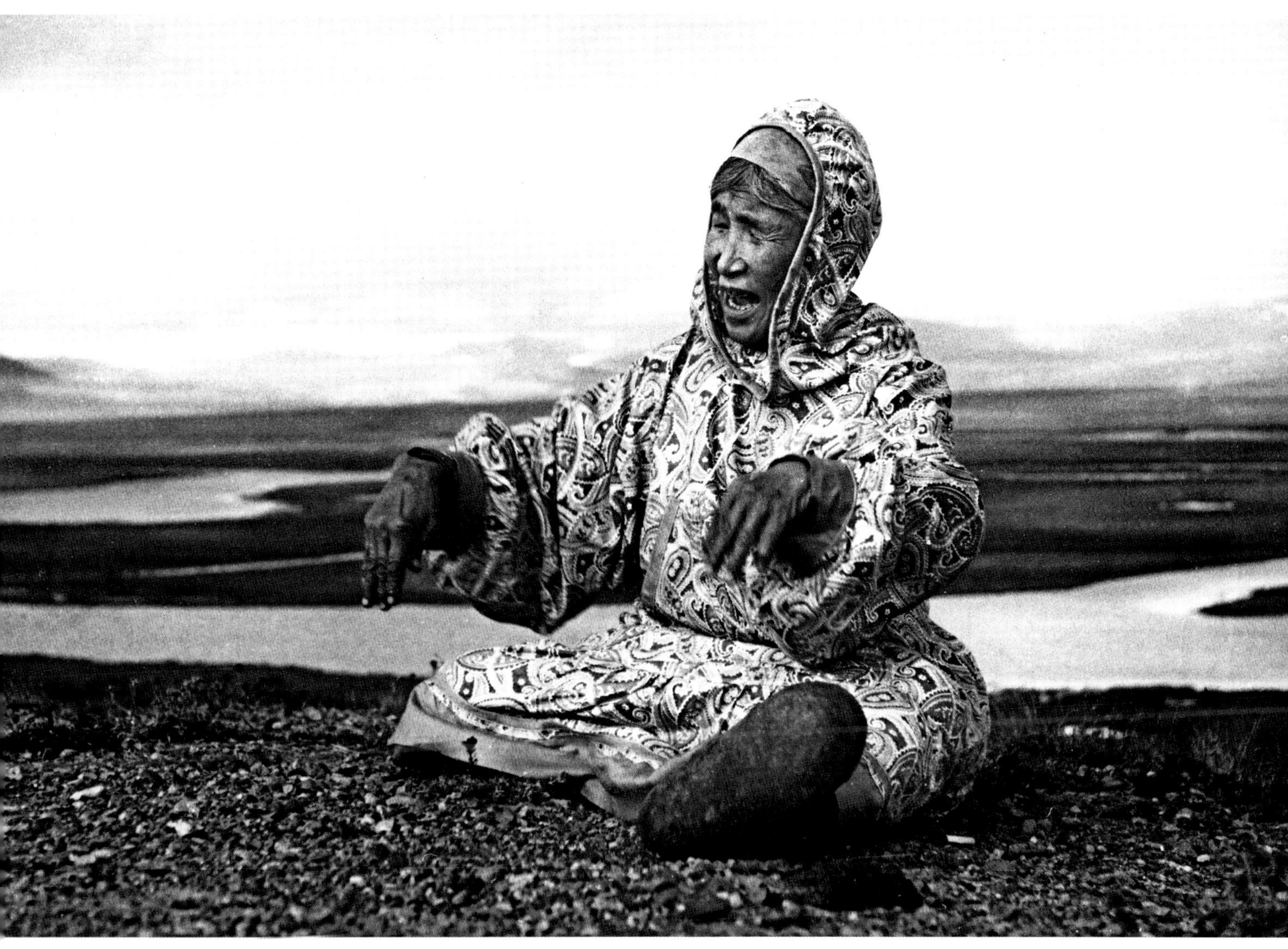

SOCIAL ORGANIZATION

Celebrations and Ceremonies

An unforgiving environment necessitates the collaboration of individuals and families to obtain food and clothing. The cooperative techniques developed by the Inuit are institutionalized through a tradition of celebrations and ceremonies. Social events where feasting, dancing, and games take place restrain anti-social conduct, strengthen community bonds, honour ancestors, and relieve tension. Communal gatherings celebrate a successful hunt, make contact with the spirits, welcome visitors, and make the time pass pleasantly. During the long winter, when the sun does not rise above the horizon, or when blizzards keep people indoors for days at a time, community activities help preserve mental and physical health.

The drum is the only instrument to accompany singing and dancing. In many communities each man has his own song, which only he has a right to sing. He can have a song partner, who is like his brother and is his closest friend, sharing everything. Song duels between antagonists

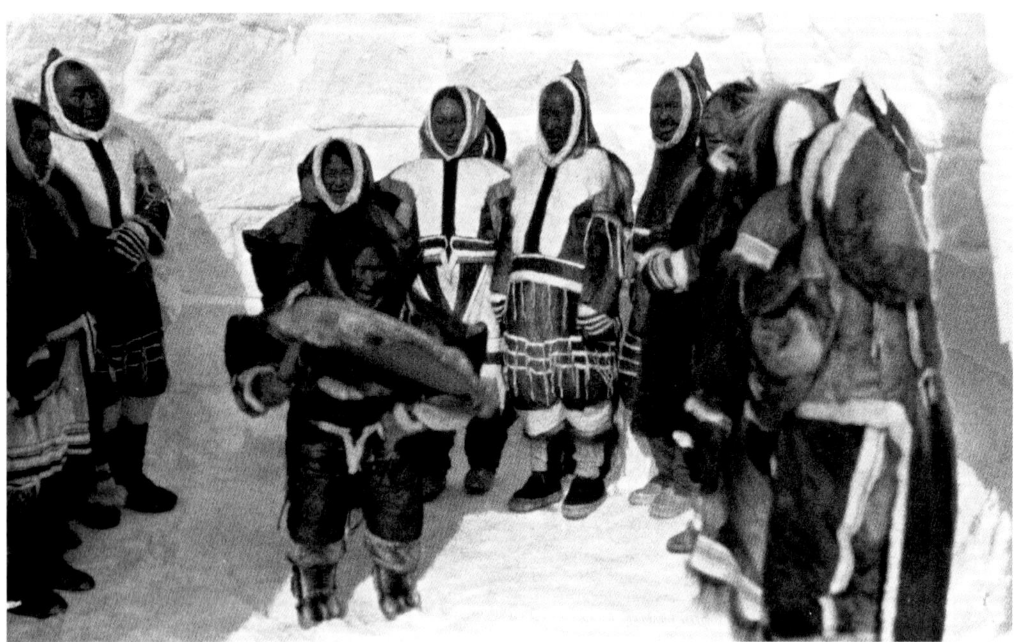

Left Dance of the Copper Inuit, Coronation Gulf area, NWT, 1931. Ikpukkuaq staged an enactment of Inuit snowhouse celebrations for Richard Finnie, a photographer with the Canadian Department of Mines and Resources (Vanast 1991, 84). In this photograph, a woman takes her turn with the drum during the dance held in the *qaggi*, the great snowhouse or tent.

Opposite above Nanulik and Ankanaun, Siberian Yup'ik of Ungaziq, Chukotka, 1971, dancing. Siberian women created dances to entice, welcome, and honour the whales. In Alaska, the whales were said to come to the whaling captain's wife who was generous in sharing the catch.

Opposite below Asykolyan, a Siberian Yup'ik of Sighinek, Chukotka, 1971, dances, wearing white over his traditional clothing during the dance ceremonies connected to the whale.

provide a socially sanctioned means to vent hostility and to disperse anger.

In former times, in the Cumberland Gulf area, in Labrador, and in many other localities, hunting success was celebrated in the *qaggi,* the great snow house or tent, particularly after the capture of a whale. The Labrador Inuit gave thanks for the whale to Torngak, a powerful spirit who lived in a cave in the high mountains near Cape Chidley. Traditional rituals of the Inuit, including the Siberian Yupiit, celebrated success in the hunt, the most important of which was the whale hunt (M. Zhornitskaya, personal communication 1990; Rainey 1947; Taylor 1985; VanStone 1985a; Zhornitskaya 1983, 1990).

A sculping or skinning dance performed by Labrador Inuit contains ethical teaching.[19] A young man dances around a seal he has just caught. (The 'seal' is a small boy covered with a shawl representing the skin.) He boasts of the valuable fur with which he will become rich and come back to the girl he plans to marry. He 'skins' the seal, crowing about the sensation he will cause in the village. As he makes the last cut, the seal jumps up, runs off, and leaves the hunter with the skin. It turns out to be worthless and the dancer, much chagrined and perplexed, leaves deeply disappointed. The story reinforces prohibitions against greed and boasting and reminds viewers of the participation of the soul of the animal in the outcome of the hunt (Hawkes 1916, 140-1).

For social and ceremonial occasions people put on their best clothes. Hunters returning to camp or visiting strangers would stop on the trail to put on personal decorations and boots fit for dancing. The traditional dancing costumes were hoodless, and special dancing caps were worn along with gloves. The Copper Inuit wore a dancing cap made of caribou and loon, trimmed with hare or other soft skin. A feathered loon's skin forms the middle of such a cap. The loon's bill is upstanding, and from it dangles a whole weasel skin. Throughout the Arctic from Siberia to Kalaallit Nunaat the loon has a mythical and symbolic significance. Because of its call, it is known as the bird of song and eloquence, and by its presence on dancing caps it takes part in the celebrations. The loon is associated with vision, both for the layperson and the shaman. In a recurring Inuit legend, the loon restores eyesight to a

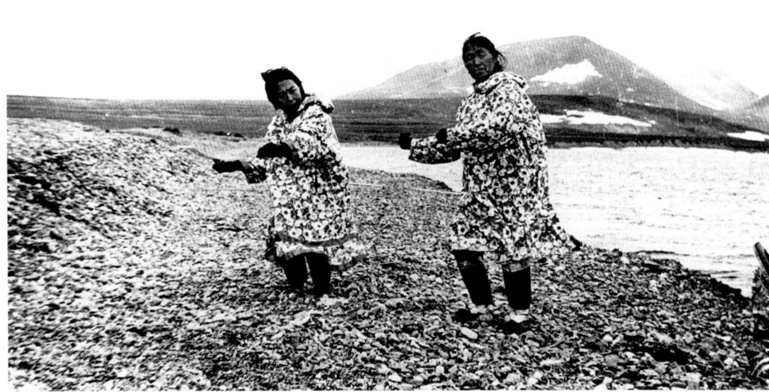

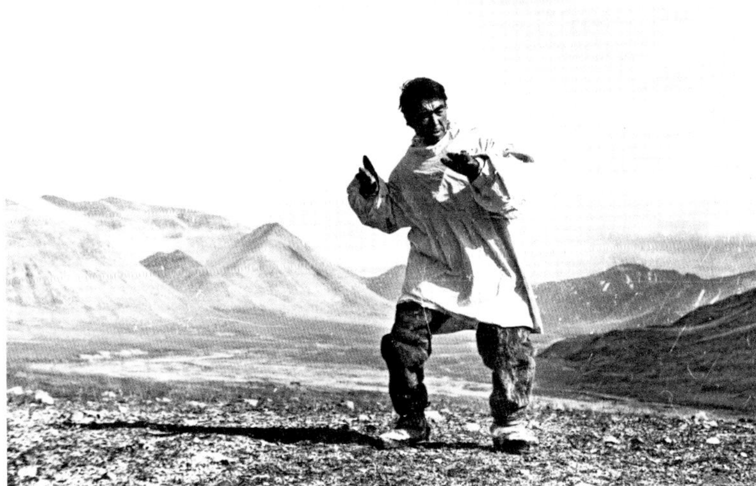

blind child. There is no faster water bird, and whoever wears a loonskin amulet will acquire the loon's speed as well as vision.[20]

The use of gutskin clothing for ceremonial and spiritual purposes is well known in Alaska and Siberia and to some extent in Canada.[21] Women in southwest Alaska wore gutskin parkas when making new sealskin kayak covers. The costume stopped evil influences from entering or affecting the kayak. Men considered that gutskins prevented bad spirits from entering the sea nets and from keeping away seals. 'Puffins' beaks hung along the shoulder and upper arm and around the wrists [of gut parkas]. That would be for the men's hunting coats, and I remember they would have feathers. They had the beaks for the reason that they would rattle and scare off the bad spirits from the hunt,' explains Rita Pitka Blumenstein of Tununak, Alaska (Hickman 1987, 23).

In Alaska, the *Kevgiq*, or Messenger Feast, emphasized the continued renewal of people, the redistribution of goods, and respect for animals (Morrow 1984, 131-5). For this celebration the *nasguq*, the feast maker, sent messengers carrying red-painted feathered wands to invite another village to be their guests. They wore newly made squirrel-skin jackets trimmed with wolverine and new caribou boots. Other envoys asked for gifts on behalf of the nasguq – for instance, the inviting community might have need of bearded seal skins to make boot soles. Once the visiting village accepted the invitation, they tried to exceed the request as a matter of honour. The ceremonies consisted of dancing, singing, feasting, and gift exchanges.

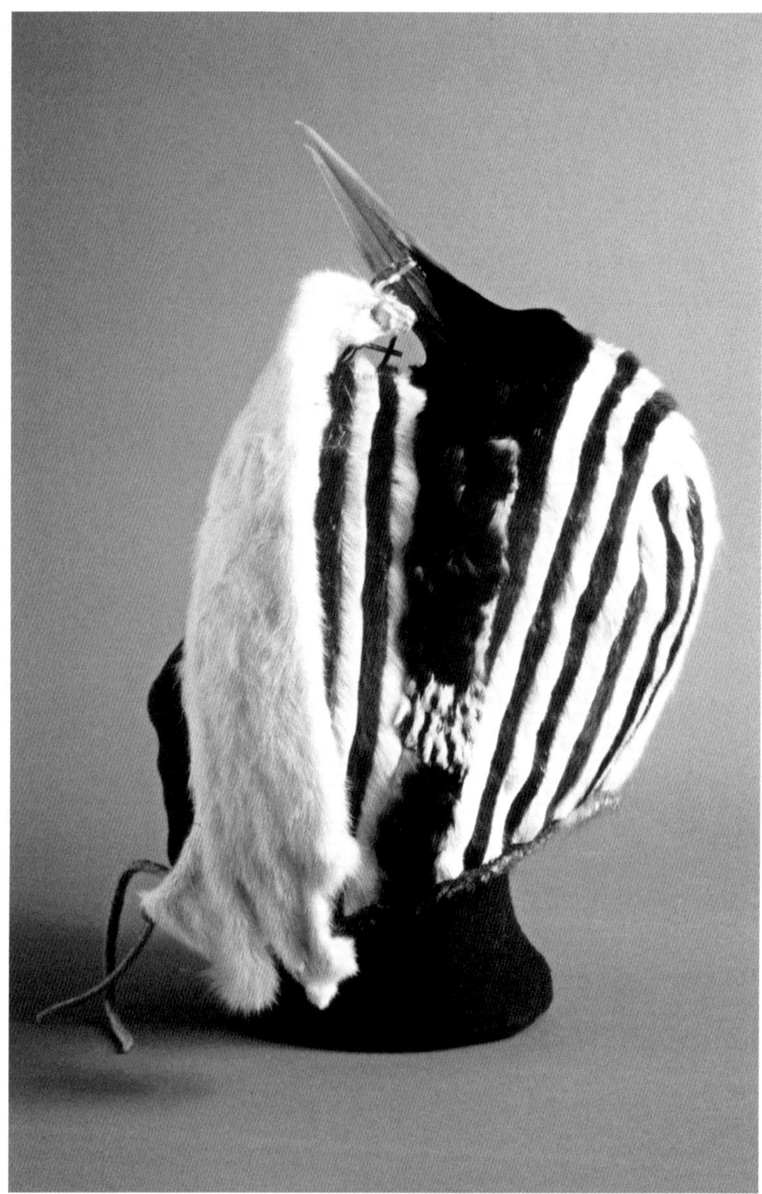

Above Dancing cap of skins of caribou, loon, weasel, and hare; beak, felt, sewn with sinew, 42 cm, Copper Inuit, ca. 1968. Collected at Qurluqtuuq, NWT, by Jean-Paul Péloquin. Because of its intricate construction, the loonskin cap is a luxury. In the course of an evening's entertainment the owner lends it freely to the participants (Jenness 1946, 28-30). The dancer moves his or her head to the rhythm of the drum, swinging the ermine skin so that it imitates the movements of loons. The kind of fine striping seen in this cap is found in women's trousers (see, for example, page 112). The androgynous costume of some Siberian shamans included women's striped trousers.

The male dancers, naked above the waist, wore headdresses, necklaces, and armlets, and manipulated feathered dance sticks.

The feast associated with Sedna, the sea goddess, took place in late fall or winter when sickness, bad hunting, and storms increased. The participants asked Sedna to release the seals so that the community could have adequate food and clothing. To protect themselves from the angry Sedna, people wore amulets at the top of their hoods, usually a part of the first garment they had worn as a baby. Some of the rituals entailed renewal symbolism such as drinking fresh water, turning toward one's birthplace, rekindling the lamp lights, which had been extinguished before the ceremonies, and exchanging gifts to represent the bounty of Sedna. The symbolic killing of Sedna and her rebirth epitomized the relationship of the Inuit to the animal world, whereby the slain animal, if treated with respect, was reborn.

During an important ceremony in the Sedna festival, two masked figures called *qailirtitaang* approached the celebrants. They appeared massive, for they wore heavy boots, several pairs of trousers, and women's amau-tiit. The actors were sometimes comical, frightening (especially to children), or lascivious. The qailirtitaang were spirit helpers of Sedna, and the men in the community acted out an attack on them. Once these monstrous figures had collapsed and their weapons had been broken, the men gave them fresh water to revive them. They then asked them about the hunt and the prospects for the coming year (Boas [1888] 1964, 195-201).

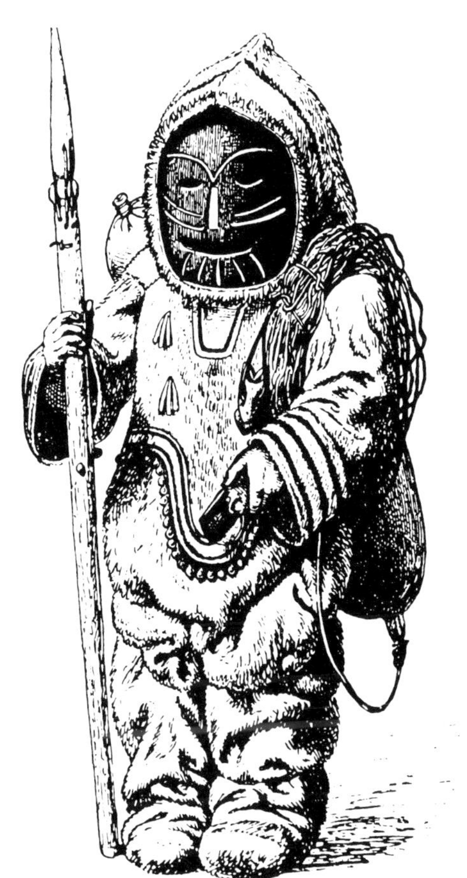

Above Qailirtitaang, a masked figure. Drawing by Franz Boas, late ninteenth century. The ensemble of the qailirtitaang, who was a man, combines male and female elements. The tattooed mask, amauti, and scraper are feminine. The harpoon and sealskin float are part of a man's hunting equipment.

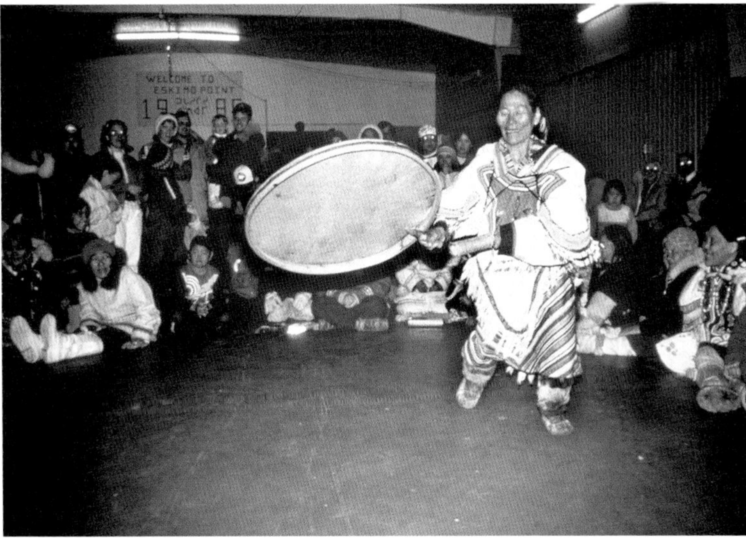

Below Drum dance at Arviat, NWT, 1990. The drummer wears a recently made skin parka.

The Asiatic Yupiit called the sea deity Samna or Sana, she-who-lives-below (Serov 1988, 243). In their mythology, Samna created people and sea animals. The Reindeer Chukchi borrowed this legend from the Siberian Yupiit, and in their version the goddess went to the tundra, where she created people and reindeer, and to the coast, where she created the sea animals.

The Sedna festival continues to be celebrated in the Contemporary Era. The *Nalauut* ritual, observed in 1976, combines elements of the Sedna legend with Christian observances on the night of the Epiphany, around Christmas (Richling 1980). In traditional times, the loss of the sun in midwinter, called *Tauvijjuaq* in Iglulik, was a sombre period of intense cold and hunting inactivity. Storytelling and games helped pass the time. The appearance of two stars called Aagjuuk (Altair and Tarazed in English) was the sign for the mid winter celebration *Tivajuut* to begin (MacDonald 1993, 19-22).

Drum dancing and festive celebrations continue to be held across the Arctic, when people put on their best wear to join together for a time of contests, singing, and dancing. Traditional costumes, masks, dance fans, and headwear live on in dance and drama performances of comic and serious purposes.

Masks

The mask is an extension of clothing and at the same time embodies in itself the functions of clothing: to cover and protect the body, to disguise, to transform.[22] Masks are bearers of the ancient culture, for they often

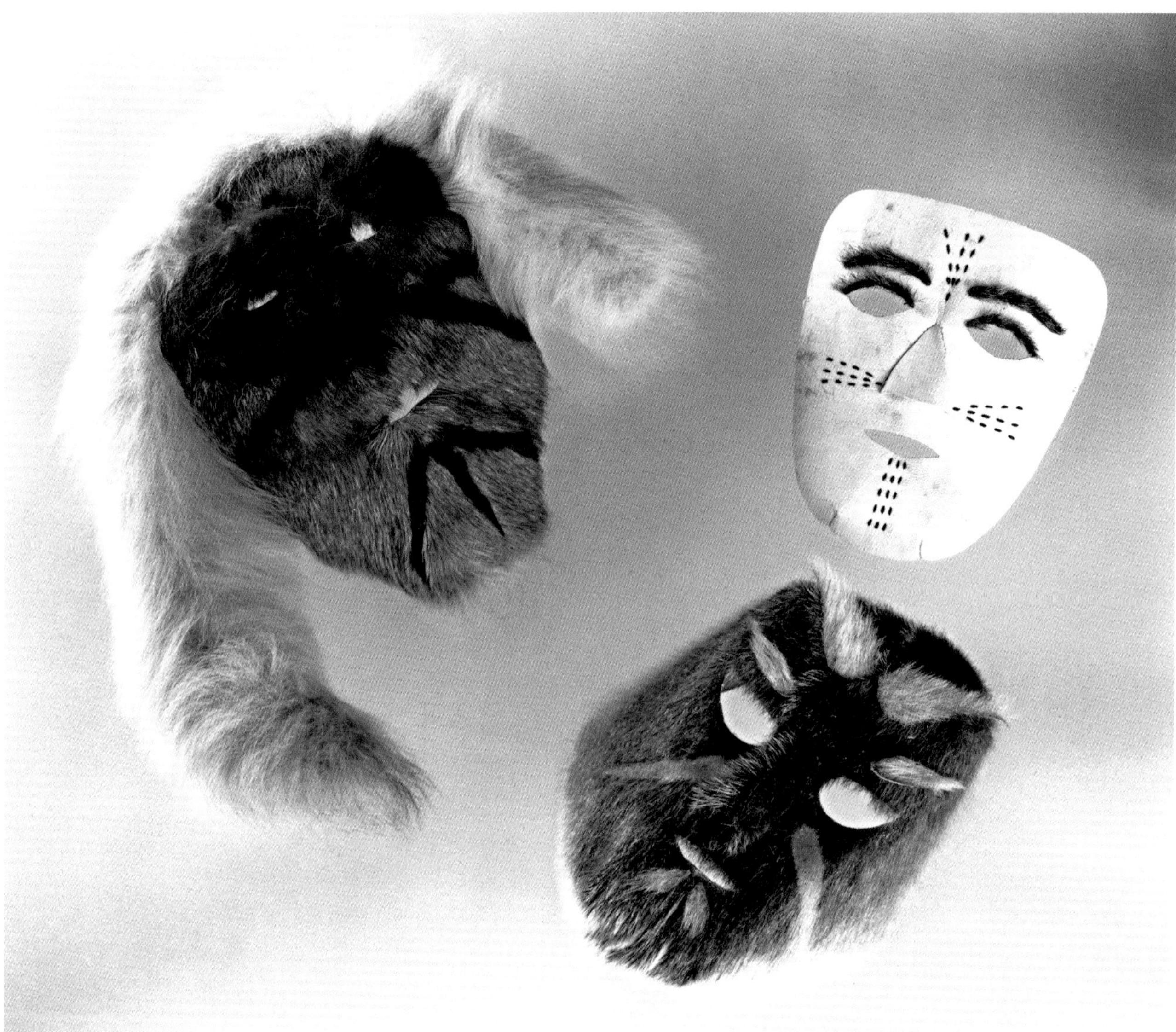

depict legendary figures and the spirits. The skin mask also functions practically as protection against the wind. Masks are used primarily during ceremonies, rituals, and entertainments by laypeople and shamans.

Masks fell into disuse for some time after the advent of missionaries and other outsiders into the Arctic. In eastern Kalaallit Nunaat, with the conversion of the population to Lutheranism by the early twentieth century, traditional ceremonies and customs were denigrated and even prohibited. Masks associated with community celebrations were no longer made, even though in Kalaallit Nunaat they had no religious significance (Gessain 1978).

Masks are made of wood or of furred or dehaired skin. Previous generations obtained wood from shipwrecks, by trade, or by gathering driftwood at the shore. Men continue to make the wooden masks, women the skin ones; each works the materials that lie in their domain. Ivory or bones of sea animals form teeth. Seal, dog, and musk-ox fur can become hair, eyebrows, eyelashes, moustache, and beard. A knot of hair at the back indicates a woman; a tuft on the forehead or on the chin denotes

Masks (clockwise from left): Caribou skin and fox (?), 33 cm, Iglulingmiut, 1971. Artisan: woman elder of the Inuit Cooperative at Iglulik, NWT. Collected at Iglulik by B. Saladin d'Anglure. Such a mask was worn during the festival of Tivajuut, which was held in deepest winter when darkness prevailed. Sealskin mask, 21 cm, Nunatsiarmiut, 1987. Artisans: Padloo Saila and Eeakuna Parr of Kinngait, NWT. Sealskin mask, 30 cm, Nunatsiarmiut, 1987. Artisans: Padloo Saila and Eeakuna Parr of Kinngait, NWT. Masks worn by men often had women's tattoo marks, which may have implied intersexuality in the characters portrayed in rituals. Incised lines, stitches, or slim furred or dehaired skin strips affixed by glue or tiny rivets compose furrows and tattoos.

a man. The masks of the Canadian Inuit are simple in comparison with the more elaborate ones of Kalaallit and Alaskans.

The Angakkuq

The role of the *angakkuq,* or shaman, was open to both men and women. Persons born with spiritual gifts were able to mediate between the community and the spirit world.[23] When people could not solve their own problems by following rules for living they turned to the shaman for help. Misfortunes could be cleared away by his or her intercession, by confessing to broken prohibitions, and by atonement.

The shaman's main duties were to cure the sick, to protect individuals and the community from evil spirits, to obtain success in the hunt, to divine tragedies, and to predict the weather. By mediation with the spirit controlling the weather, the shaman helped the community have good hunting, thus ensuring a supply of food and clothing. The male spirit of the air and weather goes under many names. Among the Netsilingmiut he is called Naarjuk or Sila (Rasmussen 1929, 71-2). Naarjuk is a giant's child, orphaned by the murder of his parents. He flew up into the sky and became the weather spirit. He could punish the community with storms by flapping his atajuq, the one-piece suit worn by children. The shaman would ascend to find the child deity, beat him, and tie his suit tightly around him, thus stopping the storm.

An Inuk became a shaman in several ways: through spiritual knowledge inherited from a parent; by being selected in youth by a shaman who had observed his or her qualities; or by undergoing religious experiences. Training with the angakkuq taught the novice techniques and a secret vocabulary. At the end of the training the apprentice received a helping spirit called a *tuurngaq,* and the necessary equipment such as a head-dress, belt, and knife (Balikci 1970, 225-38).

Women shamans are remembered in many localities, some as great and powerful, but the supernatural powers of the male angakkuq appear to have been broader: he could travel to the moon, the depths of the sea, or the afterworld. In some regions, such as the area west of Hudson Bay, a female shaman could administer only to female patients (Fainberg 1967, 254).

The shaman did not live apart from community life but continued in the role of hunter or mother. The dress therefore did not differ greatly from the rest of the community although, in the Central Arctic, the belt and headdress were distinctive from those worn by laypeople (Blodgett 1979, 155-7). The shaman might keep a piece of clothing, perhaps related to a helping spirit that in times past had aided in ceremonial duties. The spirit of a mask gave supernatural powers. A birdskin head-covering or a caribou fur headband lent majesty to shamans when they were performing spiritual rights. The shaman's belt was sometimes of caribou fur, preferably with the long white stomach fur still adhering, or of the skin of the spirit helper. Carvings and amulets on the belt assisted the shaman to help the individual or the community.

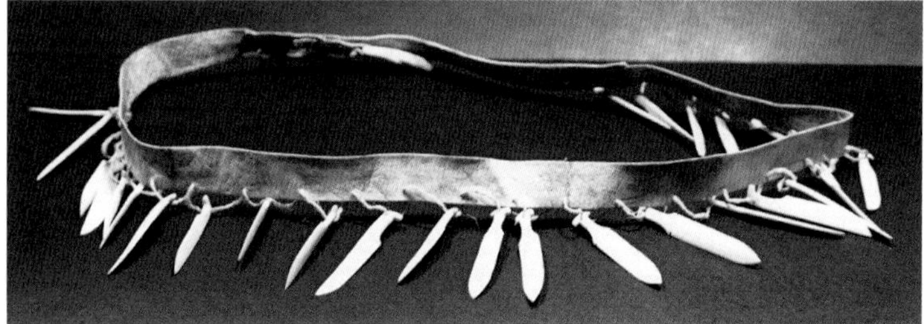

Mitts and gloves were important for use in shamanic and secular ceremonies and dances, and there are records from all over the Arctic regarding covering the hands. An account of the activities in the eighteenth century of two shamans in Naini to 'cure' an unsuccessful seal hunter describes how they sat on a seal skin with sealskin gloves on their hands (Taylor 1974b, 85). In a séance witnessed at Lake Hikoligjuaq, NWT, the shaman Igjugarjuk reached his familiar deep in the earth (Birket-Smith 1971, 189). Men, women, and children touched his covered hands. Then he placed a mitten in front of him and pressed on it with his wand. The presence underneath the ground made the wand more and more immovable. The spirit answered the shaman's questions according to whether he could raise the wand or not. The mitten thus became a surrogate hand, a link between the shaman and his helping spirit, a connection between the human and spiritual worlds.

A doll collected at Kuujjuaq in the late nineteenth century embodied the spirit of the great hunter and shaman Sa'pa, who lived on the eastern shore of Hudson Bay (Turner 1979, 32-4). It has very large mittens with a thumb and a palm that has two partitions or fingers: a possible reference to the foot of Raven.[24] From the figure's belt, made of polar bear skin, hung objects to endow alertness and great speed. The doll, dressed in shaman's clothing and accessories, thus became a spiritual proxy for the angakkuq. The local shaman would place the doll on a pole in a favourable position overlooking the territory to control the movement of animals.

The Siberian Yup'ik shaman also had no special costume, although pendants, tassels, and a tobacco pouch worn with his or her usual clothing showed the office (Hughes 1984, 256). An important amulet on the belt was a wooden figure of a swallow. The swallow protected the hunter on the sea. In winter the bird became a wolf that punished reindeer herders who did not share their meat and hides with the coastal dwellers. Siberian Yup'ik shamans did wear special white clothing, probably made of reindeer, during the whale ceremony when they foretold the weather (Serov 1988, 246-7). In Siberia, the Russian term 'kamlanie' – 'kam' means shaman – refers to the rituals of the shaman in which he or she danced and communicated with the spirits.[25] Asiatic Yup'ik shamans wore kamleikas, hooded coats made with the intestines of sea mammals, during these ceremonies. Similarly, Alaskan shamans wore gut parkas as ceremonial and spiritual garments during séances to cure people of illness or when performing miracles beneath the sea.

An important exception to the ordinary clothing worn by Canadian Inuit shamans is found in the extraordinary robe of the shaman Qingailisaq (Boas 1907; Driscoll 1983; Issenman 1985; Rasmussen 1929; Saladin d'Anglure 1983). The original costume is said to have been bought in 1902 in Iglulik by Captain George Comer on behalf of Franz Boas for the American Museum of Natural History, where it now rests. Andy Awa, a grandson of the shaman, asserted, however, that Captain Comer's persistent efforts to obtain the clothing met with

Above Shaman's belt of caribou skin, antler, ivory, and sinew, 125 cm, Netsilingmiut, 1958. Artisan: Jacob Kringorn Sissenark (ca. 1905-85) of Arviligjuaq, NWT, who donated the belt to Father Franz Van de Velde, o.m.i., in 1958. Many objects hung from the shaman's belt, some of them gifts from people helped or who hoped to receive favours. The spirits of the miniature snow knives and snow beaters on this belt fought evil spirits.

Opposite Shaman Qingailisaq's robe, caribou skin and wool, sewn with sinew, 109 cm, Iglulingmiut, reproduction 1982. Caribou-skin mitts, sewn with sinew, 27.7 cm, Iglulingmiut, reproduction 1982. The mitts have fur to the inside except for the wrist-band, which is decorated with fur mosaic. Caribou-skin hat, sewn with sinew, diameter 26 cm, Iglulingmiut, reproduction 1982. Artisans: Jeannie Arnaanuk and family of Iglulik, NWT, descendants of shaman Qingailisaq, made three reproductions of the costume based on the research of B. Saladin d'Anglure, Université Laval, in consultation with Ujuraq, the shaman's grandson. The replicas are copies of the costume in the American Museum of Natural History, 60/4440.

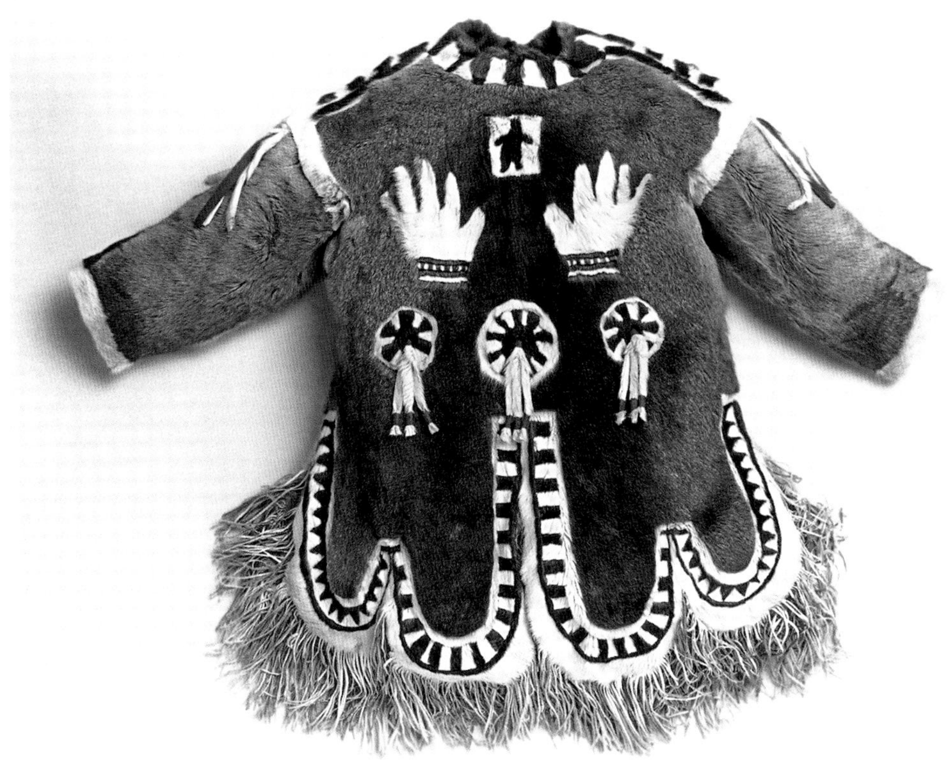

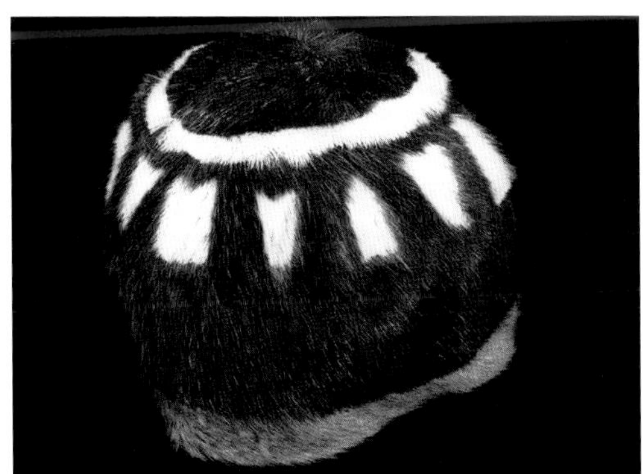

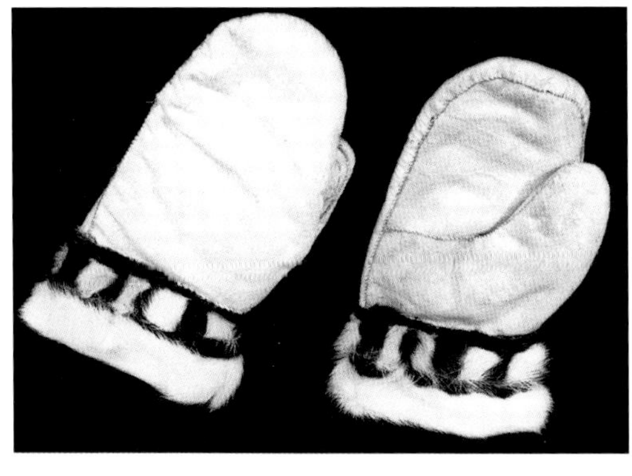

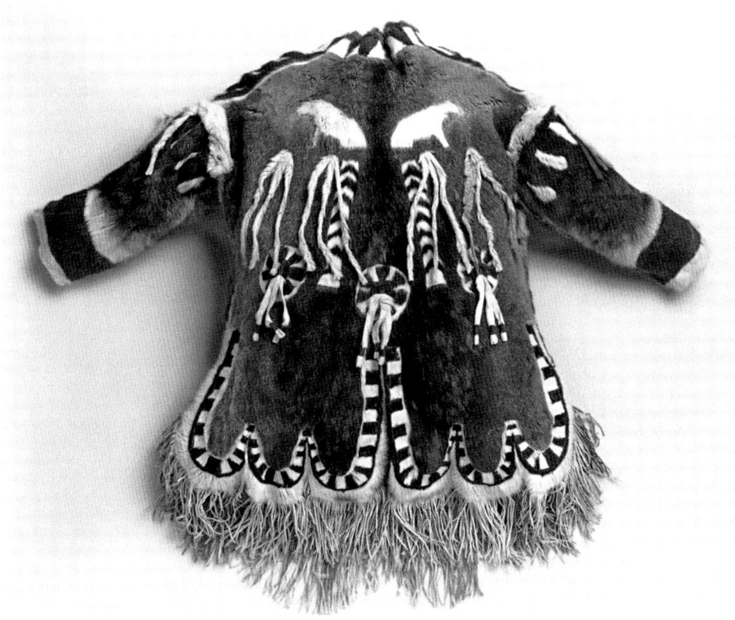

resistance from his grandfather, for to give away any spiritual object meant relinquishing its inherent power (Driscoll 1983, 212).[26] Since Qingailisaq did not like to refuse the captain, he asked his wife to make a duplicate of the costume, which consisted of coat, hat, and mitts. Awa believes that this duplicate is now in the possession of the American Museum of Natural History and that, in keeping with Inuit tradition, the original clothing was probably buried with his grandfather.[27]

The legend of the robe, as told by Awa, a son of Qingailisaq and himself a great shaman, centres on mountain spirits called *ijirqat* – or, in Kalaallit Nunaat, known as *iseraq* – who can be seen only by shamans. One day when Qingailisaq was out hunting he saw four caribou. He shot one with his arrow and soon it turned into a woman dressed in splendid clothing. She fell to the ground and gave birth to a son, and then she and the child died. The other caribou turned into men, and the eldest attacked Qingailisaq, trying to throw him down. The shaman realized that the caribou were ijirqat, the invisible mountain spirits who can transform themselves into humans. Qingailisaq talked quietly with one of them and convinced him he did not wish to harm him or his fellow spirits. The spirit instructed him to have clothing made such as the spirit-woman caribou had worn. Qingailisaq's wife did so, and placed a representation of the dead child and two hands on the front of the coat. On the back she inlaid images of giant white caribou, known as 'children of the earth.' (Ijirqat are born out of eggs below the earth's crust and live inside the earth.) Franz Boas's version of the narrative says that the purpose of the hands is to ward off evil spirits. Knud Rasmussen's rendition states that the hands show how the spirit-caribou sought to overpower the shaman. Actually the hands are gloved, an appropriate image for a shaman's hands.

The style and motifs of Qingailisaq's costume have parallels in the clothing of the Siberian Koryak. It is dress-like and hoodless. The ten scallops on the lower edge of the coat, a feature not found in Inuit clothing, have a fur mosaic border similar to the motifs on a Koryak man's funerary hood. Scallops decorate the lower edge of Koryak burial robes, although they are more numerous on the Iglulik shaman's coat. The circular designs with blade-like projections on Qingailisaq's robe, three in front and three in back, echo Koryak and Chukchi roundels.[28] The decorative strips that dangle from the circular motifs have ornamentations of red stroud such as that found in the ceremonial and shamanic clothing of the Chukchi, which was embellished with red tassels of twisted wool or fur. Red, for the Chukchi, was the colour of life. The row of chevrons that descends from each of the spirit-caribou images on the back of Qingailisaq's coat is also found on a Koryak dancing coat and a burial robe.[29]

Other individuals and institutions have now taken the place of the shaman, although some communities are reexamining the ancient beliefs of traditional society. Young people are experiencing a revival of the

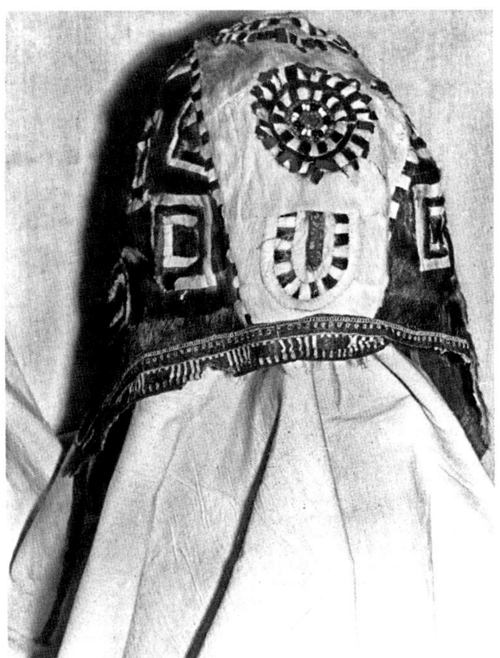

Funerary hood of reindeer skin, embroidery, and beads, sewn with sinew, Koryak, early twentieth century. Collected at Korf Bay, Koryak Okrug, CIS. The fur mosaic roundels and U-shapes on the front and back of the hood echo the motifs on Shaman Qingailisaq's robe. For an analysis of this and other Koryak funerary hoods, see Prytkova (1976, 68) and Serov (1988, 245).

shaman in the shape of Super Shamou, the Flying Inuk, a mythical figure endowed with extraordinary powers. Created by Peter Tapatai, whose birth name is Shamou, and Barney Pattunguyak of the Inuit Broadcasting Corporation, this modern shaman enters Inuit homes via the television and videotapes. Super Shamou, played by Peter Tapatai, dresses in red longjohns and a blue cape, and speaks Inuktitut. He flies above Arctic communities to save Inuit youngsters from trouble and to teach right from wrong (Fisher 1988).

Life's Stages

All peoples mark the crucial times in the life span with certain significant and socially accepted customs and ceremonies. Birth, puberty, marriage, pregnancy and childbirth, illness, and death are such occasions. In traditional Inuit society, these solemn junctures were met with appropriate, time-honoured conventions to legitimize, safeguard, and speed the person in his or her passage (Boas [1888] 1964; Dufour 1988; Freeman 1978; Jenness 1922; Nungak and Arima 1969; Rasmussen 1929, 1931; Ungalaaq 1985).

Childbirth

Childbirth among the Nunatsiarmiut, Iglulingmiut, and Netsilingmiut took place in a small temporary hut or snow house. After the birth, the mother and child lived in another separate dwelling for a month or longer, since the birth process was considered to render the mother unclean and dangerous to hunters. The Copper and Caribou Inuit, however, did not practise seclusion at childbirth.

In the temporary snow hut where birthing took place, there were no skins for rugs since the vapours would cling to the bedding. When the mother took the newborn on her lap, she did not lay it directly on her clothing, but on the soft skin of marmot, ermine, or wolf. Once she stopped bleeding she had to throw away all these skins and her old clothing. New mothers and women who had miscarried or were menstruating were forbidden to cure or work with certain skins used to make boots and mitts. These rules protected the community from offending the animals and helped ensure their return to be hunted. Strict interdictions governed the activities of women during their menses and parturition. A menstruating woman was not allowed to sew or go near hunting equipment, including stepping over a kayak. It was thought that a vapour arose from human blood that was offensive to animals and that contaminated any person or object with which it was in contact.[30] The hands of menstruating women appeared red to the souls of animals, and finding this sight unpleasant, they would not come near. Women were enjoined, for the sake of successful hunting, to advise the community of their condition by stitching or tying up the back flap of their amautiit and to observe the interdictions.

A sixty-one-year-old Netsilingmiut elder from Arviligjuaq related in 1991 that a newborn baby's umbilical cord traditionally was tied with a tassel from the kiniq, the front flap of the amauti. The tassel belonged to the woman helping the mother at the birth, usually her mother or mother-in-law. The elder mentioned as well a feature in some Arctic societies: the husband was expected to attend the birth (Henry Stewart, personal communication 1992). Godparents continue to dress the infant in the first clothing, and godparent and godchild have special responsibilities toward each other for the rest of their lives. The godparent is perceived to form the child's character. For example, a godfather calls his goddaughter *arnaliaq,* 'making you a woman.' She calls him *sanajiarjuk,* 'dear little maker' (Louis-Jacques Dorais, translation notes 1990). Traditionally the godmother is the woman who assists the mother during and after the child's birth.

In Nunavimiut society the woman who helps mother and child during and after the birth is called the *ikajurti,* 'the woman who helps.'[31] She is charged as part of her duties with making the newborn's clothing after the delivery. While waiting, the infant is swaddled in a hare skin and held on the breast of the mother under her amauti. When the new clothes are ready, the baby moves to the amaut. As the child grows and the clothing changes, the first set often becomes a keepsake. In traditional life some pieces became powerful amulets.

The sex of children, which determines their role and their clothing, was in some communities thought to be governed by the phenomenon of *sipiniq* (Birket-Smith 1929; Dufour 1975, 1988; Saladin d'Anglure 1967, 1986; Washburne and Blackmore 1976). Sipiniq, which means the act of changing sex, signifies the process at the moment of birth whereby some male infants – and, very rarely, female infants – decide to change their sex. The word, which in the plural is *sipiniit,* also denotes such a child, who during gestation was one sex and changed to the opposite at the time of exiting from the mother's body. Belief in this phenomenon is well known and endures in Iglulik, but in Nunavik only the elders remember its occurrence.

Children who are sipiniit are named after a relative or family friend who has died, at which time the soul of the deceased goes to reside in the infant. Thus children are accorded the respect given to elders and are treated with love and deference. Since names have no gender, the child can have a social sexual cognizance opposite to the biological. A child named for a deceased relative of the opposite sex wears clothes, dresses the hair, and performs tasks to conform to the role of that sex. This role change is not obligatory – the parents make the decision – and is not transvestism as known in other societies. The child incorporates the soul and functions of the person whose name is shared. If a girl receives her grandfather's name, she addresses her

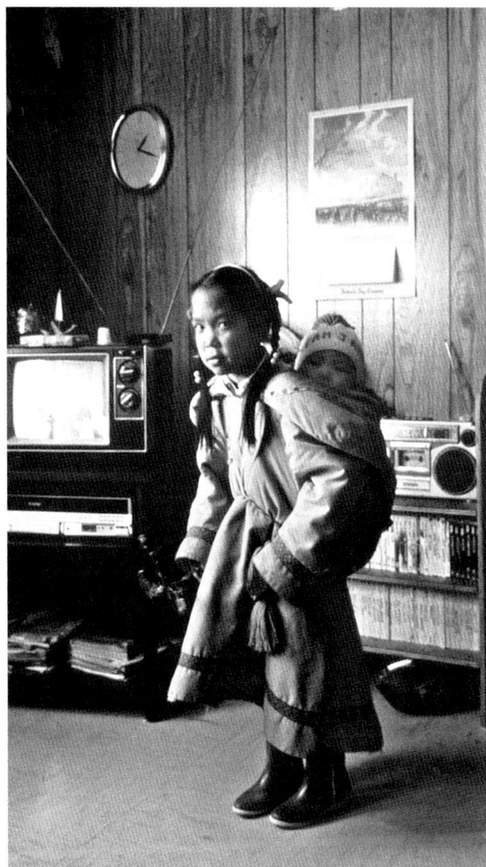

Rachel Kalliraq's granddaughter of Iglulik, NWT, 1986, holds a sibling in her amaut. A girl is gradually given tasks so that she becomes a help to her mother and grandmother. It was believed that the better seamstress a girl became, the better wife she would be. Little girls still use their amaut to carry a baby or a puppy. They play house with toys, dolls, and models made by their fathers and grandfathers.

father as 'my son,' and her father calls her 'little father.' Sometimes the young child decides when she or he wants to become the forebear and dresses appropriately (Martha Greig, personal communication 1985). A boy might say: 'Today I feel I am grandmother.' Jeela Alikatuktuk Moss-Davies noted the persistence of the tradition in 1985: 'In North Baffin Island and Iglulik area *sipiniq* is still recognized. My sister was named after my mother's father. She wore boy's clothing until she was twelve, and wore her hair clipped.'

Prior to the time when a boy caught his first seal and a girl reached her menarche, children whose sex was socially opposite to their physiology gradually began to dress and to assume the duties of their biological sex (Dufour 1975, 1981). Boys' hair was cut. Girls put aside, at least indoors, their boys' clothes and received an amauti, sometimes with a token baby-pouch. These youngsters experienced many difficulties as they moved from one way of life to another. Their parents helped them by their emotional support and by providing new clothing and training. Clothing played a key role to help the youngsters gain a new feeling about themselves and their future roles.

Childhood

Children start to learn their work in the family when they are about four years old, sometimes earlier, by participating in family tasks and in play.[32] 'We made wooden dolls and dressed them in caribou skin clothing, which we also made ... Someone would carve a baby for my dolls from a piece of ivory ... The only game the boys played was pretending to be out seal hunting, harpooning an old seal hip bone. They would take caribou hair, mat it together, and bring it back to the dolls as their catch,' describes Atoat of Ikpiarjuk (Innuksuk and Cowan 1976, 21). Parents and grandparents would make dolls for their daughters or granddaughters to play with or to carry in their amautiit. In times past, the elders believed that such dolls made possible the birth, some day, of many sons (Rose Dufour, written communication 1986).

Traditionally, if a family had only girls or only boys, a child was sometimes trained in the functions usually reserved for the opposite sex. Boys learned to sew, tend the lamp and cook, gather moss and berries, and otherwise help their mothers. Girls learned from their fathers how to fashion tools, train dogs, and how to hunt and fish: 'I had to

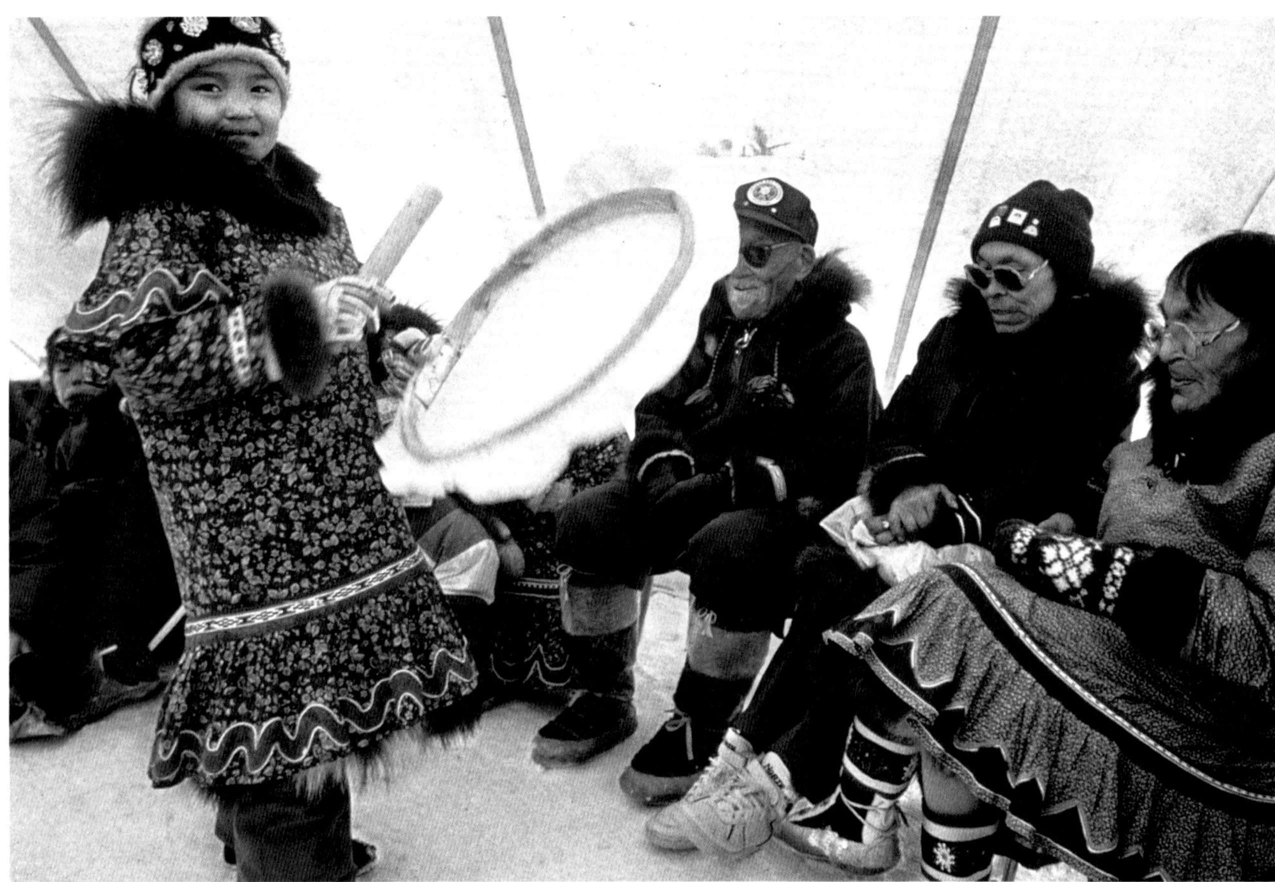

hunt seals with men since we didn't have any brothers. I went with anyone who went seal hunting but I had a hard time trying to learn the skills,' said Mary Inukpuk of Inukjuak.[33]

Puberty

The boy's first catch of a seal, caribou, or sea mammal marks his transition to manhood and is cause for celebration. In the old days a ritual for the first seal took place on the ice beside the breathing hole. The boy took off both his jackets and lay down on them with his upper body naked. His father then dragged the seal, before it died, across the boy's back, to prevent the seals from fearing him. Liivai Qumaaluk of Sanikiluaq tells of the time when he caught his first seal at the breathing hole: 'I remember how cold it was when water froze on top of my skin while the seal was being pulled' (Nungak and Arima 1969, 103).

In some communities, the mother of the boy prepares the skin of his first seal to make it white and supple for use as decoration on boots or on an amauti. 'So the skin was all ready when they sent it to the woman who was known as my wife because I was her husband's namesake ... That is how I learned the tradition of giving gifts to the widow or widower of the person you were named for,' explains Qamanirq of Ikpiarjuk (Innuksuk and Cowan 1976, 43). In the old days, when a Copper Inuit boy caught his first caribou his mother made herself a pair of trousers from the skin. In many places, on the occasion of a son's first catch, his mother added to her facial tattoos.

Traditionally, the customs observed when a girl reached puberty varied, and concerned her dress and sometimes her hairdressing and tattooing. The tail of her coat was let down or sewn longer, her hood became

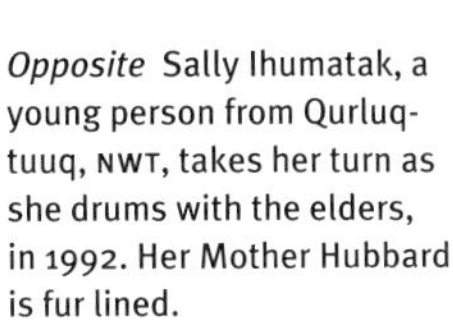

Opposite Sally Ihumatak, a young person from Qurluqtuuq, NWT, takes her turn as she drums with the elders, in 1992. Her Mother Hubbard is fur lined.

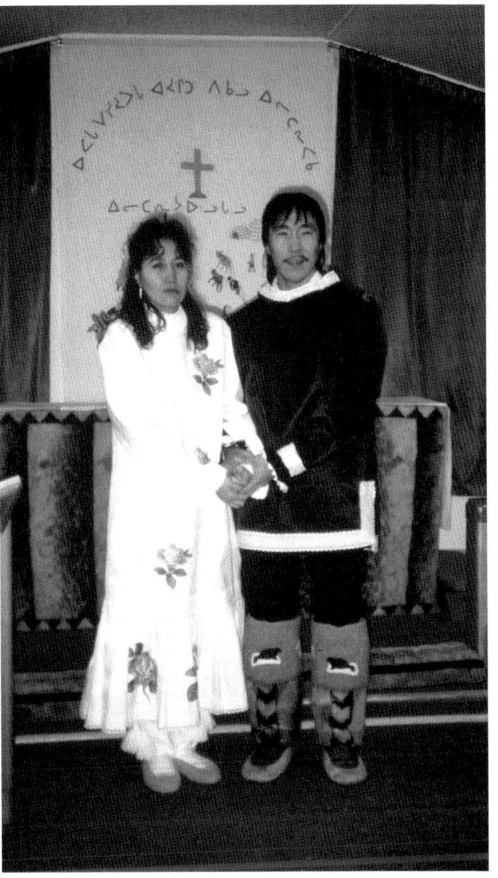

Right Linda Alookee and Inuk Charlie were married in Taloyoak, NWT, in 1995. The bride wore a white, hand-embroidered Mother Hubbard; the groom a fabric adaptation of the traditional Netsilingmiut fur parka. They are pictured here in front of the church altar, which is draped with sealskin hangings.

larger, and the amaut was either added or enlarged. Among the Caribou Inuit, the decorative pieces on the back of the amauti, which they called puberty symbols, covered the thongs that held up the lower edge of the tail. This practice signalled that the young woman was unmarried or, if married, was childless (Winifred P. Marsh, written communication, 1983). Among the Labrador Inuit the pubescent girl no longer wore her hair in braids hanging down in front on her shoulders but would loop her hair in side plaits under her ears and fasten the rest at the back. Like Kalaallit women, although the colours differed, she wore coloured ribbons to denote her status. The young girl wore pink, the married woman blue, and the widow white. Today, all over the Arctic, girls on the brink of womanhood continue to participate in family and community activities as befits their status.

Marriage

In traditional life marriage was not marked by any special ceremony, although it was an important event. The young woman took with her to her new home her ulu, lamp, needles, and sinew. Gifts from her husband-to-be could include ptarmigan socks, trousers, marrow bones, and etched tools such as a needlecase. Today, after a church ceremony, families continue to honour the couple by a feast and entertainment.

Illness and Death

In traditional society illness and accidents were deemed to be caused by someone breaking the prohibitions or by evil spirits who had to be exorcised and propitiated.[34] Among the Qangmaliit of Umingmaktuuq, dying persons dressed themselves in their best garments and met the inevitable with stoicism and dignity. Mourning ceremonies expressed grief as well as the fear of death. The spirit of the deceased lingered in the vicinity of the body for three or four days, and any violations of the rules of bereavement became a crime against the soul. Therefore no work, such as hunting or making or drying clothes, was allowed, and no sharp-edged instrument such as an ulu could be used in the vicinity of the body, for it might injure the lingering soul.

Some groups, such as the Netsilingmiut, observed the mourning period by keeping on hooded garments from morning to night and covering the hands with mittens. The body of the deceased was dressed in new clothing and often folded and wrapped in skins (as were the Qilakitsoq mummies).

Beside or inside the grave the survivors placed objects for the dead or miniatures such as tools and clothing. A woman would have her ulu and other household implements buried with her. The spirit of the dead appropriated the spirits of the grave goods and thus received an easier passage into the next world. As well, as Chuna McIntyre of Iik, Alaska, explains, 'over the face was placed a specially prepared seal gut Death Mask ... Seal gut is translucent, light, and resilient ... It was essentially a transparent shield, a window to the spirit world' (Hickman 1987, 10).

The death of children brought great sadness to the family and community. In several groups the mother who lost a child had to cover her head with a cap or a piece of skin for a year. A custom among the Pallirmiut and the Qairnirmiut governed a situation in which several infants in one family died. The next child to be born wore clothing with the fur flow on one side going up and on the other side down, or that was made half of seal skin, half of caribou. The child thus became unrecognizable to evil spirits and could grow up in peace.

Only the closest relatives attended the dead, and after the burial they had to throw away their clothing and put on newly made garments. The spirits of the dead could communicate with the living through the shaman, and told the living about their welfare in the afterlife and gave them advice. The relatives, or the shaman in some cases, put on gutskin coats during ceremonies to reach the souls of the dead. Among the Bering Sea Inupiat and Yupiit, at the Great Feast for the Dead, the namesake of the deceased dressed in new clothing. A woman would remove a tassel from the back of her best coat after the death of someone close. When a child was born in the community and was considered a replacement for the deceased, she sewed back the tassel (Fienup-Riordan 1987, 48-9).

In the past, as today, when all the observances have been made, the Inuit rest assured that the soul of their kinfolk is at peace, has completed its journey, and will be met at another time. Inuit traditions surrounding death reveal an outlook where end and beginning merge to make a wholeness of existence.

EXTERNAL RELATIONS

Documentation regarding hostilities between Inuit groups in Canada and the clothing worn during combat is difficult to find.[35] It is known, however, that the Kittegaryumiut of the Mackenzie Delta had encounters with the Qangmaliit (Nuligak 1971, 42-3). An incident related to Nuligak by his great-uncle Naoyavak, which probably occurred early in the twentieth century, reveals something about these meetings. One day Naoyavak's people, the Kittegaryumiut, were joined by some strangers. One of them, a man named Kayoktunak, put on his 'war shield,' an Arctic fox parka, although he assured the group he was not looking for a fight. The parka had been soaked in seal oil and fine sand had been smeared in the folds. After drying in the sun the coat became a horn-like shield that could not be pierced by arrows or knives. Inuit wore this kind of armour, called *ningasiq,* when they engaged in battle with other groups or with Dene.

Organized warfare in Alaska is better known.[36] Among the Yupiit of Nelson Island, a decorative reminder of a well-known battle conducted with bows and arrows adorns a man's coat. After a final hand-to-hand fight, the defeated survivors retreated. In a reminder of the successful escape, the seamstress now sews a strip of caribou skin on the shoulders of the dress parka: 'Known as the "vomit design" the skin commemorates the retreating warrior who had just eaten the rich back fat of a caribou before his pursuers commenced to chase him. As he ran, he turned first to one side and then the other, emptying his stomach of its rich contents and making his pursuers' path both slippery and treacherous' (Fienup-Riordan 1988, 15-16).

FAMILY AND COMMUNITY ORGANIZATION

From the testimony of the Inuit and early Canadian ethnologists we have obtained a view of Inuit society that recognizes leadership but has no masters who can dictate actions. The traditional ideal community shares its goods. It treats its children with kindness and a minimum of constraints. It is at one with the environment and neighbours. There is a measure of equality between men and women. These tenets, enshrined in Inuit ideals, can be seen as survival mechanisms and are related to an economic cycle in which women and men depend on each other to shoulder the responsibilities for food, clothing, shelter, and emotional sustenance.

Other reports sometimes contradict the belief in achieving consensus. Although there were no rulers or state apparatus, for example, a whaling captain in Alaskan Inuit society oversaw activities and made the decisions. In the Mackenzie Delta area earlier in the century, 'people never killed more than they needed and young hunters were taught never to kill more than they needed. Each tribe in those days had a leader or chief, and what he said went,' wrote Bertram Pokiak of Tuktuujaqtuuq about the old times as related to him by his grandparents (Pokiak 1989, 41).

Within communities, the nuclear and extended family formed loosely agglomerated bands in which various families joined or left, according to season, territory, and hunting grounds. After discussion, hunters, in particular male elders who were successful hunters, arrived at an entente that took their wives' preferences for certain foods and skins into consideration. Sharing was carried out by a system of kinship and hunting partnerships.[37] In former times, caribou skins cached during the summer were brought to the settlement in the fall. There they were distributed to the community to be dressed for the manufacture of winter clothing. The meat and skin of the bearded seal belonged to all who participated in the hunt. Since bearded seal continues to be used primarily to provide boot soles, the skin of one seal provides enough soles for a number of boots. Today, caribou skins are not considered to come under community ownership and are no longer saved until there are enough to make clothes for everyone, but are presumed to be personal property. If someone needs clothing or anything else, however, they are provided for either by helping themselves or by the permission of the owner.

Eventually some property, in addition to skins, became designated as private, including rifles, kayaks, tools, and household utensils. Norms dictate that food and other material goods are shared among the ill, the elderly, and the orphaned. The largest burden of sharing falls on the more successful and therefore wealthier hunters and their families.

The interdependence of women and men led to the cooperation essential to survival (Briggs 1974). The family as an economic unit, with complementary roles for women and men, is the basis for the mutual esteem and a measure of equality that appear to characterize most marital situations. 'Women were not to become the bosses of their husbands and if they were given good advice, they were to try to follow it The man was to be good to his wife and both were to discuss things together peacefully ... There should be absolutely no abuse of children, any children, and they should live in kindness with one another,' asserts Martha Angugatiaq Ungalaaq of Iglulik (Ungalaaq 1985, 23).

A better understanding by outsiders of this interdependence is emerging, at least with respect to Inupiaq society, in which women are considered pivotal to the hunt, epitomized by an expression of men: 'I'm not the great hunter, my wife is' (Bodenhorn 1990; Burch 1975). In this northern Alaskan society, wives play a key role, symbolically and ritually, to attract the animals.[38] As Bodenhorn explains, hunting is a sacred act. The man must treat the animal with respect. But it is the woman who attracts the animals, sometimes by entreating the moon for good hunting, by butchering and sharing the meat so that the animal is pleased and returns to be hunted anew, and by sewing the skin with artistry as a tribute to the creature's generosity in allowing itself to be killed. The seamstress performs an ancient role when she makes a second skin for her family. Her needle helps make her husband into a great hunter, for the animals are pleased by clean, beautiful clothes. A skilled artisan is of inestimable value to her family and a source of pride.

All over the Arctic, each sex can take part in activities that usually belong to the other. Some men scrape skins and can repair their clothes and boots while out hunting without their wives.[39] They have a precise knowledge about the qualities required in the different skins for the varied clothing needs. If tending the baby a man might put on his wife's amauti, so that the baby is held snugly in front or back to engage in play or sleep. Women and children help with the caribou hunt and with sealing and fishing. Indeed, some women engage in hunting with or without men.

The parka given to a bride by her husband's family contains a wealth of symbols

Above Ida Aivek of Uluksartuuq, NWT, 1988, wears a Mother Hubbard parka of fabric and fur. The community is seen in the background.

Below (Right) Woman's dress parka of skins of ground squirrel, wolf, wolverine, otter, mink, calf, elk, and salmon; beads, red yarn; lining of ground squirrel; sewn with dental floss. Yup'ik 1988. The parka was made by Eliza Chase, Master artist and teacher. She was born in Kasigluq, Alaska, and now resides in Mamterilleq. In some Alaskan parkas, the tassels of wolverine, front and back, represent the extensions of fingers. The five-fingered tassels are an expression of pride in oneself. The tassels with four fingers commemorate the deceased (Meade 1990, 231). (Left) Man's parka of skins of muskrat, calf, wolf, otter, and beaver, cloth, Yup'ik, 1988. The parka was made by Marie Lekander, Master artist and teacher. She was born and resides in Mamterilleq.

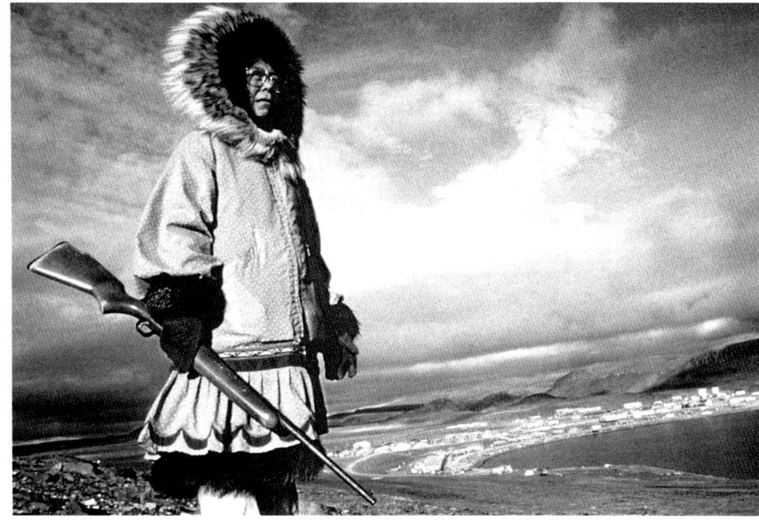

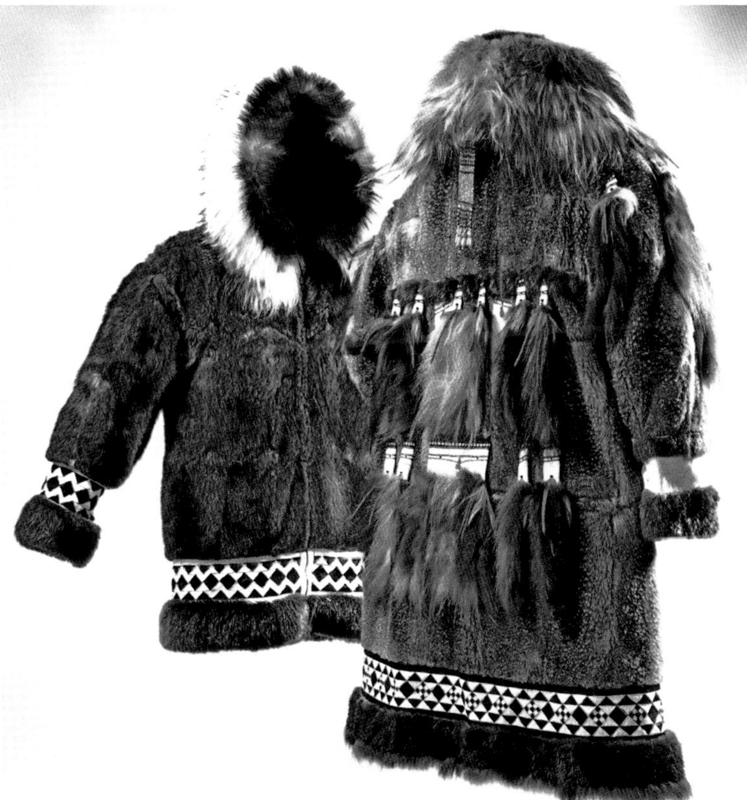

that connect the person to the kin group and to the universe (Meade 1990). The shape of the inserts, the forms of decoration in fur and beads, all tell some aspect of family and often group history.[40] One Yup'ik Kodiak elder, who still has relatives in Kamchatska, Russia, related that the panels on her new parka gave her life history (Murielle Nagy, personal communication 1992).

The essential role Inuit women have played in their economic life may mean more power for women than is seen in some non-Inuit societies. Clothing manufacture is one way for a woman to establish control over her life. She can sell some of her work and thus increase the household cash flow.

The roles of men and women have changed somewhat. Trapping and hunting is often supplemented by or is auxiliary to wage-earning activities. Skin-sewing functions have narrowed because fabric clothing makes up a substantial part of modern wardrobes. Women have moved easily into employment outside the home. Yet the traditional values expressed by eminent elder Martha Ungalaaq in 1985 continue to be held by those who aspire to be Inummariit, the real Inuit.

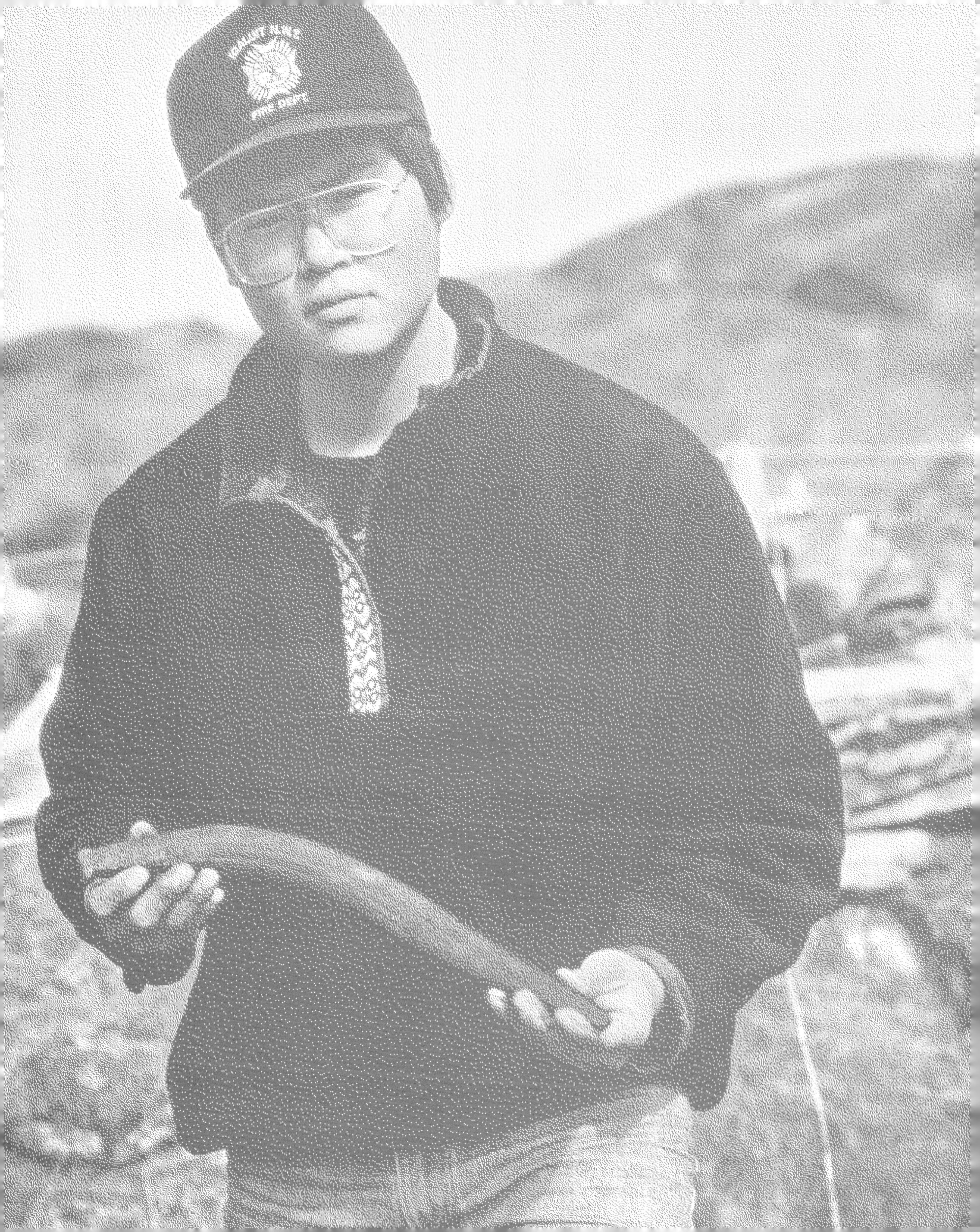

Land, God-made, ingenious planet we live in, as distinguished from other heavenly bodies, or from the dwelling place of the spirits. We, the prisoners of the earth, of whatever size, shape or form we are, all live and die, be we man, beast or fowl; we have to share the planet. Generation upon generations the land we live in never seems to change; we rise to see the glory of the skies, the setting of another day, and yet this land that is on our feet is there. Take it away, where would be the joy of living?

John Weetaltuk, 'Land' (1981)

Chapter 6

New Explorations

Two children of Iqaluit, 1987, wear caribou-fur clothing. On the right, the son of the photographer, Brent Boddie, wears a crocheted wool tuque under his hood.

Although there is now a considerable body of knowledge about Inuit dress, contributed by both Inuit and non-Inuit, there are many roads to explore. To record, collate, and examine new ground in the realm of Inuit clothing is important to both North and South. Answers to some areas of investigation could be useful in the study of human migrations, development of cultures, and even, perhaps, of human origins.

THE ROLE OF ELDERS

Clothing studies have some urgency, for the original keepers of the lore, the elders, are passing away. Because northerners no longer rely exclusively on skin clothing for survival, many of the remaining elders neither gather and prepare skins nor pass on to the young the art and skill of garment construction. The younger generation are part of a school system that until recently trained them only for a life removed from coping with the elements and left them in ignorance of their history.

Thus the Inuit way of life is in danger of eroding, in part because of overwhelming economic, political, and cultural forces from the dominant society to the South. Inuit communities have counteracted these forces over the past two decades to engender pride in their heritage and to rediscover and preserve their birthright. Clothing is an important part of that patrimony, and its future is becoming more assured. A resurgence of interest in producing clothing, and initiatives undertaken by Inuit throughout the Arctic, have helped fur clothing usage to flourish. Elijah Grey of Kangiqsualujjuaq expressed his concern (Nungak 1983, 119-20):

I would like to know which clothes are best for survival in freezing temperatures, which are most dependable and which can still be made but are no longer made. Are they no longer made because the skins are not available or because it is no longer known how to make them? Were hunters safer out in the cold with caribou hide garments? Did people die from exposure because of unsuitable clothing? Did adults stop teaching younger people how to make traditional clothes because it takes too long to make them?

It remains necessary to gather, preserve, and pass on the ancient lore before it is too late. Both non-Inuit and Inuit researchers and institutions are making valuable contributions to this goal. That fur clothing is essential in certain kinds of weather – when hunting in winter or conducting lengthy scientific experiments – is well established (Nungak 1983, 117-18, 126):

I make caribou skin parkas for my men out of the hides of caribou they kill. Caribou hides are great for cold weather. Caribou skin socks don't get damp from sweat like other materials. I still use dried grass in my boots. It keeps your feet warm and dry as toast.
Mary Pootoogee of Kangiqsuk

I still prepare skins and make them into clothes. I have sons who often go out hunting ... My sons complain how cold sheepskin boots are. When they pack what they need to take along in their hunts, I always pack pairs of caribou skin boots for them to take along, just in case.
Akinisie Novalinga of Purvirnituq

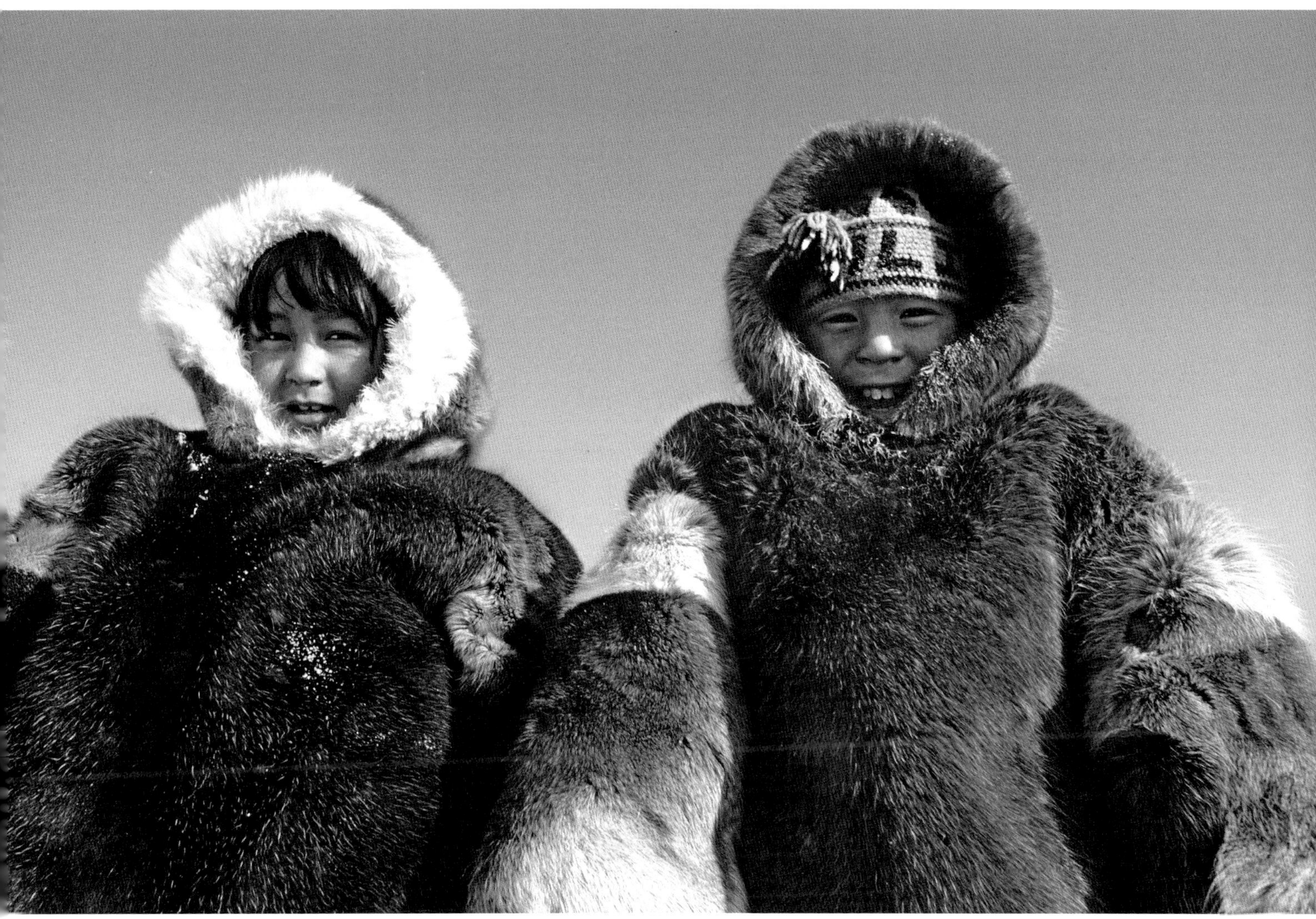

In Canada, the clothing complexes of some groups – the Copper Inuit, Netsilingmiut, Iglulingmiut, and Caribou Inuit, and to some extent the Qikirtamiut and Nunatsiarmiut – are fairly well-known in the literature, although much still remains to be written, photographed, and filmed. Major investigations still have to be undertaken about the clothing of the Inuvialuit, the Nunavimiut, and the Labrador Inuit.

In promoting the heritage it is important to understand the role of clothing as a link to enduring cultural wellsprings. Clothing, as does language, affirms a distinctive identification and can convey treasured traditions that endow a people with pride and feelings of self-worth. Furs worn in combination with imported dress demonstrate that the Inuit intend to control their lives by continuing to make appropriate choices from the past and the present.

INUIT COMMUNITIES

Many measures taken in Inuit communities are promoting a resurgence of the culture, with the Inuktitut language as well as English used in the programs. The agenda of the Pauktuutit, the Inuit Women's Organization, for example, includes programs that preserve and promote the culture through clothing. Inuit organizations

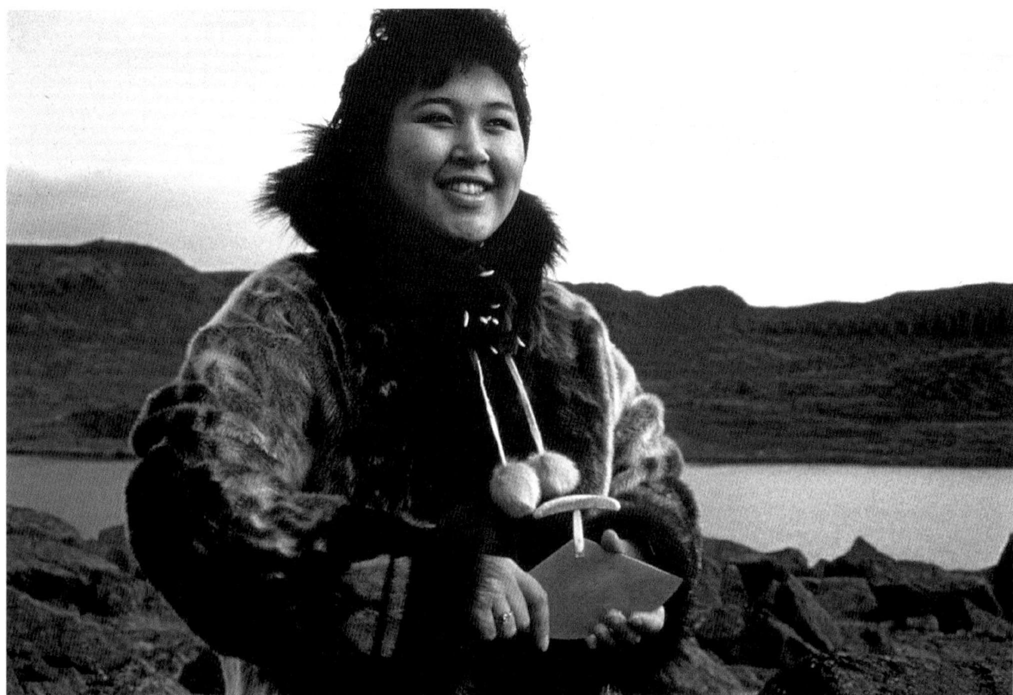

Left Judy Klengenberg of Uluksaartuuq, NWT, 1987, holds an ulu. She wears a sealskin parka with long-haired ruff and wrist trim.

Opposite above Inuit women and children at Inukjuaq, Nunavik. In the background is the main part of the Daniel Weetaluktuk Museum and Cultural Transmission Centre, built by Avataq Cultural Institute in 1992.

Opposite centre One of the sites of Avataq Cultural Institute's archaeological field school at Inukjuaq in 1995. Archaeology research in Nunavik started in a limited way in 1958. Today, the full-time program is open to Inuit and non-Inuit, some of whom come from other countries.

Opposite below Ipeelee Itorcheak, a student in the Arctic College Environmental Technology Program, Nunatta Campus, Iqaluit, NWT, 1992, displays a snow beater made of antler. It was recovered from archaeological excavations in the entry passage of a Thule culture (ca. AD 1000-1700) winter house ruin at the Tungatsivvik Site, Baffin Island.

and school boards, sometimes assisted by non-Inuit institutions, have established documentary and photographic archives (Aapak 1981; Lahti 1996). They are recording the elders' personal and group histories, legends, and wisdom about survival skills, in their own language. They are helping to train teachers, archaeologists, and museologists. Museums established in the North by the Inuit are community-based centres for education about and preservation of the traditions. Their collections and exhibitions include, of course, clothing and tools of construction. Primary schools and high schools, and five branches of Arctic College in the Northwest Territories, have established courses that teach traditional skills. 'I am really happy about the sewing programme because I am learning how to make an amautik,' says Maggie Augiak of Kangiqsuk. 'I didn't know before how to do this, so I always had to get somebody else to make one for me. Now I'll be able to teach my daughter' (Myers 1980, 116).

In Ausuittuq, students at Ummimmak school learn to make sealskin clothing as part of the Piniaqavut Arts Project, sponsored by the Baffin Divisional Board of Education (Inuit Art Quarterly 1994, 39). Some schools offer survival courses that include learning to process skins and produce fur and bird-skin clothing (Edward Miller, Joanne Miller, personal communication 1991). Avataq Cultural Institute of Nunavik coordinated courses in 1995 and 1996 to teach sewing kamiit and amautiit in several northern Québec communities. Funding was provided by the Kativik Regional Government Employment and Training Program.

In addition, the Inuit, led by their elders, are seeking to revitalize traditional knowledge to serve contemporary life (Ernerk 1993, 12). The government of the Northwest Territories, the majority of whose members are Aboriginal people, founded the Science Institute of the Northwest Territories, now called Nunavut Research Institute, which combines traditional Inuit wisdom with the knowledge of the industrial scientific community. In the same vein, Arctic College's programs lead to professions in the physical and the social

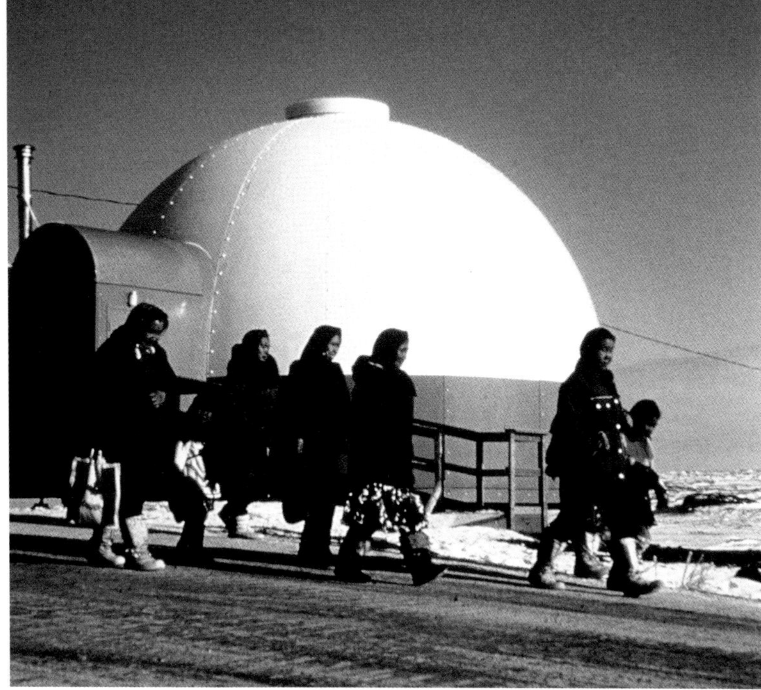

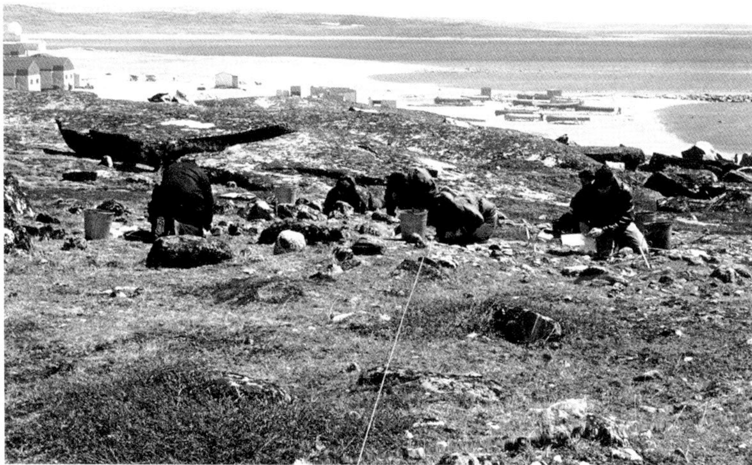

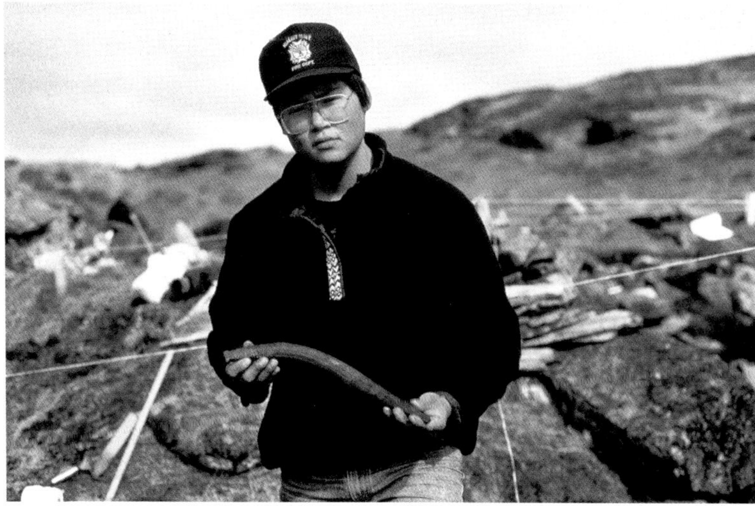

sciences, such as archaeology, anthropology, and museology. In one project, formal training in heritage research started in 1991 with the Tungatsivvik Archaeological Project. Part of the Environmental Technology Program set up by Arctic College, the program cooperates with the whole community of Iqaluit: 'Results of the project are being actively integrated into local educational and interpretive structures, as community members from elders to school children participate in "making history come alive"' (Stenton and Rigby 1995). Archaeological excavations have uncovered, from palaeolithic times through to the Thule and Historic eras, thousands of artifacts, including clothing-related tools such as blades, scrapers, uluit, and at least one thimble holder and a snowbeater. The community helps to design and carry out the research and is kept fully informed of progress by public presentations and radio. The artifacts, stored locally, and information gathered are used by the community to understand their culture and history. In the course of participating in the program, people acquire the skills needed for training in related professions (Rigby and Stenton 1992).

INTERCONTINENTAL STUDIES

The Inuit Circumpolar Conference, established in 1977, has brought a realization that the four circumpolar countries have a commonality, one feature of which is their clothing. Consciousness about Arctic clothing has been present in the South for some centuries, for artifacts from the North have

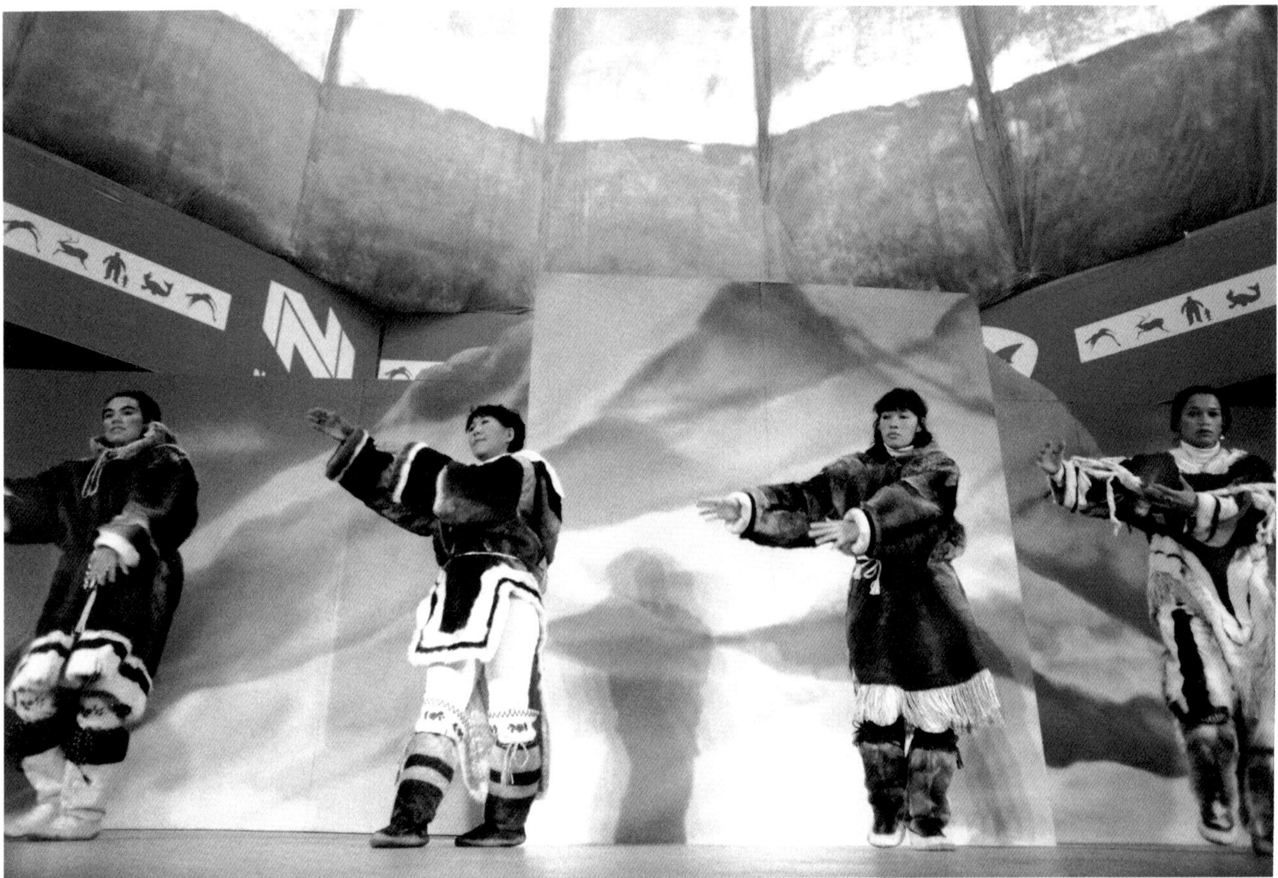

been brought back and housed in the world's museums since European contact in the sixteenth century. (See the appendix for a list of museum collections.) Inuit cognizance that they are the heirs of ancient and valuable traditions may help elders to make manifest what they take for granted: that their clothing is eminently efficient and is made beautiful according to time-honoured precepts.

The parallels and diversities in circumpolar material culture, including clothing and tools, have been elaborated on in the works of numerous writers (Birket-Smith 1929, Part 2, 234-94; Buijs 1993, 1997; Buijs and Vogelsang-Eastwood 1993; Dolgikh and Fainberg 1959; Fitzhugh and Crowell 1988; Gurvich 1979, 1986; Hatt 1934, 1969; Ivanov 1963, 1970a, 1970b; Leroi-Gourhan 1946; Levin and Potapov 1961, 1964; Mitlyanskaya 1983; Mundkur 1984; Nooter 1984; Prytkova 1976; Schuster 1951). The clothing of the Saami and of some Siberian peoples is also well documented.[1] Coordination and further research in the field and on this considerable body of literature may throw light on migrations, contacts, and the spread of clothing complexes and design typologies.

Prehistoric Carvings, Tools, and Figurines

The connections between the clothing and tools from the Saami across Siberia to Kalaallit Nunaat are unmistakable (Issenman 1997). Pendants made of mammoth ivory found at the 21,000-year-old site at Mal'ta, CIS, bear further study to compare them with bone and ivory drops found at Canadian Thule sites and in Kalaallit Nunaat, in particular those with pear-like and figure-eight shapes (Hansen 1979, 3-4; Sproull 1977, 72-9).

Opposite At the 1995 Canadian National Exhibition, Toronto, Pauktuutit Inuit Women's Organization staged choreographed presentations of men's, women's, and children's clothing designed and produced by Inuit women. The photograph shows, from left to right (designer in parentheses), Eva Sowdluapik of Arviat (Dorothy Aglukark), Susie Nakashuk of Pangniqtuuq (Women's Sewing Group of Pangniqtuuq), Rita Tikivik of Qamanittuaq (Lucy Iyago with her mother, Racheal Arnamartik), and Lucie Idlout Johnsen of Qamanittuaq (Hattie Atutuvaa).

Above Choir from East Kalaallit Nunaat singing at the Fifth Inuit Circumpolar Conference held at Sisimiut, Kalaallit Nunaat, in 1989.

Below One vitrine from the permanent exhibition 'Labrador Inuit circa 1700' at the Newfoundland Museum, St. John's, mounted in 1980. The clothing was made by Sophie Lampe of Naini, Labrador, in 1979.

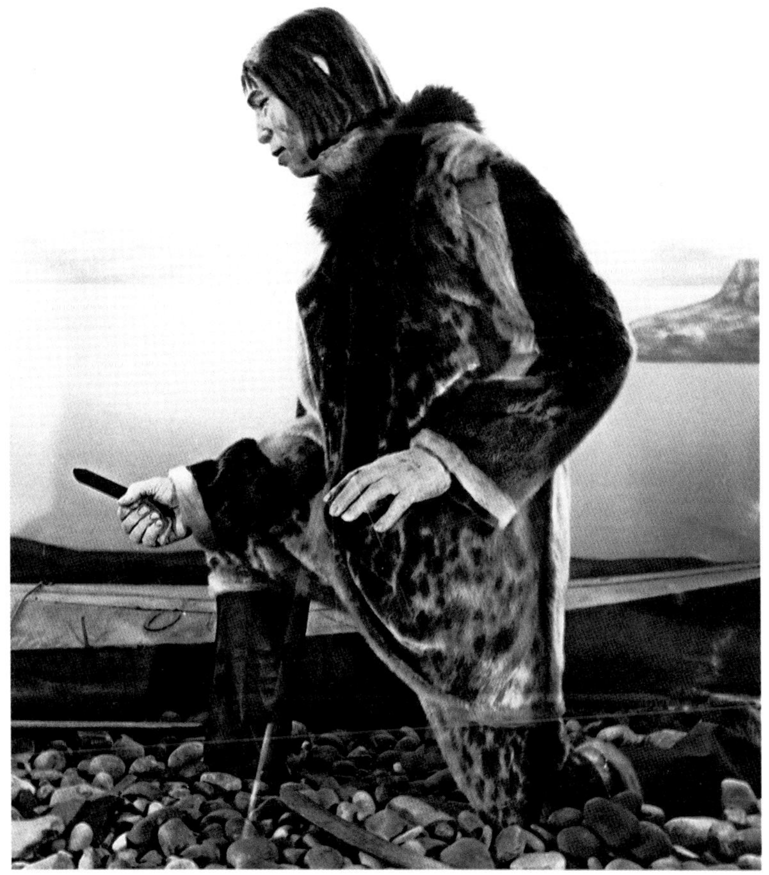

Among the artifacts found at excavations of a Bronze Age burial site on the lower Lena River was a human skeleton (Okladnikov 1970, 137). The deceased had been dressed in fur clothing, possibly made of squirrel skins, sewn with sinew. A large stone knife, triangular-shaped like an ulu, was in the right hand along with a needlecase. The tubular case, made of bone, housed a copper needle among twisted lengths of well-preserved sinew. Also with the remains were several small copper discs, possibly for clothing decoration. These Bronze Age tools and clothing, possibly belonging to ancestors of present-day Siberian Evenks or Evens, are remarkably similar to Inuit artifacts known across the Arctic from the Pre-Dorset to the Historic eras.

More extensive examination could be given to the clothing tools of different eras: the distribution and evolution of uluit, needles and their cases, thimbles and thimble holders. The forms, shapes, and materials of tools can reveal something about the civilizations of the migrants and the routes of their journeys. Definitive studies of the ulu, for example, a tool known in many cultures and in many eras, are now shedding light on history and technology and on how different forms relate to changes in material conditions, and contact through population shifts (McGrath 1992; Rankin and Labrèche 1991).

Another implement, the needlecase, is known from the Palaeolithic Age to the twentieth century and is found in the material culture of peoples across northern Scandinavia and northeastern Russia, across Siberia to Sakhalin Island, and from Alaska and Canada to Kalaallit Nunaat (Fitzhugh and Kaplan 1982, 134-5; Ivanov 1970a; Mason 1891; Nelson [1899] 1983, 103-4, 106; Nordic Arts Centre 1981, p. 9, nos. 4-9). Materials used to make the cases depended, of course, on available resources: bone, antler, and ivory from land animals, sea mammals, birds; and metals. Even the stalk of a feather could house the precious needles. Similar shapes are found in the various locales: tubular with a pull-through strap, some with a stopper at one end, and some flattened. The stopper of an unusual Chukchi bone needlecase consists of three dogs' heads. Possibly the case came to Chukotka from Alaskan Inupiat or Yupiit, since this type is unknown in Siberia (Ivanov 1970a, 202, Figure 4, no. 3).

A type of hook-shaped thimble holder found at the Utqiagvik site and dated approximately AD 1510 was also found on the site of the Sermermiut people of Kalaallit Nunaat, whose settlement existed from 1500 BC to AD 1850 (Mobjerg and Caning 1986, 182). It seems that the hook-shaped guard is not found in Canada. Instead, the fluked or anchor-shaped thimble holder, some with a bicephalous form, and the wing shaped holder are part of women's tool aggregations in the Thule and Historic periods in the areas between Alaska and Kalaallit Nunaat.

Prehistoric figurines with clothing depicted on them and other carvings teach us about possible connections between prehistoric northern peoples and later cultures characterized as Eskimo. Already discussed in Chapter 1 are the Palaeolithic figurines

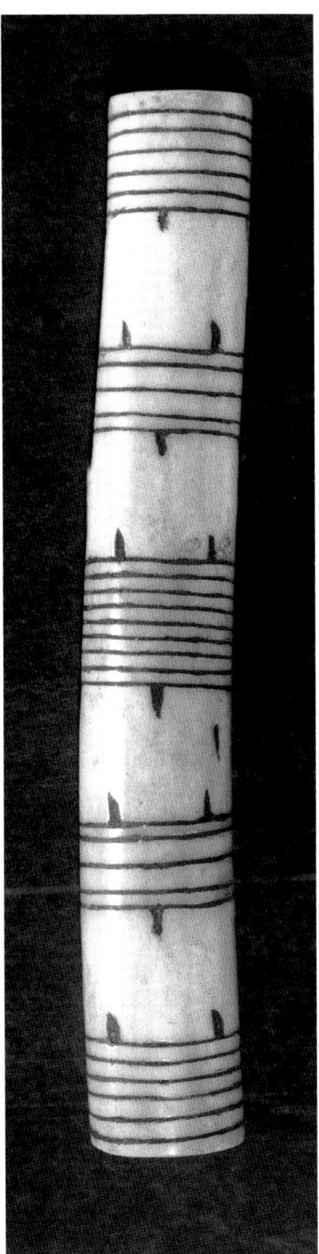

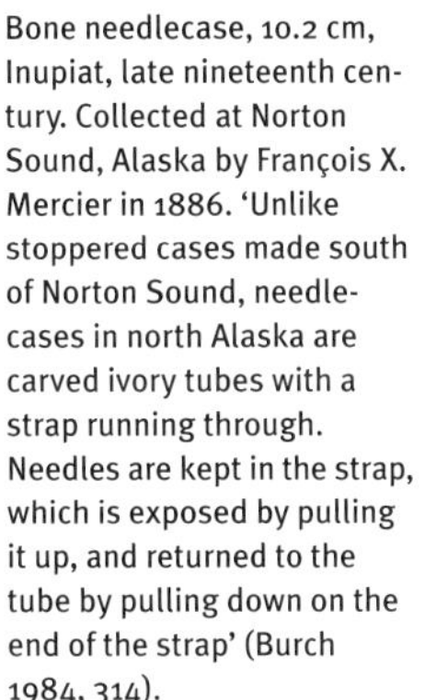

Bone needlecase, 10.2 cm, Inupiat, late nineteenth century. Collected at Norton Sound, Alaska by François X. Mercier in 1886. 'Unlike stoppered cases made south of Norton Sound, needlecases in north Alaska are carved ivory tubes with a strap running through. Needles are kept in the strap, which is exposed by pulling it up, and returned to the tube by pulling down on the end of the strap' (Burch 1984, 314).

found at Buret' and Mal'ta in the CIS. Some figurines from Mal'ta are considered to exhibit fur garments, girdles, back pouches, and headdresses (Abramova 1967, 67, 89). Could the back pouch possibly be an amaut?

Intriguing are some Dorset statuettes that gaze outward with powerful stance and wear a hoodless garment with what has been called a high collar. This style is found on figurines excavated from widely scattered areas in the eastern Arctic, and it is puzzling. The climate of the Early Dorset era, from 500 BC to 1 BC, was colder than today's, followed by some slight warming in the Late Dorset period, from 1 BC to AD 1000 (McGhee 1987, Plate 11).[2] A hoodless parka would not give adequate protection under such conditions. Does the clothing represented on these figurines actually have a collar, or has the hood been folded back to leave the wearer bare-headed? Is there some other explanation for this style of coat? Can these figurines – which are found, it seems, only in the eastern Arctic – tell us something about the origin and spread of the Dorset culture? Is it possible that Dorset hunters, who are known for their elegant iconography, sought to capture the moment when, with hood thrown back, they welcome back *Siqiniq*, the sun, after its long absence? When the sun's first rays appear over the horizon, Inuit of the twentieth century gather on a height of land, remove their gloves, toss back their hoods, and hold out their arms as a greeting to Siqiniq. The ceremony helps to ensure prosperity and salutes the many kind spirits the sun harbours (de Coccola and King 1956, 249).

Parallels in Style, Motifs, and Ornamentation

Interdisciplinary studies of frozen finds at Qilakitsoq in Kalaallit Nunaat and at the Utqiagvik site in Alaska have yielded much information about Arctic peoples. Comparisons of clothing artifacts with historical Inuit clothing could lead to some interesting discussion. The traditional Copper Inuit amauti, for example, distinctive among all Inuit clothing, may have a prototype in the Qilakitsoq woman's parka from the Thule culture bearers, with its shallow hood and sleeve that has a ninety-degree angle of fall from the shoulder and a forty-five-degree angle at the sleeve-shoulder seam.

Some frozen recoveries have not yet been studied in detail, partly because at the time of discovery the technology was not sufficiently developed to undertake the necessary research. In 1930 the American anthropologist Martin Luther found well-preserved mummies in rock caves in southern Kalaallit Nunaat. A few of these remains were brought back to the Peabody Museum at Harvard University, where they are preserved (Hansen and Gullov 1989, 70). A frozen female body dated ca. AD 400 was recovered on Sivuqaq, Alaska, in 1970 (Smith and Zimmerman 1975, 435). While no clothing was associated with the deceased, the tattooing patterns included what is interpreted as the 'flanged heart' motif. This particular design can also be likened to the double lobes and heart shapes found on Caribou Inuit clothing.

There are many examples of motifs and design typologies shared among Siberians, Arctic North Americans, and Kalaallit, as discussed in Chapter 5, but a comprehensive understanding of the similarities and dissimilarities has yet to be ventured.[3] Some symbols found on historical clothing are used from the first century through the Thule culture – the Y, parallel lines, broken (stretched) stitch, spurred lines, dots, circle and dot, tooth, and arrow shapes. Not yet clear is if the spread of motifs and styles, as exemplified in Qingailisaq's costume, resulted from collective memory, as well as direct contact via trade routes and migrations or some other reason.

A reversal of the process in which complexes moved from Siberia east to North America and Kalaallit Nunaat may be found, in one instance, in the Koryak burial robe. The tail of this robe – actually a point – was until recently considered obligatory although it had disappeared from other Siberian parkas.[4] It has been hypothesized that the Koryaks, Chukchis, and Itel'mens received this characteristic from Alaskan Yupiit (Gurvich 1979, 34).

Beads, spoons, pennies, and other decorations obtained by Inuit in trade are found on clothing, tools, and jewellery. A preliminary stylistic analysis of thirteen beads recovered at the Tungasivvik archaeological site suggests a date from the late nineteenth to the middle of the twentieth century. The tent ring from which the beads were unearthed is now assigned a period between 1900 and 1940 (Stenton and Rigby 1995, 53; Karklins 1993). This kind of study can help, for example, to determine the origin and date of arrival of beads

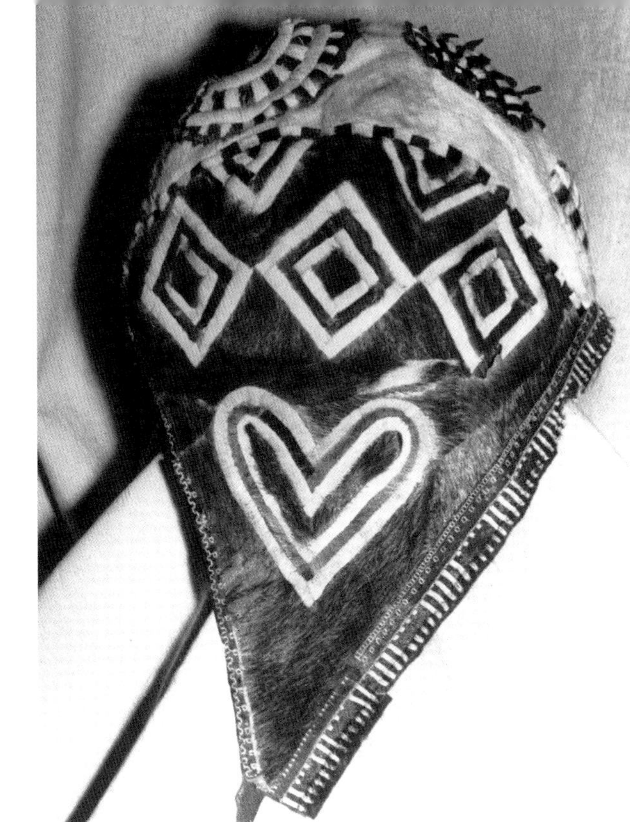

Above Funerary hood of reindeer skin, embroidery, beads, sewn with sinew, Koryak, early twentieth century. Collected at Korf Bay, Koryak Okrug, CIS.

Below Reindeer skin funerary hood Koryak, early twentieth century. The pattern of and motifs on these hoods resemble those of North American Inuit (see figure 2.1 on page 48 and photos on pages 48, 193, and 233). See Prytkova (1976, 67-8) for a discussion of this funerary hood.

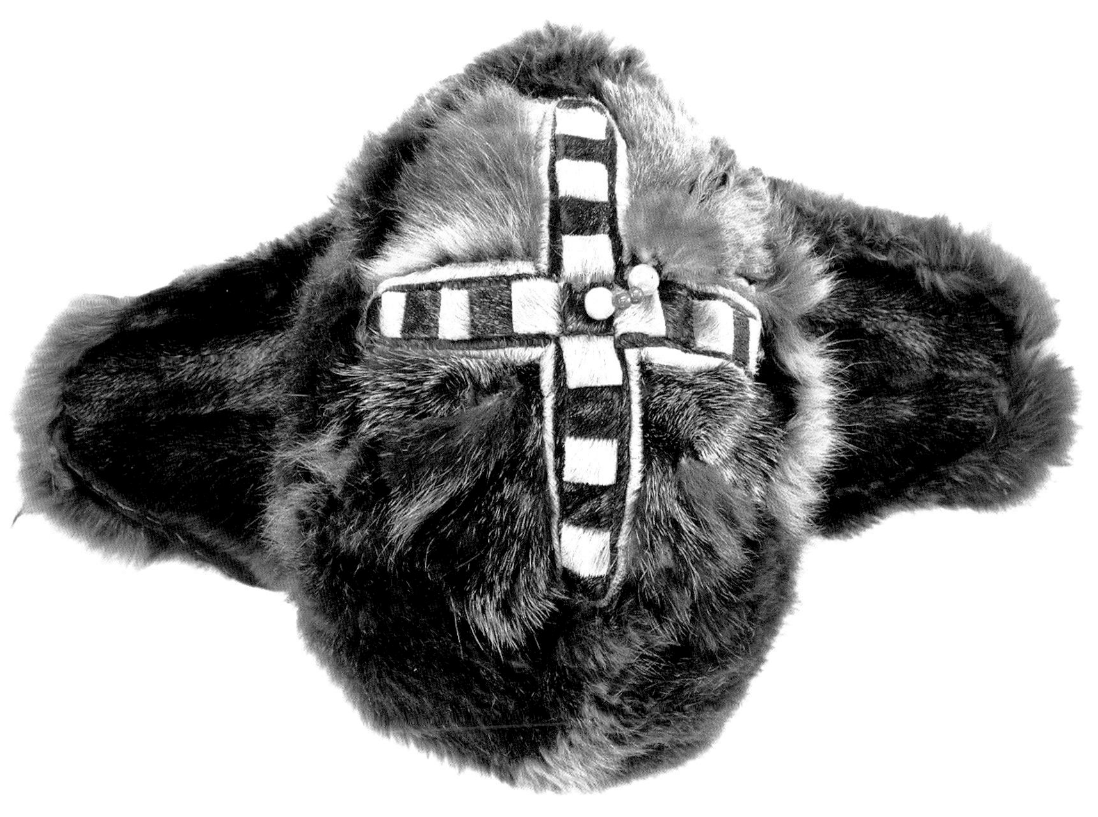

Inuit drummers at Qurluqtuuq, NWT, 1991 wear a combination of fur and fabric, using the style of the Western Arctic.

and other artifacts on clothing and tools in museum holdings, thus adding to the often sparse data in the provenance notes.

EVOLUTION OF STYLES

We now know something about the evolution and spread of styles of historical North American Arctic clothing and of the Kalaallit, but a lacuna exists in knowledge about clothing before the Thule era. The examples we have of Thule and immediate post-Thule clothing tell us that flaps characterized the early coats. Twentieth-century Kalaallit women's garments, if we compare them with the dress of the mummies of Qilakitsoq, lost the high hood, and the flaps became so small that Canadian Inuit call their Kalaallit kinfolk 'Akukitormiut' – the people of small tailpieces (Rosing 1986, 41). What caused the style changes and when?

Canadian Inuit maintained the distinctive flaps into the Contemporary era. The flaps, seams, and other features were discrete according to group so that it was and is possible to tell the origin of the wearer, although now some of the distinguishing aspects have become blurred, and the even-edged amauti is very often worn. The kayak, which appeared possibly in the Dorset culture and certainly in the Thule era (McGhee 1983, 81; 1978, 67, 79), may explain the reduction of the back flap of men's parkas and in some places its disappearance.

Traditional Copper Inuit clothing, no longer made, had many distinctive features. White caribou-fur panels covered the chest of dress and dancing garments. Some of the disadvantages of the costume were its shallow hood edged with narrow, short-haired fur that barely covered the cheekbones, a high waist that allowed wind entry, and a long narrow tail that had to be looped up for sealing and other tasks. The woman's costume suffered from the same impediments. With the high waist there was no front flap to protect the infant when removed from the amaut for elimination. The hood was built up by a series of arcs and sewn to the neck of the amauti, thus adding a seam at a point of stress. Because the Copper Inuit used lighter weight summer caribou skins for both layers of clothing, they needed a long overcoat for stormy weather, for sealing, and for travelling, a style also used by their ancestors (Inukshuk and Cowan 1976, 17; Jenness 1946, 17). They gradually gave up traditional wear for the more comfortable Alaskan and Inuvialuit styles after 1916.

Yet among the groups with which the Copper Inuit traded were the Kittegaryumiut and Inuvialuit, whom they met on Victoria Island. There they would have seen clothing resembling that of the Inupiat and Yupiit and the dress of the Inuvialuit, which gave more protection than their own. It is possible that no Copper Inuit women accompanied their mates on these long trips and that prior to 1916 they were unaware of the styles to the west of them.

The Siberian, Alaskan, and Inuvialuit women's garment, as we know it from the nineteenth and early twentieth centuries, had long, broad, U-shaped flaps. This pattern developed into the dress-like form we

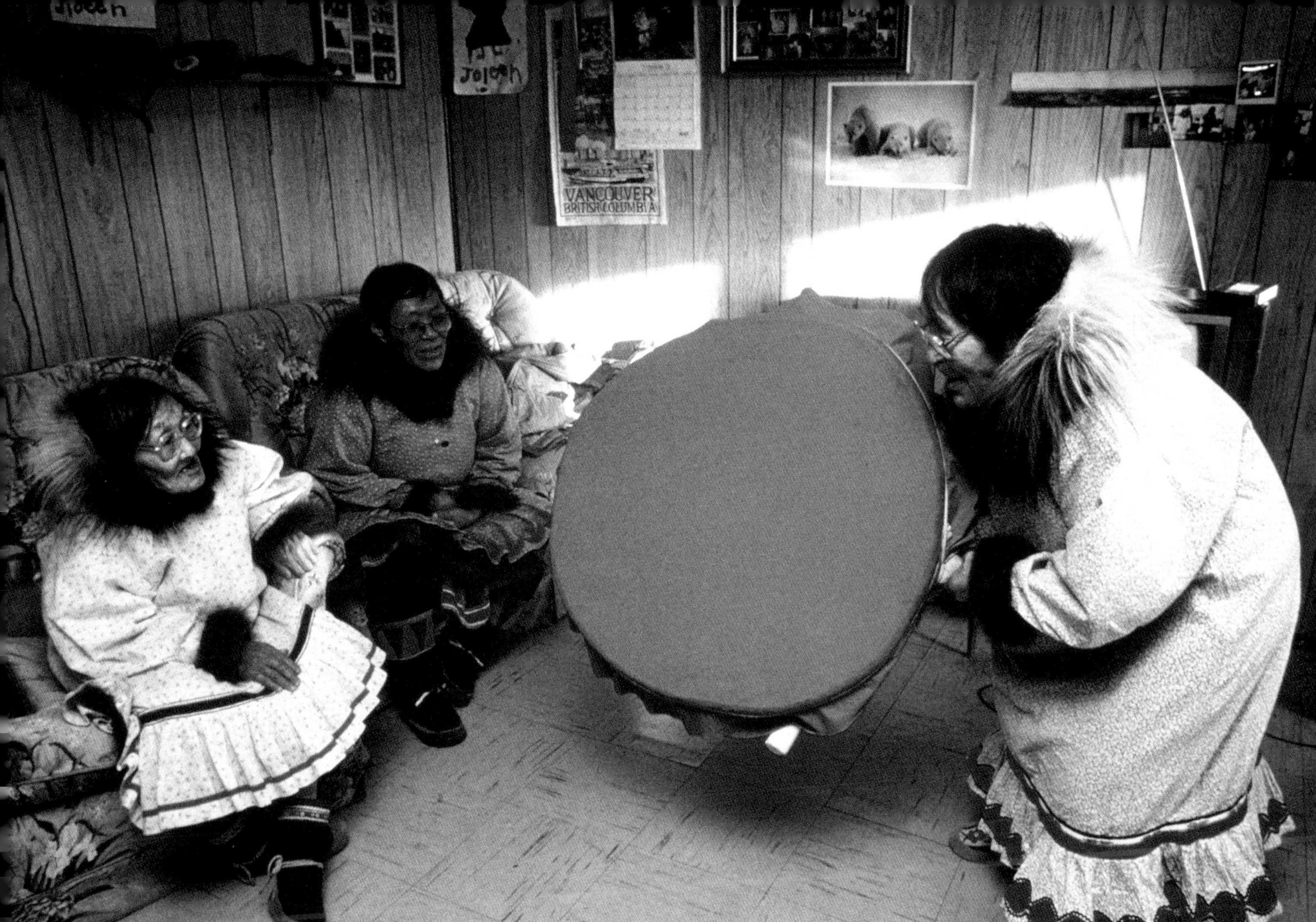

know today. Some Alaskan and Inuvialuit amautiit have a fullness built into the back to carry the child. It is unclear if the Siberian amauti pattern ever had this fullness.[5] Today's inhabitants of Sivuqaq, Alaska, who call themselves Siberian Yupiit, say that in their memory they have never had the baby pouch but have carried children in their arms or on their shoulders (Helen Siwooko Carius, personal communication 1990). Further studies may uncover the dates and the kinds of changes and the reasons for the alterations of style in western Inuit clothing.

EAST, WEST, BUT NOT BETWEEN

Some complexes appear to occur only in Siberia, the extreme west of Alaska, and Kalaallit Nunaat and are not found in the Arctic between. Excavations of a Thule culture winter site in 1978 on the east coast of Ellesmere Island showed a strong relation to cultural developments in the Bering Sea region (Schledermann and McCullough 1980, 29). The discoveries included needlecases that displayed anthropomorphic figures such as those found in Alaska. An ivory browband fragment was ornamented with Y motifs and grouped triangles common to the Thule culture and Punuk art.

Already mentioned are the technique of slit threading or weaving found among Siberians, Alaskans (VanStone 1985a), and Kalaallit, and the small knife used by Siberian and Kalaallit women to cut skin strips and mosaics for clothing decoration. To these examples of techniques known in the extreme east and west of the Arctic can be added the Kalaallit technique of sewing narrow, dyed skin strips edge to edge or overlapped, a form known, for example, among Yukaghirs and Koryaks. These forms of decoration could be the prototype of the 'Delta trim' that spread east from the Mackenzie Delta area and is now found all over the north.

An important example of a typology limited to the eastern and western Arctic occurs in a boot pattern found at Qilakitsoq and in other places in western Kalaallit Nunaat, and at Utqiagvik and Barrow in Alaska (Hansen 1969-70, 103; Murdoch 1892, 134, Figure 81; Turcy 1986, 162). The pattern has two pieces, the upper and the sole, as seen in a pair of children's boots from Kalaallit Nunaat, with a third piece to form the cuff. One seam of the upper runs down the mid-centre of the boot front and then diagonally across one side of the instep to the outer edge – left if the left foot, right if the right – of the sole. Boots from the Thule era, dated AD 1150-1350, with the same seam configuration were found on the floor of a winter dwelling on Ellesmere Island.[6] The Thule culture people replaced the Dorset on Ellesmere Island about AD 1000. They were close to Kalaallit Nunaat, and during the Little Ice Age they abandoned the island to join relatives in Kalaallit Nunaat (Schledermann 1981, 595). Is it possible that some of the boots worn by Thule culture bearers on their journey across the Arctic from Alaska to Kalaallit Nunaat had this pattern? The Kalaallit still use this boot pattern to make waterproof sealskin boots (Le Mouël 1978, 250).

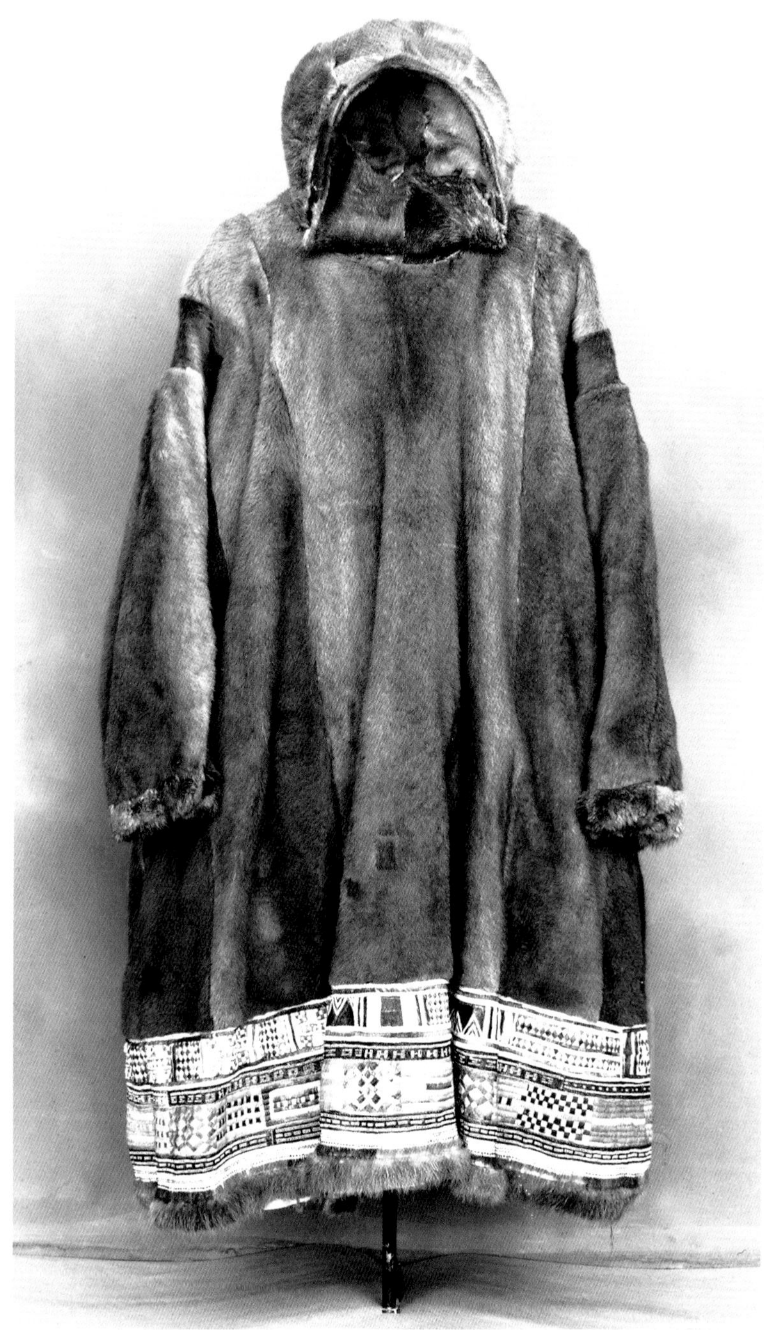

Above and opposite Dancing coat of skins of reindeer, seal, and beaver; cotton, sewn with sinew, Koryak (Alyutortsy), late nineteenth century. The elaborate decoration seen on the outer coat occurred only on ornamented coats worn at ceremonies to honour the spirits of whales brought in by Koryak hunters. The whale, if treated kindly, would gratefully return with its kin. The detail of the Koryak ceremonial coat shows the *opuvan*, a decorative band that includes slit-threading, fur mosaics, and edge-to-edge layering. 'These decorative bands are made separately from the rest of the garment and, as they are constructed, wound on reels. When a garment is worn out, the decorative elements may be detached and saved to use again on a newly made coat' (VanStone 1985a, 12).

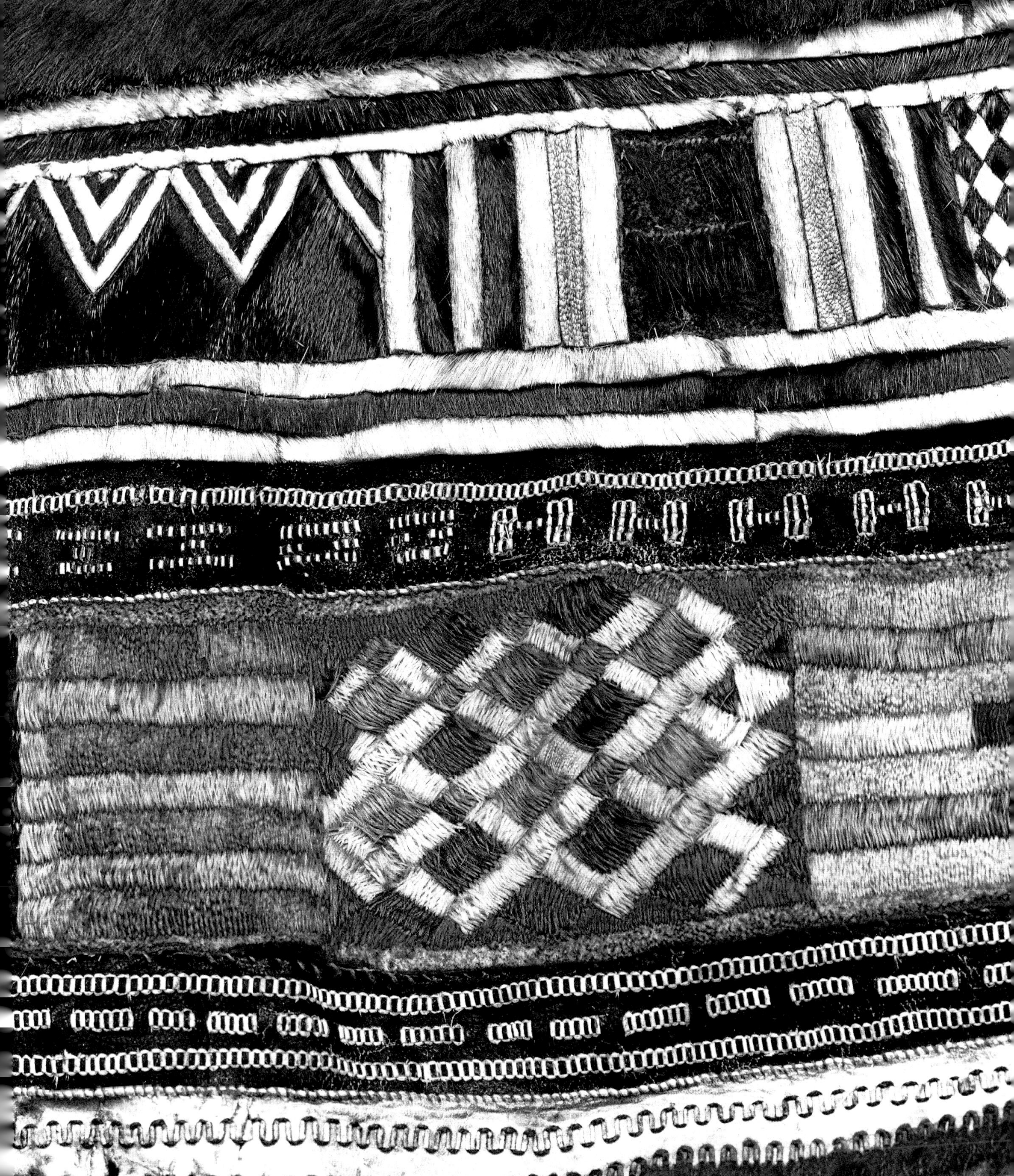

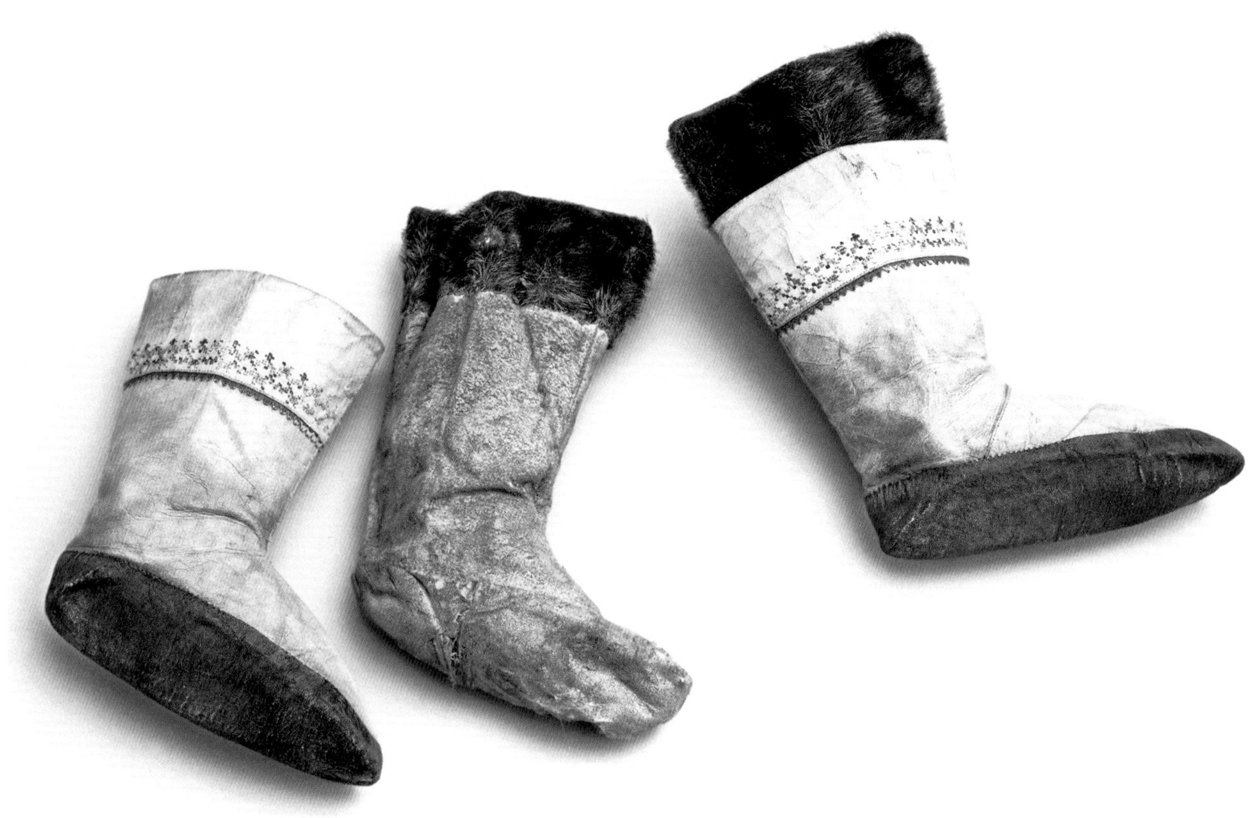

Other examples of elements found only in the western or eastern Arctic are the one-piece waterskin suit used in whaling, recorded in Alaska, Labrador, and Kalaallit Nunaat, and the 'walrus tusk' inserts in the parkas of Siberian Yupiit, Alaskans, Inuvialuit, and sixteenth-century Nunatsiarmiut.[7] What is to be made of the phenomenon of elements found only in the extreme east or west?

INUIT AND MUSEUMS

Museums and other institutions in many parts of the world have holdings, some vast, of objects originating with Native peoples, including clothing. Some institutions have documented their collections, while others still have to begin their research. Many difficulties have plagued the relationships between first peoples and museums.[8] Issues of concern to curators of ethnology and to Inuit have an impact on these clothing assemblages: the ethics of collecting; repatriation of grave goods and sacred materials; research in the Arctic and in museums; access to collections; identification of people in archival photographs, training and employment; Inuit control, as equals, of cultural interpretation in exhibitions; and power in policy-making mechanisms (Arnold 1992, Cernetig 1991).

Toward the end of the 1970s some non-Inuit museums carried forward the earlier endeavours of individual curators and began to work with Inuit to display and

Child's sealskin and dogskin (?) boots (23 cm) and stockings (27 cm), Kalaallit, early twentieth century. Collected in Kalaallit Nunaat by Christian Leden. The stocking is inside the boot on the right, but shown separately in the centre of the photo. On the boot at the right, note the seam that runs down the centre front of the upper and then to the right side to meet the sole edge.

interpret their patrimony. In 1987 the Assembly of First Nations (AFN) of Canada proposed to the Canadian Museum of Civilization that they jointly evaluate museum policies regarding the material and spiritual heritage of Aboriginal peoples (Erasmus 1988). These talks culminated in a report of a taskforce on museums and first peoples co-sponsored by the AFN and the Canadian Museums Association (CMA). The report proposed 'guidelines to develop an ethical framework and strategies by which Aboriginal Peoples and cultural institutions could work together to represent Aboriginal history and culture' (Assembly of First Nations / Canadian Museums Association 1992, 1).

Even though the idea of a museum comes from the South, the Inuit are no strangers to museum work. They have participated in acquiring for southern museums artifacts of archaeological, anthropological, historical, and artistic value.[9] An outstanding Inuit discovery was the evidence of the prehistoric culture later named Dorset in 1924. The Inuit call the people from this era the Tuniit. They arranged to send the artifacts to Diamond Jenness of the National Museum of Canada. Jenness, the brilliant, gentle archaeologist and anthropologist whom they knew and loved, studied the collection and prepared the original definition of the Dorset culture (Taylor 1971-2, 35).

The consultation process has progressed toward a partnership between Inuit and southern institutions that hold archives and stores of first peoples' material and spiritual culture. The exhibition 'Names and Lives of Nunavik,' for example, which opened in 1992 at the McCord Museum of Canadian History, Montréal, grew out of collaboration between Avataq Cultural Institute, Ludger Müller-Wille of the Department of Geography of McGill University, Taamussi Qumaq (1914-93), the first Inuk author of an Inuktitut dictionary, and the Department of Ethnology and Archaeology of the McCord Museum.

RESEARCH AND INFORMATION EXCHANGE

Inuit and non-Inuit can now gain access to documentation available in Canadian institutions about Inuit clothing and all the other artifacts of the heritage – an important resource for studies, research, and exhibitions. The sophisticated facilities of the Canadian Heritage Information Network (CHIN) store, retrieve, process, and exchange information about museum inventories.[10] Initiated under government sponsorship in the early 1970s, it now offers worldwide access to information on collections via the Internet.

Problems surround Inuit clothing data entered into the network. The paucity of funds available to curators of collections restricts staff time necessary for research that includes Inuit participation. Accession cards and records from the nineteenth and the first part of the twentieth century usually had meagre and sometimes inaccurate information. The difficulty of establishing the origin, let alone the history and date, of many artifacts is great. Significant details of garments can be missed if garments are examined only by non-Inuit. Some observations of early ethnographers, if pursued by Inuit researchers, may provide insights hitherto unknown.[11]

Lexicons that include clothing terms are numerous, but they are not inclusive or standardized. A study of the words describing the clothing in the context of the language of any one group may elucidate meanings previously hidden. A system to measure Inuit clothing, subscribed to by all those who store clothing and wish to describe it, still has to be established.[12]

Translation is also a crucial need if information is to be exchanged: from Russian, Finnish, Swedish, Norwegian, and Danish into English, French, and the Eskaleutian languages, and the reverse. One can imagine the euphoria that must have swept North American ethnographers when the 1914 work of Gudmund Hatt, that giant among researchers of Arctic skin clothing, was translated from Danish into English in 1969. There is now the hopeful announcement by the National Science Foundation Division of Polar Programmes in the United States of the start of a Russian Translation Project (Condon 1992, 1). The project will review, translate, and publish research papers written in Russian. The *Petersburg Journal of Cultural Studies,* founded in 1992, is published in English and edited by Russian Arctic linguist Nikolai Vakhtin. A special issue, 'Classics in Siberian Anthropology,' edited by Igor Krupnik of the Smithsonian Institution, is devoted to papers by renowned anthropologists originally published in Russian from the 1920s to the 1940s (Smithsonian Institution 1993, 9).

The need for annotated listings of sources from all countries for the study of Arctic clothing has also now become evident. Such sources are books, articles, tapes of personal and group histories, films and videos, photographic archives, and institutional collections and catalogues.[13]

CLOTHING AND PERSONALITY

A little known area of exploration is the relation of clothing to personality. There are some articles and books on growing up in Inuit society, but few discuss the role of clothing in character formation.[14] Has clothing had an influence on the temperament of Inuit peoples? The material conditions of northern survival have called for sensitivity to every aspect of the environment, adaptability, and an attunement to forces that must be met in cooperation with others. Upbringing in the amauti can affect feelings of security, self-worth, confidence in meeting difficulties, and closeness to others. To clothe oneself in furs can epitomize the strength of human beings as part of nature.

NORTH AND SOUTH

'Our culture must not be lost. Inuit and white people should help one another and cooperate on many things. Our land is not the same as down south, so please let's not have conflicts and fight over anything. Inuit and white men, yes, should live

Titus Alooloo, former Minister of Culture and Communications for the government of the Northwest Territories, reads the dedication at the ceremony to rebury human remains at Naujaat, NWT, in September 1991. Among those participating is Peter Ernerk, former member of the NWT Legislative Assembly.

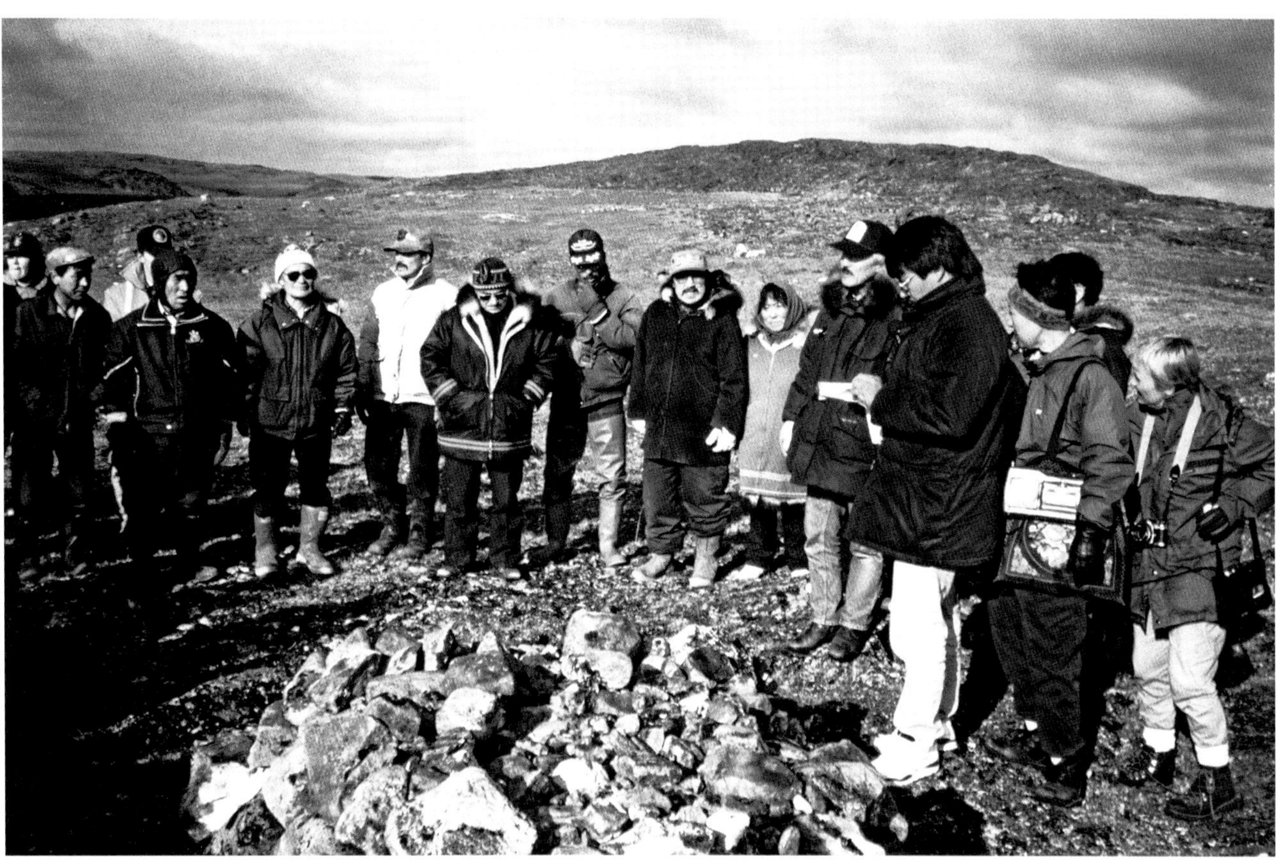

together in peace' (Ungalaaq 1985, 25). Inuit culture is a repository of the vast and intimate knowledge necessary to live and work in the North. The history of Arctic exploration has records of Inuit guides, interpreters, hunters, and seamstresses, many anonymous, on whom non-Inuit depended for survival.[15] Among the explorers and anthropologists who came to the North and entered enthusiastically into Inuit society were the members of the Canadian Arctic Expedition (1913-18) and the young Scandinavians of the Fifth Thule Expedition (1922-4). They dressed in furs, made for them by Inuit seamstresses, and lived with Inuit who taught them about their culture. Through their reports they made a major contribution to understanding the Inuit heritage.

Today, North and South are interdependent in meeting the problems of saving the environment, of developing the Arctic, and of preserving the Inuit way of life. The Inuit Circumpolar Conference (ICC) and organizations such as the Arctic Studies Center of the Smithsonian Institution in Washington are conducting studies across the North that include these issues. The ICC has an enviable record in international affairs. It is a non-governmental organization within the United Nations, which awarded it the Global 500 Environment Award in 1988 for its Inuit Regional Conservation Strategy. With the melting of the 'Siberian ice curtain' contacts in the North between the continents have begun to flourish, and the ICC has established an office in Provideniiya, Chukotka (George 1995). This recent collaboration may open the way for more intercontinental studies of Inuit clothing as part of the wider range of research now available.

The Inuit wish to maintain their hunting and trapping economy while making

Maata Pudlat, wife of Jimmy Manning, stands next to an inukshuk with their child Saimata held in the amaut, 1984. The inukshuk stands forty miles west of Kinngait, NWT.

responsible decisions about other avenues of growth. In many parts of the Arctic one will see, particularly in milder weather, no fur garments. Skin sewing functions have narrowed since fabric items make up a substantial part of modern wardrobes, although the amauti, of fabric or fur, sealskin boots, and down-filled coats are made everywhere. Women have moved easily into employment outside the home, leaving less time for traditional tasks. Prepared skins can be ordered from a resource such as the reindeer herd at Nabachtoolik near Tuktuujaqtuuq.

The activities of anti-harvesting lobbies resulted in 1983 in a crushing ban on sealskin imports by the European Economic Community. Little known is that the ringed seal, used by the Inuit for food, footgear and other pieces of clothing, tents, and formerly for bedding and exports, is the most prolific sea mammal in the Arctic, numbering in 1986 close to 5,000,000. The ringed seal is one of the most important elements in the High Arctic coastal ecosystem (Forsyth 1985, 109). Birthing takes place not on the ice, as does that of the harp seal of the Maritimes, but in a cave under the ice where the pups remain for over two months. Once the pups are weaned and leave the underwater den to forage for food with the adults, Inuit hunters harvest the animals at the breathing-holes, ice-floe edge, or open water. Wholesale slaughter, such as that practised by some Newfoundland sealers with the harp seal, does not occur.

As a result of the blow to the Arctic economy imposed by outsiders – a kind of ideological imperialism – the Inuit hunter, whether man or woman, has difficulty paying for equipment, repairs, ammunition, and gasoline to hunt for furs and country food.[16] The combined annual earnings of NWT Inuit hunters from sealskin sales are now estimated at $17,000, compared with up to $1,000,000 as recently as 1981 (Herscovici 1994). Women have curtailed activities such as sewing skins or garments that use furs, except for their own use or for sale in local cooperatives. Young Jimi Doupont Onalik sums up the feelings of Inuit. His pet peeve, he says, 'is self-righteous animal rights groups who think they can tell us what we can or cannot wear or eat.' He enthusiastically vouches for the warmth of fur clothing (Onalik 1995, 22).

The wise outsider has learned from the experiences of the early traders and from Inuit colleagues how to dress in the North. Furs worn in combination with imported dress show that the Inuit intend to make appropriate choices from the past and the present. The Inuit know that fur and skin clothing will always be needed, for protection and identity, and as a carrier of treasured traditions. By using the encyclopedic knowledge of the Inuit about, for one thing, cold weather clothing, governments and businesses that often include or are operated by Inuit are cooperating to restore jobs and incomes. A true partnership in the Arctic that matches the wisdom and skill of hunters and seamstresses with the technological and marketing facilities of industry and governments, as called for by the Science Council of Canada (Goar 1990, B3),

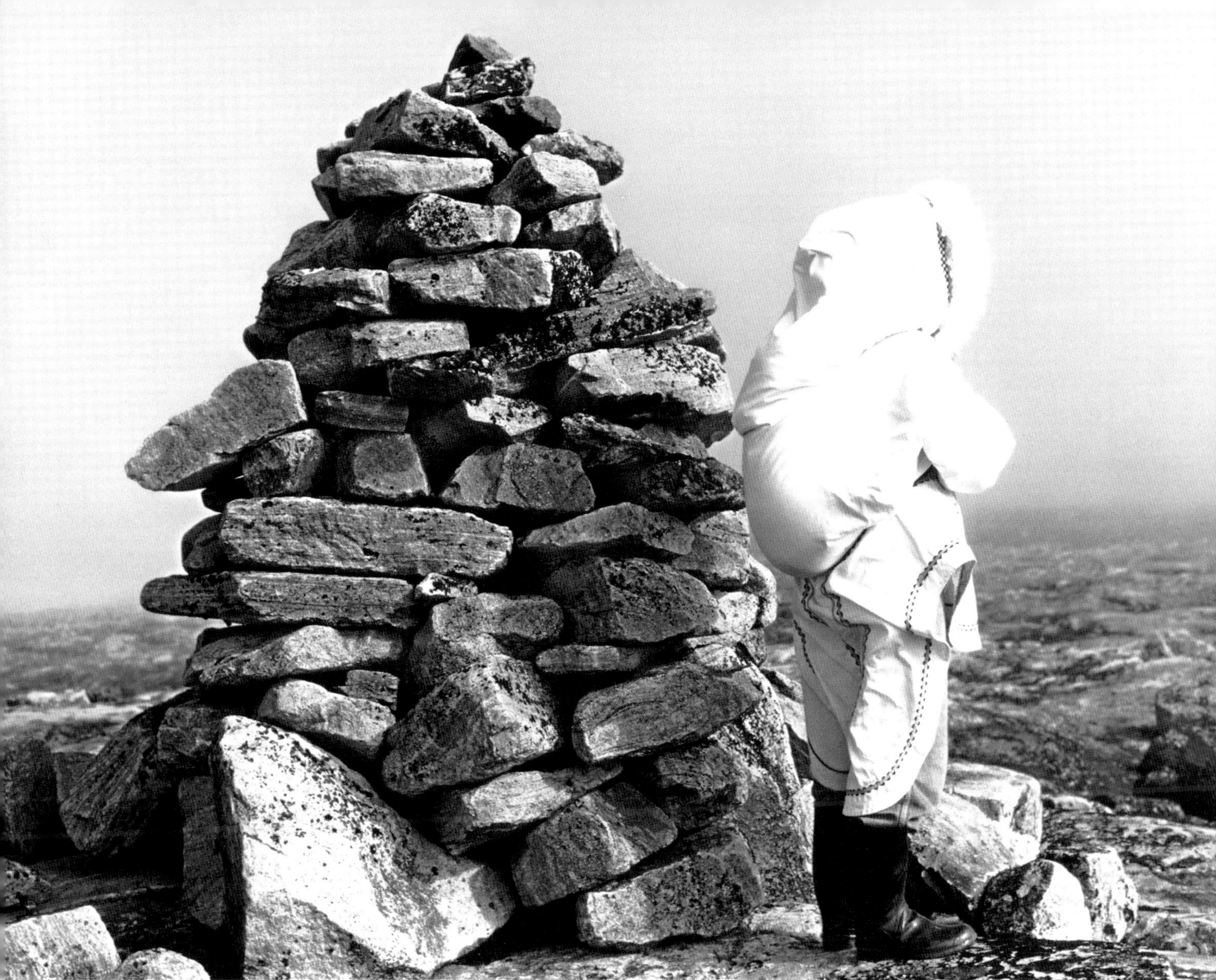

can help develop further the kind of clothing needed to survive in low temperatures. Over the past two decades southerners have cooperated with the Inuit, more and more as equal partners, to bring knowledge of northern cultures to an eager public.

The Inuit and their forebears survived over 4,000 years in the Arctic by a loyalty to their traditions and constant adaptation of their culture (Condon 1983). They retained their refined technology and developed a cosmology appropriate to their mode of life. Through contact with non-Inuit they have taken from dominant societies the components that suit them best while trying to live in the way they prefer. By wearing skin clothing the Inuit celebrate their accomplishments, show pride in being part of a rich, complex culture, and affirm their lasting connection to the natural and spiritual worlds of their ancestors.

Appendix: Collections of Inuit Clothing

Some institutions have scant stores; others have extensive, world-renowned holdings. While every effort has been made to discover which organizations have collections, the list undoubtedly is incomplete and may, in some instances, be erroneous. The author would welcome further information.

Canada

Agvituk Historical Society, Aqvituq (Hopedale), Labrador, Newfoundland
Bata Shoe Museum Foundation, Toronto, Ontario
Canadian Museum of Civilization, Hull, Québec
Daniel Weetaluktuk Museum and Cultural Transmission Centre of Avataq Cultural Institute, Inukjuaq, Nunavik (Arctic Québec)
Eskimo Museum, Kuugjuaq (Churchill), Manitoba
Fédération des Coopératives du Nouveau Québec, Baie d'Urfé, Québec and Purvirnituq, Nunavik
Glenbow Museum, Calgary, Alberta
Holman Historical Museum, Uluksaartuuq (Holman), NWT
Inuit Cultural Institute, Silattuqsarvingat, Kangiqliniq (Rankin Inlet), NWT
Inummariit Cultural Association, Iglulik, NWT
Kelowna Museum, Kelowna, British Columbia
Lower Fort Garry National Historic Park, Selkirk, Manitoba
Manitoba Museum of Man and Nature, Winnipeg, Manitoba
McCord Museum of Canadian History, Montréal, Québec
Musée Amérindien et Inuit, Godbout, Québec
Musée de la civilisation, Quebec City
Musée des Soeurs Grises, Montréal, Québec
Musée de l'Université Laval, Ste-Foy, Québec
Newfoundland Museum, St. John's, Newfoundland
Northern Life Museum and National Exhibition Centre, Fort Smith, NWT
Nunatta Sunaqutangit Museum, Iqaluit, NWT
Piulimatsivik, Moravian Mission Church Museum, Naini (Nain), Labrador
Prince of Wales Northern Heritage Centre, Yellowknife, NWT
Provincial Museum of Alberta, Edmonton, Alberta
Royal British Columbia Museum, Victoria, British Columbia
Royal Canadian Mounted Police Museum, Regina, Saskatchewan
Royal Ontario Museum, Toronto, Ontario
Saipalaseequtt Museum Society, Pangniqtuuq, NWT
Saputik Museum, Purvirnituq, Nunavik
Université Laval, département d'anthropologie, Ste-Foy, Québec
University of Alberta Clothing and Textiles Museum, Edmonton, Alberta
University of Manitoba Clothing and Textiles Museum, Winnipeg, Manitoba
Winnipeg Art Gallery, Winnipeg, Manitoba

Europe

Confederation of Independent States
Chukotka Museum, Anadyr, Chukotka
Institute of Ethnography, Moscow
Kamchatka Regional Museum, Petropavlovsk-Kamchatskii
Magadan State Museum, Magadan
Museum of Peter the Great (formerly Museum of Anthropology and Ethnology), St. Petersburg
Museye Arctic i Antartica, St. Petersburg
Provideniya Museum, Provideniya, Chukotka
State Museum of Ethnography of the Peoples of the Confederation of Independent States, St. Petersburg
State Unified Museum of Irkutsk, Irkutsk

Denmark
National Museum of Denmark, Copenhagen

Estonia
State Historical Museum of Estonia, Tallinn

Finland
National Museum of Finland, Helsinki

France
Musée de l'Homme, Paris

Germany
Deutsches Ledermuseum, Offenbach
Hamburgisches Museum für Völkerkunde, Hamburg
Institut und Sammlung für Völkerkunde der Universitaet, Gottingen
Karl-May Museum, Radebeul
Museum für Völkerkunde, Berlin
Staatliches Museum für Völkerkunde, Dresden
Staatliches Museum für Völkerkunde, Munich
Ubersee Museum, Bremen
Völkerkundemuseum, Herrnhut

Netherlands
American Museum, Cuijk
Museon, The Hague
Rijksmuseum voor Volkenkunde, Leiden

Norway
Ethnographical Department of the Historical Museum, Bergen
Tromsø University Museum, Tromsø
Trondheim University Museum, Trondheim
University Ethnographical Museum, Oslo

Sweden
Folkens Museum Etnografiska (Nordenskiöld Collection from Port Clarence, Alaska), Stockholm

Switzerland
Musée d'Ethnographie, Neuchâtel

Japan
Historical Museum of Hokkaido, Sapporo, Hokkaido
Hokkaido Museum of Northern Peoples, Abashiri City, Hokkaido
National Museum of Ethnology, Suita City, Osaka
National Museum of Tokyo, Tokyo

Kalaallit Nunaat (Greenland)

Greenland National Museum, Nuuk (now called Nunatta Katersugaasivia Allagaategarfialu)
Qaanaaq Museum, Qaanaaq, Polar Kalaallit Nunaat

United Kingdom

Anthropological Museum of Marischall College, University of Aberdeen, Aberdeen
Art Galleries and Museums, City of Dundee District Council, Dundee
Bristol Museums and Art Gallery, Bristol
British Museum Ethnography Department: Museum of Mankind, London
Hancock Museum, The University, Newcastle upon Tyne
Hunterian Museum, The University, Glasgow
Kelvin Grove Museum, Glasgow
Museum and Art Gallery, Maidstone
Manchester Museum, The University, Manchester
Merseyside County Museum, Liverpool
Moravian Museum, Fulneck, Pudsey
Perth Museum and Art Gallery, Perth
Pitt Rivers Museum, Oxford University, Oxford
Royal Museum of Scotland, Edinburgh
Scott Polar Research Institute, Cambridge
Ulster Museum, Botanic Gardens, Belfast
University Museum of Archaeology and Anthropology, Cambridge

United States of America

Alaska State Museum, Juneau, Alaska
American Museum of Natural History, New York City
Anchorage Museum of History and Art, Anchorage, Alaska
Baranof Museum, Sun'aq (Kodiak), Alaska
Brooklyn Museum, New York City
Carnegie Museum of Natural History, Pittsburgh
Dartmouth College Museum, Hanover, New Hampshire
Denver Art Museum, Denver, Colorado
Field Museum of Natural History, Chicago, Illinois
Florida State Museum, University of Florida, Gainesville, Florida
Haffenreffer Museum, Brown University, Bristol, Rhode Island
Hearst Museum of Anthropology (formerly Lowie Museum), University of California, Berkeley, California
Kotzebue Museum, Kotzebue, Alaska
Logan Museum of Anthropology, Museums of Beloit College, Beloit, Wisconsin
Mathers Museum, Indiana University, Bloomington, Indiana
Milwaukee Public Museum, Milwaukee, Wisconsin
Moravian Historical Society, Nazareth, Pennsylvania
Museum of Anthropology, University of Michigan, Ann Arbor, Michigan
Newark Museum, Newark, New Jersey
Peabody Museum of Archaeology and Ethnology, Harvard University, Cambridge, Massachusetts
Peabody Museum of Natural History, Yale University, New Haven, Connecticut
Peabody Museum of Salem, Salem, Massachusetts
Peary-MacMillan Arctic Museum, Bowdoin College, Brunswick, Maine
Robert Hull Fleming Museum, University of Vermont, Burlington, Vermont
Samuel K. Fox Museum, Dillingham, Alaska
San Diego Museum of Man, San Diego, California
Santa Barbara Museum of Natural History, Santa Barbara, California
Sheldon Jackson College Museum, Sitka, Alaska
Smithsonian Institution, National Museum of Natural History, Washington, DC
Thomas Burke Memorial Washington State Museum, University of Washington, Seattle, Washington
University of Alaska Museum, Fairbanks, Alaska
University of Iowa, Museum of Natural History, Iowa City, Iowa
University Museum, University of Pennsylvania, Philadelphia, Pennsylvania
Yugtarvik Regional Museum, Mamterilleq (Bethel), Alaska

Notes

Preface

1 'South' and 'southerners' refer to territories and peoples who live beyond Inuit lands.

2 Each of Birket-Smith's 111 Pan-Arctic tables discusses one cultural element – for example, the snow-house or the ulu. He shows its distribution, gives references for research, and adds his own descriptive comments. Missing from the tables are the needlecase and the boot-sole creaser. He also has tables of the distribution of cultural elements in Indian North America and Northern Eurasia.

3 ASTIS is Canada's only northern abstracting and indexing service. Each annual issue of the ASTIS *Bibliography* contains the full ASTIS database. Over twenty bibliographies and databases are subsets of the full database. The *Astis Bibliography* CD-ROM uses software from National Information Services Corporation, producers of the Arctic and Antarctic Regions CD-ROM.

4 A list of institutions that house Inuit clothing in their stores appears in the appendix. Lists of museum inventories of Arctic ethnological artifacts are available in, for example, Csonka (1988), Hunter (1967), the Museum Ethnographers Group (1986), Taylor (1969-70) and, most important, through the Canadian Heritage Information Network (see Chapter 6).

5 The mandate of Inuttigut Pirusiit, Avataq's documentation centre, is to collect and make available information, photographs, artifacts, documents, and other materials concerning the culture and history of the Inuit of Nunavik. Among their files are photographs or photocopies from the Archives Deschatelets, Ottawa; the Canadian Museum of Contemporary Photography, Ottawa (formerly the National Film Board of Canada); the Canadian Museum of Civilization, Hull; Margery Hinds, Victoria, BC; Frederica Knight, Winnipeg; the National Archives of Canada, Ottawa; the Père Lechat Collection, Ottawa; Queen's University Archives, the A.A. Chesterfield Collection, Kingston, Ontario; George I. Quimby, Seattle. Important among their documents and tapes are interviews with elders.

Chapter 1: The Inuit: Time and Space

1 The quotation is found in Brody (1976, 194) and is reproduced with the permission of the Minister of Supply and Services Canada.

2 This quotation is found in Ungalaaq (1985, 13).

3 Inupiat is the plural, Inupiaq the singular, also an adjective.

4 The singular of Inuit is Inuk, meaning 'person.' In this book, whenever a generic designation is needed, I use the word 'Inuit.'

5 The figure for Siberia was also provided by the late I.S. Gurvich, Institute of Ethnography, Moscow, in 1987. The population figures in the map of the Alaska Native Language Center do not include Inuit living in urban Alaska (10,300) and continental Denmark (5,000). Robert-Lamblin (1993, 92) writes that of the Kalaallit Nunaat population of 55,533, 84 per cent – or 46,650 people – are Natives. The *Canada Year Book* gives 1,600 as the number of Inuit living outside Arctic communities (Canada 1991, 90). I have added all these additional numbers together to obtain a world total.

6 Yupiit is the plural for Yup'ik.

7 Dates for these periods are still approximate and overlap, and they are not precisely the same for each locality. For Pre-Dorset, Dorset, and Thule prehistory of Canada see McGhee (1978, 1979, 1981a, 1981b, 1983, 1984); Maxwell (1960, 1973, 1984, 1985); Stewart (1989). For the contribution of Diamond Jenness to origins theory see Collins and Taylor (1970, 76-7).

8 Issenman (1997) gives an exposition of prehistoric Arctic clothing and tools.

9 References to a statuette dressed in clothing or to a clothed figurine allude to clothing depicted on the surface of the carving. I know of only one prehistoric figurine that actually wears a piece of skin that represents clothing.

10 For information on Dorset statuettes see Issenman and Rankin (1988), Meldgaard (1960), Taylor and Swinton (1967), and Thomson (1985). The photographic archives of Yolande Perrault of Montréal contain many images of Dorset carvings, some of which can be interpreted in several ways, as Thomson states (1985), including as figurines.

11 Two additional Dorset figurines with the high collar are in the collections of the National Museum of Denmark L13.730, found at Inuaarsivik by Jorgen Meldgaard; and of the Canadian Museum of Civilization, IX-C:5554, found on Mill Island by Derek O'Brien.

12 Information on prehistoric clothing tools can be found in Anderson (1984), Clark (1984), Fitzhugh (1984), Harp (1951), McElhone (1984b), McGhee (1972, 1978, 1979, 1981a, 1981b, 1984), McGrath (1992), Mathiassen (1927), Maxwell (1960, 1973, 1984), Rainey (1941), Rankin and Labrèche (1991), and Turcy (1986). See Leroi-Gourhan (1946) for a classification and distribution of tools, including including knives with transverse cutting edges such as the ulu in Asia, America, and Kalaallit Nunaat, using examples from prehistory and more recent times.

13 In addition to the double-pointed bone needles dated about AD 500, Elmer Harp Jr. found the usual ones with one point dated about AD 1-1000, Middle Dorset, at the Turngasiti-5 site, Sanikiluaq (written communication 1988).

14 Further information about winged needlecases in the Arctic is found in Ackerman (1984), Boas (1901, 1907, [1927] 1955), McGhee (1978), Mathiassen (1927, Part 1), Nelson ([1899] 1983, 103-4, Plate 44), and Sproull (1977).

15 Sinew can be plaited using three to six strands. The resulting cordage is almost unbreakable. The cord in the casing of a boot, when pulled tight, prevents ingress of wind and snow.

16 For a description of the archaeological finds, including clothing, of the Thule culture bearers of Ruin Island, see McCullough (1989).

17 Restoration was undertaken jointly by the Conservation Division, Canadian Museum of Civilization and the Archaeology Section, Canadian Conservation Institute.

18 Møller (1989) is the main source of information about the Qilakitsoq clothing. For additional insights see Ammitzbøll et al. (1989), Hansen and Gullov (1989), Kalaallit Nunaata Katersugaasivia (n.d.), and Rosing (1986).

19 Turcy (1986) is the main source of information about the Utqiagvik clothing. For reports of the whole project see Hall and Fullerton

(1990) and Lobdell and Dekin (1984).

20 The base of the Inuit hood pattern has extensions of various shapes, sometimes at both the front and back. These extensions 'root' or anchor the hood to the body of the coat, thus eliminating the need for a seam directly at the neck.

21 A three-dimensional view of the Kalaallit prisoners' clothing was published by Olearius (1656), who met the three Inuit women at Gottorp (Meldgaard 1980, 4). Tankards carved from narwhal tusk ca. 1660 bear miniature sculptures of these Inuit with naturalistic details. For a full account of the research and discussion of the clothing see Bencard (1989).

Chapter 2: From Earth, Sea, and Sky

1 This quotation is found in Rasmussen (1932, 133-4).

2 Further information on tools can be found in Balikci (1970), Hahn (1977), Mitchell and Van de Velde (1981), and Vézinet (1980), as well as in references in Chapter 1.

3 See Hickman (1987) for a full discussion of sea mammal intestines and of fish skins.

4 Kuujjuaq Research Centre (n.d.). In Nunavik the Inuit organization Angugivaq Wildlife Management works with the Canadian Wildlife Service to conserve the eider duck population.

5 Some principles of Inuit clothing manufacture were known, although incompletely, to outsiders in the eighteenth and nineteenth centuries, in particular Boas ([1888] 1964), Murdoch (1892), Parry (1824), and Turner ([1894] 1979). The most extensive documentation in the twentieth century started with Hatt (1916, 1969), Jenness (1946), Manning and Manning (1944), and Stefansson (1945, 1958). For an analysis of the principles of clothing manufacture and a summary of the literature see Stenton (1991a).

6 Parts of the Arctic can in fact be called a desert. Ausuittuq, for example, has an average total annual precipitation of 1.5 centimetres (Devine 1982, 138).

7 The caribou perspires through its footpads and maintains a balanced temperature by panting.

8 To make cords, belts, and lines, the skin of a freshly killed seal is cut around its body in bands twenty-five to thrity-five centimetres wide. The bands are then cut in spirals at a constant width, the length being determined by the width of the original ring of skin. The blubber is scraped away and the hair removed by shaving or scalding.

9 Also see note 5.

10 Also see note 5.

11 Quotation from Nungak (1983, 132). Inuit articles and school courses now give formal instruction on survival techniques. See, for example, Niviaxie (1995).

12 The word 'tailored' presents problems. In Anglo-European parlance it has come to describe clothing cut close to the body along somewhat severe lines, most often a suit. Conn (1955, 1974, 1991) aptly suggests that since the word is associated with the techniques of the European tradition, 'fitted' better describes some of the patterns of Native North Americans. The seams used in many cultures, including Inuit, are much the same where similar-size pieces are joined, where a longer piece is gathered to a shorter, or where curved parts are sewn together. If made of thin, woven fabric, the garment appears to be flat or draped, that is, two-dimensional. When made of skins, particularly if furred, the clothing can become three-dimensional.

13 In the nineteenth century and the first half of the twentieth, some men's parkas had a slit mid-front, occasionally from the base to the chest. Called an *akuitoq* (Strickler and Alookee 1988, 136, 175), this style has been noted in the areas west of Hudson Bay (Keewatin) and Baffinland, and among the Nunavimiut. Most men's parkas have side openings starting at the base, with the exception of Labrador where the male parka has no side vents.

14 Also see note 5.

15 This use of the fur has a disadvantage. While the fur flow at the front goes from top to bottom, as is usual, the fur flow at the back goes from bottom to top. The latter results in a rough surface, unpleasant to look at and to work in, that traps unwanted materials such as snow and debris.

16 Words checked by Mark Kalluak, Inuit Cultural Institute, Arviat 1986.

17 Louis-Jacques Dorais explains: 'In fact, *amaut* and *amauti* are the same word. The pouch is called *amautiup punga* – "the pouch of the amauti"' (written communication 1990).

18 See Driscoll (1980) for a comprehensive, perceptive exploration of the amauti.

19 Inuit mothers know that babies never develop diaper rash when moss is used. This spongy material can be washed and dried. Today some manufacturers of disposable diapers extract substances from sphagnum moss for use as a counter-irritant.

20 Also see note 5.

21 Also see note 5.

Chapter 3: Tools and Techniques

1 This quotation is found in Myers (1980, 17).

2 This quotation is found in Ungalaaq (1985, 6).

3 Readers may obtain more information on the ulu and other men's and women's tools in Boas ([1888] 1964), Fitzhugh and Kaplan (1982), Mason (1891), Nelson ([1899] 1983), Vézinet (1980). See Rankin and Labrèche (1991) for an extensive bibliography on uluit. See also Chapter 1, note 12.

4 Some prehistoric uluit from many cultures – including the Alaskan Northern Archaic tradition (ca. 4000 BC), the Old Whaling Culture (Alaska ca. 1300 BC), and the Dorset culture – have no true handle.

5 'Knives for cutting, skiving (paring), or slicing are usually ground on both sides. Chisels, plane irons, scrapers, and scissors are ground on one side only. The angle of the grind is determined by the hardness of the steel and the use to which the tool is put. The term "honing" applies to the finishing of the edge at a slightly greater angle than the angle of grind. Honing is accomplished by a steel, stone, or strop – the finer the grit, the sharper the edge' (D.G. Lunan, written communication 1984).

6 Further information on needlecases can be found in Birket-Smith (1929, Part 1, 248-9), Boas (1908), Fitzhugh (1984, 529), Hatt ([1914] 1969, 21), Hawkes (1916, 98, 99, 213, Plate 24a,c,e), Jenness (1946, 90-1), Maxwell (1984, 362), and Turner ([1888] 1979, 90). For a history and description from prehistoric times of needlecases of Siberian peoples see Ivanov (1970a). For Saami needlecases see Nordic Arts Centre (1981, 9).

7 An anchor-shaped thimble guard resembles a ship's anchor that has upright flukes. A flat piece of ivory, this kind of holder has flukes or posts that go up from the base at the centre or side and run parallel to the guard. Such thimble guards have been found in Thule culture assemblages and in the Historic era.

8 Sources for clothing production are found throughout the text. Some important studies are Alariaq (1975), Birket-Smith (1924, 1929), Conn (1955, 1974), Driscoll (1983), Hadlereena, Hadlari, and Jensen (1986), Hall, Oakes, and Webster (1994), Hatt (1916, 1969), Hawkes (1916), Hickman (1987), Holtved (1967), Jenness (1946), Karetak (1982), Le Mouël (1973, 1978), Manning and Manning (1944), Mathiassen (1928), Moller (1989), Oakes (1987b, 1991), Pharand (1971b, 1974, 1975), Stefansson (1914, 1945, 1958), Torngak (1973), Turcy (1986), Vézinet (1980), and Wilder (1976).

9 See Stenton (1991a, 4-15) for discussion of caribou-skin qualities. Hatt (1969) writes about several kinds of skins in the circumpolar regions in terms of qualities, dressing, and use. Arima (1984, 455) has written that in the Inuktitut language there are 'at least twenty designations for the animal distinguishing maturation, sex, fatness, coat and other features.'

10 One example is Musée de la civilisation 71-696, Quebec City. The boots are from Purvirnituq.

11 For sources on number of caribou skins required for clothing and a summary of the literature see Stenton (1991b, 19-26).

12 Vézinet (1980) and others present evidence of a group of Inuit they named Nunamiut. This group lived in Nunavik's interior, depending mainly on caribou for their subsistence. They ceased to exist as a group around 1920 due to the lack of caribou at that time in their part of the Arctic.

13 When seal skins are brought back home, the woman scrapes off the blubber and other matter to prepare them for clothing. The blubber or fat is rendered down. In the old days, seal oil provided heat and light. Now it is used in the household and medicinally to alleviate or cure physical ailments such as ear infections and gastrointestinal

disturbances, and to prevent what are known as diseases of the soul – for example, depression and malaise (Borré 1994).

14 In Alaska a gutskin parka is called a *kamleika,* a word used by Russians in Alaska to mean 'shirt.' The Inupiaq word is *imarnin.* The words used by Yup'ik speakers are *immar enin.* Nunavik elders call the intestine parka an *akuilitaq.* The Kalaallit word is *kapisaq,* and they called the half-jacket worn in the kayak that tied around the cockpit rim an *akuilisaq* (Birket-Smith 1924, 184) or *tuvilik* (Le Mouël 1978, 248).

15 For more on gut parkas see Hickman (1987), Ray (1959), Wilder (1976).

16 In Sanikiluaq intestines are still dried and used to make ropes and lines (Edward Miller, Joanne Miller, personal communication 1991).

17 Pregnant women are allowed to remove the grease and fat from skins, but scraping to make the skin supple is prohibited for fear of causing bleeding, spontaneous abortion, or worse. Skin dressing activity is accomplished from a crouched position where the woman (or sometimes the man) moves back and forth. The fetus *in utero* is thus moved excessively and the head can be crushed (Dufour 1988, 57-8).

18 One consultant, Ailsa Shimotakahara, kept skins in the freezer or refrigerator.

19 I learned about Inuit boot making in full detail from Ailsa Shimotakahara of Montréal (personal communication 1980). Shimotakahara produced boots for her family after intensive tutelage from Iqaluit elders. Comprehensive studies of Inuit boot production are found in Oakes (1987b), Oakes and Riewe (1995), and Pharand (1974, 1975). Some of Alariaq's (1975) headings for sections in her article show how complex skin preparation can be: 'Bleached skin without hair, Skin with blubber, Whitened skin, Skin with hypoderm, Skin for domestic use, Skin with blubber and hypoderm, Various uses of skin' (translation by Louis-Jacques Dorais).

20 Artifact II-V-21 at the Sheldon Jackson College Museum, Sitka, Alaska, is a waterskin collected at Barrow.

21 Information presented here is from Rosing (1986). Diklev (1988) suggested that the process of removing fat from birdskins can be described as 'sucking out' rather than 'gumming.' Also see Oakes (1992).

22 The teeth of the adult female bodies found at Qilakitsoq showed evidence of sinew making (Pedersen and Jakobsen 1989, 123-5).

23 The sinew used to sew the clothing of the frozen family at Utqiagvik was less than one millimetre in diameter and one and a half to two millimetres in circumference (Turcy 1986, 85-6).

24 When in 1978 I asked Napachee, one of the highly skilled seamstresses of the sewing cooperative at Iqaluit, NWT, if I could buy an amauti, she readily assented. She looked me over back and front, measured me across the hips with a hand spread using the span from the tip of her thumb to the tip of her middle finger. A few weeks later my amauti arrived. It fit perfectly.

25 During the exhibition IVALU: Traditions du vêtement inuit / Traditions of Inuit Clothing, held at the McCord Museum of Canadian History, Montréal, April 1988 to January 1989, Lucy Meeko demonstrated skin clothing in one of the educational programs ancillary to the exhibition.

26 The clothing of the Qilakitsoq mummies has the same alignment of fur and feathers.

27 I counted eighteen stitches of sinew to 2.5 centimetres on an amauti in the collection of the McCord Museum of Canadian History, Montréal.

28 Couching is a 'technique in which a thread of any thickness is sewn onto the ground material by means of a different and generally finer thread visible as a pattern' (Clabburn 1976, 68).

Chapter 4: Inuit Style

1 This quotation is found in Nungak (1983, 110).

2 This quotation is found in Nungak (1983, 109).

3 This quotation is found in Myers (1980, 118).

4 For an overall comparison of circumpolar clothing styles and methods of construction see Hatt ([1914] 1969) and Buijs (1997). In this text sources for Canadian groups are given for each section. For Siberia, see Menovshchikov and Shnakenburg (1964), Mitlyanskaya (1983), Nelson ([1899] 1983), and Prytkova (1976). For Alaska, see Brandford (1967), Conn (1955), Fitzhugh and Kaplan (1982), Gubser (1965), Jolles (1994). Meade (1990), Murdoch (1892), Nelson ([1899] 1983), Ray (1966), and Turcy (1986). For Siberia and North America, see Fitzhugh and Crowell (1988) and Hooper (1853). For Kalaallit Nunaat, see Bahnson (1997), de Neergaard (1987), Diklev (1988), Hansen (1979), Holtved (1967), Kaalund (1984), Kalaallit Nunaata Katersugaasivia (n.d.), Le Mouël (1973, 1978), Moller (1989), Rix (1979), and Rosing (1986).

5 Sources that describe Inuvialuit clothing are: Brandford (1967), McGhee (1974), Morrison (1990), Murdoch (1892), Nuligak (1971), Petitot ([1887] 1981), Smith (1984), Stefansson (1909, 1911, 1914), and Strickler and Alookee (1988)

6 The name Paulatuuq derives from the Inuvialuktun term for 'soot of coal.' (Inuvialuktun is a dialect spoken by some Inuvialuit.) The Inuit of this hamlet found coal locally and used it for heat.

7 Baleen, called whalebone by Europeans, is a series of plates that hang from the upper jaw of some whales. The bowhead whale can yield up to a ton of the smooth, springy substance, which sometimes measures 4.25 metres. In the nineteenth century, baleen was used by Europeans as a stiffening for hoop skirts, umbrellas, and for men's and women's corsets.

8 The first North American reindeer herd was brought from Siberia to Alaska in the early 1900s. In 1929 the Alaskan owners agreed to sell the Canadian government 3,000 animals. A Saami, Andrew Bahr, was hired to drive the herd from Nabachtoolik in western Alaska to Kittigazuit on the east side of the Mackenzie Delta area. He and Inuit travelled on foot with the animals over uncharted territory for five years. The herd became privately owned in 1972, and by 1982 grew to 13,000 (Steltzer 1985, 75).

9 Ticking belongs in the group of hardy fabrics such as denim, duck, canvas, and webbing. It has alternating stripes of coloured and white yarns. Uses include linings, harnesses, coverings for mattresses and furniture, and the base for rubberized materials (Linton 1954, 395).

10 Mary Saich, personal communication to Catherine Rankin 1983. Saich taught school in Aklaarvik, NWT. Charles Lindbergh and his pilot wife Anne Morrow stayed in Aklaarvik in August 1931 on their way to Japan and China. They flew the *Sirius* via Kuugjuaq and Qamanittuaq, where they also touched down (Lindbergh 1935, 80ff).

11 Information on Delta trim and other forms of western and Kalaallit decoration comes from Judy McGrath (written communications 1980-6).

12 In Britain and America the Mother Hubbard wrapper, sometimes called a dressing- or tea-gown, was a loose ankle-length dress gathered to a square or round yoke. It had long sleeves gathered at the cuff and could be trimmed with lace and ribbon at the yoke and sleeve top. It was worn in the nineteenth and early twentieth centuries. American missionaries brought the wrapper to Hawaii to clothe the 'pagans' (Wilcox 1969, 218, 221). See Driscoll (1980, 17) for discussion of the Mother Hubbard in the Arctic.

Calico is a cotton plain-weave cloth, usually printed. The name derives from the town of Calicut, India. On Qikiqtaruk the word *kaliko* meant any kind of woven or knitted material; *tupek kaliko* meant tent drilling; *kaliko kammik* meant woolen socks (Stefansson 1909, 225). The manifest of the whaling ship *Era,* 1903-5, included 731 yards of calico (Ross 1975, 140).

13 For further information on Copper Inuit history and trade patterns see Condon (1994, 1996), Csonka (1994), Hickey (1984), and Morrison (1991).

14 For an account of the Coppermine families of 1916 31 see Jenness (1922, [1928] 1959), Finnie (1940), and Vanast (1991). Details about Jenness's life in his family of adoption are found in Collins and Taylor (1970, 74).

15 Sources that describe Copper Inuit clothing are the works of Birket-Smith (1945), Damas (1984b), Hall, Oakes, and Webster (1994), Jenness (1922, 1946), McGhee (1972), Oakes (1991), Rasmussen (1932), Stefansson (1914), and VanStone

(1994). I studied and catalogued the Copper Inuit clothing and tools in the collection of the McCord Museum of Canadian History, Montréal, and that information is recorded in the accession notes.

16 Taylor (1974a) researched the assemblages of Netsilingmiut material gathered by Roald Amundsen in 1903-5. Other sources for Netsilingmiut clothing are Amundsen (1908), Balikci (1970, 1984), Birket-Smith (1945), Hatt ([1914] 1969), Rasmussen (1931), and Schwatka (1884).

17 Taylor (1974a) draws on Amundsen's unpublished diaries of voyages from 1903 to 1907. He traces the movements of hunters and gives population statistics, such as that in January 1905 the camp at Ursuqtuuq consisted of eighteen families with a total of sixty people.

18 Sources describing Iglulingmiut clothing and life are Igloolik Adult Education Centre (1985), Lyon (1824), Mary-Rousselière (1984), Mathiassen (1928), Parry (1824), Pharand (1974, 1975), Rasmussen (1929), and Ungalaaq (1985).

19 Pharand's work (1974, 1975) provides background for much of the discussion here.

20 'The Eskimos that inhabit this vast heap of rock call it Shugliak: the Island-Pup That is Suckling the Continent Mother-Dog. They never call it Southampton Island' (Sutton 1934, 1). Material for this discussion of the Sallirmiut comes from Boas (1901, 1907), Lyon (1824), Mathiassen (1927, Part 1), Merbs (1983), Ross (1975), and Sutton (1934). Damas (1984c, 395-6) summarizes the sources for the Sallirmiut.

21 Background for this discussion of the Caribou Inuit is found in Arima (1984), Birket-Smith (1929), Csonka (1995), Driscoll (1980, 1983), Hall, Oakes, and Webster (1994), Marsh (1976, 1987), Oakes (1991), Oakes and Karetak (1987), Rasmussen (1930), VanStone and Oswalt (1959), and Will (1971). Research notes in the Department of Ethnology, Canadian Museum of Civilization, Hull, Québec, and the Manitoba Museum of Man and Nature, Winnipeg, are invaluable.

22 Background sources for the Nunatsiarmiut are Boas (1901, 1907, [1888] 1964), Ellis ([1748] 1946), Hulton and Quinn (1964), Kemp (1984), Speck (1924a), Wakeham (1898), and Washburne and Blackmore (1976).

23 See Hulton and Quinn (1964, 43-7, 141-3, Plates 62, 63) for discussion of John White's images, their copies, and derivatives.

24 The collection of the Scott Polar Research Institute contains a 'draught excluder' from the Thule culture. The accession notes state that a piece of dog skin tied from the trousers to below the knee filled the gap between bearskin pants and the boots.

25 I have among my papers an Inuit drawing of what seems to be leggings. The lines are faint and the provenience unknown, precluding publication.

26 Consultants who shared their knowledge are Bernadette Driscoll, Leah Idlout, Lucie Kayulik, Judy McGrath, Sarah Naluktuq, Annie Napayok, and Siasi Irqumia Smiler.

27 Duffle is a woolen cloth with a thick nap, sometimes known as blanket cloth, named from the town of Duffel near Antwerp, Belgium.

28 Sources for discussion of the Nunavimiut are Alasuaq (1973), Guédon (1967), Hawkes (1916), Myers (1980), Nungak (1983), Saladin d'Anglure (1984), and Turner ([1894] 1979). Also see the resources of Avataq Cultural Institute Documentation Centre, Lachine, Québec, and Inukjuaq.

29 Bernadette Driscoll, Judy McGrath, and Annie Napayok enlightened me on this subject.

30 Sources for this discussion of the Qikirtamiut are Diklev (1988), Francis and Morantz (1983), Freeman (1978), Freeman (1983), Pharand (1971), Schwartz (1976), Trudel (1989). For information on birdskin clothing see Birket-Smith (1945), Hatt ([1914] 1969), Holtved (1967), Nelson ([1899] 1983), Nungak (1983), Oakes (1992), Rosing (1986), Saladin d'Anglure (1984), and Wilder (1976).

31 Robert Flaherty, when he was searching for minerals, met Weetaltuk on Charlton Island in 1915. Flaherty's map, published in 1918, is based on Weetaltuk's 1910 chart, and both have been reproduced in standard geography texts (Freeman 1983).

32 Sources for Labrador Inuit clothing are Borlase (1994), Hawkes (1916), Clermont (1980), McGrath (1980), Saunders (1986), Speck (1924b), Taylor (1978), and Taylor (1974b, 1979, 1984, 1985). Much of the information about Labrador and its clothing has been given to me by Judy McGrath.

33 The Moravians, a popular name for the missionaries of the Unitas Fratrum or United Brethren, were the first Europeans to establish permanent residence in Labrador. They went north of Hamilton Inlet and opened their first mission at Naini in 1771. Their foundations continued until as late as 1904, when they opened their last station at Killiniq.

34 For an account of the impact on and resulting legislation concerning the exhibition of Inuit from Labrador, see Saunders (1986). For a description of the events surrounding the kidnapping by Commodore Hugh Palliser of Mikak and her child Tutauk, with a view of the clothing, see Taylor (1983-4, 1984).

35 For a survey and discussion of various renditions of the handbill, and a translation of the text, see Sturtevant (1976, 438-40; 1980).

36 Variant spellings include cassock and cassack: 'A loosely-fitting pullover garment of animal skin, swanskin, canvas or calico, with a hood attached, worn in northern Newfoundland and Labrador; the Inuit ADIKEY, DICKY [atigi]' (Story, Kirwin, and Widdowson 1982, 87). See Firestone (1992) for variations of the word 'cossack' in connection with Labrador settlers who adopted clothing production tools, materials, and methods from the Inuit.

37 Red Bay, a Labrador community on the Strait of Belle Isle, was the site of a large whaling station in the early 1500s and is the earliest known industrial complex in Canada. It was the first centre to make cloth covers commercially. They were identical to the ones made in Kalaallit Nunaat except that the Labrador cossack has remained long and the Kalaallit one is shortened and in the 1800s developed pockets (Judy McGrath, written communication 1983).

38 Mole skin was a thick-twilled short-napped cotton with the surface shaved before dyeing. The word 'dogskin' is used in the accession notes of the National Museum of Denmark.

39 For more on inter-Native trade see Issenman (1995) and Trudel (1989). For more information about trade routes see Burch (1988), Harris (1987), and Jones (1996). Leroi-Gourhan (1946) traces the spread of artifacts from the North Pacific to the peoples of the rivers of Asia, to America, and to Kalaallit Nunaat.

40 See Vézinet (1980) for an account of the Nunamiut, the inland people of Nunavik.

41 Information on Saami clothing is found in Agren (1977), Jomppanen (1982), Manker (1962), Nilsson (1977), Svensson (1992), and Zorgdrager (1997).

42 Ellen Maarit Nakkalajarvi and Anne Nuorgam, both Saami from Oulu, Finland, showed their clothing to me and explained its features, and allowed me to make a detailed inspection of their boots in 1992. Chukchi and Koryak boots I have examined do not exhibit the waterproofing features of Inuit boots, which can be worn in water, and in melting snow and ice. See the section on Siberian clothing in the References for material on footgear.

43 Pagination for Ivanov 1963, Bronshtein 1986, and Prytkova 1976 refers to the original work in Russian. English translation courtesy of Indian and Northern Affairs Canada. See Birket-Smith (1929), Low (1906), Hawkes (1916), and Speck (1914, 1924a, 1924b, 1925, 1937, 1940). See also Birket-Smith (1929, 295-364) for documentation on culture elements in Indian North America and Northeast Asia.

44 References to similarities and dissimilarities in Amerindian and Inuit clothing appear in Birket-Smith (1929), Brandford (1967), Conn (1955, 1974), Fitzhugh and Crowell (1988), Gurvich (1979), and Hatt (1916, 1969). Leroi-Gourhan (1946) traces the routes of the spread of cultural materials. These routes include from Siberia to North America (Inuit and Indian) to Kalaallit Nunaat.

45 Backrest banners AP-1525 and AP-834 in the Glenbow Museum have the circle and dot motif. Backrest banner V-A-502 in the Canadian Museum of Civilization has the splayed blades.

46 Information about population movements is found in Boas ([1888] 1974) and Rowley (1985).

47 One model of an eiderdown-filled jacket made in Nunavik uses Gibraltar cloth, a 100 per cent nylon material: one layer inside, two layers for the outside shell (Serge Bedekian, personal communication 1988).

Chapter 5: Spiritual, Artistic, and Social Traditions

1 Caroline Palliser of Inukjuaq is the former coordinator of Language and Culture Programmes for Kativik School Board, which serves some fifteen communities in northern Québec. Her paper was originally delivered at the First Inuit Clothing Conference sponsored by the Centre for Northern Studies, McGill University, Montréal, 1988. The author would like to acknowledge the generosity of Caroline Palliser in granting permission to reprint the paper.

2 The quotation from Ivaluardjuk was drawn from Rasmussen (1929, 56). Discussion on Inuit belief systems is drawn from Boas ([1888] 1964), Borré (1994), Hawkes (1916), Hickman (1987), Jenness (1946), Lantis (1946), Maxwell (1985, 55), Morrow (1984), Nungak and Arima (1969), Rasmussen (1931), Ray (1981), Rosing (1981, 1986), Serov (1988), and Taylor (1974b, 1985).

3 For human-animal symbolism, transformation, and artistic traditions see Driscoll (1987). For dances with notes on clothing see Victor-Howe (1994), and Zhornitskaya (1983, 1990). For a discussion of the roles of the spirits and their many names in the Arctic, see Nungak and Arima (1969, 113-16).

4 The chevron is 'probably the oldest ornamental motif, originating in Palaeolithic and Neolithic line patterns ... and [among] ancient peoples has symbolized many natural forms, such as water, lightning, or a serpent' (Ware and Stafford 1974, 55). The chevron placed in serial form and linear chevrons with a line through each apex grace many small carvings from sites in the Arctic. These etchings lead to the interpretation that the skeleton is represented on the surface.

5 Much of the information about helping spirits and amulets comes from Rasmussen (1931, 258-77). See also Oosten (1992a, 1997).

6 Information about dyeing, cutting, and sewing Kalaallit 'embroideries' is available in de Neergaard (1987), Jorgensen (1974), and Rix (1979).

7 The petit-point stitch dates from before the sixteenth century and was used extensively in Tudor England. It is still used in many parts of the world for carpets, wall hangings, pillows, and upholstery.

8 One example of North Alaskan waterproof boots decorated at the top with slit weaving is found in Murdoch (1892, 134-5). Valentina Gorbatcheva, State Museum of Ethnography, St. Petersburg showed me Siberian slit threading when we examined a Koryak man's funeral garment, a Koryak festivity coat, and a 1982 Even woman's coat in 1989.

9 For an example of slit weaving found in Canada see Taylor (1974a, 54-6), where he describes Netsilingmiut browbands gathered by Amundsen at the beginning of the twentieth century.

10 For information on dyes and colours see Hatt (1969, 16), Hickman (1987), Jenness (1946, 4, 35), McGrath (1977), Taylor (1974a, 26-30), Turcy (1986, 87), and Turner (1886, 94, 113, 119).

11 Information about fringes on sealskin clothing was given to me by Jeela Alikatuktuk Moss-Davies (personal communication 1984).

12 Sources for the discussion on pendants and beadwork are: Arutiunov and Fitzhugh (1988), Boas (1907), Bockstoce (1977), de Neergaard (1987), Driscoll (1983, 1984), Dubin (1987), Francis (1988), Hansen (1979), Hawkes (1916), Hickman (1987), Israel (1971), Jenkins (1972, 1975), Kaalund (1984), Karklins (1985, 1992, 1993), McGhee (1972), Marsh (1976), Orchard (1975), Speck (1940), Turner (1979), and the accession notes on beaded amautiit at the Manitoba Museum of Man and Nature.

13 An otolith is a calcareous stone in the ear of the fish. One of the Netsilingmiut browbands examined by Taylor (1974a, 56) has forty-three otoliths sewn to it.

14 The Venetians, realizing the value of beads for trade, had established enterprises for the manufacture of glass beads as early as the eleventh century. They monopolized the industry until the 1600s, when bead factories were set up in other parts of Europe, notably Bohemia.

15 Judy McGrath and Winifred P. Marsh contributed to my understanding of Pallirmiut and Iglulingmiut designs. Marsh suggested to me in 1983 that the influence of the Voisey family played a strong role in the pictographic beadwork designs. A forebear of the Voisey family came to Labrador from Cornwall, England, and married an Inuk woman. Some of the family moved to Naujaat, later to Kangiqliniq. The four daughters – Mrs. Hayward, Grace, Rosie, and Winnie – were renowned for their artistry in creating beaded coats (Winifred P. Marsh, written communication 1983).

16 Sources for the study of motifs are Bronshtein (1986), Issenman (1985, 1986), Ivanov (1963), Jenness (1946), Kaalund (1984), Levin and Potapov (1961), Mathiassen (1928, Part, 1, 116-17, 199-200), Mundkur (1984), Prytkova (1976), Rainey (1941), Smith and Speir (1927), and Speck (1925).

17 Whether all plant-like motifs in northern clothing are imitations of flowers and leaves occurring in nature is controversial. Some beadwork designs that may be construed as leaves are found in the clothing of the Koryak, Chukchi, Yupiit, and Sakhalin Islanders.

18 The shawls of Kashmir, India, with their pine tree or cone motifs, were an item of fashion through their use by Queen Victoria. The shawl began to be manufactured by the wool merchants of Paisley, Scotland, in the nineteenth and twentieth centuries, hence the name 'Paisley shawl.'

19 Newfoundland sealers use the term 'sculp' to describe skinning a seal with the fat left adhering to the hide.

20 For a more complete exposition of the loon's significance see Rosing (1981). Nastapoka (1995) relates a legend.

21 'When people wish to communicate with the spirits, they must put on a gutskin raincoat. This is the dress of the spirits' (Hawkes 1916, 137).

22 Information about masks is found in Blodgett (1979), Fienup-Riordan (1987, 1996), Gessain (1978, 1984), Kaalund (1984), Oosten (1992b), Ray (1975), and Speck (1935).

23 Sources of information about shamanism are Balikci (1970), Birket-Smith (1971), Blodgett (1979), Driscoll (1983), Hughes (1984), Merkur (1992), Nungak and Arima (1969), Oosten (1981, 1986, 1997), Prokof'eva (1971), Rasmussen (1929, 1931, 1932), Ray (1981), Saladin d'Anglure (1983), Serov (1988), Taylor (1974b), Tein (1994), and Turner ([1894] 1979).

24 Raven was a central figure in Siberian and Alaskan Yup'ik myths (Serov 1988, 242-3). This magical bird brought light to the world by piercing the membrane between our world and the realm of the spirits. The natives of Kamchatka, CIS, say Raven taught people how to 'sew from leaves and hides, to weave fishnets, to build canoes, and to beat the drum.' The dancer Asykolyan (see page 205) wears mitts with a divided palm, a possible metaphor for Raven's feet.

25 Information about *kamlanie* comes from Valery Tishkov, in accession notes accompanying photograph 2246-133 of the State Museum of Ethnography of the Russian Federation of the CIS, St. Petersburg, 1986. Translation of the notes from the Russian into English courtesy Indian and Northern Affairs Canada.

26 Jochelson (1926, 170-4, 194-6) discusses Yukaghir shamanism. He records that when he arranged with the chief of the Yukaghir Alaseia clan to purchase the costume of shaman Igor Shamanov, the shaman left the tent in tears because his dress was the main source of his powers, of which he was now deprived.

27 American Museum of Natural History 60/4440.

28 See American Museum of Natural History 70/3212 for an example of the scallop design. American Museum of Natural History 70/3384, 70/6794b-d, and 70/6791a,b,c are examples of disk-like ornaments sewn to clothing, at least one that of a shaman, of the Koryak and the Chukchi.

29 The dancing coat is from the Field Museum of Natural History, Chicago, FM 32009.

30 Medical research has shown that women produce a hormone called prostaglandin during menses. At this time, secretions of the sweat glands and other organs give off odours, even through the hands (Robert A.H. Kinch, MD, written communication 1985). Animals whose sense of smell is acute can respond with varying degrees of aggression or avoidance.

31 The word *ikajurti* is used only on the Hudson Bay coast. On Hudson Strait and in Ungava the helping woman is called *sanaji* (Louis-Jacques Dorais, written communication 1990).

32 See Strickler and Alookee (1988)

for a discussion of dolls as a teaching device and culture bearer.

33 Mary Inukpuk, born 1902, of Inukjuaq, Nunavik, in an interview with Alicie Niviaxie 1985. The interview was translated by Sarah Naluktuk for the Inuit History Project, Avataq Cultural Institute.

34 Sources for information about customs surrounding illness and death are Birket-Smith (1929), Boas ([1888] 1964), de Coccola and King (1956), Fienup-Riordan (1987), Fitzhugh and Kaplan (1982), Hawkes (1916), Jenness (1922), and Serov (1988).

35 For more information on external conflict consult Murray (1988) and Taylor (1979).

36 Siberian and Alaskan warfare is documented in Burch (1974, 1988) and Fienup-Riordan (1988, 1990). For hide armour of Chukchi and Siberian Yup'ik warriors see Van-Stone (1983).

37 For information concerning sharing and private property see Bodenhorn (1988, 1989), Buijs (1993), and Fainberg (1967, 244-5). It appears that the hunter's wife, who cuts up and shares out the meat with the partner's family or with the community, keeps the skin (Cunera Buijs, personal communication 1994).

38 For symbolism and rituals of the hunt with references to clothing consult Bodenhorn (1990), Briggs (1974), Rainey (1947), Taylor (1974b), VanStone (1985a), and Zhornitskaya (1983, 1990).

39 In the eighteenth century the men of Naini, Labrador, were responsible for dressing skins (Taylor 1974b, 52). In nineteenth-century records of the west coast of Hudson Bay men prepared skins (Boas [1888] 1964, 170). Stefansson (1914, 149) records that in the Mackenzie Delta area men performed the fourth scraping of the skins.

40 Residents of Sitnasuaq, Alaska, told me that they could tell from the forms of the white pukiq chest inserts on caribou parkas the family of the person wearing it. A bride's new parka combined design elements from both families (personal communication 1982).

Chapter 6:
New Explorations

1 Shnirelman (1994) gives information about today's Siberian indigenous peoples. For more data on Siberian clothing, see Bogaras (1904-9), Gorbatcheva (1988), Hooper (1853), Popov (1948), Prytkova (1952, 1976), Savel'eva (1967), Simchenko (1963a, 1963b), Smolyak (1984), Sverdup (1978), and Vasilevich (1963).

2 The 'high-collared' figurines I know of come from Inuaarsivik, Kalaallit Nunaat; Shuldham Island, Labrador; Diana Island, Nunavik; Devon Island and Mill Island, NWT.

3 Additional references for the study of parallels between Native cultures of Northeast Asia and North America are Chaussonnet (1988), Gorbatcheva (1988), Gurvich (1979, 1986), Woodbury (1968), and Zhornitskaya (1983). See also Issenman (1984, 1986) and Lee (1995).

4 I was able to study this type of robe, accession number 70-3212, at the American Museum of Natural History in 1987.

5 See Fitzhugh and Kaplan (1982, 132-43) for a discussion of Alaskan styles.

6 The boots are in the collection of the Arctic Institute of North America, Calgary.

7 For further discussion of some puzzles in the area of Inuit clothing studies see Issenman (1992a).

8 Documentation about relationships between Inuit and non-Inuit institutions is contained in Andreason (1986), Arnold (1992), Assembly of First Nations / Canadian Museums Association (1992), Issenman (1991, 1992b), and Rigby and Stenton (1992). Hall, Oakes, and Webster (1994) include an exposition of the collaborative process employed to produce the exhibition, 'Threads of the Land: Clothing Traditions from Three Indigenous Cultures,' held at the Canadian Museum of Civilization, Hull, 1995-7.

9 For several examples of significant contributions of Inuit to southern institutions, see Issenman (1992b, 7-9)

10 CHIN is a program of Communications Canada, Ottawa. Among its many services it provides access to more than 120 databases and contains computer records of more than 12,000,000 heritage objects. Over 300 museums in twenty-two countries use CHIN (Bradley 1991, 69). Conscious that the speed in development of electronic data management increases daily, I refer readers to the Canadian Museum of Civilization (CMC) 'Digitization at the CMC' 1994 and Canadian Museums Association 'New Directions for CHIN' 1995. CHIN has a client services office in Ottawa, an e-mail service, and a site on the World Wide Web.

11 Jenness, for example, noted that the fur fringes on Coronation Gulf, NWT, were evenly spaced, whereas in Dolphin and Union Strait it was more usual to group the fur dangles in clusters of three and four (1946, 13). Some Copper Inuit clothing at the McCord Museum of Canadian History, Montréal, has dangles in clusters of two.

12 Examples of discrepancies underline the difficulties. I have seen the measurement of the width of the top of a parka taken from the edge of one sleeve across the chest to the edge of the other, from the seams of the dropped shoulders, or from where the cataloguer thought the person's shoulders would come. The narrow skin piece placed between the sole of some boots and the upper is called variously a joiner, inlay, strip, or intermediary tuck. The piece over the top of the foot can be named a vamp, gore, or instep. For a model of standardization of classification and terms for footwear, see Webber (1989).

13 A start in the compilation of sources is found in Issenman (1984). Surveys such as Hunter (1967) and the Museum Ethnographers Group (1986) list institutional Arctic collections and occasionally specify clothing. See also the acknowledgments section of this book for libraries, bibliographies, archives, and museums consulted.

14 Driscoll (1980) was the first to write of the significance of the amauti in child rearing. Dufour (1988) writes of the crucial nature of clothing at stages in the lives of sipiniq children. Books on growing up in Inuit society include Coles (1977, 1978), Freeman (1978, 1994), Honigmann and Honigmann (1967), Jenness (1922), Ungalaaq (1985), and Washburne and Blackmore (1976).

15 See Devine (1982), Schweger (1983a, 1983b). See Firestone (1992) for the adoption by Labrador settlers of Inuit clothing traits.

16 The Inuit consider 'country food' – food from the land – as most essential, especially seal meat for its nutritious and curative powers. See Borré (1994).

Glossary of Place Names

Inuktitut to Qallunaaq[1]

Aklaarvik	Aklavik, NWT
Akulivik	Cape Smith, Québec
Anaulirvik	Cape Wolstenholme, Québec
Arviat	Eskimo Point, NWT
Arviligjuaq	Pelly Bay, NWT
Aqvituq[2]	Hopedale, Labrador
Arviliit	Ottawa Islands, NWT
Ausuittuq	Grise Fiord, NWT
Avanersuaq Kommunia	Thule District, Greenland
Avvaq	Cape Bathurst, NWT
Chukotka	Chukchi Peninsula
Igluligaarjuk	Chesterfield Inlet, NWT
Iglulik	Igloolik, NWT
Iik	Eek, Alaska
Ikaasuk	Sachs Harbour, NWT
Ikpiarjuk	Arctic Bay, NWT
Ilulissat	Jacobshavn, Greenland
Inaliq	Diomede Islands, CIS and USA
Inuaarsivik	Inuarfissuaq, Greenland
Inukjuaq	Port Harrison, Québec
Inuuvik	Inuvik, NWT
Iqaluit	Frobisher Bay, NWT
Iqaluktuuttiaq	Cambridge Bay, NWT
Ivujivik, Nunavik	Ivujivik, Québec
Kalaallit Nunaat	Greenland
Kangiqliniq	Rankin Inlet, NWT
Kangiqlugaapik	Clyde River, NWT
Kangiqsualujjuaq	George River (Port Nouveau-Québec), Québec
Kangiqsujuaq	Wakeham Bay, Québec
Kangiqsuk	Payne Bay, Québec
Katiktalik	Cape Fullerton, NWT
Kikiaq	Rigolet, Labrador
Killiniq	Killinek (Port Burwell), NWT
Kimmiruk	Lake Harbour, NWT
Kinngait	Cape Dorset, NWT
Kuugjuaq[3]	Churchill, Manitoba
Kuujjuaq, Nunavik	Fort Chimo, Québec
Kuujjuaraapik	Great Whale River (Poste-de-la-Baleine), Québec
Lake Hikoligjuaq	Lake Yathkyed, NWT
Lluughraq	Lorino, Chukotka
Mailasikkut	Chisasibi
Mamterilleq	Bethel, Alaska
Maquuvik	Makkovik, Labrador
Mittimatalik	Pond Inlet, NWT
Naini	Nain, Labrador
Naujaat	Repulse Bay, NWT
Nulahugiuq	Bernard Harbour, NWT
Nunavik	Arctic Québec, Nouveau-Québec
Nunavut	Eastern NWT
Nuuk	Godthåb, Greenland

Oleq	Uelen, Chukotka
Paamiut	Frederikshåb, Greenland
Pangniqtuuq	Pangnirtung, NWT
Paulatuuq	Paulatuk, NWT
Purvirnituq	Povungnituk, Québec
Qaanaaq	Qânâq, Thule, Greenland
Qamanittuaq	Baker Lake, NWT
Qanartalik	Douglas Harbour, Québec
Qausuittuq	Resolute Bay, NWT
Qerre	Lavrentiya, Chukotka
Qikiqtarjuaq	Broughton Island, NWT
Qikiqtaruk	Herschel Island, Yukon
Quikirtaaluk	Diana Island, NWT
Qipuqqaq	Postville, Labrador
Quaqtaq	Koartac, Québec
Qurluqtuuq	Coppermine, NWT
Qutdligssat	Kutdligssat, Greenland
Saaqqayaaq-Qikirtasiit	Digges Island, NWT
Salliq	Coral Harbour, NWT
Salluit	Sugluk, Québec
Sanikiluaq	Belcher Islands, NWT
Shugliaq	Southampton Island
Sighinek	Sireniki, Chukotka
Sisimiut	Holsteinsborg, Greenland
Sitnasuaq	Nome, Alaska
Sivuqaq	Gambell, St. Lawrence Island, Alaska
Sun'aq	Kodiak, Kodiak Island, Alaska
Taciq	St. Michael, Alaska
Taloyoak	Spence Bay, NWT
Tasiilaq	Angmassalik, Greenland
Tikigaq	Point Hope, Alaska
Tuktuujaqtuuq	Tuktoyaktuk, NWT
Tunirmiut	Native Point, NWT
Uluksartuuq	Holman Island, NWT
Umingmaktuuq	Bay Chimo, NWT
Unangan Islands	Aleutian Archipelago
Ungaziq	Chaplino, Chukotka
Uqsuqtuuq	Gjoa Haven, NWT
Utkraluk	Baillie Island, NWT
Vaali	Happy Valley-Goose Bay, Labrador

Qallunaaq to Inuktitut

Aklavik, NWT	Aklaarvik
Aleutian Archipelago	Unangan Islands
Angmassalik, Greenland	Tasiilaq
Arctic Bay, NWT	Ikpiarjuk
Arctic Québec, Nouveau Québec	Nunavik
Baillie Island, NWT	Utkraluk
Baker Lake, NWT	Qamanittuaq
Bay Chimo	Umingmaktuuq
Belcher Islands, NWT	Sanikiluaq
Bernard Harbour, NWT	Nulahugiuq
Bethel, Alaska	Mamterilleq
Broughton Island, NWT	Qikiqtarjuaq
Cambridge Bay, NWT	Iqaluktuuttiaq
Cape Bathurst, NWT	Avvaq
Cape Dorset, NWT	Kinngait
Cape Fullerton, NWT	Katiktalik
Cape Smith, Québec	Akulivik
Cape Wolstenholme, Québec	Anaulirvik
Chaplino, Chukotka	Ungaziq
Chesterfield Inlet, NWT	Igluligaarjuk
Chisasibi, Québec	Mailasikkut
Chukchi Peninsula	Chukotka
Churchill, Manitoba	Kuugjuaq
Clyde River, NWT	Kangiqlugaapik
Coppermine, NWT	Qurluqtuuq
Coral Harbour, NWT	Salliq
Diana Island, NWT	Qikirtaaluk
Digges Island, NWT	Saaqqayaaq-Qikirtasiit
Diomede Islands, CIS and USA	Inaliq
Douglas Harbour, Québec	Qanartalik
Eastern Northwest Territories	Nunavut
Eek, Alaska	Iik
Eskimo Point, NWT	Arviat
Fort Chimo	Kuujjuaq
Frederikshåb, Greenland	Paamiut
Frobisher Bay	Iqaluit
George River (Port Nouveau-Québec)	Kangiqsualujjuaq
Gjoa Haven, NWT	Uqsuqtuuq
Godthåb, Greenland	Nuuk
Great Whale River (Poste de la Baleine), Québec	Kuujjuaraapik
Greenland	Kalaallit Nunaat
Grise Fiord, NWT	Ausuittuq
Happy Valley Goose Bay, Labrador	Vaali
Herschel Island, Yukon	Qikiqtaruk
Holman, NWT	Uluksartuuq
Holsteinsborg, Greenland	Sisimiut
Hopedale, Labrador	Aqvituq
Igloolik, NWT	Iglulik
Inuarfissuaq, Greenland	Inuaarsivik
Inuvik, NWT	Inuuvik
Jacobshavn, Greenland	Ilulissat
Killinek (Port Burwell), Labrador	Killiniq
Koartac, Québec	Quaqtaq
Kodiak, Kodiak Island, Alaska	Sun'aq
Kutdligssat, Greenland	Qutdligssat
Lake Harbour, NWT	Kimmiruk
Lake Yathkyed, NWT	Lake Hikoligjuaq
Lavrentiya, Chukotka	Qerre

Lorino, Chukotka	Lluughraq
Mackenzie Delta area	Inuvialuit Land Claims area
Makkovik, Labrador	Maquuvik
Nain, Labrador	Naini
Native Point, NWT	Tunirmiut
Nome, Alaska	Sitnasuaq
Ottawa Islands, NWT	Arviliit
Pangnirtung, NWT	Pangniqtuuq
Paulatuk, NWT	Paulatuuq
Payne Bay, Québec	Kangirsuk
Pelly Bay, NWT	Arviligjuaq
Point Hope, Alaska	Tikigaq
Pond Inlet, NWT	Mittimatalik / Inukjuaq
Port Harrison, Québec	Inukjuaq
Postville, Labrador	Qipuqqaq
Povungnituk, Québec	Purvirnituq
Qânâq, Thule, Greenland	Qaanaaq
Rankin Inlet, NWT	Kangiqliniq
Repulse Bay, NWT	Naujaat
Resolute Bay, NWT	Qausuittuq
Rigolet, Labrador	Kikiaq
Sachs Harbour, NWT	Ikaasuk
St. Lawrence Island, Gambell, Alaska	Sivuqaq
St. Michael, Alaska	Taciq
Sireniki, Chukotka	Sighinek
Southampton Island	Shugliaq
Spence Bay, NWT	Taloyoak
Sugluk, Québec	Salluit
Tuktoyaktuk, NWT	Tuktuujaqtuuq
Uelen, Chukotka	Oleq
Wakeham Bay, Québec	Kangiqsujuaq
Western Northwest Territories	Inuvialuit Land Claims area

Notes

1 Qallunaaq is the Inuit word for any non-Inuit human (Dorais, written communication 1993). I have used place-names referred to in this work by the words employed by the Inuit. In many instances the Inuit designation has become the official government appellation. The Nunatop project, originally known as the Place Names Project, sponsored by Avataq Cultural Institute of Nunavik, has gathered several thousand traditional place names that will be included in official federal and provincial maps. This project is the first such enterprise in the world initiated by Native peoples to bring back their original names to their homelands.

The greatest aid in the orthography was given by Louis-Jacques Dorais of Université Laval. Recent renditions of names have been obtained from the Inuit Tapirisat of Canada (1992, 32-3), Müller-Wille and Avataq Cultural Institute (1991, 44), and Alaska Native Language Center (1995).

2 Aqvituq is called Hupatili (Hopedale) by Labrador Inuit (Dorais, written communication 1993).

3 Kuugjuaq is called Kuujjuaraaluk (Big Kuujjuaq) by Nunavimiut and Labrador Inuit to distinguish it from Kuujjuaq (Fort Chimo), Nunavik (Dorais 1993).

References

Aapak, Kailapi. 1981. About Education. *Inuktitut* 48:7-15

Abramova, Z.A. 1967. Palaeolithic Art in the USSR. *Arctic Anthropology* 4, no. 2:1-179

Ackerman, Robert A. 1984. Prehistory of the Asian Eskimo Zone. In *Arctic,* edited by David Damas, 106-18. Vol. 5 of *Handbook of North American Indians.* Washington, DC: Smithsonian Institution

Ågren, Katarina. 1977. Samiskt draktskick i Västerbotten. *Västerbotten* 3:129-98

Alariaq, Elizabeth. 1975. Qisiliriniit Ajjigiinngittut. Different Ways of Working with Sealskins, translated by Louis-Jacques Dorais. *Inummarit* 1, no. 2:n.p.

Alaska Native Language Center. 1995. *Map of the Inuit-Yup'ik-Aleut Languages.* Fairbanks: University of Alaska

Alasuaq, A. 1973. *Guide de la couturière (Manuel scolaire en syllabique avec traduction anglaise et française).* Purvirnituq: Commission Scolaire du Nouveau-Québec

Aliyak, Moses. 1991. Qungannaqtut. *Inuktitut* 73:44-5

Ammitsbøll, T., R. Møller, G. Møller, T. Kobayashi, H. Hino, G. Asboe-Hansen, and J.P. Hansen. 1989. Collagen and Glycosaminoglycans in Mummified Skin. In *The Mummies from Qilakitsoq-Eskimos in the 15th Century,* edited by J.P. Hart Hansen and H.C. Gulløv. Man and Society no. 12. Copenhagen: Meddelelser om Grønland

Amundsen, Roald. 1908. *The North west Passage.* Vols. 1 and 2. London: Archibald Constable

Anderson, Douglas D. 1984. Prehistory of North Alaska. In *Arctic,* edited by David Damas, 80-91. Vol. 5 of *Handbook of North American Indians.* Washington, DC: Smithsonian Institution

Andreason, Claus. 1986. Greenland's Museum Laws. *Arctic Anthropology* 23, nos. 1-2:239-46

Arctic Institute of North America. *ASTIS.* Calgary: Arctic Institute of North America (annual)

—. *Bibliography.* Calgary: Arctic Institute of North America (annual)

Arima, Eugene. 1984. Caribou Eskimo. In *Arctic,* edited by David Damas, 447-62. Vol. 5 of *Handbook of North American Indians.* Washington, DC: Smithsonian Institution

Arnaujaq, Leah. 1986. *In the Days of the Whalers.* Arviat, NWT: Inuit Cultural Institute

Arnold, Charles. 1992. Archaeology in the Canadian Arctic: Past and Present. Repatriation of Skeletons to the Northwest Territories. *Information North, Arctic Institute of North America* 18, no. 3:1-7

Arutiunov, S.A. 1988. Chukchi: Warriors and Traders of Chukotka. In *Crossroads of Continents. Cultures of Siberia and Alaska,* edited by W. Fitzhugh and A. Crowell, 39-42. Washington, DC: Smithsonian Institution Press

Arutiunov, S.A., and William Fitzhugh. 1988. Prehistory of Siberia and the Bering Sea. In *Crossroads of Continents. Cultures of Siberia and Alaska,* edited by W. Fitzhugh and A. Crowell, 117-29. Washington, DC: Smithsonian Institution Press

Assembly of First Nations / Canadian Museums Association. 1992. *Turning the Page: Forging New Partnerships between Museums and First Peoples.* Ottawa: Task Force Report on Museums and First Peoples

Bacqueville de la Potherie, Claude C. Le Roy. 1722. *Histoire de l'Amérique septentrionale.* 4 vols. Paris: Nyon

Bahnson, Anne. 1997. Skin Clothing in Greenland. In *Braving the Cold: Change and Continuity in Arctic Clothing,* edited by Cunera Buijs and Jarich Oosten, 60-88. Leiden: Centre for Non-Western Studies, Leiden University

Balikci, Asen. 1970. *The Netsilik Eskimo.* New York: Natural History Press

—. 1984. Netsilik. In *Arctic,* edited by David Damas, 415-30. Vol. 5 of *Handbook of North American Indians.* Washington, DC: Smithsonian Institution

Beach, Hugh. 1994. The Saami of Lapland. In *Polar Peoples: Self-Determination and Development.* London: Minority Rights Group Publications

Belsey, William. 1986. Return to Ennadai. *Northwest Explorer* 5, no. 3:28-39

Bencard, Mogens. 1989. Two 17th-century Eskimos at Rosenborg Palace. In *The Mummies from Qilakitsoq – Eskimos in the 15th Century,* edited by J.P.H. Hansen and H.C. Gulløv, 47-55. Copenhagen: Meddelelser om Grønland

Birket-Smith, Kaj. 1924. Ethnography of the Egedesmunde District with Aspects of the General Culture of West Greenland. *Meddelelser om Grønland no. 66.* Reprint, New York: AMS Press 1976

—. 1929. *The Caribou Eskimos: Material and Social Life and Their Cultural Position. Report of the Fifth Thule Expedition 1921-24.* Vol. 5, Pts. 1-2. Copenhagen: Gyldendalske

—. 1945. *Ethnographical Collections from the Northwest Passage. Report of the Fifth Thule Expedition 1921-24.* Vol. 6, Pt. 2. Copenhagen: Gyldendalske

—. 1971. *Eskimos.* New York: Crown Publishers

Blodgett, Jean. 1979. *The Coming and Going of the Shaman: Eskimo Shamanism and Art.* Winnipeg: Winnipeg Art Gallery

Boas, Franz. 1901. The Eskimo of Baffin Land and Hudson Bay. *Bulletin of the American Museum of Natural History* 15, no.1:1-370

—. 1907. Second Report on the Eskimo of Baffin Land and Hudson Bay. *Bulletin of the American Museum of Natural History* 15, no. 2:371-570

—. 1908. Decorative Designs of Alaskan Needlecases. *Proceedings of the United States National Museum* 34:321-44

—. [1927] 1955. *Primitive Art.* Reprint, New York: Dover Publications

—. [1888] 1964. *The Central Eskimo.* Reprint, Lincoln: University of Nebraska Press. Originally published as *Sixth Annual Report of the United States Bureau of Ethnology 1884-1885,* 399-669. Washington, DC: Smithsonian Institution

—. 1984. The Eskimos of Baffin Land. *Études/Inuit/Studies* 8, no. 1:139-44

Bockstoce, John R. 1977. *Eskimos of Northwest Alaska in the Early Nineteenth Century: Based on the Beechey and Belcher Collections and Records Compiled during the Voyage of HMS* Blossom *to Northwest Alaska in 1826 and 1827.* Pitt Rivers Museum Monograph Series no. 1. Oxford: Oxford University Press

Bodenhorn, Barbara. 1988. Whales, Souls, Children and Other Things that Are 'Good to Share': Core Metaphors in a Contemporary Whaling Society. *Cambridge Anthropology* 13, no. 1:1-18

—. 1989. The Animals Come to Me, They Know I Share: Inupiaq Kinship, Changing Economic Relations and Enduring World Views on

Alaska's North Slope. PhD dissertation, Cambridge University, Cambridge

—. 1990. 'I'm Not the Great Hunter, My Wife Is.' Inupiat and Anthropological Models of Gender. *Études/Inuit/Studies* 14, nos. 1-2:55-74

Bogoras, Waldemar. 1904-9. The Chukchee. *The Jesup North Pacific Expedition 7, Memoirs of the American Museum of Natural History.* Leiden: E.J. Brill, New York: G.E. Stechert. Reprint, New York: AMS Press 1975

Borlase, Tim. 1994. *The Labrador Settlers, Métis and Kabluângajuit.* Happy Valley-Goose Bay, Labrador: Labrador East Integrated School Board

Borré, Kristen. 1994. The Healing Power of the Seal: The Meaning of Inuit Health, Practice, and Belief. *Arctic Anthropology* 31, no. 1:1-15

Bradley, Merridy. 1991. Where Do We Go from Here? CHIN/RCIP. *Muse* 9, no. 1:66-9 (English), 70-3 (French)

Brandford, Joanne Segal. 1967. Eskimo Parka and Northern Athapaskan Tunic: A Design Comparison. MA thesis, University of California at Berkeley

Brasser, Ted J. 1984. Backrest Banners among the Plains Cree and Plains Ojibwa. *American Indian Arts Magazine* (Winter):56-63

Briggs, Jean. 1974. Eskimo Women: Makers of Men. In *Many Sisters,* edited by Carol Mathiassen, 261-304. New York: Free Press

Brody, Hugh. 1976. Land Occupancy: Inuit Perception. In Vol. 1 of *Report: Inuit Land Use and Occupancy Project,* edited by Milton Freeman, 185-242. Ottawa: Indian and Northern Affairs Canada

Bronshtein, M.M. 1986. Typological Variants of Ancient Eskimo Graphic Ornamentation. (The problem of a cultural history of the Bering Sea Region during the first millennium BC [to the] first millennium AD). *Soviet Ethnography* 6:45-58, (Russian); 1-23 (Indian and Northern Affairs Canada translation, English). Pagination given in text refers to the original work in Russian.

Brower, Charles D. 1899. Sinew-Working at Point Barrow. *American Anthropologist* n.s. 1:597

Bruemmer, Fred. 1971. *Seasons of the Eskimo.* Toronto: McClelland and Stewart

Buijs, Cunera C.M. 1993. Disappearance of Traditional Meat-Sharing Systems among the Tinitekilaamiut of East Greenland and the Arviligjuarmiut and Iglulingmiut of Canada. In *Continuity and Discontinuity in Arctic Cultures,* edited by Cunera Buijs, 108-35. Leiden: Centre for Non-Western Studies, Leiden University

—. 1997. Ecology and Principles of Polar Clothing. In *Braving the Cold: Change and Continuity in Arctic Clothing*, edited by Cunera Buijs and Jarich Oosten, 11-33. Leiden: Centre for Non-Western Studies, Leiden University

Buijs, Cunera, and G.M. Vogelsang-Eastwood. 1993. *Patterns for Arctic Clothing.* Leiden: Rijksmuseum voor Volkenkunde and Stichting Textile Research Centre

Burch, Ernest, Jr. 1974. Eskimo Warfare in Northwest Alaska. *Anthropological Papers of the University of Alaska* 15, no. 2:1-11

—. 1975. *Eskimo Kinsmen. Changing Family Relationships in Northwest Alaska.* New York: West Publishing Company

—. 1988. War and Trade. In *Crossroads of Continents. Cultures of Siberia and Alaska,* edited by W. Fitzhugh and A. Crowell, 227-40. Washington, DC: Smithsonian Institution Press

—. 1994. The Inupiat and the Christianization of Arctic Alaska. *Études/Inuit/Studies* 18, nos. 1-2:81-108

Canada. 1988. *Humanities Data Dictionary of the Canadian Heritage Information Network,* compiled by the Documentation Research Group, Museum Services Canada. Ottawa: Communication Canada

—. *Canada Year Book.* 1986, 1990, 1991. Ottawa: Ministry of Supply and Services, Statistics Canada

Canadian Museum of Civilization. 1994. Digitization at the Canadian Museum of Civilization: The On-ramp to the Information Highway. Hull, PQ: Canadian Museum of Civilization

Canadian Museums Association. 1995. New Directions for CHIN. *Muséogramme. Newsletter of the Canadian Museums Association* 23, no. 4:3-4

Carlo, Jean Flanagan, and Rose Atuk Fosdick. 1988. *A Treasured Heritage: The Works of Masters and Apprentices.* Fairbanks: Institute of Alaska Native Arts and University of Alaska Museum

Cartwright, George. 1792. *A Journal of Transactions and Events, During a Residence of Nearly Sixteen Years on the Coast of Labrador: Containing Many Interesting Particulars, Both of the Country and its Inhabitants Not Hitherto Known.* 3 vols. Newark, England: Allin and Ridge

Cernetig, Miro. 1991. Inuit Reclaim Heritage Carted off by Scientists. *Globe and Mail,* 13 July, pp. A1, A4

Chaussonnet, Valérie. 1988. Needles and Animals: Women's Magic. In *Crossroads of Continents. Cultures of Siberia and Alaska,* edited by W. Fitzhugh and A. Crowell, 209-26. Washington, DC: Smithsonian Institution Press

Clabburn, Pamela. 1976. *The Needleworker's Dictionary.* New York: William Morrow

Clark, Donald W. 1984. Pacific Eskimo: Historical Ethnography. In *Arctic,* edited by David Damas, 185-97. Vol. 5 of *Handbook of North American Indians.* Washington, DC: Smithsonian Institution

Clermont, N. 1980. Les Inuit de Labrador méridional avant Cartwright. *Études/Inuit/Studies* 4, nos. 1-2:147-66

Coles, Robert. 1977. *Eskimos, Chicanos, Indians.* Vol. 4 of *Children of Crisis.* Boston: Little, Brown

—. 1978. *The Last and First Eskimos.* Boston: New York Graphic Society

Collins, Henry B., and William E. Taylor Jr. 1970. Diamond Jenness (1886-1969). *Arctic* 23, no. 2:71-81

Condon, Richard G. 1983. Modern Inuit Culture and Society. In *Arctic Life. Challenge to Survive,* edited by M.M. Jacobs and J.B. Richardson III, 149-73. Pittsburgh: Carnegie Institute

—. 1992. Editor's note. *Arctic Anthropology* 29, no. 1:1

—. 1994. East Meets West: Fort Collinson, The Fur Trade and the Economic Acculturation of the Northern Copper Inuit, 1928-1939. *Études/Inuit/Studies* 18, nos. 1-2:109-35

Condon, Richard G. with Julia Ogina and Holman Elders. 1996. *The Northern Copper Inuit: A History.* Toronto: University of Toronto Press

Conn, Richard. 1955. A Classification of Aboriginal North American Clothing. MA thesis, University of Washington, Seattle

—. 1974. *Robes of White Shell and Sunrise: Personal Decorative Arts of the Native American.* Denver: Denver Art Museum

—. 1991. Some Design Concepts of Traditional Subarctic Clothing. *Arctic Anthropology* 28, no. 1:84-91

Crowe, Keith J. 1974. *A History of the Original Peoples of Northern Canada.* Montréal and Kingston: Arctic Institute of North America and McGill-Queen's University Press

Csonka, Yvon. 1988. *Collections Arctiques.* Neuchâtel, Suisse: Musée d'ethnographie de Neuchâtel

—. 1994. Intermédiaires au long cours: Les relations entre Inuit du Caribou et Inuit du Cuivre au début du XXe siècle. *Études/Inuit/Studies* 18, nos. 1-2:21-47

—. 1995. *Les Ahiarmiut: À l'écart des Inuit Caribous.* Neuchâtel, Suisse: Editions Victor Attinger SA

Damas, David. 1984a. Central Eskimo: Introduction. In *Arctic,* edited by David Damas, 1-7. Vol. 5 of *Handbook of North American Indians.* Washington, DC: Smithsonian Institution

—. 1984b. Copper Eskimo. In *Arctic,* edited by David Damas, 397-414. Vol. 5 of *Handbook of North American Indians.* Washington, DC: Smithsonian Institution

—. 1984c. Central Eskimo: Introduction. In *Arctic*, edited by David Damas, 391-6. Vol. 5 of *Handbook of North American Indians.* Washington, DC: Smithsonian Institution

—, ed. 1984d. *Arctic.* Vol. 5 of *Handbook of North American Indians.* Washington, DC: Smithsonian Institution

de Coccola, Raymond, and Paul King. 1956. *Ayorama.* New York: Oxford University Press

Dekin, Albert A., Jr. 1984. Retrospect and Prospect: Archaeology. *Arctic Anthropology* 21, no. 1:149-51

de Neergaard, Helga Bruun. 1987. *Avittat. Gønlandske skindmønstre* (Greenland skin embroideries). Nuuk: Society of Greenlandic Women's Clubs

Devine, Marina, ed. 1982. *NWT Data Book 1982-1983.* Yellowknife: Outcrop

Dickerson, Mark O., and Karen M. McCullough. 1993. Nunavut ('Our Land'). *Information North, Arctic Institute of North America* 19, no. 2:1-7

Diklev, Torben. 1988. Birdskin Coat Manufacture in the Thule Region. Paper presented at the First Inuit Clothing Conference, Centre for Northern Studies and Research,

McGill University, Montréal, 5-7 May

Dolgikh, B., and L.A. Fainberg. 1959. Some Parallel Features in the Culture of Samoyeds and Eskimos. *International Congress of Americanists Proceedings* 33, no. 2:88-97

Driscoll, Bernadette. 1980. *The Inuit Amautik: I Like My Hood to be Full.* Winnipeg: Winnipeg Art Gallery

—. 1983. The Inuit Parka: A Preliminary Study Based on the Collections of the National Museum of Man (Ottawa); the Manitoba Museum of Man and Nature; the American Museum of Natural History; and the National Museum of Natural History, Smithsonian Institution. MA thesis, Carleton University, Ottawa

—. 1984. Sapangat: Inuit Beadwork of the Canadian Arctic. *Expedition* 26, no. 2:40-7

—. 1987. Pretending to be Caribou: The Inuit Parka as an Artistic Tradition. In *The Spirit Sings: Artistic Traditions of Canada's First Peoples,* 169-200. Toronto: McClelland and Stewart

Dubin, Lois Sherr. 1987. *The History of Beads.* New York City: Harry W. Abrams

Dufour, Rose. 1975. Le Phénomène du *sipiniq* chez les Inuit d'Iglulik. *Recherches Amérindiennes au Québec* 5, no. 3:65-9

—. 1988. *Femme et enfantement. Sagesse dans la culture Inuit.* Québec: Les Editions Papyrus

Durner, George M., and Steven C. Amstrup. 1995. Movements of a Polar Bear from Northern Alaska to Northern Greenland. *Arctic* 48, no. 4:338-41

Eber, Dorothy. 1971. *Pitseolak: Pictures out of My Life.* Toronto: Oxford University Press

—. 1973. Eskimo Penny Fashions. *North/Nord* 20, no. 1:37-9

Ellis, Henry. 1946. Eskimos of 1746. *The Beaver* 277 (June): 30-33. Extracts from *A Voyage to Hudson's Bay by the Dobbs Galley and California in the Years 1746 and 1747 for Discovering a North-West Passage.* London: H. Whitridge 1748

Erasmus, Georges. 1988. Preserving Our Heritage: A Working Conference for Museums and First Peoples. Opening address, Ottawa, November

Ernerk, Peter. 1993. Inuit Silattuqsarvingat – The Inuit University of the North. In *Social Sciences in the North,* edited by Louis-Jacques Dorais and Ludger Müller-Wille. Topics in Arctic Social Science, 1:11-14. Ste-Foy, PQ: International Arctic Social Sciences Association and le Groupe d'études inuit et circumpolaires

Études/Inuit/Studies. 1982. The Four Kalaallit Kidnapped in 1654. *Études/Inuit/Studies* 6, no. 2:2

Fainburg, L. 1967. On the Question of the Eskimo Kinship System. *Arctic Anthropology* 4, no. 1:244-56

Fienup-Riordan, Ann. 1987. The Mask: The Eye of the Dance. *Arctic Anthropology* 24, no. 2:40-55

—. 1988. Eskimo War and Peace: The History of Bow and Arrow Warfare among the Yup'ik Eskimos of Western Alaska. *Draft Papers of the Crossroads of Continents Symposium.* Washington, DC: Smithsonian Institution Press

—. 1990. Yup'ik Warfare and the Myth of the Peaceful Eskimo. In *Eskimo Essays,* edited by Ann Fienup-Riordan, 146-66. New Brunswick, NJ: Rutgers University Press

—, ed. 1996. *Agayuliyararput / Our Way of Making Prayer: Kegginaqut, Kangiit-llu / Yup'ik Masks and the Stories They Tell.* Translated by Marie Meade. Anchorage and Seattle: Anchorage Museum of History and Art and University of Washington Press

Finnie, Richard. 1940. *Lure of the North.* Philadelphia: David McKay

Firestone, Melvin. 1992. Inuit Derived Culture Traits in Northern Newfoundland. *Arctic Anthropology* 29, no. 1:112-28

Fisher, Matthew. 1988. Super Shamou Flies across the North Battling for Truth, Justice, Inuit Way. *Globe and Mail,* 28 December, pp. 1, 4

Fitzhugh, William W. 1984. Paleo-Eskimo Cultures of Greenland. In *Arctic,* edited by David Damas, 528-39. Vol. 5 of *Handbook of North American Indians.* Washington, DC: Smithsonian Institution

Fitzhugh, William, and Aron Crowell, eds. 1988. *Crossroads of Continents. Cultures of Siberia and Alaska.* Washington, DC: Smithsonian Institution Press

Fitzhugh, William, and Susan Kaplan. 1982. *Inua: Spirit World of the Bering Sea Eskimo.* Washington, DC: Smithsonian Institution Press

Forsyth, Adrian. 1985. *Mammals of the Canadian Wild.* Camden East, Ontario: Camden House Publishing

Francis, Daniel, and Toby Morantz. 1983. *Partners in Furs: A History of the Fur Trade in Eastern James Bay 1600-1870.* Montréal and Kingston: McGill-Queen's University Press

Francis, Peter, Jr. 1988. Beads and Bead Trade in the North Pacific Region. In *Crossroads of Continents. Cultures of Siberia and Alaska,* edited by William Fitzhugh and Aron Crowell, 341. Washington, DC: Smithsonian Institution Press

Franklin, U.M., E. Badone, R. Gotthardt, and B. Yorga. 1981. *An Examination of Prehistoric Copper Technology and Copper Sources in Western Arctic and Subarctic North America.* Mercury Series Paper no. 101. Ottawa: National Museum of Man

Freeman, Milton. 1983. George Weetaltuk (ca. 1862-1956). *Arctic* 36, no. 2:214-15

Freeman, Minnie Aodla. 1978. *Life among the Qallunaat.* Edmonton: Hurtig

—. 1994. Traditional and Contemporary Roles of Inuit Women. In *Inuit Women Artists,* edited by Odette Leroux, Marion E. Jackson, and Minnie Aodla Freeman, 248-50. Hull, PQ: Canadian Museum of Civilization

Freuchen, Peter, and Finn Salomonsen. 1958. *The Arctic Year.* New York: G.P. Putnam's Sons

George, Jane. 1995. Siberian Ice Curtain Melts to Let Polar Peoples Meet. *Globe and Mail,* 17 August, p. A8

Gessain, Robert. 1978. Masques Eskimo d'Ammassalik: Côte est du Groenland. *Le Courrier du Musée de l'Homme* 3

—. 1984. Dance Masks of the Ammassalik (East Coast of Greenland), edited by D.J. Ray. *Arctic Anthropology* 21, no. 2:81-107

Gilberg, Rolf. 1988. Inughuit, Knud Rasmussen, and Thule. *Études/Inuit/Studies* 12, nos. 1-2:45-55

Goar, Carol. 1990. Arctic Industry Could Be a Winner for Us. *Gazette* (Montréal), 5 January, p. B3

Goddard, John. 1987. People of the Seal. *Equinox* 6, no. 2:91-101

Gorbatcheva, Valentina. 1988. *Par le chemin des rennes sauvages.* Catalogue pour l'exposition des oeuvres d'art et d'artisanat des peuples indigènes du nord de la Russie. Moscow, Leningrad, Quebec City: Ministère de la Culture de la RSFSR, Musée ethnographie de peuples de l'URSS, Ministère des Affaires culturelles du Québec

Graves, J. 1983. Polar Bear of the Northwest Territories. *Arctic Wildlife Sketches,* edited by Ed Hall. Yellowknife: Government of the Northwest Territories

—. 1985. Barren-Ground Caribou of the Northwest Territories. *Arctic Wildlife Sketches,* edited by Ed Hall. Yellowknife: Government of Northwest Territories

Greer, Louise, and Anthony Harold. 1979. *Flying Clothing, the Story of Its Development.* Shrewsbury, UK: Airlife Publications

Gubser, Nicholas J. 1965. *The Nunamiut Eskimos: Hunters of Caribou.* New Haven: Yale University Press

Guédon, Marie-Françoise. 1967. Organisation des activités féminines dans la communauté esquimaude d'Ivujivik (Nouveau-Québec) en 1966. Maîtrise, Université de Montréal, Montréal

Gurvich, Ilja S. 1979. An Ethnographic Study of Cultural Parallels among the Aboriginal Populations of Northern Asia and Northern North America. *Arctic Anthropology* 16, no. 1:32-8

—. 1986. Ethnic Connections across Bering Strait. In *Crossroads of Continents. Cultures of Siberia and Alaska,* edited by W. Fitzhugh and A. Crowell, 17-23. Washington, DC: Smithsonian Institution Press

Hadlereena, Melanie, Attima Hadlari, and Maureen Jensen. 1986. Making Waterproof Kamiks. Artisan: Seepola Nowdluk of Iqaluit, NWT. In *A Way of Life,* edited by Ed Hall, 57-70. Yellowknife: Government of the Northwest Territories

Hahn, J. 1977. L'utilisation du bois de caribou chez les Esquimo du Cuivre sur l'île de Banks, NWT, Canada. *Méthodologie appliquée à l'industrie de l'os préhistorique.* Colloques Internationaux no. 568. Paris: Editions du centre national de la recherche scientifique

Hall, Edwin S., Jr. 1984. Interior North Alaska Eskimo. In *Arctic,* edited by David Damas, 338-46. Vol. 5 of *Handbook of North American Indians.* Washington, DC: Smithsonian Institution

Hall, Edwin S., and Lynne Fullerton, eds. 1990. Vol. 1, *The 1981 Excavations at the Utqiagvik Archaeological Site, Barrow, Alaska.* Vol. 2,

Additional Reports of the 1982 Investigations by the Utqiagvik Archaeology Project, Barrow, Alaska. Vol. 3, *Excavation of a Prehistoric Catastrophe: a Preserved Household from the Utqiagvik Village, Barrow, Alaska.* Barrow, Alaska: The North Slope Borough Commission on Inupiat History, Language, and Culture

Hall, Judy, Jill Oakes, and Sally Qimmiu'naaq Webster. 1994. *Sanatujut: Pride in Women's Work. Copper and Caribou Inuit Clothing Traditions.* Hull, PQ: Canadian Museum of Civilization

Hansen, J.P. Hart, and H.C. Gulløv, eds. 1989. *The Mummies from Qilakitsoq – Eskimos in the 15th century.* Man and Society Series no. 12. Copenhagen: Meddelelser om Grønland

Hansen, Keld. 1969-70. The People of the Far North. *Folk* 11-12:97-107

—. 1979. *Perler i Grønland.* (Beadwork in Greenland). Copenhagen: National Museum of Denmark

Harp, Elmer, Jr. 1951. An Archaeological Reconnaissance in the Strait of Belle Isle Area. *American Antiquity* 16, no. 3:203-20

Harris, R. Cole, ed. 1987. *From the Beginning to 1800.* Vol. 1 of *Historical Atlas of Canada.* Toronto: University of Toronto Press

Hatt, Gudmund. 1916. Moccasins and their Relation to Arctic Footwear. *Memoirs of the American Anthropological Association* 3, no. 3:147-250

—. 1934. North American and Eurasian Culture Connections. *Proceedings of the Fifth Pacific Science Congress* 4:2755-65

—. 1969. Arctic Skin Clothing in Eurasia and America: An Ethnographic Study. Translated by Kirsten Taylor. *Arctic Anthropology* 5, no. 2:3-132. Originally published as *Arktiske Skinddragter i Eurasien og Amerika: En Etnografisk Studie* (Copenhagen: J.H. Shultz 1914)

Hawkes, Ernest William. 1916. *The Labrador Eskimo.* Geological Survey, Memoir 91. Anthropological Series no. 14. Ottawa: Canada Department of Mines

Herscovici, Alan. 1994. Harpooning the Inuit Way of Life. *Globe and Mail,* 14 June, p. A19

Hickey, Clifford G. 1984. An Examination of Processes of Cultural Change among Nineteenth Century Copper Inuit. *Études/Inuit/Studies* 8, no. 1:13-35

Hickman, Pat. 1987. *Innerskins/Outerskins: Gut and Fishskins.* San Francisco: San Francisco Craft and Folk Museum

Hinds, Margery. 1984. Pootoogook. *The Beaver* 315, no. 2:38-43

Holm, Gustav F. 1888. Ethnologisk skizze af Angmagsalikerne (Ethnological sketch of the Ammassalik people). *Meddelelser om Grønland* 10, no. 2:43-182

Holtved, Eric. 1967. Contributions to Polar Eskimo Ethnography. *Meddelelser om Grønland* 182, no. 2

Honigmann, John J., and Irma Honigmann. 1967. Frobisher Bay Eskimo Childhood. *North.* No. QS-0006-051-EE-A-14. Ottawa: Northern Administration Branch, Department of Indian Affairs and Northern Development. Reprint, Ottawa: Indian and Northern Affairs

Hooper, William Hulme. 1853. *Ten Months among the Tents of the Tuski, with Incidents of an Arctic Boat Expedition in Search of Sir John Franklin, as far as the Mackenzie River and Cape Bathurst.* London: John Murray

Hughes, Charles C. 1984. St. Lawrence Islanders. In *Arctic,* edited by David Damas, 262-77. Vol. 5 of *Handbook of North American Indians.* Washington, DC: Smithsonian Institution

Hulton, Paul H., and David Beers Quinn. 1964. *The American Drawings of John White 1577-1590.* London: Trustees of the British Museum and Chapel Hill: University of North Carolina Press

Hunter, John E. 1967. *Inventory of Ethnological Collections in Museums of the United States and Canada.* Washington, DC: Committee on Anthropological Research in Museums of the American Anthropological Association, in collaboration with Wenner-Gren Foundation for Anthropological Research, New York

Igloolik Adult Education Centre. 1985. *Illinqaruminaqtuit.* Iglulik: Igloolik Adult Education Centre

Innuksuk, Rhoda, and Susan Cowan. 1976. *We Don't Live in Snow Houses Now.* Ottawa: Canadian Arctic Producers

Inuit Art Quarterly, eds. 1994. Update: Cultural Activities in Grise Fiord, Northwest Territories. *Inuit Art Quarterly* 9, no. 3:39

Inuit Tapirisat of Canada. 1992. Map of Canadian Inuit Communities. *Inuktitut* (75):32-3

Iqallijuq, Rose. 1972. Tuktunik Anuraliurnirmik. Les habits en peaux de caribou. *Inummarit* 1:18-21

Irving, Laurence. 1972. *Arctic Life of Birds and Mammals, Including Man.* Berlin: Springer-Verlag

Israel, Heinz. 1971. Beinschnitzerei der Eskimo. Catalogue, Dresden Museum für Völkerkunde. *Abhandlungen und Berichte des Museum* 33:1-46, 113-40

Issenman, Betty Kobayashi. 1984. Sources for the Study of Inuit Clothing. Manuscript on deposit with various libraries and in author's archives, Montréal

—. 1985. Inuit Skin Clothing: Construction and Motifs. *Études/Inuit/Studies* 9, no. 2:101-19

—. 1986. The Asian and Siberian Connection: Designs in Inuit Skin Clothing. Paper presented to the Native Arts Study Group, Ottawa: National Museum of Man, 8 January

—. 1990. Clothing for Arctic Survival. Inuit Sewing Techniques. *Threads* 27 (February-March):58-61

—. 1991. Inuit Power and Museums. *Information North, Arctic Institute of North America* 17, no. 3:1-7

—. 1992a. Inuit Clothing – Some Riddles. Paper presented at the First International Congress of Arctic Social Sciences, Université Laval, Ste-Foy, PQ, 25-31 October

—. 1992b. Inuit and Museums: Allied to Preserve the Arctic Patrimony. Paper developed from a lecture given at the First International Congress of Arctic Social Sciences, Université Laval, Ste-Foy, PQ, 25-31 October

—. 1995. Inuit Skin Clothing: Some Aspects of the Inter-Native Fur Trade in the Arctic and of the Import of Fur Clothing to Inuit and Non-Inuit. Paper presented at the Seventh North American Fur Trade Conference, St. Mary's University, Halifax, 24-7 May

—. 1997. Stitches in Time: Prehistoric Inuit Skin Clothing and Related Tools. In *Braving the Cold: Change and Continuity in Arctic Clothing,* edited by Cunera Buijs and Jarich Oosten. Leiden: Centre for Non-Western Studies, Leiden University.

Issenman, Betty, and Catherine Rankin. 1988. *Ivalu: Traditions du vêtement inuit. Traditions of Inuit Clothing.* Montréal: McCord Museum of Canadian History

Ivanov, S.V. 1963. *Ornament narodov Sibiri kak istoricheskiy istocknik* (Ornaments of the peoples of Siberia as an historical source). Moscow and St. Petersburg: Izdatel'stvo Akademii Nauka SSSR. Pagination refers to the original work in Russian (Indian and Northern Affairs Canada translation).

—. 1970a. Starinnye trubchatye igolniki narodov Sibiri (The needlecases of Siberian peoples). In *Odezhda narodov Sibiri* (The clothing of Siberian peoples), edited by S.V. Ivanov, 196-207. St. Petersburg: Nauka sbornik statei muzeia antropologii i etnografii

—, ed. 1970b. *Odezhda narodov Sibiri* (The clothing of Siberian peoples). St. Petersburg: Nauka sbornik statei muzeia antropologii i etnografii. Pagination taken from the original article

Jenkins, Michael. 1972. Trade Beads in Alaska. *The Alaska Journal* 2, no. 3 (summer):31-9

—. 1975. Glass Trade Beads in Alaska. *The Bead Journal* (Summer):23-6

Jenness, Diamond. 1922. *The Life of the Copper Eskimos.* Vol 12. *Report of the Canadian Arctic Expedition 1913-18.* Ottawa: King's Printer

—. 1946. *Material Culture of the Copper Eskimo.* Vol 16. *Report of the Canadian Arctic Expedition 1913-18.* Ottawa: King's Printer

—. 1959. *The People of the Twilight.* New York: Macmillan 1928. Reprint, Chicago: University of Chicago Press

Jochelson, Waldemar. 1926. The Yukaghir and the Yukaghirized Tungus. *The Jesup North Pacific Expedition 9, Memoirs of the American Museum of Natural History.* Leiden: E.J. Brill, New York: G.E. Stechert 1926. Reprint, New York: AMS Press 1975

Jolles, Carol Zane. 1994. Cutting Meat, Sewing Skins, Telling Tales: Women's Stories in Gambell, Alaska. *Arctic Anthropology* 31, no. 1:86-102

Jomppanen, Karen. 1982. *Lapin Kasitoita. Sami Kiehtatuoiik.* Helsinki: Werner Soderstrom Osakeyhtio

Jones, H.G. 1996. Christian Klengenberg and the Opening of Trade with the Copper Inuit. *Études/Inuit/Studies* 20, no. 2:101-8

Jorgensen, Kirsten. 1974. *Making Leather Clothes.* Cincinnati: Van Nostrand Reinhold

Kaalund, Bodil. 1984. *The Art of Greenland: Sculpture, Crafts, Painting.* Translated by Kenneth Tindall. Berkeley: University of California

Press. Originally published as *Grønlands kunst: Skulptur, brugskunst, maleri* (Copenhagen: Politiken 1979)

Kalaallit Nunaata Katersugaasivia. n.d. *Qilakitsoq*. Nuuk: Grønlands Landsmuseum

Karetak, Rhoda. 1982. Preparing Wildlife for Use. *Inuktitut* 50 (May):58-66

Karklins, Karlis. 1985. *Glass Beads. The Levin Catalogue of Mid-19th Century Beads. A Sample Book of 19th Century Venetian Beads. Guide to the Description and Classification of Glass Beads.* Ottawa: National Historic Parks and Sites Branch, Parks Canada

—. 1992. *Trade Ornament Usage among the Native Peoples of Canada. A Source Book.* Studies in Archaeology, Architecture and History. Ottawa: National Historic Sites, Parks Service, Environment Canada

—. 1993. Tungatsivvik (KkDo-3) Bead Analysis. Unpublished Report to Arctic College, Iqaluit, NWT

Kasudluak, Peter. 1995. Seasons on the Hudson Bay Coast. *Tumivut* 7 (Autumn):24-7

Kelsall, John P. 1968. *The Migratory Barren-Ground Caribou of Canada.* Ottawa: Department of Indian Affairs and Northern Development

Kemp, William B. 1984. Baffinland Eskimo. In *Arctic*, edited by David Damas, 463-75. Vol. 5 of *Handbook of North American Indians.* Washington, DC: Smithsonian Institution

Krupnik, Igor I. 1994. Interaction et changement dans l'univers inuit: Introduction. (Change, interaction and the Inuit universe: Introduction). *Études/Inuit/Studies* 18, nos. 1-2:21-47

Kuujjuaq Research Centre. n.d. *Mitiq. The Ecology, Use and Management of the Common Eider in Northern Quebec.* Kuujjuaq and Montréal: Avataq Cultural Institute

Lahti, Brian. 1996. The Nunavutians Build a Bureaucracy. *Globe and Mail*, 4 May, A18

Lantis, Margaret. 1946. The Social Culture of the Nunivak Eskimo. *Transactions of the American Philosophical Society* n.s. 35, no. 3:153-323

—. 1984. Nunivak Eskimo. In *Arctic*, edited by David Damas, 209-23. Vol. 5 of *Handbook of North American Indians.* Washington, DC: Smithsonian Institution

Lee, Molly. 1995. Siberian Sources of Alaska Eskimo Coiled Basketry. *American Indian Art Magazine* 20, no. 4 (autumn):56-69

Le Mouël, Jean-François. 1973. Préparation et utilisation des peaux de phoques chez les Eskimos Naujamiut. In *L'Homme, hier et aujourd'hui*, 173-92. Paris: Éditions Cujas

—. 1978. *'ceux des mouettes': Les Eskimo naujamiut, Groenland-Ouest.* Mémoires de l'Institut d'Ethnologie no. 16. Paris: Musée de l'Homme

Leroi-Gourhan, André. 1946. *Archéologie du Pacifique-Nord: Matériaux pour l'étude des relations entre les peuples riveraine d'Asie et d'Amérique [and Greenland].* Paris: Institut d'Ethnologie, Musée de l'Homme

Levin, M.G., and L.P. Potapov, eds. 1961. *Istoriko-etnograficheskii atlas Sibiri.* Moscow: Institut etnografii an SSSR

—. 1964. *The Peoples of Siberia.* Translated by Stephen Dunn. Chicago: University of Chicago Press. Originally published as *Narody Sibiri* (Moscow: Russian Academy of Science 1956)

Lindbergh, Anne Morrow. 1935. *North to the Orient.* New York: Harcourt, Brace and Company

Linton, George E. 1954. *The Modern Textile and Apparel Dictionary.* Plainfield, NJ: Textile Book Service

Lobdell, John, and Albert A. Dekin, eds. 1984. The Frozen Family from the Utqiagvik Site, Barrow, Alaska: Papers from a Symposium. *Arctic Anthropology* 21, no. 1

Low, Albert P. 1906. *Report on the Dominion Government Expedition to Hudson Bay and the Arctic Islands on the D.G.S. Neptune 1903-1904.* Ottawa: Government Printing Bureau

Lyon, George F. 1824. *The Private Journal of Captain G.F. Lyon of H.M.S. Hecla during the Recent voyage of Discovery under Captain Parry.* London: John Murray

McCullough, Karen M. 1989. *The Ruin Islanders: Thule Culture Pioneers in the Eastern High Arctic.* Mercury Series Paper no. 141, Archaeological Survey of Canada. Ottawa: Canadian Museum of Civilization

MacDonald, John. 1993. Tauvijjuaq: The Great Darkness. *Inuit Art Quarterly* 8, no. 2:18-25

McElhone, John P. 1984a. Inuit Rawhide Clothing. Paper prepared for Art Conservation Program, Queen's University, Kingston, Ontario

—. 1984b. The Composite Tools of the Inuit: Strategies for Their Conservation in Museums. Paper prepared for Art Conservation Program seminar, Queen's University, Kingston, Ontario

McGhee, Robert. 1972. *Copper Eskimo Prehistory.* Publications in Archaeology no. 2. Ottawa: National Museums of Canada

—. 1974. *Beluga Hunters: An Archaeological Reconstruction of the History and Culture of the Mackenzie Delta Kittegaryumiut.* Newfoundland Social and Economic Studies no. 13. St. John's: Institute of Social and Economic Research, Memorial University of Newfoundland

—. 1978. *Canadian Arctic Prehistory.* Toronto: Van Nostrand Reinhold

—. 1979. *The Palaeoeskimo Occupations of Port Refuge, High Arctic Canada.* Mercury Series, Archaeological Survey of Canada Paper no. 92. Ottawa: National Museum of Man

—. 1981a. *The Tuniit. First Explorers of the High Arctic.* Ottawa: Archaeological Survey of Canada, National Museum of Man

—. 1981b. *The Dorset Occupations in the Vicinity of Port Refuge, High Arctic Canada.* Mercury Series, Archaeological Survey of Canada Paper no. 104. Ottawa: National Museum of Man

—. 1983. Eskimo Prehistory. In *Arctic Life: Challenge to Survive*, edited by Martina Magenau Jacobs and James B. Richardson III, 73–93. Pittsburgh: Carnegie Museum of Natural History, Carnegie Institute

—. 1984. Thule Prehistory of Canada. In *Arctic*, edited by David Damas, 369-76. Vol. 5 of *Handbook of North American Indians.* Washington, DC: Smithsonian Institution

—. 1987. Peopling the Arctic. In *Historical Atlas of Canada.* Vol. 1. *From the Beginning to 1800*, edited by R. Cole Harris, plate 11. Toronto: University of Toronto Press

—. 1992. Northern Approaches. Before Columbus: Early European Visitors to the Shores of the 'New World.' *The Beaver* 72, no. 3 (June-July):6-23

McGrath, Judy. 1977. *Dyes from Lichens and Plants.* Toronto: Van Nostrand Reinhold

—. 1980. Revival of the Labrador Inuit Scene c. 1700. Translated by Bertha Kairtok. *Them Days* 5, no. 4:25-40

—. 1992. Stone to Steel: A History of the Ulu. Unpublished Report to Department of Economic Development and Tourism, Government of the Northwest Territories, Yellowknife

McGrath, Judy, and Doris Saunders, eds. 1979. *Grass Work of Labrador.* Catalogue of exhibition of same name, sponsored by Art Gallery of Memorial University, the Newfoundland Museum, and *Them Days* magazine. St. John's Art Gallery, Memorial University of Newfoundland

Manker, Ernst. 1962. *The Lapps. Guide to the Exhibits in Nordiska Museet and Skansen Open-Air Museum.* Stockholm: Malung

Manning, T.H., and E.W. Manning. 1944. The Preparation of Skins and Clothing in the Eastern Canadian Arctic. *Polar Record* 4, no. 28:156-69

Marsh, Winifred Petchey. 1976. *People of the Willow: The Padlimiut Tribe of the Caribou Eskimo.* Toronto: Oxford University Press

—. 1987. *Echoes from a Frozen Land.* Edmonton: Hurtig

Martin, Laurence. 1986. Tears Flow as Inuk Meets Soviet Kin. *Globe and Mail*, 7 June, p. B8

Mary-Rousselière, Guy. 1984. Iglulik. In *Arctic*, edited by David Damas, 431-46. Vol. 5 of *Handbook of North American Indians.* Washington, DC: Smithsonian Institution

Mason, Otis. 1891. The Ulu or Woman's Knife of the Eskimos. *Annual Report of the United States National Museum for 1890*, 411-16 and Plates 52-72. Washington, DC: Smithsonian Institution

Mathiassen, Therkel. 1927. *Archaeology of the Central Eskimos: Report of the Fifth Thule Expedition 1921-24.* Vol. 4, Pts. 1-2. Copenhagen: Gyldendalske

—. 1928. *Material Culture of the Iglulik Eskimo: Report of the Fifth Thule Expedition 1921-24.* Vol. 6, Pt. 1. Copenhagen: Gyldendalske

Maxwell, Moreau S. 1960. *An Archaeological Analysis of Eastern Grant Land, Ellesmere Island, Northwest Territories.* Anthropological Series no. 49, National Museums of Canada Bulletin 170. Ottawa: National Museum of Man

—. 1973. *Archaeology of the Lake Harbour District, Baffin Island.* Mercury

Series, Archaeological Survey of Canada Paper no. 6. Ottawa: National Museum of Man

—. 1984. Pre-Dorset and Dorset Prehistory of Canada. In *Arctic*, edited by David Damas, 359-68. Vol. 5 of *Handbook of North American Indians*. Washington, DC: Smithsonian Institution

—. 1985. *Prehistory of the Eastern Arctic*. Orlando, FL: Academic Press

Meade, Marie. 1990. Sewing to Maintain the Past, Present and Future. *Études/Inuit/Studies* 14, no. 1-2:229-39

Meldgaard, Jorgen. 1980. Ethnographic Objects in the Royal Danish Kunstkammer. In *Grønland/ Greenland*, edited by B. Dam-Mikkelson and T. Lundbaek, 1-16. Ethnographical Series no. 17. Copenhagen: Publications of the National Museum

Menovshchikov, G.A., and A.B. Shnakenburg. 1964. The Eskimos. In *The Peoples of Siberia*, edited by M.G. Levin and L.P. Potapov, 836-50. Translated by Stephen Dunn. Chicago: University of Chicago Press. Originally published as *Narody Sibiri* (Moscow: Russian Academy of Science 1956)

Merbs, Charles F. 1983. *Patterns of Activity-Induced Pathology in a Canadian Inuit Population*. Archaeological Survey of Canada Paper no. 119. Ottawa: National Museum of Man

Merkur, Daniel. 1992. *Becoming Half Hidden: Shamanism and Initiation among the Inuit*. 2nd ed. New York and London: Garland Publishing

Michael, Henry N. 1984. Absolute Chronologies of the Late Pleistocene and Early Holocene of Northeastern Asia. *Arctic Anthropology* 21, no. 2:1-66

Mirsky, Stephen D. 1988. Solar Polar Bears. *Scientific American* (March):24, 26

Mitchell, Eric, and Frans Van de Velde. 1981. *Canadian Inuit Artifacts*. Ottawa: Canadian Arctic Producers Cooperative

Mitlyanskaya, T.B. 1983. *Sel'skomu Uchitelyu o Narodnikh Khudozhestvennykh Remeslakh Sibiri i Dal'nego Vostoka* (Handbook for rural teachers of national arts and crafts of Siberia and the Far East). Moscow: Proveshchenie

Mobjerg, Tinna, and Kirsten Caning. 1986. Sermermiut in the Middle of the Nineteenth Century. *Arctic Anthropology* 23, nos. 1-2:177-98

Møller, G. 1989. Eskimo Clothing from Qilakitsoq. In *The Mummies from Qilakitsoq – Eskimos in the 15th Century*, edited by J.P.H. Hansen and H.C. Gulløv, 23-46. Man and Society no. 12. Copenhagen: Meddelelser om Grønland

Morrison, David. 1990. *Iqlulualumiut Prehistory: The Last Inuit of Franklin Bay, NWT*. Hull, PQ: Canadian Museum of Civilization

—. 1991. The Copper Inuit Soapstone Trade. *Arctic* 44, no. 3:239-46

—. 1992. *Arctic Hunters. The Inuit and Diamond Jenness*. Hull, PQ: Canadian Museum of Civilization

Morrison, Lynn. 1986. The Conservation of Seal Gut Parkas. *The Conservator* 10:17

Morrow, Phyllis. 1984. It Is Time for Drumming: A Summary of Recent Research on Yup'ik Ceremonialism. *Études/Inuit/Studies* 8, supplementary issue:113-40

Müller-Wille, Ludger. 1994. *Série de cartes toponymiques inuit*. Montréal: Institut culturel Avataq, Relevés de noms indigènes et Département de géographie de l'Université McGill

Müller-Wille, Ludger, and Avataq Cultural Institute, eds. 1991. *Nunavik: Inuit Place Name Map Series*. Inukjuaq, Nunavik: Avataq Cultural Institute

Mundkur, Balaji. 1984. The Bicephalous 'Animal Style' in Northern Eurasian Religious Art and Its Western Hemispheric Analogues. *Current Anthropology* 25, no. 4:451-82

Murdoch, John. 1892. Ethnological Results of the Point Barrow Expedition 1881-1883. In *Ninth Annual Report of the Bureau of Ethnology 1887-1888*, 19-441. Washington, DC: Smithsonian Institution

Murray, Paul E. 1988. Recollections of an Eskimo Triumph, A Cultural Analysis. *Anthropos* 83:153-9

Museum Ethnographers Group. 1986. *Survey of Ethnographic Collections in the United Kingdom, Eire, and the Channel Islands (Interim Report)*, edited by Y. Schumann. 2 vols. Occasional Paper Series no. 2. London and Oxford: Museum Ethnographers Group

Myers, Marybelle, ed. 1980. *Things Made by Inuit*. Baie d'Urfé, PQ: Fédération des Coopératives du Nouveau-Québec

Nastapoka, Abraham. 1995. How the Tuulliik [Loons] Cured the Blind Man. *Tumiuut* 6:21-22

National Museum of Denmark. 1955. *Arctic Peoples and American Indians. Guides to the National Museum*. Copenhagen: National Museum of Denmark

Nelson, Edward William. 1983. The Eskimo about Bering Strait. In *Eighteenth Annual Report of the Bureau of American Ethnology, 1896-1897*, 3-518. Washington, DC: Smithsonian Institution 1899. Reprint, Smithsonian Institution Press

Nilsson, Marianne. 1977. Pa jakt efter drakttraditioner (Saami dress and traditions). *Västerbotten* 3:199-201

Niviaxie, Davidie. 1995. A Survival Manual. Falling through the Ice. *Tumivut* 7 (Autumn):16-17

Nooter, G.W. 1984. *Life and Survival in the Arctic. Cultural Changes in Polar Regions*. The Hague: Government Publishing Office

Nordic Arts Centre, eds. 1981. *Sámi Art*. Helsinki: Nordic Arts Centre

Northern Quebec Inuit Association. 1972. *Taqramiut / The Northerners / Les septentrionaux*. Quebec: Northern Quebec Inuit Association

Nuligak. 1971. *I, Nuligak*, edited by M. Metayer. New York: Pocket Books

Nungak, Zebedee, ed. 1983. *Northern Quebec Inuit Elders Conference*. Inukjuaq: Avataq Cultural Institute

Nungak, Zebedee, and Eugene Arima. 1969. *Eskimo Stories. Unikkaatuat*. Bulletin 235, Anthropological Series no. 90. Ottawa: National Museums of Canada

Oakes, Jill. 1987a. *Inuit Annuraangit: Our Clothes, a Travelling Exhibition of Inuit Clothing*. Edmonton: Thumb Prints

—. 1987b. *Factors Influencing Kamik Production in Arctic Bay*. Mercury Series Paper no. 107. Hull, PQ: Canadian Museum of Civilization, Canadian Ethnology Service

—. 1988. Pattern Development in Eskimo Point, NWT. *Student Research in Canada's North / Les recherches des étudiants dans le Nord canadien*, 560-4. Hull, PQ: Association of Canadian Universities for Northern Studies

—. 1991. *Copper and Caribou Inuit Skin Clothing Production*. Mercury Series Paper no. 118. Hull, PQ: Canadian Museum of Civilization, Canadian Ethnology Service

—. 1992. Eider Skin Garments Used by the Ungava Inuit from the Belcher Islands, Northwest Territories: Construction and Context. *Clothing and Textiles Research Journal* 10, no. 2:1-10

Oakes, Jill, and Sally Karetak. 1987. Arctic Jewels: The Traditional Inuit Parka. *Northwest Explorer* 6, no. 2:16-21

Oakes, Jill, and Rick Riewe. 1995. *Our Boots: An Inuit Women's Art*. Vancouver: Douglas and McIntyre

Okladnikov, A.P. 1941. Paleolitich-eskaya statuetkaiz Bureti raskopki 1936g (A palaeolithic statuette from Buret: Excavations of 1936). *Materialy i issledovaniya po arkheologii* 2:104-9

—. 1964. Ancient Population of Siberia and Its Culture. In *The Peoples of Siberia*, edited by M.G. Levin and L.P. Potapov, 13-95. Translated by Stephen Dunn. Chicago: University of Chicago Press. Originally published as *Narody Sibiri* (Moscow: Russian Academy of Science 1956)

—. 1970. *Yakutia before Its Incorporation into the Russian State*, edited by Henry N. Michael for the Arctic Institute of North America. Montréal: McGill-Queen's University Press

Olearius, Adam. 1656. Vermehrte Newe Beschribung der muscowitischen und persischen Reyse. Chapter 4 of *Von den Grünländern*, 163-79. Schleswig: n.p.

Onalik, Jimi Doupont. 1995. Profile on Youth. *Uqausiksat* 2, no. 1 (March-June):22

Oosten, Jarich. 1981. The Structure of the Shamanistic Complex among the Netsilik and Iglulik. *Études/ Inuit/Studies* 5, no. 1:83-98

—. 1986. Male and Female in Inuit Shamanism. *Études/Inuit/Studies* 10, no. 1-2:115-31

—. 1992a. The Efficacy of Amulets among the Inuit of Northeast Canada. Paper presented to the First International Congress of Arctic Social Sciences, Université Laval, Ste-Foy, PQ, 25-31 October

—. 1992b. Representing the Spirits: The Masks of the Alaskan Inuit. In *Anthropology, Art and Aesthetics*, edited by Jeremy Coote and Anthony Shelton, 113-34. Oxford: Clarendon Press

—. 1997. Amulets, Shamanic Clothes and Paraphernalia in Inuit Culture. In *Braving the Cold: Change and Continuity in Arctic Clothing*, edited by Cunera Buijs and Jarich

Oosten, 105-30. Leiden: Centre for Non-Western Studies, Leiden University

Orchard, William C. 1975. *Beads and Beadwork of the American Indians.* 2nd ed. New York: Contributions from the Museum of the American Indian, Vol. II, Heye Foundation

Parry, William Edward. 1824. *Journal of a Second Voyage for the Discovery of a North West Passage, 1821-1823, in His Majesty's Ships Hecla and Fury.* London: John Murray

Pedersen, P.O., and Jan Jakobsen. 1989. Teeth and Jaws of the Qilakitsoq Mummies. In *The Mummies of Qilakitsoq – Eskimos in the 15th Century,* edited by J.P.H. Hansen and H.C. Gulløv, 112-30. Man and Society no. 12. Copenhagen: Meddelelser om Grønland

Petitot, Emile Fortuné. 1981. *Among the Chiglit Eskimos.* Edmonton: Boreal Institute for Northern Studies, Occasional Publication no. 10. Translation by E. Otto Höhn of *Les Grands Esquimaux.* Paris: E. Plon, Nourrit 1887

Pharand, Sylvie. 1971a. Notes d'observations aux Iles Belcher. Unpublished ms., Département d'anthropologie, Université Laval, Ste-Foy, PQ

—. 1971b. Accession papers for the birdskin clothing. Musée de la civilisation, Quebec City. Archives des collections, Musée de la civilisation

—. 1974. *Clothing of the Iglulik Inuit.* Research report, Canadian Ethnology Service. Ottawa: National Museums of Canada

—. 1975. Le vêtement des Inuit Iglulik. MA thesis, Université Laval, Ste-Foy, PQ

Pokiak, Bertram. 1989. Tuktoyaktuk Memories. *Inuktitut* 70:36-44

Popov, Andrei A. Nganasany. 1948. *Material'naia kul'tura.* Moscow and St. Petersburg: Nauka

Porsild, Morton P. 1915. Studies on the Material Culture of the Eskimo in West Greenland. *Meddelelser om Grønland* 51:113-250

Prokof'eva, E.D. 1971. Shamanskie Kostiumy narodov Sibiri. (Shamanistic costumes of the peoples of Siberia). *Sbornik Muzeia Antropologii i Etnografii* 27:5-100

Prytkova, N.F. 1952. Tipy verkhney odezhdy narodov Sibiri (Types of upper garments of the peoples of Siberia). *Akademiya nauk SSSR* 15:19-22

—. 1976. Odezhda chukchei, koriakov i itel'menov (Chukchi, Koryak and Itelman clothing). In *Material'naia kul'tura narodov Sibiri i severa* (Material culture of the peoples of Siberia and the North), 5-88. St. Petersburg: Nauka. Pagination refers to original work in Russian. (Indian and Northern Affairs Canada translation)

Rainey, Froelich G. 1941. The Ipiutak Culture at Point Hope, Alaska. *American Anthropologist* 43, no. 3:364-75

—. 1947. The Whale Hunters of Tigara. *Anthropological Papers of the American Museum of Natural History* 41, no. 2:231-483

Rankin, Catherine, and Yves Labrèche. 1991. Traditional Ulus and Their Prehistoric Counterparts in the Central and Eastern Arctic. *Études/Inuit/Studies* 15, no. 1:105-30

Rasmussen, Knud. 1929. *Intellectual Culture of the Iglulik Eskimos: Report of the Fifth Thule Expedition 1921-24.* Vol. 7, Pt. 1. Copenhagen: Gyldendalske

—. 1930. *Intellectual Culture of the Caribou Eskimos: Report of the Fifth Thule Expedition 1921-24.* Vol. 7, Pt. 2. Copenhagen: Gyldendalske

—. 1931. *The Netsilik Eskimos: Report of the Fifth Thule Expedition 1921-24.* Vol. 8, Pts. 1-2. Copenhagen: Gyldendalske

—. 1932. *The Intellectual Culture of the Copper Eskimos: Report of the Fifth Thule Expedition 1921-24.* Vol. 9. Copenhagen: Gyldendalske

Ray, Dorothy Jean. 1959. The Eskimo Raincoat. *The Alaska Sportsman* (November):3, 44

—, ed. 1966. The Eskimo of St. Michael and Vicinity as Related by H.M.W. Edmonds in 1899. *Anthropological Papers of the University of Alaska* 13, no. 2

—. 1975. *Eskimo Masks: Art and Ceremony.* Seattle: University of Washington Press

—. 1981. *Aleut and Eskimo Art and Innovation in South Alaska.* Seattle: University of Washington Press

Richling, Barnett. 1980. Images of the 'Heathen' in Northern Labrador. *Études/Inuit/Studies* 4, no. 1-2:233-42

Riewe, Roderick. 1975. A Lesson on Winter Survival from the Inuit. *Manitoba Nature* (Winter):24-33

Rigby, Bruce, and Douglas Stenton. 1992. Renewing the Cultural Spirit: Inuit Study Their Past Alongside Southern Archaeologists. *Arctic Circle* 2, no. 5 (March-April):34-6

Rix, Lotte. 1979. *Grønlandske Skinddragter.* Nationalmuseet Working Papers no. 11. Copenhagen: National Museum of Denmark

Robert-Lamblin, Joëlle. 1993. Socio-Demographic Situation of the Yuit and Inuit Eskimos and Chukchis of Chukotka. *Études/Inuit/Studies* 17, no. 2:73-96

Rosing, Jens. 1981. The Loon. *Folk* 23:151-60

—. 1986. *The Sky Hangs Low.* Translated by Naomi Jackson Groves. Kapuskasing, ON: Penumbra Press. Originally published as *Himlen er lav* (Arhus, Denmark: Wormianum 1979)

Ross, W. Gillies. 1975. *Whaling and Eskimos: Hudson Bay 1860-1915.* Publications in Ethnology no. 10. Ottawa: National Museum of Man

Rowley, Susan. 1985. Population Movements in the Canadian Arctic. *Études/Inuit/Studies* 9, no. 1:3-21

Saladin d'Anglure, Bernard. 1967. *L'organisation sociale traditionelle des Esquimaux de Kangirsujuaq, Nouveau-Québec: Travaux divers.* Québec: Université Laval, Centre d'études nordiques

—. 1983. Ijiqqat: Voyage au pays de l'invisible Inuit. *Études/Inuit/Studies* 7, no. 1:67-83

—. 1984. The Inuit of Quebec. In *Arctic,* edited by David Damas, 476-507. Vol. 5 of *Handbook of North American Indians.* Washington, DC: Smithsonian Institution

—. 1986. Rêve, transe, et chamanism: Au coeur du troisième sexe inuit dans l'arctique central canadien. Paper presented at the Fifth Inuit Studies Conference, McGill University, Montréal, 6-9 November

Saladin d'Anglure, Bernard, ed., with Michael Mautaritnaaq and Johanne Mark. 1979. *Tuktuit mitsaanut.* Ste-Foy, PQ: Association Inuksiutiit Katimajiit, Université Laval

Saunders, Doris. 1986. Expositions and Epidemics. *Them Days* 12, no. 1:3-19

Savel'eva, I. 1967. Narodnyi kostium: forma i funktsiia (Folk dress: design and function). *Dekorativnoe iskusstvo* 10:31-5

Schledermann, Peter. 1981. Eskimo and Viking Finds in the High Arctic. *National Geographic* 159, no. 5:574-601

Schledermann, Peter, and Karen McCullough. 1980. Western Elements in the Early Thule Culture of the Eastern High Arctic. *Arctic* 33, no. 4:833-41

Schuster, Carl. 1951. Joint Marks: A Possible Index of Cultural Contact between America, Oceania, and the Far East. Amsterdam: *Uitgave Koninklijk Instituut Voor de Tropen (Royal Tropical Institute)* 94, no. 39:2-51

—. 1964. Skin and Fur Mosaics in Prehistoric and Modern Times. In *Festscrift für Adolf E. Jensen,* 559-610. Munich: K. Renner

—. 1967. A Survival of the Eurasiatic Animal Style in Modern Alaskan Eskimo Art. In *Selected Papers of the 29th International Congress of Americanists,* edited by Sol Tax, 35-45. New York: Cooper Square

Schwartz, Fred H. 1976. Inuit Land Use in Hudson Bay and James Bay. In Vol. 1 of *Report: Inuit Land Use and Occupancy Project,* edited by Milton M.R. Freeman, 115-20. Ottawa: Department of Indian Affairs and Northern Development

Schwatka, Frederick. 1884. The Netschilluk Innuits. *Science* 4, no. 98:543-5

Schweger, Barbara F. 1983a. Documentation and Analysis of the Clothing Worn by Non-Native Man in the Canadian Arctic prior to 1920 with an Emphasis on Footwear. MSc thesis, University of Alberta, Edmonton

—. 1983b. Clothing the Early Expeditions: An Essential Contribution by the Native Seamstresses. Paper presented at the Yukon Historical and Museums Association, MacBride Museum, Whitehorse, Yukon, 15 November

Segal, Martha, and Charlotte Newton. 1990. The Conservation of Archaeological Skin Artifacts from the Canadian Arctic. *Journal of the International Institute for Conservation Canadian Group* 15:23-30

Serov, S.I. 1988. Guardians and Spirit-Masters of Siberia. In *Crossroads of Continents: Cultures of Siberia and Alaska,* edited by W. Fitzhugh and A. Crowell, 241-55. Washington, DC: Smithsonian Institution Press

Shnirelman, Victor A. 1994. Hostages of an Authoritarian Regime: The Fate of the 'Numerically-Small Peoples' of the Russian North under Soviet Rule. *Études/Inuit/Studies* 18, nos. 1-2:201-23

Simchenko, I.B. 1963a. Nganasanskie

ornamenty (Nganasan ornamentation). *Sovetskaya etnografiia* 3:166-71

—. 1963b. Prazdnik Any'o-dialy u Avamshikh Nganasan (The Any'o-dialy feast of the Avam River Nganasans). *Akademiia nauk SSSR. Instutii etnografii Trudy* n.s. 84:168-79

Smith, Derek G. 1984. Mackenzie Delta Eskimo. In *Arctic*, edited by David Damas, 347-58. Vol. 5 of *Handbook of North American Indians*. Washington, DC: Smithsonian Institution

Smith, Dorothy, and Leslie Spier. 1927. The Dot and Circle Design in Northwestern America. *Journal de la Société des Américanistes de Paris* n.s. 19:47-55

Smith, George, and Michael R. Zimmerman. 1975. Tattooing Found on a 1600 Year Old Frozen Mummified Body from St. Lawrence Island, Alaska. *American Antiquity* 40, no. 4:433-7

Smithsonian Institution. 1993. Ethnography at the Center. *Arctic Studies Center Newsletter* 2:8-9

Smolyak, A.V. 1984. *Traditional Economic and Material Culture of the Peoples of the Lower Amur and Sakhalin*. Moscow: Nauka

Speck, Frank Gould. 1914. *The Double Curve Motive in Northeastern Algonkian Art*. Geological Survey Memoir 42, Anthropological Series no. 1. Ottawa: Canada Department of Mines

—. 1924a. Eskimo Collection from Baffin Land and Ellesmere Land. *Indian Notes* 1, no. 3:143-9

—. 1924b. Collections from Labrador Eskimo. *Indian Notes* 1, no. 4:211-17

—. 1925. Central Eskimo and Indian Dot Ornamentation. *Indian Notes* 2, no. 3:151-72

—. 1935. Labrador Eskimo Mask and Clown. *The General Magazine and Historical Chronicle* 37, no. 2:159-73

—. 1937. Analysis of Eskimo and Indian Skin-Dressing Methods in Labrador. *Ethnos* 2, no. 6:345-53

—. 1940. Eskimo Jacket Ornaments of Ivory Suggesting Function of Bone Pendants Found in Beothuk Sites in Newfoundland. *American Antiquity* 5, no. 3:225-8

Sproull, Jane. 1977. Towards a Definition of Styles and Patterns in Thule Decorative Art. MA thesis, Carleton University, Ottawa

Stefansson, Vilhjalmur. 1909. The Eskimo Trade Jargon of Herschel Island. *American Anthropologist* n.s. 11, no. 2:217-32

—. 1911. Food and Clothing of the Copper and Mackenzie Eskimo. Field notebook dated 31 December, Stefansson Collection, Dartmouth College Library, Hanover, NH

—. 1913. *My Life with the Eskimo*. New York: Macmillan

—. 1914. The Stefansson-Anderson Arctic Expedition: A Preliminary Ethnological Report. *Anthropological Papers of the American Museum of Natural History* 14, Part 1

—. 1945. *Arctic Manual*. Prepared under the direction of the Chief of the Air Corps, US Army. New York: Macmillan

—. 1949. Cold Weather Clothing. Unpublished ms, Stefansson Collection, Dartmouth College Library, Hanover, NH

—. 1958. Clothes Make the Eskimo. In *The Experience of Writing*, edited by W.D. Baker and T.D. Strandness, 41-8. Englewood Cliffs, NJ: Prentice-Hall

Steltzer, Ulli. 1985. *Inuit: The North in Transition*. Chicago: University of Chicago Press

Stenton, Douglas. 1991a. The Adaptive Significance of Caribou Winter Clothing for Arctic Hunter-Gatherers. *Études/Inuit/Studies* 15, no. 1:3-28

—. 1991b. Caribou Population Dynamics and Thule Culture: Adaptations on Southern Baffin Island, NWT. *Arctic Anthropology* 28, no. 2:15-43

Stenton, Douglas R., and Bruce G. Rigby. 1995. Community-Based Heritage Education, Training and Research: Preliminary Report on the Tungatsivvik Archaeological Project. *Arctic* 48, no. 1:47-56

Stewart, Henry. 1989. The Arctic Small Tool Tradition and Early Canadian Arctic Palaeo-Eskimo Cultures. *Études/Inuit/Studies* 13, no. 2:69-101

Story, C.M., W.J. Kirwin, and J.D.A. Widdowson. 1982. *Dictionary of Newfoundland English*. Toronto: University of Toronto Press

Strickler, Eva, and Anaoyok Alookee. 1988. *Inuit Dolls: Reminders of a Heritage*. Toronto: Canadian Stage and Arts Publications

Sturtevant, William C. 1976. First Visual Images of Native America. In *First Images of America: The Impact of the New World on the Old*, edited by Fredi Chiappelli, 417-57. Berkeley: University of California Press

—. 1980. The First Inuit Depiction by Europeans. *Études/Inuit/Studies* 4, no. 1-2:47-9

Sutton, George Miksch. 1934. *Eskimo Year*. New York: Macmillan

Sverdrup, Harald U. 1978. *Among the Tundra People*. Translated by Molly Sverdrup. La Jolla, CA: Scripps Institute of Oceanography. Originally published as *Hos Tundra-Folket* (Oslo: Gyldendal Norsk Forlag 1938)

Svensson, Tom G. 1992. Clothing in the Arctic: A Means of Protection, a Statement of Identity. *Arctic* 45, no. 1:62-73

Swann, June. 1982. *Shoes*. London: B.T. Batsford

Taylor, Helga R. 1978. Source Materials for a Reconstruction of Traditional Labrador Inuit Clothing. Unpublished report prepared for the Newfoundland Museum, St. John's

Taylor, J. Garth. 1969-70. Inventory of Eskimo Ethnological Collections from the Canadian Eastern Arctic based on a Survey of Museum Collections in the United States and the United Kingdom. Unpublished Report to the National Museums of Canada, Ottawa

—. 1974a. *Netsilik Eskimo Material Culture: The Roald Amundsen Collection from King William Island 1903-1905*. Oslo: Norwegian Research Council for Science and the Humanities

—. 1974b. *Labrador Eskimo Settlements of the Early Contact Period*. Publications in Ethnology no. 9. Ottawa: National Museum of Man

—. 1979. Inuit Whaling Technology in Eastern Canada and Greenland. In *Thule Eskimo Culture: An Archaeological Retrospective*, edited by Allen P. McCartney, 267-77. Mercury Series, Archaeological Survey Paper no. 88. Ottawa: National Museum of Man

—. 1983-4. The Two Worlds of Mikkak. Parts 1 and 2. *The Beaver* 314, no. 3 (Winter):4-13; 314, no. 4 (Spring): 18-25

—. 1984. Historical Ethnography of the Labrador Coast. In *Arctic*, edited by David Damas, 508-21. Vol. 5 of *Handbook of North American Indians*. Washington, DC: Smithsonian Institution

—. 1985. The Arctic Whale Cult in Labrador. *Études/Inuit/Studies* 9, no. 2:121-32

Taylor, William E., Jr. 1971-2. Found Art and Frozen. *artscanada* (December-January):32-47

Taylor, William E., Jr., and George Swinton. 1967. Prehistoric Dorset Art. *The Beaver* 298:32-47

Tein, Tassan S. 1994. Shamans of the Siberian Eskimos. Translated and introduced by Dimitri B. Shimkin. *Arctic Anthropology* 31, no. 1:117-25

Thomson, Callum. 1985. Dorset Shamanism: Excavations in Northern Labrador. *Expedition* 27, no. 1:37-49

Torngak, Agatha. 1973. Ugjugaviniq. La peau de phoque barbu. *Inummarit* 1:22-6

Trudel, François. 1989. Les Inuit de l'est de la Baie d'Hudson et la traite à Fort George (1837-1851). *Études/Inuit/Studies* 13, no. 2:3-32

Tuck, John, Jr. 1954. The Baffin Island Reindeer Experiment. Unpublished ms, Stefansson Collection, Dartmouth College Library, Hanover, NH

Turcy, Beth Louise. 1986. Traditional Kakligmiut Skin Clothing. MA thesis, State University of New York, Binghamton

Turner, Geoffrey. 1976. *Hair Embroidery in Siberia and North America*. Pitt Rivers Museum Occasional Papers on Technology no. 7. Oxford: Oxford University Press

Turner, Lucien M. 1886. *Contributions to the Natural History of Alaska*. Washington, DC: US Government Printing Office

—. 1979. *Ethnology of the Ungava District, Hudson Bay Territory. Indians and Eskimos in the Quebec-Labrador Peninsula*. Quebec City: Presses Comeditex with Association Inuksiutiit Katimajiit and Université Laval. Originally published as *11th Annual Report of the Bureau of American Ethnology for the Years 1889-1890*, 159-350 (Washington, DC: Smithsonian Institution 1894)

Ungalaaq, Martha Angugatiaq. 1973. Caribou Garments. *Inummarit* 2, no. 1:6

—. 1985. *Recollections of Martha Angugatiaq Ungalaaq*. Autobiography Series no. 1. Arviat, NWT: Inuit Cultural Institute

Vanast, Walter J. 1991. The Death of Jennie Kanajuq: Tuberculosis, Religious Competition and Cultural Conflict in Coppermine, 1929-31. *Études/Inuit/Studies* 15, no. 1:75-104

Van Deusen, Kira. 1997. Protection and Empowerment: Clothing Symbolism in the Amur River Region of the Russian Far East. In *Braving the*

Cold: Change and Continuity in Arctic Clothing, edited by Cunera Buijs and Jarich Oosten, 149-68. Leiden: Centre for Non-Western Studies, Leiden University

VanStone, James W. 1983. Protective Hide Armor of the Historic Chukchi and Siberian Eskimos. *Études/Inuit/Studies* 7, no. 2:3-24

—. 1984. Sealskin Bags of Unusual Construction from the Bering Strait Region. *Field Museum of Natural History Bulletin* 55, no. 2:23-6

—. 1985a. Ornamental Coats of the Koryak. *Field Museum of Natural History Bulletin* 56, no. 6:8-15

—. 1985b. An Ethnographic Collection from Northern Sakhalin Island. *Fieldiana: Anthropology* n.s. 8

—. 1989. Nunivak Island Eskimo (Yuit) Technology and Material Culture. *Fieldiana: Anthropology* n.s. 12

—. 1994. The Noice Collection of Copper Inuit Material Culture. *Fieldiana: Anthropology* n.s. 22

VanStone, James W., and Wendell H. Oswalt. 1959. The Caribou Eskimos of Eskimo Point. *Northern Coordination and Research Centre* NCRC 59-2. Ottawa: Department of Northern Affairs and Natural Resources

Vasilevich, G.M. 1963. Tipy obuvi narodov Sibiri. (Types of footgear of the peoples of Siberia). *Sbornik Muzeye antropologii i etnografii* 21:3-64

Vézinet, Monique. 1980. *Les Nunamiut, Inuit au Coeur des Terres.* Québec: Ministère des Affaires culturelles

Victor-Howe, Anne-Marie. 1994. Songs and Dances of the St. Lawrence Island Eskimos. *Études/Inuit/Studies* 18, nos. 1-2:173-82

Wakeham, William. 1898. *Report of the Expedition to Hudson Bay and Cumberland Gulf in the Steamship 'Diana.'* Ottawa: Queen's Printer

Ware, Dora, and Maureen Stafford. 1974. *An Illustrated Dictionary of Ornament.* New York: St. Martin's Press

Washburne, Heluiz Chandler, and Anauta Ford Blackmore. 1976. *Land of the Good Shadows: The Life Story of Anauta, an Eskimo Woman.* New York: John Day Company 1940. Reprint, New York: AMS Press 1976

Webber, Alika Podolinsky. 1989. *North American Indian and Eskimo Footwear: A Typology and Glossary.* Don Mills, ON: Bata Shoe Museum Foundation

Weetaltuk, John. 1981. Land. In *Paper Stays Put,* edited by Robin Gedalof, 41-3. Edmonton: Hurtig

Whitehead, G. Kenneth. 1972. *Deer of the World.* London: Constable and Company

Wilcox, R. Turner. 1969. *The Dictionary of Costume.* London: B.T. Batsford

Wilder, Edna. 1976. *Secrets of Eskimo Skin Clothing.* Anchorage: Alaska North-West Publishing

Will, George S., ed. 1971. *Inuit.* Winnipeg: Manitoba Museum of Man and Nature

Woodbury, Anthony C. 1984. Eskimo and Aleut Languages. In *Arctic,* edited by David Damas, 49-63. Vol. 5 of *Handbook of North American Indians.* Washington, DC: Smithsonian Institution

Woodbury, Robert L. 1968. Clothing, Its Evolution and Development by the Inhabitants of the Arctic. *Archives of Environmental Health, American Medical Association* 17, no. 10:586-91

Wright, J.V., and Roy L. Carlson. 1987. Prehistoric Trade. In *Historical Atlas of Canada*. Vol. 1. *From the Beginning to 1800,* edited by R. Cole Harris, plate 14. Toronto: University of Toronto Press

Zhornitskaya, Maria Y. 1983. *Narodnoye Choreograficheskoye Iskusstvo Korennogo Nasyelyeniya Severo-Vostoka Sibiri* (Choreographic art of the Native people of Northeast Siberia). Moscow: Nauka

—. 1990. Traditional and Modern Dances of the Eskimo Peoples of the USSR. Paper presented at the Seventh Inuit Studies Conference, University of Alaska, Fairbanks, 19-24 August

Zorgdrager, Nellejet. 1997. Saami Clothing and Saami Identity. In *Braving the Cold: Change and Continuity in Arctic Clothing*, edited by Cunera Buijs and Jarich Oosten, 131-48. Leiden: Centre for Non-Western Studies, Leiden University

Illustration credits

Photographs

In photographic captions, an object's given measurement is of its greatest dimension – height, length, or width – in centimetres. The following institutions have kindly granted permission for the images to be reproduced.

Arctic Studies Center, National Museum of Natural History, Smithsonian Institution, Washington, DC: p. 92, NMNH T-1676

Avataq Cultural Institute, Inukjuaq, Nunavik, and Lachine, PQ: p. 157, photograph by Marion Cirefice, 1990; p. 227, photograph by Steven Hendrie, 1992; p227, 1995

Bata Shoe Museum, Toronto: p. 81, P81.330.2, photograph by Ray Webber; p. 157, P82. 157AB; p. 186, photographs by Ray Webber, P82.132.2

Bibliothèque Nationale du Québec: p. 153, Bacqueville de la Potherie (1722, 1:81)

Boas (1964 [1888], 198): p. 207

British Library, London: p. 164, Department of Printed Books

British Museum, London: pp. 35, 85, and 215, photographs by J.C.H. King, 1986; p. 70, MM 025977; p. 126, Am19 11, 1986, Am10 14; p. 127, MM026945; p. 132, MM029549, photograph by J.C.H. King, 1986, p. 134, MM034003/33, photograph by Geraldine Moodie, 1908; p. 141, MM02582; p. 144, Department of Prints and Drawings, PS-131736, 199.a.3; p. 145, Department of Prints and Drawings, 40470

Canadian Guild of Crafts Quebec, Montréal: p. 67 (needles); p. 157, 1950

Canadian Museum of Civilization, Hull, PQ: pp. 12, RbJr-1:198c; p. 13, SgFm-4:312, photograph from Arctic Institute of North America; p. 13, IX-C:2626, photograph from the McCord Museum of Canadian History; p. 15; p. 16, IX-C:509; p. 17, IX-C:5271, TkAu-1:2, neg. no. 95-1067; p. 19, SfFk-4:510, photograph from the Arctic Institute of North America; p. 19, RBJR-1:993, RbJr-1:1000, RbJr-1:990, neg. no. 95-1084, photograph by Richard Garner; p. 46, IV-C:758; pp. 77, 78, and 80, photographs by Judy Hall, 1993; p. 105, 51439; p. 112, 38993, 38994, photographs by R.N. Anderson, 1916; p. 128, IV-C-3533, photograph by Serge Gilbert; p. 146, IV-C-5255a,b, photograph by Judy Hall; p. 189; p. 202, IV-D-2024; p. 211 (mitts and hat), IV-C-5139a,b, IV-C-5138; p. 231, IV-E-589

Canadian Museum of Contemporary Photography, Ottawa: p. 78, 64-4405, photograph by Gar Lunney, 1964

Department of Resources, Wildlife, and Economy, Government of the NWT, Baffin Region: p. vi, D0051; p. 129, D0078, photograph by Mike Beedell, 1987; p. 225, D0028, photograph by Brent Boddie, 1987

Eskimo Museum, Kuugjuaq, MB: p. 16, C58.2-1, photograph by Lorraine Brandson; p. 37, C59.23-2, photograph from the McCord Museum of Canadian History; p. 210, C58.1-3, photograph by Lorraine Brandson

Fédération des Coopératives du Nouveau-Québec, Baie d'Urfé, PQ: p. 86, photograph by Werner Zimmerman, 1979; p. 89, photograph by Optic Nerve, 1978; p. 156, photograph by Amy Yanagi, 1988, *Threads*, Taunton Press, Newtown, CT

Field Museum of Natural History, Chicago: pp. 236, 237, 32007

Glenbow Museum Archives, Calgary: p. 139, NA-2306-9, photograph by Geraldine Moodie, ca. 1915; p. 175, NC-1-6, photograph by Lomen Brothers

Greenland National Museum, Nuuk: pp. 21, 22, and 23, ED 28, ED 12, ED 4, and ED 3, photographs from the National Museum of Denmark by John Lee; pp. 33, 196, photographs from the McCord Museum of Canadian History

Indian and Northern Affairs Canada: p. 8, LH 20A88 2, photograph by John Paskievich, 1988; p. 243, CD 63PH84 60, photograph by Jimmy Manning, 1984

Institute of Ethnography, Photography Archives, Moscow: p. 54, VDNX Collection 656442, photograph by E. Balahnov, 1988; p. 202, 73-121-22, photograph by S.N. Ivanov, 1974; p. 203, 73-127-24, photograph by S.N. Ivanov, 1974; p. 205, photograph by M. Zhornitskaya, 1971; p. 205, photograph by A. Maslov, 1971

Inuit Cultural Institute Collection held at the Prince of Wales Northern Heritage Centre, Yellowknife, NWT, formerly with Inuit Art Section, Indian and Northern Affairs Canada: p. 184, 2.71.234, photograph from Indian and Northern Affairs Canada

Inuktitut, Inuit Tapirisat of Canada: p. 229, photograph by John Bennett, 1989

© Inuvialuit Social Development Program, Yukon North Slope Cultural Resources Survey: p. 108, 1991

B.K. Issenman: pp. 51, 61, 151, 181

Rosemarie Kuptana, Photography Archives, Ottawa: p. 73, Rosemarie Kuptana and *Inuktitut Magazine* ITC-KUP-2

Lyon (1824, 54): p. 132

McCord Museum of Canadian History, Montréal: p. 16 (uluit), ME987x.56, M21040, MEL983.163.243; p. 17, M18589.2, MEL983.163.14 Hugh A. Peck Collection, ME930.39.14; p. 32, ME987x.71; p. 41, Ian Lindsay Collection, ME983.184; p. 47, ME966x.127.2, photographs by Amy Yanagi, 1988, *Threads*, Taunton Press, Newtown, CT; p. 47, ME966x125.2, photograph by Marilyn Aitken; p. 49, ME983x.51.1-2; p. 51, Tom Humphry, Notman Photographic Archives; p. 52, ME967x.32.1-2, ME983x.74, ME982x.327; p. 52, ME966x.128.1-2, ME965.194.1-2 gift of Mrs. Arthur Schwartz, M1203.1-2 gift of Mme Georges Languedoc; p. 53, ME931.5.2.1-2 gift of Mrs. W. Molson; p. 61, Tom Humphry, Notman Photographic Archives; p. 62, ME930.19, ME983x.94, ME930.39.15; p. 63, M21015.1-2; p. 64, ME930.20, M21048, ME982x.320; p. 65, ME982x.79.17, M4936 donated by Mrs. J.B. Learmont; p. 67, ME982x.99.1-3, M12164 donated by the Montréal Natural History Society, ME987x.71; p. 67 (thimbles), ME982x.157.4, ME982x.155.1-2, Canadian Guild of Crafts Quebec, Montréal; p. 68, ME982x.188, MEL984.207.9.1-2 gift of Ian Lindsay, Ottawa; p. 70, ME967x.37; p. 72, M5836; p. 83, ME942.28; p. 90, ME966x.127.1, ME942.29, photographs by Amy Yanagi, *Threads*, Taunton Press, Newtown CT; p. 91, ME965.194.1-2, photographs by Amy Yanagi, *Threads*, Taunton Press, Newtown, CT; p. 101, ME930.1.25, photographs by Marilyn Aitken; p. 102,

ME927.1.98; p. 111, ME966x.127,1-2; p. 115, ME967x.35.1, ME967x.36.1; p. 135, M978.76.26, M13071, M13076.1-2; p. 146, Notman Photographic Archives; p. 147, M5835.1-2; p. 148, M5836; p. 148, Notman Photographic Archives MP 245/75 (874); p. 149, ME983x.67; p. 150, Notman Photographic Archives MP 245/75 (255); p. 151 (front), MEL988.17.1-3; p. 154, M5837; p. 157, Ian Lindsay Collection, ME983.184; p. 170, ME982x.187.1-2; p. 173, Notman Photographic Archives MP598 (121), photograph by G.E. Mack, August 1921; p. 182, photograph by Marilyn Aitken, ME967x.43; p. 183, ME966x.127.1-2, ME966x.124.1-2; p. 185, ME984.277; p. 190, ME937.3; p. 192, M5836; p. 193, ME937.3; p. 194, M12164; p. 201, ME930.1.23.1-2; p. 206, ME976.148; p. 208 (right), ME987.215, ME987.214; p. 238, ME983x.69.1-4, gift of Canadian Guild of Crafts Quebec

Judy McGrath, Photography Archives, Pakenham, ON: p. 217, photograph by Steve Alookee, 1995

Chuna McIntyre, Photography Archives, Iik, Alaska: p. 6, photograph by Kerry Richardson

Musée de la civilisation, Quebec City: pp. 94-95, 72-22; p. 160 (inner and outer amauti), 72-23

Musée de l'Université Laval, Quebec City: p. 211 (robe), U.L.I. photograph from the McCord Museum of Canadian History

Museum of Peter the Great (formerly Museum of Anthropology and Ethnology), St. Petersburg: pp. 48, 187, and 189, Forshtein Collection from Chukotka, CIS, 4211-10, 4211-6a.b, 4211-16, photographs by E. Balahnov, 1988; p. 100, Photography Archives 3164, photograph by S.N. Ivanov, 1974; p. 233, 1681-2

Mystic Seaport Museum, Mystic, CT: p. 134, Comer Collection 63:1767:67

National Archives of Canada, Ottawa: p. 57, PA 112079, photograph by Richard Harrington, 1950; p. 103, C5109, photograph by Ernest Brown; p. 104, R.M. Anderson Collection, C-23642; p. 106, PA175729, S.J. Bailey / Indian and Northern Affairs Canada Collection; p. 116, PA-172882, R.S. Finnie Collection; p. 119, PA99350, photograph by L.T. Burwash, 1926; p. 153, C 84717, photograph by Graham Drinkwater; p. 165, C-95201; p. 167, CX-124432; p. 182, PA 114690, photograph by Richard Harrington, 1953; p. 204 PA 101172, photograph by R.S. Finnie, 1931

National Museum of Denmark, Copenhagen: pp. 8, L.211, photograph by Th. N. Krabbe, 1909; p. 28, N.38cl; p. 45, P.29.1, P.29.20a-b, P.29.20e-f, P.145, P.52; p. 80, Lc.46; p. 120, P.29.2, P.29.13, P.29.27a-b, P.29.27c-d, P.29.27e-f, P.143; p. 121, P.29.10, P.29.18, P.29.28a-b, P.29.28c-d; p. 168, P.230a,b,c,d,e; P.231a,b,c; P.229a,b,c,d,e,f; p. 194, Ld.103, Ld.102, Ld.108

Newfoundland Museum, St. John's: p. 12, IdCq-22:145, photograph by Antonia McGrath

Novosti Press Agency, Moscow: p. 7

NWT Archives, Government of the Northwest Territories, Yellowknife: p. 46, photograph by Tessa Macintosh, 1988; pp. 54, 117, 122, 123, 177, and 216, 7425, 7295, 7361, 7350, 7426, 7355, 7298, photographs by Tessa Macintosh, 1992; p. 141, 5266, photograph by Tessa Macintosh, 1987; p. 142, photograph by Valerie Conrad, 1990; p. 151, photograph by Tessa Macintosh, 1992; p. 207, 6210, photograph by Valerie Conrad, 1990; p. 221, 2089, photograph by Tessa Macintosh, 1988; p. 226, photograph by Tessa Macintosh, 1987; p. 235, 6694, photograph by Tessa Macintosh, 1991; p. 241, 1991

Pauktuutit Inuit Women's Organization: p. 228, photograph by Sally Qimmiu'naaq Webster, 1995

Prince of Wales Northern Heritage Centre, Government of the Northwest Territories, Yellowknife: p. 198, 977.37.38, 977.37.37; p. 199, 977.37.34; p. 200, 977.37.35 Royal Canadian Mounted Police Museum, Regina: p. 48, 34.6.5, photograph by Gerald Downes; p. 139, 34.6.3, photograph by Canadian Conservation Institute

Royal Ontario Museum, Toronto: pp. 34 and 155, HC2300, HC2265, photographs from the McCord Museum of Canadian History

B. Saladin d'Anglure: Collection, Quebec City: pp. 55, 56, 75, and 131, BSA I.D.10, BSA I.D.3, BSA III.B.I, BSA 1.A.16(a)1 and (a)2, photographs from McCord Museum of Canadian History; p. 208 (left) BSA 1.E.1(e). Photography Archives, Quebec City: pp. 37, 85, and 156, photographs by S. Pharand and B. Saladin d'Anglure, 1971; p. 160 (inner amauti), photographs by S. Pharand and B. Saladin d'Anglure, 1971, Musée de la civilization, 72-23; p. 161, photograph by S. Pharand and B. Saladin d'Anglure, 1971

State Museum of Ethnography of the Russian Federation of the CIS, St. Petersburg: p. 213, 2246-133 (sections of Prytkova's text translated courtesy of Indian and Northern Affairs Canada and by the late Nina Farmer); p. 233, 2246-133

Douglas Stenton, Photography Archives, Iqaluit: p. 227, photograph by Douglas Stenton, 1992

Them Days Archives, Vaali, Labrador: p. 169, Collection of Jerry and Regina Sillet; p. 229 photograph by Antonia McGrath, 1980, with the permission of the Newfoundland Museum, St. John's

Threads, Taunton Press, Newtown, CT: pp. 90, 91, and 92, photographs by Amy Yanagi, 1988

Université de Québec à Montréal, Laboratoire d'archéologie: p. 12, 15,063, photograph by Patrick Plumet; p. 16 (needle), 3059

University of Alaska, Fairbanks: p. 75, Archives, Alaska and Polar Regions Department, Otto Geist Collection, 64-98-688N; p. 221, University of Alaska Museum EC13

University Museum, University of Pennsylvania, Philadelphia: p. 107, NA239, photograph from McCord Museum of Canadian History; p. 130, NA 2844

Utqiagvik Archaeology Project, State University of New York at Binghamton: pp. 25, 27, and 183, BAR2-44-55710, BAR2-44-54150, BAR2-44-54739, BAR2-44-54140, photographs from the Department of Archaeology by Bruce Wrighton

Figures

Figs. 1.1, 1.2, based on blueprints from Greenland National Museum, Nuuk, ED 28 KNK 999 x 14/28, ED 12 KNK 999 x 20/12; Figs. 1.3, 1.5, 1.6, based on drawings by Beth L. Turcy (1986, 143, 156, 162); Fig. 1.4, based on drawing by John Murdoch (1892, 117); Figs. 2.1, 2.3, based on drawings by T. B. Mitlyanskaya (1983, 41, 42); Figs. 2.2, 2.4, based on drawings by Tuumasikadlak, translation from Inuktitut to English by La Fédération des Coopératives du Nouveau-Québec (Saladin d'Anglure 1979, 205, 206, 207); Fig. 3.1, based on drawing by Mrs. Rhoda Karetak, 1986; Figs. 3.2, 3.4, based on drawings by Donna Kern, reprinted with permission from *Threads,* no. 27 (1990):63, 60 by Taunton Press, Newtown, CT; Fig. 3.3, based on drawings by Sylvie Pharand (1971), Archives des collections, Musée de la Civilisation, Quebec City, 72-22; Fig. 3.5, Beechey Collection, Pitt Rivers Museum, Oxford University Museum no. A.M.655, Museum no. A.M.654, illustration by John R. Bockstoce, reprinted with permission from the Publications Department, Pitt Rivers Museum, University of Oxford, UK; Figs. 4.1, 4.2, 4.3, 4.4, 4.5, Dorothy K. Burnham, Canadian Museum of Civilization, Hull, PQ, IV-D-960, IV-D-944b, IV-C-665a.b, IV-C-924, IV-C-628, reproduced by permission of D.K. Burnham and the Canadian Museum of Civilization; Fig. 5.1, Margaret Issenman, after Ivanov (1963): (1) Pl.75:4; (2) Pl.75:6; (3) Pl.17:2; (4) Pl.101:10; (5) Pl.149:20; (6) Pl.149:14; (7) Pl.101:8; (8) Pl.149:17; (10) Pl.105:17; (11) Pl.233:9; (12) Pl.265; (13) Pl.273, after Prytkova 1976, fig. 9, p. 67, after Levin and Potapov 1961, table 14, 386

Sponsors

Avataq Cultural Institute
Although not a part of the James Bay and Northern Québec Agreement, Avataq has emerged in the process of Inuit self-determination that occurred in the 1970s as the vehicle by which the region of Nunavik may preserve traditional values and objects of historical importance while at the same time promote and sponsor activities of a cultural nature throughout the region. The institute began its operations on 1 November 1980 and is duly registered as a cultural, non-profit organization. It is the Inuit Elders of Nunavik who mandate Avataq on its programs and projects, through the regular Inuit Elders Conferences. Avataq has its headquarters in Inukjuaq, Nunavik.

Canadian Inuit Art Information Centre, Department of Indian Affairs and Northern Development
The Canadian Inuit Art Information Centre of the Department of Indian Affairs and Northern Development is dedicated to facilitating and supporting all aspects of the development and promotion of Inuit arts and crafts created in the Northwest Territories, Northern Québec, and Labrador. The centre maintains artist files and publishes biographies of Inuit artists and artisans, maintains the world's foremost Inuit art research library, and collects slides and other audio-visual materials. The centre provides research assistance to museums and the academic community, gives advice and information to artists and the Inuit art marketing network, and responds to requests for information about Inuit art and artists from the general public. The centre has produced educational publications and a video, and is currently working on a multimedia presentation on Inuit art.

Fur Council of Canada
The Fur Council of Canada is an umbrella organization representing all segments of the fur industry, including trappers, fur farmers, auction houses, dressers and dyers, designers, manufacturers, and retailers. The objectives of the Fur Council and its member organizations are to promote industry based on the sustainable use of renewable resources. Aboriginal people were the founders of the fur trade in North America and still account for about half of all Canadian trappers. The First Nations are also increasingly involved in processing, manufacturing, and designing, and other sections of the industry. Long known as a source for the world's finest furs, Canada now also produces designers who are also making a name for themselves in the fashion capitals of the world. The North American Fur and Fashion Exposition, which is held and organized by the Fur Council of Canada each May in Montréal, is one of the biggest and most important fur fairs in the world.

Fur Institute of Canada
The Fur Institute of Canada is a national, multi-stakeholder organization with a mandate from the Wildlife Ministers Council of Canada to establish a standard of excellence for the optimum development and conservation of the fur resources of Canada. Institute membership includes trappers, fur ranchers, Aboriginal organizations, conservation agencies, animal welfare groups, auction houses, manufacturers, retailers, national and international support groups, and the federal, provincial, and territorial governments.

Fur Program, Department of Indian Affairs and Northern Development
It is with great pleasure that the Department of Indian Affairs and Northern Development has agreed to be a co-sponsor of *Sinews of Survival: The Living Legacy of Inuit Clothing*. In our increasingly urbanized society, people who think of themselves as environmentalists can be heard promoting the use of synthetic materials over the use of natural products such as seal skin and fur. This book reminds us of what it really means to say 'sustainable use of natural resources' when the only clothing materials available come from the animals found running across the tundra or swimming under the polar ice.

Hydro-Québec
Hydro-Québec is a publicly owned electric utility constituted in April 1944. It generates, transmits, and distributes most of the electricity consumed in Québec. Ninety-three percent of its generating facilities are hydroelectric, a feature unique among large power systems. Hydro-Québec is dedicated to the total satisfaction of its customers' needs as well as to sustainable development. It consistently engages in research and seeks a wide variety of partnerships, including many with Aboriginal communities and nations in Québec.
Hydro-Québec est une société d'Etat qui a été constituée en avril 1944. Elle produit, transporte, et distribue la quasi-totalité de l'électricité consommé au Québec. Son parc de production de plus de 31 000 MW est formé à 93% de centrales hydroélectriques, une caractéristique unique au monde dans les réseaux de cette ampleur. Hydro-Québec est vouée à la satisfaction des besoins de ses clients et au développement durable. Elle consacre des efforts soutenus à la recherche et multiple les formes de partenariat dont plusieurs avec les communautés ou nations autochtones du Québec.

Inco Limited
Inco Limited, a Canadian company with operations in twenty-three countries, is the world's largest producer of nickel. Inco's premier position was assured for years to come when, in 1996, the company acquired the rich nickel-copper-cobalt ore body at Voisey's Bay in Labrador. Inco has always worked in harmony with the people who live near its mining operations, and Voisey's Bay will be no exception. In addition to proceeding in accord with stringent environmental and land-use legislation, Inco's subsidiary – Voisey's Bay Nickel Company Limited – is engaged in effective dialogue with representatives of Labrador's Aboriginal groups to ensure Native concerns are resolved promptly and with a sense of fair play. In that same spirit, Inco is pleased to be a sponsor of Betty Kobayashi Issenman's important manuscript, *Sinews of Survival: The Living Legacy of Inuit Clothing*.

Jackman Foundation
Established in 1964 by Henry R. Jackman, the Jackman Foundation assists organizations to answer the needs of Canadian society. The foundation offers grants to a variety of charitable organizations ranging from major Canadian institutions to small grassroots groups. Their concerns vary from theatre to medicine, from the environment to day care. Through these groups, the Jackman Foundation endeavours to preserve the values of traditions of Canadian culture while responding to both the new and the ever-present requirements of citizens. The Jackman Foundation is pleased to

support the publication of *Sinews of Survival: The Living Legacy of Inuit Clothing* as part of its objective of preserving the values and traditions of Canadian culture.

Kativik School Board
The Kativik School Board, an Inuit-governed school board, was created by the James Bay and Northern Québec Agreement in 1975 to serve the people living in the fourteen communities of Nunavik (Northern Québec, north of the fifty-fifth parallel). The school board is guided by a dual mandate: to develop a curriculum that embraces Native traditions, culture, and language, and to prepare students for active participation in the modern world. The Kativik School Board develops programs and teaching materials, and provides primary and secondary education for 2653 students in Inuktitut, English, and French; offers academic upgrading, and technical-vocational education to the adult populations; trains Inuit teachers to meet provincial standards; and provides on-the-job training for school board employees and employees of other Nunavik organizations.

Lytton Minerals Limited
Lytton Minerals Limited (TSE: LTL) is an independent Toronto-listed mining and exploration company that has focused its activities in the Northwest Territories. The company has successfully carried out a massive exploration program over the last four years extending over thirteen million acres covering the northern part of the Slave territory. Some of the resulting discoveries are moving into the development phase. Lytton's aim is to contribute to the economic life of the Northwest Territories by continuing to develop its mineral interests in the area while maintaining the highest environmental standards.

Makivik Corporation
Makivik Corporation is the non-profit Inuit-owned business-development corporation created to manage the 1975 James Bay and Northern Québec Agreement compensation moneys. In the Inuktitut language, 'Makivik' means 'advancement' – a fitting name for an organization whose main goal is to develop not only the economy, but the political and social landscape as well. In keeping with its ongoing concern with educational and cultural issues, Makivik Corporation is proud to support the publication of *Sinews of Survival: The Living Legacy of Inuit Clothing*.

Nunavut Tunngavik Incorporated
The objective of the Nunavut Tunngavik is to constitute an open and accountable forum, organized to represent Inuit of all the regions and communities of Nunavut in a fair and democratic way, that will safeguard, administer, and advance the rights and benefits that belong to the Inuit of Nunavut as an Aboriginal people, so as to promote their economic, social, and cultural well-being through succeeding generations.

Nunavut Wildlife Management Board
The Nunavut Wildlife Management Board (NWMB) is an institution of public government established under the terms and conditions of the Nunavut Land Claims Agreement, effective 9 July 1993. The NWMB is the main instrument of wildlife management in the Nunavut Settlement Area and the main regulator of access to wildlife resources, subject only to the ultimate responsibility of government in matters pertaining to wildlife management. The NWMB will strive to enable and protect the beneficial utilization of wildlife for and by the beneficiaries of the Nunavut Land Claims Agreement and to manage wildlife consistent with the principles of conservation, sustainability, and ecosystemic integrity.

Placer Dome Canada Limited
Placer Dome Canada is one of the country's largest gold producers. The company is committed to integrating the efficient extraction of mineral resources with responsible environmental stewardship and to creating and maintaining positive relationships with its Aboriginal neighbours in the communities in which it operates. As a member of Canada's Arctic community, Placer Dome is proud to support the publication of *Sinews of Survival: The Living Legacy of Inuit Clothing*. We hope that this unique volume will secure, and at the same time share, many years of Inuit knowledge and experience with Inuit and non-Inuit people alike. Congratulations on achieving this important milestone.

Telesat Canada
Telesat is Canada's national satellite communications company providing telecommunications and broadcast distribution services throughout North America via its fifth-generation Anik E satellites. Telesats's satellites carry television and radio broadcasting, voice communications, and data communications networks. Created in 1969, Telesat was the first company in the world to establish and operate a domestic satellite telecommunications network and, since the mid-1970s, has provided consulting services on virtually every aspect of the satellite industry from the ground up. Telesat is pleased and honoured to support Northern communities in projects such as *Sinews of Survival: The Living Legacy of Inuit Clothing*.

Index

Note Page numbers in **bold** indicate captions for illustrations. Where illustrations and captions are on separate pages, the page cited refers to the caption description.